Beginning Ubuntu Linux

Fifth Edition

Emilio Raggi, Keir Thomas,
Trevor Parsons, Andy Channelle,
Sander van Vugt

Beginning Ubuntu Linux, Fifth Edition

ISBN-13 (pbk): 978-1-4302-3039-7

ISBN-13 (electronic): 978-1-4302-3040-3

Printed and bound in the United States of America 9 8 7 6 5 4 3 2 1

President and Publisher: Paul Manning
Lead Editor: Frank Pohlmann
Technical Reviewers: Bruce Byfield, Richard Hillesley
Editorial Board: Clay Andres, Steve Anglin, Mark Beckner, Ewan Buckingham, Gary Cornell, Jonathan Gennick, Jonathan Hassell, Michelle Lowman, Matthew Moodie, Duncan Parkes, Jeffrey Pepper, Frank Pohlmann, Douglas Pundick, Ben Renow-Clarke, Dominic Shakeshaft, Matt Wade, Tom Welsh
Coordinating Editor: Tracy Brown
Copy Editors: Corbin Collins, Damon Larson
Compositor: Mary Sudul
Indexer: John Collin
Artist: April Milne
Cover Designer: Anna Ishchenko

Distributed to the book trade worldwide by Springer Science+Business Media, LLC., 233 Spring Street, 6th Floor, New York, NY 10013. Phone 1-800-SPRINGER, fax (201) 348-4505, e-mail orders-ny@springer-sbm.com, or visit www.springeronline.com.

For information on translations, please e-mail rights@apress.com, or visit www.apress.com.

Apress and friends of ED books may be purchased in bulk for academic, corporate, or promotional use. eBook versions and licenses are also available for most titles. For more information, reference our Special Bulk Sales–eBook Licensing web page at www.apress.com/info/bulksales.

The source code for this book is available to readers at www.apress.com.

To my wife, Pim, and my two children, Camilo and Dante

Contents

About the Authors

■ **Emilio Raggi** lives in Buenos Aires, Argentina, and has been managing IT Projects for the past 12 years. He was very much a Windows fanboy, until one day he had to manage an Ubuntu desktop deployment project. He was highly qualified as Microsoft implementer, holding certificates as an MCP and MCSE, and was a consultant for an MS Partner. Still, Ubuntu had its charms and won him over. He is now an avid fan, user, and promoter, to the benefit of his family, friends, and colleagues. He is also an avid student of philosophy.

■ **Keir Thomas** is an award-winning author who has written several best-selling Linux titles for Apress. A former computer magazine editor, he has been writing about computers, operating systems, and software for a decade. He has also served as editor on several computer books. His works have been translated into many languages. Thomas works as a full-time author and has written five books for Apress. He lives on the side of a mountain in England, and his hobbies include hiking and playing musical instruments.

■ **Trevor Parsons** has been using free software for a decade, and was founding editor of the UK's *Linux User* magazine. When he's not writing, editing, and breaking computers, he sidelines as a drummer and fiddle player. Even then there's always an Ubuntu Flash drive in his violin case.

■ **Andy Channelle** is a lead instructor and web systems coordinator at the University of the West of England specializing in journalism and new media. He has written for a variety of technology magazines including *Linux Format* and *Mac Format* over the last ten years and has also managed a few large web projects based on free software and open principles.

Andy lives in the UK and enjoys writing, playing the guitar and drums, and sitting out in the sun reading books.

■ **Sander van Vugt** is an independent Linux expert, living in the Netherlands. He delivers his Linux training courses worldwide and is specialized in Linux performance issues. Sander is the author of many books, including *Beginning Ubuntu Server* and *Pro Ubuntu Server*. Sander can be reached at his e-mail address, mail@sandervanvugt.nl.

About the Technical Reviewers

■ **Bruce Byfield** is a journalist who specializes in writing about free and open source software. He has been a contributing editor at *Linux.com*, and his articles have appeared on the *Datamation, LWN, Linux Developer Network, Linux Journal*, and *LinuxPlanet* sites. He also writes a monthly column for the *Linux Journal* web site and a weekly blog called "Off the Beat" about the free software community for *Linux Pro* magazine. In addition to his online publications, he has published in such magazines as *Linux Journal, Linux Pro* magazine, *Maximum Linux, The New Internationalist*, and *Ubuntu User*. Although he long ago lost count, he has sold over 750 articles in his career.

Before becoming a journalist, Byfield was marketing and communications director at Progeny Linux Systems, and product manager at Stormix Technologies. His book *Witches of the Mind* is considered the definitive work on the American fantasist Fritz Leiber. He also designs elearning courses and is a marketing and communications consultant.

Byfield lives in Burnaby, Canada. In addition to free and open source software, his interests include parrots, aerobic exercise, science fiction, listening to punk-folk music, and collecting Northwest Coast art.

■ **Richard Hillesley** writes about free software and lives in the southwest of England.

Introduction

Linux applies an alternate philosophy to computing that revolves around the sharing of not only software but also knowledge. To use Linux is to become part of a huge global community of people who have caught on to a phenomenon that is changing the world.

Ubuntu (http://www.ubuntu.com) is the natural continuation of these goals. It's a project founded by entrepreneur businessman Mark Shuttleworth with the intention of bringing a freely available, high-quality operating system to the world. To this end, Shuttleworth invested $10 million of his own money to guarantee that this will be the case for many years to come. In 2010, the project has moved closer to becoming self-sustaining as Ubuntu becomes part of the mainstream for desktop, Netbook, and server users.

The fundamental concept is that Ubuntu is available for use by anyone in the world, no matter who or where they are. As such, many different languages are supported, and the operating system can also be accessed by those with disabilities, such as partial sight or hearing. Ubuntu might just as easily be found on a Wall Street banker's laptop as on a battered old computer in a Brazilian *favela*.

Ubuntu is built around one of the most established versions of Linux: Debian (http://www.debian.org). The Debian Project was started back in 1993, shortly after the very first version of the Linux software was released, and has become one of the pioneering varieties of Linux. Ubuntu and Debian Linux both share common goals and are closely allied, but Ubuntu focuses largely on the desktop. For example, it provides a powerful office suite by default, as well as some excellent pieces of Internet software. Only recently has a dedicated server version become available.

It's also very easy to use. Ubuntu works straight out of the box. As soon as it's installed, you should be ready to start using it without any further work. In addition, tasks such as updating your software are as easy under Ubuntu as they are under Windows—in many cases, easier. Above all, however, Ubuntu is designed to be shared. You can take the DVD-ROM included with this book and install Ubuntu on as many computers as you want. You can also copy it as many times as you want and give those copies to your friends. We're serious! This isn't some kind of trick, either—Ubuntu isn't a trial version that will quit running in a month. You will never find yourself having to pay a fee further down the line, even if you want to install additional software. Ubuntu, and much of the software that runs on top of it, will always be free of charge.

Since its inception in 2004, Ubuntu has literally taken the world of Linux by storm and has even broken out of the technically demanding world of open source software. It's consistently voted the most popular desktop Linux and has even garnered a handful of celebrity users along the way: Jamie Hyneman of the popular TV show *MythBusters* is a fan, as is novelist and blogger Cory Doctorow. Within some Internet communities, such as Digg.com and Reddit, you may struggle to find individuals who don't use Ubuntu.

Ubuntu's popularity has risen as the software appears on desktop and laptop computers from the likes of Dell and HP, and it is finding its way into many users' hands through Netbooks.

What You'll Find in This Book

Beginning Ubuntu Linux, Fifth Edition is divided into five parts, each of which contains chapters about a certain aspect of Ubuntu use. These parts can be read in sequence, or you can dip in and out of them at will. When a technical term is mentioned, it is defined on first use in the chapter, or a reference is made to the chapter where the term is explained.

Part 1 examines the history and philosophy behind Ubuntu and the Linux operating system. We aim to answer many of the common questions about Linux. Such knowledge is considered to be as important, if not more so, than understanding the technical details on how Linux works. But although these chapters should be read sooner rather than later, they don't contain any technical information that you absolutely require to get started with Ubuntu.

Part 2 covers installing Ubuntu on your computer. An illustrated guide is provided, and all installation choices are explained in depth. Additionally, you'll find a problem-solving chapter to help, just in case anything goes wrong.

Part 3 focuses on getting started with Ubuntu. It covers setting up the Linux system so that it's ready to use. First we explore the graphical interface, so you know where to go to perform the most basic tasks. One chapter is dedicated to setting up common hardware devices, such as printers, and another explains how you can secure your system. You'll also learn how to fully personalize Ubuntu so you feel more at home with it, and how to work with your files.

In Part 4, we take a look at how you can use Ubuntu to perform your day to day tasks. We list the most common Ubuntu applications as an introduction for users more acquainted with Windows. Then we take a look at working with text files and with OpenOffice.org, the complete office suite built into Ubuntu. Then we explore ways to get connected with other people through e-mail or instant messaging. A whole new chapter takes a look at hot topics like social networks and cloud computing, and how Ubuntu can help you make the most of them with minimal effort. We also look at working with audio, movies and multimedia, and digital photos. And we finish Part 4 by going over different options for playing games with your Ubuntu PC.

Part 5 is dedicated to give you the skills necessary to keep your system running smoothly. You'll learn how to install new software, manage users, optimize your system, back up essential data, schedule tasks, and access computers remotely.

Finally, Part 6 contains four appendixes. The first is a full introduction to the command-line prompt, and includes a quick reference to the most used commands. Appendix B is a glossary of Linux terms used not only in this book but also in the Linux and UNIX worlds. The third appendix explains how to get further help when using Ubuntu, and the fourth explains how to use the DVD and the differences between the various versions of Ubuntu.

What's New in the Fifth Edition

The original edition of *Beginning Ubuntu Linux* was the first English-language book to provide a guide to using Ubuntu, and it remains one of the best. Successive editions of the book have tracked the changes within the Ubuntu project and have improved each time.

This edition of *Beginning Ubuntu Linux* has been thoroughly updated and revised to take into account improvements with the 10.04 release of the software, code-named Lucid Lynx. The previous edition covered the 9.04 release. This version of Ubuntu has incorporated a new level of integration with social networks. A new cloud service, Ubuntu One, helps you keep your files and personal information synchronized to multiple PCs. Ubuntu 10.04 also simplified, with Ubuntu Software Center, the way you can search for and install new applications. And it is a Long Term Support release, meaning that you will be given support and updates for your desktop installation for three years.

About the DVD-ROM Supplied with This Book

The DVD-ROM attached to the book is completely new, compared to that offered with previous editions. This edition offers a double-sided DVD-ROM that contains virtually every official release of Ubuntu 10.04, including not only the main Ubuntu release, but also Kubuntu, Xubuntu, and releases for servers and Netbooks.

By booting from Side A of the DVD-ROM you can opt to install Ubuntu or run in "live" mode, which means that the entire operating system boots from the disc and doesn't touch your hard disk. This can be useful for those who want to "try out" Ubuntu.

The contents of the DVD-ROM are explained in detail in Appendix D.

Conventions Used in This Book

The goal when writing *Beginning Ubuntu Linux* was to make it as readable as possible while providing the facility for readers to learn at their own pace.

Throughout the book, you'll find various types of notes and sidebars complementing the regular text. These are designed to provide handy information to help further your knowledge. They also make reading the book a bit easier.

▓ **Note** A note is designed to provide an important piece of information that you should know and that will help your understanding of the topic being discussed.

▓ **Tip** A tip is something that will help when you need to perform the task being described. Alternatively, it might be something that can make your life easier when using Ubuntu.

▓ **Caution** A caution is something you should certainly pay attention to, because it warns of a hidden danger or particular caveat that applies to the topic being discussed.

In the sidebars, we take a moment to explain something that you should know, but that isn't vital to an understanding of the main topic being discussed. You don't need to read the sidebars there and then; you can return to them later if you like.

Apress®

Apress License Agreement (Single-User Products)

PART 1

■ ■ ■

Introducing the World of Linux

CHAPTER 1

■ ■ ■

Meet Ubuntu Linux

Because you're holding this book in your hands, there is a good chance that you have heard of Ubuntu Linux before. Maybe someone suggested it to you or you have read about it in the media. Anyway, we will try to show you how you can use it to make your life easier. First we point out ten (though there are certainly more) good reasons why you should give it a try. Then we talk about Ubuntu Linux in more detail, showing what it is and what it is like to work with.

We will be happy if, by the end of this chapter, you feel confident enough to install Ubuntu Linux on a PC. Of course, you'll get the maximum benefit from it by reading the rest of the book. Without proper guidance you may sometimes feel that Linux is a wild jungle, but this book can help you become an expert user.

Ten Reasons to Try Ubuntu Linux

In our experience there are at least ten good reasons to try Ubuntu Linux right away:

- You want your computer to boot really fast and to be fully functional after that.

- You want to use a sleek and modern operating system (OS) but are reluctant to buy a Mac.

- You are an idealist who thinks that software should be free ("free as in free speech").

- You are a materialist who would rather have software for free ("free as in free beer").

- You have seen Ubuntu Linux installed in a friend's PC and want the same "wow" computer experience for yourself.

- You are tired of being exposed to hackers and malicious users every time you open Internet Explorer.

- You just bought a netbook and it either (a) comes loaded with an old OS, or (b) has a brand new OS that limits you on what you can do.

- You have an old PC that you don't want to throw away just yet, but which is nearly useless under the latest versions of Windows.

- You are a hardcore Linux user who wants to figure out why Ubuntu has been chosen the best Linux desktop distribution so many times.

- You have been asked by your boss to evaluate Ubuntu Linux as a replacement for Windows on your organization's desktop computers. Or maybe you are the boss and want to motivate your crew with a great project.

This list could go on; we all have good reasons to try Ubuntu Linux on our PCs. More reasons will occur to you once you get to know it.

Of course, if you're already using an older version of Ubuntu (and taking into account that, in Ubuntu's terminology, "older" means six months), you don't need us to point out its virtues, right?

What Is Ubuntu Linux Anyway?

Ubuntu Linux can be defined in many ways and from different angles. First off, it is an operating system (usually shortened to OS). Ubuntu is a distribution of Linux, based on Debian, and that gives it some characteristic features. But to describe it only as an OS would be nothing short of unfair: it also has a wide range of pre-installed applications and many more readily available at the click of the mouse, and an ever-growing user community. Let's talk about what Ubuntu is in a little more depth.

Ubuntu Linux Is an Operating System

Ubuntu Linux, as an OS, is, very simply, what makes your computer work.

A computer is much more versatile than a TV or DVD player. You can plug different input devices into it, run applications, and expect it to do a lot of stuff. To be able to do all this, your computer needs an OS, the underlying software that instructs it in how to perform all its functions.

An OS tells your computer what to do when it starts, for example. Without it, your computer would beep and wait in annoyance when you turned it on. The OS also communicates with your computer's hardware, and with the applications that you use to perform your work. The OS glues together all aspects of your computer.

The first and most important of those components is you, the user. You're the one who chooses which applications to run, what actions to take, and whether the PC should be turned on or off. The OS needs input from you and needs to communicate to you the result of your actions.

Usually, you work with applications, which enable you to do specific tasks, such as writing documents or browsing the web. Applications also need to communicate with your OS, to interact with other applications, and to make the computer's hardware work. How they do this varies by operating system, which is why most Windows applications will not work out of the box with Linux. But, as we will see later, that shouldn't deter you from using Linux.

You also have data, the information you need to perform your work. You might save photos, documents, and other files. In this respect, the OS should provide a means to access storage capacity, whether it is local (a hard disk attached directly to your computer), removable (USB drive), or remote (a file server or online storage system). Data comes in different formats, and each format is usually tied to a specific application, which may even be registered as proprietary. For example, a document with the extension ".doc" or ".docx" has been written and saved with Microsoft Word. This is why interoperability—the ability to use different data formats with various applications—is important. As an analogy, think about a thermometer reading 64° F. We can say that temperature itself is the data, and the measurement unit the format. You can change the format (to degrees Celsius) while keeping the same data, but you can't have measurement of temperature without a measurement unit. An interoperable application would be able to read the temperature whether it is in degrees Fahrenheit or Celsius.

Last but not least, you have the hardware, such as graphic and sound cards, printers, scanners, and many other devices. Usually, to make a specific piece of hardware work, the OS needs a driver, a special piece of code that handles communication with the device. Maybe the greatest challenge you'll face when using Ubuntu Linux will be getting all your hardware up and running. Although most devices should run out-of-the-box with Ubuntu, you might have to follow some additional steps to make some specific pieces of hardware work. That's why we pay so much attention in this book to this topic.

As you can see, an OS does a lot of stuff. On desktop computers, the most popular OS is Microsoft Windows, with Windows 7 being the latest incarnation.[1] Windows is a closed and proprietary OS, which means that nobody outside Microsoft can view or modify its source code (unless you are given permission to do so by Microsoft, and even then you must sign a Non-Disclosure Agreement). It is also "non-free" in the sense that you must pay for it, and depending on the version Windows can be really expensive.[2]

But, as with any other component of your computer, the OS can be swapped out for a better one. Welcome to Ubuntu Linux.

Ubuntu Is a Distribution of Linux, Based on Debian

Ubuntu, as an OS, is part of the larger family of Linux distributions.

You'll find out more about that in Chapter 2. For now, suffice it to say that Ubuntu uses Linux as its kernel. The *kernel*[3] is the portion of the OS that performs the most basic functions, such as memory and process management. Linux is an open and free kernel, strongly based on concepts first sketched up for UNIX, Linux's honorable ancestor. That's why it is said that Linux is a UNIX-like OS.

Linux is one of the flagship developments of the free and open source software movement. It is a very versatile and powerful OS that runs on many different hardware platforms. Although widely adopted in devices such as servers and smartphones, it hasn't yet earned great market share on desktop computers. But that might be about to change—thanks in part to Ubuntu Linux.

Because Linux is just a kernel, it usually needs other programs to run as a full OS. Different Linux distributions (or *distros* for short) package all the other software needed to make an OS, each with a different philosophy in mind. More often than not, there are organizations behind each distribution, and these organizations often drive the development of new packages.

Ubuntu Linux is one such distribution, but it isn't completely original, which is to say it wasn't created from scratch. It is in fact an adaptation of Debian. Debian has been around almost as long as Linux itself, having been founded in 1993, just two years after Linus Torvalds[4] made his initial announcement of the Linux kernel. Debian is widely respected within the Linux community and has some claim to be the definitive Linux distribution.

The Debian project was started by a computer scientist named Ian Murdock, and its name comes from a combination of his Christian name with that of his girlfriend Deborah—hence Deb-Ian (sort of like Brangelina).

Debian is well known for its strict adherence to the spirit of free and open source software, which is embodied in the Debian Social Contract and the Debian Free Software Guidelines (DFSG). These documents[5] lay down rules for the governance of the decentralized worldwide community that is Debian.

Debian is not, like many other Linux distributions, sponsored by any company, but rather by a not-for-profit organization called Software in the Public Interest.[6]

---

[1] Windows is of course very popular as a server OS also.

[2] At the time of this writing, the full version of Windows 7 ranged from $199 to $319 (http://www.microsoft.com/windows/buy/default.aspx). This price did not include Microsoft Office.

[3] The kernel is commonly presented alongside with the shell, the latter being the interface between the user and the kernel. The traditional shell for Linux is based on the command line.

[4] Linus Torvalds is the original creator of the Linux kernel. See Chapter 2 for more details.

[5] Available here: http://www.debian.org/social_contract

[6] http://www.spi-inc.org/

Debian is also well known for how it manages its software. Part of the Debian project is to maintain an online database and repository of software, which is available to all Internet users. Today, more than 25,000 free applications are in there, and much care has been taken to make software installation and upgrade as easy as possible.

Ubuntu Linux Is a Full Desktop Solution

But to talk about Ubuntu Linux as just an OS would be unfair. It is much more than that.

Ubuntu Linux is built upon the sound foundation of Debian, and by all standards they are very much alike; however, they do differ in their approaches. Although supremely flexible, Debian is mostly used on servers. Ubuntu, on the other hand, is primarily a desktop distribution, although it also has a Server edition. In terms of their approaches to releasing new software, Debian is extremely cautious and issues a release only after a through bug-testing procedure. In contrast, Ubuntu is very aggressive, which allows it to include more modern software, though sometimes in not-so-stable versions.

Building upon Debian's premise, Ubuntu Linux is a full-featured desktop solution that comes with tons of applications ready to install and use. It is not just the OS that is free and open: you also get, pre-installed, the full productivity suite OpenOffice.org, a browser, a photo manager, mail and messaging clients, and much, much more. Once you install Ubuntu Linux, you will seldom need an application that is not found in its repositories. It's like being granted unrestricted access to a warehouse full of goodies!

Computers can be money pits. But with Ubuntu Linux, you can stop worrying about how much software costs and start thinking what you want to do and how to use the right tools to do it.

The Ubuntu Linux Experience

When you replace your OS, many things change with it. The interface might not look the same, the applications can be different, and you may not be able to ask the same people for help. So you may ask: "What would it be like to work with Ubuntu Linux? What would I be getting into?"

Those are good and legitimate questions. We will try to give you a preliminary impression, but the answers can be truly obtained only when you use Ubuntu yourself for the first time.

"Linux for Human Beings"

If you have heard about Linux before, you might think it is a dull and text-based OS that can only be used by computer geeks. But although the command-line shell has a central role to play, there are many different flavors of Linux (called distributions, as you will see in Chapter 2), and Ubuntu is aimed at being easy to use.

One of the nicknames for Ubuntu is "Linux for human beings."[7] This means that when the developers get together to analyze future directions for the OS, they talk about what people want to use the computer for.

Many of the improvements of Lucid Lynx, the latest version of Ubuntu Linux, are in the area of integration with social networks. It is not that the development team has any special relationship with those applications; it's just that they acknowledge that a great part of our activities with a computer today involves using sites like Facebook and Twitter. Services that so many people use should be simple and straightforward.

Another area of great improvement has been application installation. There is a new concept regarding how applications should be looked for and installed. With other operating systems, you

---

[7] https://help.ubuntu.com/10.04/about-ubuntu/C/

normally go to the store and buy a box. Then you go home, pull the DVD from the box, and figure out how the software is installed. You even have to store a paper with information about licensing for the rest of your life! The whole process is cumbersome and prone to problems. Ubuntu, with its Software Center, has a completely different approach. Installing applications is as easy as browsing categories and selecting which application best suits your needs. Then it is installed and ready to use. For free.

Those are just two examples of the OS being designed "for human beings." It means, in short, that the user interface is easy and simple and that its features are there only to be of use to you. The ultimate goal of Ubuntu Linux is to make your life easier.

Ubuntu is also meant to communicate in the local language of the user, and that's human-friendly too. It takes into consideration that different people have different abilities. And, as you'll read later in this chapter, it makes you part of a broad community of people sharing knowledge and trying to help other people.

If you take a look at the Table of Contents of this book, you will find that there is no single chapter devoted to working with the command-line shell. Strange in a Linux book, right? It's not that we forgot to write about it! But we think that Ubuntu Linux is such a user-oriented OS that access to the shell can be reduced to a minimum.

■ **Note** Of course, the command-line shell is still an important part of Ubuntu Linux, and it makes a lot of sense to learn about it in depth if you want to become a true guru. We devote an appendix to the subject, and there are also many books on the shell available from Apress if you want to learn more.

A Powerful yet Flexible Operating System

Maybe you're wondering whether Ubuntu Linux is a stable and versatile OS or just one that is free and... you know... better not examined too thoroughly. After all, haven't we all been told that anything free is worth what you paid for it?

If that is your concern, you should worry no further. Ubuntu, as we stated before, is a distribution of Linux. And Linux is running on quite a lot of computing devices, from tiny ones to gigantic ones. One of the smallest computers in the world, CompuLabs fit-PC,[8] runs Ubuntu, and so do many phones. On the other end of the spectrum, the Jaguar,[9] the world's most powerful supercomputer, runs Linux as well. That means it is both flexible and powerful. If you look at the computer market as a whole, it seems that desktop computers are the last stronghold outside of the hands of Linux (the reason for that lies elsewhere, not in technical limitations).

Is it powerful? Of course it is! Of the 500 most powerful computers, as measured by the TOP500 organization in June, 2010,[10] 91% run some version of Linux. Microsoft Windows runs on just 1% of those computers. This dominance wouldn't be possible if Linux weren't a stable and efficient OS.

Once upon a time z/OS, a proprietary OS from IBM, was the only option for the powerful mainframe computers in use today for mission-critical operations in many industries; now, more and more use Linux on System z, accounting today for roughly one third of the mainframes running worldwide.

Linux also drives almost half of the servers that make up the Internet.[11] Together with the Apache HTTP server, the MySQL database engine, and programming languages like PHP, Python, and Perl,

---

[8] http://www.fit-pc.com/web/

[9] http://www.nccs.gov/jaguar/

[10] http://www.top500.org/stats/list/35/osfam

[11] https://ssl.netcraft.com/ssl-sample-report//CMatch/osdv_all

Linux forms an open source bundle collectively known as LAMP, which is a free alternative to proprietary (and expensive) solutions. And LAMP is not just for low-traffic web sites: the mighty Wikipedia runs on Linux—on Ubuntu Linux, in fact[12]).

Linux is also hard to beat when it comes to flexibility. It not only runs huge servers hidden in datacenters; many Linux derivatives found their ways into the smartphone market, Google's Android being the most popular but not the only one (and there are plans to use it on more devices, such as TV sets). And after HP's acquisition of Palm in late April, 2010, it has plans to use WebOS, which uses the Linux kernel as well, as a platform for its Tablet PCs and connected mobile devices.[13] This flexibility is what allows Linux to be a serious contender—many would say the perfect option—in the netbook market.

When the first generation of netbooks came out, the concept was nothing short of a revolution. Until that moment, PC manufacturers had thought that users would always be willing to spend money on ever-more powerful computers with a lot of unnecessary software. Windows Vista was the logical conclusion of that line of thought: a bloated OS, hungry for hardware resources. Microsoft seemed to hope that people would buy a new and expensive computer just to be able to run its latest OS, which was full of functionality many did not want or need. What happened was just the opposite: to avoid having to do that, many stuck to Windows XP or turned to Linux. And some even went one step further, by replacing big desktops and notebooks with the smaller netbooks. The unthinkable had happened: people actually wanted *less* than what the market had been providing. What they wanted was a "good enough" computer that allowed them to do their work, while being cheap enough to be affordable in a time of economic uncertainty.

Microsoft was startled. It was obvious by then that Windows Vista was not designed for that kind of device, so it allowed netbook manufacturers to install Windows XP and wait for Windows 7 to save the day. Now that Windows 7 is out, what netbooks have is an artificially reduced version of the Windows OS—reduced not to accommodate the simpler hardware imprint, but to make you pay extra money if you want all the functionality.

Ubuntu Linux sees things differently. Because it is free, it doesn't have to be limited for commercial purposes. Because it needs fewer hardware resources to run, it is natively better suited to small netbooks, and can run more applications on them as a result. And because it is relatively safe, it doesn't need antivirus software running constantly in the background, consuming valuable processor cycles and disk I/O on a computer with limited hardware resources.

Continuous Improvements

One of the things you have to get used to is the frequency with which new versions of Ubuntu Linux appear, each with new features and hardware support. The release cycle of Ubuntu Linux is every six months. The development team follows a time-based release cycle, not a feature-driven one. What does this mean?

Some operating systems, including Microsoft Windows, are launched only when all the planned and committed features are ready. At the beginning of the development cycle, the list of proposed features for the product is set. The company then starts selling the idea of the future product, full of new toys. Because of this, they must finish programming all the new features before launching the product, and a delay in any feature (no matter whether it is important or not) can slow down the whole project. That's why Microsoft Windows delays are so common and launch day announcements are so widely publicized. Sometimes features go live half baked, just to avoid pushing the date still further back, and then a maintenance update has to be made available just after launch.

---

[12] http://en.wikipedia.org/wiki/Wikipedia#Software_and_hardware

[13] http://www.hp.com/hpinfo/newsroom/press/2010/100428xa.html?jumpid=reg_R1002_USEN

Things are different with Ubuntu Linux. From the very beginning, the development team made a commitment to release a new version every six months.[14] Release dates are usually scheduled for April and October. That's why a relatively young OS (born in 2004) is now, six years later, on its 12th release.

How does Ubuntu do this? Are its programmers more responsible or better at project management? Well, that could be part of the explanation, but not all of it. The reason Ubuntu can do it this way is because it follows a completely different release philosophy.

Instead of basing releases on features, Ubuntu bases them on *time*. It is a fine example of the "timebox" method[15] of agile software development. Ubuntu sets a release date for a new version of the OS long before it actually happens, and some guiding goals are given for that version. After that the development works entirely differently, because Ubuntu Linux depends on many unrelated teams of developers working together on some specific piece of software. Those teams have no relationship with Ubuntu or Canonical. They can be as disparate as the GNOME team (developers of the GNOME desktop environment used by Ubuntu), Mozilla (maintainers of the Firefox web browser), and Oracle (home of the OpenOffice.org project).

Canonical, the company behind Ubuntu, can't enforce a release schedule for all those projects. So, as the launch date approaches, Ubuntu enters a "feature freeze" state. All packages are updated to the latest stable version and bundled together to test compatibility. Most problems are fixed, and the product is released right on schedule.

This means that sometimes, if a team is delayed, the price of timely release is that the latest functionality of a certain product will not be included. That is a shame, sure, but then again, with a release cycle of just six months, the updated functionality will be available to Ubuntu Linux users almost immediately when it's ready. And upgrades, like Ubuntu itself, are completely free of charge—and easy to apply as well.

■ **Note** It has become customary that Ubuntu releases are named after animals, preceded by an adjective that suggests the philosophy behind the particular version. At the time of writing, for example, the latest releases were Jaunty Jackalope, Karmic Koala, and Lucid Lynx. The OS also uses a version number that references the year and month of the update. So 10.04 means 2010, April release.

Make features available when they are ready. Have a state-of-the-art OS release every six months. This is such a common-sense approach! Too bad Microsoft will never be able to use it with Windows. Do you think they could convince anybody to buy a new version of Windows every six months?

The Product Family

Since Vista, one of the odd things about Microsoft Windows has been the number of different editions on offer. Windows Starter, Home Basic, Home Premium, Professional, Enterprise, Ultimate... the diversity seemed to be there just to confuse consumers.

But no, that wasn't the goal: it was there to make them pay more. Like a used car salesperson, they first tell you that it is cheap, based on the price of the Starter edition. And then, when you ask why you

---

[14] http://www.ubuntu.com/project/about-ubuntu

[15] There is plenty of information about timeboxing in the web—for example, here:
http://www.davecheong.com/2006/07/26/time-boxing-is-an-effective-getting-things-done-strategy/

can't do a certain thing, they say: "Oh, for that you need another edition, available for just a few more bucks." Suddenly you find yourself going up the editions stairway, "few bucks" after "few bucks," ending up having to pay quite a few hundred bucks for the whole experience.

Ubuntu Linux, too, comes in many different editions, but the rationale is quite different. First off, all editions of Ubuntu are free. Technically speaking, these are not different editions of Ubuntu, but derivatives. A *derivative* of Ubuntu means that some people packaged things differently to produce an OS targeted at a specific set of users. For example, some people find the KDE desktop environment more appealing than GNOME. So Canonical provided a new derivative of Ubuntu, which installs KDE by default instead of GNOME. There's nothing more to it than that. It's for simplicity's sake. To make your life easier. Linux for human beings, remember?

There are a lot of derivatives. Some are maintained by Canonical, and some are not. The most common are:

- *Ubuntu:* The well-known, GNOME-based OS.

- *Kubuntu:* Like Ubuntu but with the KDE desktop environment.

- *Edubuntu:* A special derivative loaded with applications for educational purposes.

- *Ubuntu Netbook Remix:* A special version, targeted at mini notebooks. The desktop is somewhat redesigned to fit smaller screens, and special care is taken to have it preloaded with web-enabling technologies such as the Flash plug-in.

But there are many others. There are Ubuntus for Christians and for Muslims, Ubuntus in Chinese and in Italian, Ubuntus for anthropologists and for designers. There is even an Ubuntu for Google employees, called Goobuntu. Because Ubuntu is a full desktop solution with a staggering number of applications, anyone can mix the ingredients the way he likes and share what he has done with the rest of the world.

Just to be clear: it is not that a derivative blocks some features the way Windows Starter does. It's just a customization. If you want KDE, for example, you can start with Ubuntu, install the required packages, and end up with the exact same desktop as you would have if you installed Kubuntu in the first place.

The Ubuntu Linux Community

One of the arguments Microsoft uses to try to scare you away from Linux is that you will have no support. That there's nobody "on the other side of the line" when you have a problem.

It's totally the other way around. Linux is much more than a computer OS. It's an entire community of users all over the globe. When you start to use Linux, you become part of this community (whether you like it or not—although you will!).

One of the benefits of membership is that you're never far from finding a solution to a problem. The community likes to congregate online around forums and newsgroups, which you can join in order to find help.

Your initial placement in the ranks of the community is "*newbie.*" This is a popular term for someone who is new to Linux. Although it may sound derisive, it actually helps when you talk to others. Advertising your newbie status encourages people to take the time to help you—after all, they were newbies once upon a time.

There is another reason not to be disheartened by your newbie tag: you'll outgrow it very quickly. By the time you reach the end of this book, you'll be on your way to the other end of the spectrum: guru. You'll be one of those giving out the advice to those newbies, and you'll be 100% confident in your skills.

But being part of a community is not just about getting free technical support. It's about sharing knowledge. Linux was created to be shared among those who want to use it. There are no restrictions, apart from one: any software changes you make and distribute must also be available to others.

The spirit of sharing and collaboration has been there since day one. One of the first things Linus Torvalds did when he produced an early version of the Linux kernel program was to ask for help from others. And he got it. Complete strangers e-mailed him offering to contribute their time, skills, and effort to help him with his project. This has been the way Linux has been developed ever since. Thousands of people around the world contribute their own small pieces, rather than one big company being in charge. And the same concept applies to Linux knowledge. When you learn something, don't be afraid to share this knowledge with others. "Giving something back" is an important part of the Linux community, and that doesn't mean just creating programs—people contribute artwork, documentation, and time to help others.

To understand why Linux is shared, it helps to understand its history, as well as the history of what came before it. You'll learn more about this in Chapter 2.

Praise for Ubuntu Linux

By now, you know a lot of reasons to begin using Ubuntu Linux. We'll wrap up the chapter by highlighting why is wise to stop using Windows and try Ubuntu Linux instead. Many of the topics touched on in this section have already been mentioned; now you have them all together in one place to help you argue with Windows die-hards.

Should I Stop Using Windows?

This question could be split into two smaller problems: why would I want to stop using Windows? And, is it a wise move? There are many reasons to stop using Windows, some of which are:

- *It is insecure:* Security is only a recent concern for Microsoft. And in spite of the many efforts the company claims it is making, new security flaws are detected each and every month, making "patch Tuesday" a nightmare for many system administrators. The lax security also necessitates expensive antivirus programs, which consume precious hardware resources.

- *It is expensive:* Although Windows often comes pre-installed on new computers, its cost is built into the computer price, and it may be in only a limited version. You have to pay more for the advanced versions, for upgrades when a new version is released, and for any additional software you want to install.

- *It is full of bugs:* In his 1999 essay "The Cathedral and the Bazaar," Eric S. Raymond, an open source advocate, stated Linus' Law that goes like this: "Given enough eyeballs, all bugs are shallow." This means that software is less likely to have bugs when more people can review its code. Microsoft Windows is closed source software, so only its own developers get to view the source code. When they overlook a bug, there is no way of detecting it until a problem actually happens. It is not that there are no bugs in open source software, but they are more likely to be found and corrected in a timely manner. You can try to find them yourself!

Now, is it wise to stop using Windows and start using Ubuntu? Let's answer some of the most common questions regarding the move to Ubuntu Linux:

- *I won't be able to run my applications!* This is true at some point, but it has three workarounds: first, you *can* use Windows applications with Wine, an implementation of the Windows API. Second, there are a lot of replacement applications that also happen to be free. And third, there is a strong tendency for applications to become web-based, so what's important then is the web browser, not the API.

11

- *I need to use Windows for my job!* There are plenty of workarounds if you really can't get away without using Windows from time to time. You could set up dual-booting and use both on one computer. You could use Ubuntu for your everyday tasks and Windows to keep yourself up-to-date with that technology, or you could install Windows in a virtual PC inside Ubuntu with VirtualBox.[16] This way you get the best of both worlds—but remember that you'll need a valid Windows license for either of those scenarios.

- *I will need to get help sometimes!* We have already mentioned the Linux community. Think about it this way: Microsoft has a monopoly over Windows support. Because its source code is closed, they are the only ones that can help you at certain problems. And they are often unwilling to do so, maybe because your product is no longer supported, or because "your problem will be resolved with the next service pack." And what would happen to your support if Microsoft went out of service?

There are many reasons to drop Windows, and there is no good reason to be afraid of doing so. It should be painless if you do it properly.

Ubuntu Linux and its Strengths

"Okay, so I should stop using Windows. Why should I start using Ubuntu and not another operating system?" you might ask. Because:

- *Ubuntu is the best Linux distribution for desktops:* It is Linux, which means it is stable and secure; it is derived from Debian, so it is free, open source, and has a lot of applications available; and it is Ubuntu, a distribution oriented to human beings.

- *It is beautiful:* The aesthetic aspects of the interface are well polished, so your friends will be really surprised by its looks! It is a "wow" operating system.

- *It will make your life easier:* A lot of work has already been done for you. Applications have been catalogued and published. The interface has been tweaked. Hardware has been made compatible. Communities have been formed. All this social capital is there for you to take advantage of it. Wouldn't it be foolish not to?

If we have convinced you to try Ubuntu Linux, let us be your guide on your first baby steps. On the journey, you will feel your strides growing stronger chapter after chapter. By the end of it, you should be able to stand by yourself and on your way to becoming a senior member of the community!

But first let us tell you some more about the history of Ubuntu Linux. That is the subject of Chapter 2, which completes Part I of this book.

Summary

In this Chapter, the first in the book, we introduced you to Ubuntu Linux and pointed out some of its salient features. You learned how it is an OS based on Linux and derived from Debian. We talked about how Ubuntu is developed and why are many different versions or editions, such as Kubuntu or Edubuntu. Finally, we analyzed reasons for making the change to Ubuntu Linux.

---

[16] http://www.virtualbox.org/wiki/VirtualBox

CHAPTER 2

■ ■ ■

GNU "slash" Linux

We talk in this chapter about some of the major driving forces behind Ubuntu Linux. Although it is a young operating system (OS), it has a history and a family to be proud of, because it is the heir of a tradition dating back to the late 1960s, and even before.

If, after reading Chapter 1, you started wondering, how could it all be free of charge? Where's Linux Corp. and how does it make a profit? Who are the members of the Linux community that answer my questions without expecting anything in return? If you are asking yourself those questions, then you should read this chapter.

UNIX

We start our history at a rather arbitrary point in time: the birth of UNIX in the late 1960s. Our rationale for doing so is quite straightforward: Linux is a UNIX-like OS, designed and written specifically with the aim of reproducing UNIX's core functionality.

UNIX is an extremely successful OS, originally developed in 1969 at Bell Labs, New Jersey, by a group of AT&T employees. Its creators, who included Ken Thompson, Dennis Ritchie, and Brian Kernighan, are ranked today as some of the most prominent personalities in computer history and are even idolized by some UNIX gurus. UNIX was, and still is, a very modern, portable, multi-tasking OS.

MS-UX?

Did you know that there was a Microsoft version of UNIX? In 1979, Microsoft acquired a license from AT&T and produced a derivative of UNIX for microcomputers. It was called Xenix, and for a time was the UNIX version with the largest installed base, piggybacking on the x86 processor success.

To produce Xenix, Microsoft worked with The Santa Cruz Operation, which later retained the rights and produced SCO UNIX. In recent years, this company has been actively fighting other UNIX and Linux manufacturers over the ownership of the rights to UNIX and related intellectual property issues. Several judicial proceedings are being held in the U.S. over those issues.

In the late 1970s and early 1980s, UNIX had a tremendous preeminence in academic circles. It was highly respected by computer scientists of the day and became the basis for many subsequent variants made by different companies. Operating systems such as HP-UX, Solaris, and IBM AIX were a result of those efforts.

The Rise of the IBM PC... and of Microsoft

In 1981 IBM introduced the IBM PC in an attempt to gain share in the microcomputer market. It was such a huge success that in the end it turned against its creator and undermined IBM's market dominance. What IBM did at the time was sharply at odds with its previous corporate culture. To shorten the development cycle, it chose to integrate components from different vendors instead of using proprietary components from IBM itself. It also published detailed documentation of the PC's internal architecture, so other companies were able to create their own expansion modules. There's nothing wrong with those practices, except when they clash with (or even undermine) your own business model.

One of those components was the CPU: IBM used the Intel 8088 microprocessor. This allowed other computer manufacturers to create compatible computers, collectively known as PC clones.

And there was also the operating system: MS-DOS, from Microsoft. Bill Gates and his company had a brilliant idea: instead of selling their OS to IBM, they only licensed it. They thus reserved their right to license the OS to other hardware makers—namely the ones that were already cloning the IBM PC.

So the only identifiable components that remained the same across all these computers were the processor and the OS. Eventually the "Wintel" duo (short for Windows and Intel) began replacing "IBM PC" as the brand of the new revolution. The dream of "a PC on every desktop" running Microsoft software spun off in a thousand directions from that point onwards.

Independence from any particular hardware provider and the freedom to license its OS to different manufacturers has been the foundation of Microsoft's success with Windows. The hardware and the OS evolved, from XT to Pentium, and from MS-DOS to Windows, but the underlying business model remained the same (with an ever-stronger arm to force deals as Windows became more popular). Microsoft became one of the most salient examples of a closed and proprietary software business model.

RMS on Free Software

Speaking out against the practice of proprietary and closed software was an MIT Lab programmer called Richard Matthew Stallman, or RMS as he prefers to be called.

Working at MIT labs, several episodes warned him about how proprietary and closed software was imposing severe limits to their users' freedoms. He believed that users should be free: free to create, to study, to use, to reproduce, to share, to modify, and to do with software what they wanted. The principles of free software were born.

Sometimes people get confused about what "free" means in this context. RMS has often explained that what he means by "free" is "free as in free speech," not "free as in free beer." That is, free software should not *necessarily* be given away for free, but it definitely should not limit in any way what the user can do with it.

He set himself the task of creating an OS and enough applications to make proprietary software unnecessary, in a collaborative project he called GNU. This is a recursive acronym (and programmer's in-joke) that means "GNU's Not Unix!" Although the goal was to make it UNIX-like, it was meant to be entirely free and rigorously excludes any UNIX code. The project was first announced on September, 1984, and started development a few months later.

They had to write the core of the OS, or kernel (which was given the name HURD), and a set of applications that reproduced the operation of UNIX. The latter part advanced swiftly, but development of the kernel stalled. It soon reached a point in which the only part missing from the free UNIX-like utopia was the kernel.

As part of his efforts, Stallman also created the Free Software Foundation, which, as its name implies, advocates for the use of free software.

RMS VS. BILL G

There are hardly two people more at odds than Richard Stallman and Bill Gates. A few anecdotes may help illustrate their different attitudes towards software and life in general. Here they are, the Harvard dropout and the MIT hacker, face to face:

- In 1975, Paul Allen and Bill Gates licensed a version of BASIC to the company MITS, for use with its newest creation, the Altair Computer. After seeing that computer sales were strong, but BASIC's were lagging, they discovered that many hobbyists from a club in Palo Alto were making illegal copies of the OS and installing it on their own. Bill Gates then wrote an infuriated letter in which he defended the right of software makers to earn profits by selling their products for a price. He asserted that widespread adoption of such software without proper payment would discourage developers from producing quality software. (Maybe if he opened the code to the hobbyists, the Altair BASIC would have improved from their collaboration!)

- In 1977, RMS was a programmer working at MIT's AI Laboratory. When the authorities tried to enforce password-protected access, Stallman convinced many users to set a blank password in order to re-enable anonymous access. He linked freedom to anonymity; today, he recommends not using a cellphone or a key card, so your movements cannot be tracked.

- In 1980, a new printer arrived at the AI Lab, and RMS requested access to its source code. He and some fellow hackers had successfully modified the code for the previous printer in order to enhance user experience. He was denied, and the printing with the new device was worse than with the previous one. That confirmed to him that people should have the right to access and modify the programs they use, in order to better them.

Copyleft

Two questions Richard Stallman had to answer when laying the foundation for free software development were whether it should be licensed and, if so, how.

There was a problem with the original idea of free software, a hole through which a malicious company could profit from the efforts of altruistic programmers. If a person, organization, or community writes an application and gives it away for free, making it part of the public domain and granting all rights in an unrestricted fashion, then what prevents a greedy user from registering the application under his name and trying to profit from the copyright? That type of practice had to be somehow avoided without limiting user freedom.

Something like that happened to RMS. He was asked to write an application; he agreed to do it and to make it public domain, and was later denied access to the modified version as updated by the same people who had requested it in the first place.

But he disliked the idea of copyright, because he thought it was inherently limiting. It gave an author excessive power over his work, letting him or her define what the user could or could not do with it. Copyright was not the solution for RMS. But somehow he had to play by the rules in order to avoid being deprived of the results of his work once again.

So he conceived the idea of "copyleft" as a special kind of copyright which imposes limits on one thing only: the right to prevent sharing. Works registered under copyleft licenses can be used, studied, shared, modified, and redistributed as anyone likes; but every modification or addition *must* be licensed under similar copyleft terms. That way everyone benefits from the work of others, even the original author. It's also called a "viral" license, because it is transmitted from person to person. No one has the right to prevent others from sharing the software.

Because copyleft granted users the right to modify the work, an important side effect was that the source code had to be released together with the application.

Stallman decided that a copyleft type of license was ideal for the GNU project and so created the GNU Public License, or GPL. Today, much of the work from the open source community is licensed under the GPL or other licenses inspired by the same concepts.

The Quest for a UNIX-like Operating System

Richard Stallman was not the only one with the idea of making a UNIX-like operating system. In fact, in the 1980s the technical superiority of UNIX was widely recognized, so everyone expected it to become the dominant force in the PC market recently created by IBM and its clones.

But that wasn't happening. Disputes over copyright issues spread among UNIX companies in what became known as the "UNIX wars." The HURD (the kernel of the GNU project, remember?) was nowhere near finished (even today there is still no stable release). And MS-DOS continued to gain popularity, a Microsoft trend that later intensified with the graphical interface of Windows.

As an exception, from the BSD version on, UNIX spawned a little derivative that today, after years of evolution, is giving Microsoft people more than one headache: the Mac OS. That's right: the sleek operating system from Apple (now in the version Mac OS X) shares a foundation with Linux as a UNIX-like operating system.[1]

Meanwhile, in the Netherlands, a computer science professor named Andrew Tanenbaum was writing a classic book called *Operating Systems: Design and Implementation.* He decided that for it to be more didactic, the book should be accompanied by a complete operating system, including its source code. The result of this work was MINIX, short for "minimal UNIX." It was developed for compatibility with the IBM PC models available at the time and included a kernel (the core of the OS, remember), a memory manager, and a file system—pretty much the most important components of any OS. The book became very popular, and MINIX became the learning tool of many students worldwide. Linus Torvalds was one of them.

Linus Torvalds and His Little Project

In 1991 Linus Torvalds was a student at the University of Helsinki, Finland, when he purchased an Intel 80386-based IBM PC, which he intended to use as a terminal emulator for remotely connecting to the University's lab.

The main choices at that time for a PC operating system were MS-DOS and MINIX. He was rapidly disappointed with MS-DOS, and given his respect for UNIX and his willingness to learn, his choice was the latter. But his dissatisfaction with some technical aspects of MINIX encouraged him to create his terminal emulator from scratch, although based on MINIX. He also wanted his version to be noncommercial, which MINIX, although inexpensive, was not. The terminal emulator soon evolved into a full OS kernel he first called "Freax" (a combination of "free," "freak," and the "X" that identified it as a

---

[1] As we are writing this, Apple's market cap just surpassed Microsoft's: http://gizmodo.com/5548460/apple-is-now-bigger-than-microsoft-the-most-valuable-tech-company-in-the-world

UNIX-like system), but in the end "Linux" (yes, standing for "Linus") became popular because that's how a friend named the folder in which the files were stored and shared.

Torvalds then decided he wanted his OS to do more things, but he needed outside collaboration so he didn't have to do all the hard work. It was due to a bit of laziness that he posted a message to the MINIX user group which started with the less-than-visionary statement: *"I'm doing a (free) operating system (just a hobby, won't be big and professional like gnu) for 386(486) AT clones."*

LINUX 0.01

The first version of Linux, dubbed Linux 0.01, was extremely limited. It only ran on AT 386 machines and even then only a small subset of the hardware worked. Because for a long time he was a lonely coder hiding from the Finnish winter, it was as though the hardware required for making Linux work was... Linus Torvalds' own PC! Even having a Finnish keyboard was recommended.[2]

What followed was his "accidental revolution." Soon more and more developers were following his lead in the development of the Linux kernel, starting what is now considered the most important collaborative effort in computing history. He even had a fierce debate with Andrew Tanenbaum, who declared in the same user group that "Linux is obsolete" as early as 1992. In the end, of course, Linus prevailed.

Today, Linus Torvalds lives with his wife Tove and their three daughters in California, supervising the Linux kernel development and directing The Linux Foundation, a not-for-profit organization sponsored by individuals and companies that advocate the use of free software and Linux in particular. He is seen by the community as their leader, and is often called the "benevolent dictator of planet Linux," even though he likes to describe his own position as the "hood ornament" of Linux.

GNU "slash" Linux

But Linux wasn't a complete OS. It was just a kernel, unable to do anything useful without programs running in top of it.

So Linux was in search of programs already available for free that emulated the working environment of a UNIX-like computer... which was exactly what the GNU project was producing. Meanwhile the GNU project was struggling to develop a free, open source, UNIX-like kernel... which was exactly what Linus Torvalds and his crew were doing. So a perfect match was found.

It is not that both teams merged into one. The GNU project continued with its development of the HURD. It's just that for practical purposes, if one person wanted to have a complete OS, he needed both parts: the Linux kernel and the GNU applications.

That was the origin of a very fruitful relationship between Linux and GNU. Today many free software advocates call the OS by the full name GNU/Linux (pronounced "GNU slash Linux"). Richard Stallman even proposed the name "Lignux" one time. It you ever come across a discussion as to whether the OS should be called "Linux" or "GNU/Linux," you should know that the latter name is defended by the followers of Richard Stallman who think his applications are as important as the kernel itself.

---

[2] http://www.kernel.org/pub/linux/kernel/Historic/old-versions/RELNOTES-0.01

The Linux Diaspora

For a Linux newbie, one of the most disorienting aspects is: why are there so many versions? You just want to use Linux, but which one? Linux itself seems to be nowhere—all there are to be found are distributions.

That is quite true, but the real question you should be asking yourself is: what do I want to do with Linux? Anwer that question, and the perfect distribution (or at least a short list of them) should emerge naturally.

Distributions appeared at first as a way to make Linux installation easy by integrating all the required software plus additional applications that made that distribution unique. There were some original distributions, and then many that spawned from there in order to achieve a particular goal, and this makes Linux history resemble a tree-like structure. There are commercial distributions, sponsored by companies that sell services associated with their products, and there are completely free distributions. There are even free distributions that are almost 100% copies of commercial distributions! Thus Linux is a never-ending story, like human history, because there will always be new objectives and goals. This dispersion is not a liability for Linux, but one of its major strengths: you'll always have a distribution that matches your exact needs... and if not, you can create your own!

WHAT ABOUT THE PENGUIN?

The penguin is the official mascot of the Linux kernel and was suggested by Linus Torvalds himself. He had quite a fixation with penguins, and even claimed to have been bitten by one in Australia, which caused, according to him, dreams of penguins for several days.

In 1996, Torvalds said the mascot should be a penguin—a contented penguin with its stomach stuffed with herring and about to burp. He used the words "cuddly" and "cute" to describe what he was thinking. He preferred that Linux be associated with a cute little animal instead of a ferocious one, because he wasn't in the arena to fight but to have fun and making a great OS.

The idea of having an animal as a mascot, he also reasoned, gave people freedom to change the logo while retaining the link nonetheless. This proved to be true. We have today a lot of variations of the penguin that still makes us think of Linux.

The penguin's name is Tux, which can be explained as meaning (T)orvalds (U)ni(X), and as a reference of the tuxedos penguins seem to be wearing.

Table 2-1 lists some (but by no means all) of the most popular Linux distributions in use today.

Table 2-1. *Linux Distributions*

Distro	Brief Description
Slackware	One of the first Linux distributions and the oldest in active maintenance, which intends to keep its design simple often to the detriment of its usability. First released in 1993.
Debian	A free Linux distribution that emphasizes the principles of free software and collaborative development through the Debian Constitution and a Social Contract. Debian is released with access to a load of free applications available online. It was created by Ian Murdoch in 1993, the name being a combination of Debra, the name of his girlfriend, and his own.
SuSE Linux	A Linux distribution based originally on Slackware and created by four German students in 1994. It is very popular in Europe and in academic circles. In 2004 it was acquired by Novell and later divided into a free and developmental version (openSuSE), and two commercial ones (SuSE Linux Enterprise Server and SuSE Linux Enterprise Desktop). Novell has an interoperability agreement with Microsoft (which is a source of a lot of scorn towards SuSE in the free software community) and leads several projects that aim at being friendly with Windows shops (such as the Mono project or the Evolution mail and calendar client).
Red Hat	One of the first and most popular commercial versions of Linux. First launched in 1994, Red Hat gave Linus Torvalds shares of stock when it went public, allowing him to make a small fortune (he hadn't profited much from Linux before). In 2003 it spawned the Fedora project to take advantage of external and community developers instead of relying exclusively from internal programmers. It now sponsors both a free distribution, Fedora, and Red Hat Enterprise Linux, available only through a subscription.
Mandriva	A French distribution, derived from Red Hat and formerly known as Mandrake Linux. Is very popular in France and focuses on ease of use.
CentOS	CentOS is a distribution based almost exclusively on Red Hat Enterprise Linux. As the source code of that OS is entirely available for free, it can be packaged to create another distribution, and that's what CentOS does after stripping it of Red Hat branding and logos. Even its version schema exactly follows that of Red Hat.
Ubuntu	A distribution based on Debian and the main focus of this book. It has also some derivatives like Kubuntu (that uses KDE instead of GNOME), Edubuntu (for the academic public), and even Goobuntu, a version developed by Google employees for internal use in the company. It was first launched in 2004 and is maintained by Canonical, a UK-based company.
Chrome OS	An OS developed by Google which is designed to work only with web applications. Based on Linux and launched in 2010, it runs only on specialized hardware.

Open Source

Open source is a concept often associated with Linux and free software.

Linux is an open source project, which means that its source code is available for anyone to see. That's different from, say, Microsoft's development model, which is *closed source.* Microsoft's source code is not widely available, and if you're granted access to it (if you are, for example, a partner), you have to sign a nondisclosure agreement. Linux is also free and licensed under the GPL.

Open source as a development practice has a lot of advantages over closed source. One of them is what is known as Linus' Law: "Given enough eyeballs, all bugs are shallow." If source code is open, everybody can see it, and thus errors have more chances of being detected and corrected in a timely fashion.

There are currently many open source projects that, although they run on top of other operating systems besides Linux, are mostly associated with it. Some examples can be found in Table 2-2.

Table 2-2. *Free and Open Source Software*

Application	Brief Description
Apache	A free and open source web server maintained by the Apache Software Foundation, it serves the majority of web sites on the Internet today.
MySQL	A free and open source relational database now owned by Oracle (after the purchase of Sun Microsystems, its former owner). MySQL is used in conjunction with Apache and programming languages such as Python, PHP, and Perl to create powerful web sites. This bundle is commonly called LAMP (Linux, Apache, MySQL, and the programming language, which all start with P).
OpenOffice.org	A free and open source office productivity suite, with a word processor (Write), a spreadsheet (Calc), a database (Base), a presentation software (Impress), a vector graphic editor (Draw), and a tool for creating and editing mathematical formulas. It is sponsored by Sun Microsystems (now owned by Oracle), which also also sells a "pro" version called StarOffice, with more functionality.

Some years ago, the open source concept became more institutional and often collides with that of free software, at least in the heads of their leaders. In 1998, the Open Source Initiative (OSI) was founded with the aim of making this family of software more appealing to commercial organizations, which may be scared by the concept of software being free. The open source model of development, the founders thought, had its own merits, whether the software produced was free or not. OSI tries to sell the business case for open source as a pragmatic solution, without the moral philosophy entanglement of free software.

But the two concepts are often linked, giving rise to the acronyms FOSS ("Free and Open Source Software") and FLOSS (the "L" from *libre,* Spanish for "free").

The South African Factor

At the time of this writing, recent events have put the Republic of South Africa in the spotlight. In 2010, the World Cup, one of the most prestigious and popular sports championships in the world, is taking place in South Africa. Clint Eastwood's 2010 movie *Invictus* depicts some turning points in recent South

African history. *District 9*, another motion picture, directed by South African director Neill Blomkamp, takes place in an alternate reality of a Johannesburg hosting a race of extraterrestrial refugees.

And then there is Mark Shuttleworth. After earning half a billion dollars in the late 1990s and traveling to space, Mark Shuttleworth, a young South African entrepreneur, found himself with a lot of money in his pockets and in search of a cause.

He found it in Linux and the free software promise. Mark had been a Debian programmer in the 1990s, but this time his mission was somewhat different and more ambitious: he envisioned a world in which the PC market was upside down. Instead of users having to pay for the OS, as people do with Windows, he wanted it to be possible and sustainable to give the OS away for free and profit from services such as consulting, customization, and support. He thought that Linux was an already mature platform and a perfect fit for this business model. And he aimed at the heart of Microsoft: the desktop computer. But, unlike many others, he understood that for users to massively embrace his product, it would not only have to be free, but also exciting, easy to use, and complete. There had to be a "wow" factor in place for his plan to succeed.

The name *Ubuntu* was a perfect choice to reflect both free software principles and South Africa's cultural heritage. *Ubuntu* (pronounced "oo-BOON-too") is a Bantu word with synonyms in many other African languages. Although it has been described as too beautiful to be translated into English, the word reflects the idea that you only became truly human through other human beings. There is a Zulu saying that goes: *umuntu ngumuntu ngabantu* ("a person is a person through (other) persons"). It has also been defined as "humanity through others." By emphasizing fraternal bonds between human beings, the name Ubuntu takes free software principles one step further, connecting it to a broader humanistic view of the world. It is not just that open source software is better programmed, or that an individual has the right to use the software as he likes: it sees humanity as a collective endeavor that will only attain its goal if we treat our fellow humans as companions on a trip instead of just customers or providers. Ubuntu the OS attempts to be a means by which *ubuntu* the philosophy can thrive. Mark Shuttleworth believes that if Ubuntu succeeds, he really will be changing the world. It's not a small goal he set for himself!

Mark then founded Canonical Ltd., the UK-based company behind Ubuntu, in 2004, with initial funding of $10 million. He believes Ubuntu will grow to be a sustainable business over the years, and not just the whim of a billionaire. Its revenue, Shuttleworth disclosed in an interview a couple of years ago, was $30 million a year. Still far from the billions Microsoft earns by selling Windows, but pretty good for a company that gives away its main product!

The Year of the Linux Desktop

There is an old, so-far-unfulfilled prophecy about "the Year of the Linux Desktop." Many have predicted that Linux would eventually replace Windows as the de-facto desktop OS, but so far it hasn't happened.

Might things be changing? Could the long-awaited "Year" finally be here?

We're not about to do any prophecy. We don't know. But then again, Linux is not about market share, but just plain sharing. To share, say, an apple with you means giving it to you. You can eat it, give it away, or store it for later use. That's what sharing means; otherwise something is expected in return. Proprietary software makers want you to take the apple, pay for it in advance, feel that you need to eat the apple right away, and then sell you a knife to peel it (and it's even better if only *their* knife works with that particular apple). They polish the apple and put a sticker over the worm hole so you don't see it until it's too late. Their revenues derive from this method.

The aim of this book is not to follow the "Year of the Linux Desktop" hype, but to tell you that you can make the personal choice of opting for Ubuntu Linux and its application stack without fear, and even with some hope.

Having said that, there are a few signs that this might be, really, the "Year of the Linux Desktop"! We mention in Chapter 1 that trends in the desktop computing market can lead one to think that the very foundation on which the Microsoft Windows success story is based might be shaking right now, among them the emergence of web-based applications and the "good enough" revolution in hardware.

Microsoft's mission of battling piracy can also be a force driving Ubuntu Linux adoption. Believe it or not, on desktops, the second most installed OS behind legitimate copies of Microsoft Windows is... illegal copies of Microsoft Windows. But if Microsoft increases its pressure on pirates (as it's already doing), people might turn to free alternatives rather than keep paying for Windows. And if more users turn to Linux, anything could happen. With only 1% of the market share for desktop computers, the Linux community produced something as good as Ubuntu; it's difficult to imagine where the limit will be if that figure increases.

Ubuntu is now a mature desktop OS in its 12th release, and it is reportedly being used by more than 12 million users worldwide.[3] That makes it the most popular Linux distribution for desktops; in fact, it has been chosen as distribution of the year many times. Red Hat and Novell, with Red Hat Enterprise Linux Desktop and SUSE Linux respectively, are aiming at the corporate market and have made some advances there that push forward the overall Linux community.

There might never be a "Year of the Linux Desktop." There might be, after Microsoft Windows, another "big thing" that changes the landscape and poses a new challenge to Linux. But Ubuntu and Linux have already been successful in raising the bar when it comes to what we expect to receive for each dollar we spend in software.

Summary

This chapter closes the introductory part of the book. We've discussed the history of Ubuntu, starting from the creation of UNIX in the 1970s, to the rise of IBM PC and Microsoft's DOS in the 1980s, and gone from the initial call for collaboration from Linus Torvalds to the reality of free and open source software that is Ubuntu.

Along the way we met characters such as Richard Stallman and Linus Torvalds, the founding fathers of the GNU/Linux OS. We also reviewed the concepts of copyleft, free software, and open source, which are part of understanding the world of Linux and Ubuntu.

---

[3] http://www.internetnews.com/dev-news/article.php/3875296/Ubuntu-Preps-Lucid-Lynx-Hits-12M-Users.htm

■ ■ ■

## PART 2

Installing Ubuntu

CHAPTER 3

■ ■ ■

Pre-installation

Now that you know a bit about where Ubu...
want to use it, it's time to get Ubuntu runn...
included with this book. Most computers...
Windows themselves. They have no need...
Windows pre-installed. By contrast, it's r...
any other flavor of Linux on them. There...
supplies excellent hardware to customer...
And even Dell has been known to offer U...
inexpensive Inspiron Mini 10 netbook.

But for most of us, getting Ubuntu means installing...
prospect if you haven't done it before. However, Ubuntu makes this job as easy...
installation routines are very advanced compared to previous versions of Linux and even compared to
other current distributions.

What does saying that you're going to install Ubuntu actually mean? It involves three things:

- Somehow, all the files necessary to run Ubuntu are going to be put onto your hard
  disk.

- The PC will be configured so that it knows where to find these files when it first
  boots up.

- The Ubuntu operating system will be set up so that you can use it.

However, in order to do all this and get Ubuntu onto your PC, you must undertake some
preparatory work, which is the focus of this chapter.

Understanding Partitioning

Chances are your PC already has Windows installed on it. This won't present a problem. In most cases,
Ubuntu can live happily alongside Windows in what's called a *dual-boot setup*, which enables you to
choose which operating system to run at your computer's startup. However, installing Ubuntu means
that Windows must make certain compromises. Windows is forced to cohabit on your hard disk with
another OS—something it isn't designed to do.

■ **Note** Even if you intend to install Ubuntu on a completely blank hard disk, it's still important that you
understand partitioning.

---

is that Windows needs to shrink and make some space
a second hard disk, which is discussed later in this chapter). In
separately defined part of the disk, which is referred to as a
automatically by the Ubuntu installation routine, but it's important
hat you know what to do in the unlikely event of anything going wrong.

stall Ubuntu within the Windows file system too, as an alternative to dual-booting. That's

disks are split into partitions, which are large chunks of the disk created to hold operating
nd data (just as a large farm is partitioned into separate fields). A partition is usually multiple
es in size, although it can be smaller.

■ **Note** If you use a Macintosh, don't feel left out! The next chapter includes a sidebar explaining the options for installing Ubuntu on your Mac.

You can view your disk's partitions by using the Disk Management tool in Windows XP, 2000, Vista, and 7, as shown in Figure 3-1. You can access this tool by right-clicking Computer in the Windows Start menu and selecting Manage. This brings up the Computer Management window, where you will find Disk Management under Storage.

Most desktop PC systems have just one partition, unless the user has specifically created additional partitions. As mentioned, Ubuntu needs a partition of its own. During installation, Ubuntu needs to shrink the main Windows partition and create two new partitions: one for the operating system itself, and an extra one to hold the swap file.

In addition, the Ubuntu installation routine writes a new boot sector (also known as a *boot loader*). The *boot sector* is located at the very beginning of the disk and contains a small program that then runs another program that lets you choose between operating systems (and therefore partitions) when you first boot up.

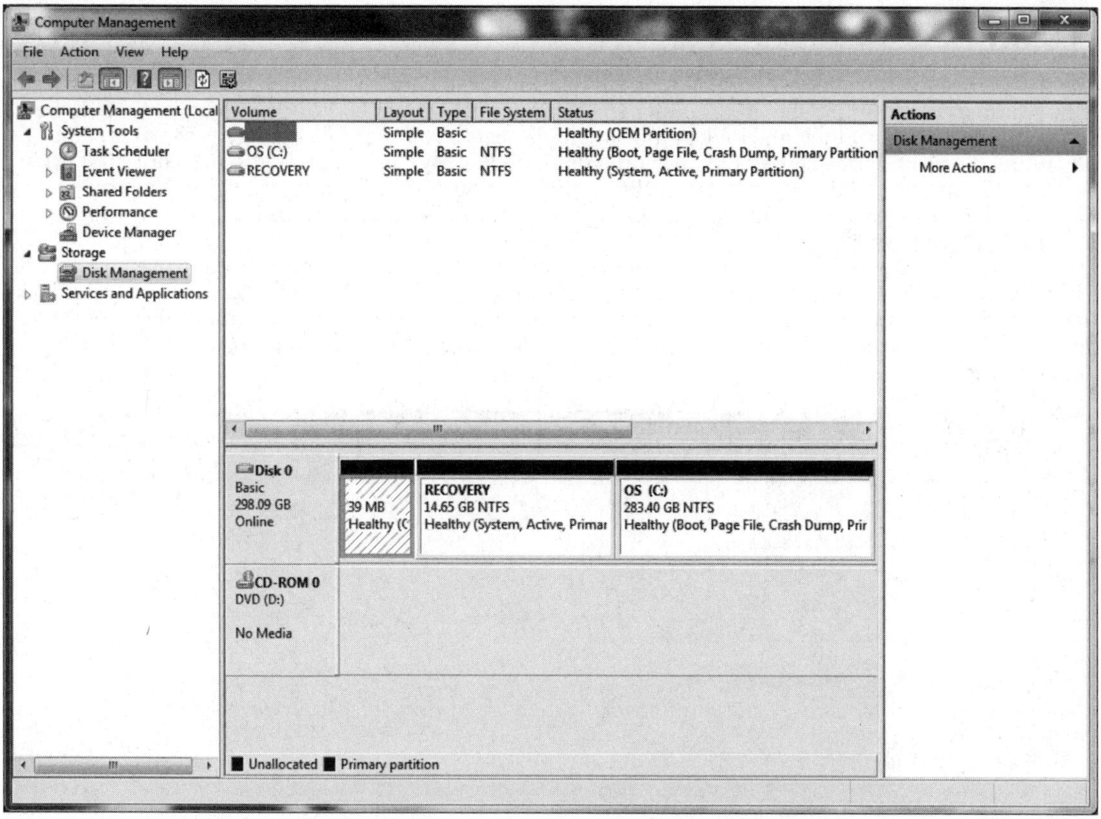

Figure 3-1. You can view your disk's partitions by using Windows' Disk Management tool.

■ **Note** Partitioning a laptop for dual-booting can present some tricky decisions. Manufacturers often create multi-partition setups including a recovery partition to make it very easy to reset Windows to factory defaults. It's tempting to delete this recovery partition and devote the space to Linux. If you decide to do this, make sure you have a full set of Windows recovery disks before you start!

Of course, Ubuntu cannot shrink a Windows partition that is packed full of data, because no space is available for it to reclaim. Therefore, one of the first preparatory steps is to ensure that enough space is free.

Freeing Up Space

The first step before installing Ubuntu alongside Windows is to check how much free space you have in your Windows partition. To see the amount of free space you have under Windows Vista or 7, click the Start button, click Computer, and look at the bar graph next to your hard disk drive, as shown in Figure 3-2. With older versions of Windows, you should double-click My Computer, right-click your boot drive, and select Properties. The free space is usually indicated in purple on a pie chart.

In both cases, look for how much free space you have. In Windows Vista and 7, this is the first figure underneath the bar graph.

You need to have at least 3GB of free space in your Windows partition for Ubuntu to use, but 3GB is a bare minimum and should be considered only if you have no other choice (that is, your computer lacks free disk space). You'll need more space than that if you wish to install a lot of programs. If you don't have enough free space, you have several options: reclaim space, remove Windows, or use a second hard disk.

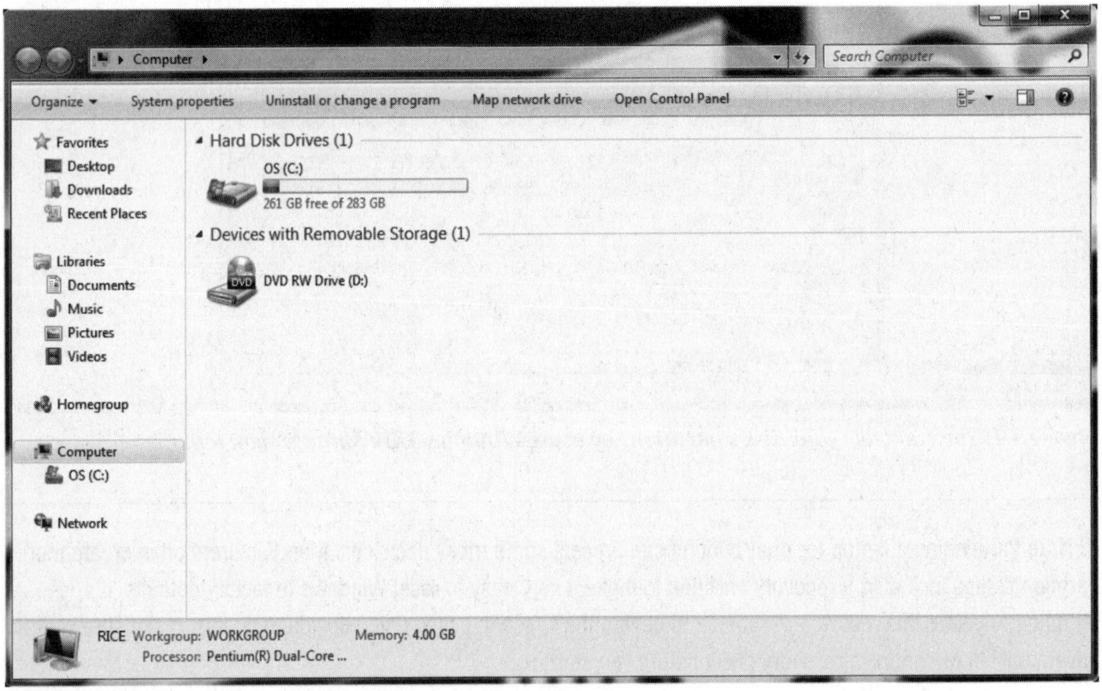

Figure 3-2. Ubuntu needs free disk space in which to install, so you might need to clean up your Windows partition.

Reclaiming Space

In Windows 7, Vista, and XP, you can run the Disk Cleanup tool to free some space on your hard disk. Under Windows 7 and Vista, click Start ➤ Computer and right-click the icon representing your hard disk. Select Properties from the menu that appears and then click the Disk Cleanup button. On Windows XP, click the Disk Cleanup button beneath the pie chart showing the free disk space. Disk Cleanup is also accessible by clicking Start ➤ All Programs ➤ Accessories ➤ System Tools ➤ Disk Cleanup.

You might also consider turning off System Restore. This consumes a lot of disk space, which you can reclaim. However, deactivating System Restore means you lose the possibility of returning your system to a previous state should anything go wrong (although you can always manually back up your data, of course). To access System Restore under Windows 7 and Vista, click the Start button and then right-click Computer in the menu. Select Properties and click the System Protection link on the left of the window that appears. In Windows 7, select the drive (usually C:) for which you want to deactivate System Restore and click Configure. Select Turn Off System Protection in the window which appears, and confirm your change by clicking OK here and in the underlying System Protection window. In Windows Vista, remove the check alongside the drives under the Available Disk list, confirm that you want to turn off System Restore, and click the OK button on the System Properties dialog box. Under Windows XP, right-click My Computer, click Properties, and then click the System Restore tab. Next, put a check alongside Turn Off System Restore on All Drives, and click OK.

If you still cannot free up enough disk space, consider uninstalling unused software via the Add/Remove Programs applet within Control Panel. If you have any large games installed, consider removing them first, because they usually take up substantial amounts of hard disk space. You might also consider deleting movie and MP3 music files, which are renowned for eating up hard disk space. The average MP3 is around 4MB, for example, and one minute of video typically takes up 10MB of disk space!

Removing Windows

Some users might prefer a second, more radical option: getting rid of Windows completely and letting Ubuntu take over the entire hard disk. If you feel confident that Ubuntu will fulfill your needs, this is undoubtedly the most straightforward solution. You'll be able to do this during installation. However, this will also mean that any personal data you have will be lost, so you should first back up your data (as described shortly).

■ **Caution** You should be aware that installing Windows back onto a hard disk that has Ubuntu on it is troublesome. Windows has a Darwinian desire to wipe out the competition. If you attempt to install Windows on an Ubuntu hard disk, it will overwrite Linux.

Using Another Hard Disk

A third option for making room for Ubuntu is attractive and somewhat safer in terms of avoiding the potential for data loss: fitting a second hard disk to your PC. You can then install Ubuntu on this other hard disk, letting it take up the entire disk. Unlike some versions of Windows, Ubuntu doesn't need to be installed on the primary hard disk and is happy on a secondary drive.

A second hard disk is perhaps the best solution if you're low on disk space and want to retain Windows on your system. However, you'll need to know how to install the new drive or find someone to do it for you (although step-by-step guides can be found on the Web—just search using Google or another search engine). In addition, if your PC is less than 12 months old, you could invalidate your warranty by opening up your PC.

If you have an old PC lying around, you might also consider installing Ubuntu on it, at least until you're sure that you want to run it on your main PC.

VIRTUALIZATION

If you don't want to repartition your disk or add another disk drive, there's another way you can run Ubuntu under Windows: using virtualization software.

Put simply, *virtualization* software lets you run a "computer within a computer" (or, in fact, several computers within a computer!). It does this by cleverly sharing system resources between the real computer and the one that's being virtualized in software.

When the virtualization software is run, the virtual computer appears in a program window. A BIOS-like startup screen appears, just as on a real computer, and then the virtual hard disk (usually a file on the main hard disk) is booted. An operating system may then be installed onto the virtual hard disk or, alternatively, it's possible to download entire virtual machines from various sites, for which the hard work of installing the operating system has been done for you!

There are a wide variety of virtualization software packages available, both proprietary and freely available open source. Undoubtedly the best open source rendition is VirtualBox (www.virtualbox.org), which is sponsored by database giant Oracle. Perhaps the best proprietary packages are those offered by VMware, including VMware Server and VMware Player. Both products are entirely free of charge and can be downloaded from www.vmware.com. Another version of VMware, called Workstation, which is available for a charge, is also highly praised by many.

Also popular with many is QEMU (www.nongnu.org/qemu/), although it doesn't quite offer the performance of the software already mentioned. However, should you decide to give it a try, also worth downloading is QEMU Manager, which provides a GUI-based configuration front end for QEMU: see www.davereyn.co.uk/download.htm.

If you have an Apple computer, you'll also be able to run Ubuntu virtually, using the open source choices of VirtualBox and QEMU, or the paid-for proprietary options of VMware Fusion and Parallels Desktop. Software developers who need to test their work on all three major operating systems often run Linux and Windows virtualized on OS X, partly because Apple hardware is very powerful and therefore capable of running virtual machines with ease, and partly because Apple makes it technically and legally difficult to virtualize Mac OS X on non-Apple hardware.

Using a virtualized computer is a great way to try out Ubuntu before you commit yourself to anything more drastic, but you have to be aware of the drawbacks as well. Operating systems running within virtual computers tend to operate more slowly compared to running natively on a computer, and the virtualized hardware is often very simple (virtual machines have only recently gained the ability to access your computer's 3D graphics hardware, for example). Setting up a virtual computer can be difficult for those who are new to it, and you'll require a powerful PC with at least 2GB of memory (and more like 3–4GB for optimum results).

One final note: virtualization software is also available for Ubuntu, which means you could install and run Windows within a virtual machine running on Ubuntu. This is an excellent way to go if you still need access to a few legacy Windows programs. QEMU, mentioned previously, runs on Ubuntu, as does VirtualBox and the various VMware products.

Backing Up Your Data

Whichever route you decide to take when installing Ubuntu, you should back up the data currently on your computer beforehand. Possibly the easiest way of doing this is to burn the data to recordable CD or DVD discs by using a program such as Nero or Infrarecorder and a CD-R/RW or DVD-R/RW drive.

If you take the coexistence route, installing Ubuntu alongside Windows, you should back up your data anyway for insurance purposes. Although the people behind Ubuntu test all their software thoroughly and rely on community reporting of bugs, there's always the chance that something out of your control will go wrong. Repartitioning a hard disk is a major operation and carries with it the potential for data loss.

If you intend to erase the hard disk when installing Ubuntu (thereby removing Windows), you can back up your data and then import it into Ubuntu.

Table 3-1 shows a list of common personal data file types, their file extensions, where they can be typically found on a Windows system, and notes on importing the data into Ubuntu. Note that earlier versions of Windows (95, 98, and Me) may differ when it comes to data storage locations.

Table 3-1. *Data That Should Be Backed Up*

Type of File	File Extensions	Typical Location (Windows 7)	Typical Location (XP)	Notes
Office files	.doc, .docx,.xls, .xlsx, .ppt, .pdf, etc.	\Users\ <username>\ Documents	\Documents and Settings\ <username>\ My Documents	Microsoft Office files can be opened, edited, and saved under Ubuntu using the OpenOffice.org suite. PDF documents can be viewed with the Evince program.
E-mail files	N/A	N/A	N/A	The Evolution mail client used by Ubuntu cannot import data directly from Microsoft Outlook or Outlook Express. However, there is a convoluted but effective workaround, described in the next section.
Digital images	.jpg, .bmp, .tif, .png, .gif, etc.	\Users\ <username>\ Pictures	\Documents and Settings\ <username>\ My Pictures	Ubuntu includes a variety of programs to catalog, view, and edit image files.
Multimedia files	.mp3 , .mpg , .avi , .wma , etc.	Various within Documents	Various within \ My Documents	With some additional downloads, programs under Ubuntu can play most audio and movie file formats.

Type of File	File Extensions	Typical Location (Windows 7)	Typical Location (XP)	Notes
Internet Explorer Favorites	None	\Users\ <username>\ Favorites	\Documents and Settings\ <username>\ Favorites	Your Favorites list cannot be imported into Ubuntu, but the individual files can be opened in a text editor in order to view their URLs, which can then be opened in the Ubuntu web browser. Better still, install Firefox, have it import your favorites, and then follow the instructions in the next table item.
Mozilla Firefox Bookmarks	.html	N/A	N/A	If you use Mozilla Firefox under Windows, you can manually export your bookmarks for import under Firefox when Ubuntu is installed. Click Bookmarks ➤ Organize Bookmarks, click the Import and Backup button on the toolbar of the window that appears, and then select the Backup option from the menu that appears. To import the bookmarks into Ubuntu's version of Firefox, repeat the steps, but click the Restore ➤ Choose File option on the menu instead and then locate the .html file you saved. Alternatively, take advantage of Firefox's new syncing capability by setting up a Mozilla Weave account in Preferences. This can be used to securely share your bookmarks, passwords, and more between copies of Firefox running on any system anywhere.
Miscellaneous Internet files	Various	Various	Various	You might also want to back up web site archives or instant messenger chat logs, although hidden data such as cookies cannot be imported.

Backing Up E-Mail Files

Microsoft e-mail cannot be easily imported into Ubuntu. Most e-mail programs use the MBOX format, and this is true of Ubuntu as well as programs created by the Mozilla Foundation (the organization behind the Firefox web browser). However, Microsoft uses its own DBX file format for Outlook Express and PST format for Outlook.

As a workaround, you can download and install the free Mozilla Thunderbird e-mail client (available from www.getthunderbird.com) on your Windows system. In Thunderbird, choose Tools ➤ Import to import your messages and contacts from Outlook, Outlook Express, or even the popular Eudora mail client. You will then be able to back up Thunderbird's mail files and import them into Evolution under Ubuntu, as described in Chapter 14.

To find where the mail files are stored, in Thunderbird choose Tools ➤ Account Settings, and then look in the Local Directory box. Back up each file that corresponds to a folder within your mail program (for example, Inbox, Sent, and so on). Note that you need to back up only the files without file extensions. You can ignore the .sdb folders as well as the .msf files.

■ **Tip** To quickly go to the location of the Thunderbird e-mail files under Windows, copy the address in the Local Directory text box. Then, under Windows XP, click Start ➤ Run, paste the address straight into the Open box, and click OK. Under Windows Vista or 7, paste the address into the Start Search text box and press Enter. Bear in mind that some of the folders are classified as system folders and are therefore hidden. You will need to activate the View Hidden Files option within My Computer.

Making Notes

When you're backing up data, a pencil and paper come in handy too. You should write down any important usernames and passwords, such as those for your e-mail account and other online services.

In addition, don't forget to jot down essential technical details, such as your IP address if you are part of a network of computers using static addresses (this will usually be relevant only if you work in an office environment).

■ **Tip** If you've forgotten any passwords, several freeware/shareware applications are able to "decode" the asterisks that obscure Windows passwords and show what's beneath them. A good example is Asterisk Password Reveal, which you can download from www.paqtool.com/product/pass/pass_001.htm. Shareware sites like www.download.com offer similar applications.

Note that you don't need to write down information such as hardware addresses, because hardware is configured automatically by Ubuntu. Howe making a note of the make and model of some items of internal hardware, s and sound card. This will help if Ubuntu is unable to automatically detect y a situation is fairly unlikely to arise. Under Windows Vista and 7, you can fin clicking the Start button and right-clicking Computer. Click Properties in the

...r link on the left of the window that appears. Under Windows XP, right-click My
...op (or on your Start menu), select Properties, and click the Hardware tab. Then
...er button.

...everything down, you might consider taking a screenshot by pressing the Print
...your favorite image editor to print it.

...with a wide variety of hardware, and in most cases, it will automatically detect your system
components. ...re in any doubt, you can consult the forums at http://ubuntuforums.org—in particular, the
Hardware Help forums under the Main Support Categories heading. You might also consider subscribing to one or
more of the Ubuntu mailing lists at https://lists.ubuntu.com. Remember that an important element of Ubuntu
is its community of users, many of whom will be very willing to answer any questions you might have!

When you're certain that all your data is backed up, you can move on to the next chapter, which
provides a step-by-step guide to installing the operating system.

Summary

The aim of this chapter has been to prepare both you and your computer for the installation of Ubuntu.
You've looked at how your hard disk will be partitioned prior to installation and the preparations you
should make to ensure that your hard disk has sufficient free space. You also learned about the types of
files you might choose to back up, in addition to vital details you should record, such as usernames and
passwords for your online accounts.

In the next chapter, we move on to a full description of the Ubuntu installation procedure. The
chapter guides you through getting Ubuntu onto your computer.

CHAPTER 4

■ ■ ■

Installing Ubuntu

It's now time to install Ubuntu. In the dim and distant past, installation was sometimes difficult, but the developers now have it down to a fine art, so it should take only 30 minutes or so on a modern PC. It's also relatively simple, with very few decisions to make throughout, and lots of hand-holding.

However, you should examine all the options you're offered to make sure they're correct. Installing an operating system involves a couple of serious processes that have the potential for data loss. Read and consider every warning message you see, and be sure to keep your wits about you. Above all, make a backup of your data beforehand, as described in the previous chapter.

An Overview of the Installation Process

The DVD-ROM disc supplied with this book is double-sided. This means it's like a vinyl LP record. To play Side A, simply insert the disc with the Side A label topmost. To play Side B, insert the disc with the Side B label topmost.

Side A contains the current Long term support (LTS) release version of Ubuntu, 10.04, code-named Lucid Lynx. This is the most recent version of Ubuntu at the time of writing. Side B contains the following:

- ISO image files of the 32-bit and 64-bit versions of Ubuntu 10.04, which you can burn to a blank CD-R/RW disc by following the instructions in Appendix D. This is included in case you want to give copies of Ubuntu to your friends, or if you want to try the Wubi Windows installer (see the "Installing Ubuntu Inside Windows" sidebar), which isn't included with the DVD version of Ubuntu 10.04 for technical reasons.

■ **Note** You can also freely duplicate the DVD supplied with this book and give copies to friends if you want. In fact, this is encouraged.

- The 32-bit "Alternate Install" version of Ubuntu 10.04, which can be useful for setting up automated deployments, upgrading from older installations without network access, LVM and/or RAID partitioning, and installing on systems with less than about 256MB of RAM.

- The 10.04 (Lucid Lynx) releases of Kubuntu and Xubuntu, which provide alternative Desktop environments if Ubuntu's default Desktop environment, GNOME, does not suit your taste, and Edubuntu, which provides a layer of educational content on top of the standard Ubuntu installation. For more details on these versions of Ubuntu, see Appendix D.

- An image of the Ubuntu Netbook Edition, which presents a simplified interface which its developers feel is more suited to the smaller screens found on Netbooks.

If you want to try one of the installers on Side B of the DVD, you will first need to burn it onto a CD (or DVD, in the case of the Edubuntu image). This procedure is discussed in Appendix D.

However, most readers will want to install the default version of Ubuntu. So to start things rolling, insert Side A into the DVD-ROM drive and boot your computer. You might have to set your BIOS to boot from DVD, as explained in stage 2 of the installation guide in this chapter.

If you've ever installed Windows from scratch on a computer, you might be used to working with the Windows installation program. This appears when you boot from a Windows CD or DVD or run the setup.exe program from the Desktop, and it guides you through installing Windows onto your hard disk.

Ubuntu is a little different. After you've booted from the DVD-ROM, a menu will appear. You can choose the Install Ubuntu option, and the DVD will continue booting to a graphical installer. Alternatively, you can choose the Try Ubuntu option. This allows you to run Ubuntu from the DVD-ROM, effectively trying it out without making any changes to your computer.

Using Ubuntu without installing it to the hard disk is referred to as running in *live distro mode*. Although this is a great way to take a sneak peak at what Ubuntu offers, there are a few things to be aware of, as discussed in the sidebar titled "Running in Live Distro Mode."

To install Ubuntu on your computer, simply select the Install Ubuntu option from the Welcome window. This will run the dedicated installation program, which will work through a few stages to get Linux on your computer's hard disk. During the installation stages, you'll be asked a handful of essential questions and will be taken through the process of creating space on your computer for the new OS. After this, Ubuntu is installed onto your hard disk.

At the end of the procedure, your PC will boot straight into the Ubuntu login screen, and you're set to go. There's no need to mess around configuring hardware, because for almost everything, that's done automatically. Neat, eh?

In most cases, the installation process will run smoothly without a hitch. But if you do run into problems, head over to Chapter 5, which addresses many of the most common issues and provides solutions.

RUNNING IN LIVE DISTRO MODE

If you don't want to install Ubuntu just yet, you can try it out by booting the operating system straight from the DVD supplied with this book. You might want to do this, for instance, to highlight any potential hardware issues or if you're visiting friends and want to boot up into a familiar Desktop on their PC. To do this, simply insert the DVD-ROM and then reboot your computer. Make sure the computer is set to boot from DVD (see stage 2 of the installation guide in this chapter to learn how), and select the Try Ubuntu 10.04 option. After a few moments, the Ubuntu Desktop will appear. Depending on the speed and memory capacity of your computer, this process can take some time, so be patient. You can follow most of the chapters in this book when running in live distro mode, and you can even save data (documents, downloads, and so forth) to a USB drive. However, you should be aware of the following issues:

- *Settings:* Any changes you make to the system will be forgotten as soon as you shut down your PC or reboot. In other words, each time you run in live distro mode, it will be as if Ubuntu has been freshly installed. For example, if you've configured a network card or rearranged the Desktop, those changes will be lost. There are ways around losing settings on each reboot, but they require partitioning your hard disk, which, frankly, is as much effort as installing Ubuntu from scratch. So there's little to be gained by doing so.

- *Performance:* Because the data must be read from DVD-ROM, running Ubuntu in live distro mode is a slow and, therefore, frustrating experience. It can also be noisy if your DVD-ROM is a model that makes a whirring noise as it spins.

- *System:* As strange as it sounds, Ubuntu is largely unaware of when it's running in live distro mode. For example, if you were to follow the instructions in Chapter 8, which discuss how to update your system, Ubuntu will attempt to update, even though it's running in live distro mode! Of course, it can't do this, because, as far as it is concerned, the DVD-ROM is the hard disk, and it's therefore impossible to write data to it. This can create confusing error messages.

- *Risk to data:* When running in live distro mode, you're given practically unlimited power over the system. This means that you could potentially repartition the hard disk, for example, or even wipe the hard disk entirely, all without any password prompt or warning. This can be useful in certain circumstances—you can attempt to "rescue" a hard disk that's having problems using the live distro mode of the Ubuntu disc. But using it for everyday tasks is a huge risk, and the potential for accidental damage is high.

In short, we recommend that you use live distro mode sparingly and only to get a taste of what Ubuntu is like. If you intend to use Ubuntu for any significant period of time, take the plunge and install it to your hard disk.

A Stage-by-Stage Installation Guide

As outlined in Chapter 3, you shouldn't start the installation process until you've made sure there is enough space for Ubuntu on your hard disk and you have backed up all your data. With those preparations complete, you're ready to install Ubuntu. The remainder of this chapter guides you through the process.

Stage 1: Prepare the Windows Partition for Resizing

If you're installing Ubuntu on a computer that already contains Windows, it's a good idea to perform three additional steps before actually installing Ubuntu. These steps will ensure that Ubuntu will be able to resize the Windows partition successfully.

If your computer doesn't contain Windows, or if you're installing Ubuntu onto a second hard disk, you can skip straight to stage 2.

The following are the steps for preparing the Windows partition for resizing:

1. Scan the disk for errors.

2. Defragment the hard disk.

3. Ensure that Windows is shut down correctly.

To scan the disk, open My Computer (or Computer if you're running Windows Vista or 7), right-click your Windows drive (usually C:\) and select Properties. In the window that appears, click the Tools tab and then click the Check Now button under the Error Checking heading. Ensure that there's a check alongside Automatically Fix File System Errors, and click the Start button. You will then be prompted to schedule the disk check the next time your computer restarts. Select to do so and reboot your computer, so the disk check can take place.

When the computer has rebooted, it's time to defragment your disk. Windows can be untidy with how it stores data on the disk. Over time files get broken into pieces and scattered all over your Windows partition. Defragmenting the partition will not only make Windows run more quickly, but will also consolidate your files at the beginning of the partition, enabling you to shrink it further and create a larger partition for Ubuntu in the freed space. Repeat the previous steps to view the Tools tab of the drive's Properties dialog box, and click the Defragment Now button. Then work through the defragmentation program's options in order to defragment the Windows disk (shown in Figure 4-1); usually this involves simply clicking the Defragment button (labeled Defragment Now under Windows Vista or Defragment Disk under Windows 7).

After that has completed—it may take several hours if your computer has not been defragmented before—shut down the computer as usual and proceed to stage 2 of the installation process.

It's vital that the computer shuts itself down properly. If the computer doesn't cleanly shut down, Ubuntu's installation program might stop with an error message about not being able to resize the partition.

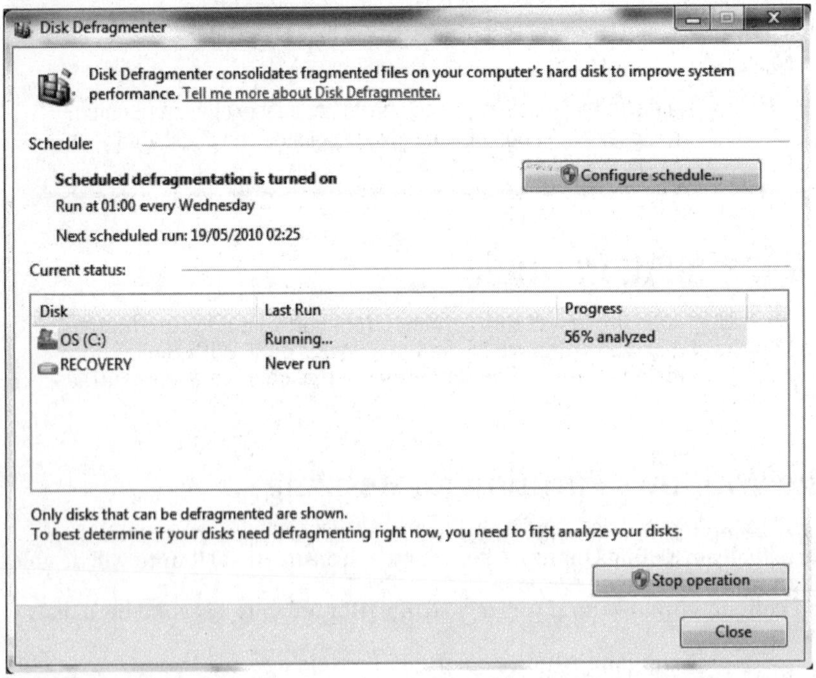

Figure 4-1. *Before installing Ubuntu, it's essential to scan the Windows partition for errors and to defragment it.*

INSTALLING UBUNTU INSIDE WINDOWS

Ubuntu includes a clever piece of software called Wubi that lets you install Ubuntu within the Windows file system. In other words, there is no need to repartition your hard disk. Aside from this, there is no major difference between a partitioned installation and a Wubi installation.

Wubi works by creating a loopback file system—that is, it creates a single large file within the Windows file system, and that file is then used as the Ubuntu file system.

Wubi is a nice way to try out Ubuntu on a more permanent basis than using the live distro mode. The biggest issue is that Wubi requires at least 256MB of memory and 5GB of hard disk space, although this shouldn't present any problems for relatively modern computers. However, users have reported performance degradation compared to a dedicated Ubuntu installation in its own partition, and you'll also find that Ubuntu's useful Hibernate power-saving mode (what Windows refers to as Suspend to Disk) isn't supported.

Unfortunately, for technical reasons Wubi isn't included on the DVD release of Ubuntu, as supplied on Side A of the DVD-ROM disc that comes with this book. To use it, you'll need to burn your own CD-R/RW disc from the installation ISO image of Ubuntu provided on Side B of the disc. To learn how to do this, follow the instructions in Appendix D.

To use Wubi, insert the CD while Windows is up and running. In the dialog box that appears, click the Install Inside Windows button. If the dialog box doesn't appear, navigate to the contents of the CD and double-click wubi.exe. In the next dialog box, you are presented with a series of drop-down lists. Using these, you can choose which drive to create the Ubuntu file system on, if you have more than one hard disk or partition, and you can choose the size of the loopback file system you want to create. In most cases, the default options are fine. You will need to enter a username and password in the boxes provided. These will form your Ubuntu login details. When you're finished, click the Next button.

Wubi will then create the loopback file system. When it has finished, you'll be invited to reboot your computer. After the computer is up and running again, you'll be presented with a boot menu from which you can choose either Windows or Ubuntu. Choosing Ubuntu will then start the installation routine, which will complete automatically. Following this, you'll be prompted to reboot. From then on, selecting the Ubuntu option from the boot menu will start Ubuntu. To start Windows, simply choose the Windows option from the menu.

To remove the Ubuntu file system from your Windows hard disk, navigate to C:\ubuntu from within Windows and double-click Uninstall-Ubuntu.exe. Don't be tempted to just delete the Ubuntu folder, because doing so will not remove the boot menu component.

Stage 2: Boot from the DVD-ROM

With your computer booted up, insert the Ubuntu disc into the DVD-ROM drive, with Side A topmost. Close the tray and reboot your computer. The disc might automatically run under Windows, opening a menu where you can click to find out more about Ubuntu, but you can ignore this.

Because you need to boot from the DVD-ROM disc in order to run the Ubuntu installer, the first step is to make sure your computer's BIOS is set correctly.

Many modern computers let you press a particular key during the initial boot phase of your computer, during the memory testing and drive identification period, to make a boot menu appear. Often this is F8, Delete, or Esc, but you should keep an eye on the boot messages to identify the correct key. On the boot menu, you can choose to boot from the CD or DVD drive from the list.

If you do not have an option to boot from the CD/DVD drive, you'll need to enter the BIOS setup program and change the boot priority of your computer. To do this, press the Delete key just after the computer is first activated. Again, some computers use another key or key combination, and your boot screen should indicate which key to press.

When the BIOS menu appears, look for a menu option such as Boot and select it (you can usually navigate around the screen of the BIOS menu using the cursor keys, and select options by pressing Enter). On the new menu, look for a separate entry such as Boot Device Priority or perhaps Boot Sequence. Make sure that the entry for the CD/DVD-ROM is at the top of the list. Arrange the list so that CD/DVD-ROM is followed by the floppy drive and then your main hard disk. You can usually press the F1 key for help on how the menu selection system works.

After you've made the changes, be sure to select the Save and Exit option. Your PC will then reset and boot from the Ubuntu DVD-ROM, and you'll be greeted by the Ubuntu DVD boot menu.

■ **Note** After Ubuntu has been installed on your computer, you might choose to repeat this step and rearrange the boot order once more to make the hard disk appear at the top of the list. Then your computer won't waste time checking the DVD-ROM drive for a boot disc every time it starts.

Stage 3: Try or Install

When the DVD-ROM boots, for a few seconds you'll see a purple background with two small icons—a keyboard and an accessibility symbol—at the bottom of the screen, hinting that accessibility features such as a screen reader can be reached by pressing any key on the keyboard. Most people can just leave the boot sequence to continue.

You will then be entertained by a progress indicator for a minute or so, depending on the speed of your machine, after which the installer window will appear (Figure 4-2).

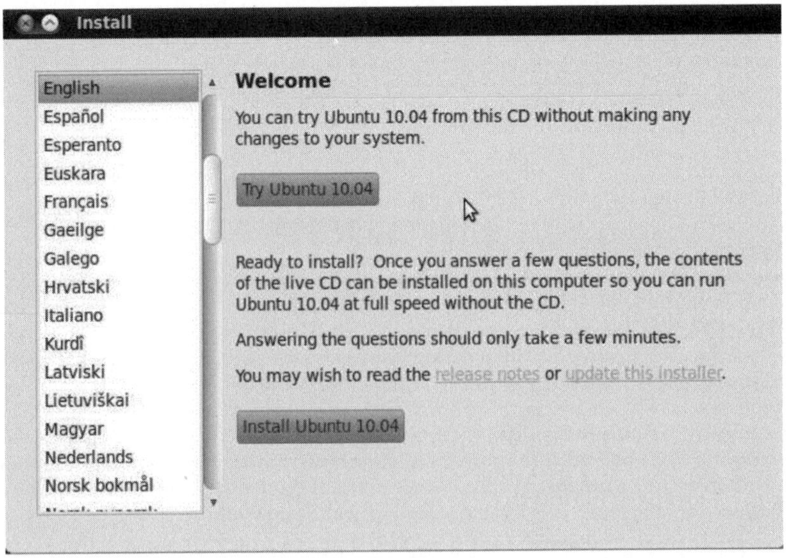

Figure 4-2. The Welcome screen of the installer: choose to test the system out, or install it.

English is the default language for the installer, but a selection list on the left of the window offers the choice of more than 60 other languages, reminding us what an amazingly international project Ubuntu is.

The two main options offered by the Welcome window are as follows:

Try Ubuntu 10.04: This option lets you run Ubuntu "live" from the DVD-ROM disc, so you can try out its features, albeit in a slightly limited state (see the "Running in Live Distro Mode" sidebar). If you've never seen Ubuntu up and running, choose this option and play around. You can always click the install icon on the Desktop when you're ready to take the plunge.

Install Ubuntu 10.04: This will start Ubuntu's installation routine. Choose this if you want to get straight on with installing Ubuntu on your PC now.

Text links on this window also offer you the opportunity to read the release notes for Ubuntu 10.04 and to update the installer itself. It's not essential to do either of these.

■ **Note** Pressing a key when the purple background first appears on booting the DVD-ROM will bring up an alternative boot menu. This allows you to activate accessibility features, test your computer's memory, or start a text-mode installer, in case the standard graphical installer has problems displaying on your hardware. Chances are you won't need any of these options.

Stage 4: Select Your Location and Time Zone

Ubuntu will next ask you to choose your time zone. If your PC is already connected to the Internet, Ubuntu may already have detected your location correctly. You can select your time zone manually by clicking your location on the world map that's displayed or by selecting the nearest city from the drop-down lists at the base of the page.

When you click the map, you'll see that the time zone is highlighted in green, and you can click near your location within this band. You'll also see a live clock showing the time in that location. See Figure 4-3 for an example.

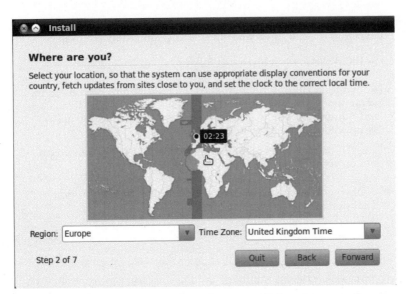

Figure 4-3. Select the time zone from the map and then you can refine your options by using the drop-down lists at the bottom of the page.

The city you choose doesn't matter a great deal—the purpose of this step is to ensure that Ubuntu selects the correct time zone for your location, which it does by looking up the city in a database of time zones.

After you've made your selection, click the Forward button.

Stage 5: Confirm Your Keyboard Layout

Next you'll be asked to confirm the keyboard layout you'll be using, as shown in Figure 4-4. This should correspond to your language and locale settings, and will be automatically selected, so you can just click the Forward button. If you're unsure whether Ubuntu has guessed the correct keyboard layout, you can click the test text field and type in some characters before continuing. You can also manually set your preferred keyboard layout by clicking the Choose Your Own radio button and selecting as appropriate from the country and layout lists.

■ **Note** Keyboard layouts can differ from country to country even if they speak the same language. This is to allow for local necessities. The UK keyboard layout has the pound sterling symbol (£) above the number 3, for example, and swaps around the locations of a handful of other symbols, too.

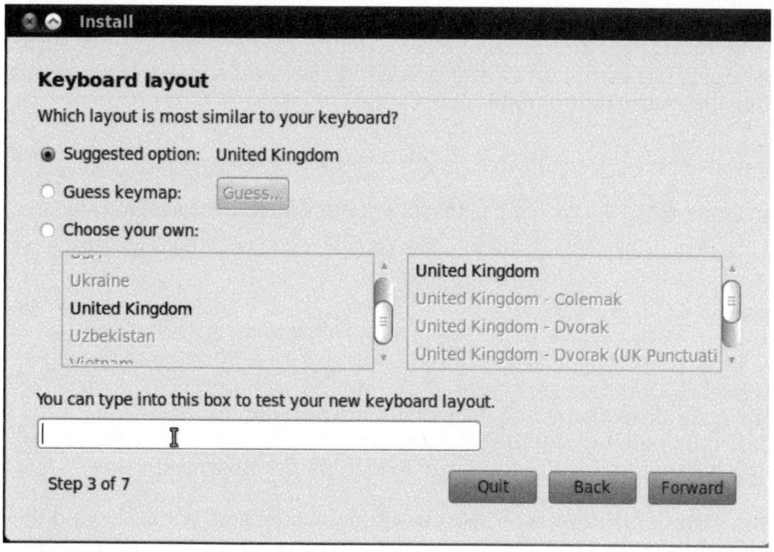

Figure 4-4. *Ubuntu will guess your keyboard layout, but you can test it to make sure by typing in the test text field at the bottom of the dialog box.*

Stage 6: Repartition Your Hard Disk

Partitioning the disk is one of the most important steps during installation, but, unfortunately, it's one that can be couched in difficult terminology. Partitioning is the process of dividing up a hard disk into sections so that different operating systems or one operating system and some data can exist on the same computer and convince the computer that more than one disk exists. Though it's a complex subject, Ubuntu does its best to make partitioning easy.

The Ubuntu installation routine offers several options for disk partitioning:

- Resize the existing partition on the hard disk and install Ubuntu alongside it in the newly created free space. (This option is not offered if the disk has no existing partitions.)

- Use the entire disk, whether it already has some contents or not (that is, if the computer or hard disk is new or if you want to overwrite your Windows installation).

- Use the largest free space that might already exist on the hard disk, for example if you've already manually repartitioned the disk. (This option is not offered if the disk has no existing partitions.)

- Manually edit the partition table—that is, resize/delete any existing partitions by hand and create the Ubuntu partitions. This is suitable only for expert users.

Most people who are installing Ubuntu on a computer that already has Windows on it will want to resize the main partition, as described next.

If you're installing Ubuntu on a computer that has no operating system installed or one that you would like to completely erase from the computer, follow the instructions under the upcoming "Use Entire Disk" section. However, be aware that this will completely wipe any data from that disk.

Resize the Main Partition

This is the default partitioning option if your computer already has Windows installed on it. Ubuntu will detect the main Windows partition and suggest the amount of resizing.

■ **Caution** If there's not enough free space within the Windows partition, you won't be able to resize it to make space for Ubuntu. If this is the case, the Ubuntu installer will tell you. See Chapter 3 for suggestions for freeing up space.

By default, Ubuntu attempts to grab as much space for itself as possible, without shrinking the existing partition too much. In our example in Figure 4-5, the installation program has decided to split the disk roughly 50/50, giving both operating systems a decent amount of space. This is shown in the bar display: the right part of the bar represents Windows, and the left part represents the new Ubuntu partition.

Ubuntu's default choice is normally fine, but you can also click and drag the grab bar in the middle of the partitioning display bar to increase or decrease the sizes of the Windows and Ubuntu partitions. You may want to give Windows a little more space if you plan to divide your time between Windows and Ubuntu. Bear in mind that, while Ubuntu can read files on the Windows partition, Windows refuses to do vice versa, so if you want to access your files locally from both operating systems, those files should be stored in the Windows (NTFS or FAT) partition.

The Ubuntu installer is intelligent enough not to let you set an impossible value for shrinking the existing partition. The Ubuntu installer is also clever enough to know that Windows needs some free space within its partition to operate effectively—to write temporary and system files and user-created files such as Word documents, for example. So you shouldn't be able to make changes that are too extreme. On a test system, we couldn't set a size for the existing partition lower than 10 percent of the entire disk, because the existing data on the partition occupied about 10 percent of the space. You can override this protection by manually partitioning, as described in the "Manually Edit the Partition Table" section of this chapter. Similarly, the installer shouldn't let you create an inadequate amount of free space for Ubuntu when dragging the slider to the right.

The next time you start Windows, having resized your Windows partition, it's very likely that Microsoft's disk checking program will run. This is quite normal. Typically it will complete without finding any errors.

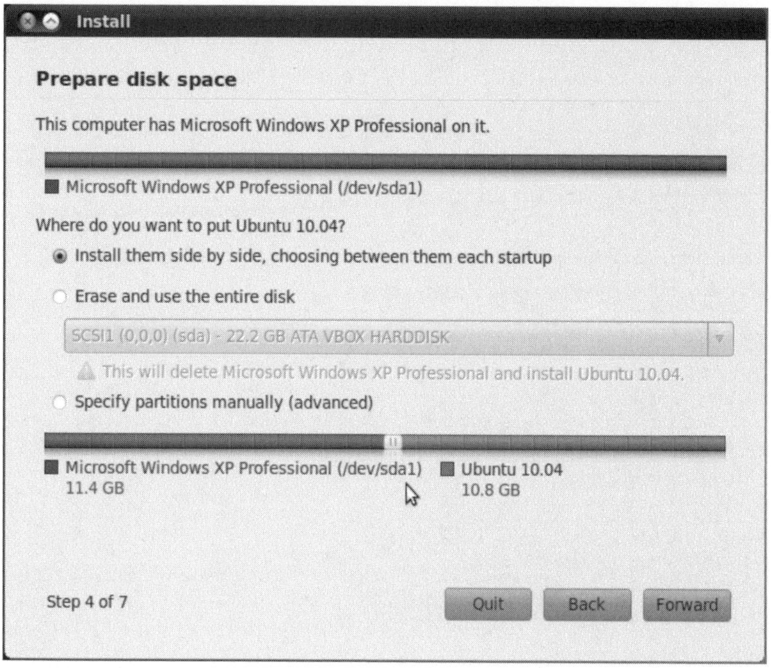

Figure 4-5. *The installer will take as much space as Ubuntu needs, without shrinking the existing partition too much.*

After you've made your selection, click the Forward button. After a warning message asks whether you really want to take this irreversible step, the installer will resize the partition. This might take a few moments.

■ **Caution** If you're resizing a partition on a laptop or notebook computer, ensure that you have the main power connected. If the power goes off during the resizing procedure because of a failing battery, there's a very good chance your Windows partition will be destroyed.

Use Entire Disk

If the hard disk is empty, or if you've decided to eradicate Windows and use only Ubuntu on your computer, you can choose the "Erase and use the entire disk" option, as shown in Figure 4-6.

If the disk does have contents, this option will remove them and then use the entire disk to install Ubuntu. As mentioned in Chapter 3, before undertaking this move, you should back up essential data from the Windows partition (or any others on the hard disk). There is no easy way of undoing the partition erasure, so you should proceed with caution.

After you've made the choice, click the Forward button. The deletion should take place quickly, after which you can proceed straight to the next stage in this guide.

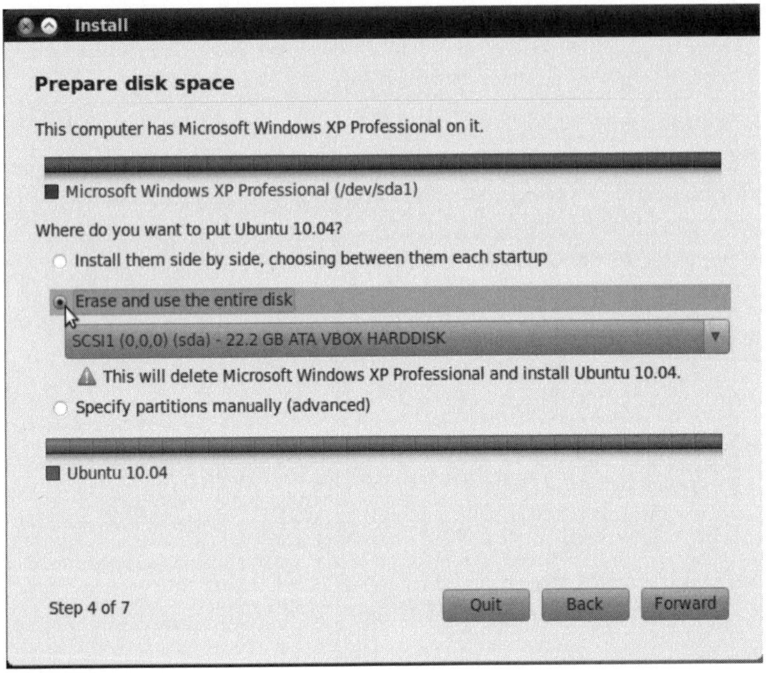

Figure 4-6. *If you have an unused disk or are getting rid of Windows entirely, choose the "Erase and use the entire disk" option.*

Use the Largest Continuous Free Space

If you've already repartitioned your hard disk by using a third-party utility, or if you deliberately created a smaller Windows partition in order to leave free space for another operating system, you can select the "Use the largest continuous free space" option (note that this option won't appear unless there is free space on the hard disk). Then the Ubuntu installation program will use the *largest amount of free space* for the Ubuntu partitions. This is an important point: if you have more than one area of free space, the largest will be used.

If you do have more than one amount of free space, the Ubuntu installation routine is unable to automatically use any smaller amounts of free space. If you want this to be the case, the only option is to manually partition, as described in the section "Manually Edit the Partition Table." However, only advanced users will need to do this.

After you've made your choice, click the Forward button and proceed to the next stage in this guide.

Use a Second Hard Disk

If your computer has more than one hard disk—a new hard disk you've added for Ubuntu, as described in Chapter 3, or a second hard disk already installed in your computer—you should select it under the Use the Entire Disk option. The way Ubuntu identifies your hard disks might seem a little complicated at first, but is actually straightforward.

If your computer is relatively new, chances are it has a SATA-based hard disk. If so, the first hard disk will be identified as sda, the second as sdb, the third as sdc. All that changes in each case is the last letter: a, b, c, and so on.

If your computer uses IDE-based hard disks, the drives will also be identified as sda, sdb, and so on. The primary master drive in the system is identified as hda, the primary slave as hdb, the secondary master as hdc, and so on. The drive will also be identified by make and model, which may help you identify it.

Assuming the second IDE hard disk is installed as a slave on the primary channel, as is the standard configuration for an additional hard disk, it will be identified as hdb, so make that selection. If the disk is installed as the slave on the secondary channel (that is, the same channel as the DVD-ROM drive), it will be identified as hdd.

After you've selected the disk, click the Forward button.

Manually Edit the Partition Table

If, for any reason, you find that Ubuntu's default partitioning choices are not for you, you can opt to manually edit the partition table. For example, you may want to separate the operating system installation from your /home folder. This separation makes doing a fresh installation of Ubuntu or another Linux easy, because the data is left untouched. There are essentially two stages to work through if you choose this option:

- You're given the chance to repartition the disk manually. You can resize or delete any existing partitions and create the partitions Ubuntu needs.

- While creating/editing the partitions, you'll be asked to assign *mount points.* You'll be prompted to tell Ubuntu which of the partitions on the disk it should use for the *root file system* (that is, the main partition for Ubuntu's use) and which should be used for the *swap partition.*

Manually partitioning offers ultimate flexibility but requires a relatively high level of knowledge of how Ubuntu works. Therefore, we recommend that only experts undertake this step, unless you have no other choice because the default Ubuntu partitioning choices do not offer what you need or do not work properly for you.

In the following steps, we explain how to resize an existing partition, create the new partitions that Ubuntu needs, and assign mount points so that Ubuntu is able to use them.

■ **Tip** GParted is a graphical partition tool that you can use to add, edit, and delete partitions easily. GParted looks similar to the third-party commercial partition tools you may have already used. You can run this utility by starting Ubuntu in live distro mode and choosing System ➤ Administration ➤ GParted from the menu. After you have made the desired changes with this partition editor, you can reboot and start the Ubuntu installer again. Then when you manually edit the partitions in the installer, you need to set mount points only on the partitions that you created in GParted.

Prepare Partitions

When the disk partitioning choices appear, click the "Specify partitions manually (advanced)" radio button and click Forward. The Prepare Partitions window will appear, as shown in Figure 4-7. This window lists the hard disks detected by Ubuntu and their corresponding partitions. Each item has the following properties:

- *Device:* This is the logical representation of the hardware device in Ubuntu. See the previous section for an explanation of the drive identification, but note that here the drive references are preceded with /dev. You can ignore this. The numbers at the end refer to the order of partitions. For example, sda1 refers to the first partition of the first hard disk, and sda2 refers to the second partition of the first hard disk.

- *Type:* This specifies the file system type of the partition. For example, NTFS and VFAT are Windows file systems, ext4 indicates the Ubuntu partition, and swap indicates a swap file partition.

- *Mount Point:* A mount point is a location within Ubuntu's file system where Ubuntu will "see" a partition. At least one partition needs to be mounted as root, denoted with a single /. Mounting is discussed further in Chapter 10.

- *Format?:* This indicates whether the partition will be formatted during installation. Formatting will destroy any data on a partition, so ensure that you have backups of important data and that you really do want to format.

- *Size:* This determines the disk space of the partition, in megabytes. Note that the strict definition of the word *megabyte* is used, meaning 1,000,000 bytes, rather than the more widely used 1,024,000 bytes (1,024KB). To confuse matters, the 1,024KB definition is used in the rest of the installation program. (From its next release, Ubuntu is due to switch entirely to the SI standard, that is, 1MB (megabyte) = 1,000 KB).

- *Used:* This determines how much disk space has been consumed, in megabytes.

At the bottom of the window are buttons to manipulate the hard disk as a whole or each individual partition. For the hard disk, you can opt to create a new partition table. This effectively returns the disk to as-new status, with no partition information, so creating a new partition table is tantamount to erasing the whole hard disk. Be sure you know what you're doing! For unallocated free space, you have an option to add a new partition. For an existing partition, you have an option to change its properties (this option lets you resize the disk and assign a mount point) or delete the partition to accumulate free disk space. You also have a revert option to undo all hard disk changes, which applies to all desired changes except resizing a partition, because resizing is carried out as soon as you select to do so, unlike the other changes, which are carried out after working through all the installation stages.

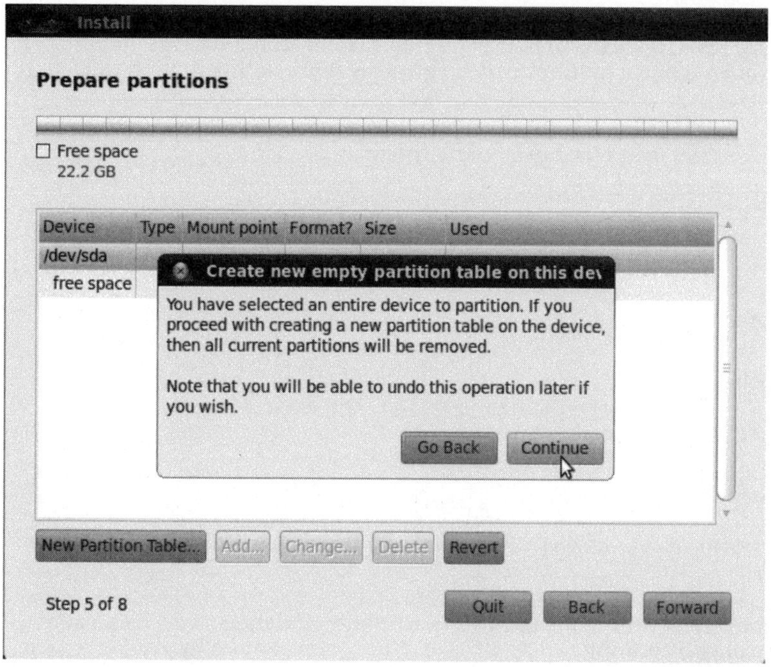

Figure 4-7. *Creating a new partition table has the same effect as completely wiping the contents of a disk. Use with extreme care.*

So you want to resize the main NTFS (Windows) partition. Search for that partition in the partition type list; it will be shown as ntfs.

Determine Windows Partition Size

After you have found the NTFS partition, you should determine how much space should be retained in your Windows partition so that Windows will still function properly while providing a sufficient amount of space for Ubuntu. The bare minimum disk space required for a Windows partition varies between 2GB for Windows XP and 16GB for Windows 7, though these minimums will give you very little space for documents or other data.

You should free up as much space as possible for Ubuntu. But if disk space is a concern, you will need to determine the minimum of disk space that should be put aside for the main and swap partitions of Ubuntu.

The main partition will contain the Ubuntu operating system itself. This partition should have at the very least 3GB of disk space (2GB for the base installation, and the rest for new applications, software upgrades, and your data).

The swap partition is similar to the swap file under Windows (sometimes referred to as *virtual memory* or the *paging file*), except that it resides on its own partition. The traditional purpose of a swap partition is to act as additional memory should the main memory become full. Accessing the hard disk takes longer than accessing the RAM, so using the swap partition for this purpose is a last resort. The swap file is also used by Linux for storing "anonymous pages," that is, data that exists in memory only and not on disk. Without swap, there would be nowhere for anonymous pages to go when Linux wants to use the memory space they're taking up. Additionally, the swap file is used to store the contents of the physical memory when the computer enters Hibernate (Suspend to Disk) power-saving mode.

The ideal size for the swap partition is a subject of endless debate. Recommendations usually depend on the size of your physical RAM. If you want to use the Hibernate feature on your computer, your swap partition size must be at least equal to the size of the physical RAM, or hibernation will fail. See Table 4-1 for some suggestions.

Table 4-1. Suggested Swap Partition Sizes for a Desktop Ubuntu System

Physical RAM Size	Swap Partition Size[a]
512MB	1,024MB
1,024MB (1GB)	1,024MB
2,048MB (2GB)	2,048MB
3,072MB (3GB)	3,072MB
4,096MB (4GB)	4,096MB

[a] *Swap partition sizes have been adjusted to take into account the strict definition that 1 megabyte = 1,000,000 bytes, as stated in the Create Partition dialog box.*

After you have determined the size of your main and swap partitions, total their sizes. This is how much free space you need to allocate for Ubuntu.

Edit Partition Properties

In the Prepare Partitions window, select the NTFS partition and click Change to edit its properties. Figure 4-8 shows how to edit a partition. In the Edit Partition dialog box, you can edit three partition properties:

- *New Partition Size in Megabytes:* This allows you to adjust the size of the selected partition. If you reduce the size of the selected partition, the remaining space will be allocated for free space. For example, if you have an NTFS partition with a size of 104,847MB and you would like to allocate 8,192MB for Ubuntu, you would need to reduce the size of the NTFS partition to 96,655MB. Adjust the size of the NTFS partition as you determined in the previous step.

- *Use As:* This either changes or displays the file system of the selected partition. The current file system is NTFS, because you are editing a Windows partition, so select ntfs from the list if it isn't already displayed. Be careful not to select any of the other entries from the list, because this could damage your Windows setup irreversibly.

- *Mount Point:* Ubuntu makes non-Linux file systems (such as Windows) available by *mounting* them. You can either select one of the default suggestions (on our test system, these were /dos and /windows) or type your own path (but only if you know what you're doing).

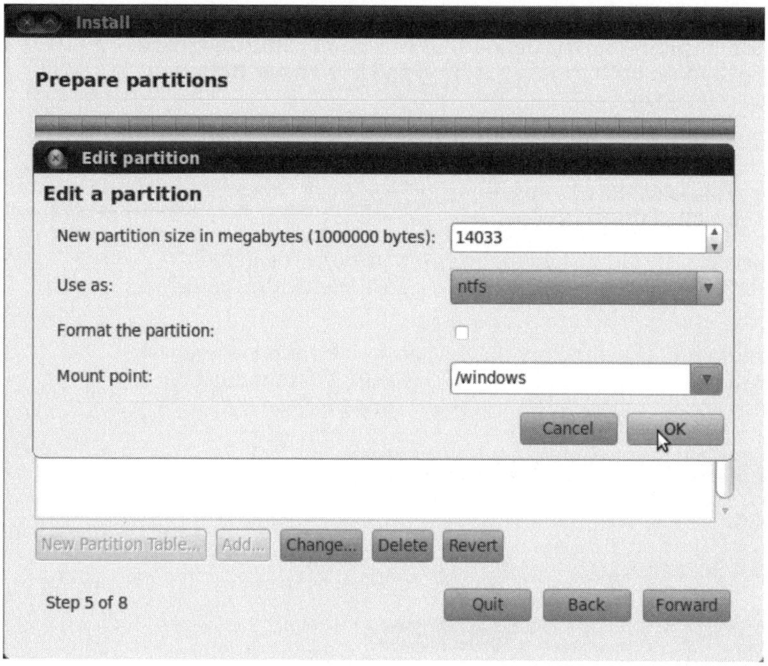

Figure 4-8. *With manual partition editing you can shrink a Windows (NTFS) partition and choose a mount point where it can be accessed from your new Ubuntu system.*

After you're satisfied with your choices, click the OK button. At this point, you are prompted to confirm that your desired changes will be made to the disk. It's a good idea to read through the summary carefully, because after you click Continue, there's no going back. Any data on the disk will be lost. Click Continue when you're ready to start the resizing process. After the process is finished, you will have free space to allocate for Ubuntu.

If you see an error message while trying to resize the partition, it's likely that Windows was not shut down correctly. To fix this situation, exit the Ubuntu installer, reboot Windows, and opt to check the disk. Then reboot so the check can take place. After that, reboot again, ensuring that Windows is properly shut down. Then you can return to the Ubuntu installer.

Create Main and Swap Partitions

The next step is to create partitions with the free space. Select the new free space you have created and click the Add... button. The Create Partition dialog box will appear, as shown in Figure 4-9. This dialog box has five options:

- *Type for the New Partition:* This option allows you to set the partition as primary or logical. Unless the hard disk has more than one operating system installed, you should select the Primary option. With primary partitions, you can divide your hard disk up to only four partitions. If you need more than four partitions, or if there are already three partitions on the disk, select the Logical option, and create the further partitions you need within the new logical partition.

- *New Partition Size in Megabytes:* This option sets the number of megabytes that will be allocated to the new partition. The default value takes all of the free space, but since you are going to make both a main partition and a swap partition, you should adjust the size accordingly.

- *Location for the New Partition:* This option specifies whether the new partition will be created on the beginning or end area of the free space. It's recommended that you use the beginning. This way, the free space can be seen easily, because it always appears just below all of the partitions.

- *Use As:* This option specifies the file system of the new partition. The default option of Ext4 Journaling File System is fine when you are creating the main partition.

- *Mount Point:* The mount point is a directory that will act as a location where you can make a disk accessible. The main partition you create for Ubuntu must be mounted as root. This is always represented as a single forward slash (/).

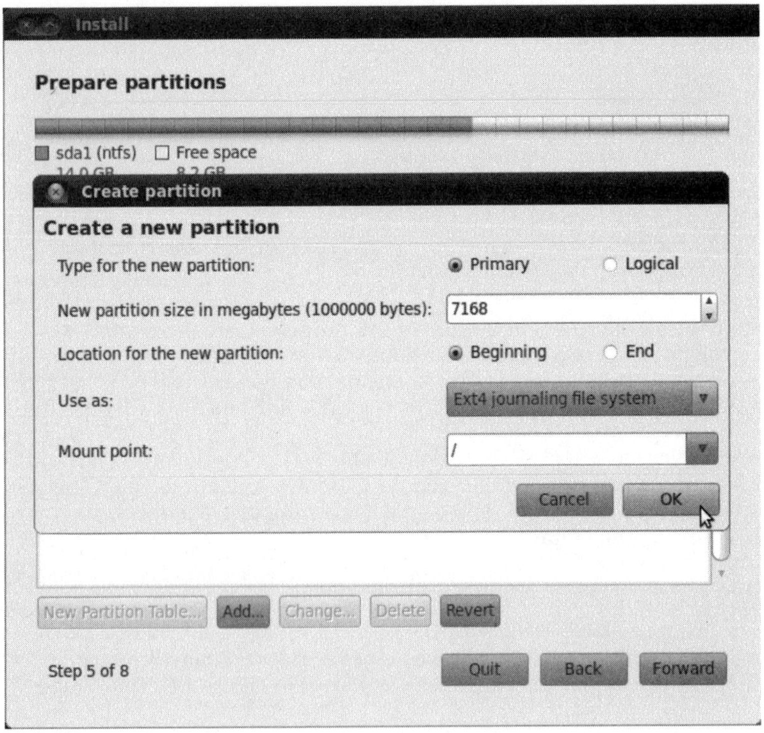

Figure 4-9. You can create a new partition as long as there is free/unallocated space available.

To create the main partition, where the operating system and data will all be stored, reduce the new partition size to leave enough space for swap, choose Ext4 as the format from the Use As drop-down menu, and then set the Mount Point to the forward slash (/) to specify that this partition is the main partition or root file system. Your dialog box should look similar to the one shown in Figure 4-9. Click the OK button to continue.

Next we'll create the swap partition. If you calculated the main partition size correctly, you can just accept the remaining space for use as swap. Change the Use As option to Swap Area. Leave the rest of the options untouched (note that the swap partition doesn't need a mount point). For example, if the size of the physical RAM is 1GB, the partition size for the swap partition should be set to 1,024MB, as shown in Figure 4-10. Click OK to continue.

You should now have partitions ready to go, as shown in Figure 4-11. Note that you may also have an NTFS partition visible if you're dual-booting with Windows. Click Forward to continue.

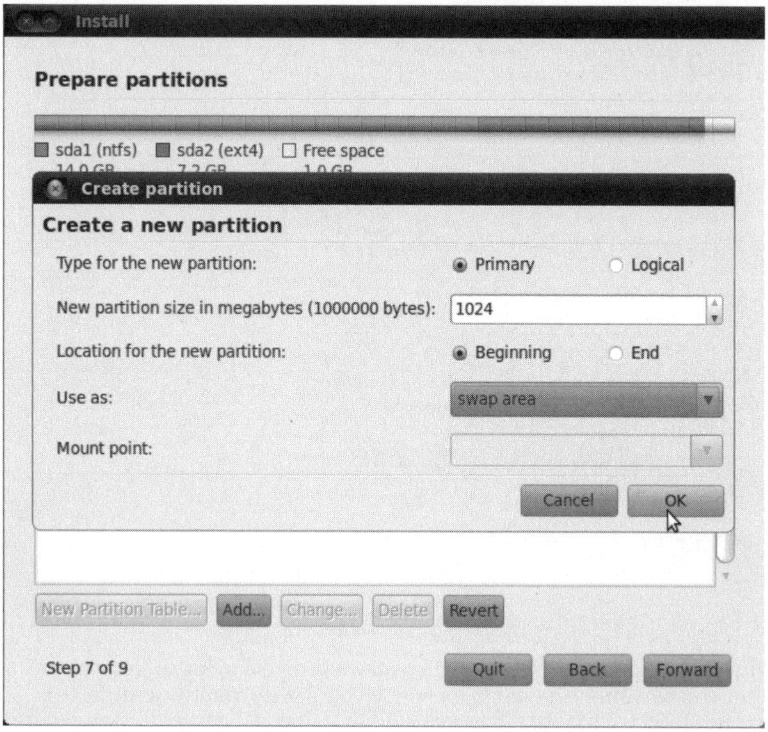

Figure 4-10. *If you've done your sums right, the remaining space on the disk should be what you calculated that you wanted for swap.*

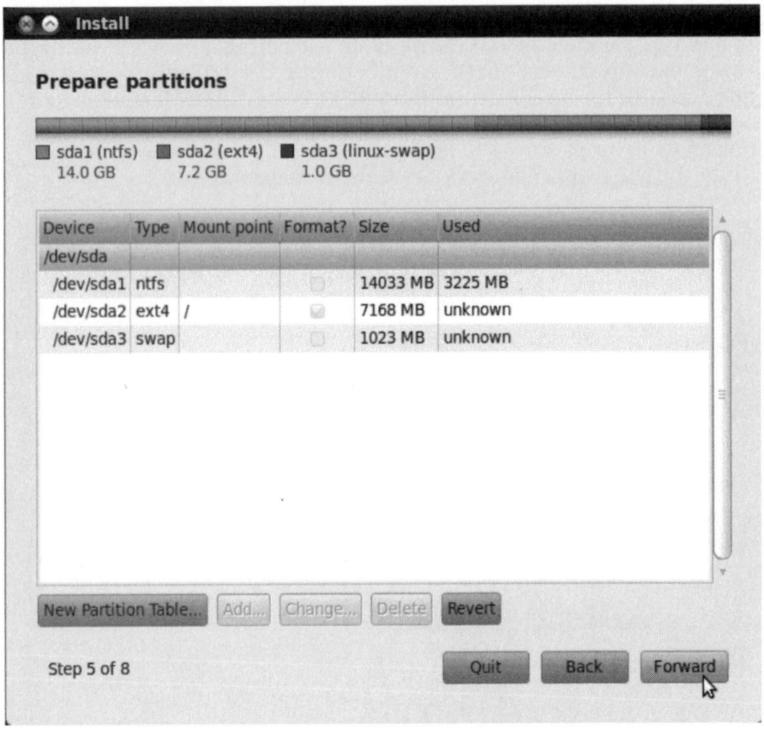

Figure 4-11. With your partitions configured, you're ready to move on.

Stage 7: Set Up a User

Next you'll be prompted to say who you are and choose the name you want to use to log in. In answer to the question What Is Your Name? you can enter the name by which you'll be formally identified on the system to anyone who uses it. The standard practice is to use your first and last names, separated by a space.

Next, you'll be asked for the name you want to use to log in. This username needs to be unique; two users on the same computer cannot have the same username. Also, it must follow these rules:

- The username should be one word without any spaces in it.

- You can choose any username consisting of uppercase and lowercase letters and numbers, but not symbols or punctuation.

- The username cannot begin with an uppercase letter, although you can use uppercase in the rest of the name.

The simplest procedure for choosing a username is to use your own first name, typed entirely in lowercase letters. For example, in Figure 4-12, we've set the full name to Trevor Parsons and the login name to trevor. Helpfully, Ubuntu will add the first part of the full name to the username space automatically.

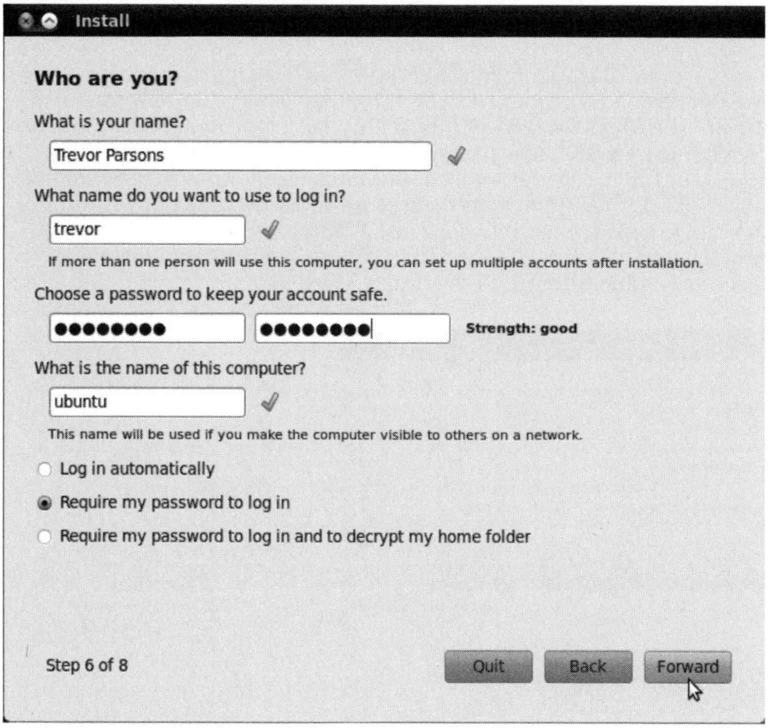

Figure 4-12. You should enter an ordinary name, a login name, a password, and, if you want, a name to give your computer.

Following the username, enter a password. Here, the rules are the inverse of those for your username. A good password contains numbers, uppercase and lowercase letters, punctuation marks, and anything else you can get in there! This helps make your password almost impossible for someone else to guess, and thus makes your system more secure. (If you want to be really secure, create a password that's ten or more characters long.) You'll need to enter the password twice; the second time confirms that you didn't make a typo the first time around.

The What Is the Name of This Computer? text box contains the hostname for the computer. This is how the computer is identified on certain types of networks, if you choose to share files or resources with other computers. Ubuntu will fill in this field automatically based on your username, but you can replace that with something else more personal. The rules for the hostname are broadly similar to those for the username; it cannot contain spaces or symbols. For example, if your computer is a Dell PC, you might type **Office_Dell** (note that you can use an underscore character in place of a space character).

After you're finished, click the Forward button.

Stage 8: Import Documents and Settings

The next step is to migrate accounts by importing documents and settings of existing user accounts from your Windows partition to Ubuntu. (You won't be prompted to do this if you're installing Ubuntu on a fresh hard disk or have chosen to overwrite your Windows partition.) Just select the items you would like to import to your account, as shown in Figure 4-13. Then click the Forward button to continue.

This is certainly a handy feature to be offered by the installer, but think twice about whether to use it. If you have a large amount of data, such as music and video, stored on your Windows partition, there is little point in using the migration tool to copy it over onto your new Ubuntu partition. You would be merely duplicating large amounts of data on the same disk, which makes little sense given that your Windows partition will in any case be accessible from your new Ubuntu system.

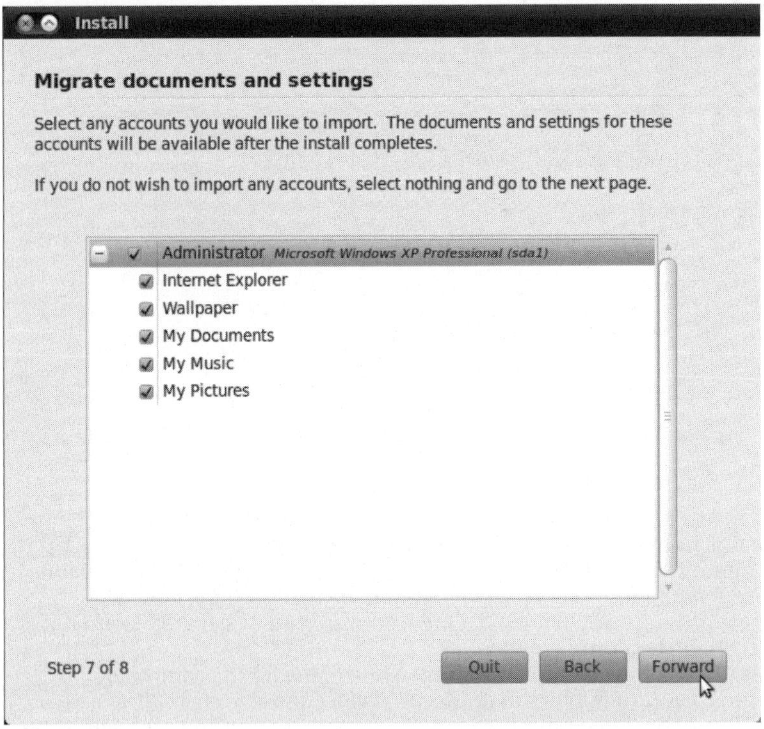

Figure 4-13. Select the items you would like to migrate from Windows to your account.

Stage 9: Confirm Installation Choices

At this point, you'll see the Ready to Install window, which lists the choices you've made, as shown in Figure 4-14. It's a good idea to check to make sure everything is correct before clicking the Install button.

When you're ready to install Ubuntu, click the Install button. This will start the installation procedure. The new partitions you created will be formatted, and the Ubuntu files will be copied.

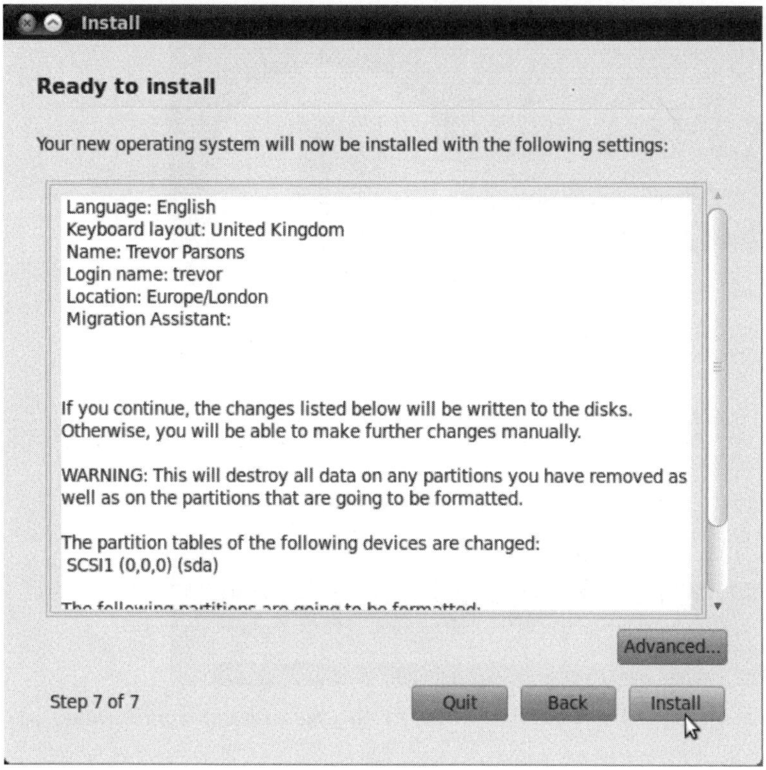

Figure 4-14. *Confirm the installation choices, and click the Install button to format the new partitions and copy the Ubuntu files.*

If you click the Advanced button (which isn't required), you will be prompted to customize the boot loader and set a network proxy if you have one. For the boot loader settings, you have the option not to write the boot loader to the disk. The option makes sense if you already have an existing boot loader, perhaps from another Linux installation, and you would prefer to use it as the primary boot loader for all the operating systems installed on your computer.

Stage 10: Perform Installation

Now all you have to do is wait! The Ubuntu installation routine will copy the necessary files and install Ubuntu, as shown in Figure 4-15. It won't require any further input from you, unless something goes wrong. For example, if you've created partitions that are too small in the previous section, this is the point at which you'll be told. If you do encounter an error, the installation program will quit, and you will need to start it again by clicking the icon on the Desktop, this time altering your choices accordingly.

Installation should take no more than 30 minutes. It completed in half that time on most of our test systems.

Installing system

Entertainment with music and movies

- Ubuntu is ready to play music and videos from the web, from CDs and DVDs.

- The Rhythmbox Music Player lets you organize your music, listen to Internet radio, and purchase a variety of songs. Manage your podcast subscriptions and automatically download new episodes.

- Discover popular, DRM-free music available for purchase from the Ubuntu One Music Store, a cloud-enabled digital music store. Purchases are automatically stored in the cloud and synchronised across all of your computers.

- Plug in an MP3 player to start synchronizing your music collection, or insert a CD to copy songs to your computer.

Copying files...

45%

Figure 4-15. *While the Ubuntu files are copied, you can read about its nifty features and applications.*

Stage 11: Reboot and Enjoy Ubuntu!

When installation has finished, a dialog box will appear telling you to restart the computer (see Figure 4-16). After you click the Restart Now button, the DVD will be ejected automatically. It's important that you remove it so that you don't accidentally boot Ubuntu's installer again when the machine restarts. In fact, Ubuntu will prompt you to remove the disk and press Enter to confirm the removal.

Following this, the system will restart. If you've installed Ubuntu on a computer that contains Windows, you'll first see the Grub boot menu. This offers a number of choices, including the chance to boot Ubuntu into recovery mode, which can help fix your computer (discussed in Chapter 5). You can also choose to boot into Windows. You can switch between the menu choices by using the arrow keys; press Enter to make your selection.

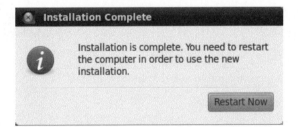

Installation Complete

Installation is complete. You need to restart the computer in order to use the new installation.

Restart Now

Figure 4-16. *You're almost ready to get started with Ubuntu.*

You can also run Memtest86 to test your system's memory. However, most users can simply press Enter when the menu appears, which will select the topmost entry, thereby booting Ubuntu in normal mode. Alternatively, after 10 seconds, the default choice will be automatically selected.

If you installed Ubuntu onto a computer or hard disk without any other OS, the system will start up directly, without displaying a boot menu (although this can be accessed if desired by holding down Shift during startup).

After a few seconds have passed while Ubuntu loads, you'll see the Ubuntu login screen, as shown in Figure 4-17 (unless you set up Ubuntu to log you in automatically). From here, you can progress to Chapter 6 to learn how to get started. Alternatively, if you've run into any problems, see Chapter 5.

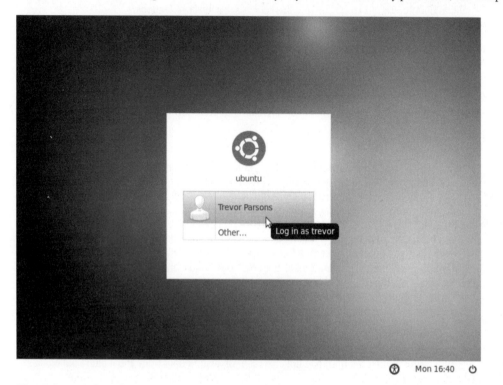

Figure 4-17. When the computer has rebooted after installation, the standard Ubuntu login screen will appear.

INSTALLING UBUNTU ON AN APPLE MAC

Ubuntu can also run on Apple Macintosh computers, as well as PCs. However, the instructions vary depending on the processor installed in your Macintosh. To find out which type of processor your Mac uses, click the Apple menu and select About This Mac. In the summary dialog box, look for the Processor heading. If your computer is more than four years old, the line will probably read "PowerPC," and you should refer to the instructions under that heading. If yours is a more recent Mac, and the line contains "Intel" in combination with any other words, such as "Intel Core i5," continue with the following instructions.

Intel

If your Mac contains an Intel processor, you might be able to boot from the DVD-ROM supplied with this book and use it to install Ubuntu. However, some extra steps are necessary. If you're using Mac OS X 10.5 "Leopard" or 10.6 "Snow Leopard," you can use Apple's Boot Camp utility (located in Applications ➤ Utilities) to resize the existing Mac OS X partition. Boot Camp is also used to provide a boot menu to let you switch between Mac OS X and Ubuntu. However, Boot Camp is designed to allow Windows to be installed alongside Mac OS X, so some additional steps are necessary to make it work with Ubuntu. A full guide is provided at the official Ubuntu wiki: `https://help.ubuntu.com/community/MacBook`.

If you're running Mac OS X Tiger (10.4), you may want to look into using third-party boot menu software called rEFIt (`http://refit.sourceforge.net`). This utility can also be used in Leopard and Snow Leopard in place of Boot Camp.

After the computer has been correctly configured by following the guide, you can boot from the DVD-ROM and follow the instructions in the rest of this chapter. Hold down the C key (or Cmd+Shift+Option+Delete on older systems) when the Apple symbol appears during booting to boot from the DVD-ROM disc.

PowerPC

Ubuntu also works on a Mac based on a PowerPC processor, although a special version must be used. Note that Canonical, the company that sponsors Ubuntu, no longer provides official releases of Ubuntu on this architecture. Current versions are supported solely by the community. The PowerPC version of Ubuntu 10.04 can be downloaded from `http://cdimage.ubuntu.com/ports/releases/lucid/release/`. Choose the link entitled `Mac (PowerPC) and IBM-PPC (POWER5) desktop CD`. Once you've saved this ISO image to disk, you'll need to manually burn it to a blank CD-R or CD-RW, and then boot from it to install Ubuntu. However, first you must create some free space on the hard disk, so you can install Ubuntu alongside your existing OS (assuming you want to dual-boot Mac OS X and Ubuntu; if you want to let Ubuntu use the entire hard disk, the Ubuntu installer will be able to wipe the existing partitions, and no further action is necessary). Boot from the Mac OS X installation DVD-ROM and quit the installer. Then use Disk Utility from the menus to resize the hard disk in order to make space.

To create the Ubuntu installation CD in Mac OS X, insert a blank CD-R or CD-RW, and then start Disk Utility. Choose Images ➤ Burn, navigate to the `ubuntu-10.04-desktop-powerpc.iso` file you downloaded and then click the Burn button. When the burn has finished, use the disc to boot from and install Ubuntu, following the instructions provided in this chapter. Hold down the C key (or Cmd+Shift+Option+Delete on older systems) when the Apple symbol appears during booting to boot from the CD.

The Virtual Option

Many owners of Apple computers choose to run Ubuntu in a virtual machine running on OS X, rather than install and run it natively. As discussed in the "Virtualization" sidebar in Chapter 3 (where we list the main virtualization software options for Mac OS X), this can be a convenient and risk-free choice, whether you're an ordinary user who wants to experiment with Ubuntu or a software developer who wants access to OS X, Linux, and Windows on a single machine. Virtualizing is a compromise, though, both in performance—because Ubuntu has to compete for hardware resources with the host operating system—and in the heavy dependence you will still have on proprietary software. The choice is very much yours!

Summary

By following the steps outlined in this chapter, you should now have Ubuntu installed on your computer. We've tried to provide you with enough information to get around certain problems, and explain each step of the installation.

Alas, it's still possible that you encountered hurdles that weren't addressed here. In the next chapter, you'll find solutions to common problems associated with Ubuntu installation.

CHAPTER 5

■ ■ ■

Solving Installation Problems

There's a very good chance that your Ubuntu installation will go smoothly, and you'll find yourself with a first-rate operating system up and running within just a few minutes. However, issues do sometimes arise, so we've drawn together a list of common problems alongside their solutions, which should get you out of any tight spot. These problems are organized by when they occur: (A) before you start Ubuntu's live distro mode; (B) while running the installation program; and (C) after the installation, when you boot for the first time. The final section of the chapter describes how to configure the graphical subsystem with the X.org configuration utility, which can be useful if graphical glitches arise. The latest version of Ubuntu has an all-encompassing recovery mode, which should assist in solving many problems.

A. Preinstallation Problems

Some problems might arise before you even boot Ubuntu's live distro mode in order to run the installation program. This section addresses such issues.

The Disc Doesn't Boot

When I boot from the Ubuntu DVD-ROM, the drive spins up as if something is happening, but I see either nothing or strange graphics on the screen.

Solution

The DVD-ROM disc might be either dirty or faulty. Examine its surface for scratches or try removing dust from it with a soft, lint-free cloth. A typical indicator of a dirty or damaged disc is that the drive spins up and then instantly spins down several times in succession—listen to the whir of the drive's motor to tell whether this is the case.

If the disc seems okay, it might be that your computer is not set to boot from the DVD or is unable to display the Ubuntu boot menu. In the former case, you'll need to redefine the boot order in the computer's BIOS, as covered in Chapter 4. To get around the latter problem, when you see the blank screen or graphical corruption, press the Escape key twice. Then press Enter. You'll see the word boot: at the top left of the screen, along with a prompt where you can enter commands. Type **live** and press Enter.

The Computer Is Having a Kernel Panic

The DVD starts to boot, but then the computer freezes and eventually displays a message along the lines of "Kernel Panic."

Solution

Kernel Panic errors occur when Ubuntu cannot continue to load for various reasons. In this context, it's likely that either the DVD is faulty (or dirty) or that the PC has a hardware problem.

First, check to make sure that the DVD is clean and not scratched. If possible, try it on a different computer. If it works, then it's clearly not at fault, and your computer most likely has a hardware issue. In particular, bad memory can cause problems. Does the computer already have an operating system installed? Does it run without problems? If not, consider replacing your memory modules.

To thoroughly test your computer's memory, boot from the Ubuntu DVD, press any key when you first see an Ubuntu logo, and select the Test Memory option on the menu (use the arrow keys to move up or down in the list, and press Enter to make a selection). This will run the Memtest86 program, and any problems with your memory will be reported in the Errors column on the right side of the program screen. For more details about how to use Memtest86, see `www.memtest86.com`.

The DVD Starts to Boot, but the Screen Goes Blank or Corrupted

Soon after the DVD starts to boot, the computer looks like it has crashed—the screen goes blank or the display looks scrambled!

Solution

Your graphics card may be incompatible with either the framebuffer graphical mode used by Ubuntu's boot routine, or the new kernel-mode-setting technology which is now enabled by default on most common video chipsets. You can overcome these problems by following these steps:

1. Reboot the computer. As soon as you see the purple background, with two small icons at the bottom of the screen —a keyboard and an accessibility symbol—press any key to access the boot menu. Choose your language and then press F6. This will bring up a list of kernel boot options. Press Escape to dismiss this menu.

2. You should then see a cursor at the end of a line of text which starts with the words `Boot Options`. Using the Backspace key to delete `quiet splash` from the end of the line, as shown in Figure 5-1. Then press Enter.

If the problem persists, reboot, press a key to access the boot menu, choose your language, and press F6 again to bring up the boot options. This time use the arrow and spacebar/Enter keys to select nomodeset from the list. Press Escape, and then Enter.

Additional boot options which you can try adding manually include:

`i915.modeset=0` (for older Intel graphics adapters)

`xforcevesa`

`fb=false`

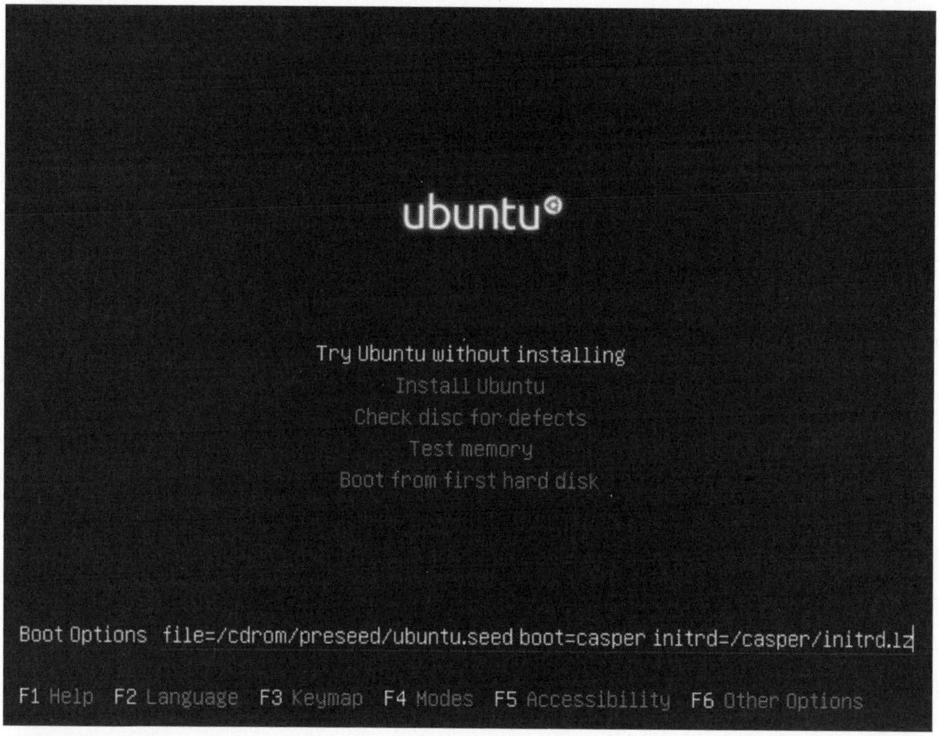

Figure 5-1. Pressing F6 in the boot menu gives you the chance to choose from a menu of kernel options or edit the options manually.

The Computer Freezes During Installation

After I've selected the Install Ubuntu option on the menu, the status bar appears, but then the computer freezes.

Solution

It's possible that the power-saving feature or the advanced programmable interrupt controller (APIC) in your computer is causing problems. Boot the DVD again, and as soon as you see the purple background, with two small icons at the bottom of the screen—a keyboard and an accessibility symbol—press any key. Choose your language and then press F6 to bring up a list of kernel boot options. Using the arrow keys to navigate, and spacebar/Enter to select or deselect options, make sure that the following three options are selected:

    acpi=off

    noapic

    nolapic

Then press Escape to dismiss the boot options menu, and Enter to boot Ubuntu.

Installer "Unrecoverable Error" Message

Booting the DVD fails with the message "The installer encountered an unrecoverable error. A desktop session will now be run so that you may investigate the problem or try installing again."

Solution

Two solutions which can fix this problem are:

- Ubuntu's release notes suggest that you reboot the DVD, access the boot menu by pressing any key at the splash screen (when you see the two small icons at the foot of the screen), select "Try Ubuntu without installing," and then use the "Install Ubuntu 10.04" icon when the live Desktop appears.

- Go into your computer's BIOS settings and disable the floppy disk. Alternatively, if your computer has a floppy disk controller but no floppy disk drive connected, and you may want to use that ancient technology occasionally, install a floppy disk drive and reboot.

My Notebook Display Looks Corrupted During Installation

I'm attempting to install Ubuntu on a notebook computer. After I select the Install Ubuntu option and press Enter, the screen is filled with graphical corruption, and it looks like Ubuntu has crashed. (Alternatively, the screen looks squashed, or some elements are off-center or off the edge of the screen.)

Solution

When the Ubuntu boot menu appears, press the Escape key twice and then press Enter. At the boot: prompt, type **live vga=771**. Then press Enter. This starts the live mode in a safe, VGA resolution. You should be able to change the resolution after the system has loaded.

I'm Using a KVM, and the Screen Looks Wrong

I'm using the same keyboard, mouse, and monitor across several computers, courtesy of a keyboard, video, and mouse (KVM) switch. When Ubuntu boots, the resolution is wrong and the graphics are corrupted. (Also, my keyboard or mouse doesn't work correctly.)

Solution

A KVM switch may not allow Ubuntu to correctly probe the attached hardware. Consider attaching the keyboard, monitor, and mouse directly to the computer for the duration of the installation. After installation is accomplished, you can reintroduce the KVM, and things should be fine.

NONE OF THESE SOLUTIONS WORK!

If you run into installation problems for which you can't find a solution here, you can try using the Alternative Installer. This will need to be burned to a CD as an image and booted as before.

We've provided an ISO image of a CD version of Ubuntu that uses the Alternative Installer. This can be found on Side B of the DVD-ROM. You can learn more about it in Appendix D.

Unfortunately, there isn't space to provide a full installation guide here, although most installation options should correspond loosely to those discussed in Chapter 4.

During the three-year support lifetime of Ubuntu 10.04 Desktop Edition, updated versions known as "point releases" will be made available every six months—labelled 10.04.1, 10.04.2, 10.04.3 and so on—incorporating bug fixes and updates. If you're having trouble installing the version supplied in our DVD, or you are preparing to install Ubuntu 10.04 some time after this book was published, check http://releases.ubuntu.com/lucid/ for the latest point release. The bug that is causing you installation problems may have been fixed, and you will also avoid having to download and apply hundreds of megabytes of updates after installation.

B. Installation Problems

After the DVD-ROM has booted in live distro mode, and you've run the installation program, you may get error messages or experience other difficulties. This section offers some solutions to common installation problems.

I'm Offered Only a Text Login

I've partitioned my disk and clicked to start the installation, after which the Installing System progress bar appears. However, it stops at a certain percentage with an error message. If I click the Continue button, everything continues, and at the end I'm offered the chance to reboot into the new installation. However, when I reboot, the Ubuntu Desktop doesn't appear. Instead, all I see is a black screen with a text-mode login prompt.

Solution

For some reason, vital Ubuntu software hasn't been correctly copied to the machine. Make sure the DVD is in your computer's drive and, at the aforementioned text-mode login prompt, type your username and press Enter. Type your password when it's requested and press Enter. Note that you will not see any characters, masked or otherwise, as you type your password. Then, at the command prompt, type the following, pressing Enter or Return after each line:

```
sudo apt-get update
    [At this point you'll need to type your password; do so]
sudo apt-get -f install
sudo apt-get install ubuntu-desktop
```

If this doesn't work, follow the instructions in the "None of These Solutions Work!" sidebar, and install Ubuntu using the Alternate Installer.

The Computer Can't Find My Hard Disk

When the Ubuntu installation program gets to the Prepare Disk Space stage, it reports that it can't find any hard disk in my computer.

Solution

There are many possible reasons for this, but here are three potential solutions that you might try in sequence:

1. Select "Specify partitions manually" and click the Forward button. You should see a list of hard disks with each of its partitions displayed, and you should then be able to follow the instructions under the "Manually Edit the Partition Table" heading in Chapter 4.

2. Ensure that the jumpers are set correctly on the hard disk (consult the hard disk's documentation if necessary). This is particularly worth checking if you have more than one hard disk installed in your computer. If this doesn't solve the problem, and your second hard disk is nonbootable (that is, it's used only for data storage), try temporarily removing it and then installing Ubuntu. Reconnect it after installation has completed.

3. See the "None of These Solutions Work!" sidebar to learn how to use the Alternate Installer. This contains an older installation program that many consider more reliable on some problematic computers.

I See Lots of Hard Disks in the Partitioner

When I try to install Ubuntu, the Prepare Partitions screen shows one (or several) additional small hard disks, usually identified as /dev/sda or similar, followed by a number.

Solution

If you have a USB memory stick inserted, or a memory card reader with a card in it, it will be identified by the Ubuntu installer in this way. You can ignore this or, if you want to avoid confusion, quit the installer, remove the memory stick or card reader, and restart the installer program. Note that many computers that ship with Windows Vista or Windows 7 may have a System Restore partition on the main hard disk, which will also show up here.

I Have Too Many Partitions

When manually partitioning, I see an error message to the effect that I can't have more than four primary partitions.

Solution

This is a limitation in how hard disks work, not an issue with Ubuntu. A hard disk can contain only four primary partitions, but this can be extended by subdividing these further into logical partitions, as covered in Chapter 4. To resolve the problem, when creating a new partition, select Logical as the type of partition.

For more details about primary and extended hard disk partitioning, see http://en.wikipedia.org/wiki/Disk_partitioning.

C. Postinstallation Problems

Problems might also occur after you install Ubuntu. This section addresses several possible postinstallation problems. This section covers only problems that appear immediately after installation—those that prevent Ubuntu from working correctly immediately after its first boot. Issues surrounding the configuration of hardware or software are dealt with in Chapter 7.

My Monitor Resolution Is Not Recognized

I use a widescreen monitor (or a widescreen notebook). When I boot to the desktop, the resolution is set too low. When I try to switch resolutions (by clicking System ➤ Preferences ➤ Monitors), the resolution my monitor usually runs at isn't available in the list.

Solution

In a minority of cases, the open source drivers for ATI and Nvidia cards can't support certain resolutions on particular monitors, especially widescreen ones. One solution is to install proprietary graphics drivers, as discussed in Chapter 7, although you should also update your system online as soon as possible (see Chapter 8) to see if the open source graphics drivers have been updated and improved. In both cases, you'll need to configure your computer to go online, which is also explained in Chapter 7.

My Keyboard or Mouse Isn't Working

After booting up, my USB mouse and/or USB keyboard are not recognized.

Solution

Try unplugging the keyboard and/or mouse, and then reattaching them. You might also try cleaning the connections with a dry cloth or compressed air. If you find they now work, log in to Ubuntu and perform an online system upgrade. See Chapter 8 for more information about this task.

If that fails to solve the problem, you can configure your BIOS to pretend your mouse and keyboard are traditional PS/2-style devices, as follows:

1. Enter the BIOS setup program by pressing Delete during the initial stages of your computer boot routine (while memory testing and drive identification are still taking place). Some computers might use a different key combination to enter BIOS setup, such as Ctrl+Insert, but that information will be displayed on your screen.

2. Use the arrow keys to navigate to the Integrated Peripherals section and then look for an entry along the lines of USB Legacy Support. Set it to Enabled.

3. Press Escape to return to the main menu, and opt to save the changes.

4. Reboot the computer.

The Computer No Longer Boots

When I boot for the first time, I see an error message along the lines of "No operating system could be found on the hard disk."

Solution

It seems that, for whatever reason, the Grub boot loader wasn't installed correctly. Boot from the DVD-ROM and select Try Ubuntu Without Any Change to Your Computer when prompted. When the Ubuntu desktop appears, click Applications ➤ Accessories ➤ Terminal. This opens a command-prompt window. Type the following command:

```
sudo grub-install sda
```

You will be prompted for your password. Type it and press Enter. Almost immediately you will be returned to the command prompt. You can then close the Terminal window and restart Ubuntu (click the power button icon in the top right corner of the screen and choose Shut Down). Ensure that you remove the DVD-ROM when prompted. You should find that the Ubuntu boot menu now appears when you boot.

Ubuntu Is Working, but Windows Won't Boot

After I've installed Ubuntu, Windows will no longer boot, although Ubuntu works fine. After I select Windows from the boot menu, the Windows boot procedure either freezes when "Starting Windows . . ." appears or the boot status bar is shown, but the Desktop never appears.

Solution

Try repairing your Windows disk by using the Windows command-line tool chkdsk. This can be done from the recovery mode of the Windows installation CD/DVD, but the instructions for how to do this vary depending on whether you're running Windows Vista or XP.

Windows Vista and Windows 7

If you're running Windows Vista or 7, follow these steps to run chkdsk:

1. Insert the Windows Vista or 7 installation DVD and select to boot from it. For details on how to configure your computer to boot from the DVD, see stage 2 of the Ubuntu installation guide in Chapter 4.

2. You'll see the message "Windows is Loading Files," along with a progress bar. After this has cleared, select your language/locale settings from the Install Windows dialog box, and then click Next.

3. On the next screen, don't click the Install Now button. Instead, click the Repair Your Computer link at the bottom-left corner of the window.

4. In the System Recovery Options dialog box, select your Windows Vista or Windows 7 partition and then click Next.

5. On the next screen, select Command Prompt.

6. In the command-prompt window that appears, type the following (this assumes Vista or 7 is installed on drive C:):

   `chkdsk c: /R`

7. Wait until the check has completed, and then type **exit** at the prompt.

8. Back in the System Recovery Options dialog box, click Restart. This will reboot your computer. Be sure to eject the Windows Vista DVD before doing so.

Windows XP

If you're running Windows XP, follow these steps to run chkdsk:

1. Insert the Windows XP installation CD and select to boot from it. For details of how to configure your computer to boot from the CD, see stage 2 of the Ubuntu installation guide in Chapter 4.

2. You'll see status messages that Windows is loading driver files. Eventually, the Windows Setup menu will appear. Press R to start the Recovery Console.

3. You'll be asked to confirm which Windows installation you would like to boot into; do so.

4. You're then prompted for the administrator's password. If you don't have one, simply press Enter.

5. At the command prompt, type the following:

   `chkdsk c: /R`

6. Wait until the check has completed, and then type **exit** at the prompt. This will reboot your computer. Be sure to eject the Windows XP CD before rebooting.

You can also use Super Grub Disk (`www.supergrubdisk.org`) to boot the computer and examine the boot process to find and fix the problem.

I Can See Only a Text Login Prompt

When I boot for the first time, all I see is a black screen with some text at the top reading, "Ubuntu 10.04 LTS [hostname] tty1" and beneath that, "[hostname] login:."

Solution

For some reason, the automatic configuration of your graphics card failed during installation. See the following section for instructions on configuring your GUI manually.

Graphical Problems

Although Ubuntu is extremely adept at automatically detecting and configuring your PC's graphics hardware, it sometimes gets things wrong. Such problems are characterized by one of the following:

- Ubuntu freezes when the Desktop would usually appear.

- You see onscreen graphical corruption of either text or graphics.

- The resolution is set too low or too high, and you can't change it to the correct resolution because it isn't offered.

- You see a black screen with only a text login prompt.

■ **Tip** If the Desktop is off-center, and the menus can't be accessed to change the resolution, right-click somewhere on the panel and temporarily add a new main menu applet. You'll then be able to access the Preferences section from this.

Troubleshooting graphical problems has never been as easy as in the latest versions of Ubuntu. Ubuntu has added a system component which ensures that X.org (Ubuntu's graphical subsystem, often referred to simply as X) will run in low-graphics mode should X.org fail to start with the current display settings. In other words, it's a lot like Safe Mode that you might be used to with Microsoft Windows.

Low-graphics mode uses 640×480 or 800×600 resolution, 16 or 256 colors, and a VESA driver to operate the graphics card. Obviously, these are not optimal settings for using the Desktop, but they're chosen for their wide compatibility with most graphics hardware.

Ubuntu also features a recovery mode that will attempt to fix common problems such as poor graphics performance and broken packages. Normally when Ubuntu boots on a computer with only one operating system installed, the Grub boot loader menu is hidden from you. To use recovery mode, you will have to access the boot menu, which you do by holding down the Shift key as soon as your computer's BIOS screen has finished displaying. From the boot menu, use the arrow keys to select the second Ubuntu option, labeled Recovery Mode, and press Enter. The Linux kernel will start up in text mode, after which a Recovery Menu will appear, on a blue background. For graphics issues, choose the fourth option on the list, `failsafeX`. This will present you with options to run Ubuntu in low-graphics mode temporarily, reconfigure your graphics settings, and troubleshoot the error.

■ **Note** On a technical level, Lucid uses the latest version of X.org, 7.5. This version of X.org is able to autodetect and autoconfigure monitors, graphic cards, and mice, which means manual customization of display settings—long the bane of Linux users around the world—is rarely necessary.

Additionally, if your computer utilizes a recent Nvidia or ATI 3D graphics card, you can try installing the proprietary drivers. This is best done when the system is up and running, so follow the instructions here to get a workable graphical system and then follow the instructions in the "Installing 3D Drivers and Activating Desktop Visual Effects" section of Chapter 7. Installing a proprietary driver might be the only way to get visual desktop effects working and utilize the full resolution of a widescreen monitor.

In Ubuntu's Monitors settings (System ➤ Preferences ➤ Monitors), you can experiment with different resolutions for your monitor, as shown in Figure 5-2. Table 5-1 shows the most common monitor resolutions. Note that flat (LCD) screens generally have only one "native" resolution at which the display is sharp, in contrast to the old CRT monitors, which can support a variety of resolutions.

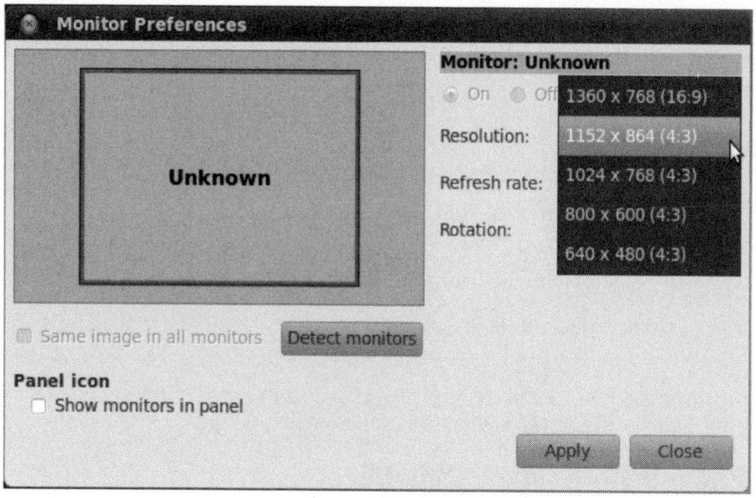

Figure 5-2. You can experiment with different resolutions in the Monitor Preferences section.

Table 5-1. Typical Monitor Resolutions

LCD Screens	Resolution
15 inches	1024×768
17 inches	1280×1024
19 inches	1280×1024, 1366×768 (widescreen), 1440×900 (widescreen)
20 inches	1600×900 (widescreen), 1680×1050 (widescreen)
21 inches	1600×1200
22 inches	1680×1050 (widescreen), 1920x1080 (widescreen)
23 inches	1920×1080 (widescreen)
23 inches	1920×1200 (widescreen)
24 inches	1920×1200 (widescreen), 1920×1080 (widescreen)
26 inches	1366×768 (widescreen), 1920×1200 (widescreen)
27 inches	1920×1080 (widescreen), 1920×1200 (widescreen)
28 inches	1920×1200 (widescreen)
30 inches	2560×1600 (widescreen)
40 inches	1366×768 (widescreen)

CRT Monitors	Resolution
14 inches	800×600, 640×480
15 inches	800×600, 640×480
17 inches	1024×768, 800×600, 640×480
19 inches	1280×1024, 1024×768, 800×600, 640×480
20 inches	1600×1200, 1280×1024, 1024×768, 800×600, 640×480

Note that if you've installed proprietary drivers for an Nvidia or ATI graphics card, you'll see a different display configuration screen. The Nvidia options are shown in Figure 5-3.

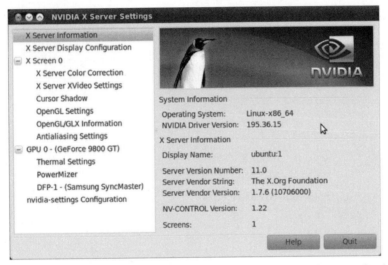

Figure 5-3. Nvidia users see a different set of options for configuring displays.

Summary

This chapter's goal was to address problems that might occur during the installation of Ubuntu. It discussed preinstallation, installation, and postinstallation issues. It also covered some of the graphical problems you may encounter.

You should now have Ubuntu installed. The next part of this book focuses on helping you get everything up and running. You'll learn essential skills and become a confident Linux user.

The No-Nonsense Getting Started Guide

CHAPTER 6

■ ■ ■

Booting Ubuntu for the First Time

Now that Ubuntu is installed, you'll no doubt want to get started immediately, and that's what Part 3 of this book is all about. In later chapters, we'll present specific details of using Ubuntu and getting essential hardware up and running. We'll also show you how to personalize the desktop so it works in a way that's best for you on a day-to-day basis. But right now, the goal of this chapter is to get you doing the same things you did under Windows as quickly as possible.

This chapter explains how to start up Ubuntu for the first time and work with the desktop. It also shows how some familiar aspects of your computer, such as using the mouse, are slightly enhanced under Ubuntu.

Starting Up

If you've chosen to dual-boot with Windows, the first Ubuntu screen you'll see is the boot loader menu, which appears shortly after you switch on your PC. If Ubuntu is the only operating system on your hard disk, you need to hold the Shift key during system startup to access this boot menu, but you won't need to do so unless you want to access the recovery mode boot settings. In fact, if Ubuntu is the only operating system on your computer, you can skip to the next section of this chapter.

■ **Note** The boot loader is actually a separate program called Grub, which has been updated to version 2 since Ubuntu 9.10. This program kicks off everything and starts Ubuntu.

The boot loader menu you see when your PC is set to dual-boot has three or four choices, as shown in Figure 6-1. The top one is what you need to boot Ubuntu. The Ubuntu option will be selected automatically within 10 seconds, but you can press Enter to start immediately.

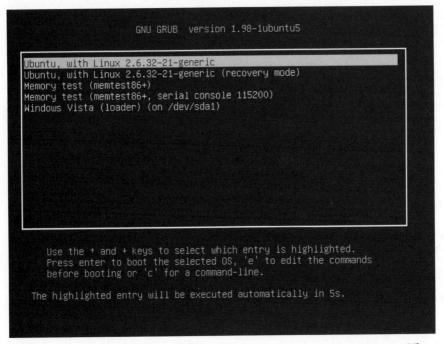

```
                    GNU GRUB   version 1.98-1ubuntu5

Ubuntu, with Linux 2.6.32-21-generic
Ubuntu, with Linux 2.6.32-21-generic (recovery mode)
Memory test (memtest86+)
Memory test (memtest86+, serial console 115200)
Windows Vista (loader) (on /dev/sda1)




         Use the ↑ and ↓ keys to select which entry is highlighted.
         Press enter to boot the selected OS, 'e' to edit the commands
         before booting or 'c' for a command-line.

      The highlighted entry will be executed automatically in 5s.
```

Figure 6-1. The default choice is fine on the boot menu, so press Enter to start Ubuntu.

You should find that you also have an entry for Windows, located at the bottom of the list and labeled with whichever version of the OS you have installed. To boot into Windows, simply use the cursor keys to move the selection to the appropriate option and then press Enter.

You should also see an entry ending in "(recovery mode)." This is a little like Safe Mode within Windows. If you select recovery mode, Ubuntu will boot to a text mode menu with six options:

resume—Resume normal boot: This option allows you to boot normally, as if you didn't need to fix anything at all. However, the big difference with this option compared to a graphical boot is that Ubuntu boots in text mode, in which system messages scroll past as Ubuntu is starting up. If you have problems with booting Ubuntu, you can run in recovery mode and choose this option to find error messages in the boot process.

clean—Try to make free space: This option forces the boot loader to try to make free space on the disk.

dpkg—Repair broken packages: This option tries to repair the software installed on your computer.

Grub—Update Grub loader: Forces Grub (the program that presents you this boot menu) to query the operating systems installed in your hard disks and to recreate the list it presents at startup.

netroot—Drop to shell prompt with networking: Like the option "root" but with the networking features fully functional.

root—Drop to root shell prompt: This option boots with conservative system settings and then presents you with a command-line prompt in administrator mode (you run as the *root user*—a special user account that has absolute power over the entire system, so try to avoid booting to this option if you can do so, and be very careful when you don't have any other option but to use the root shell prompt). The typical usage for this prompt is to change the passwords of users if they forget their passwords, to free up disk space to run normally, and to uninstall buggy software to bring back system stability. The system commands that can be used for recovery are passwd (to change passwords), mv (to move files and folders), rm (to delete files and folders), cp (to copy files and folders), mkdir (to create a new folder), and dpkg (to install or remove software). These and other commands are discussed further in Appendix A.

When you update your system software, you might find that new entries are added to the boot menu list. This is because the kernel has been updated. The *kernel* is the central system file that Ubuntu relies on, and essentially, the boot menu exists to let you choose between different kernels. Almost without exception, the first (topmost) entry is the one you'll want each time to boot Ubuntu, because this will always use the most recent version of the kernel, along with the latest versions of other system software. The other entries will start the system with older versions of the kernel and are provided in the unlikely situation that the latest kernel causes problems.

■ **Note** All operating systems need a boot loader, even Windows. However, the Windows boot loader is hidden and simply starts the OS. Under Ubuntu, the boot loader usually has a menu so you can select Linux or perhaps an option that lets you access your PC for troubleshooting problems. When you gain some experience with Ubuntu, you might choose to install two or more versions of Linux on the same hard disk, and you'll be able to select among them by using the boot menu.

Logging In

After Ubuntu has booted (and much effort has been put into reducing the time Lucid Lynx takes to do it), you should see the login screen, as shown in Figure 6-2. Here you enter the username and the password you created during the installation process. If during installation you selected to be automatically logged in at startup, then you will not see this screen and will be presented with the desktop right away.

Clicking the Shutdown Options button in the bottom-right corner of the screen brings up a menu from which you can opt to reboot the system or shut it down. Next to this button are the clock and the Universal Access Preferences button, which allows you to enable accessibility features such as the on-screen keyboard and the magnifier.

The user account you created during installation is similar to what Windows refers to as an *administrator* account. This means that the within the account you use on a day-to-day basis you can also change important system settings and reconfigure the system. However, the main difference between Ubuntu and Windows is that you'll need to enter your password to make any serious changes, rather than clicking in a confirmation dialog box, as with Windows Vista or Windows 7 (of course, Windows XP doesn't have any kind of confirmation requirement at all!).

Don't worry about damaging anything accidentally; trying to reconfigure the system or access a serious system setting will invariably bring up a password prompt. You can simply click the Cancel button if you don't want to continue.

■ **Note** Unlike some versions of Linux, Ubuntu doesn't encourage the user to use an actual root (administrator) account. This is even disabled by default. Instead, it operates on the principle of certain ordinary users adopting superuser privileges that allow them to administer the system when they need to. Those are called *sudoers*. In UNIX terms, *sudo* is short for *superuser do*, meaning to perform a task as the superuser. A sudoer is a user account enabled to execute sudo for certain tasks, as defined in the sudoers file. The user account you create during setup has these privileges.

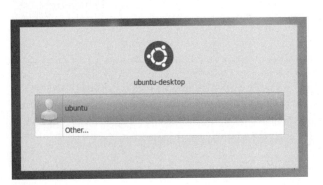

Figure 6-2. Select or type your username, enter your password, and then press Enter to log in.

Exploring the Desktop

After you've logged in, you'll see the welcoming theme of the Ubuntu desktop, as shown in Figure 6-3. Feel free to click around and see what you can discover. There's little chance of your doing serious damage, so let yourself go wild and play around with your new OS! However, be careful if any dialog boxes ask you to type your password—this indicates that you've clicked an action that has the potential to change the system in a fundamental way.

Figure 6-3. *A clean Ubuntu desktop—this is your first view of the new OS.*

First Impressions

The first thing you'll notice is that the desktop is clean compared to Windows. You don't have a lot of icons littering the screen.

Of course, you can fill the desktop with all the icons you want. As with Windows, you can save files to the desktop for easy access. In addition, you can click and drag icons from any of the menus onto the desktop in order to create shortcuts.

BEHIND THE DESKTOP: GNOME

Although we refer to the *Ubuntu desktop*, the fundamental software behind it is created by GNOME: the Free Software Desktop Project. This is one of the most well-established organizations currently producing desktop interfaces for Linux, as well as for other versions of UNIX. Its home page is http://www.gnome.org.

Although it's based on GNOME, Ubuntu's desktop has its own set of individual features and programs, as well as a unique look and feel. That said, it works in an almost identical way to versions of GNOME that are used in other Linux distributions, such as Fedora.

The nature of open-source software—whereby anyone can take the source code and create a new version of a program—makes Ubuntu's remodeling of the GNOME desktop possible. Unlike with Windows software, more than one current version of a particular program or software suite can exist, each usually tailored to the particular needs of one of the various Linux distributions.

There are also versions of Ubuntu built around KDE (http://www.kde.org) and Xfce (http://www.xfce.org), two similar desktop environments. They're called Kubuntu and Xubuntu, respectively, and they're supplied on the DVD-ROM that comes with this book. For more details, including installation instructions, see Appendix D.

■ **Note** If you're dual-booting with Windows, you might see an icon at the top left of the Ubuntu desktop that will let you access your Windows files. On one system, it was identified as sda1. Double-click the icon to view the Windows file system. Similarly, if you have a memory card reader or digital camera plugged in your PC, you might see desktop icons for them too, and any inserted CD/DVD discs will also be represented by desktop icons.

Along the top of the desktop, you see three menus:

Applications: This menu is the equivalent of the Windows Start ➤ All Programs menu. Here you'll find access to all the software available under Ubuntu, categorized for easy finding.

Places: This menu is somewhat like My Computer in Windows, in that it gives quick access to locations within the file system. The Places menu also provides access to network locations, such as file servers (this is probably be important only if you use Ubuntu in a business context). You can add and remove folders and files here for quick access to your favorite places, and also search for files.

System: This menu is a little like the Windows Control Panel, in that it allows you to change various system settings. The Preferences submenu lets you change trivial system settings, such as the screen saver, or start new system services, such as the remote desktop service that lets you view your desktop across a network connection. The Administration submenu lets you change underlying system settings, such as configuring new hardware (like printers) and installing software.

The mouse works mostly as it does in Windows, in that you can move it around and click on things. For the most part, single- and double-clicking work exactly as they do in Windows. You can also right-click virtually everything and everywhere to bring up context menus, which usually let you alter settings. And you should find that the scroll wheel in between the mouse buttons lets you scroll windows.

Something that might catch your attention the first time you open a window in Lucid Lynx is the placement of the familiar Maximize, Minimize, and Close buttons. They are placed to the left of the top bar, instead of to the right as is customary in Windows and OS X. Clicking the Close button ends each program, as in Windows.

Whenever Ubuntu is busy, an animated, circular icon appears that is similar in principle to the hourglass icon used in Windows. It also appears when programs are being launched.

■ **Caution** Bear in mind that Ubuntu isn't a clone of Windows and doesn't try to be. Although it works in a similar way—by providing menus and icons and containing programs within windows—there are differences and refinements that may trip you up as you explore.

WRONG RESOLUTION!

You might find when you boot up that Ubuntu has defaulted to the wrong resolution—in other words, everything might be a little too large or too small. You might have trouble reading text, for example, or you might find that program windows fill the screen to the extent that their contents partially disappear off the edges.

Changing the resolution is simple. Choose System ➤ Preferences ➤ Monitors from the menu (at the top of the screen). In the Resolution drop-down list, select the appropriate setting for your monitor. For a 17-inch CRT monitor, the standard resolution is 1024×768. Most 17-inch TFT screens run at 1280×1024 resolution. A 15-inch TFT screen will usually run at 1024×768 resolution. For laptops, 13-inch to 15-inch LCD panels typically run at 1280×800 resolution. If you have a 15-inch CRT monitor (common on PCs made before 2000), you'll probably find 800×600 a maximum setting; others prefer 640×480. More recent wide-screen monitors can be pushed up to 1920×1080 resolution, but this is likely to demand a higher-end graphics card to work well. If you're in doubt about your monitor's resolution, consult its manual for more information.

If the resolution you want isn't available, Ubuntu might have incorrectly set up your graphics card and monitor. See the "Graphical Problems" section in Chapter 5 to learn how to reconfigure the graphical subsystem.

Exploring the Panels

Central pieces of the Ubuntu desktop are the *panels*. Those are the strips that you find at the top and at the bottom of your desktop. They are extremely useful and highly customizable. Most of the operations you will ever need to access on Ubuntu are available through those panels, so mastering them early on is of great help (to read more about personalizing panels, refer to Chapter 9). You will encounter the following default elements in the panels:

Main menus: The three menus at the top left of the screen provide access to most of Ubuntu's functionality. As noted earlier, the Applications menu provides access to programs; the Places menu provides access to the file system; and the System menu provides access to configuration settings. You can click and drag practically every menu entry onto the desktop in order to create a shortcut.

Application launchers: Beside the main menus you'll find icons that represent applications. By default the Firefox web browser and the Ubuntu help find their home here. Some applications add a launcher here when you install them, or you can create your own launchers for existing applications. When you click one of those icons, the corresponding application starts.

Off button: The right-most item in the top panel is the Off button, about which more details are given later in this chapter. You will notice sometimes that the Off button changes its color to red. This is an indication that a change has been made to the system that requires you to reboot the computer. This can happen, for example, when you install the latest updates to Ubuntu.

Me menu: A new element introduced with Lucid Lynx—the Me Menu, indicated by your username on the panel and located to the left of the Off button—allows you to easily set your status for various IM clients and post to social network sites like Facebook or Twitter without having to log in to them. Its functionality is explained in depth in Chapter 15.

Clock: The clock is located at the top right of the screen. Clicking it brings up a handy monthly calendar and a drop-down panel that contains a miniature world map, regional time, and weather for several locations. Click it again to hide this display. Right-clicking the clock brings up a context menu. On this menu, the Preferences option lets you alter the way the date and time are displayed and enables you to define a default location for weather information (displayed in the system tray to the left of the clock). The Adjust Date & Time option lets you change the time and/or date if they're incorrect.

Indicator applet: The Indicator applet, represented by an envelope icon next to the clock, allows you to configure instant message (IM) and mail accounts, and is used by those same accounts to inform you when a change has occurred, such as new incoming mail or an IM from one of your contacts.

Notification area: This is similar to the Windows system tray. Programs that like to hang around in memory, such as the Rhythmbox media player or Skype, add icons in this top-right area to allow quick access to their functions. The Software Update Notifier appears in this area to let you know that software updates are available (similar to Windows Update). Network Manager displays an icon here when you are connected to the network. The Volume Control applet is here too. Usually, you simply need to click (or right-click) their icons to access the program features.

■ **Tip** The small bar marks the leftmost boundary of the notification area. To resize the notification area, right-click this bar and remove the check from the Lock to Panel menu entry. Then you can click and drag the bar to a different size. This might be handy if the notification area starts to fill up with icons!

Notifications: In addition to the notification area, Ubuntu also has a pop-up, short-term notification system that is used to keep you informed of changes to your system's volume, screen brightness, network availability, IM friend status, and other useful things. You might want to disable some notifications if they start to annoy you.

Hide Windows button: At the bottom left is the Hide Windows button that instantly minimizes all open windows to give access to the desktop underneath.

Window List: The largest portion of the panel at the bottom of the screen is occupied by the Window List, which shows the programs that are currently running (if any). As with Windows, you can simply click the button for any program to bring that window "to the top." Alternatively, you can right-click each entry to instantly minimize or maximize that particular window. It's also possible to switch between running applications on the Window List by pressing Alt+Tab.

Trash: To the extreme right of the bottom panel is the Trash icon. Dragging files or folders into this icon causes them to be moved to the trash. From here you can also empty the trash or view its contents.

■ **Note** There's one important difference between the Recycle Bin in Windows and Ubuntu's Trash. By default, the Recycle Bin uses only 10 percent of the remaining space on a hard disk. After this, the oldest items are automatically deleted. With Ubuntu's version, the only limit on the contents is the remaining free space on the disk. Nothing will ever be removed from the Trash unless you specifically choose to remove it.

Workspace switcher: Beside the Trash icon is the Workspace switcher, used to move between virtual desktops, described later in this chapter.

Shutting Down or Restarting Ubuntu

You can shut down or reboot your PC by clicking the Off button in the top-right corner of the screen. On many laptops and desktops, you can also briefly press the on/off button on the computer. The former method presents you with a selection of options in a drop-down list, while the latter launches a dialog box showing icons for various options, as shown in Figure 6-4.

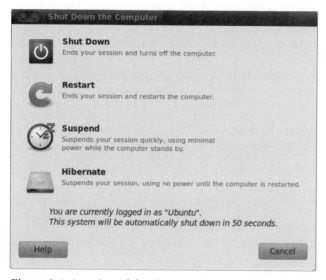

Figure 6-4. A variety of shutdown operations are available, some allowing for a quick resumption later on.

Note that not all the options appear if you use the hardware method to close down. The options in the drop-down list are as follows:

Lock Screen: This enables the screen saver and password-protects the system. The only way to leave Lock Screen mode is to enter the user's password into the dialog box that appears whenever you move the mouse or press a key.

Guest Session: This launches a new guest session of the desktop. It is ideal for employees who are temporarily using a company's PC, for example, or for friends who visit and want to check their e-mail or Facebook without leaving any trace on your PC. Any files downloaded on a guest account are deleted when the user logs out.

Switch User…: If multiple users are defined on the system (Chapter 21 discusses how to add user accounts), this option allows others to log in without closing down the original user's account. To switch back to the original user, choose Switch User again or log out the second user. The original user will need to enter their password to regain access.

Log Out: This option logs you out of the current user account and returns you to the Ubuntu login screen. Any open programs will be shut down automatically.

■ **Caution** During shutdown or logout operations, Ubuntu sometimes automatically shuts down applications that contain unsaved data without prompting you, so you should always save files prior to selecting any of the options here.

Sleep: This uses your computer's suspend mode, in which most of the PC's systems are powered down except for the computer's memory. Suspend mode is designed to save power and allow a quick reactivation of the PC. Not all computers support suspend mode, however, so you should experiment to see if your computer works correctly. Ensure that you save any open files before doing so. If your PC goes into suspend mode but fails to wake up when you shake the mouse or push keys, you may need to reboot. This can often be done by holding down the power button for about five seconds.

Hibernate: This saves the contents of the computer's memory to the hard disk and then completely powers down the computer. When the computer is reactivated, the user chooses to start Ubuntu as normal, and the memory contents are read in from disk. This allows a faster startup and allows users to resume from where they were last working. For the hibernate feature to work, the swap file needs to be as large as or larger than the main memory. Ubuntu's installation program should have automatically done that, but if you didn't dedicate enough disk space to Ubuntu when repartitioning, it might not have been able to do so. The only way to find out is to attempt to hibernate your system and see whether it works.

■ **Caution** Some users have reported that their computer is sometimes unable to "wake" from hibernation, so you should save any open files before hibernating as insurance against the unlikely prospect that this happens. We've seen this happen a few times, although hundreds of other times it's worked fine.

Restart: This option shuts down Ubuntu and then restarts the computer.

Shut Down: This shuts down Ubuntu and then powers off your computer, provided its BIOS is compatible with the standard shutdown commands. (All computers bought within the past five years or so are compatible; if you find that the computer hangs at the end of the Ubuntu shutdown procedure, simply turn it off manually via the power switch.)

Only the last four of these options are available in the Shut Down the Computer dialog box, opened via the hardware shutdown button or by pressing the Ctrl+Alt+Del combination of keys. If you leave the computer after pushing this button, it will pause for 60 seconds and then shut down.

Quick Desktop Guides

Refer to Figure 6-5 for an annotated diagram of the desktop. The figure includes an open menu, browser window, and program window, so you can get a sense of what it's like working from the desktop.

As another handy reference, Table 6-1 compares standard Windows desktop features to similar functionality on the Ubuntu desktop.

Figure 6-5. *The Ubuntu desktop is broadly similar to the Windows desktop, with a few minor differences.*

Table 6-1. *Ubuntu Equivalents of Windows Desktop Features*

Windows Function	Description	Ubuntu Equivalent
My Computer/ Computer	Double-clicking the My Computer/Computer icon gives you access to the PC system. In particular, it lets you browse the file system.	Click Places ➤ Computer to see all the drives attached to the computer in the file browser window. If you want to browse the file system. double-click File System in the list on the left side of the file browser window.
Recycle Bin	The Recycle Bin is the repository of all deleted files.	Click the small Trash icon located the bottom-right corner of the Ubuntu desktop.
Start menu	The Start menu provides access to the many computer functions, as well as a list of the programs installed on the system.	This function is split between the Applications and System menus. The Applications menu provides access to software installed under Ubuntu. The System menu lets you configure and administer the system, similar to the Windows Control Panel.
Quick Launch toolbar	Located just to the right of the Start button, these small icons let you launch popular programs with a single click.	Similar icons are located to the right of the main menus at the top of the Ubuntu desktop. You can add your own entries here by clicking and dragging program icons from the Applications menu or by right-clicking, selecting Add to Panel, and choosing an Application launcher.

87

Windows Function	Description	Ubuntu Equivalent
My Network Places/ Network Neighborhood	This icon is used to access network services, usually within a business environment (on newer versions of Windows, this icon is often hidden by default).	To browse the local network, click Places ➤ Network .
My Documents/ Documents	The My Documents/Documents folder, accessed via its icon on the Windows desktop, is a storage space set aside for a user's documents.	The user's Home folder serves this purpose and can be accessed clicking Places ➤ Home Folder.
Control Panel	The Windows Control Panel, located off the Start menu, enables the user to change system settings and preferences.	Similar functionality can be found under the System ➤ Administration and System ➤ Preferences menu options. If you'd like a more Windows-esque control panel, press Alt+F2 and type **gnome-control-center**. This presents a familiar-looking grid of icons from which you can select all of the configuration options for the OS.
Find Files/Start Search	Located on the Start menu, the Find Files/Start Search function lets a user search the file system for missing items.	To find files, click Places ➤ Search for Files. You can also add the Deskbar applet to any of your panels (right-click the panel, select Add to Panel, and choose Deskbar from the list).
Shutdown/Restart	At the bottom of the Start menu within Windows is the Shutdown/ Restart button.	Clicking System ➤ Quit brings up a dialog box that is almost identical to the one displayed in Windows XP and offers the same options as the Windows Vista shutdown submenu.
Windows Update	Located in the system tray, the Windows Update program checks for and downloads software updates, and then notifies you that the updates are ready to be installed at your command.	The Software Update Notifier checks for software updates and then notifies you when updates are available. Clicking the Update Manager icon pops up a window from which you can download and install updates. In contrast to the Windows system, Ubuntu keeps track of the majority of software installed on your PC and can upgrade almost any application or system file when new versions become available.
Switch User	This option is available when you choose to log off from Windows. You can keep the login session of the current user alive, while allowing another user to log in to Windows.	The User Switcher is located on the left side of the notification area. Click the username or real name, select another user to log in to the system, and supply the correct password. The current user's session is locked, and a new session is activated for the new logged-in user.

It takes some time to get used to the look and feel of Ubuntu; everything may initially seem a little unusual. You'll find that the onscreen fonts look a little different from those in Windows, for example. The icons also aren't the same as you're used to in Windows. This can be a little disconcerting, but that feeling will quickly pass, and everything will become second nature. You'll look at how to personalize the desktop in Chapter 9.

UBUNTU FOR MAC OS X USERS

Migrating to Ubuntu from Mac OS X shouldn't present too many surprises. In some ways, Ubuntu has more in common with OS X than it does with Windows. After all, both Linux and OS X are versions of UNIX. Here is a list of OS X functions alongside details of where they can be found within Ubuntu:

- *Finder (file browsing):* Finder under OS X offers access to files, applications, and much more and is represented on the Dock by the Mac smiley face icon. In terms of file browsing functionality, clicking Places ➤ Home in Ubuntu is all that's needed for similar behavior.

- *Finder (applications):* The Applications option within Finder shows a list of all installed programs. Exactly the same thing can be found by clicking the Applications button in Ubuntu, although the programs are arranged into submenus to make finding what you're looking for easier.

- *Finder (network locations):* Clicking the Network button in Finder enables the user to browse the local area network or access remote file servers. This functionality can be found on the Places menu: click Places ➤ Network Servers to browse the local network and Places ➤ Connect to Server to access a remote server, such as FTP (this function also allows the user to connect to local servers by specifying their addresses).

- *Macintosh HD:* Double-clicking this icon on the desktop allows the user to access the root of the Macintosh file system. To access the root file system under Ubuntu, click Places ➤ Computer, and then click the File System link in the left pane of the file browsing window.

- *Dock:* There is no direct analogy to the Mac OS X Dock under Ubuntu, but the Quick Launch icons to the right of the Applications/Places/System menus offer quick access to the web browser, e-mail client, and help system. You can add more programs to the Quick Launch toolbar by clicking and dragging them from the Applications menu. The Window List controls the active window. Additional software can be used to mimic the look and feel of the Dock if you're a big fan.

- *Trash:* Located on the Dock, the Trash icon lets OS X users salvage deleted files. The same functionality is offered by the Ubuntu Trash folder icon, which is located at the bottom-right corner of the screen.

- *System Preferences:* Located on the Dock and in the Applications menu, the System Preferences icon offers access to all of OS X's configuration utilities. Similar functionality can be found on the System ➤ Preferences and System ➤ Administration menus.

- *Spaces (version 10.5 and above):* Spaces allow you to unclutter your desktop by arranging your applications into separate workspaces. Similar functionality is available by using virtual desktops, which are located at the right side of the Window List.

- *Spotlight (version 10.4 and above):* Spotlight allows users to search their hard disk for files. To access Ubuntu's search function, click Places ➤ Search for Files. You can also click the Deskbar applet, located to the left of the notification area, or the Tracker search tool icon, located in the notification area, to search for files.

Running Programs

Starting a new program is easy. Just click the Applications menu and then choose a program from the list, just as you would in Windows using the Start ➤ Programs menu. The Applications menu, shown in Figure 6-6, is split into various subcategories of programs, such as office tools, graphics programs, and even games!

If you want to start the web browser or e-mail client (arguably two of the most popular programs offered by Ubuntu), you can click their icons on the top panel bar, just to the right of the menus at the top of the screen (see Figure 6-6).

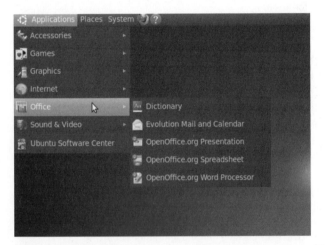

Figure 6-6. The programs on the Applications menu are split into various categories.

Working with Virtual Desktops

Windows works on the premise of everything taking place on top of a single desktop. When you start a new program, it runs on top of the desktop, effectively covering up the desktop. In fact, all programs are run on this desktop, so it can get a bit confusing when you have more than a couple of programs running at the same time. Which Microsoft Word window contains the document you're working on, rather than the one you've opened to take notes from? Where is that My Computer window you were using to copy files?

Ubuntu overcomes this problem by having more than one desktop area. By using the Workspace Switcher tool, located at the bottom right of the desktop, you can switch between two or more virtual desktops. This is best explained by a demonstration:

1. Make sure you're currently on the first virtual desktop (click the leftmost square on the Workspace Switcher), and start up the web browser by clicking its icon at the top of the screen (the globe icon located to the right of the menus).

2. Click the second square on the Workspace Switcher. This switches you to a clean desktop, where no programs are visible—desktop number two.

3. Start up the file browser by selecting the Places ➤ Home menu option. A file browser window appears.

4. Click the first square in the Workspace Switcher again. You should switch back to the desktop that is running the web browser.

5. Click the second square, and you switch back to the other desktop, which is running the file browser.

■ **Tip** Right-clicking any of the program entries in the Window List brings up a menu where you can move a program from one virtual desktop to another. Just select Move to Another Workspace.

See how it works? You can create up to 36 virtual desktops, in fact! To set the number of workspaces, right-click the Workspace Switcher and select Preferences. In the window that appears, select the number of workspaces and the number of rows in which they will be arranged (see Figure 6-7). You can even label the different workspaces and make Ubuntu show the name in the Workspace Switcher to better identification. The default is four workspaces arranged in a single row, but you can increase the number of workspaces and the number of rows.

Figure 6-7. Four virtual desktops are set up by default, but you can have as many as 36.

■ **Tip** Putting your mouse over the Workspace Switcher and scrolling the mouse wheel switches among the various virtual desktops instantly. Or you can hold down Ctrl+Alt and press the left and right cursor keys to switch between virtual desktops.

If you want to keep one application—for example, a web browser—instantly available regardless of the workspace you happen to be on, you can right-click it in the Window List and click the Always on Visible Workspace button. Now as you navigate your various workspaces, that particular button will follow you.

You can also click and drag the small representations of an application window from one workspace to another in the Switcher itself, though this is quite fiddly. The Workspace Switcher provides a way of organizing your programs and also reducing the clutter. You can experiment with virtual desktops to see whether you want to organize your work this way. Some people swear by them. Experienced Ubuntu users may have more than ten virtual desktops, although clearly this will appeal only to organizational geniuses! Other users think multiple desktops are a waste of time. We thnk they're certainly worth trying out to see whether they suit the way you work.

Using the Mouse

As noted earlier, the mouse works mostly the same under Ubuntu as it does under Windows: a left-click selects things, and a right-click usually brings up a context menu. Try right-clicking various items, such as icons on the desktop or even the desktop itself.

■ **Tip** Right-clicking a blank spot on the desktop and selecting Create Launcher lets you create shortcuts to applications. Clicking Create Folder lets you create new empty folders.

You can use the mouse to drag icons on top of other icons. For example, you can drag a file onto a program icon in order to run it. You can also click and drag in certain areas to create an "elastic band" and, as in Windows, this lets you select more than one icon at once.

You can resize windows by using the mouse in much the same way as in Windows. Just click and drag the edges and corners of the windows. In addition, you can double-click the title bar to maximize and subsequently restore windows.

Ubuntu also makes use of the third mouse button for middle-clicking. You might not think your mouse has one of these but, actually, if it's relatively modern, it probably does. Such mice have a scroll wheel between the buttons, and this can act as a third button when pressed.

In Ubuntu, the main use of the middle mouse button is in copying and pasting, as described in the next section. Middle-clicking also has a handful of other functions; for example, middle-clicking the title bar of any open window will switch to the window underneath.

■ **Tip** If your mouse doesn't have a scroll wheel, or if it has one that doesn't click, you can still middle-click. Simply press the left and right mouse buttons at the same time. This emulates a middle-click, although it takes a little skill to get right. Generally speaking, you need to press one button a fraction of a second before you press the other button.

Cutting and Pasting Text

Ubuntu offers two separate methods of cutting and pasting text. The first is identical to Windows. In a word processor or another application that deals with text, you can click and drag (or double-click) the mouse to highlight text, right-click anywhere on it, and then choose to copy or cut the text. In many programs, you can also use the keyboard shortcuts of Ctrl+X to cut, Ctrl+C to copy, and Ctrl+V to paste.

However, there's a quicker method of copying and pasting. Simply click and drag to highlight some text and then immediately click the middle mouse button where you want the text to appear. This copies and pastes the highlighted text automatically, as shown in Figure 6-8.

This special method of cutting and pasting bypasses the usual clipboard, so you should find that any text you've copied or cut previously should still be there. The downside is that it doesn't work across all applications within Ubuntu, although it does work with the majority of them.

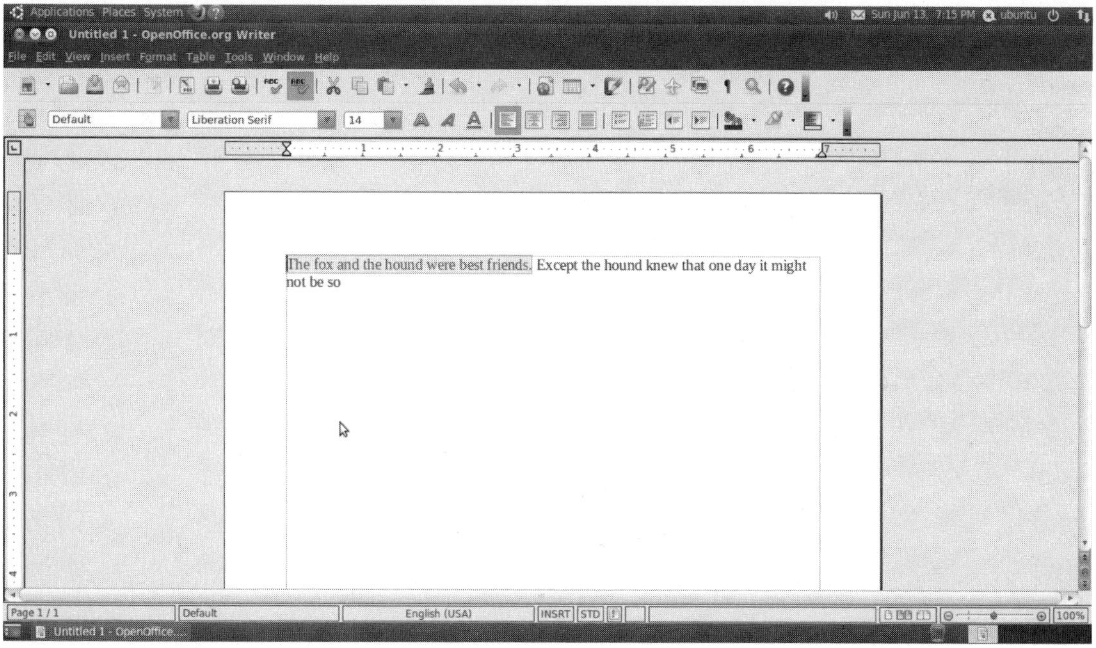

Figure 6-8. Highlight the text and then middle-click to paste it instantly.

Summary

This chapter covered booting into Ubuntu for the first time and discovering the desktop. We looked at starting programs, working with virtual desktops, using the mouse on the Ubuntu desktop, and much more. You should be confident in some basic Ubuntu skills and ready to learn more!

In the next chapter, you'll look at getting your system up and running, focusing on items of hardware that you may encounter in day-to-day use.

■ ■ ■

## CHAPTER 7

Getting Everything Up and Running

This chapter guides you through setting up all the essential components of your Ubuntu installation. This includes hardware configuration, as well as setting up e-mail. It covers the post-installation steps necessary to get your system up and running efficiently.

Like all modern Linux distributions, Ubuntu is practically automated when it comes to setting up key hardware and software components. Key software will work from the start, and most hardware will be automatically configured. However, you might need to tweak a few settings to make everything work correctly. Read on to learn more.

Will Ubuntu Support My Hardware?

The age-old criticism that the Linux OS lags *way* behind Windows in terms of hardware support is long dead. The majority of connectable devices, such as digital cameras and printers, will work with Ubuntu immediately, with little, if any, configuration.

Most underlying PC hardware is pre-configured during installation without your knowledge and without requiring further work, so with luck there will be less hunting around for drivers than you might be used to with Windows. Your graphics and sound cards should work without a hitch, for example. In addition, nearly all USB and FireWire devices you plug in after installation will be supported. (Table 7-1 lists some online sources of information about hardware support for Ubuntu). You'll be surprised at how many user manuals now have a section for Linux—often given equal weight to Mac OS. Documentation for Netgear routers is one example.

However, it's still the case that a substantial number of devices are not supported by Ubuntu. Generally, it's a black or white situation: Ubuntu either works with a piece of hardware or it doesn't.

The types of hardware that Ubuntu doesn't support are often esoteric devices that rely on custom software provided by the hardware manufacturer, but even in mass-market areas such as printers, scanners, and wireless adapters, some manufacturers are still frustratingly uninterested in publishing their own Linux drivers, and even refuse to provide details about the hardware to volunteer programmers who offer to write free and open source drivers at no expense to the company. It's also sometimes the case that brand-new models of hardware won't work with Ubuntu when they first hit the market. Companies prioritize developer resources, so Windows drivers generally get written before Linux drivers. However, as soon as a new piece of hardware comes out, work is usually undertaken to ensure that Linux is made compatible with it, by the company, the community, or a combination of the two. This is especially true of hardware such as printers and scanners, and it's one more reason why you should regularly update your system online.

■ **Tip** Before you hit the stores to buy a new piece of hardware, it's a good idea to do a little research. Compatibility with Linux is sometimes listed on the hardware box or at the manufacturer's web site (even if you sometimes need to search through the FAQ section to find out about it). And, of course, others may have tried your particular small object of desire, so searching **<hardware name> + Linux compatibility** in Google may provide enlightenment.

Table 7-1. Hardware Information Sources

Hardware	Web Sources
Graphics cards	`http://xorg.freedesktop.org/wiki/Projects/Drivers`
Sound cards	`http://linux-sound.org/hardware.html`
Printers	`www.linuxfoundation.org/en/OpenPrinting`
Scanners	`www.sane-project.org/sane-supported-devices.html`
Cameras	`www.gphoto.org/proj/libgphoto2/support.php`
Wi-fi cards	`www.hpl.hp.com/personal/Jean_Tourrilhes/Linux/`
Laptops	`http://tuxmobil.org`

Unfortunately, unlike with Windows, it's not very common to find Linux drivers on the CD that comes with the hardware. Even if you do find a Linux driver supplied, chances are that it will work with only certain enterprise-oriented versions of Linux, such as Red Hat Enterprise Linux or SUSE Linux Enterprise Desktop. Some drivers are usable but imperfect or lack features that are available in their Windows counterparts. At the time of this writing, Ubuntu has yet to gain the kind of momentum that leads manufacturers to specifically produce drivers for it, but this may change in the future, especially as more users encounter the system via Netbooks and mobile devices. Various OEMs have dipped their toes in the open source water. Dell and Shuttle are the biggest names currently bundling Linux with some of their desktop offerings, with smaller specialist companies like System 76 competing with excellent pre-installed offerings.

■ **Note** It's possible to use a program called alien to convert software installation packages designed for other distributions into Ubuntu installation files. Doing so isn't complicated but may not work well with driver files because of the subtle differences in where system files are stored across different Linux distributions. You can find more information about alien at `http://kitenet.net/~joey/code/alien/`. It's contained within the Ubuntu software repositories and can be downloaded using the Ubuntu Software Center or Synaptic Package Manager. A graphical front end to alien is available at `http://code.google.com/p/foxoman/wiki/PackageConverter`.

Using Proprietary vs. Open Source Drivers

As discussed earlier in this book, Linux is an open source OS. This means that the source code underlying Linux programs is available for study and even reuse. This is a good thing when it comes to hardware drivers, because bugs in the code can be spotted and repaired by anyone with an interest in doing so. If you consider that a bug in a graphics driver could mean your PC crashes every 5 minutes, the value of such an approach is abundantly clear.

Unfortunately, some hardware manufacturers don't like to disclose how their hardware works, because they want to protect their trade secrets. This makes it impossible for them to release open source drivers, because such drivers would expose exactly how the hardware operates. Because such companies are aware that growing numbers of people use Linux, they release *proprietary drivers*, whose source code is not made publicly available (in the same way that Windows code is not released to the public).

Aside from ethical issues surrounding not being able to study the source code, the biggest issue with proprietary drivers relates to bug fixing. To use a proprietary driver is to be at the mercy of the hardware manufacturer's own development and release schedule. If the driver has a serious bug, you'll either have to work around it or put up with troubling issues until the manufacturer offers an update. A few years ago, a proprietary driver for a 3D graphics card stopped any computer it was installed on from going into hibernation mode (that is, suspending to disk). Those using the drivers had to wait months until the fix was released.

Despite this, and although the folks behind Ubuntu strongly support free and open source software, they realize proprietary drivers need to be used in certain situations. For example, it's impossible to use the 3D graphics elements of some graphics cards unless you have a proprietary driver, and this means that visual effects will be unavailable to users who happen to have hardware that isn't currently fully supported by open source drivers.

Because of this, Ubuntu automatically installs wi-fi proprietary drivers by default if no open source alternative exists (or if the open source version is not yet good enough). It also offers the opportunity to easily install some proprietary graphics card drivers if they provide more functionality than the open source versions.

■ **Note** Linux sees hardware in a technical way, rather than in the way humans do. If you attach something such as a USB CD-R/RW drive, Linux will recognize the drive hardware and attempt to make it work. It won't try to find a driver for that specific make and model of CD-R/RW drive. Thus, Linux is able to work with a wide range of hardware, because a lot of hardware is similar on a technical level, despite the differences in case design, model names, and even prices!

WHAT HARDWARE WORKS?

The question of what hardware works under Ubuntu is one that's not easily answered. However, you can take a look at http://wiki.ubuntu.com/HardwareSupport to see if your hardware is listed. This is an informal list created by the Ubuntu community, and it's not comprehensive (which is to say that there may be hardware that works fine that isn't mentioned). Nor is the list guaranteed to be 100 percent accurate. But it's certainly worth a look.

A search engine such as Google is your best friend if the Ubuntu hardware list doesn't help. Simply search for the brand and model of your hardware and add **Ubuntu** to the search string. This should return results, usually from the Ubuntu forums (http://ubuntuforums.org) or blogs, written by those who have found a way to make that type of hardware work.

Installing Device Manager

When using Windows, you might have come across Device Manager, the handy tool that lists your PC's hardware and provides access to various properties. Ubuntu offers a similar piece of software, as shown in Figure 7-1, but it isn't installed by default.

After you can connect to the Internet (following the instructions in the "Getting Online" section of this chapter), you can install Device Manager by using the Synaptic Package Manager (see the "Installing Software" section of this chapter), as follows:

1. Choose Applications ➤ Ubuntu Software Center.

2. Your cursor is automatically in the search field, so go ahead and type **device manager**.

3. A list of programs will appear. Click Device Manager and then click the Install button that appears. Enter your password when asked.

4. A progress bar will show that the software is installing. When it's done, a green tick will appear by the program's icon. You can now close the Ubuntu Software Center window.

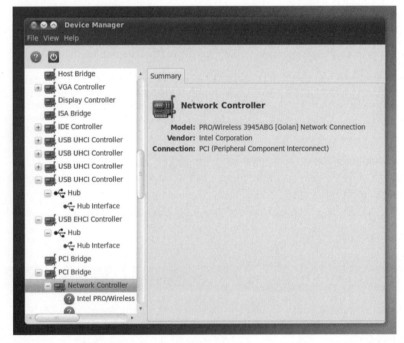

Figure 7-1. Ubuntu's Device Manager program can display just about everything you need to know about attached hardware.

If your computer is not yet online, you'll need to use a computer that is online (perhaps another computer, or Windows if you dual-boot) to download the software, and then copy it across to your Ubuntu computer for installation. To download the software, visit the following two addresses in your browser. You will be prompted to download a file after typing each address:

```
http://us.archive.ubuntu.com/ubuntu/pool/universe/g/gnome-device-manager/gnome-device↵
-manager_0.2-3_i386.deb
```

```
http://us.archive.ubuntu.com/ubuntu/pool/universe/g/gnome-device-manager/libgnome↵
-device-manager0_0.2-3_i386.deb
```

After the files are downloaded, copy them to the Desktop on your Ubuntu machine, using a USB memory stick or similar storage device. Right-click the icon for `libgnome-device-manager0_0.2-3_i386.deb` and select the first choice in the context menu, Open With Gdebi Package Manager. A Package Installer window will appear. Click the Install Package button and supply your password when asked. Close the window when the package has finished installing. Next, right-click the other icon, for `gnome-device-manager` itself and repeat the same procedure.

After you've installed Device Manager, you can open it by choosing Applications ➤ System Tools ➤ Device Manager. You'll need to click View ➤ Device Properties to ensure that Device Manager adds the useful (but occasionally overwhelming) Properties tab.

You should be aware of a few important differences between the Windows and Ubuntu versions of Device Manager. Though the aim of Ubuntu's Device Manager is to manage hardware devices, the project is still in its infancy and can provide only hardware information at the time of this writing. On the other hand, Ubuntu's list is far more comprehensive than that in Windows. In Ubuntu, Device Manager thoroughly probes the hardware to discover its capabilities.

Perhaps the biggest difference, however, is that just because a piece of hardware is listed within Ubuntu's Device Manager doesn't mean that the hardware is configured to work with Ubuntu. In fact, it doesn't even imply that the hardware will *ever* work under Ubuntu. Device Manager's list is simply the result of probing devices attached to the various system buses (PCI, AGP, USB, and so on) and reporting the data.

Nonetheless, Device Manager is the best starting place if you find that a certain piece of hardware isn't working. If a piece of hardware is listed, then it proves, if nothing else, that the system recognizes that the hardware is attached. For example, later in this chapter, we describe how you can use Device Manager to discover crucial details about wireless network devices, which you can then use to install drivers.

Configuring Ubuntu

Unlike some versions of Linux, Ubuntu doesn't rely on a centralized configuration software package. Instead, it uses smaller programs to configure hardware. For example, to configure the network, you'll use the NetworkManager program, and printers are configured using a separate printer configuration program. Because using some of the configuration software involves reconfiguring your entire system, doing so requires administrator privileges. Therefore, you'll be prompted for your login password each time you use some of the programs. In some cases, after you've made changes, you'll need to click the Apply button to put the changes into effect. When you've finished configuration, simply close the program window by clicking the Close button.

■ **Note** Ubuntu remembers your password for 5 minutes after you enter it. Therefore, if you open the same application or another that requires administrator privileges within that amount of time, you won't be prompted to enter your password again.

GETTING HELP FROM THE COMMUNITY

Configuring hardware is one area where the value of the Ubuntu community becomes very apparent. If you run into a problem, it's unlikely your situation will be unique. Others will probably have encountered the same problem and may have figured out a solution. If so, they may have posted it online. If nothing else, you might find sufficient clues to be able to solve the problem by yourself. Sharing information in this way is part of the spirit of Ubuntu and also Linux.

We've tried to provide complete guides to most hardware configuration in this chapter, but if you run into problems, your first port of call should be the Ubuntu forums, at www.ubuntuforums.org. This is the central meeting place for the Ubuntu community. You can search through existing forum postings or start your own thread asking for help. We explain a little more about the protocols of asking for help in Appendix C. The key advice is to try to spend time solving a problem yourself before you ask other people for help.

Also worth visiting in times of trouble is the community-written wiki, which can be found at https://help.ubuntu.com/community. Here you'll find a range of guides to help configure various aspects of Ubuntu. A *wiki* is a kind of community web site that anyone can edit or contribute to. The idea is that it's constructed and maintained by its readers.

We also recommend taking a look at the Ubuntu Guide, at http://ubuntuguide.org, which is also community written. The Ubuntu Guide can be concise and often expects a relatively high degree of technical knowledge, but it is also comprehensive.

Finally, don't forget that you're a member of the community too. If you encounter and subsequently solve a configuration problem, share the solution with others. You can do this by editing the Ubuntu wiki or posting to the forums.

Configuring Input Devices

Mouse and key repeat speeds are personal to each user, and you may find the default Ubuntu settings not to your taste, particularly if you have a high-resolution mouse such as a gaming model. Fortunately, changing each setting is easy. You'll find the relevant options under the System ➤ Preferences menu.

Configuring Mouse Options

Choose System ➤ Preferences ➤ Mouse to open the Mouse Preferences dialog box, which has General and Accessibility tabs. On a laptop, you might also see the Touchpad tab.

General Mouse Settings

On the General tab of the Mouse Preferences dialog box, shown in Figure 7-2, you can configure several options.

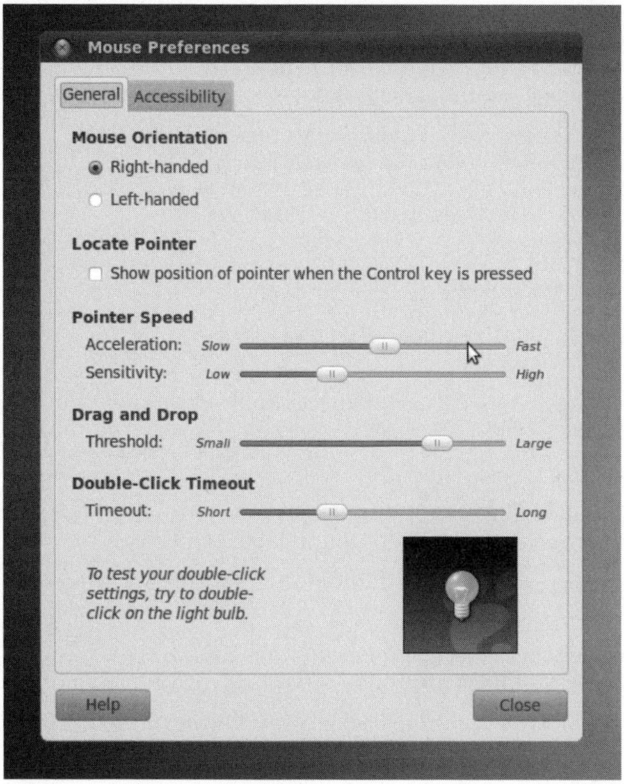

Figure 7-2. The Mouse Preferences dialog box lets you tame that mouse.

These options are as follows:

Mouse Orientation: This option lets you set whether the mouse is to be used by a left-handed or right-handed person. Effectively, it swaps the functions of the right and left buttons.

Locate Pointer: This option allows you to show where the mouse is by displaying a ripple surrounding the mouse pointer when you press the Ctrl key. This can be useful for partially sighted people who may not be able to locate the cursor on a busy Desktop.

Acceleration: This setting controls how fast the mouse pointer moves. Whenever you move the mouse, the pointer on the screen moves a corresponding amount. However, the cursor actually increases in speed the more you move your hand (otherwise, you would need to drag your hand across the desk to get from one side of the screen to the other). This is referred to as *acceleration*. If you set the acceleration too high, the pointer will fly around the screen, seemingly unable to stop. If you set it too slow, you'll need to swipe the mouse several times to make it go anywhere.

Sensitivity: This setting controls how quickly the acceleration kicks in when you first move the mouse. Choosing a higher setting means that you can move the mouse relatively quickly before it starts to accelerate and cover more screen space. A low setting means that acceleration will begin almost as soon as you move the mouse. Higher sensitivity settings give you more control over the mouse, which can be useful if you use image-editing programs, for example.

Drag and Drop: This setting determines the amount of mouse movement allowed in a dragging maneuver before the item under the cursor is moved. It is designed for people who have limited dexterity and who might be unable to keep the mouse perfectly still when selecting an item. In such cases, a large threshold value may be preferred.

Double-Click Timeout: This is ideal for those who are less physically dexterous, because the double-click speed can be slowed down. On the other hand, if you find yourself accidentally double-clicking items, you can speed it up. Test your settings by double-clicking the lightbulb image.

Changes are made as each setting is adjusted, so to test the new settings, simply move your mouse.

Accessibility Settings

The settings on the Accessibility tab can help people with physical disabilities use the mouse. However, to enable these features, you need to enable Assistive Technologies in Ubuntu first, as follows:

1. Open the Assistive Technologies Preferences dialog box (System ➤ Preferences ➤ Assistive Technologies).

2. Select the Enable Assistive Technologies check box and then click the Close and Log Out button (this is necessary to start the background services).

3. Select Log Out in the Shutdown dialog box, and then log back in again when prompted.

4. After logging in, return to the Accessibility tab of the Mouse Preferences dialog box (System ➤ Preferences ➤ Mouse).

From the Accessibility tab, you can enable Simulated Secondary Click and dwell click options. Selecting the "Trigger secondary click by holding down the primary button" check box simulates a right-click after you hold the left-click for a certain amount of time (useful for those having trouble right-clicking). The right-click actually occurs when you release the mouse button, for instance bringing up a context menu if you're clicking on a file icon. The amount of time you have to hold down the mouse button can be configured by moving the Delay slider to the left for a faster response or to the right for a longer delay.

A *dwell click* allows you to simulate a mouse-click action after the mouse pointer has been left idle for a certain amount of the time so, for instance, hovering over an icon for a few seconds could double-click it to launch an application. To enable this feature, select "Initiate click when stopping pointer movement." You can set the length of the idle time by moving the Delay slider to the left for less idle time or to the right for a longer delay. The Motion Threshold setting determines the amount of pointer movement allowed while the mouse is still considered idle (useful for those who might be unable to control small movements of their hands). Moving the Motion Threshold slider to the left makes the mouse pointer sensitive; moving it to the right makes the pointer less sensitive. You can choose two types of dwell click:

Choose type of click beforehand: This option automatically clicks the mouse when the mouse pointer is idle. If you want to choose the type of mouse click each time, put a check in the box beside Show Click Type Window. This will show a floating window, from which you can select various types of clicks, such as single-click, double-click, and so on. Alternatively, you can choose the mouse click from the Dwell Click applet instead. (Applets are discussed in the "Working with Applets" section later in this chapter.)

Choose type of click with mouse gestures: This option allows you to choose the type of mouse click to execute when the mouse movement is idle by moving the mouse in a certain direction, usually up, down, left, or right. Just wait until the mouse turns into a cross and then move the mouse. After you've performed the movement, the mouse will return to its original location before it was moved. All the mouse movements can be customized by changing the gestures in the drop-down lists for Single Click, Double Click, Drag Click, and Secondary Click.

■ **Note** Orca, GNOME's screen reader software, also includes a tool that magnifies the area under the mouse pointer. It is available under System ➤ Preferences ➤ Assistive Technologies. Select the Preferred Applications option and set Orca to "run at start." The software can be used to both magnify an area of the screen under the mouse and, using a speech synthesizer, read onscreen elements out loud.

Touchpad Settings

The Touchpad tab appears on laptops only. You can set the following options:

Disable touchpad while typing: It's easy to brush against the touchpad accidentally with the ball of your thumb while you're typing. This option, which is enabled by default, eliminates the problem by disabling the touchpad momentarily after each keypress.

Enable mouse clicks with touchpad: This allows you to simulate a mouse click by tapping the touchpad. Depending on the sensitivity of your touchpad, this is either great or the most annoying thing in the world.

Scrolling options: Like a scroll wheel on a mouse, your laptop's touchpad can be used to scroll pages and images up and down, or even left and right. By default, vertical edge scrolling is enabled, so that running your finger up and down the right edge of the touchpad will scroll web pages up and down. If you enable horizontal scrolling, you will additionally be able to scroll left and right by running your finger along the bottom edge of the touchpad. The two-finger scrolling option disables edge scrolling, and instead makes the touchpad scroll if you have two fingers moving on it at the same time. If you don't like any of these features, you can choose to disable scrolling completely.

Changing Keyboard Settings

Choose System ➤ Preferences ➤ Keyboard to open the Keyboard Preferences dialog box. This dialog box has five tabs: General, Layouts, Accessibility, Mouse Keys, and Typing Break.

General Settings

The General tab offers Repeat Keys settings and a Cursor Blinking slider. You can alter the rate of key repeat, which can be useful if you often find yourself holding down the Backspace key to delete a sentence; a shorter setting on the Delay slider and a faster setting on the Speed slider can help. However, if you make the delay too short for your typing style, you may find double characters creeping into your documents; typing an *f* may result in *ff*, for example.

Modifying the Cursor Blinking slider setting may help if you sometimes lose the cursor in a document. A faster speed will mean that the cursor spends less time being invisible between flashes.

Layouts Settings

On the Layouts tab, you can choose your keyboard model, add an alternative keyboard layout, and configure layout options, as shown in Figure 7-3. Typically, the generic keyboard works fine for most setups. However, if you want to make full use of the extra keys on your keyboard, such as Mail, Web, Power, Sleep, Suspend, and so on, you should select your keyboard model.

If you write in two different languages on your keyboard, it may be helpful to be able to switch between them. Click the Add button, and select the second language from the list. To switch from one language to another, you can add the Keyboard Indicator applet in a panel and toggle from one language to another by clicking the applet.

The Keyboard Layout Options dialog box, accessed by clicking the Options button, lets you select from a multitude of handy tweaks that affect how the keyboard works. For example, you can configure the Caps Lock key to act like a simple Shift key, or you can turn it off altogether. You can configure the Windows key so that it performs a different function too. Put a check alongside the options you want after reading through the extensive list.

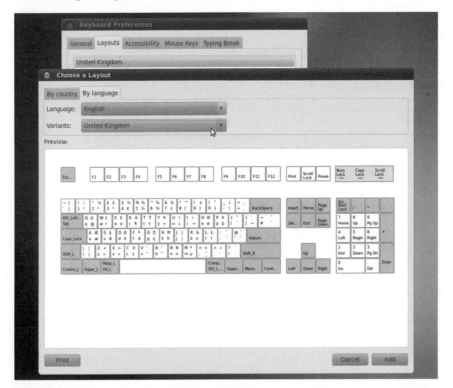

Figure 7-3. *You can have more than one language setting in place for a keyboard, which is handy if you need to type in a foreign language.*

Accessibility Settings

As with the mouse, there are also accessibility options for keyboard users to help people with physical disabilities. On the Accessibility tab, you can configure the following settings:

> *General:* You have an option to enable/disable ("toggle") accessibility features with keyboard shortcuts. This is disabled by default.

■ **Caution** Do not check the box labeled "Accessibility features can be toggled with keyboard shortcuts" unless you are sure you need it. Once enabled, if you happen to hold down the Shift key for eight seconds, or tap the Shift key five times, a dialog window will appear asking whether you want to enable the Sticky or Slow Keys features. This can be a source of confusion!

> *Sticky keys:* Some people are unable to hold down more than one key at a time, which is a problem if you want to type a keyboard shortcut such as Ctrl+S to save your work. As its name suggests, the sticky keys feature "holds down" keys such as Shift, Ctrl, and Alt while you press another key on the keyboard. To enable sticky keys, select the Simulate Simultaneous Keypresses check box. You can test sticky keys by running the File Browser (Places ➤ Home Folder). Try pressing Alt and F sequentially; Nautilus will open the File menu as if you pressed those keys simultaneously. If you would like to disable sticky keys on the fly, without having to use this dialog box, select "Disable sticky keys if two keys are pressed together." You can test this by pressing Ctrl+Alt. A Sticky Keys Alert dialog box will appear to prompt you to disable sticky keys.

> *Slow keys:* This feature controls the reaction rate of keys. By moving the Delay slider to the left, the reaction rate of the keys becomes faster. By moving the slider to the right, the reaction rate of the keys becomes slower, to the point that you would need to hold the key for a certain amount of time for it to be considered as a key press. This has obvious uses for people with limited dexterity in their fingers, but most people will not want this enabled.

> *Bounce keys:* This feature controls the repetition of letters on the screen when the same key is accidentally pressed. By moving the slider to the left, the repeat rate will be quicker; moving it to the right adds time for the key to be repeated.

At the bottom of the dialog box is a text box for typing to test the settings you've just configured. You can also enable sound notifications by clicking the Notifications button. These notifications will let you know when the keyboard accessibility features have been enabled or disabled. You can set sound alerts for accessibility in general, sticky keys, slow keys, and bounce keys.

Mouse Keys Settings

The mouse keys feature lets you use your numeric keypad to control the mouse pointer. By selecting the "Pointer can be controlled using the keypad" check box and pressing the Num Lock key, you can move the mouse pointer by typing from the numeric keypad.

With mouse keys enabled, the 5 key both simulates a mouse click and acts as the center of a directional wheel surrounding it. The 1, 2, 3, 4, 6, 7, 8, and 9 keys simulate mouse direction. Some numeric keypads have arrows on them to indicate this.

You can move the Acceleration slider to adjust the time it takes while pressing the mouse keys for the mouse movement to reach full speed.

The Speed slider sets the distance offset of the mouse pointer when you press a mouse key. By moving the Speed slider left, the mouse pointer covers a smaller distance when you press a mouse key, giving you the illusion that the mouse movement is slower. By moving the Speed slider right, the mouse pointer covers a larger distance when you press a mouse key, giving you the illusion that the mouse movement is faster.

The Delay slider determines the amount of time to press the mouse keys before the mouse pointer starts to move. You can set the delay by moving the Delay slider to the left for a quicker response time and to the right for a longer delay.

Typing Break Settings

The Typing Break tab features a function that can force you to stop typing after a predetermined number of minutes, to give your fingers and wrists a rest. It does this by blanking the screen and displaying a "Take a break!" message. Note that a notification area icon will appear before the break time to give you advanced warning of the lockout.

Creating Keyboard Shortcuts

Ubuntu lets you define your own keyboard shortcuts for just about any action on the system. To create a shortcut, choose System ➤ Preferences ➤ Keyboard Shortcuts. In the dialog box, search through the list for the action you want to create a shortcut for, click it, and then press the key combination you want to use. For example, you might locate the Volume Up and Volume Down entries in the list, click each, and press Ctrl+left arrow and Ctrl+right arrow. Then you will be able to turn the volume of your sound card up or down by holding down Ctrl and tapping the left or right arrow key, respectively.

■ **Caution** Be careful not to assign a shortcut to a popular key. It might be nice to make Totem media player appear when you hit the spacebar, for example, but that will mean that it will start up several times whenever you type a sentence in a word processor! Also be aware that some key combinations are used by applications. Within OpenOffice.org's Writer, for example, the Ctrl+left/right arrow key combination moves you from word to word in a paragraph. If you define those combinations as shortcuts, you will no longer have this functionality.

An example of a handy shortcut is to configure your Home folder to appear whenever you press Ctrl+Home. This can be done by locating the Home Folder option under the Desktop heading.

Getting Online

Getting online is vital in our modern Internet age, and Ubuntu caters to all the standard ways of doing so. Linux was built from the ground up to be an online operating system and is of course based on UNIX, which pioneered the concept of networking computers together to share data back in the 1970s. However, none of this is to say that getting online with Ubuntu is difficult! In fact, it's easy.

Regardless of whether you use a mobile broadband connection, a standard wired Ethernet network device or a wireless network device, the same program, NetworkManager, is used to configure your network settings under Ubuntu. Support for many makes and models of equipment is built in, so in most cases, all you need to do is enter a few configuration details.

■ **Note** Linux runs about 60 percent of the computers that make the Internet work! If you use Google, Facebook, or Wikipedia, you're using Linux. As your Linux skills increase, you'll eventually get to a stage where you, too, can run your own Internet servers. It sounds difficult but can be quite easy.

Using NetworkManager

NetworkManager lets users easily manage wireless (also known as wi-fi) and wired connections, as well as mobile broadband connections. An icon for this utility sits in the notification area at the top right of the Desktop and changes according to the type of connection currently active (up/down arrows for wired network, radio waves for wireless network, and so on). NetworkManager automatically detects any wireless networks that are in range, as well as if you're currently plugged in to a wired network. If you automatically connect to a network, a black notification box will appear on the top right of your screen for a few seconds and then fade away.

Clicking the NetworkManager icon will show a list of networks detected. By selecting an entry in the list, you can then connect to the network, and you'll be prompted to configure WEP/WPA protection, if applicable.

■ **Caution** At times we have been prompted for the *wrong kind* of wireless protection—for example, we were asked for a 128-bit WEP key rather than a 64-bit key when trying to connect to a network. In other words, it pays to check that you're being prompted for the right thing, and to select the correct option if you're not. Failure to do so might result in frustration! If you are really stuck, make sure to read your wireless router documentation.

Following this, the NetworkManager icon will display the signal strength of the connection for as long as you're connected. By clicking it, you'll be able to see at a glance what network you're connected to and any others within range. If you want to switch networks, just click the NetworkManager icon and select a different network in the list. If it's a secure network, you'll be prompted for a password before you're granted access.

■ **Tip** By right-clicking the NetworkManager icon, you can opt to completely disable your network hardware if you wish. This is quite useful if you don't need a network and would like to conserve your laptop battery.

NetworkManager settings persist across reboots, provided the network that was last configured is in range. This means that NetworkManager is ideal for all kinds of wireless network users, from those who frequently switch between different networks (that is, mobile workers) to those who just use a single wireless network connection, such as that provided by a wireless network broadband router in a home/small office environment. NetworkManager will also let you switch to a wired (Ethernet) connection, if and when you attach one to your computer.

NetworkManager will automatically detect networks and the type of connection. If you want to manually supply details, such as the IP address and gateway, or the name of the wireless base station—which might be necessary if your base station doesn't broadcast its name or if you need to connect to a specialized setup—you can do so by editing the connection.

Configuring Wired Networking

Every conventional desktop or laptop computer comes with an Ethernet port which is used to make a wired network connection to a router, hub, or switch.

Wireless networking as an alternative is extremely popular, particularly of course for portable devices such as laptops, but connecting via a cable offers advantages in speed, reliability and security. For these reasons wired Ethernet connections are still the standard in office environments. Even at home, if you have a desktop computer located close to your router, you may as well connect them using the Ethernet cable that came with your router.

In most cases, NetworkManager will sense a wired Ethernet connection and automatically connect using the Dynamic Host Control Protocol (DHCP). This means that your computer receives its IP address, gateway, subnet mask, and Domain Name System (DNS) addresses automatically. All routers manufactured today are set up to automatically use DHCP out of the box.

■ **Tip** If a DHCP server is not available, Ubuntu will attempt to set up a network automatically using the Zeroconf (or Zero Configuration Networking) system, just like Microsoft Windows systems. (Microsoft refers to this as Automatic Private IP Addressing, but it's also known as *link-local*.) In other words, if a bunch of computers plug into a hub or router on an ad hoc basis, without being configured and without a DHCP server operating, they will be able to network with each other. To make this work, each computer randomly assigns itself a unique IP address that starts with 169.254 with a subnet mask of 255.255.0.0.

If you need to manually specify network details such as IP and router addresses, perhaps because you work in an office environment with nonstandard systems, start by speaking to your system administrator or technical support person to determine the settings you need. Ask the administrator for your IP address, DNS server addresses (there are usually two or three of these), your subnet mask, and the router address (sometimes called the *gateway address*). The settings you will get from your system administrator will usually be in the form of a series of four numbers separated by dots, something like 192.168.0.233. After you have this information, follow these steps:

1. Right-click the NetworkManager icon in the notification area and select Edit Connections from the menu.

2. Select the Wired tab from the tab bar and click the Add button. This launches the new network configuration screen, where you can create a profile for the wired network.

3. Provide a name for the new connection. Then select the IPv4 Settings tab and change the Method drop-down from DHCP to Manual.

4. Click Add and supply the IP address, subnet mask, and gateway address for the device. You should also fill in the areas for DNS Servers and Search Domains. You can add more than one address to these sections by separating each one with a comma. Figure 7-4 shows an example of these settings. Click Apply after filling in the information. The network will be added to the list.

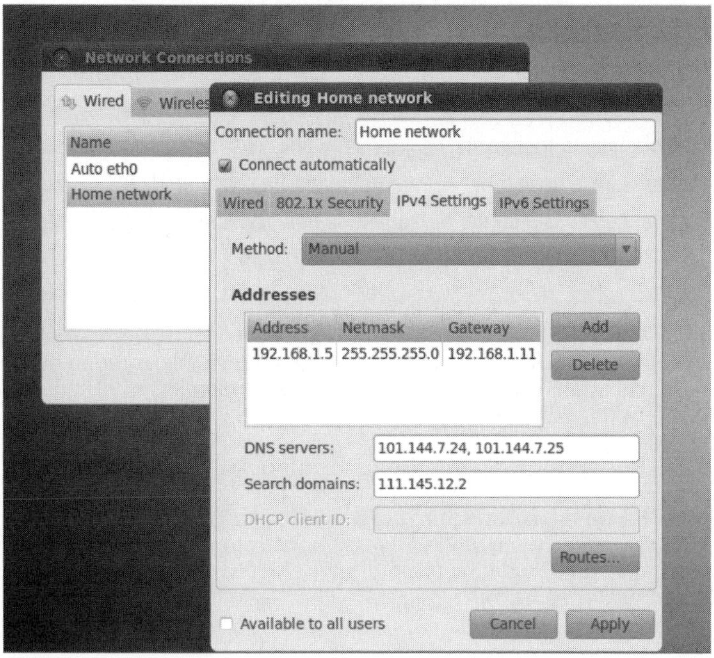

Figure 7-4. Ubuntu will automatically work with DHCP networks, or you can define a static IP address.

■ **Tip** If you're using a static IP address with a router, such as that provided by a DSL modem, the DNS address is often the same as the router/gateway address.

Your network connection should now work. If you now have more than one wired network connection set up, you can switch between them by clicking on the NetworkManager icon and selecting the appropriately named connection under Wired Networks. If your newly set up connection isn't working, try rebooting. However, if your system administrator mentioned that a proxy must also be configured, you'll need to follow the instructions in the "Working with a Proxy Server" section later in this chapter.

Connecting to a Wireless Network

A wireless (wi-fi) network is, as its name suggests, a network that does away with cabling and uses radio frequencies to communicate. It's more common for notebooks and handheld computers to use wireless connections, but some desktop computers also do. Indeed, it's increasingly the case that many workplaces are switching to wireless networking, eschewing old-fashioned, cable-based networking.

■ **Note** Slowly but surely, wi-fi is replacing wired Ethernet networks. However, sometimes wi-fi networks are impractical or simply undesirable. For example, the metal infrastructure in some buildings means the signal becomes unreliable. Wi-fi is also considered too insecure for some companies, as the wi-fi signal often spreads to the street outside the building. Although such transmissions are nearly always secured and WPA2 is considered secure, wi-fi security implementations have been broken. Ethernet might be considered old technology, but trying to steal data from physical cables is an order of magnitude more difficult, to the point of being practically impossible.

Notebooks and PDAs typically use built-in wireless network devices, with an invisible antenna built into the case. However, some older notebooks might use PCMCIA cards, which have an external square antenna, and some desktop computers might use PCI-based wireless cards or USB dongles, which have external rubber/plastic antennas, in the style of old cell phones.

Ubuntu includes support for most wireless network devices. However, it's possible to use Windows wireless network device drivers for unsupported hardware. Also, sometimes Ubuntu appears to support a wireless network device, in that it identifies it and lets you configure it, but you might find that it simply doesn't work (or works very badly, perhaps with an intermittent connection). In this situation, you can also try installing Windows drivers. See the "Installing Windows Wireless Network Device Drivers" section later in this chapter for details.

■ **Note** Ubuntu is rare in the Linux world in that it uses some proprietary (closed source) wireless device drivers by default. Ubuntu is, after all, an open source OS and is committed to the goals of free and open source software. The use of proprietary drivers is considered a necessary evil because not all devices have open source drivers right now, and not all open source drivers support all the functions you might be used to (typically, they might not support the WPA functionality of your wi-fi device, for example). The use of proprietary drivers is regarded as a stopgap measure, and it's hoped that manufacturers will realize that it is in their interests to support open source driver development, making proprietary drivers redundant.

Connecting to a wireless network device is easy with NetworkManager. Just click the NetworkManager icon, and you will see the available wi-fi networks in the Wireless Network list. Networks protected with WEP/WPA have a padlock in the wireless icon to the right of the name, as shown in Figure 7-5. Those that are "open" don't have this padlock.

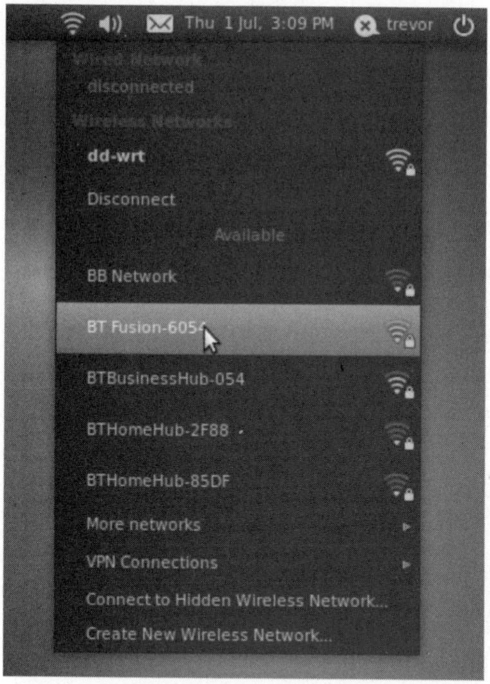

Figure 7-5. Clicking the network icon displays a list of available wireless networks.

You might see many wi-fi networks listed, depending on your location. The wireless base stations are identified by their Service Set Identifier (SSID) or sometimes ESSID, with *E* standing for *Extended*.

If the SSID you would like to connect to is not listed by NetworkManager, it could mean that your wireless base station isn't set to broadcast its SSID or, worse, Ubuntu's wi-fi drivers aren't functioning correctly. If it's the former, all you need to do is right-click the NetworkManager icon and select Connect to Other Wireless Network. Then, in the new dialog box, type the SSID under Network Name, set Wireless Security to None or the appropriate security type, fill in the other information depending on the type of wireless security you selected, and click Connect. If it's the latter, you may need to use a Windows driver, as described in the next section.

■ **Tip** If you are not offered any wireless networks at all, ensure that the wireless hardware is switched on. Some notebooks have a keyboard combination to turn it off to save battery power. Others have a little switch located on one of the edges of the notebook. Right-click the NetworkManager icon and ensure that Enable Networking and Enable Wireless are both selected.

To connect to a wi-fi network, select the wireless base station you want to connect to in the list. If it isn't protected by WEP/WPA, you will be connected to it automatically.

If the wi-fi network you wish to connect to is protected with WEP or WPA, a dialog box will appear, prompting you for the password/passphrase, as shown in Figure 7-6. In the Wireless Security field, make sure the correct type of security for the wireless network is selected—it's usually right, but don't assume it's automatically correct! By default, the password/passphrase is obfuscated by circle characters so that anyone looking over your shoulder can't see what you're typing. If it helps (and if your shoulder is clear), check the Show Password box. This can be really handy when you're typing a particularly long passphrase.

■ **Note** WEP keys come in either hexadecimal (hex) or plain text (passphrase) varieties. Hex keys look similar to this in their 128-bit form: CB4C4189B1861E19BC9A9BDA59. In their 64-bit form, they will be shorter and may look similar to 4D9ED51E23. A passphrase will take the form of a single short sentence. In home and office environments, WPA networks are usually protected with passphrases. In larger corporate or academic environments, you might find that the network is protected with a WPA certificate.

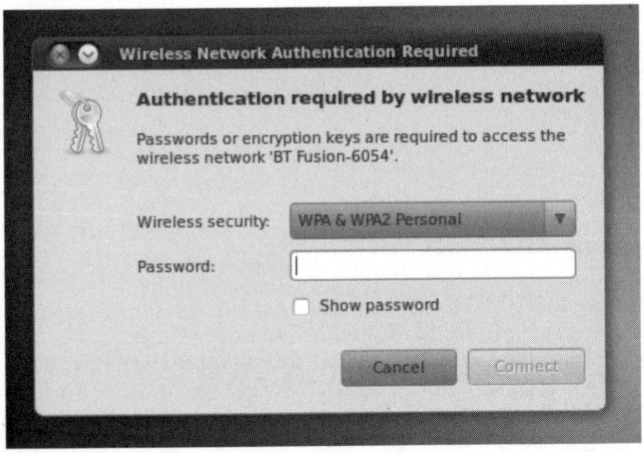

Figure 7-6. Ubuntu is able to join WPA-protected wireless networks.

When you're finished, click the Connect button. You should see the NetworkManager icon start to animate as the program attempts to connect and find an IP address. After a few seconds, when the animation finishes and the icon switches to display signal strength, you should find yourself online.

If your computer doesn't seem to connect, try rebooting. If the hardware doesn't work after this, it might be that the drivers Ubuntu installed by default are incompatible with your network device. In this case, you can try using a Windows wireless network device driver, as described in the next section.

Should you find yourself in the unusual situation of needing to specify the IP address, subnet mask, and gateway for a wireless connection, you can do so using the manual configuration mode of NetworkManager, as outlined in the "Configuring an Ethernet Network Device" section earlier in this chapter. Simply follow the instructions in that section, but select the Wireless Connection entry in the list rather than Wired Connection. In the dialog box that appears, you'll see additional areas for entering your SSID and WEP/WPA protection details.

WEP VS. WPA

Most wireless networks are protected using either the Wired Equivalent Privacy (WEP) or Wi-Fi Protected Access (WPA) systems. WPA is effectively an updated version of WEP and offers much stronger protection. There are two versions of WPA: WPA and WPA2. WPA2 is newer and corrected several security flaws in WPA. Both work in roughly the same way.

WEP and WPA encrypt the data being transmitted on the network, the idea being that it cannot be stolen by crackers with special equipment. Also, people can't join the wireless network unless they know the encryption key, which is basically an access code or password that prevents unauthorized people from accessing the network. As with other situations where security is important, you should choose a strong password containing letters of both cases, punctuation, and numbers.

Of the two, you should ideally configure your wi-fi base station to use WPA, because, sadly, WEP can be compromised within 5 minutes by using easily available software. However, the situation isn't quite so clear-cut for some Ubuntu users. Not all of Ubuntu's built-in wi-fi drivers support WPA. Some might claim to support it, but you might find they don't work reliably. Unfortunately, the only way you will be able to find out whether this is the case for you is to try to configure your network device and see what happens.

If you fall into the camp of not having good WPA support on your Ubuntu PC (and only a small percentage of users will), you might find WEP is your only reliable option, and you might therefore need to reconfigure your base station to use it. Our experience has shown that WEP has a very high success rate under Ubuntu. However, sometimes 128-bit WEP won't work on some troublesome wi-fi devices, and you might need to switch your network to 64-bit WEP instead.

WEP is a compromise in security terms, but try to remain realistic when considering your immediate environment. If your wireless network is within your home, is it likely that the couple living next door will have the know-how to crack a wireless network connection? Are they likely to want to do so?

On the other hand, if you live in an apartment block with several other computer-literate people, or if you work in an office, the risk might be considerably higher. Some people suggest that breaking into wireless networks is almost a sport for certain individuals. If this is the case, and you feel you simply can't use WEP, consider installing Windows drivers using NdisWrapper, as explained later in this chapter.

But whatever the case, bear in mind that confidential Internet connections, such as those for banking and shopping sites, are independently protected using a separate technology. See the sidebar titled "Secure Connections on the Net" later in this chapter for details.

Installing Windows Wireless Network Device Drivers

NdisWrapper is effectively an open source driver (technically described as a *kernel module*) that allows Linux to use standard Windows XP drivers for wireless network devices. You might describe NdisWrapper as being a translation layer between the Linux kernel and the Windows drivers, which can be installed by using NdisWrapper's configuration tools.

You should use NdisWrapper in only one of two situations:

> *Your wireless network hardware simply isn't recognized by Ubuntu:* All you see when you click the NetworkManager icon is a Manual Configuration option; you don't see any wireless networks listed. Of course, you should first ensure

that the wireless hardware in your computer is switched on—some notebooks offer the facility to deactivate it to save battery life.

Your network hardware is recognized by Ubuntu but fails to work correctly or adequately when you configure it: Perhaps it is unable to associate with wireless base stations, or maybe you can't connect to WPA-enabled base stations and consider WEP too insecure for your surroundings. If this is the case, in addition to installing NdisWrapper, you'll need to undertake an additional step in order to blacklist the existing Ubuntu driver.

Using NdisWrapper is relatively simple, and just a handful of commands are required. However, getting hold of the necessary Windows driver files is harder work because, unfortunately, NdisWrapper isn't designed to work with the usual method of driver distribution: .exe files. Instead, NdisWrapper needs the specific .inf and .sys files that constitute the driver—effectively, the Windows system files. These are contained within the .exe file and must be manually extracted.

■ **Note** Sometimes drivers are distributed as .zip files, in which case the relevant files are easy to get at. Keep your fingers crossed that this will be the case for your particular hardware!

NdisWrapper is far from perfect. Not all wireless devices have been proven to work with it, and it's not necessarily the case that a driver available for Windows will work under Linux. Sometimes trial and error is required. Annoyingly, Windows drivers sometimes appear to work but then prove unreliable. Some might stop working. Some might even crash your system. The best plan is simply to give it a try.

■ **Tip** NdisWrapper gets better and better with every new release. This is why it's a good idea to update your system on a regular basis.

In the instructions in this section, we explain how to make an Atheros AR5008 wireless network device that's built into an Apple MacBook work under Ubuntu using NdisWrapper. The instructions remain essentially the same for all types of wireless network hardware. However, some specific details, such as download addresses, will obviously differ.

First, you'll need to install the NdisWrapper software and then you can install the necessary Windows drivers. These steps will make your wireless network device available under Ubuntu. Then you can follow the instructions in the previous section to connect to that wireless network.

Installing the NdisWrapper Configuration Tools

NdisWrapper consists of two components: a kernel module and configuration tools. The kernel module comes as part of the default kernel package, so is installed by default, but you will need to install the configuration tools manually.

To do so, ensure you are online using a wired connection to your router have an active wired network connection, following the previous "Configuring an Ethernet Network Device" section. Then start up the Ubuntu Software Center, which you'll find under Applications. Do a search for **windows wireless** and install the Windows Wireless Drivers package which will come up in the search results. You will need to enter your password when prompted. Installing this package automatically installs not only the graphical Windows wireless driver installation tool, but also the underlying packages ndiswrapper-utils and ndiswrapper-common.

Installing the Windows XP Drivers

After the NdisWrapper configuration software is installed, you can install the Windows XP wireless network device drivers. There are several parts to the procedure:

- Identify the wireless network hardware and then source the appropriate Windows driver. If you're dual-booting with Windows, the drivers may already be available on your Windows partition.

- Extract the necessary .sys and .inf files from the driver archive (and possibly .bin files, although this is rare).

- You may need to "blacklist" (that is, tell the system to ignore) the built-in Ubuntu driver, so that NdisWrapper can associate with the hardware.

- Use the NdisWrapper configuration tool to install the Windows driver.

These steps are covered in the following sections. You will need another computer that's already online to download some files and check the NdisWrapper web site for information. If your computer dual-boots, you can use your Windows setup to do this, or if you have an Ethernet port on your computer, you could plug into a wired network.

Identifying Your Wireless Network Hardware and Sourcing Drivers

To identify the wireless network hardware for use with NdisWrapper, you need two pieces of information: the make and model of the hardware and the PCI ID number. The former is the make and model of the hardware as identified by Ubuntu as a result of system probing, rather than what's quoted on the packaging for the wireless network device or in its documentation. These details discovered by Ubuntu will usually relate to the manufacturer of the underlying components, rather than the company that assembled and marketed the computer. The PCI ID is two four-digit hexadecimal numbers used by your computer to identify the device internally (such as 168c:001c). The same PCI ID numbering system is used by both Windows and Ubuntu, which is why it's so useful in this instance.

You can find both the PCI ID and the make/model information by using the Device Manager tool. Follow the instructions in the "Installing Device Manager" section earlier in this chapter if you haven't already installed this program. Then follow these steps:

1. Choose Applications ➤ System Tools ➤ Device Manager. In the left column, find the entry that reads Network Controller, Networking Wireless Control Interface, or WLAN Interface. You might also look for USB Interface, PCI Bridge, or 802.11 to exhaust your search. Then look at the corresponding summary in the right column, where you'll find the make and model of the hardware listed under the Vendor and Model headings. If no useful details are listed, you might need to click the parent entry in the list. On one test system, we found the WLAN Interface entry, but saw the make and model details only after we clicked the Ethernet Controller parent entry in the list on the left.

2. Write down the make and model shown in Device Manager. For example, on a test notebook containing an Atheros wireless network device, the make and model read AR5001 Wireless Network Adapter. Remember that these details don't relate to those listed in the instruction manual or computer packaging (our notebook's specification lists the hardware simply as Built-in AirPort

Extreme Wi-Fi). This is because Ubuntu is identifying the hardware generically, reading information from its component hardware.

3. Click the Properties tab of Device Manager (if this isn't visible, click View ➤ Device Properties) and look through the information there for a line that begins `info.udi`. Look at the end of the line and make a note of the two sets of characters that are separated by an underscore and preceded by `pci_`. Look at Figure 7-7 for an example taken from our test machine. Yours may differ, but the line should always end with `pci_` and then the digits. If it doesn't, you have selected the wrong entry in the list of devices on the left. Try examining a different entry, such as the parent of the entry in the list.

4. Write down the characters following `pci_` at the end of the `info.udi` line. Written alongside each other, the two sets of digits that are separated by an underscore form the all-important *PCI ID number*. In written form, they're usually separated by a colon. If either of the sets of letters or numbers is fewer than four characters long, simply add zeros before them in order to make four characters. In our test machine, the end of the `info.udi` line reads `168c_1c`. We add two zeros before 1c, making a complete PCI ID of `168c:001c`. On another PC, the end of the line reads `168c_13`. Adding two zeros before 13 gives a PCI ID of `168c:0013`.

5. Using another computer that's able to go online, visit `http://sourceforge.net/apps/mediawiki/ndiswrapper/`. Under the Documentation heading, click the "List of known working devices" link. This is a community-generated listing of the wireless network devices that have been proven to work with NdisWrapper.

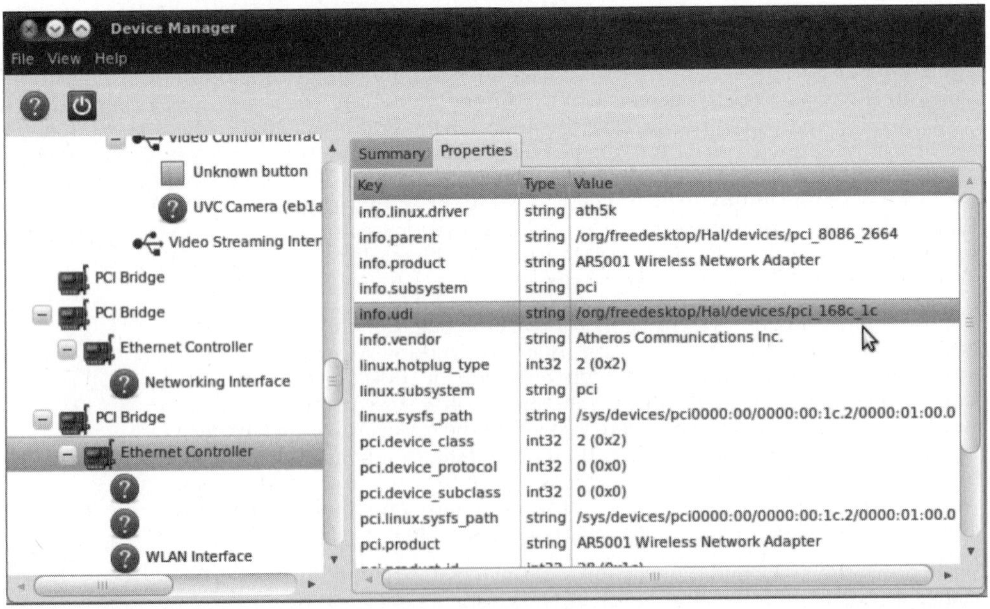

Figure 7-7. Find the PCI ID of your wireless network hardware by looking at the end of the `info.udi` *line.*

> ■ **Tip** The URL in step 5 was correct as this book went to press. If you find it no longer accurate, search Google, using **NdisWrapper list** as a search term.

6. The "known to work" cards are grouped in alphabetical order. Select the appropriate list based on the card manufacturer's name. (Remember to use the name you discovered using Device Manager in steps 1 and 2, and *not* the official name in the computer's manual or packaging.)

7. Using the search function of your browser (Ctrl+F within Firefox), look for the PCI ID number you noted earlier, in the format described in step 4. For the example in Figure 7-7, we would search for **168c:001c**. In the list, look to match the following things, presented in order of importance:

   a. The PCI ID

   b. The model name of the wireless hardware, as reported by Device Manager (listed on the Summary tab)

   c. The manufacturer and model of the notebook, as mentioned on its case or within its documentation

   It's likely many entries in the list may match your PCI ID, so search until you find the one that best matches the model of the hardware. If there are *still* many matches, search until you find an entry that matches the manufacturer and model of the notebook. You might not be lucky enough to find an exact match for the notebook manufacturer and model, however, and you might need to select the most likely choice. Use your common sense and judgment. If your notebook is manufactured by ASUS, for example, but you can't find the drivers for the exact model, then choose drivers for another ASUS model.

> ■ **Caution** Watch out for any mention of x86_64 in the description of the driver file. This indicates that the entry in the list relates to 64-bit Linux. The version of Ubuntu supplied with this book is 32-bit. If you encounter an entry relating to x86_64, keep searching.

8. Look within the entry in the list for a direct link to the driver file. Sometimes this isn't given, and a manufacturer web site address is mentioned, which you can visit and navigate through to the driver download section (usually under the Support section on the web site). Download the Windows XP driver release.

Extracting the Driver Components

After downloading the drivers, you'll need to extract the .sys and .inf files relevant to your wireless network hardware. These are all that NdisWrapper needs, and the rest of the driver files can be discarded. However, extracting the files can be hard to do, because often they're contained within an

.exe file. (Most driver .exe files are actually self-extracting archive files.) Additionally, the driver file might contain drivers for several different models of hardware, and it's necessary to identify the particular driver .inf file relevant to your wireless network device.

If the driver you've downloaded is a .zip file, your task will probably be much easier. Simply double-click the downloaded .zip file to look within it for the directory containing the actual driver files.

If the driver is an .exe file, it's necessary to extract the files within it. With any luck, you might be able to do this by using an archive tool like WinZip (www.winzip.com), assuming that you've downloaded the file using Windows. Simply open the archive by using the File ➤ Open menu option within WinZip. You may have to select All Files from the File Type drop-down list in order for the .exe file to show up in the file list. However, if you're using Windows, we recommend an open source and free-of-charge program called Universal Extractor, which can be downloaded from www.legroom.net/software/uniextract. This program can extract files from virtually every kind of archive, including most driver installation files. After it is installed, simply right-click the installation .exe file, and select UniExtract to Subdir. This will then create a new folder in the same directory as the downloaded file, containing the contents of the installer file.

After you've extracted the files within your downloaded driver file, look for the files you need. The driver files will likely be contained in a folder called something like Driver or named after the operating system, like Win_XP. After you've found the relevant directory, look for .inf, .sys, and .bin files (although you may not find any .bin files; they're used in only a handful of drivers). You can ignore any other files, such as .cab and .cat files. Click and drag the .inf, .sys, and .bin files to a separate folder.

The task now is to find the .inf file for your hardware. If there's more than one, you'll need to search each until you find the one you need. You need to look for text that corresponds to the PCI ID you noted earlier. Open the first .inf file in a text editor (double-clicking will do this in Windows) and, using the search tool, search for the first part of the PCI ID, as discovered earlier. For the example in Figure 7-7, we would search for **168c**. If you don't find it within the file, move on to the next .inf file and search again. When you get a search match, it will probably be in a long line of text and to the right of the text VEN_. Then look farther along that line to see if the second part of the PCI ID is mentioned, probably to the right of the text that reads DEV_. In the case of the driver file we downloaded for the example, the entire line within the .inf file read as follows (the two component PCI ID parts are shown in bold):

%ATHER.DeviceDesc.001B% = ATHER_DEV_001B.ndi, PCI\VEN_**168C**&DEV_**001C**

If you find both component parts of the PCI ID in the line, as in this example, then you've found the .inf file you need. (In fact, you'll probably find *many* lines matching what you need, which is fine.)

You must now transfer the .inf file, along with the .sys and .bin files (if any .bin files were included with the driver), to the computer on which you want to install the drivers. This can be done by putting them onto a floppy disk, CD, or USB memory stick. Create a new directory called driver on the Desktop and save them there.

Your procedure from this point depends on whether Ubuntu recognized your wireless networking device when you first booted but was unable to make it work correctly. If it did, you will need to blacklist the built-in driver so that NdisWrapper can associate with the hardware. If the device wasn't recognized, you can skip straight to the "Using NdisWrapper to Install the Drivers" section.

Blacklisting Existing Drivers

To blacklist the existing built-in driver that didn't work with your wireless device, you need to find out the name of the kernel module and then add it to the /etc/modprobe.d/blacklist file. Here are the steps:

1. Open Device Manager (System ➤ Administration ➤ Device Manager) and then select the entry in the list for your wireless network device. This is the one you discovered in steps 1 and 2 earlier, in the "Identifying Your Wireless Network Hardware and Sourcing Drivers" section.

2. Click the Properties tab (if this isn't visible, click View ➤ Device Properties) and look for the line that begins info.linux.driver. Then look in the Value column and make a note of what's there. For example, on one of our test notebooks, the Value column read ath5k. Close Device Manager.

3. Hold down the Alt key on your keyboard and press F2. This will bring up the Run Application dialog. Type the following to open the blacklist configuration file in the Gedit text editor:

   gksu gedit /etc/modprobe.d/blacklist.conf

4. Click Run and enter your password when prompted.

5. At the bottom of the file, type the following on a new line:

   blacklist modulename

   Replace modulename with the name of the module you discovered earlier. For example, on our test system, we typed the following (as shown in Figure 7-8):

   blacklist ath5k

6. Save the file and then reboot your computer.

You should now find that the wireless network device is no longer visible when you click the NetworkManager icon, and all you see is a Manual Configuration option. This is good, because it means the hardware no longer has a driver attached, and you can now tell NdisWrapper to use the hardware.

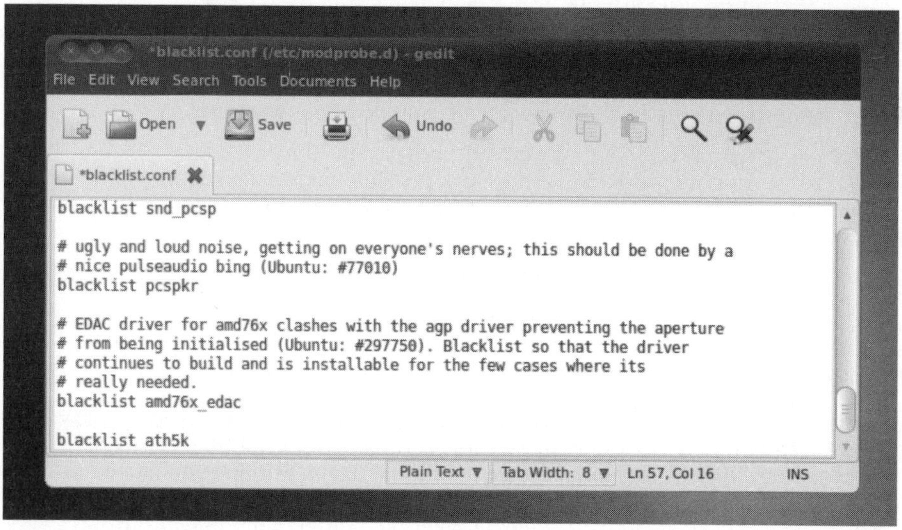

Figure 7-8. To stop Ubuntu from loading its own drivers, you may need to blacklist the module.

Using NdisWrapper to Install the Drivers

On the Ubuntu computer on which you want to install the drivers, you should now have the .inf file from the previous steps, plus the .sys and possibly .bin files that constitute the driver. You should have copied these files from the removable storage device into a new folder on your Desktop named driver.

■ **Note** If you've used a USB memory stick to transfer the files, its icon should appear automatically on the Desktop as soon as it's inserted. When you've finished with it, right-click it and select Unmount. You must do this before physically removing any kind of USB memory device, as explained later in this chapter.

To install the driver by using NdisWrapper, follow these instructions:

1. Click System ➤ Administration ➤ Windows Wireless Drivers. Enter your password when prompted.

2. Click the Install New Driver button.

3. The Install Driver dialog box appears, prompting you to select the .inf file for your wireless device. Click the Location drop-down list to open a file-browsing dialog box.

4. Navigate to the .inf file you copied to your system, which you have placed in the driver folder on your Desktop. Double-click the Desktop folder and then double- click the driver folder listed in the right column. Select the .inf file you copied in the driver folder and then click the Open button.

5. Back in the Install Driver dialog box, click the Install button.

6. At this point, you should see the driver listed at the left column of the Wireless Network Drivers dialog box. It specifies the name of the driver installed and whether the hardware is installed. If it says the hardware isn't installed, you've probably selected the wrong .inf file, or might be using the wrong driver file. Return to the previous sections and try to get an alternative Windows driver.

7. No reboot is necessary, and your wireless network card should work immediately. To test whether the driver works, click the NetworkManager icon and see if there are wireless networks listed. If it works, click Close to exit the Wireless Network Drivers dialog box.

Following this, you should find that the network device is available for configuration. Follow the earlier instructions for connecting to a wireless network.

Removing NdisWrapper Drivers

As mentioned earlier, although NdisWrapper can solve a lot of headaches with nonworking wireless hardware, it isn't perfect. You might find that the Windows driver you install simply doesn't work. In such a case, you can download a different version of the driver and try again. But first you'll need to remove the existing driver.

Choose System ➤ Administration ➤ Windows Wireless Drivers and enter your password when prompted. In the Windows Network Drivers dialog box, select the driver you want to remove in the left column and click Remove Driver. Click Yes when prompted to confirm the removal. Click Close to exit the tool.

SECURE CONNECTIONS ON THE NET

For home users, the use of online banking services requires the transfer of confidential data. So is this a good reason to use the strongest form of wireless network encryption with your broadband router? No, it isn't. In fact, it makes no difference.

This is because the transfer of confidential or financial data across the Web—to and from online banking sites, for example—is nearly always protected by Secure Sockets Layer (SSL) HTTP. This works across any type of network connection, including wireless and Ethernet, regardless of whether the connection has its own protection.

You can tell you're browsing a site that's using SSL because the address will begin with `https`. Additionally, most browsers display a padlock symbol at the bottom of the screen (the Firefox browser will also turn the background of the address bar yellow). Accessing such sites should be safe, even if your wireless network connection is "open," which is to say it isn't protected with either WEP or WPA.

Similarly, although online shopping sites might not use SSL while you're browsing, when it's time to pay, they always use SSL. This ensures that your credit card details are encrypted. If the store doesn't adopt an `https://` address when you click to visit the virtual checkout, you shouldn't shop there!

So do you even need WEP or WPA protection if you simply use your wireless connection to browse the Internet? Yes. In addition to the risk of unauthorized users hopping onto your connection if it isn't protected, some web mail services transfer your username and password "in the clear," which is to say without using SSL. This means your information could be picked up by an eavesdropper. In the case of Hotmail and Yahoo! Mail, you can select secure login, but it isn't activated by default. Google Mail appears to use SSL all the time for login, but after this, your e-mail messages are transmitted across the Internet in the clear and, in theory, anyone can eavesdrop on them.

Connecting to a Mobile Broadband Network

Many countries now have widespread 3G cellular networks capable of delivering data at broadband speeds to mobile devices. Smartphones now come with 3G capability by default, with 3G USB adapters ("dongles") to plug into your notebook now commonplace on pay-as-you-go or contract arrangements. Higher-end notebooks and Netbooks now come with mobile broadband adapters built as standard.

Ubuntu offers excellent support for mobile broadband devices, whether you want to connect via a 3G USB adapter plugged into your notebook, an inbuilt 3G adapter, or your 3G-enabled cellphone connected ("tethered") via USB cable.

You can set up your mobile broadband device as follows:

1. Connect your 3G device (dongle or cellphone) to your notebook:

   • A dongle connected via USB cable should be instantly recognized.

   • Cellphones will generally need to be switched into modem mode, and you will need to consult your manufacturer's documentation for details. For example, when you plug a Nokia smartphone into a notebook, a dialog will appear on the phone giving you the option of switching to Mass Storage Mode or PC Suite Mode. Select the latter to make it act as a modem.

   • If your notebook has a built-in 3G device, make sure it's switched on.

2. Click the NetworkManager icon in the top panel of your Ubuntu Desktop. If your 3G device has been recognized, you should see a extra heading of Mobile Broadband, and under it "New Mobile Broadband (GSM) connection," which you should click on to start the New Mobile Broadband Connection setup wizard.

3. The three simple steps in this wizard are:

   • *Choose Your Provider's Country:* This will probably be correctly set already, based on the regional and language choices you made when you installed Ubuntu, but check it anyway before you click Forward.

   • *Choose Your Provider:* You should see a list of all the 3G providers operating in your country. Choose yours. In the unlikely event of your provider not being listed, you can enter the name manually. Click Forward.

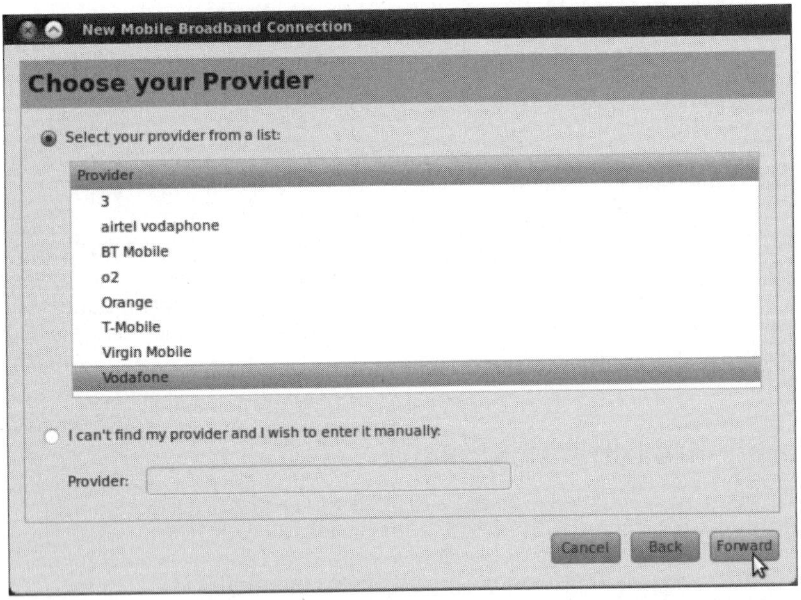

Figure 7-9. Ubuntu's mobile broadband connection wizard makes it straightforward to set up a 3G link.

   • *Choose Your Billing Plan:* Several pre-set options will be shown in the "Select your plan" drop-down. For Vodafone UK, for example, the options are Contract, Prepaid, TopUp, and Go. The correct plan name for your 3G device should be there, but if it's not, there is an additional option of "My plan is not listed," which will let you set the APN (Access Point Name) manually. (You will have to ask your provider for this information). Click Forward, check the settings, and click Apply.

If you're within a 3G coverage area, your mobile broadband device should now make a connection, and all necessary settings such as IP address, gateway, and domain name servers should be automatically configured.

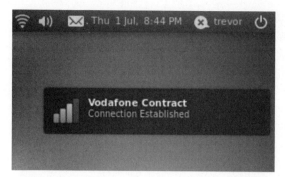

Figure 7-10. *Uh-oh. Now that you're set up with a high-speed mobile broadband connection, your boss will expect you to be hard at work wherever you are!*

Working with a Proxy Server

Some networks in offices, schools, and universities require that you use a web proxy (often referred to as an *HTTP proxy*). A *proxy* is a server computer that provides additional security by providing a single portal to all web pages. It also helps speed up Internet access by storing frequently accessed pages. This means that if ten people request the same web page, there's no need to get the same ten pieces of data from the Internet. The proxy computer can send them its own copies.

You'll need to speak to your system administrator to see whether your location uses a proxy. If it does, your administrator will most likely give you an address, which may take the form of a web address (a URL) or an IP address. When you have this information, follow these steps to configure the proxy:

1. Open Network Proxy Preferences (System ➤ Preferences ➤ Network Proxy).

2. On the Proxy Configuration tab, choose one of the three types of proxy configuration:

    • By default, the Direct Internet Connection option is selected, meaning that network traffic is routed directly, without using a proxy.

    • Manual Proxy Configuration enables you to set the proxy servers and respective ports for HTTP Proxy, Secure HTTP Proxy, FTP Proxy, and Socks Host. You can fill in this information based on the settings you received from your system administrator. If you were provided with one proxy for Internet access, select the Use the Same Proxy for All Protocols check box and fill in the details for the HTTP proxy and port, as shown in Figure 7-11. If your proxy uses authentication, click the Details button. In the HTTP Proxy Details dialog box, select the Use Authentication check box and then supply the username and password. Click the Close button.

    • Automatic Proxy Configuration allows you to enter the link (URL) to discover the proxy settings at your location.

3. On the Ignored Hosts tab, you can set the list of sites that will bypass the proxy. By default, any site hosted on your own computer is bypassed. You can add and remove sites as well. You normally add intranet (internal) web sites to this list.

4. Click the Close button after you're finished making changes to the proxy settings.

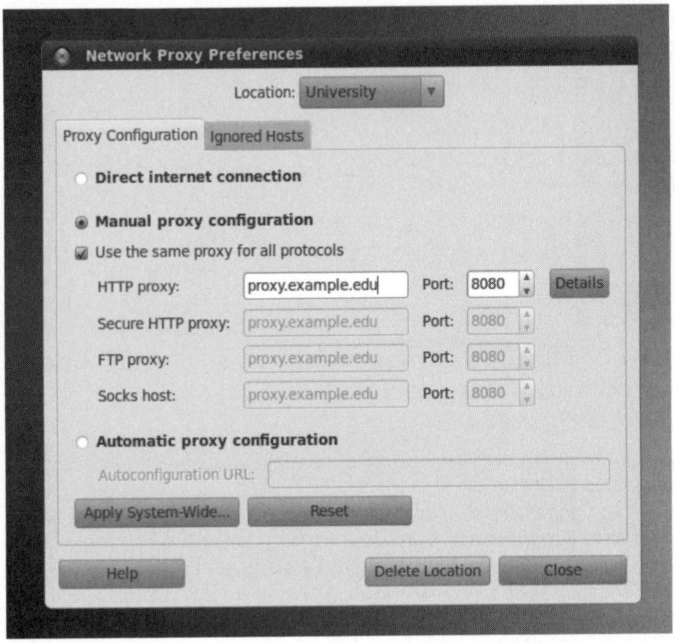

Figure 7-11. Proxy settings can be configured for a variety of locations.

If you have a laptop that is used in various locations, you can set up a series of proxy configurations that can then be selected whenever you move around. To create a new one, select New Location from the Location drop-down at the top of the window, input a name, and then set the appropriate values. After it is saved, each configuration remains available under the Location drop-down.

■ **Tip** Some ISPs run proxy servers too. However, unlike proxies in offices, it's typically up to you whether you choose to use them. You might find that using a proxy speeds up your connection, especially when you access popular sites, so it's worth trying out. To find out whether your ISP offers a proxy, visit its technical support web pages or phone its technical support line.

Adding a Printer

Ubuntu supports a wide variety of printer models— everything from laser printers to color ink-jet models, and even some of the very old dot-matrix printers.

If you work in an office environment, you might be expected to access a shared printer. Sharing a printer is usually achieved by connecting the device directly to the network. The printer itself typically has special built-in hardware to allow this to happen. Alternatively, the printer might be plugged into a Windows computer, such as a Windows server (or even simply someone's desktop PC), shared so that other users can access it—a setup known as *Windows printer sharing*. Ubuntu will work with network printers of both types.

■ **Caution** The vast majority of printers are now supported by Linux and work brilliantly. However, several manufacturers are still reluctant to release information about how their printers work, making Linux support difficult or impossible. If you're in the market for a new printer, and you want it to work with your Ubuntu system, be sure to check the OpenPrinting printer listings at `www.openprinting.org/printers` so as to avoid buying an expensive paperweight.

Configuring a Local Printer

A *local printer* is one that's directly connected to your computer, typically via USB. Any printer you attach to your computer will be configured by Ubuntu automatically and ready to use immediately, as shown in Figure 7-12.

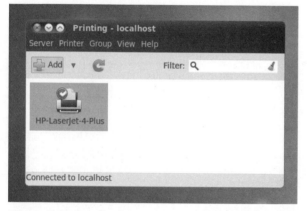

Figure 7-12. Any local printers are automatically configured when you connect them to the computer and then turn them on.

However, if the printer malfunctions when printing, such as churning out paper when a print job is sent to it, printing garbage, or not working at all, you can attempt to configure it yourself. To set up a local printer, follow these instructions:

1. Click System ➤ Administration ➤ Printing. In the Printer configuration window, click the Add button. You'll see the message "Searching for Printers." This might take a few moments to work through.

2. In the New Printer dialog box, you need to select which printer to configure. The printers that Ubuntu detected are listed under Devices. Click the printer you want to use and then click the Forward button to continue. You'll see the message "Searching for Drivers."

3. Select the printer manufacturer. By default, Ubuntu selects the manufacturer that best fits your printer, but you can select another manufacturer from the list. Alternatively, you can provide the PostScript Printer Description (PPD) file if the built-in drivers cannot operate your printer. When you've finished, click Forward.

■ **Tip** You can find PPD files on the CD that came with your printer or download them. OpenPrinting (www.openprinting.org) and Adobe (www.adobe.com/products/printerdrivers/winppd.html) offer many printer drivers for download.

---

4. Ubuntu again selects the detected model and corresponding driver for your printer, but you can change these selections. If the default driver simply doesn't work correctly, try a similar but different model. Select the appropriate model in the Model list in the left column and then select the appropriate driver for your printer from the Drivers list in the right column. Click the Forward button to continue.

5. You'll be invited to give the printer a name. The default should be OK. You can fill in the Description and Location fields if you want, but these are necessary only if you intend to share the printer across a network. Click Apply when you've finished.

■ **Tip** Sharing your printer on the network so that other computers can use it is simple: open the Printer configuration window (System ➤ Administration ➤ Printing), select Settings from the Server menu, and put a check in the Publish Shared Printers Connected to This System box. Then click the OK button.

After installation has finished, the printer will then appear in the Printer Configuration window. To see whether it's working correctly, double-click to see the printer properties, as seen in Figure 7-13, and then click the Print Test Page button at the base of the window.

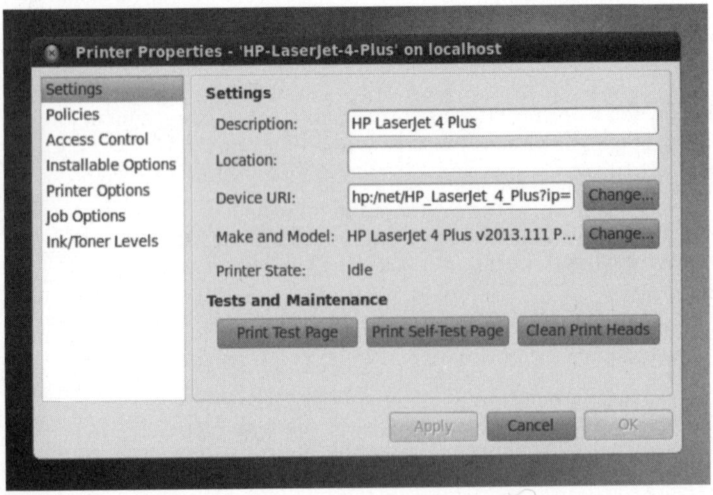

Figure 7-13. After the printer is configured, you can see its properties and test it by printing a test page.

If the printer is installed correctly, you should find yourself with a test page showing color gradations.

If the printer hasn't been installed correctly, it either won't work at all or will start spewing out page after page of junk text. If this is the case, click Cancel Tests (where the Print Test Page button used to be) and then turn off the printer. Delete the printer driver by selecting the printer in the list on the left and clicking the Delete button at the top of the Printer configuration window. Then repeat the installation steps, this time trying different settings.

Configuring a Network Printer

A network printer is one that is not directly connected to your computer. Instead, it connects to the network via an Ethernet cable, or sometimes via a wi-fi adapter. In this way, all computers in the office will be able to use it. It's also possible to share a printer that's attached to your computer to other computers on the network. The sharing is typically done using the Windows networking protocol (SMB). In this case, follow the instructions in the next section.

Some printers have the required server hardware built in, but others might use a special print server module that attaches to the printer's USB or parallel printer port. Ubuntu can work with both types of hardware.

Ubuntu is compatible with UNIX (LPD), HP JetDirect, and Internet Printing Protocol (IPP) server types. These are the most ubiquitous types currently in use for stand-alone printer servers.

Before beginning, you'll need to find out the printer's network (IP) address and, if relevant, the queue name or the port number. You should be able to find out these details by speaking to your network administrator or the person who configured the printer. If it's up to you to configure the network printer, consult its manual to find out how to set a static IP address.

Follow these steps to configure a network printer:

1. Click System ➤ Administration ➤ Printing. In the Printer configuration window, click the Add button.

■ **Tip** You can add as many printers as you want. You could configure a local printer (that is, one attached to your computer) and then configure a network printer.

---

2. Recent models of network printer will be detected automatically and shown in the Devices list. If so, select the printer name and click Forward and proceed to step 5.

3. If your printer isn't automatically detected, you can use the Find Network Printer facility to query the printer across the network and discover which printing protocol it prefers. To do this, click Find Network Printer, enter the network address of the printer in the Host field, and click Find. If all is well, a new entry will be made in the Devices listed, and you can click Forward and proceed to step 5.

4. Older printers often aren't discoverable by the preceding methods, in which case you can set the printing protocol manually in the Devices list. If you're unsure of which to choose, try Internet Printing Protocol (IPP). If you wish to connect to a Hewlett Packard (HP) printer with an HP print server attached, select AppSocket/HP JetDirect. (You could also choose LPD/LPR Host or

Printer, but this has long been replaced by IPP.) In the Host field, enter the network address of the printer. In the case of HP JetDirect, the default port number should work, unless you have been specifically told to enter a different number. Depending on which server option you chose, you may also need to enter the queue name. If it's IPP, you need to provide the host and printer queue, but Ubuntu makes it easy to set this up. Just type the network address in the Host field, and then click Find Queue. The IPP Browser dialog box will pop up and display a list of printer queues. Select a printer queue and then click OK. Ubuntu will update the entries in the Host and Queue fields automatically. Click the Verify button to check whether you can access the printer with the updated settings. If it fails, try changing the Host field to the printer's network address. After you have the correct settings, click Forward.

5. As prompted, choose the printer manufacturer, printer model and driver, and printer name, just as if you were configuring a local printer. See steps 3, 4, and 5 in the previous section for guidance. Click the Apply button after you've made your selections.

6. When the printer is installed, select the printer from the list in the Printer configuration window and then click Print Test Page.

If the printer doesn't work, it's likely that you set the wrong server type. Try an alternative type; if you chose IPP the first time, try App Socket/HP JetDirect the second time. Many print servers can emulate a variety of modes, so trying a different setting may work.

If the printer starts spewing out page after page of text, you likely selected an incorrect printer driver. Cancel the job at the printer by clicking Cancel Tests. Next, select the printer in the list on the left and click the Delete button at the top of the window to remove the printer. Then repeat the installation steps, this time trying an alternative driver.

Configuring a Windows/SMB Shared Printer

A Windows (or SMB) printer is one that's directly connected to a computer and then made available across the network via the network sharing function of the OS. Effectively, the computer acts as the printer server. Often, in corporate environments, such printers are attached to server computers, but an individual may share the printer attached to a workstation.

In a home situation, a Windows/SMB share is an excellent and inexpensive way of sharing a printer among many computers. The printer is attached to one PC, and, as long as that computer is switched on, the printer will be available to the other computers in the household.

Assuming that the printer has been correctly set up to be shared on the host computer, connecting to a Windows/SMB printer share is easy. In fact, you may find that Ubuntu finds the printer in the background and sets it up automatically! If you find the printer is available when you choose to print from an application, try it out and see if it works.

However, more likely, you'll need to add it manually. Follow these steps to set up a Windows/SMB shared printer:

1. Click System ➤ Administration ➤ Printing. In the Printer configuration window, click the New Printer button.

2. In the Devices list, select Windows Printer via SAMBA.

3. Click the Browse button to probe the network to see whether any printer shares are available. More than one might appear, so navigate through the printer shares until you find the desired printer. Select the printer and click the OK button. If you cannot find the printer share listed in the SMB Browser

dialog box, you may need to enter the details in the smb:// field manually, as shown in Figure 7-14. This entry will probably take the form of the address followed by the printer name (for example, officepc/epson). Speak to your system administrator or the individual in charge of the shared printer to find out what these are.

4. Click the Verify button to check whether the printer is accessible. If it succeeds, skip to step 6. If it fails, you may need to supply the username and password to access the shared printer, as described next.

5. Select the Authentication Required check box. In the Username and Password fields, type the username and password required to access the shared printer. These can be the login details of any user of the computer or, if the shared computer and printer are configured for Guest access, you can try typing **Guest** for the username and leaving the Password field blank. After the details have been filled in, click Forward.

6. As prompted, choose the printer manufacturer, model, driver, and name, just as if you were configuring a local printer. See steps 3, 4, and 5 in the "Configuring a Local Printer" section for guidance. Click the Apply button after you've made your selections.

7. When the printer is installed, select the printer from the list in the Printer configuration window and then click Print Test Page.

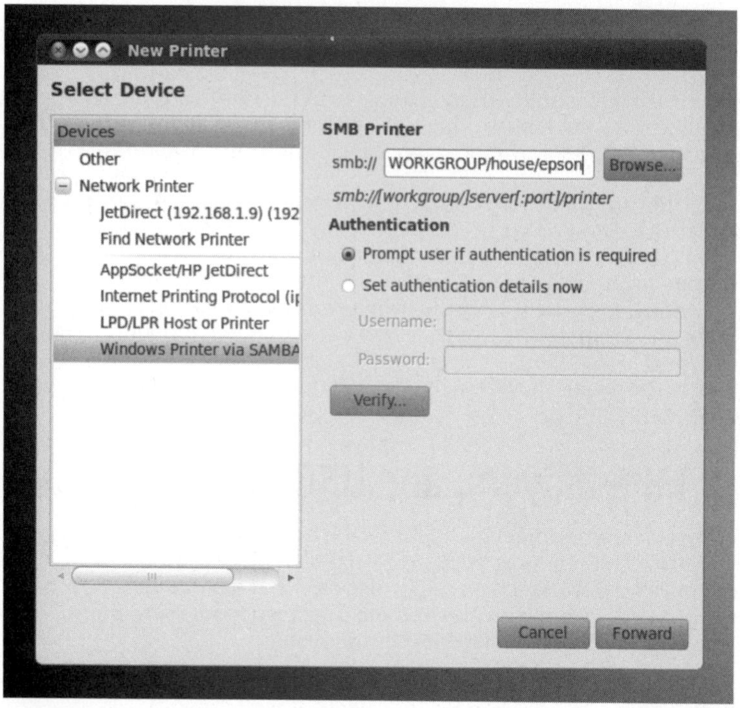

Figure 7-14. Ubuntu should be able to automatically detect any Windows or SMB shared printers on your network.

If the printer makes a noise as if to start printing but then decides not to, you might need to change a setting on the Windows machine. Click Start ➤ Printers and Faxes and then right-click the shared printer's icon. Select Properties and click the Ports tab in the Properties window. Remove the check in the Enable Bidirectional Support box and then click OK. Then restart both the Windows and Ubuntu computers.

If the printer starts spewing out page after page of text instead of the test page, it's likely that you selected the wrong printer driver. Cancel the job at the printer by clicking Cancel Tests. Next, select the printer in the list and click the Delete button at the top of the Printer configuration window to remove the printer. Then repeat the installation steps, this time using an alternative driver.

Administering a Printer

Like Windows, Ubuntu uses the concepts of print queues to handle printing. When you print from an application, the print job is held in the print queue. If the queue is empty, the job is printed immediately. If there are already jobs waiting to be printed, or if a print job is already in progress, the new job is added to the queue.

■ **Tip** If you have more than one printer installed (maybe you have a printer attached to your PC but also print to a network printer), you can set one as a default, which will automatically be chosen whenever you choose to print. Click System ➤ Administration ➤ Printing. Your current default printer is indicated by a tick in a green circle. If you'd like to make another printer your default, right-click its icon and select Set As Default.

When you print a document, the Document Print Status icon appears in the notification area (it looks like a printer). Single-click the icon to view the jobs waiting to be printed, if any. Right-clicking a job displays a context menu that lets you cancel, delete, hold, and release the job, and even move it to a different printer.

When you print from applications, Ubuntu will display a unified printer interface, as you might be used to in Windows. You will find similarities when you print in Gedit, GIMP, and Firefox. The only exception is OpenOffice.org, which offers its own simplified print dialog box.

Most applications that use the unified print dialog box will provide additional unique options related to that particular application. For example, the F-Spot photo manager offers settings useful for photographs, such as laying up multiple images on a single page, whereas Gedit offers functions related to basic text printing.

Ensure that you select your printer in the list on the left of the print dialog box (on the General tab) in order to see all the available options.

Using Digital Cameras, MP3 Players, and USB Memory Sticks

Removable storage is the term applied to peripherals that you might attach to your computer and that contain their own storage. Examples include USB memory sticks, external hard drives, MP3 players, digital cameras, and photographic memory card readers. You might also find that devices such as mobile phones are treated as removable storage devices when you attach them directly to your computer.

When you attach any removable storage device, Ubuntu does the following:

- Displays an icon on the Desktop, which you can double-click to view the removable storage device contents.

- Automatically opens a File Browser window showing the contents of the device.

- Adds an icon for the device to the File Browser's Places list, which is also accessible via Places on the top panel.

- If the removable storage device contains digital images (if it's a digital camera, for example), a bar will appear towards the top of the File Browser window with a button which will enable you to import the images to the F-Spot photo library program. You'll learn more about this in Chapter 18, which provides a concise guide to cataloging and manipulating your digital images. Similarly, if your device contains audio files, Ubuntu will detect this and a button will be added enabling you to open these files in the Rhythmbox audio player.

The contents of the removable storage device will be accessible in exactly the same way as any other files on your system. You should be able to copy, delete, and create files on the device, provided the device isn't read-only (if the read-only switch isn't set on a USB memory stick, for example). If the device contains MP3 tunes, you should be able to double-click them to play them, provided the playback codecs are installed (see Chapter 14).

However, a very important rule must be followed when you've finished with removable storage devices under Ubuntu (or indeed any operating system): the device must be *safely removed* (or in technical terms *unmounted*) before you physically remove it. This applies also to memory cards that are inserted into a card reader—before removing any card from the card reader, it must be safely removed.

Safely removing is quite simple to do. Just right-click the icon on the Desktop or within the Computer window and select Safely Remove Drive, as shown in Figure 7-15. Make sure you save and close any files that you may have been working on before you do so, or you may see an error. You'll need to close any File Browser windows that might have been browsing the storage device too.

Following this, you can safely physically remove the card or unattach the device. Reinserting it will make it available once again.

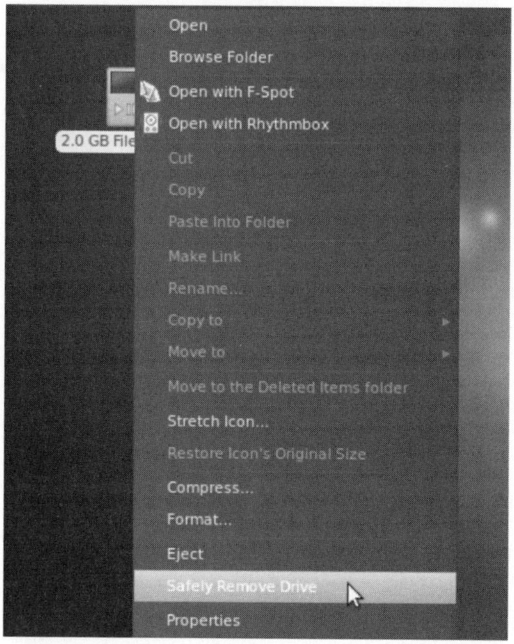

Figure 7-15. *You may be tempted to whip out a USB drive as soon as you've copied files to it, but it should be unmounted properly in order to protect your data.*

■ **Caution** Be very careful not to remove a memory card from a card reader while you're writing to or reading from it on your PC. This will most likely damage the card irreparably. At the very least, it will wipe the contents of the card.

Configuring a Scanner

Scanners may seem like archaic machines that have been superseded by digital cameras or absorbed into multifunction devices, but they're still the best method of transcoding nondigital images and textual documents into a digital format.

A lot of flatbed scanners can be made to work under Ubuntu, but not all types are supported. You can check the list of currently supported scanners by visiting www.sane-project.org. Additional models are added to the list all the time, and this is another reason to make sure your system is completely up-to-date (see Chapter 8, which explains how to update your system software).

The best test of whether your scanner is supported under Ubuntu is simply to see whether it will work. Scanning within Ubuntu is handled by the Simple Scan utility. This is a stand-alone program that operates like the TWAIN drivers that you might have used under Windows.

To configure a scanner and scan images, follow these steps:

1. Choose Applications ➤ Graphics ➤ Simple Scan. On startup, the program attempts to detect your scanner. If it finds a compatible model, Simple Scan will start. If the scanner isn't recognized, a dialog box will appear telling you so.

2. Using Simple Scan is as simple as its name suggests. Just lay your original on the scanner and click the Scan button. There's no preview. Simple Scan will go ahead and scan your original at full resolution and display the resulting image. You can then crop, rotate and save the image to disk using the controls in the toolbar. The file types which Simple Scan supports are PNG (lossless), JPEG (compressed), and PDF.

3. Under Document ➤ Preferences, you can alter the scan resolution for text and photos, according to your scanner's capabilities, and also set the default page size.

Simple Scan should be good enough for most purposes, but if you'd like a little more control over your scanning, with capabilities such as adjusting gamma, contrast and brightness, you might consider installing Xsane, which is available in the Ubuntu Software Center.

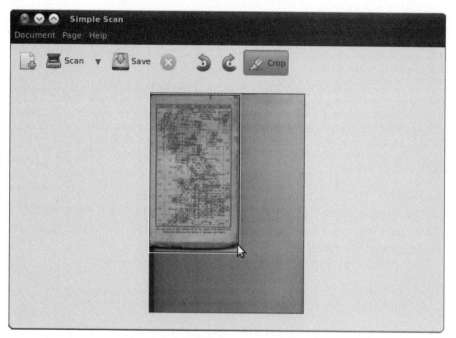

Figure 7-16. The Simple Scan program makes scanning really easy.

Installing 3D Drivers and Activating Desktop Visual Effects

The modern trend is for operating systems to incorporate flashy graphical effects into ordinary Desktop functions. For example, when windows are minimized in Windows Vista, they physically shrink and fade down to the Taskbar. Under Mac OS X, program windows appear to be "poured" into the Dock when minimized. In Windows Vista and Windows 7, when you press Alt+Tab to switch through open programs, the program windows are previewed vertically in a graphical arrangement, and you can flick through them, rather like searching through a card index. These effects are achieved using the 3D processing power of the computer's graphics card, even though the effects aren't necessarily 3D in nature.

■ **Note** On a technical level, the technique is known as *compositing*. What you see on the screen is first drawn in the graphics card memory and then transferred to the screen, rather than everything simply being drawn directly onto the screen.

Ubuntu includes similar Desktop visual effects, courtesy of a system called Compiz (www.compiz.org). However, all Desktop visual effect systems have a couple requirements, and these apply to Ubuntu as well:

- For Desktop effects to work, your graphics card (or motherboard graphics chipset) must be comparatively recent. Examples include the ATI Radeon, Nvidia GeForce, and Intel GMA product lines. Most graphics cards manufactured within the last five years with a graphics processing unit (GPU) should be adequate, and very recent models definitely will work.

- The correct graphics drivers must be installed. Currently, Intel GMA and some ATI Radeon graphics cards are supported by default because Intel and ATI provide open source 3D-capable drivers. For other hardware, including Nvidia cards, the manufacturer has not assisted development of open source drivers, and you may need to manually install a proprietary driver. Even for Nvidia cards, the picture is improving, with the open source Nouveau drivers now considered good enough for Ubuntu to install by default.

■ **Note** For most graphics cards, the open source graphics drivers will now support 3D Desktop effects. You will probably only need to install the proprietary driver if you want high performance from intensive 3D applications such as Google Earth and first-person shooter games.

Some proprietary 3D graphics drivers are provided under Ubuntu, but *only* if open source equivalents are missing. It is hoped that open source drivers will one day replace the need for proprietary drivers.

So do you actually need to install new drivers? If you find that Desktop effects are working, the correct drivers are already installed. A good way to test this is to hold down Ctrl+Alt and then tap the left or right arrow key. This will switch to the next virtual Desktop. If the entire desktop physically slides out of the way, Desktop effects are activated. If the Desktop remains static, and a small dialog box appears in the center of the screen to let you choose a virtual Desktop, then Desktop effects are not activated.

A utility called Hardware Drivers lets you manage proprietary drivers for your graphics card. This should appear automatically in the notification area immediately after installation if your hardware requires proprietary drivers.

Follow these instructions to activate the proprietary graphics driver:

1. Click the Hardware Drivers icon to run the Hardware Drivers program. If it's not visible, click System ➤ Administration ➤ Hardware Drivers.

2. Supply your password in the authorization dialog box and click OK.

3. In the Hardware Drivers window, select the Enabled check box beside your graphics card device driver.

4. A dialog box appears, asking you to confirm that you want to enable the driver. It explains that enabling the driver enables visual effects on your Desktop. Click the Enable button.

5. The Summary dialog box appears to tell you what new software will be installed. Click the Apply button.

6. The driver is downloaded and installed. Then the Changes Applied dialog box appears to tell you that the changes are completed. Click the Close button.

7. In the Hardware Drivers window, click the Close button.

8. You need to restart the computer so that Ubuntu will use the new driver. Click the session menu (the Power button at the top right of the screen), select Restart, and confirm.

After the new graphics driver is installed, Desktop visual effects should start working immediately, as shown in Figure 7-17. If you experience seemingly random systemwide crashes or freezing after installing a 3D graphics driver, consider reverting to your old setup by using the Hardware Drivers program (System ➤ Administration ➤ Hardware Drivers) to disable the new driver. Unfortunately, in a small minority of cases, the proprietary driver can prove buggy.

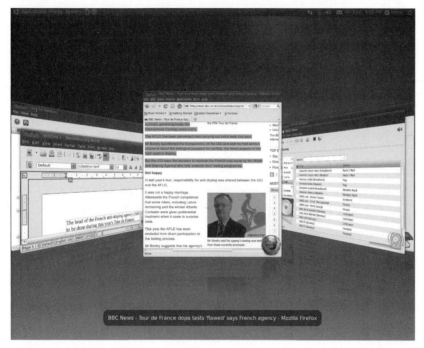

Figure 7-17. Using the correct graphics drivers can add sophisticated effects to your desktop.

Two modes of operation are available for Desktop visual effects: Normal and Extra. Normal is the default and provides a good subset of the available effects: menus fade into view, program windows shrink when minimized, and so on. Extra provides a lot more effects, some of them rather extreme, such as wobbling when you click and move a window, and windows appearing to explode to the corners of the screen when maximized. To switch between the two settings, right-click the Desktop, select Change Desktop Background, and then click the Visual Effects tab in the dialog box that appears. If you would like play with individual effects, install Simple CompizConfig Settings Manager in the Ubuntu Software Center, and then run System ➤ Preferences ➤ CompizConfig Settings Manager. The effects are divided into logical sections and can be easily activated and assigned keyboard shortcuts to your taste.

Configuring Bluetooth

Bluetooth is the short-range networking facility that allows various items of hardware to work with each other wirelessly. You can use Bluetooth for everything from file transfers between a mobile phone and computer to employing a wireless keyboard or mouse with your desktop computer.

For Bluetooth to work, both devices need to have Bluetooth support. Many mobile phones come with Bluetooth nowadays, as do an increasing number of notebook computers. It's also possible to buy very inexpensive Bluetooth USB adapters.

Bluetooth support is built into Ubuntu and should activate automatically if Bluetooth hardware is present on your PC. You will know if this is the case because a Bluetooth icon will appear in the notification area. This is used to administer all Bluetooth devices that you might want to connect to your computer.

Pairing Bluetooth Devices

When two pieces of Bluetooth-compatible hardware need to communicate on a regular basis, they can get together, a process also known as *pairing* or *bonding*. This means that they trust each other, so you don't need to authorize every attempt at communication between the devices. Indeed, some devices won't communicate unless they're paired in this way.

Pairing is simple in practice and works on the principle of a shared personal ID number (PIN). The first Bluetooth device generates the PIN and then asks the second Bluetooth device to confirm it. After the user has typed in the PIN, the devices are paired. Pairing is easily accomplished under Ubuntu and doesn't require any additional software.

As an example, the following are the steps for bonding a mobile phone to an Ubuntu PC. Bonding for devices without a user interface, such as keyboards, is handled differently, as explained in the "Using a Bluetooth Keyboard or Mouse" section a little later in the chapter.

1. Ensure that the Ubuntu PC is visible, which is to say that other Bluetooth devices can detect it. Click the Bluetooth icon in the notification area, select Preferences, and make sure that the Always Visible radio button is selected. Click Close.

2. You can pair up two devices from either end, but we're going to begin using Ubuntu. To do this, click the Bluetooth icon in the notification area and select "Set up new device." This launches the Bluetooth New Device Setup. Click the Forward button.

3. The device setup probes the ether and finds any connectable devices. These will appear first as a series of numbers and then using their friendly names, as shown in Figure 7-18.

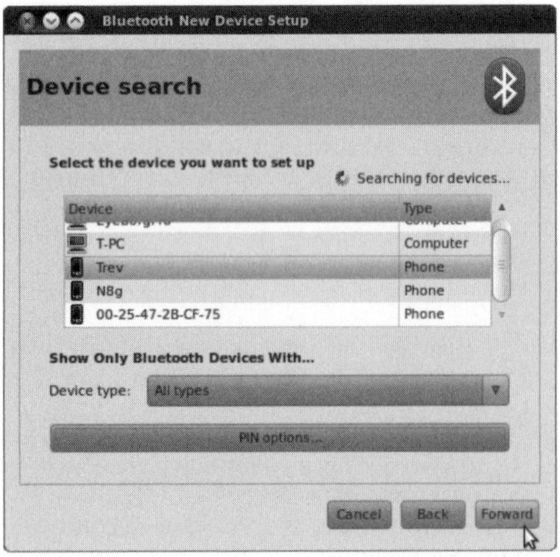

Figure 7-18. A pairing request is easily accomplished through the Bluetooth applet.

4. Select the device you want to connect to and click Forward. By default a random five-digit PIN code is created and transmitted, although if you want you can create a custom one by clicking PIN options. The setup window will display this number, and you should receive a prompt on the phone showing the same number and asking if you want to pair with this as a trusted device. Confirm that on your phone and click the Matches button in the Ubuntu setup (fairly soon or it will time out!). The two devices will now be paired.

If you subsequently want to remove the pairing, click the Bluetooth icon and select Preferences. In the list of Devices at the bottom of the dialog box, select the entry for your Bluetooth device and click the Delete button. Don't forget to remove the pairing on the Bluetooth device too.

Transferring Files Between Bluetooth Devices

If you own a Bluetooth-equipped camera phone, you might be used to transferring pictures to your computer using Bluetooth. It's by far the easiest way of getting pictures off the phone and avoids the need for USB cables or card readers. To transfer files via Bluetooth, you can use the Bluetooth applet.

■ **Note** Some phones refuse to transfer files unless the phone and computer are paired, so follow the instructions in the previous section first. Phones such as like the Nokia 6680 don't need pairing for file transfer, although each transfer must be confirmed manually.

Browsing Files on a Remote Device

The easiest way to get files to or from a device is to use Nautilus:

1. Click the Bluetooth icon in the notification area and select Browse Files on Device.

2. Choose your phone (or other device) from the list and click Browse. You may need to confirm the action on your phone by selecting Yes.

3. The File Browser opens up with the folders available on the device (see Figure 7-19). You can then navigate through these and copy files to your Desktop in the usual drag-and-drop fashion. You can also add files to the phone in the same way.

Figure 7-19. You can use the File Browser to access a Bluetooth device.

Sending Files from an Ubuntu PC to Another Device

There are two ways to send files to another Bluetooth device from your Ubuntu PC. The first is to use the Bluetooth applet. The second is to right-click the file in question and select Send To. The second method is useful if you want to send many files at once, and you will have the option of automatically zipping the files into a single archive (but bear in mind that the Bluetooth device receiving the file will need to be able to subsequently unarchive the file).

Using the Bluetooth Applet

Follow these steps to use the Bluetooth applet to send files:

1. Click the Bluetooth icon in the navigation area and click Send files to device.

2. In the Choose Files to Send dialog box, navigate to the file you want to send and click Open.

3. In the Select Device to Send To dialog box, select the target Bluetooth device and click the Send To button.

4. The target Bluetooth device might prompt you to accept or deny a file transfer request from Ubuntu. Choose to accept it.

5. After the file has been received by the Bluetooth device, click Close.

Using the Send To Option

To send one or more files using the Send To option on the context menu in the File Browser or on the Desktop, follow these steps:

1. Either right-click an individual file or folder, or select several files and click one of them. Right-click and select Send To.

2. In the Send As drop-down list in the dialog box that appears, select Bluetooth (OBEX Push). In the Send To drop-down list, ensure that your Bluetooth device is selected.

3. If you're sending several files, you can put a check in the Send Packed In check box. This will create a new single .zip archive and add the files to it automatically. Otherwise, each file will simply be sent one after the other. If you are sending a folder, the Send Packed option is already checked and cannot be unchecked.

4. Click the Send button. You may be prompted to authorize receipt of the files on the Bluetooth device, so do so. Bear in mind that transfer of many files may take some time because Bluetooth is not a particularly speedy form of data transfer.

5. After the file transfer is complete, click the Close button.

Using a Bluetooth Keyboard or Mouse

Your Bluetooth-equipped keyboard or mouse may work automatically under Ubuntu. However, if not, you may need to pair it to your PC, as follows:

1. Ensure that the Ubuntu PC is set to be discoverable. Click the Bluetooth icon in the notification area, click Preferences, and make sure that the "Make computer visible" check box is selected. Click Close.

2. Switch your keyboard or mouse to discoverable mode. Read the instructions for your device to find out how this is done. On an iGo Stowaway keyboard we used during testing, this required pressing the Ctrl+blue Fn+green Fn keys simultaneously.

3. While you're reading the manual, find out whether the device has a default passkey. Mice almost certainly will (and it's nearly always 0000), but keyboards might require you to type one manually when it comes to the pairing request.

4. Click the Bluetooth icon and select Preferences. Click the Set up new device button. Ubuntu will search for your input device. In you're surrounded by multiple Bluetooth devices, you might find it useful to narrow down the search to input devices using the Device Type drop-down.

5. You should find that your keyboard or mouse is detected automatically and appears in the list below the Select Device heading (if not, ensure that it is still in discoverable mode and hasn't switched itself off). Click the entry for the keyboard or mouse, and then click the Forward button.

6. A comment box should pop up on the Ubuntu computer, notifying you of a pairing request between Ubuntu and the keyboard or mouse. Click the Enter Passkey button.

7. What happens next depends on whether you're trying to connect a keyboard or mouse. Bear in mind that the process of pairing quickly times out on the Ubuntu computer, so you need to complete the following steps without hesitation:

   • In the case of a mouse, enter the passkey that you read earlier in the manual for the mouse. As mentioned, this is usually 0000. After you click OK, the mouse should be paired and should start working.

   • Some keyboards also use a default passkey of 0000, and, if so, you can enter that, and the keyboard should be paired. However, some Bluetooth keyboards might require you to enter a passkey created on the computer. In the Authentication Request dialog box on the Ubuntu PC, type a random four-digit passkey—something like **1234** (although for security reasons, you might want to choose something that's slightly less easy to guess). Click OK. On the Bluetooth keyboard, type the same number and press Enter. Following this, you should find that the keyboard is paired with the computer and will work.

8. Click Close in the Bluetooth Preferences dialog box.

If the keyboard or mouse does not work after a reboot, try turning it on and off again. If that doesn't work, deactivate the Bluetooth functionality on the PC, perhaps by momentarily unplugging the Bluetooth dongle or, on a notebook, using the relevant keyboard combination to turn off and on again the Bluetooth system.

Configuring Sound Cards

Generally speaking, your sound card shouldn't require any additional configuration and should work immediately after you install Ubuntu. The icon for the volume control applet is located at the top right of the Ubuntu Desktop, and it offers a quick way to control the master volume.

However, if you want to change your balance or microphone level, or if your sound card offers more than stereo output, such as multiple-speaker surround sound, then it might be necessary to take some simple steps to allow full control of the hardware:

1. Click the volume control icon (the one that looks like a speaker). A simple volume control will open underneath.

2. Click Sound Preferences below the volume slider.

3. The Sound Preferences dialog box appears. On most computers, you will have just one simple stereo sound card shown in the Hardware tab, and there won't be much to configure. In the Output tab, you will be able to adjust the balance, should you ever need to, while in the Input tab you can unmute your microphone and adjust the input volume. If your computer has more than one sound card—for example, onboard sound and an external USB 5.1 sound card—you can set which card is active in the Hardware tab and then switch to the Output tab to adjust volume sliders for balance, fade, and subwoofer, as shown in Figure 7-20. On a notebook that has a sound card featuring pseudo-surround sound, we could add a control to alter the intensity of the effect.

When you've finished, click the Close button.

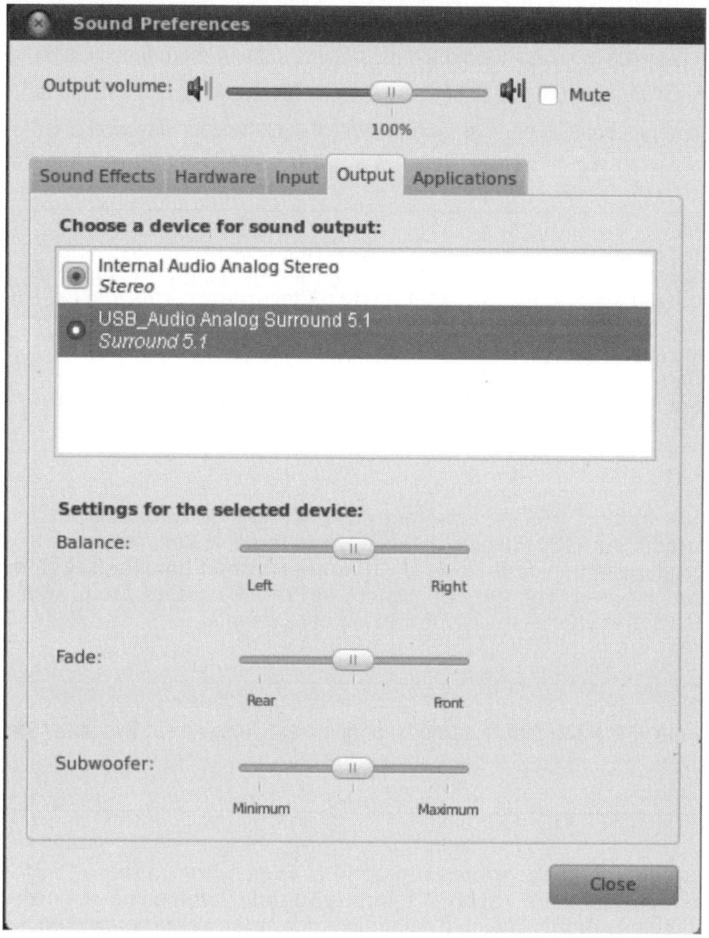

Figure 7-20. In Sound Preferences you can control all aspects of your sound card's output.

Using Power-Management Preferences

Depending on the degree to which your computer supports power-saving functionality, Ubuntu will let you configure your display to go into standby mode after a certain amount of time and will also allow you to configure your notebook to enter sleep (standby) mode. In addition, if you use a notebook computer, Ubuntu might let you configure additional aspects, such as the display brightness. These functions are controlled by using the Power Management Preferences. To start this, click System ➤ Preferences ➤ Power Management. If Ubuntu is installed on a notebook computer, you'll see three tabs in the program window: On Mains Power, On Battery Power, and General. If Ubuntu is installed on a desktop computer, you'll see just the On Mains Power and General tabs.

■ **Note** Not all PCs are created equal when it comes to power-saving features. Some support more functionality than others. In addition, Ubuntu is compatible with most but not all power-management systems, and it might not be able to support certain power-management functionality on your system, even if such functionality works under Windows.

Notebooks have the additional tab because it's possible to define two separate power management profiles: one for when the computer is plugged in and one for running on battery power. This makes sense, because you might never want your display to switch off when connected to an outlet, but it's advisable that it should deactivate within, say, 15 minutes of inactivity if the computer is running on battery power (to extend the life of the battery).

The three tabs of the Power Management applet are explained in the following sections.

On Mains Power

If your computer is a desktop PC without a battery, you'll see two options under the On Mains Power tab: Put Computer to Sleep When Inactive For and Put Display to Sleep When Inactive For. The dropdowns next to each of these options allow you to define one of a number of preset time limits before each feature kicks in, including the option of Never. There is also a check box which enables you to spin down the hard disks when possible, at the same time as the computer is put to sleep.

■ **Note** The sleep mode can be to either suspend to RAM (that is, standby) or hibernate. You can set this under the General tab.

If your computer is a notebook computer, you'll see some extra options. Depending on the technology used in your computer, you might see a Set Display Brightness To slider, which you can use to set the brightness of the screen when the power is connected. Whenever mains power is connected, the display brightness will be changed to match this setting.

You may see a When Laptop Lid Is Closed option, with a drop-down list. As it suggests, this will control what happens when the notebook is closed. Depending on the hardware contained in your computer, you might have the choice of doing nothing, blanking the screen, suspending the computer (shutting down all systems but RAM), hibernating (suspending RAM to disk and turning off the notebook), and shutting down the computer. However, not all computers support each of these modes, so the choices you see might vary.

Additionally, you may see a Dim Display When Idle check box, which you can select to conserve power by dimming the screen when your system is idle.

On Battery Power

The options under the On Battery Power tab, present only on a notebook computer, are largely the same as those under the On Mains Power tab, as you can see in Figure 7-21. These settings come into operation the instant the mains power is disconnected from your notebook and the battery kicks in.

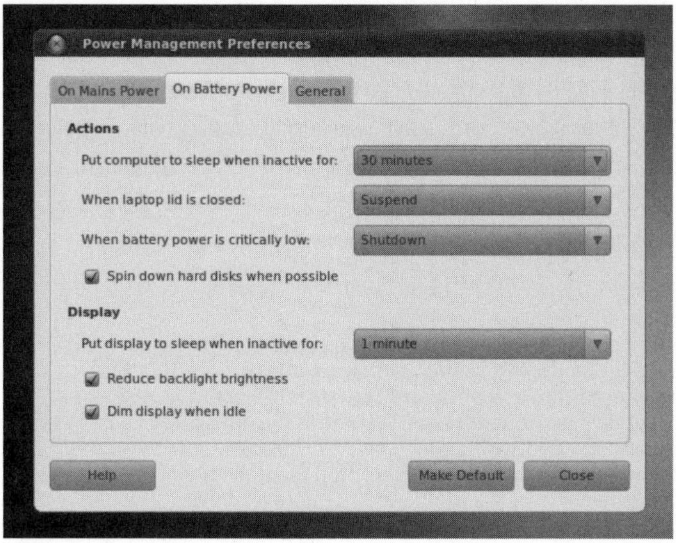

Figure 7-21. *Notebook users can define an additional power profile that will kick in when the battery is in use.*

An extra option appears as the last item in the Actions section: When Battery Power Is Critically Low. Here you can opt to automatically suspend, hibernate, or shut down the notebook when the battery power is nearly gone.

The check boxes at the bottom of the Display section could help save battery power considerably. You may select the Reduce Backlight Brightness option, which as it suggests, sets backlight brightness to a lower setting when you run on battery power. As with On Mains Power, the Dim Display When Idle option may also be available for battery power.

■ **Caution** Be aware that sleep mode requires a little battery power to work and will eventually drain your battery, especially if it's already on its last legs.

General

Under the General tab, you have options to customize button actions and notifications. These settings persist whether the computer is on mains or battery power.

In the Actions section, you can set what happens when the power button is pressed and the computer is active. Effectively, this controls whether pressing the button when Ubuntu is running should shut down the computer, suspend it, or hibernate it. You can select Ask Me, which will cause the standard Quit dialog box to appear (that is, the same dialog that appears if you click the Session Menu icon in the top-right corner of the screen). You can also customize the action for the suspend button. The available actions are to do nothing, suspend, or hibernate. Hibernate writes the contents of RAM to the hard disk and then shuts down the computer. Suspend shuts down most systems of the computer except for the RAM, which is kept active. Then, when you press a key or move the mouse, the computer wakes up almost instantly as the subsystems are reactivated.

■ **Caution** Hibernate doesn't work on all systems. The best plan is to test it by bringing up the Session Menu (top-right corner of the screen) and selecting Hibernate. Even if Hibernate appears to work, there are reports of it being unreliable. Some users report that their computer occasionally fails to wake up, causing a loss of data. Therefore, you should always save any open files before using the hibernate function or before leaving your computer unattended for any period in which hibernate mode might kick in automatically. Hibernate will definitely not work unless your swap partition is at least as large as your RAM.

The General tab also lets you select whether the power icon is visible in the notification area. If you're using a notebook, you can choose to display the icon only when the battery is nearly drained, when your battery is charging or discharging, or regardless of the battery state. Desktop PC users will probably opt not to display the power icon at all. The most fuss-free option is perhaps Only Display an Icon When Charging or Discharging, which is selected by default.

Finally, there's also an extra option you can select to play sounds when error events occur.

■ **Tip** The power icon in the notification area will give you an indication of the charge status of your battery if you're using a laptop. If you click it and select Laptop Battery Discharging, a Power Statistics window will be displayed, giving you masses of information about your mains adapter, battery, and processor.

POWER SAVING: IS IT WORTH IT?

The amount of power drawn by our computers varies tremendously, from 25 watts or so for a netbook to 250 watts or more for a desktop computer and monitor. Even 250 watts may not sound much, but most of us are running our machines for hours at a time, and energy isn't getting cheaper. So it's worth considering employing power-saving techniques, even if only to save yourself money, let alone the global considerations of how fast the power stations are gobbling up non-renewable resources and pumping out CO_2.

Try to avoid leaving your computer turned on overnight or when you're away from it for long periods. At a minimum, get used to suspending your system. It only takes half a minute to wake up fully. As well as saving power, switching off your computer avoids wear and tear on its components, extending its life. Although the CPU can work 24×7 without trouble, it's cooled by a fan that's a simple mechanical device. There are other fans in your computer too, such as the graphics card fan and case fan. Each of these will eventually wear out. If your graphics card fan stops working, the card itself will overheat and might burn out. The same is true of the CPU fan. However, by shutting down your computer overnight, you can effectively double the life of the fans and radically reduce the risk of catastrophic failure. Isn't that worth considering?

Summary

In this chapter, you learned how to set up the common types of hardware you might have attached to your computer. Additionally, you looked at configuring various software components that are vital for Ubuntu's correct functioning.

You stepped through getting online with Ubuntu (including joining a wireless network), adding a printer, connecting to a digital camera, configuring a 3D graphics card, and much more.

In Chapter 8, we move on to look at how you can ensure that your system is secure and protected.

CHAPTER 8

■■■

How to Secure Your Computer

Linux is widely considered one of the most secure operating systems available. On a basic level, Linux is built from the ground up to be fundamentally sound, and it allows users to work securely without their even noticing it. For instance, it enforces the system of ordinary users who are limited in what they can do, thus making it harder for security breaches such as virus infections to occur.

In addition, Linux contains a firewall that is hardwired into the kernel, called `iptables` (http://www.netfilter.org). The firewall is considered among the best solutions by practically all computer security experts. Not only that, but it can protect your home PC just as well as it can protect the most powerful supercomputer.

Like many Linux components, `iptables` can be managed the hard way or the easy way. The hard way requires in-depth knowledge of how networks operate and an ability to hack configuration files, both of which are beyond the skills of many ordinary computer users. Fortunately, several programs act as interfaces to `iptables` and make it simple to operate (or at least as simple as any equivalent Windows-based software firewall, such as ZoneAlarm from Check Point Software Technologies).

In Ubuntu, this built-in firewall is turned off by default. This is because the developers don't think that Ubuntu requires a firewall, and on a technical level, they're correct. Unlike Windows, Ubuntu has no Internet-facing services (programs that wait for connections from the Internet or local area network). It was just such a service on Windows XP that allowed the Blaster worm to bring the Internet to its knees in 2003 (see http://en.wikipedia.org/wiki/Blaster_worm). Expressed metaphorically, the theory is that without any windows or doors, Ubuntu is difficult, if not impossible, for hackers to break into (or for viruses or worms to infect). However, configuring the firewall with a program like Firestarter, which we examine later in this chapter, can be done so quickly and with such little effort that, in our opinion, there's no reason not to use the Linux firewall.

In addition, as with most versions of Linux, Ubuntu doesn't come with antivirus protection out of the box. This is because there are practically no viruses affecting Linux, and it is reasoned that there simply isn't a need for virus protection. However, as with a firewall configuration program, installing an antivirus program is easily done, and we explain how in this chapter. But first, we spend some time examining more-basic security concepts. Following that, we look at how to set up encryption for files and e-mail so they can be opened only by the intended recipients. Then we cover some elementary steps that you can take to protect your system.

Windows Security vs. Linux Security

If you've switched to Ubuntu from Windows, there's a very good chance that the security failings of Windows featured in your decision. Windows 7 contains many improvements, but Microsoft's record on security over the past few years has not been great. New and serious security warnings have appeared on an ongoing basis, and even now, new and devastating viruses and Trojans make news headlines with worrying frequency (usually described as a *PC virus* rather than what it actually is—a Windows virus).

One argument is that Windows is the target of so many viruses merely because it's so popular. Although it's true that some of those who write viruses do so because they dislike Microsoft, there's also little doubt that Windows has more than its fair share of security issues.

Many people are still critical of Microsoft's approach to security. For example, from Vista onwards, Windows includes User Account Control (UAC) dialog boxes that appear whenever a system-affecting action is required. However, they are so common that many people stop reading what they warn about and simply click OK by reflex. Many even switch them off. Compare that to Ubuntu: Similar dialog boxes appear whenever a system-affecting action is required, but the Ubuntu password dialog boxes have more of an impact because they appear far less frequently than UAC dialog boxes. Also, here the user's password must be entered. This forces the user to stop and think rather than simply click a mouse button.

Although Windows 7 offers reasonable security, Windows XP, Microsoft's most popular operating system (OS) to date, is considered an easy target for hackers and virus writers. Upon installation, the default user is given administrative privileges. True, a handful of tasks can be performed only by the genuine administrator, but the default user can configure hardware, remove system software, and even wipe every file from the hard disk. Although you would never intentionally damage your own system, computer attackers use various techniques to get you to run malicious software (by pretending it's a different file, for example) or they simply infect your computer across the Internet without your knowledge, which is how most worms work.

Viruses and worms also usually take advantage of security holes within Windows software. As just one example, an infamous security hole within Outlook Express a couple of years ago allowed a program attached to an e-mail message to run when the user simply clicked a particular message to view it. In other words, infecting a Windows machine was as easy as sending someone an e-mail message!

It's a different story with Linux. Viruses and worms are far rarer than they are on Windows. In fact, the total number of viruses and worms that have been found in the wild infecting Linux systems is likely less than 1,000 (one report published in 2005 put the number at 863, and the number is unlikely to have grown much since then). As strange as this may sound to a Windows user, you can have a PC without viruses.

■ **Caution** Linux fans constantly note that viruses can't cause a problem on their system because the core of the OS is well protected. However, you should remember that the most important part of any computer system is, arguably, the data on it, so it's worth devoting time and effort to protecting this too. (See the upcoming "Encryption" section for more information.)

But although we would love to say that security holes are not found on Linux, the sad truth is that they're a fact of life for users of every OS. Many so-called *rootkits*—specialized software toolkits that aim to exploit holes within the Linux OS and its software—are available.

The bottom line is that although writing a virus or worm for Linux is much harder than doing the same thing on Windows, all Linux users should spend time securing their system and never assume that they're safe.

Root and Ordinary Users

Although users are the subject of another chapter, allow us to introduce the distinction between the root user account and ordinary users, because this distinction is the foundation on which much of the security model is based. For a more in-depth discussion on the matter, refer to Chapter 21. Linux makes use of something called the *root* user account. This is sometimes referred to as the *superuser* account, and that gives you an idea of its purpose in life: the root user has unrestricted access to all aspects of the system. The root user can delete, modify, or view any file, as well as alter hardware settings. Because everything on a Linux system is a file, this gives the root user immense power.

Linux systems also have *ordinary* user accounts, which are limited in what they can do. Such users are limited to saving files in their own directory within the /home directory (although the system is usually configured so that an ordinary user can read files outside the /home directory too). But an ordinary Ubuntu user cannot delete or modify files outside of their /home directory unless explicitly given this permission by the root user.

The user account you created during the installation of Ubuntu is a limited account, but on some Linux systems, it's possible to type root at the login prompt and, after providing the correct password, actually log in as root and perform system maintenance tasks. Ubuntu is slightly different in that the root account is disabled by default, and users are instead able to borrow superuser powers whenever they're required, in a similar way to Mac OS X. For this to happen, they simply need to provide their own login password. With desktop programs, a password prompt dialog box appears automatically.

Although the root account is disabled, most key operating system files "belong" to the root user, which is to say that only someone with superuser powers can alter them. Ordinary users are simply unable to modify or delete these system files. This is a powerful method of protecting the OS configuration from accidental or even deliberate damage.

■ **Note** Along with the root and ordinary user accounts, there is a third type of Linux account, which is similar to a limited user account, except that it's used by the system for various tasks. These user accounts are usually invisible to ordinary users and work in the background. For example, the CD/DVD-ROM subsystem has its own user account that Ubuntu uses to access the CD/DVD-ROM hardware. The concepts of users and file permissions are discussed in more depth in Chapter 21.

ARE YOU A CRACKER OR A HACKER?

Linux users are often described as *hackers*. This doesn't mean they maliciously break into computers or write viruses. It's simply using the word hacker in its original sense from the 1970s, when it described a computer enthusiast who was interested in exploring the capabilities of computers. Many of the people behind multinational computing corporations started out as hackers. Examples are Steve Wozniak, cofounder of Apple Computer, and Bill Joy, cofounder of Sun Microsystems.

The word *hacker* is believed to derive from model train enthusiasts who "hacked" train tracks together as part of their hobby. When computing became popular in the early 1970s, several of these enthusiasts also became interested in computing, and the term was carried across with them.

However, in recent years, the media has subverted the term hacker to apply to an individual who breaks into computer systems. This was based on ignorance, and many true hackers find the comparison extremely offensive. Because of this, the term cracker was coined to clearly define an individual who maliciously attacks computers.

So, don't worry if an acquaintance describes herself as a Linux hacker or tells you that she has spent the night hacking some PHP code. Many Linux types use the term as a badge of honor.

Encryption

Encryption is a means of protecting data by encoding it in such a way that the casual observer can't view it without a password/passphrase or a special file known as a *cryptographic key* (normally abbreviated to *key*). Encryption is used for privacy purposes and also to verify the identity of the person who originated a file or an e-mail message.

Two types of encryption are normally utilized on home computers and offered by Ubuntu:

File encryption: Files can be encrypted so that they require a secret passphrase to be decrypted. Alternatively, you can encrypt files so that they can be decrypted only by a particular individual.

E-mail encryption: E-mail messages can either be encrypted, so that only the recipient will be able to read them, or signed, so that the recipient can be sure the e-mail genuinely originated from you and not a third party.

Ubuntu's e-mail program, Evolution, supports the digital signing of e-mail as well as full encryption of e-mail sent to others or decryption of e-mail sent to you. The Nautilus file manager can also be used to encrypt files for personal use or so that only a particular individual will be able to decrypt them. Password encryption is also available in applications such as OpenOffice.org, which may be used to write or organize sensitive data such as accounts or confidential correspondence.

■ **Note** Although Evolution supports encryption, you don't have to use it. Indeed, many Ubuntu users don't utilize public key encryption, although power users often go this route. And, in general, relatively few people use e-mail encryption.

Underpinning Ubuntu's encryption system is a *public key encryption system*. Two keys are generated by an individual: the *private key* and the *public key*. The private key is kept private by the individual who generated it, while the public key is passed around to anyone who wants it (or even published on Internet databases). The two keys are related in that one key can encrypt data so that only the corresponding key can decrypt it.

For example, you could encrypt a file or e-mail message intended for Jane by using her *public* key, and only Jane would be able to decrypt it, by using her *private* key. However, and crucially, you would not be able to subsequently decrypt the file, even though you had encrypted it in the first place—data encrypted with a public key cannot then be decrypted with that same public key. Only the private key can decrypt it. If Jane wanted to encrypt a file so that only you could decrypt it, she would need to use *your* public key. You would then use your *private* key to decrypt it. No one else would be able to decrypt it after it was encrypted.

When utilized in an e-mail program, public key encryption works in two ways. Someone sending you a message can encrypt it and any attached files with your public key so that only you can read it. This ensures confidentiality. In the same way, you can encrypt a message sent to others by using their public key, so that only they can read it. Alternatively, and more commonly, a digital signature can be added to an e-mail file, even though the e-mail itself is sent unencrypted. This signature is generated from your private key along with the body of the message, and it is decrypted at the other end by using your public key, therefore proving the e-mail could have come only from you. This is known as *signing* an e-mail message, because it is as if you personally signed it in your own handwriting, thereby vouching for its authenticity. The e-mail is sent in plain text in case the recipient doesn't use public key encryption.

Setting Up for Encryption

To manage your encryption keys, you use the Seahorse application, which comes with Ubuntu. You first generate a *key pair* (your private key and the public key), and then you can export or publish the public key so others can use it.

Generating a Key Pair

Regardless of whether you want to use Evolution's encryption/signing feature or Nautilus's file-encryption abilities, you must first create a key pair. Here are the steps for doing so:

1. Click Applications ➤ Accessories ➤ Passwords and Encryption Keys. This will run the Seahorse application, as shown in Figure 8-1.

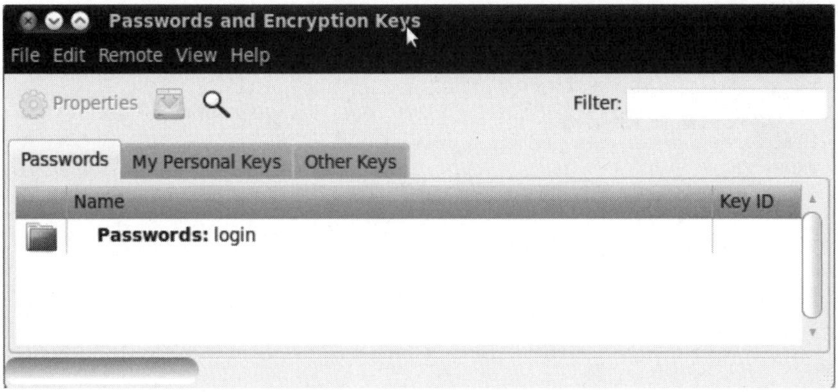

Figure 8-1. Seahorse is an easy-to-use management tool for passwords and encryption keys.

2. Click File ➤ New and select PGP Key from the available options, as shown in Figure 8-2. PGP, which stands for Pretty Good Privacy, is an industry-standard public key encryption system and is typically used to secure e-mails or files. The Secure Shell key is used as an extra security measure when connecting to remote machines, as discussed in Chapter 25. The Password Keyring can act as a kind of wallet for securely storing a collection of passwords that would then be accessible with a single password. Use the Stored Password option to store a text password in a keyring.

Figure 8-2. Choose PGP Key to create a key pair for e-mail or file encryption.

3. The New PGP Key dialog box appears. Fill in a full name, e-mail address, and, optionally, a comment, as shown in Figure 8-3. The e-mail address you use for your PGP key should be the one you will be using for sending e-mails with Evolution (see Chapter 14 for instructions on creating an e-mail account in Evolution). You may also set three advanced options, available in the Advanced Key Options drop-down list:

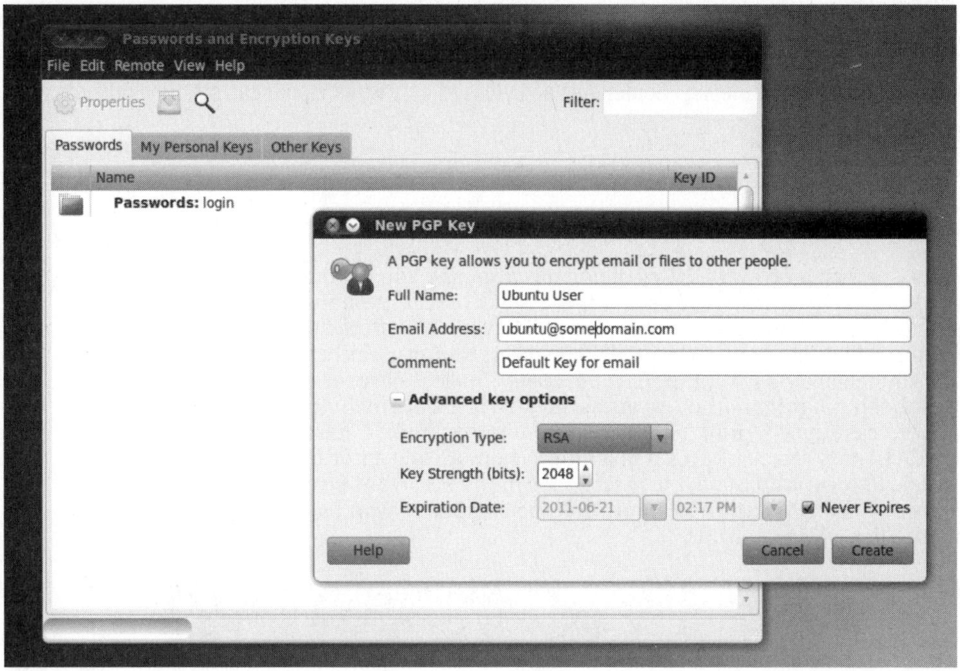

Figure 8-3. Fill in the fields in the New PGP Key dialog box and optionally set advanced options for your keys.

- Encryption Type lets you choose the type of cipher for your new keys. The default is RSA—RSA along with DSA Elgamal are the best choices because they enable you to encrypt, decrypt, sign, and authenticate files and e-mail. DSA (sign only) and RSA (sign only), on the other hand, can only sign files and e-mail.

- The Key Strength option specifies the strength of your key, set in bits. The lower the key strength, the faster it is to encrypt and decrypt, but choosing a lower strength will make it easier for others to crack the encryption. Increasing the key strength means slower encryption, but this should be weighed against the fact that it reduces the chance of your messages being intercepted—to the point where larger keys of 2,048+ bits are currently considered unbreakable. This is why the default is set as 2,048 bits, which is a sensible compromise.

- The Expiration Date option sets an expiration date on your keys. The default is that the keys are set to never expire. An expiration date is useful if you suspect your private key might fall into the wrong hands (for example, if you use a laptop that could get stolen), as the key will be useful only until the expiration date. If you decide to assign an expiration date, you must create a new key before the old one expires and use the old key to sign your new one, in order to maintain authentication.

■ **Note** The Key Strength option aids in strengthening your key, because the key strength is based on the type of cipher used together with the size of the key. Sometimes a key based on a weak cipher can still be made into a strong key by increasing the key length.

---

4. Click the Create button to create the keys.

5. The Passphrase for New PGP Key dialog box appears. You need to create a passphrase for your new PGP key. This is a block of text (perhaps a sentence or simply a long stream of characters) that will have to be entered when decrypting files you have encrypted while using Nautilus, and encrypted e-mails you receive via Evolution. The best passphrase is easy for you to remember but hard for others to guess; ideally, it should include uppercase and lowercase letters, punctuation, and numbers to make it harder for a brute force dictionary attack (that is, a machine systematically entering real words) to break. Enter your passphrase twice: once in the Password box and again in the Confirm box. As shown in Figure 8-4, the characters won't appear on the screen. Click OK to continue.

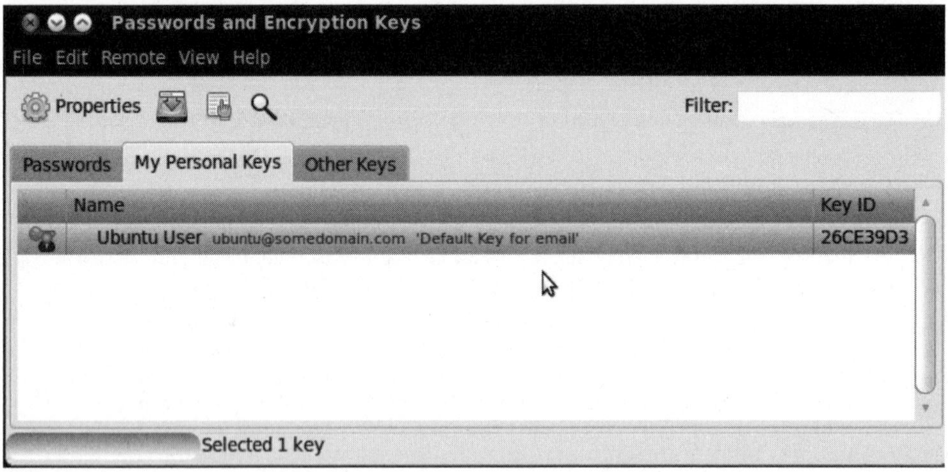

Figure 8-4. After the PGP key has been generated, it will be listed on the My Personal Keys tab.

6. Wait while the PGP key is being created. Depending on the key length you've chosen, this may take some time. After the process is finished, your new PGP key will be listed in the My Personal Keys tab of the main Seahorse window, as shown in Figure 8-4.

7. It's possible to redefine your passphrase at a later date without affecting the actual encrypted files. Right-click the PGP key in the My Personal Keys tab and select Properties. Click the Change Passphrase button and, after you've entered the existing passphrase, you'll be able to add another one. The small + icon shown on the left edge of Figure 8-5 allows you to tag a key with a photo or icon from your system.

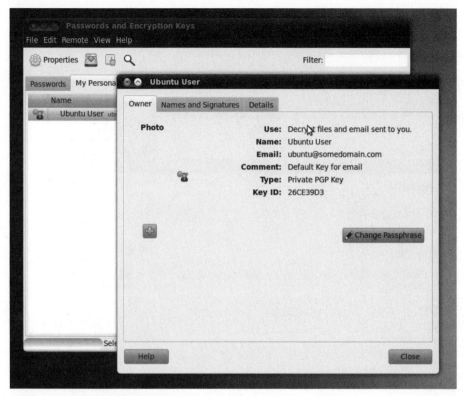

Figure 8-5. *You can change your passphrase anytime by using the Properties box. You'll need your original passphrase to do it, though.*

Exporting Your Public Key

As mentioned earlier, your public key must be shared with others if you want them to be able to encrypt messages or files so that only you can access them, or if you want them to authenticate any signed e-mail messages you send them. To do this, you use Seahorse to export your public key—effectively, to make it available as a file that can be e-mailed to others, or perhaps stored in a flash disk that is given to other people.

■ **Note** If recipients of signed e-mail don't have your public key, they won't be able to authenticate your e-mail signature, but they will still be able to read the message and access any attached files. The signature will probably show up as a .pgp file attached to the e-mail. Have you ever received an e-mail message with a file called something like signature.pgp attached? Now you know what it is!

Exporting the key is as simple as running Seahorse (Applications ➤ Accessories ➤ Passwords and Encryption Keys), selecting your key in the My Personal Keys tab, and then clicking the Export button. You'll be prompted to save the file to your preferred location, as shown in Figure 8-6. After the file is saved in your /home directory, you can distribute it in any way you like.

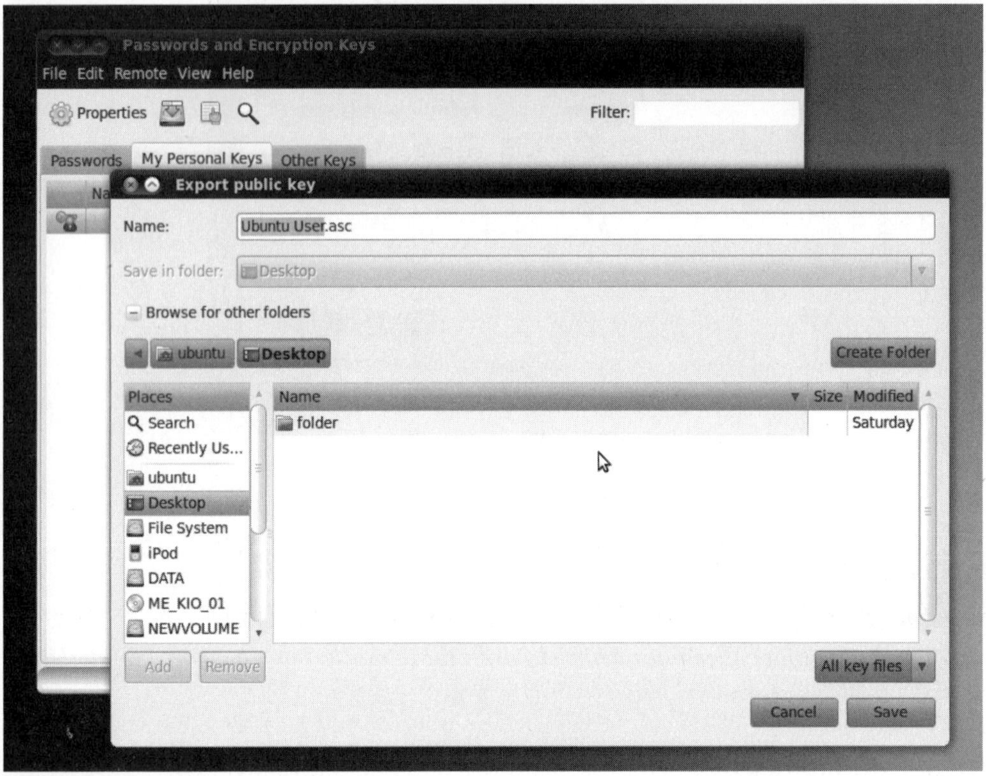

Figure 8-6. Using Seahorse, you can export your public key for distribution.

Publishing Your Public Key

For wider distribution of your public key, you can publish it in a public key server. This makes it easily available to anyone with Internet access, and it is the preferred method of sharing public keys. The steps to publish your key are as follows:

1. Run Seahorse (Applications ➤ Accessories ➤ Passwords and Encryption Keys) and click Remote ➤ Sync and Publish Keys.

2. The Sync Keys dialog box appears, as shown in Figure 8-7. To be able to sync your key, you first need to click the Key Servers button and specify where your key will be published.

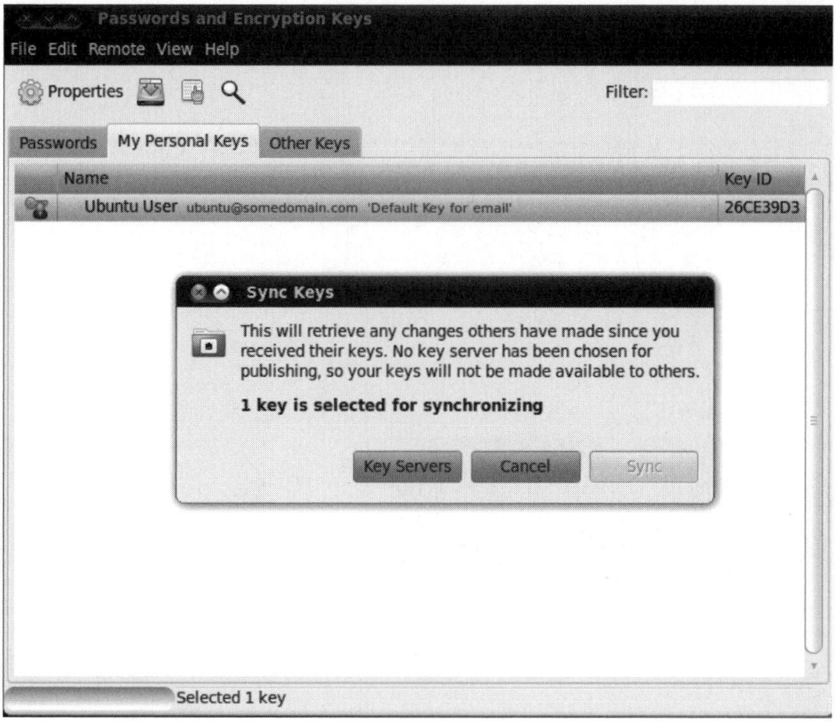

Figure 8-7. *You need to edit your key server settings to be able to sync your public key to your preferred key server.*

3. You will be taken to the Key Servers tab of the Preferences dialog box to customize key server settings. Here you can specify where to look for keys and where to publish your key. The most popular key server to use is pgp.mit.edu, which you can select from the Publish Keys To drop-down list, as shown in Figure 8-8. Choose your server and then click the Close button.

4. Back in the Sync Keys dialog box, click the Sync button to publish your key.

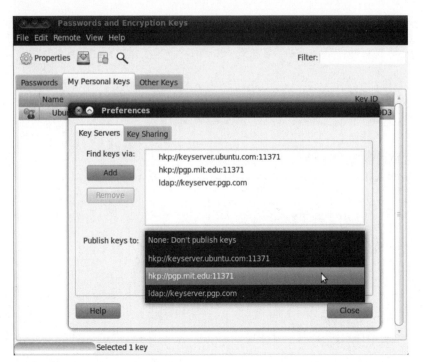

Figure 8-8. Click the Publish Keys To combo box to select where your key will be published.

Importing and Signing Public Keys

To be able to encrypt e-mail or files for others, and also verify their signatures, you need to import and then trust *their* public keys. You can obtain a public key from the person who created it or from other people who have that person's public key, or look it up from a key server.

If you've obtained the public key file personally (maybe on a floppy disk or via a USB flash drive) and it is accessible on your computer, you can import the key by running Seahorse (Applications ➤ Accessories ➤ Passwords and Encryption Keys) and choosing File ➤ Import. In the file dialog box that appears, browse your folders for the public key file that you would like to import, select that file, and click the Open button. To verify that the key was imported, in the Passwords and Encryption Keys dialog box click Other Keys and make sure that the key you just imported appears in the list.

You can also look for the key from the key server, which is perhaps easier and preferred by most people. To do so, click the Find Remote Keys… button in the Passwords and Encryption Keys dialog box. The Find Remote Keys dialog box appears. In the Search for Keys Containing text box, type the name of the person you are looking for and click the Search button. In the search results area, select the key you want to import and then click the Import button.

■ **Caution** When importing keys from a public key server, you cannot be so sure that these keys are actually owned by persons you want to communicate with in a secure manner. However, one solution for this is the so-called *web of trust*, whereby people can vouch for the authenticity of a key by signing it. See http://en.wikipedia.org/wiki/Web_of_trust for more information.

After the imported key is in the Other Keys tab, you need to sign the key to be able to send encrypted e-mail messages to the person who owns the key. In this way you are telling the system that you trust that the key is valid. You can also use the imported key to verify the authenticity of the e-mail messages you have received from that person. To do so, follow these steps:

1. Select the key to sign in the Other Keys tab. So far the key is marked with a Validity value of Unknown. This means that Seahorse has information about the key, but it doesn't know if it is valid or not. Click the Sign public Key button and the Sign Key dialog box appears, as shown in Figure 8-9.

    You can answer the question "How carefully have you checked this key?" based on how you verified the key: Not At All, Casually, or Very Carefully.

2. Your choice for "Others may not see this signature" affects the credibility of the key when you subscribe and sync your relationships to the key server. If you don't select this check box, your trust relationship will be manifested on the key server for the public to see, which is basically saying that you are vouching for the authenticity of this person's key to the public. This is helpful and convenient in reducing the number of keys to sign by others, by trusting the keys signed by you.

3. The "I can revoke this signature at a later date" option allows you to revoke the key. This lets you invalidate your trust with the key for reasons such as: the key has been compromised and misused, or if you discover the key is actually a fake.

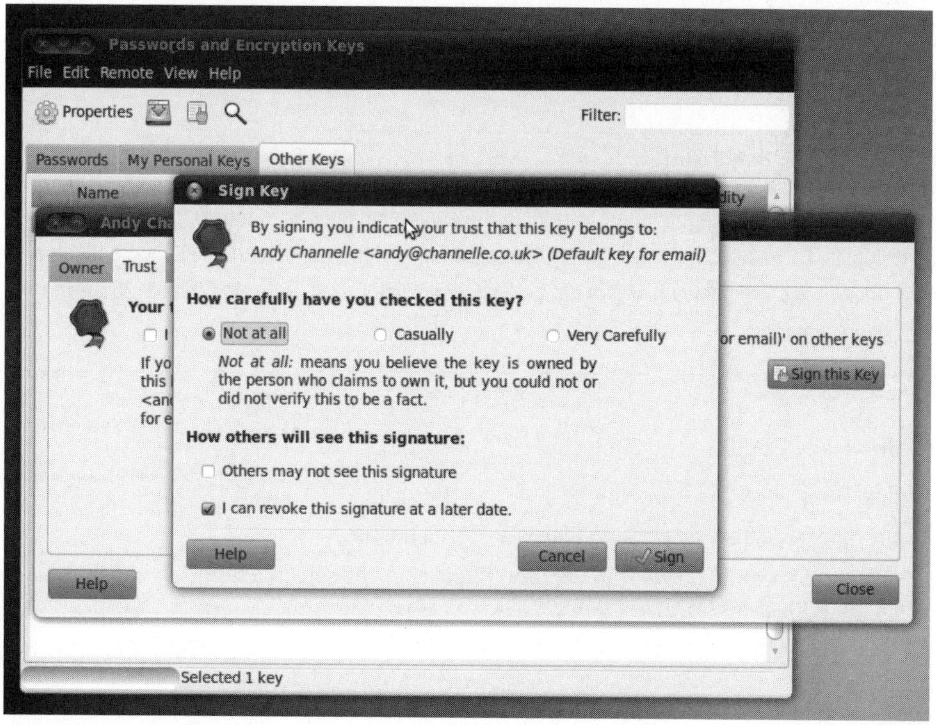

Figure 8-9. Signing a key is a way of vouching for the key's authenticity.

4. After making your selections in the Sign Key dialog box, click the Sign button to continue.

5. The Enter Passphrase dialog box appears. You need to provide the password you have entered when you created your PGP key. Supply that password and click OK. At this point, the key has been signed and is now listed with a Validity value of Full in the Other Keys tab.

■ **Tip** To reduce the number of keys to sign, you can trust the keys signed by the key that you trust. Click the Other Keys tab in Seahorse and then double-click the key to view the key's properties. When the key's properties appear, click the Trust tab and select the option "I have checked that this key belongs to <*name*> and I trust signatures from <*name*> on other keys." Click Close. The key will have a value of Full in the column Trust in the Other Keys tab. When you import new keys that are trusted by this key, those keys will automatically be part of the trusted list in the Trusted Keys tab.

Encrypting and Decrypting Files

After you've set up your encryption keys, you start encrypting files, either to store them in encrypted form within your own system or to pass them on to others. You can also decrypt your own encrypted files or files encrypted by others that are intended for you. These features are integrated into Nautilus, which makes encryption and decryption easy to accomplish.

■ **Tip** In order to be able to encrypt and decrypt files, you need to install the package seahorse-plugins. This will expand the capabilities of Nautilus, the file manager, by adding the encryption options to the context menus when you right-click a file or folder. To install the plug-in, go to Ubuntu Software Center and search "seahorse plugins." An application named Decrypt File will show up. If it is not yet installed, click Install. Refer to Chapter 20 for more information about installing software.

Encrypting a File

To encrypt a file, follow these steps:

1. Open your /home directory by clicking Places ➤ Home Folder.

2. Select a file or folder that you want to encrypt. Right-click the selected item and select Encrypt..., as shown in Figure 8-10.

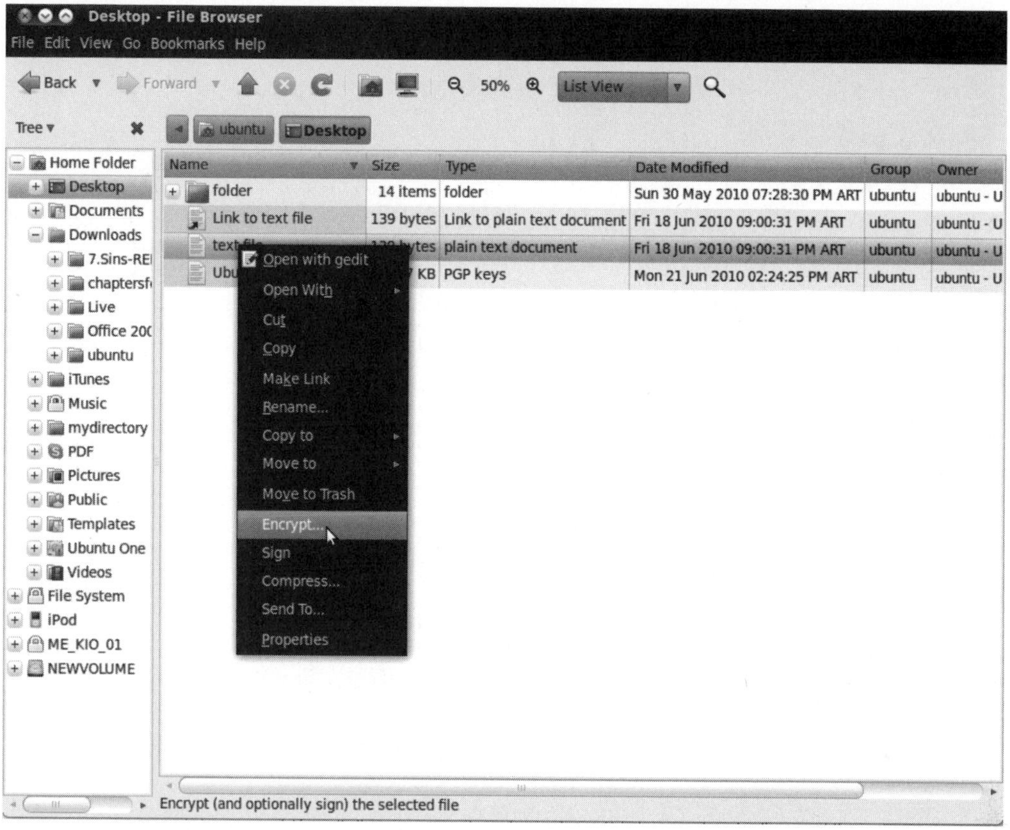

Figure 8-10. Encrypting a file or folder is a context menu option in Nautilus.

3. Select the recipients of the encrypted file, as shown in Figure 8-11. To encrypt
    a file for yourself, put a check alongside your own key. To encrypt for others,
    put a check alongside their names. Remember that file encryption is
    performed with the recipient's public key, so you will need to have imported it
    beforehand. Click OK to continue.

■ **Caution** Remember that the persons you select will be the only ones able to decrypt the file. After the file is
encrypted for someone else, *you* won't be able to decrypt it!

---

4. If you selected to encrypt more than one file, the Encrypt Multiple Files dialog
    box will appear, as shown in Figure 8-12. You can opt to encrypt each file
    separately or have the multiple files packed together in an encrypted
    compressed file, with the compression type of your choice. Select your
    preferred settings and then click OK to continue.

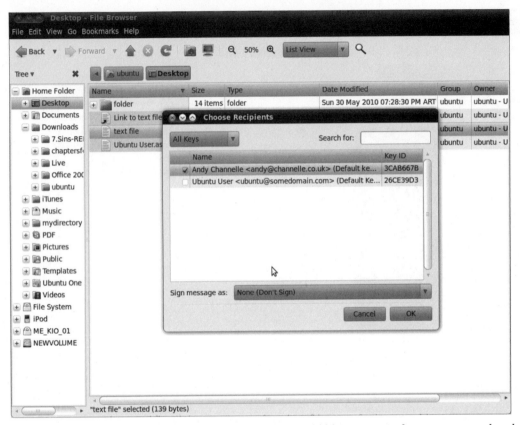

Figure 8-11. *Select recipients of the files or folders you would like to encrypt from your created and imported keys.*

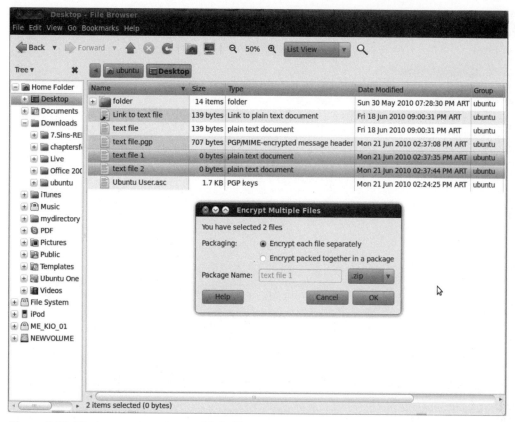

Figure 8-12. If you are encrypting multiple files, you can opt to encrypt each file or store all files in a compressed file and have that compressed file encrypted.

5.   After a file or folder has been encrypted, it will appear on your file system as a new file with a .pgp extension, as shown in Figure 8-13. This can then be passed on to your contact, if the file was encrypted with her public key, or filed away for storage if it was encrypted using your private key. For instructions on how to decrypt the file, see the following section.

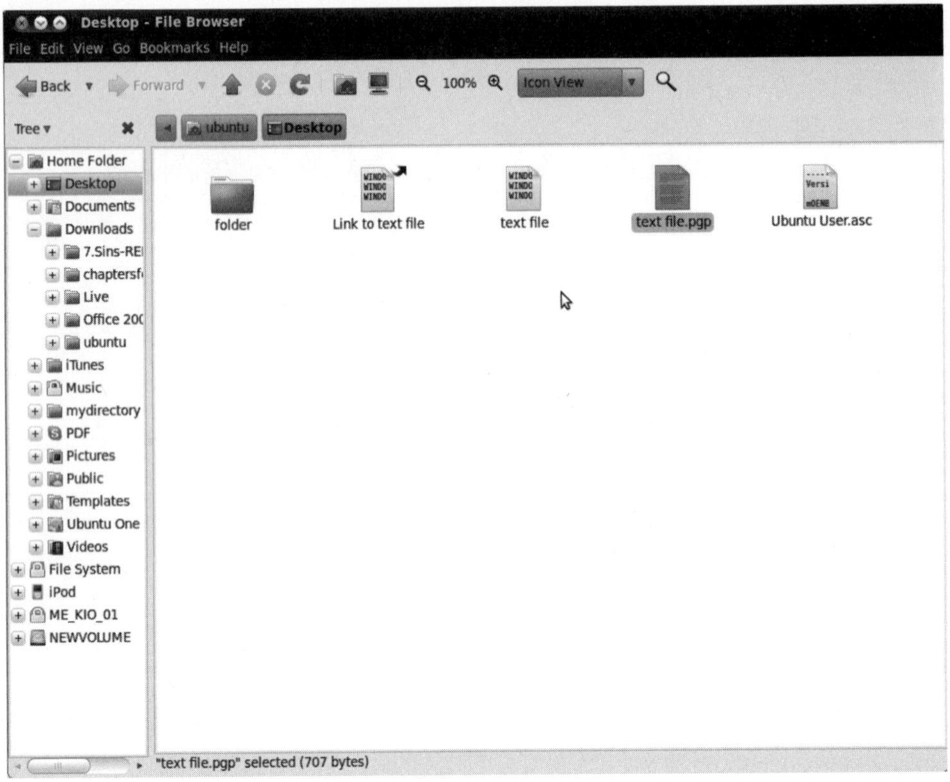

Figure 8-13. The encrypted file has the extension of .pgp.

Decrypting a File

To decrypt a file, do the following:

1. Open your /home directory by clicking Places ➤ Home Folder.

2. Select the file that you want to decrypt. The file extension is typically .pgp.

3. Double-click the file.

4. Type the passphrase that you entered when creating your key earlier.

5. The file will then be decrypted in the folder where the encrypted file is stored. It will have its original filename.

Signing and Encrypting E-Mail

After you've set up your encryption keys, you can send e-mail with your digital signature to signify the authenticity of your e-mail, as well as encrypt e-mail so that the intended recipient is the only one capable of reading your mail, and vice versa. As long as you've configured your PGP key, imported keys to trust, and configured your Evolution account, integrating this kind of security is seamless.

To sign and/or encrypt an e-mail message in Evolution, do the following:

1. In Evolution, choose File ➤ New ➤ Mail Message to compose a new e-mail message.

2. The Compose Message dialog box appears. Fill in the To field, Subject field, and the message.

3. Click Security. To mark the e-mail for signing, select the PGP Sign check box. To mark the e-mail for encryption, select the PGP Encrypt check box.

4. Click the Send button to send the e-mail.

5. If you chose to sign the message, the Enter Passphrase dialog box appears. Enter the password you assigned when you created your PGP key and then click OK.

Your e-mail will be sent, signed, and encrypted as you specified.

Validating E-Mail

To be able to validate signed e-mail messages you have received from other people, you need to import their public keys and then trust them using Seahorse. When you receive signed e-mail messages, a note indicating the authenticity of the e-mail signature is placed at the very bottom of the message.

Decrypting E-Mail

To decrypt e-mail received from other people, your PGP key needs to be configured in Seahorse. You will need to use your key to decrypt the e-mail.

Just select the e-mail message you want to decrypt, and you will see the Enter Passphrase dialog box. Enter the password to your PGP key and click OK. You will now be able to view the e-mail in plain text form.

Commonsense Security

As you start to understand how Ubuntu works, you'll become more and more aware of commonsense methods that will protect your system. However, we'll outline a few of these now to get you started:

Entering your password: Be very wary if you're asked to enter your password (outside of initial login, of course). You'll be asked to provide your password when following many of the configuration steps within this book, for example, and this is acceptable and safe. But if you're asked to do so out of the blue, you should be suspicious. If the root password prompt dialog box (shown in Figure 8-14) appears when you run a file that shouldn't really need root permissions, such as an MP3 or OpenOffice.org file, you should treat the situation with caution.

Creating perfect passwords: Setting up good security inevitably involves having a good, strong password. The challenge is to create something easy to remember but hard to crack, so it should involve punctuation, numbers, and an assortment of uppercase and lowercase letters. Perhaps you could base a password on a favorite song. For instance, TiaLTNGO@TQiD1986-4:02 is a great password. To remember it, I just need to know that "There is a Light That Never Goes Out" was a track on *The Queen is Dead* released by The Smiths in 1986, and it was 4 minutes and 2 seconds long. In contrast, password, password4, and andy1302 are poor because they are open to dictionary attacks, in the case of the first two, or personal information attack in the third case.

Installing new software: Be careful in choosing programs to download and install. Because Linux works on the basis of open source code, theoretically, anyone can tamper with a program and then offer it for download by the unwary. This rarely happens in real life. Even so, it's wise to avoid downloading programs from unofficial sources, such as web sites you find online via a search engine and whose authenticity you cannot totally trust. Instead, get software from the web site of the people who made it in the first place or, ideally, from the official Ubuntu software repositories (discussed in Chapter 20).

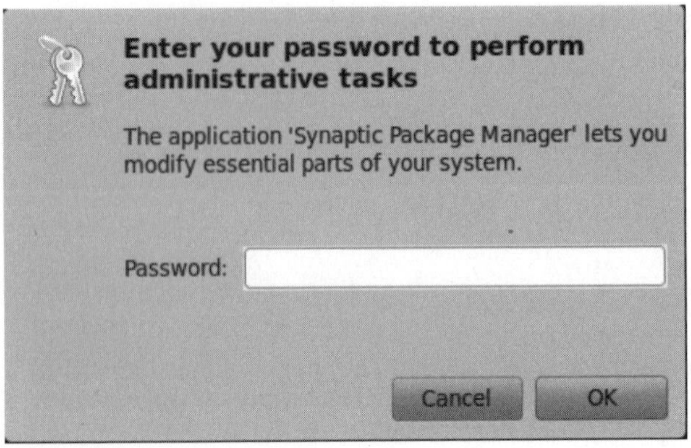

Figure 8-14. *Beware if you're asked to type your password out of the blue and for no apparent reason.*

Updating your system: Always ensure that your system software is completely up-to-date. As with Windows, many Ubuntu programs have bugs that lead to security holes. Crackers target such vulnerabilities. Downloading the latest versions of Ubuntu software ensures that you not only get the latest features, but also any patches for critical security holes. As with most versions of Linux, updating Ubuntu is easy, and, of course, it's also free of charge. You'll learn how to get online updates in the next section.

Locking up your PC: Attacks can be either remote or local, so in addition to online security, you should limit who has physical access to your computer. Any Ubuntu system can be compromised by a simple floppy boot disk, or even by just selecting the rescue mode entry on the boot menu, which provides the user with root access to the computer. This is for obvious reasons; the idea of a boot disk or the rescue mode is to let you fix your PC should something go wrong, and you cannot do this if you're blocked from accessing certain files. When Linux is used on servers that hold confidential data, it's not uncommon for the floppy and CD-ROM drives to be removed, thus avoiding booting via a boot disk. Such computers are also usually locked away in a room or even in a cupboard, denying physical access to the machine. Another option might be to add a BIOS password to the computer, meaning you'll be prompted for it during the boot process. The method for setting this up depends on your computer type, but generally, look for the BIOS Setup option when the computer is booting. Obviously, make sure you never forget a BIOS password, because a computer that doesn't boot is not very useful.

Online Updates

The Ubuntu notification area (the equivalent of the Windows system tray) at the top right of the screen contains a program that automatically monitors the package repositories and tells you when updates are available. This is the Update Manager. If you haven't yet updated your system, this icon will have probably turned into a white arrow pointing down, enclosed in an orange star, informing you that updates are available. In addition, each time you boot, you will see a speech bubble telling you that updates are available. When your system is completely up-to-date, the icon is not visible.

Clicking the Update Manager icon opens the Update Manager window, as shown in Figure 8-15. To go online and grab the updated files, simply click the Install Updates button at the bottom-right side of the window. You will probably be asked to enter your root password, because system files will need to be altered.

Figure 8-15. *You'll be informed if your system is in need of updates, and the Update Manager program can take care of everything for you.*

Be aware that some updates are large and may take some time to download, particularly if you're doing it for the first time after installing Ubuntu.

After the downloads have finished, you probably won't need to reboot unless the kernel file has been updated. If you do need to reboot, or if the update requires you to take any other action (such as logging out and then back in again), the Update Manager icon in the notification area will turn into an information icon, or into two encircled arrows. You should then click the icon to see what action you're advised to take.

APPLICATION SECURITY WITH APPARMOR

A sad fact of computing life is that all software applications have bugs of some kind. Some of these are not serious (in fact, they may remain invisible), but some might lead to abnormal program termination, data corruption, or even system failure. The worst bugs provide "back doors" into your system that can be used by crackers to wreak havoc.

Software developers fix reported bugs as quickly as possible (and one benefit of the open source approach is that solutions can come from third parties, speeding up the process), but the gap between discovering the bugs and providing a fix is a time when systems are vulnerable to attack. Taking advantage of such a vulnerability is called a *zero-day exploit*.

Fortunately, Ubuntu and several other types of Linux distributions have a clever built-in security mechanism called AppArmor, which oversees software applications and ensures that they don't do things that they shouldn't. Effectively, AppArmor "sandboxes" applications so they go only where they should within the system.

AppArmor was included in Ubuntu for the first time with version 7.04 (Feisty Fawn), three years ago. Although it's integrated into the underlying systems, AppArmor has yet to be made easily available to the user for configuration. Currently, the only way to configure AppArmor under Ubuntu is by using the command line. This will probably change in the future.

AppArmor is primarily intended to protect server systems—large computers that store and distribute data to others. As such, AppArmor is not particularly aimed at desktop users, although there is no reason why the intrepid desktop user can't make use of it.

The software works on the principle of *least privilege*, which means that each application is granted only the bare minimum of system resources it requires to run properly. Should the application prove to have a flaw that allows it to be compromised, the damage would therefore be limited in scope.

AppArmor implements this scope by way of *profiling* each application. A profile is a configuration file that contains details about what the application may do. AppArmor profiles are stored in /etc/apparmor.d. Profiles can be added by using the Synaptic Package Manager to install the package apparmor-profiles. Additionally, new applications you install may come with their own AppArmor profiles. After additional profiles are installed, they are automatically utilized.

Each application can run in one of two modes:

- *Enforce mode*: In this mode, AppArmor implements the permissions and capabilities listed in the profile. If the application tries to access a file or use a capability that is not listed in the profile, the operation will not be permitted.

- *Complain mode*: In this mode, AppArmor records the violations incurred by an application when it violates the rules imposed in the profile and stores them in the system log. These logs can be used later for creating or updating a profile of an application.

To determine which profiles and programs are running in enforce or complain mode, open a terminal window (Applications ➤ Accessories ➤ Terminal) and issue the command sudo apparmor_status.

To learn more about how to use AppArmor with Ubuntu, including how to create your own application profiles, see https://help.ubuntu.com/community/AppArmor.

Configuring the Ubuntu Firewall

A *firewall* is a set of programs that protects your PC when it's online. It does this by watching incoming and outgoing connections between your PC and the Internet and allowing through only what it is sure is secure (which usually is what you've asked for). It also attempts to close off various aspects of your Internet connection, so that crackers don't have a way in should they target your system.

The benefit of configuring the firewall is that even if your system has security vulnerabilities because of buggy software, crackers will find it a lot harder to exploit them across the Internet. When someone attempts to probe your system, it will appear to be virtually invisible.

■ **Caution** Although software firewalls such as the one built into Linux offer a high level of protection, it's best to use them in concert with a hardware firewall, such as that provided by most DSL/cable broadband routers (curiously, some of these routers actually use Linux's `iptables` software as well). Many security experts agree that relying solely on a software firewall to protect a PC affords less than the optimal level of protection.

Although Ubuntu includes a powerful firewall in the form of `iptables`, you'll also need a program that can manage it. Here we show you how to use Firestarter, available from the Ubuntu software repository, for this purpose. The configured built-in firewall really does provide very strong protection.

■ **Note** Power users might choose to configure Ubuntu's firewall without installing Firestarter. The command-line tools `iptables` and `ufw` are installed by default and are preferred by some system administrators. `Iptables` is a configuration tool used to manage Netfilter, the feature in the kernel that handles the firewall. Unfortunately, with `iptables`, you need to understand how TCP/IP works and learn cryptic commands to be able to make full use of it. But armed with that knowledge, you can turn your PC into a full-fledged, budget software router with features that rival or surpass hardware routers. `Ufw` (for *uncomplicated firewall*) is a configuration tool that also manages the Netfilter firewall. It's easier to use than `iptables` because a firewall rule in `ufw` is usually terse and readable by humans.

Installing Firestarter

Let's get started by downloading and installing Firestarter. Follow these steps:

1. Choose System ➤ Administration ➤ Ubuntu Software Center. In the Search box type **firestarter** as a search term. In the list of results, locate the program and click Install. Enter your password when prompted.

2. After the desktop is back up and running, choose System ➤ Administration ➤ Firestarter, or Application ➤ Internet ➤ Firestarter. When you run Firestarter for the first time, you'll be prompted for your password. Then a wizard will start to take you through the setup.

3. Click the Forward button to continue the wizard beyond the introductory page.

4. The first step asks which network interface Firestarter should configure, as shown in Figure 8-16. If you use an Ethernet card, have a wireless card, or attach a broadband modem directly to your computer, the answer will probably be eth0 or wlan0. However, if you use a modem, the answer is ppp0.

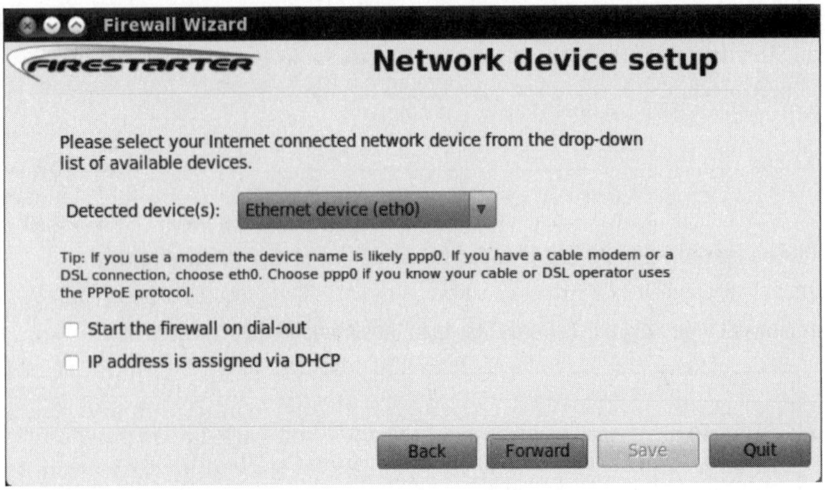

Figure 8-16. Firestarter includes a wizard to walk you through the basics of firewall configuration.

5. Put a check in the "IP address is assigned via DHCP" box, unless you're using a dial-up modem. If you are using a dial-up modem, select "Start the firewall on dial-out" check box. After making your choices, click the Forward button.

You're asked whether you want to enable Internet connection sharing. This allows you to turn your computer into an Internet router and can be very useful in certain circumstances. You can activate this later on by running the wizard again. Click Forward to continue.

■ **Note** To rerun the wizard, simply click Firewall in Firestarter's main window and then click Run Wizard.

---

6. The wizard will finish. Click the Save button to save your settings to disk. In addition, ensure that the Start Firewall Now check box is selected. After this, the Firestarter main window opens, and the software is active. You'll also see a new icon appear in the notification area of the desktop. This tells you that the firewall is running and will react to different types of threats or connections.

Configuring Firestarter

Firestarter works by controlling the data that goes into and out of your computer via your Internet or network connection. By default, it blocks every type of uninvited inbound connection but allows every type of outbound connection.

Whenever you click a link on a web page, your computer sends a request for data to the web server hosting the web page. Within a few milliseconds, that data is sent to your computer. This is an inbound data connection. The Linux firewall is clever enough to realize that the data was requested by you, so it is allowed through. However, any uninvited connections are turned away. If, out of the blue, someone attempts to connect to your computer via the popular Secure Shell (SSH) tool, as just one example, he won't be allowed to make that connection. This is a good thing, because it makes your computer secure. Crackers are turned away whenever they try to connect, no matter how they try to connect.

But in some circumstances, allowing uninvited connections is useful. For example, if you create a shared folder for other computers in your office to connect to, they will frequently make uninvited inbound connections to your computer whenever they want to grab a file. Protocols such as BitTorrent, too, rely on many incoming connections. Also, if you want to make use of SSH to connect to your computer remotely, you will need to allow such incoming connections. Therefore, Firestarter lets you allow certain types of inbound connections through.

In the terminology of Firestarter (and many firewall programs), *outbound traffic* is any kind of data originating on your computer that is sent out on the network and/or Internet. By default, Firestarter allows out all data, no matter what it is. This is described as a *permissive policy*. But Firestarter can be configured to block all outgoing connections apart from those you configure Firestarter to allow. This is a *restrictive policy* and can be useful in blocking certain types of programs that "phone home" with personal data about you, such as spyware.

■ **Note** Unlike with Windows, we've never heard of a Linux program that contains spyware that "phones home" in this way. Nevertheless, a cautious attitude often pays dividends.

A restrictive policy can also prevent certain types of viruses and worms from spreading. The downside of a restrictive policy is that you must configure Firestarter to take into account every type of outgoing data connection that you do want to allow through, such as those for web browsers, instant messaging programs, and so on.

You can configure Firestarter by clicking the Policy tab in the main program window. Click the Editing drop-down list and choose to configure either the inbound traffic policy or the outbound traffic policy.

■ **Note** Firestarter is used only to configure the built-in firewall and doesn't need to be running for the firewall to work. After you've finished configuration, you can quit the program. You'll need to use it again only if you want to reconfigure the firewall.

Setting Inbound Rules

For most users, Firestarter's default inbound traffic policy is perfectly acceptable. It configures the firewall to disallow all uninvited incoming data connections, apart from certain diagnostic tools, such as ping, traceroute, and so on. You can choose to disallow those as well, as described shortly in the "Turning Off Diagnostic Services" section.

You may want to allow an incoming connection if you intend to connect to your computer via SSH from a remote location or if you have a shared folder created for other computers in your office. It's a must if you're running the BitTorrent file-sharing application. Additionally, if you run a web server, e-mail server, or other type of server on your computer, you will need to allow the correct type of incoming connection here.

Here's how to set inbound connection rules:

1. In the Firestarter main window, click the Policy tab. Select Inbound Traffic Policy in the Editing drop-down list.

2. Right-click in the second box on the Policy tab (with the headings Allow Service/ Port/For) and then select Add Rule.

3. The Add New Inbound Rule dialog box appears. In the Name drop-down list, select the type of outgoing connection you want to allow, as shown in Figure 8-17. To allow others to access shared folders on your computer, select Samba (SMB). To allow SSH or BitTorrent connections to your computer, select the relevant entry from the list. Selecting the service will automatically fill in the Port box, which you shouldn't alter unless you know exactly what you're doing.

4. If you know the IP address of the computer that's going to make the incoming connection, you can click the IP, Host, or Network radio button, and then type in that address. However, the default of Anyone will allow anyone using any IP address to connect to your computer.

5. Click Add. Back in the main Firestarter window, click the Apply Policy button on the toolbar.

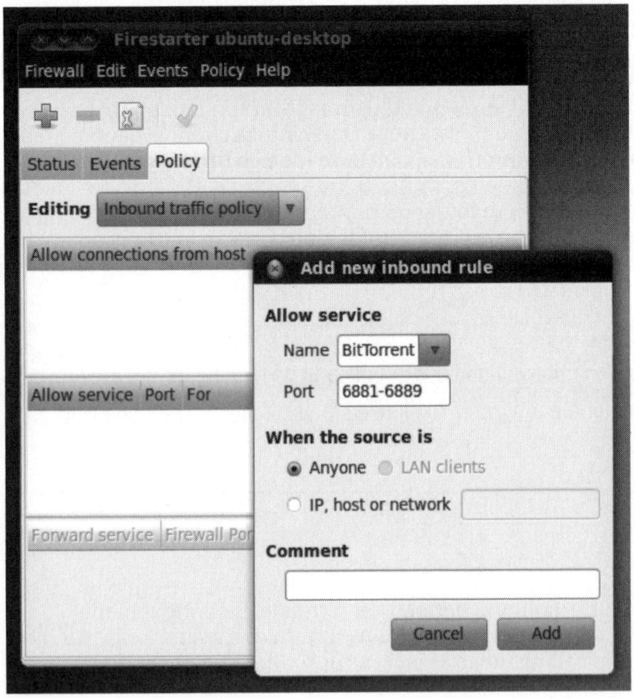

Figure 8-17. Creating an inbound rule enables computers to connect to your PC uninvited, but only if they meet the conditions of the rule.

■ **Note** You'll need to return to Firestarter whenever you activate new services on your computer. For example, in Chapter 10, you will look at accessing Windows shares across a network, and you'll need to enable SMB incoming and outgoing access for this to work. In Chapter 25, you will look at using the SSH service, which will have to be allowed through the firewall. In other words, securing your computer isn't something you can do once and then forget about. It's a continual process.

Setting Outbound Rules

By default, Firestarter allows all types of outgoing connections and, as with its incoming connections policy, this is by no means a bad choice for the average user. It's certainly the option that involves the least fuss. However, by opting to go with a restrictive traffic policy, you can completely control what kind of data leaves your computer. Any type of data connection that isn't authorized will be refused; as far as the program sending the data is concerned, it will be as if your computer did not have a network or Internet connection.

Here's how to set outbound connection rules:

1. In the Firestarter main window, click the Policy tab. Select Outbound Traffic Policy in the Editing drop-down list.

2. Click the "Restrictive by default, whitelist traffic" radio button. This option means that by default all outbound traffic will be blocked. You need to add to a "whitelist" the traffic that you want to allow.

3. In the second empty box at the bottom of the Policy tab (which has the Allow Service/ Port/For headings), right-click and select Add Rule.

4. The "Add new outbound rule" dialog box appears. In the Name drop-down list, select the type of data connection you want to allow. At the very least, you should select HTTP. This will allow your web browser to operate correctly (it's also needed to allow the Ubuntu Software Center and Update Manager programs to work). HTTPS should also be allowed—this is the secure version of HTTP used to access the likes of online banking sites, online shopping services, and some online e-mail services. You should also add a rule for POP3 and another for SMTP, without which your e-mail program won't work. Selecting the type of service will fill in the Port box automatically. You shouldn't alter this unless you know what you're doing.

■ **Note** You can add only one rule at a time. You'll have to repeat steps 3 and 4 several times to add rules for each service you want to allow.

5. Click the Add button to add the rule. Back in the Firestarter main window, click Apply Policy.

6. Test your settings with a program that uses the services you've just authorized.

■ **Caution** If you created an inbound rule, you'll need to create a matching outbound rule. If you created an incoming rule for BitTorrent, for example, you'll need to create an outgoing rule for BitTorrent too.

You can delete both incoming and outgoing rules by right-clicking their entries in the list and selecting Remove Rule.

Turning Off Diagnostic Services

Certain network tools can be misused by crackers to break into a computer or just cause it problems. In the past, the traceroute and ping tools, among others, have been used to launch denial-of-service (DoS) attacks against computers.

Ubuntu is set to allow these tools to operate by default. If you want to adopt a belts-and-suspenders approach to your computer's security, you can opt to disable them. If you don't know what ping and traceroute are, you're clearly not going to miss them, so there will be no harm in disallowing them. Here's how:

1. In the Firestarter main window, click Edit ➤ Preferences.

2. On the left side of the Preferences window, click ICMP Filtering. Then click the Enable ICMP Filtering check box, as shown in Figure 8-18. Don't put a check in any of the boxes underneath, unless you specifically want to permit one of the services.

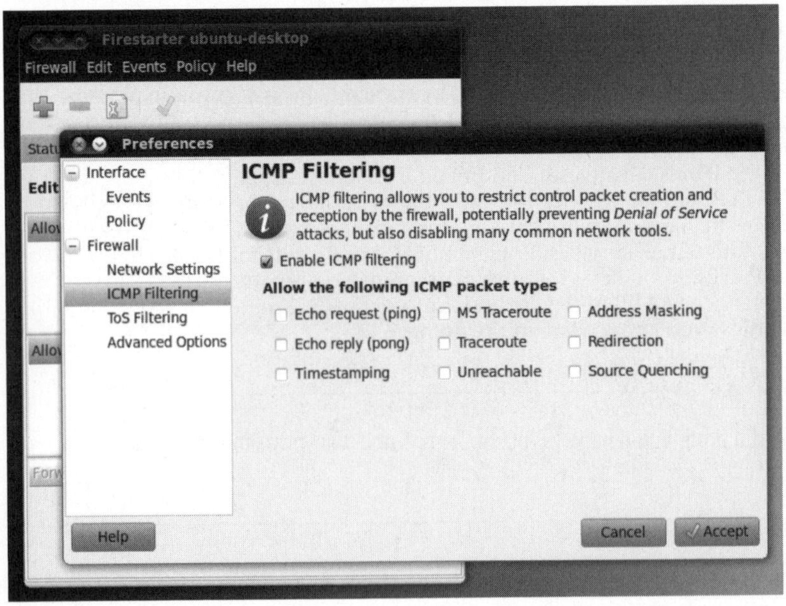

Figure 8-18. *By deactivating* traceroute, ping, *and other services, you can add extra protection to your PC.*

3. Click the Accept button to finish.

PARANOIA AND SECURITY

There's a fine line between security and paranoia. Using Firestarter gives you the opportunity to ensure that your system is secure, without needing to constantly reassess your system for threats and live in fear.

When considering your system security, remember that most burglars don't enter a house through the front door. Most take advantage of an open window or poor security elsewhere in the house. In other words, when configuring your system's security, you should always select every option and extra layer of security, even if it might not appear to be useful. You should lock every door and close every window, even if you don't think an attacker would ever use them.

If a security setting doesn't impact your ordinary use of the computer, you should select it. For example, deactivating the ping response of your computer might sound like a paranoid action, but it's useful on several levels. First, it means your computer is less easy to detect when it's online. Second, and equally important, it means that if there's ever a security flaw in the ping tool (or any software connected with it), you'll be automatically protected.

This illustrates how you must think when configuring your system's security. Try to imagine every situation that might arise. Remember that you can never take too many precautions!

Adding Virus Scanning to Ubuntu

As mentioned in the chapter introduction, Linux (and therefore Ubuntu) is not currently affected by many viruses. Nobody knows the true number of viruses affecting Linux, but it is probably less than 1,000, and that's the total since Linux was created back in the early 1990s! At the time of this writing, there are relatively few Linux viruses in the wild, which is to say, actively infecting computers.

However, there can be no room for complacency. It's probable that virus writers will turn their attention to Linux in the coming years as it becomes a popular desktop solution. It's also important to be vigilant because your Ubuntu system may be interacting with Windows computers and may act as a carrier of Windows viruses.

This section describes how to use ClamTk, which is a graphical front end for the Clam AntiVirus (ClamAV) program (http://clamtk.sf.net). ClamAV is an open source, industrial-strength antivirus scanner designed to work on all kinds of computers and operating systems. It detects Windows and even Macintosh viruses, as well as Linux and UNIX viruses. This has obvious benefits if you share files with Windows users—you can inform your friends and colleagues if any files they give you are infected (and bask in the warm feeling that arises when you realize the viruses can't affect your system!).

ClamAV's only drawback is that it is limited to virus scanning. It isn't able to disinfect files, like the more sophisticated virus scanners available for Windows. However, it should be noted that disinfection rarely works very well, as discussed in the ClamAV FAQ (http://clamtk.sf.net).

Installing ClamTk

You can install ClamAV and ClamTk through the Ubuntu Software Center, as follows:

1. Choose System ➤ Administration ➤ Ubuntu Software Center.

2. In the Search text box enter **clamtk** as a search term.

3. In the list of results, locate the program Virus Scanner and click the Install button. Enter your password when prompted.

4. The whole antivirus system involves a 26MB download.

5. Close the Ubuntu Software Center.

Updating the ClamAV Database

Before you scan for viruses, you should update the virus database. You should do this every time you scan, using the ClamTk program.

> ■ **Note** When you installed ClamAV, it added a background service called freshclam, which periodically downloads updates for ClamAV's database. However, manually updating before scanning is also a good idea, to ensure that you're always using the very latest version of the database at the time of scanning.

In order to update the database, ClamTk needs to access system files, so it needs to be run with root powers. To do this, open a terminal window (click Accessories ➤ Terminal), type **gksu clamtk** and press Enter. Enter your password when prompted. (gksu is like sudo, in that it gives the program you specify administrator powers, except it's used for GUI applications.) Click Help ➤ Check for updates. A new window will open, in which you should click "Check for updates" again. It will check for updates to both the virus definition database and the GUI. You might see a warning that your GUI version is out-of-date. This is because the Ubuntu packages are sometimes a version or two behind the main release. However, this isn't a significant issue, and ClamAV can still scan for viruses, and virus definitions will stay up-to-date. When ClamAV is first installed, it automatically grabs the latest database file, so ClamTk will probably report it's already up-to-date the first time an update is run.

If you want to update the GUI to the latest version anyway, you could go to ClamTk's webpage at SourceForge.net (http://clamtk.sf.net) and download the .deb file. For more information on how to install programs directly from .deb packages, refer to chapter 20. In brief, when the file finishes downloading, you will be asked if you want to open it with GDebi package manager. Yes, that's what you want to do. It will let you know that there is an older, more supported version of the same application in Ubuntu's own repositories. Click the Install button... at your own risk!

To run ClamTk as a normal user, you can just go to Applications ➤ Accessories ➤ Virus Scanner and perform the operation to update the signatures.

Scanning for Viruses

With Windows virus scanners, you might be used to performing whole system scans. This isn't advisable with ClamAV, because it simply isn't designed for that task. Instead, ClamAV is designed to scan user files, such as documents.

> ■ **Note** ClamAV is actually primarily designed to be used in concert with a mail server and to scan incoming or outgoing mail attachments. See the About page at the ClamAV web site (http://www.clamav.org/about).

You can try performing a full system scan, but in our tests, several false positives were identified, meaning that ClamAV identified innocent files as containing viruses. Because of this, it's best to use ClamAV to scan just your personal files for viruses, which is to say, those within your /home directory. Bear in mind that this is where all files you import to your computer will likely be installed, so this is where an infection is most likely to be found.

To scan your personal files, follow these instructions:

1. Start ClamTk by clicking Applications ➤ System Tools ➤ Virus Scanner. On the initial launch, you can define whether antivirus signatures are updated for a single user or for all users. If you have a multiuser system, you should choose the latter.

2. Before starting the scan, it's useful to ensure that hidden files are scanned. After all, a virus is likely to try to hide, rather than make its presence obvious! This can be done by clicking Advanced ➤ Preferences and checking the Scan files beginning with a dot (.*) box.

3. Although there's a button on the toolbar that lets you scan your /home directory with a single click, it won't scan recursively. That means it won't scan any folders (or folders of folders) within your /home directory, so it isn't of much use. To perform a recursive scan of your /home directory, click File ➤ Recursive Scan. Then click the OK button in the Select a Directory (Recursive) dialog box. This will select your /home directory. Of course, you can also select any other folders to scan at this stage.

4. The scan will start. Depending on the quantity of files in your /home directory and their sizes, it may take some time. You'll see a live status report beneath the toolbar, showing which file is currently being scanned. When the status line reads "Scanning Complete," the scan has finished. Running along the bottom of the window will be a complete status report, showing the number of files scanned and the number of viruses found, if any. See Figure 8-19 for an example. If any viruses are found, move on to the next section.

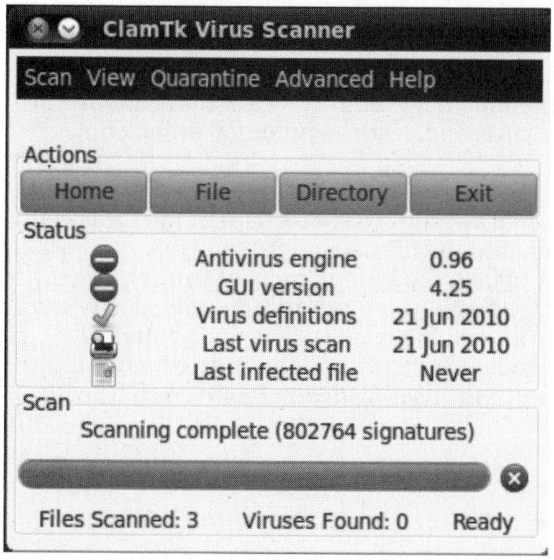

Figure 8-19. *You'll see a live status report detailing which files are being scanned below the toolbar in the ClamTk program window.*

Dealing with Infections

If any viruses are found, they will be listed in the ClamTk program window. The type of virus that's allegedly infecting the file will be listed in the Status column.

Be aware that ClamTk sometimes reports a virus when it simply can't access a particular file, perhaps because of file permission problems. If this is the case, you'll see Access Denied or Can't Open Directory in the Status column. You can ignore these files.

■ **Tip** If you really want to scan files that require superuser permissions, you can run ScanTk with superuser powers. Open a terminal window (Applications ➤ Accessories ➤ Terminal) and type `gksu clamtk`.

Entries in the list can be right-clicked and quarantined or deleted. Quarantining moves the file to a special directory for inspection or deletion later on. You can manage quarantined files by using the Quarantine ➤ Maintenance menu.

Although your impulse might be to simply delete the file, you should be cautious. Be aware that ClamTk might be reporting a *false positive*—a file that it thinks is infected with a virus, but which isn't. This is rare but can happen. If you do find a file you know is a false positive, right-click it and select Quarantine. Then click Quarantine ➤ Maintenance. In the list, select the file and click False Positive. This will ensure it's ignored next time you scan.

So what should you do if you find that a file is infected? First, don't panic. Remember that practically all viruses that ClamAV is likely to find are targeted at Windows systems and don't affect Linux.

■ **Note** If we assume there are 140,000 viruses for Windows and fewer than 1,000 for Linux, then in theory, there's a better than 99% chance that any virus ClamAV finds will be a Windows virus!

Next, find the name of the virus in the Status column and look it up online to learn more about it. This is the point at which you'll learn whether it's a Linux virus and, if so, its potential impact on your system.

You can hover your mouse over the filename in the scanner window to see its path. If the file is located in your Firefox cache, there's nothing to worry about, and the file can be deleted with impunity—just right-click and select Delete from the menu. In fact, the Firefox cache is where you're most likely to find virus infections, because this is where all the files are temporarily downloaded when you're browsing the web (including HTML files, images, and so on). But, once again, you should remember that most nefarious web sites that attempt to spread virus infections are targeted at Windows users, usually via security holes within Internet Explorer. As a Linux user using the Firefox web browser, you have far less to worry about.

WEB BROWSER SECURITY

It's not enough to rely on antivirus software for safe web browsing. In Firefox, you can tweak settings to enhance the security of browsing. However, note that improved security sometimes equates to reduced features, which can be quite frustrating.

To set security options in Firefox, choose Edit ➤ Preferences. Settings on the following tabs affect browser security (see Figure 8-20):

- *Content*: You can disable pop-up windows and disable JavaScript. Note that it's quite unlikely that you would want to completely disable JavaScript, because many modern web sites make heavy use of it (including online shopping sites and web-based e-mail, such as Google's Gmail). You could use a third-party plug-in called NoScript (http://noscript.net). This tool allows you to disable JavaScript, Java, Flash, and other plug-ins that could potentially be harmful to Firefox on all web sites by default. You can easily re-enable these scripts on each web site that you trust through the NoScript applet, located in the lower-right corner of the browser window.

- *Privacy*: You can customize retention of browser history, cookies, and private data. If privacy is of utmost importance, you can select the option "Use custom settings for history" and check the "Clear history when Firefox closes" check box.

- *Security*: You can customize attack site and forgery detection, passwords, and warning messages. You should customize these settings based on how you use the Web. For example, it's obvious that the "Warn me when sites try to install add-ons" check box should be selected, since malware is distributed this way. And if you transact business on the Web, the "Block reported web forgeries" option offers added protection from getting duped.

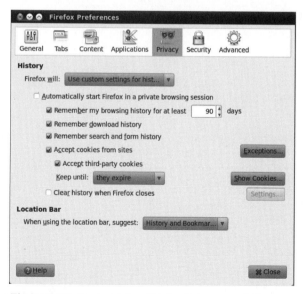

Figure 8-20. Customizing Firefox Privacy settings.

Summary

In this chapter, you've looked at what threats your system faces and how security holes can be exploited by malicious interests. You learned about measures you can take to protect your system, such as updating it online, using AppArmor to guard against errant applications, configuring the system's firewall, using encryption for e-mail and file privacy and authentication, installing an antivirus program, and customizing web browser security. We also discussed some commonsense rules you can follow to keep your system safe.

In the next chapter, we move on to looking at how your Ubuntu system can be personalized and how to set up everything to suit your own preferences.

CHAPTER 9

███

Personalizing Ubuntu: Getting Everything Just Right

If you've read this book from Chapter 1, by this stage you no doubt have become comfortable with Ubuntu. You've started to realize its advantages and are on the way to making it your OS of choice.

But things might still not be quite right. For instance, you might find the color scheme is not to your taste. Or maybe your login picture is not entirely satisfactory. Maybe you simply want to get away from the default theme and stamp your own identity on the desktop. That's what this chapter is all about: personalizing Ubuntu so you're completely happy with your user experience. To do this, you will thoroughly examine the GNOME desktop and explore its potential. You'll also add some panache to that most important application, the web browser, so it fits perfectly into your desktop.

Changing the Look and Feel

Ubuntu is similar to Windows in many ways, but the developers behind it introduced improvements and tweaks that many claim make the software easier to use. For example, Ubuntu offers multiple virtual desktops (also called workspaces)—long considered a very useful user interface feature that hasn't found favor in Microsoft's designs.[1]

■ **Note** The virtual desktop feature also passed by Apple for a long time. However, it was included in OS X Leopard three years ago, in the form of Spaces.

The Ubuntu desktop also moves the Programs menu (known in Ubuntu as the Applications menu) to the top of the screen, leaving the whole width of the screen at the bottom to display taskbar buttons. This is very sensible, because the buttons don't look cramped when more than a handful of applications are open. However, if you're not satisfied with Ubuntu's out-of-the-box look and feel, almost every aspect of the desktop experience is available for tweaking.

---

[1] The Desktops tool from Sysinternals can add similar but limited functionality to Windows; see
http://technet.microsoft.com/en-us/sysinternals/cc817881.aspx.

You might be used to changing the desktop colors or wallpaper under Windows, but Ubuntu goes to extremes and lets you alter the look and feel of the entire desktop. Everything from the styling of the program windows to the desktop icons can be altered quickly and easily.

Altering the Theme

Ubuntu refers to the look of the desktop as a *theme*. Whether you opt to use GNOME or KDE as your main desktop, Ubuntu allows you to radically personalize the whole visual experience. Several themes come with the distribution, and you can download many more. Each lets you change the way the windows look, including the buttons, scrollbars, window decoration, and icon set (although some themes come without additional icons). There is also a small selection of *assistive themes* designed to improve the desktop experience for partially sighted users.

However, unlike Windows themes, GNOME themes don't usually change the fonts used on the desktop, and the background will probably remain broadly the same. You can change these manually, as described in the "Setting Font Preferences" and "Changing the Desktop Background" sections a bit later in this chapter. The other difference is that GNOME has these facilities built in—you won't need to buy or install extra software just to change the desktop appearance.

To alter the theme, choose System ➤ Preferences ➤ Appearance. Then it's simply a matter of choosing a theme from the list on the Theme tab in the Appearance Preferences dialog box, as shown in Figure 9-1. Each selection has a small thumbnail to show you what the theme looks like. When you select one, it will be applied immediately to the desktop, including any open applications and windows. To get a really good idea of how the theme looks, you can open a Nautilus window by choosing Place ➤ Home Folder. This will give you a feel for how the icons, window decorations, and widgets such as scrollbars and menu bars look in a real-world context.

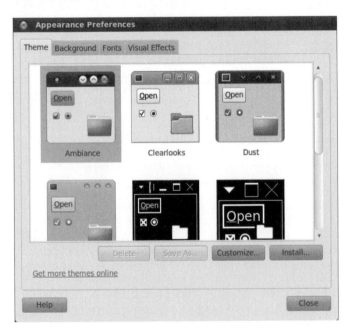

Figure 9-1. Ubuntu comes with several theme choices.

■ **Note** The default Ubuntu themes until Lucid Lynx were branded as Human and were designed to represent the skin tones of the world's population. This brand was based on the tagline "Linux for Human Beings." With Lucid, a new brand called Light was developed. Among other reasons, this name was chosen because Ubuntu is light and represents "a break with the bloatware of proprietary operating systems."[2]

The default theme in Ubuntu is called Ambiance. Radiance is a similar theme, but with a different color palette. Remember that you'll be working with the theme on a daily basis, so it should be practical and not too distracting. Those miniature Close, Minimize, and Maximize buttons might look stylish, but they're useless if they're so small that you can't reliably click them with your mouse; and if your eyes are constantly wandering to a beautiful but overpowering title bar, you won't be concentrating on your work or play. Depending on the theme you select, the Close, Minimize, and Maximize buttons can be in different places in the top bar of each window. Ambiance in particular sets them to the left in the following order (from left to right): Close, Minimize, and Maximize, whereas Clearlooks uses a more traditional, Windows-like positioning and order.

In addition to changing the overall theme, you can also modify individual theme components and even download more theme components.

Changing Individual Theme Components

You can alter the five aspects that constitute a GNOME theme: the controls (sometimes known as widgets), color scheme, window borders, icons, and mouse pointer. To make changes to a theme, select it on the Theme tab of the Appearance Preferences dialog box and then click the Customize button. You will see the Customize Theme dialog box, as shown in Figure 9-2.

---

[2] You can read the details about the change of brand here: https://wiki.ubuntu.com/Brand.

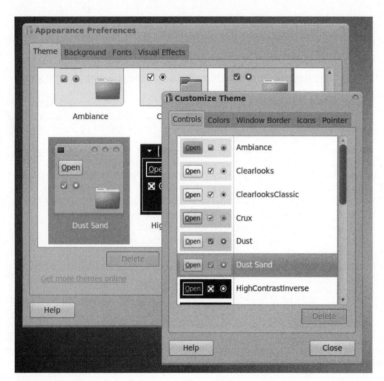

Figure 9-2. *You can customize a theme by choosing your own controls, colors, window border, icons, and mouse pointer.*

Click each tab to see your choices:

Controls: These are the elements you click within dialog boxes and windows: buttons, scrollbars, check boxes, radio buttons, and so on. The chief difference between one set of controls and another relates to their 3D effect—some are inset against the background, and some appear to be prominent. Some controls are shiny, and some appear flat. Additionally, some are rounded and some are square. Rounded controls feel more friendly, maybe even playful, while square controls tend to feel more businesslike.

Colors: You can set the background and text color of windows, input boxes, selected items, and tooltips. However, note that controls nearly always come with their own color schemes, which override any changes you make to color settings. A few controls not only override color settings, but also do not support tweakable color schemes. Examples include the HighContrastInverse and HighContrastLargePrintInverse controls. If you adjust these, ensure that you have enough contrast between the various elements; otherwise, you may end up with eye strain or a headache!

Window Border: The options on this tab control the borders of program windows and dialog boxes. Particular attention is paid to the top of the window, where the program name appears along with the Close, Minimize, and Maximize buttons.

Icons: This tab lets you control which icon set is in use. An icon set includes icons for everything you see on the screen or in menus, including folders, the Trash, programs, hard disks, network servers, and so on. Selecting a new icon set will change all icons.

■ **Note** The Icons tab of the Customize Theme dialog box doesn't let you change the icons for *specific* desktop items. You can do this by right-clicking the icon, selecting Properties from the menu that appears, and then clicking the icon preview button at the top left of the dialog box. Note that most stock icons are stored in /usr/share/icons, but if you've downloaded a particularly fine icon into your Home folder, click the Browse button and locate that. Any icons you change individually in this way won't be affected by changes made to the icon set.

Pointer: On this tab, you can set the appearance of the mouse pointer. Aside from the pointer's design, you can change its size (although this is not supported on all mouse pointers) by adjusting the Size slider. A larger mouse pointer might help the visually impaired. A small mouse pointer would be appropriate for low-resolution or small screens like those on ultraportable laptops.

If you change any of these options, the Theme thumbnail will change to the first one in the Appearance Preferences window, labeled Custom. To preview the effects fully, the best policy is to keep a Nautilus window open (Places ➤ Home Folder).

When you've made your choices, you can save the theme for further use. Click Close in the Customize Theme dialog box, and then click the Save As button on the Theme tab of the Appearance Preferences dialog box. You'll need to give the theme a name and, if you wish, a short description for future reference. By putting a check in the Save Background Image check box, the theme will also remember the background that's in use. Once saved, the theme will be available for selection from the Theme tab, where the themes are listed in alphabetical order. If you selected the Save Background Image check box, when you select the theme in the future, the background will be suggested at the bottom of the Theme tab. To select it, just click the Apply Background button.

If you don't save the theme, as soon as you select another one, the changes you made will be lost.

Installing Additional Components

If you get tired of the built-in possibilities, you can download additional theme components, such as window borders and controls, to enhance your desktop experience. Two popular web sites (among others) that you can visit are GNOME Art (http://art.gnome.org) and GNOME-Look (http://gnome-look.org). The GNOME Art web site is officially supported and is opened when you click the "Get more themes online" link on the Theme tab of the Appearance Preferences dialog box. GNOME-Look tends to be driven more by enthusiasts. Both offer a massive choice of theme components.

■ **Caution** Be warned that some of the backgrounds available from GNOME-Look display artistic nudity.

The GNOME Art site, shown in Figure 9-3, gives you access to just about every theme ever created for GNOME. In fact, the site also contains background selections, icons, and much more. All of the offerings are free to use.

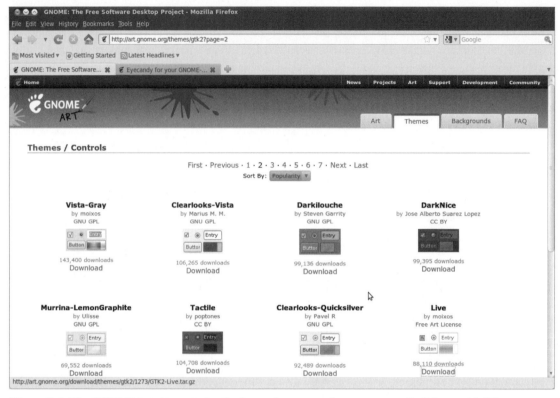

Figure 9-3. *The GNOME Art site contains the latest themes, and you can use all of them with Ubuntu.*

Installing new theme components is easy, and the instructions here work just as well for the GNOME-Look site. If you wish to install a new window border, for example, click the link to browse the examples, and when you find one you like, click to download it. It will be contained in a `.tar.gz` or `.tar.bz2` archive, but you don't need to unpack it (be sure to select the Save File option from the Firefox dialog box). Simply choose System ➤ Preferences ➤ Appearance, and click the Install button on the Theme tab. Then browse to the downloaded theme and click Open. You can also just drag the `.tar.gz` or `.tar.bz2` file onto the Theme tab of the Appearance Preferences dialog box for an instant installation. Either way, you'll be asked whether you want to use the new theme component immediately. You can say yes, or choose it later from the Customize Theme dialog box (opened by clicking the Customize button in the Appearance Preferences dialog box), where it will be available on the relevant tab.

You can delete the downloaded file when you're finished, because the information will be copied automatically to the correct place.

■ **Note** The same principle of sharing that underlines the GPL software license is also usually applied to themes. This means that one person can take a theme created by someone else, tweak it, and then release it as a new theme. This ensures constant innovation and improvement.

Changing the Desktop Background

It's easy to switch backgrounds under Ubuntu. You can also add your own images and set background size, or select a background color if you don't wish to use an image. These changes can be made from the Background tab of the Appearance Preferences dialog box (System ➤ Preferences ➤ Appearance), as shown in Figure 9-4.

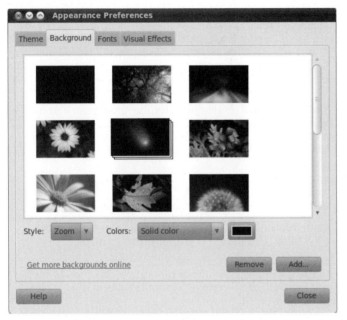

Figure 9-4. *Backgrounds can be zoomed or scaled to fill the screen by using the Style drop-down list (this figure includes backgrounds from the package).*

Switching and Adding Background Images

On the Background tab, you can select from a short list of images. You can choose any of the installed images or, by selecting the thumbnail at the top left, opt for no image at all. In the case of the latter, you can use the drop-down toward the base of the window to choose the color background style (detailed in the following options), and the colors to include by using the selector(s). You have the following options:

Solid color: This option fills the desktop with one uniform color. You are provided one color button to set the color.

Horizontal gradient: This option fills the desktop with one color on the left, blending with another color from the right. You are provided two color buttons to specify both colors.

Vertical gradient: This option fills the desktop with a color on top, blending with another color at the bottom. You are provided two color buttons to specify both colors.

To specify the color or colors that will be used, click the color buttons beside the Colors drop-down list. The Pick a Color dialog box will appear. Select a color by clicking or dragging the color wheel. You can also use the eyedropper tool to obtain any color displayed on your screen, including anywhere on the desktop or in open windows. Simply click the tool on the color.

If none of this works for you, you can manually provide the hue, saturation value (HSV); red, green, blue (RGB) values; or color name by specifying the combination of hexadecimal digits (this will be familiar to web designers).

A preview of your selection is shown at the bottom left of the dialog box, in the right color preview bar. The previous color that you selected is shown in the left color preview bar. Click the OK button after you've chosen your preferred color.

■ **Tip** You can right-click the desktop and choose Change Desktop Background to access the same menu of background choices.

If you want to use a picture of your own as the desktop background, click the Add button and then browse to the picture's location. In contrast to theme element installation, your own images are not copied to a new location, so if you delete a picture used for a background, the background image will disappear and be replaced with the normal background color.

Choosing a Background Style

From the Style drop-down list on the Background tab, you can select from the following choices:

Tile: If the picture is smaller than the desktop resolution, this option simply repeats the picture (starting from the top left) until the screen is filled. This option is primarily designed for patterned graphics.

Zoom: This option forces the picture to fit the screen, without any borders at the top and bottom. It avoids altering the aspect ratio. If the wallpaper isn't the correct aspect ratio, parts of the top/bottom or left/right of the image may be cropped off.

Center: This option places the picture in the center of the screen. If the image is not big enough to fill the screen, a border appears around the edge. If it's bigger than the screen, the edges of the picture are cropped off.

Scale: This option enlarges the image if it's too small or shrinks it if it's too big, but it maintains the aspect ratio, thus avoiding distortion. However, if the picture is in a different aspect ratio than the monitor, it may have borders at the edges.

Stretch: This option forces the picture to fit the screen, including squashing or expanding it if necessary (known as altering its aspect ratio). If the picture isn't in the same ratio as the screen, it will look distorted. Most digital camera shots should be OK, because they use the same 4:3 ratio as most monitors (although if you have a widescreen monitor with a 16:9 ratio, a digital camera picture will be stretched horizontally).

Span: This option is new in Lucid Lynx. When you have multiple monitors, select this option to have the wallpaper centered between them.

Setting Font Preferences

Ubuntu lets you change the fonts that are used throughout the desktop and applications (referred to as *system fonts*). You can also alter how they're displayed, which is useful if you want to get the best image on an LCD monitor.

To change a system font, open the Appearance Preferences dialog box (System ➤ Preferences ➤ Appearance) and click the Fonts tab, as shown in Figure 9-5. Click the button next to the system font you want to change, and then choose from the list. You can also set the font point size, perhaps to make the labels beneath icons easier to read.

By clicking the entries in the Rendering section of the Fonts tab, you can change how fonts look on your monitor. This will alter the antialiasing and hinting of the font. Antialiasing softens the edges of each letter to make them appear less jagged. Hinting affects the spacing and shaping of the letters. Used together, they can make the on-screen text look more pleasant and easier to read. Try each Rendering setting in sequence to see which looks best to you (the text in the dialog box will update automatically to show the changes). Nearly everyone with a TFT-based screen, including notebook users, finds the "Subpixel smoothing" option best.

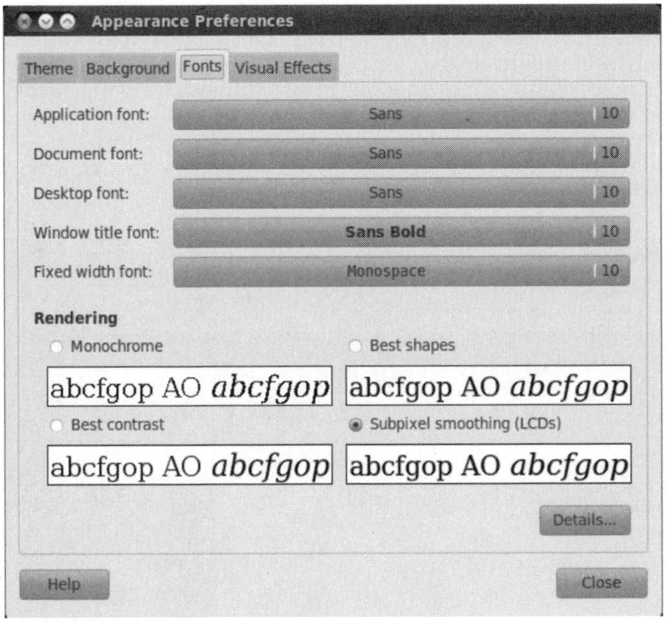

Figure 9-5. *You can alter the way fonts appear on the screen by using the Fonts tab of the Appearance Preferences dialog box.*

Using Desktop Visual Effects

Provided your computer is compatible with enabling these effects and is utilizing the correct graphics card drivers (see the "Installing 3D Drivers and Activating Desktop Visual Effects" section in Chapter 7), you can introduce a range of cool, useful—and occasionally, just plain weird—effects to your computer desktop.

Three basic settings for desktop visual effects are available: None, Normal, and Extra. You can switch between them by clicking System ➤ Preferences ➤ Appearance, and then selecting the Visual Effects tab of the Appearance Preferences dialog box.

As you might expect, the None option turns off the effects. This can be useful if your computer slows down when the effects are in use or if you're using older hardware. The Normal setting implements the standard set of effects, offering subtle but not overly noticeable changes to the interface, and is the default choice if your computer is capable of effects. The Extra setting adds more effects, largely for fun but also with some offering productivity benefits. Additionally, you can opt to install some extra software that gives you even more fine-grained control over what effects are used. The following sections discuss each of these choices for visual effects.

Using the Standard Visual Effects

The standard visual effects, used when the Normal setting is chosen, add shadows to windows and also add minimize animations so that programs literally appear to shrink into the panel. You might also notice that inactive windows and their title bars are translucent. Additionally, when a window is opened or closed, the window will appear or fade away, respectively.

There are several more subtle visual effects, requiring particular key combinations, as follows:

Tools for the visually impaired: To zoom into any area of the screen, press the Windows key and turn the mouse wheel to adjust the zoom level. You can also press Windows+1, 2, or 3 to zoom into three different levels, respectively. Additionally, you can invert the colors (like a photographic negative) either for the entire desktop or just for the current program window. Press Windows+N to toggle the current window as a negative, as shown in Figure 9-6. Press Windows+M to toggle the entire screen as a negative. Use the same combination to restore the original colors. Ubuntu also includes an advanced Zoom tool, which is activated via the CompizConfig Settings Manager, which provides facilities comparable to the leading Windows application for the partially sighted.

Figure 9-6. You can filter colors of windows or the entire screen as a visual aid.

Virtual desktops: If you use virtual desktops, as described in Chapter 6, you'll be pleased to know that the desktop effects system enhances the experience. Press Windows+E to get a miniature view of your virtual desktops arranged in a grid, as shown in Figure 9-7. To switch to a virtual desktop, just point your mouse to the virtual desktop of choice and double-click, or use the cursor keys and Windows+E once more. You can also switch from one virtual desktop to another from the desktop by moving the mouse pointer to an empty area of the desktop and then turning the mouse wheel, which will cause the desktops to slide sideways out of view. Press Ctrl+Alt+arrow key for the same effect. As you navigate from one virtual desktop to another, a grid in which each cell represents each virtual desktop will appear in the center of the screen, and a cell will be highlighted for a short period of time to let you know which virtual desktop you are on.

Figure 9-7. Pressing Windows+E gives you a miniature view of your virtual desktops.

Application Switcher: As well as moving between virtual desktops, you can navigate through applications with the Application Switcher. Just press Alt+Tab to see the list of running applications in miniature view, arranged horizontally in the center of the screen, as shown in Figure 9-8. Press the Tab key repeatedly until you find the desired application at the center of the list. Release the Alt key to switch to the desired application. Minimized applications are represented by their application icon, because Ubuntu doesn't have the option of grabbing a live screen of them. Releasing the Alt key on a minimized window will open it out.

Figure 9-8. *To use the Application Switcher, hold the Alt key and press the Tab key until you find the desired application at the center of the list.*

Using the Extra Visual Effects

By selecting the Extra option from the Visual Effects tab of the Appearance Preferences dialog box, you can enable a handful more visual effects. These include all the features of the Normal effects and then some. For starters, you will notice that when you drag or maximize a window, the window becomes "wobbly"—part of it will linger behind the rest of the window, as if affected by momentum. The Application Switcher effect is also enhanced and will display previews of open programs in 3D form when you press Windows+Tab, as shown in Figure 9-9. This obviously requires you to have the graphics power to render, but if you do have it, the 3D switcher will even play live video in the previews.

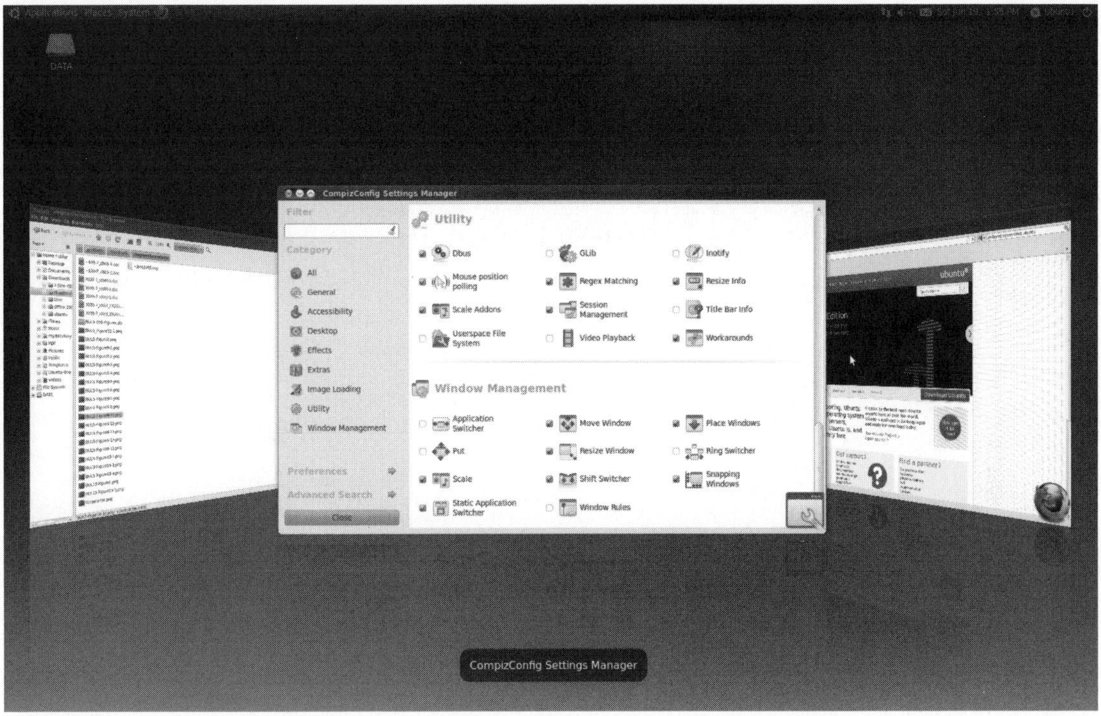

Figure 9-9. The 3D Application Switcher is displayed by pressing Windows+Tab.

Personalizing Visual Effects

If you are unsatisfied with the default choices for visual effects, you can install the CompizConfig Settings Manager tool. This gives you complete control over the Compiz Fusion system, which provides Ubuntu's visual effects. Bear in mind that some of these settings are very technical, and little provision is made for those who are new to the effects subsystems.

You can install the tool by using the Ubuntu Software Center (Applications ➤ Ubuntu Software Center). Then enter compizconfig-settings-manager as a search term in the search box. In the list of results, locate the program Advanced Desktop Effects Settings and click Install. You'll need to enter your password when prompted.

After the tool is installed, choose System ➤ Preferences ➤ CompizConfig Settings Manager. The CompizConfig Settings Manager window will appear, as shown in Figure 9-10.

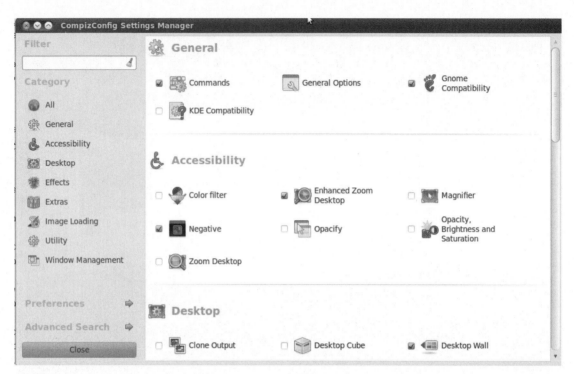

Figure 9-10. *The CompizConfig Settings Manager tool offers advanced customization of visual effects in Ubuntu.*

Compiz Fusion works by packaging each effect as a plug-in, and CompizConfig Settings Manager simply lets you switch these plug-ins on and off, as well as change their settings. One of the most important settings you can change for most plug-ins is the keyboard combination that activates them.

On the right side of the main window is the list of plug-ins grouped into logical sections. You can enable them by selecting the check box beside them. You can also change the settings of the plug-in by clicking the plug-in name and icon. This opens the settings page for the plug-in, with a single or few tabs containing configuration settings. You'll also see a brief description of the effect on the left side of the program window. When you've finished, click the Back button.

In the left column, you can use the Filter text box at the top to search for a particular plug-in; the search results will be displayed on the right side of the window. Beneath the Filter section is the Category listing, which groups the plug-ins by purpose. Clicking any category will update the list of plug-ins on the right side of the window. To return to the main program window, click the Back button. The categories are as follows:

All: All available plug-ins will be displayed in the main window.

General: This section contains just the General Options plug-in, which provides configuration settings for keyboard shortcuts for some of the effects, virtual desktop size, display settings, transparency settings for windows, and more. Some of the settings are quite technical and are perhaps best left alone unless you know what you are doing.

Accessibility: This section contains plug-ins that will help people with physical disabilities use the desktop more conveniently with visual aids. It contains plug-ins to make the active window more visible, magnify the screen for visibility issues, change colors, and assist in finding the mouse pointer. To find out what keyboard combination is required to activate any particular effect, click the plug-in's icon to change its settings and look to the button alongside each heading. Note that when a setting specifies Button 2 or Button 3, these relate to the mouse, and the super key is commonly known as the Windows key on a standard keyboard.

Desktop: This section contains plug-ins that enhance desktop behavior. If you use virtual desktops, plug-ins such as Desktop Cube and Rotate Cube can turn these into sides of a 3D cube that rotates when you switch desktops, as shown in Figure 9-11. Desktop Wall and Desktop Plane render these workspaces as if they were part of one surface. You might notice that some plug-ins have the same functionality; CompizConfig Settings Manager will offer to disable any that do when you select a new option. Plug-ins such as Viewport Switcher and Expo make it easier to preview and navigate workspaces. Show Desktop and Fade to Desktop add special effects to clear the desktop of clutter. Like many effects plug-ins, these tie in with the existing features of Ubuntu—in this case, the Show Desktop feature and button, located at the bottom left of the desktop by default.

Effects: This section contains plug-ins that add special effects to certain aspects of the desktop. Some you have already seen, such as Wobbly Windows, which is part of the Extras scheme. But others are more extreme. For example, there are several plug-ins that add eye candy to windows, such as Blur Windows, Animations, Fading Windows, and Window Decoration Reflection. 3D Windows, Cube Gears, and Cube Reflection add decorations as you traverse the 3D cube. Other plug-ins affect the entire screen, such as adding water puddles and wipers with the Water effect or adding fire on the screen with the Paint Fire on the Screen effect. Some need keyboard combinations to activate them—to find out what these are, click the plug-in icon.

Figure 9-11. *The rotating desktop cube is just about the coolest special effect you'll see on a computer desktop.*

Extras: This section includes effects useful for developers, as well as some plug-ins that simply could not be filed elsewhere. These include displaying the Compiz Fusion splash screen after logging in, benchmarking the performance of Compiz Fusion, viewing a thumbnail of a window by pointing the mouse at its entry on the Taskbar, and taking a screenshot. One notable plug-in is Annotate, which enables you to draw on the screen. This can be useful for demos and presentations when stressing key points.

Image loading: These plug-ins are technical and are required in the background to load image formats and text that will be used by other plug-ins for rendering. Do not disable them.

Utility: This section contains mostly plug-ins that work behind the scenes and a few that work externally. Unless you know what you are doing, you shouldn't change any of these settings or disable any of the plug-ins. If you have a fairly powerful machine, enable the Video Playback option, which puts live previews where application thumbnails are generated.

Window management: These plug-ins enhance window management functionality. For example, some of the plug-ins project the Taskbar in different ways, such as in 2D, in a ring, and in a 3D ring. Another example is the Group and Tab Windows plug-in, which you can use to group and tab windows. Fans of the Vista application switch method should go into Shift Switcher, look under the Appearance tab, and change Cover (which is very Apple-esque) to Flip (as in Figure 9-12).

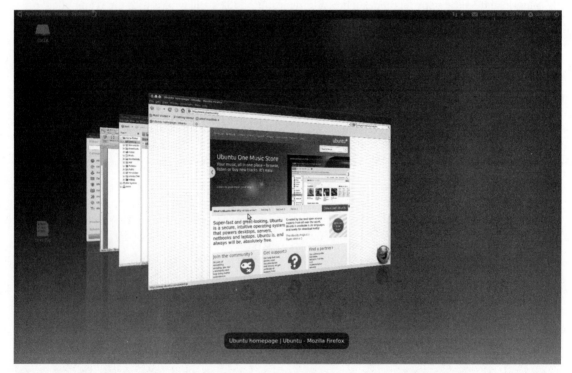

Figure 9-12. The Flip Switcher might make Windows Vista converts feel more at home.

Beneath the Categories list is the Preferences option, which is used for adjusting internal settings of Compiz Fusion, such as the back-end profile, and including and excluding plug-ins. You can leave these settings untouched.

Finally, the Advanced Search option allows you to search through options within plug-ins. The search results will first be narrowed down to a list of plug-ins in the main window. After selecting from the list of plug-ins, a new list will be displayed with narrowed-down results containing a list of grouped options. After selecting from the list of grouped options, you'll see a narrowed-down list of options that you can use to configure the plug-in's settings.

USING DESKTOP WIDGETS

If you are a fan of Windows Vista's Sidebar, Macintosh OS X's Dashboard, or Yahoo's widgets, you can use something similar under Ubuntu, called *screenlets*. To use these, you need to install the Screenlets package. This requires you to first install CompizConfig Settings Manager, as described in the main text. Finally, use the Ubuntu Software Center (Applications ➤ Ubuntu Software Center) to search for and install the Screenlets package.

Run Screenlets by clicking Applications ➤ Accessories ➤ Screenlets. After the Screenlets Manager window appears, select the screenlet you would like to enable by clicking it and then clicking the Launch/Add button. Following this, you should be able to click and drag the screenlet. Right-click a screenlet and select Properties to change its settings.

You have two choices regarding how and when the screenlet appears:

- Keep the widget on the screen at all times (the default), perhaps arranging widgets on the right side of the screen as with Windows Vista or the Google Sidebar (which can also, by the way, be used on Linux).

- Add the widget to the widget layer which is just like OS X's Dashboard and will appear only when you press F9 (and will subsequently disappear when the mouse is clicked). To add the widget to the Widget Layer, right-click it, select Window, and then click Widget.

Of course, you can have the best of both worlds, keeping some widgets on the screen and putting lesser-used items on the Widget Layer.

If you would like to add more screenlets than those available by default, go to http://screenlets.org. Under the Downloads heading, click the "third-party screenlets" link. After you've downloaded the screenlet, you can install it by clicking Install Screenlet in the Screenlets Manager window and then navigating to the downloaded screenlet.

Dressing Up Firefox

You'll likely spend quite a lot of computer time looking at Firefox, the web browser. For this reason, it's a nice idea to take as much care over the look of this vital application as your desktop. Firefox has been themeable since the first version was released, but the Mozilla project, which oversees development of the application, has since added *personas* to the application's features, enabling you to instantly change the look and feel of the application. To get started, visit the project's web site (http://www.getpersonas.com) and click the Get Personas button. This will download a small extension and ask you to restart your browser. After the browser has relaunched, you'll be presented with a very different-looking browser, as in Figure 9-13. You can change the skin by clicking the fox mask icon at the bottom left of the browser window and selecting a new one. This is a live list, so it is updated constantly. Changes should be almost instant, meaning you can reskin your browser depending on your mood.

If nothing in the list takes your fancy, create your own skin and share it with the world. See https://personas.services.mozilla.com for more.

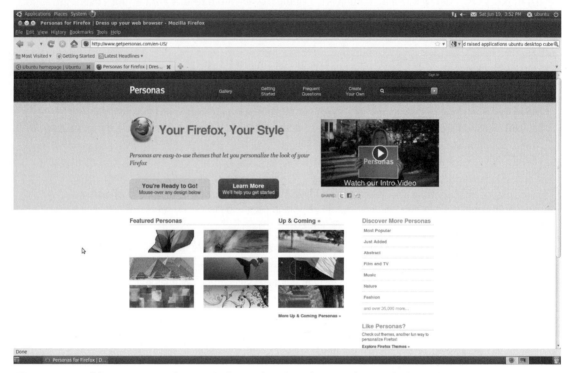

Figure 9-13. *Add some personality to Firefox and make it fit in with your desktop theme.*

Firefox also has a large collection of other extensions that can alter the way the browser looks or works. For instance, Tree Style Tabs arranges your open tabs in a treelike structure on the left edge of your browser.

Changing Your Login Picture

The login screen will display a picture alongside your name. You can click this and type your password to log in. You might be familiar with a similar system under Windows or Mac OS X.

Users can choose their own login pictures by clicking System ➤ Preferences ➤ About Me. The About Me dialog box, shown in Figure 9-14, is designed for users to enter their personal details, such as their addresses, but they can also simply use it to choose photographs of themselves or to add pictorial icons. To do this, click the empty square alongside your name at the top of the dialog box. You'll be shown a file list of default icons to choose from, and you can also navigate to your own. Ideally, the image you choose should be square and 96×96 pixels, although if the picture is too large, it will be automatically scaled down. Click OK when you've finished.

Figure 9-14. The About Me dialog box

Adding and Removing Desktop Items

Virtually the entire Ubuntu desktop can be redesigned and restructured. You can move the Applications menu from the top of the screen to the bottom to be more like Windows, for example, or you can add numerous desktop shortcuts to popular applications and/or files.

Adding a Shortcut

Ubuntu's nearest equivalent to a Windows-style desktop shortcut is a launcher, and you can create a launcher that points to a program or a file. If a launcher is created for a file, Ubuntu will automatically launch the correct program to display the file. If you create a launcher to a .jpg file, for example, Ubuntu will know to launch the Eye of GNOME image viewer when the launcher is double-clicked.

Creating a Launcher

You can create a launcher two ways. One way is to simply click and drag an icon from one of the main menus to the desktop. This effectively copies the menu's launcher to the desktop, rather than creating a new launcher, but the effect is the same.

The other way to create a launcher is to right-click the desktop and select Create Launcher. In the Create Launcher dialog box, select whether you want to create a launcher to a file or application from the Type drop-down list (the second option, Application in Terminal, will open a terminal window and run the program within it; this is only for specialized use). Then fill in the Name and Command fields.

Alternatively, if you don't know the exact name and path of the file, click the Browse button, use the file browser dialog box to navigate to the file or program, and click to select it. (If you are creating a launcher to a program, you'll probably find it in /usr/bin, which stores most of the Linux programs you use from day to day.) The Comment field can be left blank. If it's filled in, it forms the tooltip text that will appear if you hover the mouse cursor over the launcher icon.

To choose an icon for your launcher, click the icon button on the left side of the Create Launcher dialog box. You can select from several predefined icons, as shown in Figure 9-15, or choose your own picture by clicking the Browse button and navigating to the location of a saved icon. As with desktop backgrounds and themes, there are many icon sets available at http://art.gnome.org. Additional icon sets can be added by choosing System ➤ Preferences ➤ Appearance and looking under the Theme tab. In the bottom-right of the window, select Customize. You can drag and drop downloaded icon packs to the Icon tab, and they will be installed immediately. If you don't choose an icon, a stock GNOME icon is used.

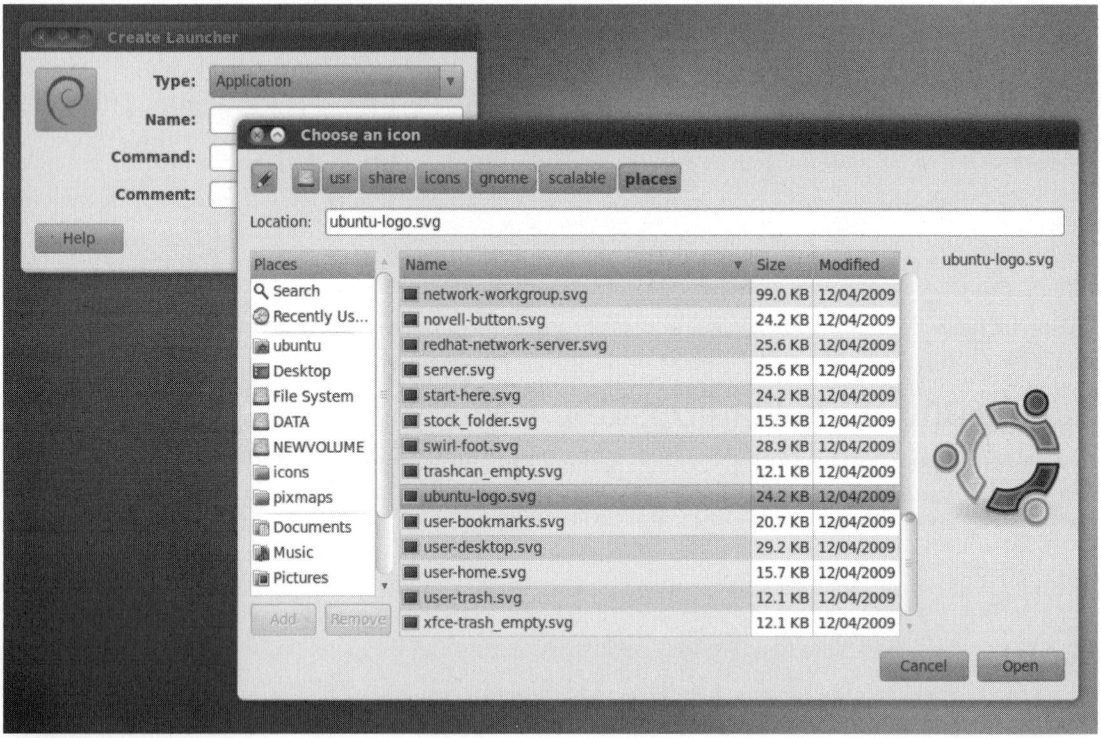

Figure 9-15. Creating a launcher is easy. Just fill in the Name and Command fields, and choose an icon.

Using Ubuntu Tweak

If you've used Windows extensively, you may have come across an application called Tweak UI, which lets you perform some useful desktop operations. Well, Ubuntu has its own version, which is perfect for adding an icon to your /home folder, the computer, or the Deleted Items folder on the desktop. It can do lots of other things, but desktop icons are what we're interested in here.

To install the application, go to http://ubuntu-tweak.com and select the option Download Now! A package will be downloaded and opened with GDebi, which is a graphical application installer. Click

Install Package, and after the package is installed, it will be available via Application ➤ System Tools ➤ Ubuntu Tweak. There are lots of options in here, including another way of finding and installing applications, but the section you need to look under is labeled Desktop. In here, select the icons you'd like to see, and they will appear as you click the buttons, as in Figure 9-16. Deselect to remove. You can also rename the icons without renaming the actual folders, which could be useful.

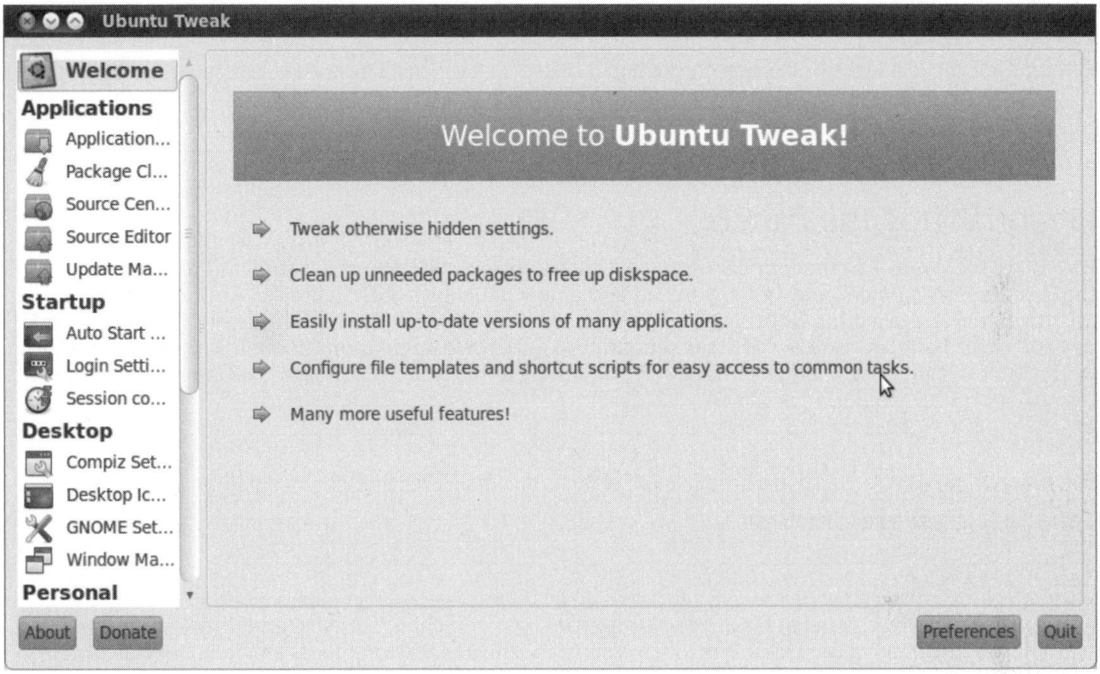

Figure 9-16. *If you're familiar with the desktop icon scheme in Windows, you can add your favorites by using Ubuntu Tweak.*

Creating a Link

Launchers have one failing: they're recognized only by GNOME (and other desktop environments, such as KDE). You can't create a launcher to an application and use it from the command line or the Alt+F2 run application box, for example. In technical terms, a launcher isn't recognized by the underlying Linux file system.

The solution is to create a *link* to the file or program. This will actually create a symbolic link to the file. A link is very similar to a launcher, except it works on a file-system level.

■ **Note** Actually, Linux offers two types of link: a *symbolic link*, which is the most common type of link used under Linux, and a *hard link*, which is a cross between copying a file and creating a shortcut.

To create a link, locate the file you want to create the link to, right-click it, and select Make Link. The link will be created in the same directory as the original file, and you can then click and drag the new link to wherever you want it to appear, such as the desktop. You don't need to choose an icon, because the link inherits the icon of the original file. For example, if it's a picture link, it will inherit the thumbnail preview icon.

■ **Note** If you find the Make Link option grayed out, it's likely that you don't have sufficient permissions to write the link to the directory in question.

Personalizing the Panels

Panels are the long strips that appear at the top and bottom of the Ubuntu screen and play host to a choice of menus, applets, and icons. You can add a new panel by right-clicking a blank spot on an existing panel and selecting New Panel. The new panel will appear on one of the sides of the desktop. If you add a third one, in addition to the two default panels, it will appear on the right side of the desktop, vertically. You can also remove a panel by right-clicking it and selecting Delete This Panel.

■ **Caution** If you delete a panel, the arrangement of items it contains will be lost. Of course, you can always re-create the collection on a different panel.

By right-clicking a panel and selecting Properties, you can change its size and dimensions. For example, by unchecking the Expand box, you can make the panel shrink to its smallest possible size. Then, when you add new components (or, in the case of a panel containing the Window List, when a new program is run), the panel will expand as necessary. This can be a neat effect and also creates more desktop space. (This effect is a little like the Mac OS X Dock, and might help make OS X users feel more at home.)

Selecting the Autohide feature will make the panel slide off the screen when there isn't a mouse over it. Choosing "Show hide buttons" will make small arrows appear on either side of the panel so that you can click to slide it off the side of the screen when it's not in use. Both techniques create more desktop space.

You can also change the panel's alignment to top, bottom, left, or right by changing the selection in the Orientation drop-down list.

Adding and Removing Menus

You can add either just the Applications menu or the entire set of menus (Applications, Places, and System) to the panel at the bottom of the screen. This can help those who long for the Windows Start button approach to access programs.

Adding All the Menus to a Panel

To add the Application, Places, and System menus to the panel at the bottom of the Ubuntu desktop, follow these steps:

1. Right-click a blank spot on the bottom panel and select Add to Panel.

2. In the dialog box that appears, click the Menu Bar option to add all three menus. You'll find this under the Utilities heading in the list; you'll need to scroll down to see it.

3. Click the Add button at the bottom of the dialog box.

4. Click the Close button.

Adding a Start-Like Button to a Panel

As an alternative to the Applications, Places, and System menus, you can add a Start-like button that offers submenus for all three menus. Here's how to add this button:

1. Right-click a blank spot on the bottom panel and select Add to Panel.

2. In the dialog box that appears, click the Main Menu option, as shown in Figure 9-17. You'll find this under the Utilities heading in the list; you'll need to scroll down to see it.

3. Click the Add button at the bottom of the dialog box.

4. Click the Close button.

Figure 9-17. Use the Main Menu applet to add a Windows-like Start button to any panel on your screen.

Deleting a Menu

Creating new instances of the menus won't delete the old ones. If you create a new Applications menu at the bottom of the screen, for example, the old Applications menu will remain at the top of the screen. In fact, you can have as many instances of the menus on the desktop as you wish, although this won't be a good use of desktop space!

To delete any menu, simply right-click anywhere on that menu and select Remove from Panel.

■ **Tip** You can personalize the Applications and System menus by right-clicking either and selecting Edit Menus. This will start the Main Menu program (also accessible from the System ➤ Preferences menu). Simply check or uncheck existing entries to add or remove them from the menus, or click the New Item button to create new entries. New application entries can be created as with the launchers discussed earlier.

Modifying the Menus

You can modify how your menus are displayed by right-clicking on one of them and selecting the option Edit Menus. You should be aware that the configuration is the same for all the menus in your desktop, if you have more than one.

You will be presented with a three-part window. To the left you will see the menu items, or categories. If you select one of those categories, its contents will be displayed in the Items section, in which you can check the items you want displayed on the menu, and uncheck those that are of no use to you. You can hide categories or individual applications. For example, select Applications in the Menus section, and uncheck the item Games. The next time you expand the Applications menu, the Games category will not be shown. But if you select the Applications ➤ Accessories menu and uncheck the item Calculator, the Accessories category will be displayed, but the Calculator won't.

You can create custom direct access for your own categories or applications. Just select in the Menus section the location of your new element, and click New Menu to create a new category, or New Item to create an application launcher inside the current category.

Click Close to save the changes, which will be effective immediately.

Moving Panel Items

To move a panel item, right-click it and select Move. Then drag the mouse to the new location and click the mouse button once to set the item in place. All panel items can be moved, including menus, and items can be moved between different panels. Any item that's in the way will be shifted to make space.

If the Move option is grayed out, right-click it and ensure that Lock to Panel doesn't have a check alongside it. This is especially relevant if you're trying to move an item into the space occupied by something else—if the other item is locked, it won't automatically shift out of the way!

Working with Applets

Almost everything you see on the desktop is considered by the GNOME desktop to be an applet, with the exception of application/file icons and the panels. A menu is a form of applet, for example, as is the Workspace Switcher.

■ **Note** Applets are completely separate from screenlets, which were discussed earlier in this chapter. Applets are built into the GNOME desktop to provide essential functionality. Screenlets are provided by the Screenlets subsystem and "float" on top of the desktop. However, there are often overlaps in terms of the functions offered by applets and screenlets.

Ubuntu provides many more applets that you can choose to add to the desktop to provide a host of useful or entertaining functionality. To add an applet, right-click a blank spot on a panel and select Add to Panel. Some applets require configuration when they're added, so you may need to right-click them and select Properties. For example, you'll need to set your location in the Weather Report applet's properties so it can provide accurate forecasting. Table 9-1 describes some of the most useful desktop applets. To remove an applet, simply right-click it and select Remove from Panel.

Table 9-1. Ubuntu Desktop Applets

Applet	Description	Configuration*
Battery Charge Monitor	Shows the battery level on notebooks and whether outlet power is in use.	None needed.
Character Palette	Displays a palette of accented or unusual characters; click a character to insert it into the text.	None needed.
Clipboard Text Encryption	Allows you to decrypt, encrypt, or sign contents of the clipboard, provided encryption is set up (see Chapter 8).	Click to encrypt, sign, decrypt, or verify clipboard contents.
Clock	Displays the time and date (active by default).	None needed.
Connect to Server	Lets you quickly connect to remote servers, such as FTP (the equivalent of clicking Places ➤ Connect to Server).	None needed.
Dictionary Lookup	Displays a text box that will look up words according to online dictionaries.	None needed.
Disk Mounter	Lets you quickly mount and unmount removable disks.	None needed.
Drawer	Displays a drawer icon that, when clicked, "slides out" to reveal yet more applets.	Right-click and select Add to Drawer to add applets.
Dwell Click	Displays a selection of mouse actions to choose from for the dwell click feature (see the "Accessibility Settings for the Mouse" section earlier in this chapter).	Click the preferred mouse action.

Applet	Description	Configuration*
Eyes	Displays two eyes whose pupils follow the mouse cursor.	None needed.
Fish	Adds a couple of fish to the panel that, when clicked, will spout wisdom.	None needed.
Force Quit	Lets you quit a crashed program.	None needed.
Inhibit Applet	Allows you to temporarily switch off automatic power saving, such as hard disk spin-down.	Click to forbid/allow automatic power saving.
Invest	Adds a text-based scrolling stock ticker to the panel.	Right-click and select Preferences to add individual stock symbols to the list.
Lock Screen	Adds an icon that, when clicked, blanks the screen and displays a password prompt.	None needed.
Log Out…	Adds an icon that allows you to log out of the current session and log in as a different user.	None needed.
Main Menu	Lets you add a single-icon Start-like system menu.	None needed.
Notification Area	Adds a notification area to the panel (active by default).	None needed.
Run Application	Adds an icon that, when clicked, makes the Run Application dialog box appear.	None needed.
Search for Files	Provides one-click access to Nautilus's search mode.	None needed.
Separator	Simply inserts a graphical separator—useful for making several applets alongside each other look neater.	None needed.
Show Desktop	Minimizes all desktop windows (active by default).	None needed.
Shut Down	Shuts down the computer.	None needed.
Sticky Notes	Lets you create virtual sticky notes.	None needed.
Switch Off…	Adds a button to shut down the computer.	None needed.
System Monitor	Adds a small graph that shows system resource usage.	Right-click and select Preferences to choose system areas to be monitored.

Applet	Description	Configuration*
Terminal Server Client Applet	Provides one-click access to locations set up within the Terminal Server program (see Chapter 25).	None needed.
Tomboy Notes	Lets you add sticky notes to the desktop.	None needed.
Trash	Adds the Trash icon to the panel, where files can be dropped for removal to the Trash.	None needed.
Weather Report	Adds an icon that shows current weather conditions.	Right-click, and select Preferences and then the Location tab to set your location.
Window List	Adds a list of windows, which you can use to switch between currently running programs (active by default).	None needed.
Window Selector	Adds an icon that, when clicked, switches between currently open windows (alternative to Window List).	None needed.
Workspace Switcher	Shows the virtual desktop selector.	None needed.

* Nearly all applets have configuration options that can be used to tweak them in various ways. This column indicates only whether immediate configuration is needed.

Summary

In this chapter, you learned how to personalize Ubuntu to your own tastes. You looked at changing the theme so that the desktop has a new appearance.

In addition, you learned how to add and remove applets from the desktop in order to add functionality or simply make Ubuntu work the way you would like.

In the next chapter, you will look at what programs are available under Ubuntu to replace those Windows favorites you might miss.

CHAPTER 10

■ ■ ■

Managing Your Data

Files are what make the world of Linux go round. They're the currency of any kind of operating system, because every time you use your computer, you generate new files, even if they're only temporary.

In this chapter, we explain how you can manage your files—that is, pictures, documents, videos, MP3s, and so forth—under Ubuntu. Linux also manages file and folder security, as does Windows, but since permissions always have associated user and group accounts, you'll have to wait until Chapter 21 to learn about the details. However, this chapter provides enough information for you to understand how the system works, and where and how you should store your data. First, we go through an introduction to Nautilus, Ubuntu's flagship file browser. Then you learn some concepts regarding the file system and how it differs from that of Windows. And last, once you have mastered Nautilus and begun to understand the file system, you will be able to perform some more advanced tasks, such as administering your disks and sharing information over a network, among others.

Using Nautilus

Nautilus is the name of the default file browser in Ubuntu. It's similar to My Computer or Windows Explorer under Windows, in that in its default view mode it presents a list of files on the right side of the window and a series of shortcuts to popular locations within the file system on the left side.

Starting Nautilus is simply a matter of clicking the Places menu and choosing a location. The main components of Nautilus are shown in Figure 10-1.

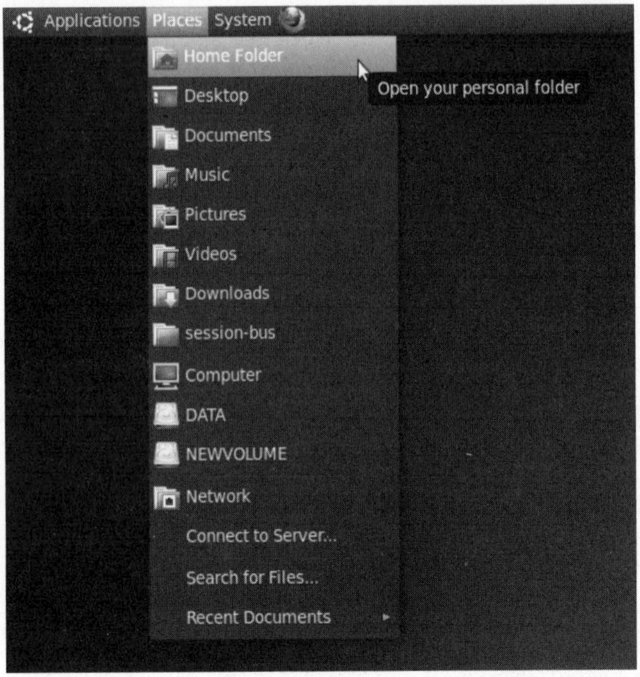

Figure 10-1. The Nautilus file explorer.

The Nautilus window consists of several elements:

Menu bar: The Nautilus menu bar has File, Edit, View, Go, Bookmarks, and Help menus. The File menu allows you to open a new tab or a new window, create files or folders, and see the current item's properties. The View menu offers options for controlling the way files are displayed in the Nautilus window, as well as the look and feel of Nautilus itself. The Edit menu lets you manually cut, copy, and paste files (operations that can also be done with the traditional Ctrl+X, Ctrl+C and Ctrl+V combinations). The Go menu lets you quickly jump to other locations in the file system or on a remote server. Using the Bookmarks menu options, you can create web browser–like shortcuts to certain file system locations or servers, so you can access them instantly. There are also some ready-made bookmarks for folders in your /home directory: Documents, Music, Pictures, Videos, and Downloads.

Toolbar: As in a web browser, the toolbar enables you to quickly move backward and forward from place to place in your browsing history. In addition, you can reload the file listing, in order to reflect any changes that might have taken place since the Nautilus window opened, quickly navigate to popular file system locations, such as your /home directory, and change the way files are displayed.

Location bar: This feature, located beneath the toolbar, is unique to Nautilus. It shows individual directories as buttons on the location bar and lets you see where you are in your file system at a glance, as well as quickly and easily move through your file-browsing history. For example, if you start in /home/andy (displayed as the andy button), and then browse to /home/andy/Pictures/holiday/disneyworld, clicking the Pictures button will return you to /home/andy/Pictures. The other folders listed on the location bar (holiday and disneyworld in this example) won't disappear and will still have buttons, so you can return to those as well. It's best demonstrated by example, so give it a try!

Zoom controls: Zoom controls are in the toolbar. These make the icons representing the files bigger or smaller. When you're browsing a lot of files at once, shrinking them will fit more in the window. On the other hand, when you're viewing photo thumbnails, it can be handy to increase the zoom setting so you can see more detail in the pictures. This also works for text files, where you'll see a portion of the text contained within the file.

View As Icons/List: To the right of the zoom controls is a drop-down list that switches between Icon, List, and Compact view. List view shows details about the files, such as file size, the type of file, its permissions, and so on. Icon view presents the files as a series of large icons. In many cases, the icons give a clue as to the nature of the file; for example, audio files appear with musical note graphics. If the folder you're browsing contains image files (or certain document files, such as PDFs), these will be automatically thumbnailed—the icon will be a small version of the contents of the file, as shown in Figure 10-2. By default Nautilus displays only previews of local files smaller than 10MB, but you can change this by choosing Edit ➤ Preferences and looking under the Preview tab. If you change any of these settings to Always, it could have an impact on performance when you're browsing remote directories. The preview is very handy when browsing pictures for printing or editing. Compact view lists the files in columns, like List view, but without the details. This means that several columns of files can usually fit within a single file-browsing window.

Places pane: The Places pane on the left in Figure 10-2 lists the most popular locations within the file system, as well as any locations that you've bookmarked. Clicking each icon takes you to that location instantly. Clicking the File System entry takes you to the root of the file system (/). There are also bookmarks for your floppy drive (if you have one), the Trash folder, any attached removable storage, and any servers available on the local network.

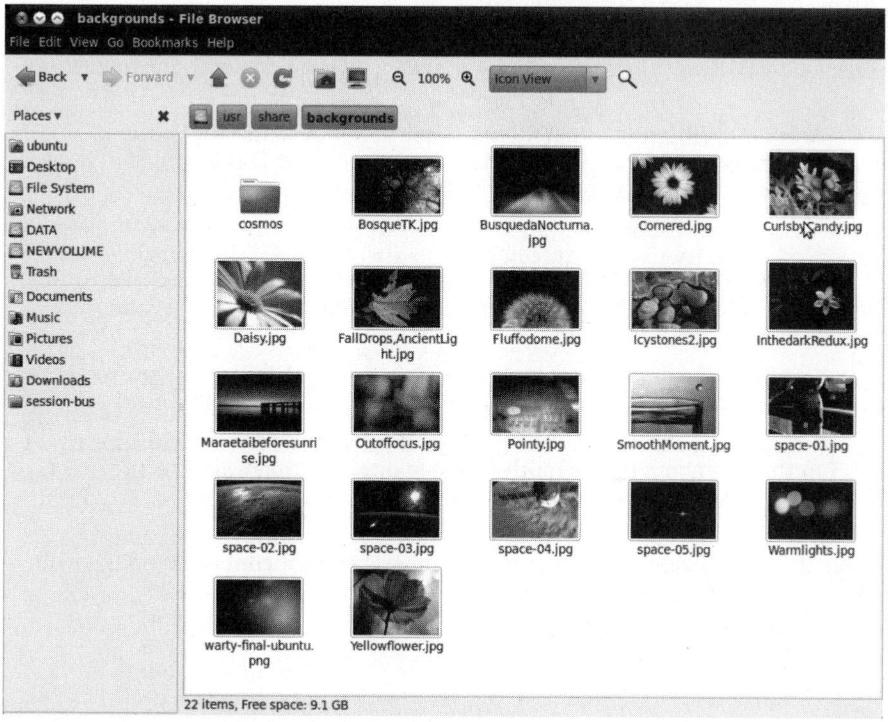

Figure 10-2. *Whenever you view a folder full of pictures in Icon view, they are automatically thumbnailed.*

■ **Tip** To bookmark a location, drag a folder to the blank area beneath the currently bookmarked folders in the Places pane. This new location will then appear with other bookmarks in the main Places menu.

As in Windows, you can right-click each file in the file browser window to see a context menu with options to rename the file, delete it, open it with particular applications, and so on. The Properties option on the context menu lets you view information about the file and alter certain aspects of it, such as its access permissions (we discuss file permissions in Chapter 21). You can even add some text notes about the file if you want!

■ **Caution** You should never delete your /home folder. Doing so will most likely destroy your personal Ubuntu configuration and prevent you from logging in, because many personal system and program settings are also stored in your /home folder.

Changing the View Mode

Nautilus comes equipped with several different view modes, which alter what appears in the sidebar on the left of the program window. The default mode—Places—is described in the preceding section, but several others can be selected by clicking the drop-down list at the top of the side pane. The modes are as follows:

Information: This displays simple information in the side pane about the currently browsed directory, including the number of files it contains and its date of creation. This is similar to how Windows file-browsing windows looked in the Windows 98 and Me releases.

Tree: This option shows a complete list of directories in the file system, along with the complete contents of directories within the user's /home directory. Each directory has a chevron alongside it that, when clicked, unfolds that directory so its contents become visible within the side pane (only directories are shown in the side pane). This view is very similar to how file-browsing windows operated back in Windows 95.

History: This view shows a list of the directories that you've visited, with the newest at the top and the oldest at the bottom. To switch to one of the directories, simply double-click its entry in the list.

Notes: This is another informational display mode. However, this time a text entry field appears, in which you can enter information about the currently browsed directory that will be recorded for future reference. This can be useful in a very large file system.

Emblems: This shows a list of icons that can be clicked and dragged onto any file or directory as a method of identifying or organizing the file for future reference. See the upcoming "Working with File and Folder Icons" section for more information.

Searching for Files

Nautilus includes a simple search tool. Click the Search button (represented by a magnifying glass) on the toolbar, and you will see a text box below the toolbar. In this text box, type any part of the filename you want to find. For example, typing **festival** will return any filenames with *festival* in them.

By clicking the plus sign icon next to the Reload button after a search, you can specify an exact file type. To do this, click the drop-down list that appears and ensure that File Type is selected. Then click the drop-down list alongside this and select the particular file type you want to find. For example, suppose you're searching for a picture taken at a festival, and you know the filename contains the word *festival*. You also have various documents you created related to attending the festival, and their filenames also contain the word *festival*. In this case, to find only photo files, you can select Picture from the drop-down list. The list, including the Picture type, is shown in Figure 10-3.

You can also restrict the search to a particular location in your file system. Simply click the plus sign icon next to the Reload button again and select Location in the drop-down list. Click the drop-down list beside this one and browse for the location in which you think your files might be.

■ **Note** The simple search tool in Nautilus is not as powerful as the Search for Files option, available from the Places menu.

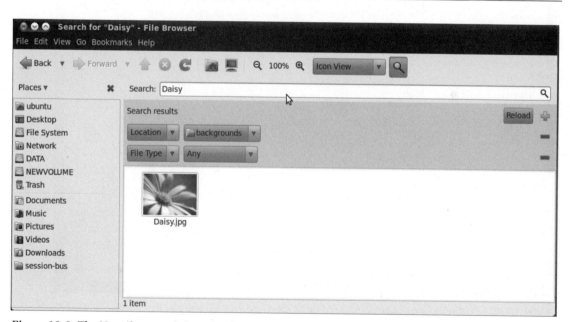

Figure 10-3. The Nautilus search function lets you filter by file type and by location.

Working with File and Folder Icons

Files and folders can have *emblems* assigned to them. These are smaller icons that are "tagged on" to the larger icons in both List view and Icon view. Emblems are designed to give you quick clues about the nature of the file. To apply an emblem, right-click the file or folder, select Properties, and then click the Emblems tab. As shown in Figure 10-4, a range of icons is available; in fact, any file or folder can have several emblems applied at once. Simply put a check in the box beside the icons you want to apply. Pick the ones that are meaningful to you. For example, a "cvs-conflict" emblem will probably be of interest only to programmers.

Nautilus makes use of a handful of emblem icons for its own needs too. For example, a square with an X in it indicates that you don't have permissions to access that file or folder at all—not even to view it. A padlock indicates a file or directory is read-only. In most cases, the file system emblems are self-explanatory.

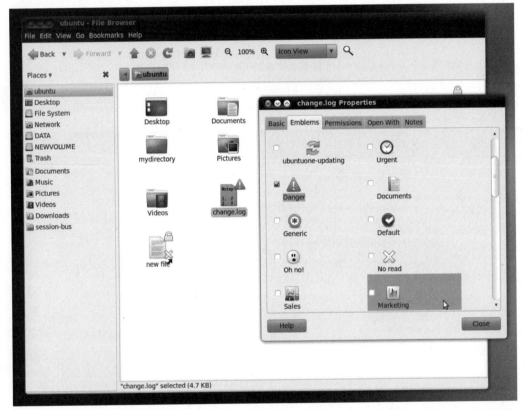

Figure 10-4. A variety of miniature emblems can be applied to an icon to aid recognition of the file.

Special Nautilus Windows

As well as letting you view your files, Nautilus has a number of object modes. This is a complicated way of saying that Nautilus lets you view things other than files.

The most obvious example of this is the Computer view of your file system, which presents an eagle's eye view of your storage devices. To access this view, click Go ➤ Computer. If you have a card reader attached, it will appear here, as will any Windows partitions that may be on your hard disk. Double-clicking each item opens a standard Nautilus file browser window (for this to work with Windows partitions, they must be set up correctly, as described in the "Accessing Windows Files" section later in this chapter).

Object mode comes into its own when viewing network locations. Clicking Go ➤ Network brings up the browsing Network object view, for example, which is a little like Network Neighborhood or My Network Places under Windows. You can also browse to FTP sites by clicking Go ➤ Location in a file browser window and entering an FTP address (prefacing it with ftp://).

■ **Note** You might be used to dragging and dropping files onto program windows or taskbar buttons within Windows in order to open the file. This only works in some programs within Ubuntu. Generally, the best policy is to try it and see what happens. If the program starts but your file isn't opened, it obviously didn't work.

HIDDEN FILES AND DIRECTORIES

When you view your /home directory via Nautilus, you're not seeing every file that's there. Several hidden files and directories relating to your system configuration also exist. You can take a look at them by clicking View ➤ Show Hidden Files in the Nautilus menu. Clicking this option again hides the files and directories.

You may notice something curious about the hidden items: they all have a period before their filenames. In fact, this is all that's needed to hide any file or directory: simply place a period at the front of the filename. There's no magic involved beyond this.

For example, to hide the file partypicture.jpg, you could simply right-click it and rename it .partypicture.jpg. You'll need to click the Reload button on the toolbar for the file view to be updated and for the file to disappear. As you might expect, removing the period unhides the file.

Files are usually hidden for a reason—for instance, they're not supposed to be editable or are used to configure application elements—and it's no coincidence that most of the hidden files are system files. In addition, every program that you install, or is installed by default, will usually create its own hidden folder for its system configuration data. Deleting such files by accident usually results in losing your personal settings for that particular program.

The Nautilus file manager has an additional method of hiding files. Any filename that ends with a ~ symbol does not appear in Nautilus file-browsing windows or on the desktop. For example, partypicture.jpg~ would be invisible. This method is primarily used to make temporary files created by GNOME applications invisible, but any user can also use it to hide sensitive files. Be aware that this technique is respected only by some GNOME applications, and the files will be entirely visible at the command line.

Launching Files and Running Programs

As with Windows or Mac OS X, most of the programs on your Ubuntu system automatically associate themselves with various file types that they understand. For example, double-clicking a picture will automatically open the Eye of GNOME image viewer application, and double-clicking a .doc file will start OpenOffice.org Writer.

Ubuntu is automatically set up to view common file types. Table 10-1 shows which programs are required for viewing certain types of documents.

■ **Note** Whenever you install new software from the installation CD or the official software repositories, it should add an entry to the Applications menu. If for some reason it doesn't, you can create a shortcut by using the techniques explained in Chapter 9.

Table 10-1. Common File Types

File Type	File Extension	Viewer	Location on Applications Menu
Word processor document	.doc, .rtf, .odt	OpenOffice.org Writer	Office ➤ OpenOffice.org Word Processor
Spreadsheet	.xls, .ods	OpenOffice.org Calc	Office ➤ OpenOffice.org Spreadsheet
Presentation	.ppt, .odp	OpenOffice.org Impress	Office ➤ OpenOffice.org Presentation
PDF file	.pdf	Document Viewer	Not on Applications menu[a]
Compressed file	.zip, .tar, .gz, .bz2, and others	File Roller	Not on Applications menu[a]
Image file	.jpg, .gif, .bmp, and others	Eye of GNOME	Not on Applications menu[a]
HTML file	.htm, .html	Firefox	Internet ➤ Firefox Web Browser
Text file	.txt	Gedit	Accessories ➤ Text Editor
Audio file	.wav, .mp3, .ogg[b]	Rhythmbox	Sound & Video ➤ Rhythmbox
Music Player Video file	.mpg, .mpeg, .avi[b]	Totem	Sound & Video ➤ Movie Player

[a] *Evince, File Roller, and Eye of GNOME are not present on the Applications menu. If you wish, you can add your own shortcuts for these applications by following the instructions in Chapter 9.*
[b] *Playback of many media files is possible only after extra software is installed. See Chapters 16 and 17 for more information.*

If you want to temporarily open a file type with a different program, right-click the file. The context menu will display a set of options; for example, for an image, you will have Image Viewer (or Eye of the Gnome), Firefox, or F-Spot. Or you can select Open with Other Application and choose other program. From that point on, every time you right-click, you'll be offered the choice of that program to open the file.

To make Nautilus automatically and permanently use the application to open the file type, right-click it, select Properties, and then click the Open With tab. Click the Add button to locate the application you want to use if it's not in the list. Finally, ensure that the radio button alongside the program you want to use is highlighted (you may need to click twice for this to happen), as shown in Figure 10-5, and then click the Close button. This will change the program association for all the files with the same extension.

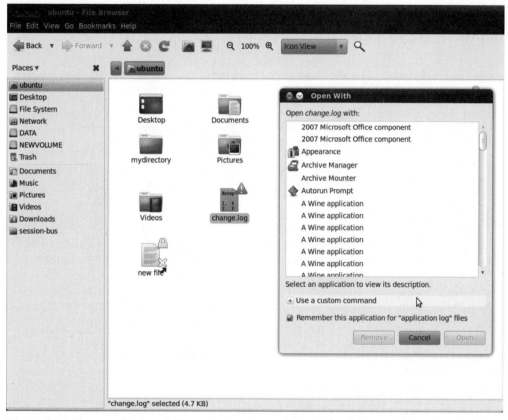

Figure 10-5. *You can change which program opens a file by right-clicking, selecting Properties, and clicking the Open With tab.*

■ **Note** In Windows, you can use Windows Explorer to launch program executables by just browsing to their locations within Program Files and double-clicking their .exe files. It's technically possible to run programs by using Nautilus to browse to their locations, but this is discouraged. One reason is that Ubuntu doesn't store all of its programs in one central folder, as Windows does. However, most programs that are used on a daily basis can be found in /usr/bin. If the program itself isn't stored in /usr/bin, the folder will contain a symbolic link (effectively, a shortcut) to the program's genuine location on the hard disk, which means it's usually possible to launch an application either by typing its name into the terminal or by pressing Alt+F2 and typing the name.

Viewing File Sizes and Other Information

Using Nautilus you can use the List view to check file size and other information. By default, the file name, size, type, and date modified are shown for each file on the current folder. Nautilus selects which unit of measure (bytes, KB, MB, or GB) are most appropriate to display each file.

In order to get an idea of which are the largest files and which are the smaller, you can click the Size column label to sort files by size. Click it again and the order is reversed. You'll see a little arrow head next to the column name. When the arrow head is pointing up, the largest file is at the top of the list; when it is pointing down, the smallest file will be displayed at the top.

You can also display additional information for each of the files. To add a column to the view, simply select View ➤ Visible Columns… inside Nautilus when the List View is selected. Just check the box next to the name of the column you want to see.

Tips and Tricks for Nautilus

Although ostensibly simple, Nautilus is packed with features, and it can be a rewarding experience working through the menus to see what you can find. Here are a handful of the more useful Nautilus features that can help optimize workflow:

Tabbed browsing: You might have used tabbed browsing with the Firefox web browser, enabling you to visit more than one site simultaneously. The same principle applies to tabbed browsing in Nautilus: pressing Ctrl+T opens a new tab, which appears at the top of the program window and enables you to browse to a different location in the file system. Files can be dragged and dropped between tabs—just click and drag them to a different tab—and tabs can be reordered by clicking and dragging them. Many tabs can be open at any one time, and the only practical limitation is the width of the program window. To close a tab, click its X button.

Matched selection: Imagine you're working on a large project and have generated a great many files. However, lacking foresight, you failed to create a special project folder and mixed all the files in with others in your Documents folder. The project files have a unique characteristic: they all have the name of the project within them. But some filenames contain other text, and there are varying types of files among the collection (images, documents, and so forth). Nautilus's matched selection feature, available on the Edit menu (click Select Items Matching), provides a solution: it lets you select files based on key text within the filenames. With the example quoted previously, you could type the project name into the Pattern dialog box that appears, surrounded by the asterisk wildcard (that is, *projectname*), which indicates that any number of characters can appear before or after the keyword. After you click OK, any filenames matching the text will be automatically selected, and you can then click and drag them to a new location or perform any other operation on them.

E-mailing files: By right-clicking a file and selecting the Send To option, you can instantly send a file by e-mail. Ensure that Evolution is selected in the Send As drop-down list in the dialog box that appears, and enter the e-mail address within the Send As text field. Under the Compression heading, you can optionally choose to compress the file first.

Extensions: As with Firefox, it's possible to add extensions to Nautilus. There are extensions to open a file as the system administrator (nautilus-gksu), resize a picture (nautilus-image-converter), or set an image as the desktop background (nautilus-wallpaper), and these can be installed through Ubuntu Software Center. You'll find most of them by simply typing **nautilus extension** in the search bar, as in Figure 10-6.

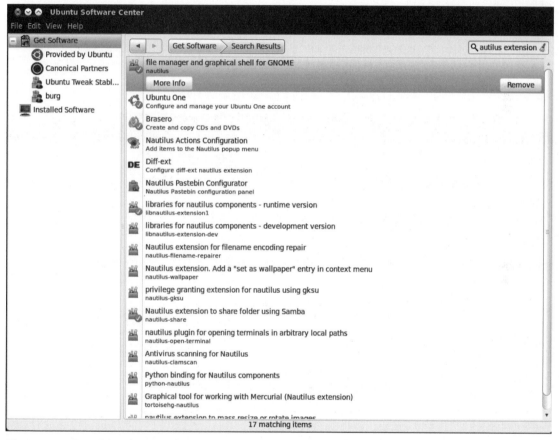

Figure 10-6. Searching for Nautilus extensions in Ubuntu Software Center

The Home Folder

Under Windows, you have access to the entire hard disk. You can write, read, or delete files anywhere (unless the system has specifically been configured otherwise). You can save your personal files in C:\Windows, for example.

Under Ubuntu, the file system is a harder place for ordinary users. They can browse most of the hard disk, but they aren't able to write files to the majority of folders (in some cases, they can't even access files). For them, most folders are like somebody else's land. It is. It is the land of the root.

As an ordinary user, instead of being allowed to prowl the entire disk, you've been given your own private parcel of storage in which you can keep your stuff securely and privately. This is a directory located within the /home directory, and its name is taken from your username. If your login name is louisesmith, your place for storing files will be /home/louisesmith. You can find it as the first item in the Places pane in Nautilus and in the Places menu also. Figure 10-7 shows an example of a user's /home directory.

■ **Note** Linux generally uses the terms *directory* and *subdirectory* for the places you put files, whereas Windows refers to them as folders. It's merely a matter of semantics. However, within the Nautilus file browser, directories are pictured as folders and are referred to as such.

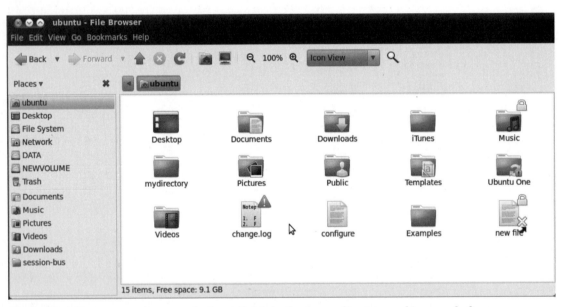

Figure 10-7. Your personal area on the hard disk is in the /home directory and is named after your username.

Your parcel will be decorated from the very start with several default directories created with the purpose of organizing your information in a logical manner. This is not very different from Windows, as you can see just by reading the names of most of those default directories or by looking at Table 10-2.

Table 10-2. Default Home Folder Subdirectories

Directory	Purpose
Desktop	This folder has the content of your desktop. Every document you place in this folder will appear on your desktop. This is like the Windows' Desktop folder.
Documents	Like Windows' My Documents folder, this is the default directory for storing personal documents. OpenOffice.org saves its documents in this directory.
Downloads	This is the folder where the files you download with Firefox are stored.
Music	A folder to store music files, like the Windows' My Music folder. Those files can be opened with Rythmbox.
Pictures	A folder to store pictures. Equivalent to the Windows' folder My Pictures.
Public	A special folder in which you can store content to be shared with your family or colleagues. It is not shared by default, but you can follow the instructions given later in this chapter in order to make those files accessible through the network.
Templates	Folder to store templates for OpenOffice.org's applications.
Videos	Folder to store video files that can be opened with the Movie Player.
Examples	This folder is actually a link to /usr/share/example-content, where you can find OpenOffice.org's sample documents, ogg audio files, and more.

Some programs might utilize those subdirectories in your /home directory in order to store and organize their output. For example, a digital camera program might utilize the Pictures directory within your /home directory. It's up to you whether you use these or change those settings in the application.

Other applications may create a hidden folder in your home. If you instruct Nautilus to show hidden files (you already know how), you will see several folders that were hidden by default, where applications store their data, For example, the .mozilla folder is where the Firefox information is stored, and the Evolution files are in .evolution.

Files within Ubuntu remember who owns them. If user johnsmith creates a file, he can make it so that only he can read or write the file (see Chapter 21 for more details on file permissions). The default setting is that other users will be able to read the file, but not write any new data to it. Directories, too, are owned by people, and the owner can set access permissions. By default, all users on a system can access each other's /home directories and read files, but they can't change the files or write new files to any directory within /home that isn't theirs.

■ **Note** Any user with superuser powers has access to all of the system and can create, edit, and delete files in all directories. This is so the superuser can perform essential system maintenance.

Understanding File System Concepts

Now that you have been playing with Nautilus for a little while and found it to be very much like Windows Explorer, you might be wondering whether the file system concepts in both operating systems are exactly the same.

Just like Windows, Ubuntu has a file system that is shared between software components and your own personal data, which you generate with your applications or download from the Internet. However, Ubuntu differs from Windows in a couple of important ways.

The File System Explained

You might already have ventured beyond the /home directory and wandered through the file system. You no doubt found it thoroughly confusing, largely because it's not like anything you're used to. The good news is that it's not actually very hard to understand. If nothing else, you should be aware that nearly everything can be ignored during everyday use.

■ **Note** The Ubuntu file system is referred to as a *hierarchical* file system. This means that it consists of a lot of directories that contain files. Windows also uses a hierarchical file system. Ubuntu refers to the very bottom level of the file system as the *root*. This has no connection with the root user, or the directory named /root, which is the personal file storage area for the root user.

You can access the root of the file system by clicking File System in the Places pane in Nautilus.

Only users with administrative powers can write files to the root of the file system. This is to prevent damage, because most of the directories in the root of the file system are vital to the correct running of Linux and contain essential programs or data.

Most directories allow all users to browse them and access the files within. You just can't write new files there or delete the directories themselves. You might be able to modify or execute programs contained within the directory, but this will depend on the permissions of each individual file.

Table 10-3 provides a brief description of what each directory and file in the Ubuntu root file system contains. This is for reference only; there's no need for you to learn this information. The Ubuntu file system broadly follows the principles in the Filesystem Hierarchy Standard[1], as do most versions of Linux, but it does have its own subtleties.

---

[1] The Filesystem Hierarchy Standard, or FHS, is a standard maintained by the Linux Foundation and defines the main directories and their content for the Linux OS.

Table 10-3. *Directories and Files in the Ubuntu Root File System*

Directory	Contents
bin	Vital tools necessary to get the system running or for use when repairing the system and diagnosing problems.
boot	Boot loader programs and configuration files. (The boot loader is the menu that appears when you first boot Linux.)
cdrom -> media/cdrom	Symbolic link (shortcut) to the entry for the CD- or DVD-ROM drive in the /dev folder. (Accessing this file lets you access the CD- or DVD-ROM drive.)
dev	Virtual files representing hardware installed on your system.
etc	Central repository of configuration files for your system.
lib	Shared system files used by Linux as well as the software that runs on it.
lost+found	Folder where salvaged scraps of files are saved in the event of a problematic shutdown and subsequent file system check.
media	Where the directories representing various mounted storage systems are made available (including Windows partitions on the disk).
mnt	Directory in which external file systems can be temporarily mounted.
opt	Software that is theoretically optional and not vital to the running of the system. (Many software packages you use daily can be found here.)
proc	Virtual directory containing data about your system and its current status.
root	The root user's personal directory.
sbin	Programs essential to administration of the system.
selinux	Commands used in the SELinux security subsystem.
srv	Configuration files for any network servers you might have running on your system.
sys	Mount point of the sysfs file system, which is used by the kernel to administer your system's hardware.
tmp	Temporary files stored by the system.
usr	Programs and data that might be shared with other systems (such as in a large networking setup with many users).[a]

Directory	Contents
Var	Used by the system to store data that is constantly updated, such as printer spooling output.
vmlinuz -> boot/ vmlinuz-2.6.32- 16-generic	Symbolic link to the kernel file used during bootup.

[a] The /usr directory contains its own set of directories that are full of programs and data. Many system programs, such as the X11 GUI software, are located within the /usr directory. Note that the /usr directory is used even if your system will never act as a server to other systems.

TYPES OF FILE SYSTEMS

Linux is all about choice, and this extends to the technology that makes the file system work. Unlike with Windows, where the only real choice these days is NTFS, Linux offers many types of file system. The basic features of every file system are present in all these types, but each is optimized for a different set of tasks. Most are *scalable*, however, which means that they will work just as happily on a desktop PC as on a massive cluster of computers.

Ubuntu uses the ext4 file system. This is a popular choice among distros, and nearly all home- or office-oriented distros use it. That said, people are constantly arguing about which file system is best. The principal measuring stick is performance. Your computer spends a lot of time writing and reading files, so the faster a file system is, the faster your PC will be overall (although, in reality, the hardware is of equal importance).

Note that what we're talking about here is the underlying and invisible technology of the file system. In day-to-day use, the end user won't be aware of any difference between ext4, reiserfs, or another file system technology (although when things go wrong, different tools are used to attempt repairs; their selection is automated within Ubuntu).

Here are the various types along with notes about what they offer:

- *ext4:* Understandably, and logically, this is an extension of ext3. Among other things, it features support for much larger hard disks and is also faster.

- *reiserfs:* This is another journaling file system, which claims to be faster than others and also offers better security features. It has fallen out of favor in recent years.

- *jfs:* This is a journaling file system created by IBM. It's used on industrial implementations of UNIX.

- *xfs:* This is a 64-bit journaling file system created by Silicon Graphics, Inc. (SGI) and used on its own version of UNIX as well as Linux.

- *zfs:* Another new file system technology (like ext4), its main benefit is support for huge storage systems. This is because of its 128-bit approach. It is used in the Sun Microsystems Solaris and OpenSolaris operating systems.

Drive References

Perhaps the most important differences between Linux and Windows are the following:

- The Linux file system doesn't use drive letters.
- The Linux file system uses a forward slash (/) instead of a backslash (\) in filename paths.

In other words, something like /home/john/myfile is typical in Ubuntu, as opposed to C:\Documents and Settings\John\myfile in Windows. The root of the hard disk partition is usually referred to as C:\ in Windows. In Ubuntu, it's referred to simply with a forward slash (/).

If you have more than one drive, the drives are usually combined into one file system under Linux. This is done by *mounting*, so that any additional drives appear as virtual folders under the file system. In other words, you browse the other hard disks by switching to various directories within the main file system.

■ **Note** If you're used to Mac OS X, the Ubuntu file system shouldn't come as much of a surprise, because both OS X and Ubuntu are based on UNIX and utilize similar concepts.

Names of Files

Another important difference between Ubuntu and Windows is that filenames in Ubuntu are case sensitive. This means that MyFile is distinctly different from myfile. Uppercase letters are vitally important. In Windows, filenames might appear to have uppercase letters in them, but these actually are ignored when you rename or otherwise manipulate files.

Because of this case sensitivity, you could have two separate files existing in the same place, one called MyFile and another called myfile. In fact, you could also have myFile, Myfile, MYFILE, and so on, as shown in Figure 10-8.

As with Windows, filenames can have spaces within them. This means it's possible to have file or folder names like Pictures from Disneyland or party at bob's house.jpg.

■ **Note** You might notice that some Linux old-hands avoid using spaces in filenames and use an underscore character (_) or a hyphen (-) instead. This is because it's tricky to manipulate filenames with spaces in them at the command prompt.

Unlike with Windows, filenames can include virtually any symbol, including an asterisk (*), backslash (\), question mark (?), less-than/greater-than signs (< and >), and so on. The only symbol that's prohibited is the forward slash (/), and that's because it has a special use in file paths, as described in the previous section. Be aware, however, that if you want to share files with colleagues running Windows, you should stick to Windows conventions to avoid incompatibilities and refrain from using the following symbols: \/:*?"<>|.

We have already stated that folders and files starting with a dot (".") are managed as hidden so they are not displayed in Nautilus or in the terminal window.

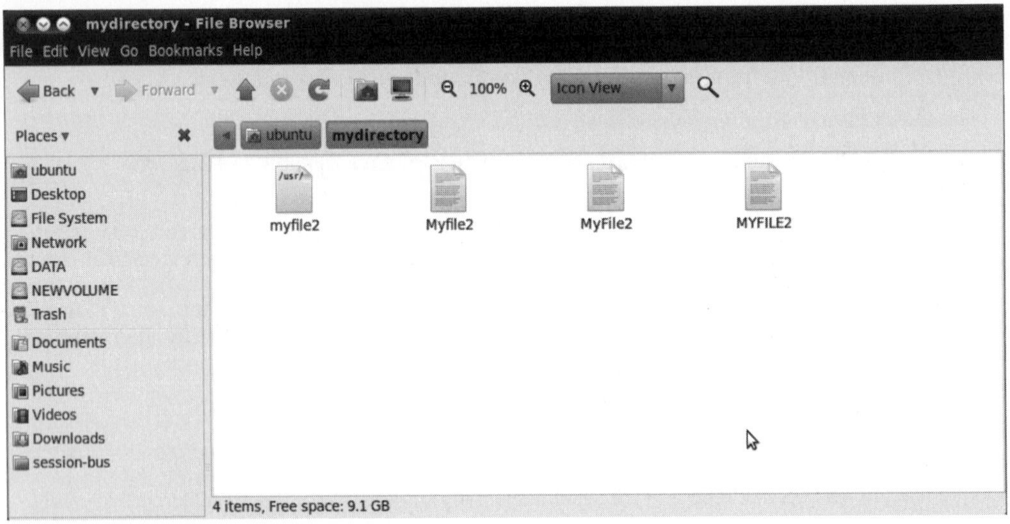

Figure 10-8. Ubuntu filenames are case sensitive, so many similar filenames can exist, differing only in which letters are capitalized.

■ **Note** If you try to copy a file with illegal symbols in its name to a Windows machine across a network, Ubuntu simply won't let you, and will report an Invalid Parameters error. In our experience, it *will* let you copy a file with illegal symbols in its name to a Windows partition, however. This results in the file being inaccessible from within Windows, so be careful!

Real Files and Virtual Files

Linux sees virtually everything as a series of files. This might sound absurd and certainly requires further explanation.

Let's start with the example of plugging in a piece of hardware. Whenever you attach something to a USB port, the Linux kernel finds it, sees whether it can make the hardware work, and if everything checks out okay, it usually makes the hardware available as a file under the /dev directory on your hard disk (dev is short for *devices*). Figure 10-9 shows an example of a /dev directory.

The file created in the /dev directory is not a real file, of course. It's a file system shortcut plumbed through to the input and output components of the hardware you've just attached.

■ **Note** As a user, you're not expected to delve into the /dev directory and deal with this hardware directly. Most of the time, you'll use various software packages that will access the hardware for you or use special BASH commands or GUI programs to make the hardware available in a more accessible way for day-to-day use.

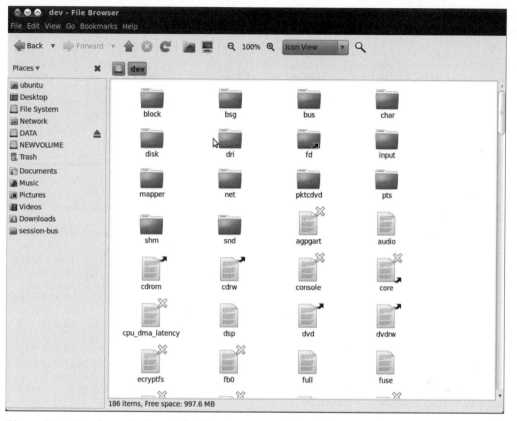

Figure 10-9. Hardware devices under Linux are accessed as if they were files and can be found in the /dev folder.

Here's another example. Say you're working in an office and want to connect to a central file server. To do this under Linux, you must *mount* the files that the server offers, making it a part of the Ubuntu file system. We discuss how this is done in the "Mounting" section later in this chapter.

■ **Note** Bear in mind that, in most cases, Ubuntu takes care of mounting automatically, as discussed later in this chapter. For example, when you try to connect to a shared folder by clicking Places ➤ Network Servers, Ubuntu automatically handles the mounting of the shared folder.

After the network server is mounted, it is treated exactly like a directory on your hard disk. You can copy files to and from it, just as you would normally, using the same tools as you use for dealing with any other files. In fact, less-knowledgeable users won't even be aware that they're accessing something that isn't located on their PC's hard disk (or, technically speaking, within their Ubuntu partition and file system). By treating everything as a file, Linux makes system administration easier. To probe and test your hardware, for example, you can use the same tools you use to manipulate files.

Working with Disks and Volumes

So far you've learned how to work with Nautilus and what the file system is. This is what is known as the *logical* side of data – but there is a *physical* side as well, that is composed by the disks and removable media attached to your computer on which the file system rests. Without disks, there could be no file system, no directories, and no files. But it is not enough to attach the disk or plug in the removable media; you need also to make it available to the OS through an operation called *mounting*.

Mounting Volumes

Described in technical terms, *mounting* is the practice of making a file system available under Linux. Whereas Windows uses drive letters to make other file systems available in Windows Explorer, Linux integrates the new file system within the root file system, usually by making the contents appear whenever a particular directory is accessed.

The mounted file system could be a partition on your hard disk, a CD-ROM, a network server, or many other things.

Mounting drives might seem a strange concept, but it makes everything much simpler than it might be otherwise. For example, after a drive is mounted, you don't need to use any special commands or software to access its contents. You can use the same programs and tools that you use to access all of your other files. Mounting creates a level playing field on which everything is equal and therefore can be accessed quickly and efficiently.

Most of the time, external storage devices are mounted automatically by the GNOME desktop software used under Ubuntu; a GNOME background service runs constantly and watches for the user attaching any storage devices to the PC. If this occurs, the external storage device is *automounted* by the GNOME desktop, usually in a folder named after the device's label within the /media directory (in other words, a USB memory stick with the label KINGSTON will be mounted at /media/KINGSTON). An entry appears on the Places menu, and an icon for the device appears on the desktop, pointing to the *mount point* (the directory used to mount the device).

In the case of mounting network storage, such as those accessed by clicking Places ➤ Network, a system called gvfs-fuse mounts the devices. Upon being mounted, these also appear on the Places menu and are given a desktop icon, but you can access them from Nautilus by browsing the hidden .gvfs directory within your /home directory. Should you access shared storage on Bluetooth hardware devices, these will also appear within the .gvfs directory.

Note that the contents of the mounted file system are made available in a virtual way. The files are *not* literally copied into the directory. The directory is merely a conduit that allows you to read the mounted file system contents.

There aren't any special commands used to work with drives that have been mounted. File managers such as Nautilus have no trouble browsing their contents.

■ **Note** The root file system is itself mounted automatically during bootup, shortly after the kernel has started and has all your hardware up and running. If you look within the special file /etc/fstab, used to tell Ubuntu Linux which partitions to mount, you'll see that it too has its own entry, as does the swap partition. Every file system that Linux uses must be mounted at some point.

Viewing Disk and Volume Information

Because Ubuntu organizes all files and folders in a single hierarchy, it is often easy to forget that you might have more than one disk attached, and that they can be of different types. It is hard to tell the physical layout of your data just by using Nautilus. You might even forget you have available space in one of your disks that is just not partitioned, because unpartitioned space is just not shown in Nautilus.

So when the time comes for doing some administration on your disks, you must use a different tool from Nautilus. Fortunately, and as you might already have guessed, Ubuntu includes such a tool: the Disk Utility, available at the System ➤ Administration menu. You can take a first look at it by examining Figure 10-10. Don't be scared!

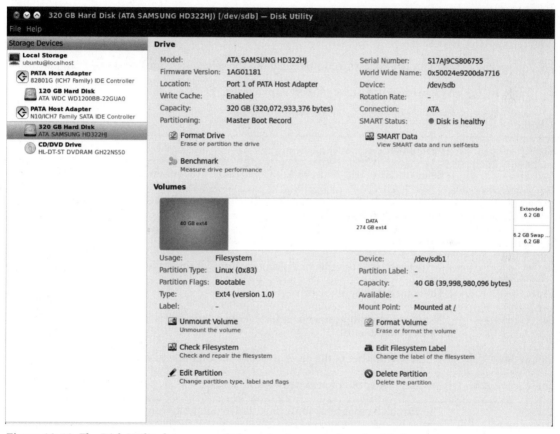

Figure 10-10. *The Disk Utility lets you see disks and volumes and work with them.*

By using the Disk Utility, you will be able to view your disks from a different angle. If Nautilus shows you the logical distribution of files and folders within a hierarchy starting at the root directory ("/"), the Disk Utility displays the physical disks where your information is actually stored. The file system hierarchy does not stand by itself; it is stored on disks, on which there are partitions, mounted in a mount point. You can use this tool to view such disks and create partitions. You will also be able to perform advanced tasks such as checking file system health.

The left pane of the Disk Utility window is named Storage Devices and is where the disks are listed. At the top is the Local Storage container, namely your computer. You can also connect to another computer by using the File ➤ Connect to Server… option, in which case the list of disks displayed will correspond to the remote computer.

The second level of entries corresponds to each of your disk controllers. It tells you how your disks are connected to your computer. Whether they are IDE or USB drives, they will be grouped under the controller they are attached to.

The third level corresponds to the drives themselves. If you select a disk, the details of the disk and its partitions will be displayed in the main pane.

As was shown in Figure 10-10, the main pane is divided into two sections: the Drive section above and the Volumes sections below. Each of those has information about the selected drive or volume and actions you can execute on it.

Managing Disks

The top section of the main pane shows information about the selected disk and tasks you can perform on it.

Table 10-4 gives you a reference of the properties of a drive.

Table 10-4. Drive Properties

Name	Description
Model	Refers to the model of the disk, as specified by the manufacturer.
Firmware Version	The level of the firmware installed. The firmware is a special program that instructs the hardware itself how to work.
Location	Controller and port to which the drive is attached.
Write Cache	Write cache is a function of disks that improves the drive write performance.
Capacity	The total capacity of the drive.
Partitioning	The type of partition scheme selected when the drive is formatted. The default is Master Boot Record.
Serial Number	The serial number of the drive, as set by the manufacturer.
World Wide Name	An unique identifier for some types of drives.
Device	The virtual file that represents the drive in the file system. The first portion will always be /dev. The second part will depend on the type of drive and the amount of disks in your system.
Rotation Rate	The speed at which the disk rotates.
Connection	The type of connections.
SMART Status	SMART is a diagnostic mechanism (you can view SMART Data by pressing the button with that name). SMART Status should be healthy if everything is okay.

On a disk, the main operation you can perform is to format it. To do it will ERASE ALL DATA CONTAINED IN THE DISK (and this cannot be emphasized enough) and make its space available to create new volumes. Please be very careful when formatting a disk. This operation is IRREVERSIBLE, so there's no way to recover the information after it.

If you are sure nonetheless that you want to format a disk, select the disk from the navigation pane and click the Format Drive button shown in the Drive section of the main pane. Leave the default selection for now and click Format.

Managing Volumes

A disk is graphically shown as a big block in the Volumes section. When you format a drive, all space is labeled Free, meaning that it is available to create volumes.

A drive without volumes is of little or no use. You cannot store files directly on the disk, nor create folders. So you need to create volumes before you do anything else. To create a volume, just select any space labeled as Free and click the Create Partition button. You will be prompted with a dialog box asking you the size, the type, and the name of the new volume. For now, you should select the Ext4 type. Click Create.

Once you have created your volume, you can:

Mount Filesystem: This will make the volume available for use, by default in the /media directory.

Unmount Volume: When you unmount a volume, its data is not actually lost, but it is only made unavailable. Mount the volume again and see that the files are still there! This command is especially useful for removable drives which need to be unmounted before physically extracting them from the PC. If you're currently browsing the mounted directory, you'll need to leave it before you can unmount it. The same is true of all kinds of access to the mounted directory. If you're browsing the mounted drive with Nautilus, or if a piece of software is accessing it, you won't be able to unmount it until you've quit the program and closed the Nautilus window (or browsed to a different part of the file system).

Format Volume: This operation erases all the information in your volume (not on your entire disk!).

Check Filesystem: Verifies its integrity. The volume must be unmounted.

Edit Filesystem Label: If you haven't changed the default when creating the volume, it will be called New Volume, and this is hardly a descriptive name. By default the mount point—that is, the folder at which the volume will be made available—is /media/LABEL. For example, a volume named NEWVOLUME will be mounted at /media/NEWVOLUME.

Edit Partition: You can mark the volume as bootable, for example.

Delete Partition: Use when you no longer need the partition. This erases all your data in the volume but, unlike formatting it, it will mark the space as Free instead of making it available again.

Advanced File Operations

Running Ubuntu on your PC may mark you as more adventurous than the majority of Windows users, but it's likely that you'll need to access Windows files on a regular basis. If you've chosen to dual-boot with Windows, you might want to grab files from the Windows partition on your own hard disk. If your PC is part of a network, you might want to access files on a Windows-based server or workstation on which a shared folder has been created. You may simply work with others who send you Windows files via e-mail.

> ■ **Note** Accessing shared printers attached to Windows computers is explained in Chapter 7, in the "Configuring a Windows/SMB Shared Printer" section.

Working with Files in Windows Partitions

If you've chosen to dual-boot Ubuntu with Windows on the same hard disk, Ubuntu allows you to access your Windows partition. An icon for it should appear on the Places menu, where it will be identified by its size (for example, if the Windows partition is 100GB in size, the icon will read 100GB Media). Selecting this should show your Windows partition contents, although you'll need to type your password when prompted in order to mount it.

After the partition has been made available, an icon for it will appear on the desktop, and it will be listed as a shortcut on the left of any file-browsing window.

> ■ **Note** You can write to or edit files in an NTFS partition. However, be aware that you could easily destroy your Windows partition, because on Ubuntu all Windows files (even the system-critical files) can be overwritten without warning. On the positive side, this feature allows you to easily recover your files from Windows if it has crashed.

Accessing Networked Files

The easiest way to access shared folders on Windows workstations or servers over a network is to click Places ➤ Network. This starts Nautilus, which attempts to search for Windows machines on your local network, just as with Network Neighborhood and My Network Places on the various versions of Windows.

If you've ever used the network-browsing services under Windows, you might already know how unreliable they can be—some computers simply don't appear in the list, others appear eventually after a wait, and others appear but then prove to be mysteriously inaccessible.

A far quicker and more reliable method of accessing a Windows shared folder is to manually specify its network name or IP address. The *network name* is simply the name of the computer that's used during networking. The *IP address* is the computer's identifying number and usually takes the form of four octets separated by periods, like this: 192.168.1.100.

You should try using the network name first when connecting to a computer. If that proves unreliable, try using the IP address instead. You can discover the network name and IP address as follows:

Network name: You can discover the network name of a Windows 7 computer by clicking Start and right-clicking Computer on the menu. Click Properties on the menu, and in the window that appears look at the value of the Computer name field. For example, the name of our test PC is WINPC. To discover the network name in Windows XP, right-click My Computer, select Properties, and then click the Computer Name tab in the window that appears. Look under the Full Computer Name heading.

IP address: To find out the IP address, open an MS-DOS command prompt. To do this in Windows XP, click Start ➤ Run, and type **cmd**. In Windows Vista or 7, click the Start button and type **cmd** into the Start Search text box. Type **ipconfig** at the prompt. Then, in XP, look for the line that reads *IP*

Address and note the details. In Windows Vista or 7, look for the line that reads *IPv4 Address* and note the number (on our test computer, we had to scroll up the window to see the line). To access a shared folder, open a Nautilus file browser window (Places ➤ Home Folder) and then click Go ➤ Location. In the box, type the following:

```
smb://computer name/
```

Alternatively, if you want to use the IP address as shown in Figure 10-11, type the following:

```
smb://IP address/
```

Obviously, in both cases, you should replace `computer name` and `IP address` with the details you noted earlier. You may also be prompted to enter a username and/or password to access the shared folder.

To create a permanent desktop shortcut to the Windows folder, right-click a blank spot on the desktop and create a launcher. In the Command text box, enter **nautilus**, followed by the full network path to the share. You can discover this by using Nautilus to browse to the shared directory, as described previously, and then clicking the icon next to the location bar to switch to the text-mode view of the path. Then cut and paste the text into the Command box. For example, on our Ubuntu setup, we created a shortcut to the `winshare` directory on the computer `WINPC` by typing the following into the Command box:

```
nautilus smb://WINPC/winshare
```

For more information about creating desktop launchers, see Chapter 9.

When using the launcher after rebooting your Ubuntu system, you might notice that the folder takes a few seconds to appear. This is normal and merely the result of the time Ubuntu takes to log on to the computer sharing the files.

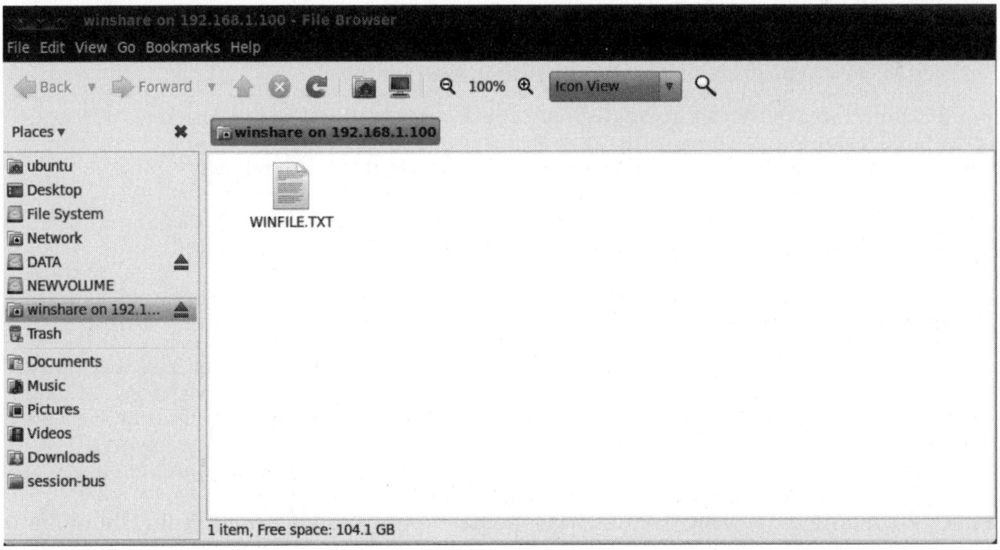

Figure 10-11. If the shared folder requires a username and/or password, you'll be invited to enter these.

Sharing a Folder from Within Ubuntu

In addition to accessing the shared files of other Windows users, you can also set up your own shared folder under Ubuntu for Windows users to access (or, indeed, other Ubuntu computers). To do this, follow these steps:

1. Right-click the folder you want to share and select Sharing Options from the menu.

2. In the dialog box that appears, put a check in the Share This Folder check box. If this is the first time you've shared a folder, a dialog box will appear telling you the sharing service software is not installed. Click the Install Service button to add it.

   You'll be prompted to type your password because some additional software needs to be installed. Following this, Ubuntu will automatically download and install the Samba file-sharing components. You'll be prompted to restart your session after it's finished (that is, log in and out again), so save any open files and restart.

3. When the desktop reappears, repeat the first step—right-click the folder you want to share, and select Sharing Options. Then put a check in Share This Folder again.

4. In the Share Name text box, type a name by which the share will be identified by other computers on the network. At the bottom of the dialog box you might see some warning messages. However, we found some of these were wrong or simply didn't make sense. This is obviously a bug, and our advice is to ignore them. If you genuinely do something wrong, like type too long a share name, Ubuntu will tell you later on.

5. By selecting the Allow Other People to Write in This Folder check box, the shared folder will be made writeable, rather than read-only.

6. At this point, you can click the Create Share check box, and the folder will then be shared. However, anybody who wants to access the folder will need to type your username and password to do so (they will be prompted automatically when they attempt to access it). By putting a check in the Guest Access check box, you can allow anybody on the network to access the shared folder in read-only mode. Then they won't need a username and password. After the shared folder is created, Windows users can access the shared folder by using My Network Places/Network Neighborhood, where it should be "detected" alongside other Windows computers.

There are caveats, however. When we tried to access a "guest access" shared folder from a Windows computer, the username and password prompt still appeared, even though none was required. To gain access, we typed gibberish into the Username field and left the Password field blank. However, we were then unable to access any other shared folders on that computer for which we needed to log in as authorized users (that is, enter the Ubuntu username/password) without logging out and then back in to the Vista computer, which serves all existing network connections.

A separate issue is privacy: by using the preceding method to share a folder within your Ubuntu login, you must reveal to others on the network your username and password details. If you don't want this to happen, you can create a *dummy account* under Ubuntu that exists solely to share folders across the network. This is possible because you don't have to be logged in to a user account for the folders to be shared—they're shared so long as the PC is up and running (even if no user is logged in). We discuss creating new user accounts in Chapter 21; you only need to create a standard nonadministrator user account. After the dummy account is set up, log in to it and create the shared folders, as described earlier. Then log out and return to the standard user account, where you can subsequently access the shared folders by clicking Go ➤ Network—your own computer's shared folders will appear alongside those on other computers on the network. You will need to provide the username and password details of the dummy account, just as if you were logging in across the network.

■ **Note** To access the shared folder from another Ubuntu computer, you might need to specify its IP address. To find out the IP address, open a GNOME Terminal window (Applications ➤ Accessories ➤ Terminal) and type **ifconfig**. Then look for the numbers alongside the `inet addr` entry.

Accessing Removable Storage Devices

Ubuntu automatically makes available any CDs or DVDs you insert into your computer, and they'll appear instantly as icons on the desktop. The same is true of any card readers or USB memory devices that you use. Alternatively, you can access the storage devices by clicking their entries on the Places menu, where entries for them will appear automatically upon attachment, or by clicking Places ➤ Computer.

Working in the Computer Window

In the Places ➤ Computer window, you'll find icons for all the storage devices attached to your computer, including the floppy disk drive if your computer has one, as shown in Figure 10-12. However, because of the way floppy disk drives work, Ubuntu isn't able to automatically detect that a floppy has been inserted. Instead, you'll need to double-click the icon, as with Windows.

■ **Note** In days of old, special tools were used to access MS-DOS floppies under Linux, and you might hear some Linux old-hands talking about them. Nowadays, you can simply use Nautilus without needing to take any special steps.

Whenever you double-click any entry in the Computer window, it opens a Nautilus file browser window. You can copy files by clicking and dragging, and right-clicking files offers virtually all the options you could need.

■ **Tip** You don't need to use Places ➤ Computer each time to access your floppy, CD, or DVD drive. These drives are mounted in the `/media` folder on your hard disk. Just browse to `/media/floppy` and `/media/cdrom`.

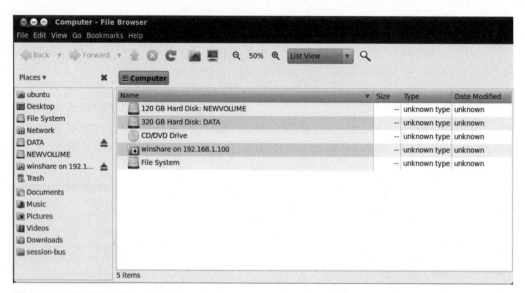

Figure 10-12. Select Places ➤ Computer to access your removable storage drive and network shares.

Ejecting Media

Ubuntu isn't quite like Windows when it comes to ejecting or unplugging removable storage devices. In practically all cases, devices must be unmounted, which is to say that you need to tell Ubuntu that you're finished with the device in question and that you're about to unplug it.

In the case of CD or DVD discs, you can simply press the Eject button on the drive itself. Ubuntu is able to detect that the disc is being ejected and automatically unmounts the drive. If the disc ever refuses to eject, right-click its icon on the desktop or within Computer and select Eject.

In the case of floppy disks, USB memory sticks, and other USB storage devices, you should always right-click the icon and select Unmount Volume. When unmounting, you may need to wait a short while for any file operations to complete on the drive. If this is the case, you'll receive a notification in the system tray. Then you can unplug or remove the device. This also applies when you're removing a memory card from a card reader—before pulling out the card from the reader, it needs to be unmounted.

■ **Note** It's necessary to close any files that were open on the device before unmounting, and even close any file browser windows that were accessing the device.

If you fail to unmount the device, Ubuntu will still believe the device is attached. This shouldn't cause too many problems, but it could crash any programs that were accessing the device. It might also mean the card isn't recognized properly when you reinsert it. In rare instances, data loss can occur.

Summary

This chapter has led you on your first steps in exploring the Linux file system. The file system is vitally important to how Linux works, and we go into it in much depth in upcoming chapters.

Here you were introduced to elementary concepts, such as where personal files are stored and the basic rules that govern what you can and cannot do with files. You also looked at the principal method of accessing files via the GUI: the Nautilus file manager. Additionally, you learned how to run programs manually, as well as how to access any Windows partitions or files that may exist on your hard disk or across a network.

And finally, you learned how to access files in heterogeneous systems, by opening Windows partitions and sharing data over the network.

## PART 4

Working and Playing with Ubuntu

CHAPTER 11

■ ■ ■

A World of Applications

Ubuntu is a thoroughly modern operating system and, as such, includes a comprehensive selection of software for just about every day-to-day task. Regardless of whether you want to write letters, edit images, or listen to music, Ubuntu offers something for you.

This chapter introduces the software under Ubuntu that performs the tasks you might be used to under Windows. It's not a detailed guide to each piece of software. Instead, this chapter aims to get you up and running with the Ubuntu replacement as quickly as possible. The chapter gives the name of each piece of software, where you can find it on Ubuntu's menus, and a few basic facts about how to use it. In many cases, these applications are covered in far more depth later in the book.

Available Software

Table 11-1 lists various popular Windows programs alongside their Ubuntu counterparts. You'll find most of the programs listed on the Applications menu. Table 11-1 also includes a number of other mainstream alternatives, most of which aren't installed by default under Ubuntu but are available from the Ubuntu online software repositories. You might want to try these later on. As you might expect, they're all free of charge, so you have nothing to lose.

■ **Note** Table 11-1 lists only a fraction of the programs available under Linux. There are quite literally thousands of others, including some that have similar facilities as those mentioned. The programs listed here are those that work like their Windows equivalents and therefore provide an easy transition.

Table 11-1. *Ubuntu Alternatives to Windows Software*

Type of Program	Windows	Ubuntu	Alternative Choices
Word processor	Microsoft Word	OpenOffice.org Writer	AbiWord (www.abisource. com) KOffice Kword[a] (www.koffice.org/kword)
Spreadsheet	Microsoft Excel	OpenOffice.org Calc	Gnumeric (www.gnome.org/projects/gnumeric) KOffice KSpread (www.koffice.org/kspread)
Presentations	Microsoft PowerPoint	OpenOffice.org Impress	KOffice Kpresenter (www.koffice.org/kpresenter)
Drawing (vector art)	Adobe Illustrator	OpenOffice.org Draw	Inkscape (www.inkscape.org) KOffice Karbon 14 (www. koffice .org/karbon)
Database	Microsoft Access	OpenOffice.org Base[b]	Knoda (www.knoda.org)
Web page creation	Microsoft FrontPage	OpenOffice.org Writer	KompoZer (http://kompozer.net/) Amaya (www.w3.org/Amaya)
E-mail	Microsoft Outlook	Evolution ———————	Mozilla Thunderbird (www.mozilla.com) KMail (http://kontact.kde.org/kmail)
Contacts manager/ calendar	Microsoft Outlook	Evolution	Kontact (www.kontact.kde.org)
Web browser	Microsoft Internet Explorer	Mozilla Firefox	Konqueror (www.konqueror.org) Chromium (www.google.com/chrome) Midori (www.twotoasts.de) Opera (www.opera.com)[c]
CD/DVD burning	Nero	Brasero	K3b (www.k3b.org)
MP3 player	Winamp	Rhythmbox	Aqualung (http://aqualung.factorial .hu) Banshee (http://banshee-project.org)

Type of Program	Windows	Ubuntu	Alternative Choices
CD player/ripper	Windows Media Player	Sound Juicer	Grip (http://nostatic.org/grip)
Movie/DVD player	Windows Media Player	Totem media player	VLC (www.videolan.org) MPlayer (www.mplayerhq.hu/homepage)
Photo Editor	Adobe Photoshop	F-Spot	GIMP, Shotwell
Image editor	Adobe Photoshop	GIMP	KOffice Krita (www.koffice.org/krita)
Video editor	Premiere Elements	PiTiVi	OpenShot, Kdenlive (www.kdenlive.org)
Zip files	WinZip	File Roller	Rar, Unrar, KArchiver (http://pagesperso-orange.fr/coquelle/karchiver)
MS-DOS prompt	cmd.exe/ command.exe	GNOME Terminal	Xterm (www.x.org)[d]
Calculator	Calc	Calculator	Too many to mention!
Text editor/ viewer	Notepad	Gedit	Kate (www.kate-editor.org)
Desktop games	Minesweeper/ Solitaire	Mines/AisleRiot Solitaire	Too many to mention!

[a] Some of the applications here are based on KDE. When using the standard Ubuntu GNOME desktop, you will have to install the core KDE libraries in order to use these. Installing software via Ubuntu Software Center should ensure that these issues are taken care of.

[b] Base isn't installed by default but is easily installed via the openoffice.org-base package. This database tool is tightly integrated with the rest of the OpenOffice.org suite.

[c] Opera is a proprietary product, rather than open source; however, it is free of charge.

[d] Xterm is part of the X.org package, so it is installed by default under Ubuntu. To use it, type **xterm** in a GNOME Terminal window. See Chapter 9 to learn how to create a permanent desktop launcher for Xterm.

LINUX HAS IT ALL

The Ubuntu software archives contain thousands of programs to cover just about every task you might want to accomplish on your computer. Diversity is vitally important within the Linux world. For example, rather than just one e-mail program, you'll find many available. They compete with each other in a gentle way, and it's up to you which one you settle down with and use.

Part of the fun of using Linux is exploring what's available. Of course, the added bonus is that virtually all this software is free of charge, so you can simply download, install, and play around. If you don't like a program, just remove it from your system. However, don't forget to revisit the program's home page after a few months; chances are the program will have been expanded and improved in that short period, and it might be better at meeting your needs.

A Quick Start with Common Ubuntu Programs

The remainder of this chapter outlines a handful of the programs listed in Table 11-1. Our goal is to give you a head start in using each program and point out where most of the main functions can be found. You'll find more details about some of them later in this book.

Keep in mind that Ubuntu doesn't aim to be an exact clone of other operating systems. Some of the programs will work in a similar way to what you're used to, but that's not true of all of them. Because of this, it's easy to get frustrated early on when programs don't seem to work quite how you want or respond in strange ways. Some programs might hide functions in what seem like illogical places compared with their counterparts on another OS. Some patience is required, but it will eventually pay off as you get used to Ubuntu.

Word Processing: OpenOffice.org Writer

OpenOffice.org is an entire office suite for Linux that was built from the ground up to compete with Microsoft Office. Because of this, you'll find that much of the functionality of Microsoft Office is replicated in OpenOffice.org, and the look and feel are also similar to pre-2007 releases of Office. The major difference is that OpenOffice.org is open source and free of charge.

OpenOffice.org Writer (Applications ➤ Office ➤ OpenOffice.org Word Processor), shown in Figure 11-1, is the word processor component. As with Microsoft Word, it's fully WYSIWYG (What You See Is What You Get), so you can quickly format text and paragraphs. This means the program can be used for quite sophisticated desktop publishing, and pictures can be easily inserted (via the Insert menu).

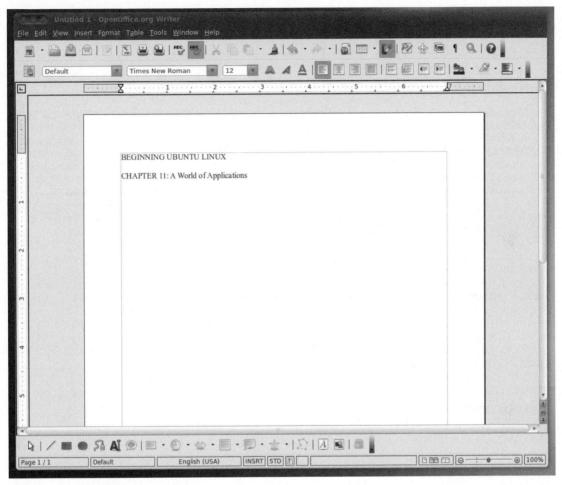

Figure 11-1. *OpenOffice.org Writer*

Writer's toolbars provide quick access to the formatting tools, as well as to other common functions. The vast majority of menu options match those found in Word. Right-clicking the text itself also offers quick access to text-formatting tools.

A number of higher-level functions are provided, such as mail merge and spell-checking, (found on the Tools menu). You can perform spell-checking on the fly, with incorrect words appearing underlined in red as you type.

As with all OpenOffice.org packages, Writer is mostly compatible with Microsoft Office files, so you can save and open .doc and .docx files. Just click File ➤ Save As, and click the arrow alongside File Type to choose a document format. The only exception is password-protected Word files, which cannot be opened. You can also export documents as PDF files (by choosing File ➤ Export As PDF), so they can be read on any computer that has Adobe Acrobat Reader installed.

■ **Note** OpenOffice.org is covered in more detail in Chapter 13.

Spreadsheet: OpenOffice.org Calc

As with most of the packages that form the OpenOffice.org suite, Calc (Applications ➤ Office ➤ OpenOffice.org Spreadsheet) does a good impersonation of its proprietary counterpart, Microsoft Excel, both in terms of powerful features and the look and feel, as you can see in Figure 11-2. However, it has only limited support for Excel's Visual Basic for Applications (VBA) macros at present. Instead, Calc and other OpenOffice.org programs use their own macro language, called OpenOffice.org Basic (for more information, see http://development.openoffice.org).

Calc has a vast number of mathematical functions. To see a list, choose Insert ➤ Function. The list on the left side of the dialog box includes a brief explanation of each function to help you get started. Just as with Excel, you can access the functions via the toolbar (by clicking the Function Wizard button) or you can enter them directly into cells by typing an equal sign and then the formula code. Calc is intelligent enough to realize when formula cells have been moved and recalculate accordingly. It will even attempt to calculate formulas automatically and can work out what you mean if you type something like **sales + expenses** as a formula.

As you would expect, Calc also provides automated charting and graphing tools (under Insert ➤ Chart). In Figure 11-2, you can see an example of a simple chart created automatically by the charting tool.

You can format cells by using the main toolbar buttons, or automatically apply user-defined styles (choose Format ➤ Styles and Formatting).

■ **Tip** In all the OpenOffice.org applications, you can hover the mouse cursor over each button for one second to see a tooltip showing what it does.

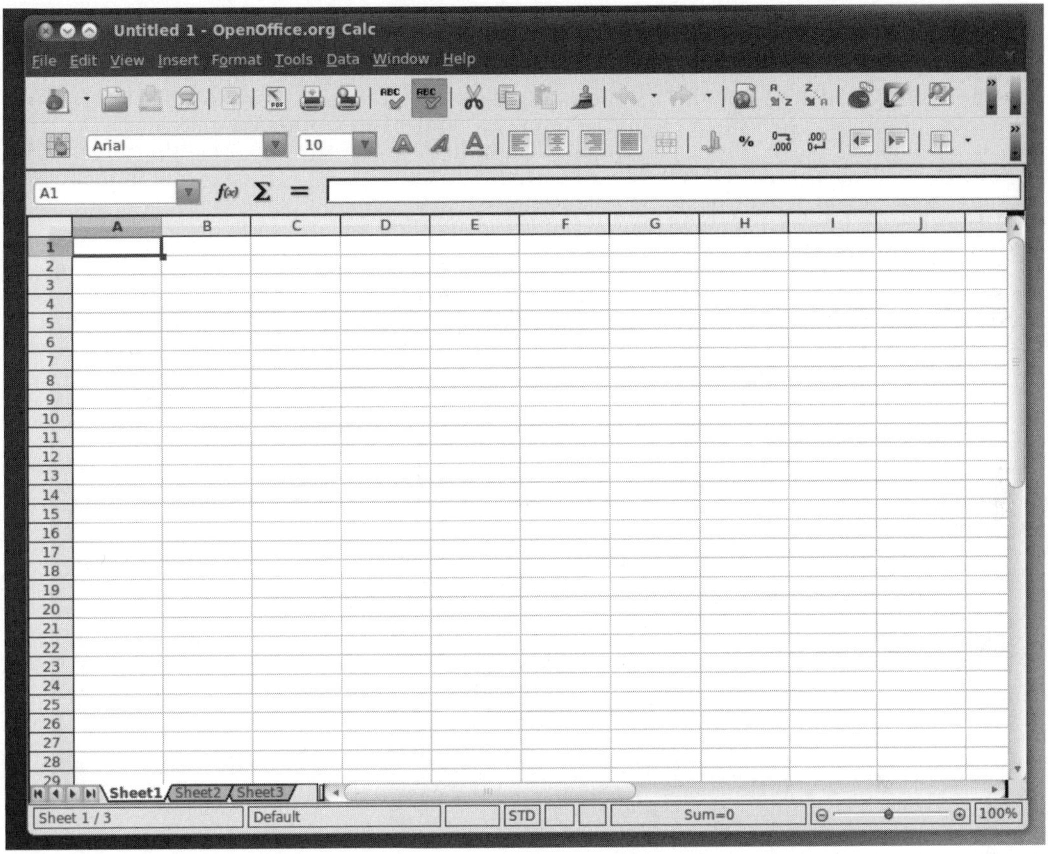

Figure 11-2. OpenOffice.org Calc

If you're a business user, you'll be pleased to hear that you can import databases to perform serious number crunching. Use Insert ➤ Link to External Data to get the data, and then employ the tools on the Data and Tools menu to manipulate it.

As with all OpenOffice.org programs, compatibility with its Microsoft counterpart—Excel files in this case—is pretty good. You can also open other common data file formats, such as comma-separated values (CSV) and Lotus 1-2-3 files.

OpenOffice.org Calc is covered in more detail in Chapter 13.

Presentations: OpenOffice.org Impress

Anyone who has used PowerPoint will immediately feel at home with Impress, OpenOffice.org's presentation package (Applications ➤ Office ➤ OpenOffice.org Presentation), shown in Figure 11-3. Impress duplicates most of the common features found in PowerPoint, with a helping of OpenOffice.org-specific extras.

The program works via templates into which you enter your data. Starting the program causes the Presentation Wizard to appear. This wizard guides you through selecting a style of presentation fitting the job you have in mind. At this point, you can even select the type of transition effects you want between the various slides.

After the wizard has finished, you can choose from the usual Normal and Outline view modes (available from the View menu, or by clicking the tabs in the main work area). Outline mode lets you enter your thoughts quickly, and Normal mode lets you type straight onto presentation slides.

You can format text by highlighting it and right-clicking it, by using the Text Formatting toolbar that appears whenever you click inside a text box, or by selecting an entry on the Format menu. Impress also features a healthy selection of drawing tools, so you can create quite complex diagrams. These are available on the Drawing toolbar along the bottom of the screen. You can also easily insert pictures, other graphics, and sound effects.

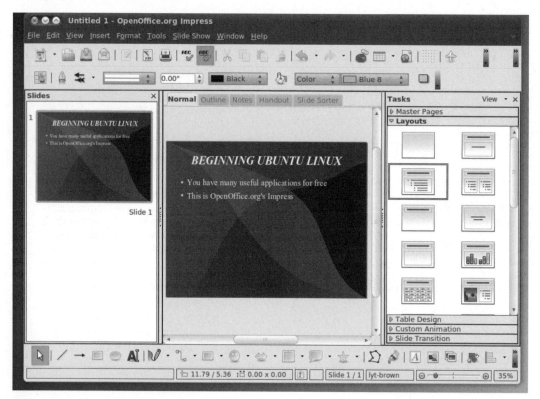

Figure 11-3. OpenOffice.org Impress

You can open and edit existing PowerPoint (`.ppt`) files and, as with all OpenOffice.org packages, save your presentation as a PDF file. Impress also lets you export your presentation as a Macromedia Flash file (`.swf`). This means that anyone with a browser and Macromedia's Flash plug-in can view the file, either online or via e-mail. Simply click File ➤ Export, and then choose Macromedia Flash (SWF) from the File Format list.

Along with slide presentations, Impress also lets you produce handouts to support your work. OpenOffice.org Impress is covered in more detail in Chapter 13.

Database: OpenOffice.org Base

Base, shown in Figure 11-4, allows you to create relational databases by using a built-in database engine, as well as interface with external databases. Base is not installed by default, so you will need to install the `openoffice.org-base` package by using Applications ➤ Ubuntu Software Center. Then you can access it by clicking Applications ➤ Office ➤ OpenOffice.org Database.

Base is very similar to Microsoft Access in look and feel, although it lacks some of Access's high-end functions. For most database uses, it should prove perfectly adequate. If you know the fundamentals of database technology, you shouldn't have any trouble getting started with Base immediately. This is made even easier than you might expect, because when the program starts, a wizard guides you through the creation of a simple database.

As with Access, Base is designed on the principles of tables of data, forms by which the data is input or accessed, and queries and reports by which the data can be examined and output. Once again, wizards are available to walk you through the creation of each of these, or you can dive straight in and edit each by hand by selecting the relevant option.

Each field in the table can be of various types, including several different integer and text types, as well as binary and Boolean values. Forms can contain a variety of controls, ranging from simple text boxes to radio buttons and scrolling lists, all of which can make data entry easier. Reports can feature a variety of text formatting and can also rely on queries to manipulate the data. The queries themselves can feature many functions and filters in order to sort data down to the finest detail.

You learn more about Base in Chapter 13.

Figure 11-4. *OpenOffice.org Base*

E-Mail/Personal Information Manager: Evolution

Evolution is a little like Microsoft Outlook in that, in addition to being an e-mail client, it can also keep track of your appointments and contacts. You can start Evolution by clicking Applications ➤ Office ➤ Evolution Mail and Calendar.

Before using the program, you need to set it up with your mail server settings, as detailed in Chapter 14. Evolution is compatible with POP/SMTP, IMAP, Novell GroupWise, Hula, Microsoft Exchange, and a handful of UNIX mail formats rarely used nowadays.

After the program is up and running, as shown in Figure 11-5, you can create a new message by clicking the New button on the toolbar. To reply to any e-mail, simply select it in the list and then click the Reply or Reply To All button, depending on whether you want to reply to the sender or to all the recipients of the message.

To switch to Contacts view, click the relevant button on the bottom left. If you reply to anyone via e-mail, they're automatically added to this Contacts list. You can also add entries manually by either right-clicking someone's address in an open e-mail or right-clicking in a blank space in the Contacts view. Clicking the Calendars view shows a day-and-month diary. To add an appointment, simply select the day and then double-click the time you want the appointment to start. You can opt to set an alarm when creating the appointment, so that you're reminded of it when it's scheduled.

Finally, by clicking the Tasks and Memos buttons, you can create a to-do list and jot down quick notes, respectively. To add a task, click the bar at the top of the list. After an entry has been created, you can put a check in its box to mark it as completed. Completed tasks are marked with a strikethrough, so you can see at a glance what you still need to do. To add a memo, click the bar at the top of the memo list and simply type what you want to remember.

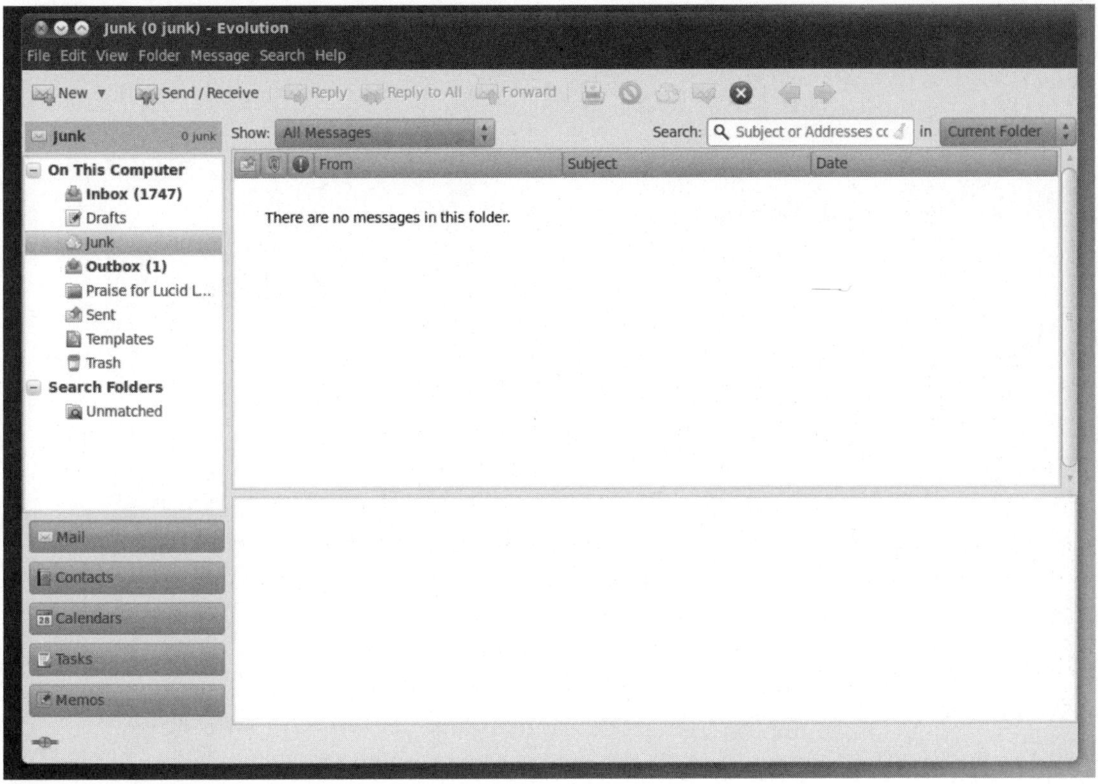

Figure 11-5. Evolution

Web Browser: Firefox

You might already know of Mozilla Firefox under Windows, where it has firmly established itself as the alternative browser of choice. The good news is that the Linux version of Firefox is nearly identical to its Windows counterpart. Start it by choosing Applications ➤ Internet ➤ Firefox Web Browser.

When the program starts, as shown in Figure 11-6, you can type an address into the URL bar to visit a web site. If you want to add a site to your bookmarks list, click Bookmarks ➤ Bookmark This Page. Alternatively, you can press Ctrl+D.

Searching is easy within Firefox. You use the search bar at the top right of the window. By default, Firefox uses Google for searches. To choose from other search engines, click the small down arrow on the left side of the search box. You can even enter your own choice of site if your favorite isn't already in the list—click Manage Search Engines and then click the Get More Search Engines link in the dialog box that appears.

Firefox popularized the principle of tabbed browsing, which means you can have more than one site open at once. To open a new tab, press Ctrl+T. You can move between the tabs by clicking them.

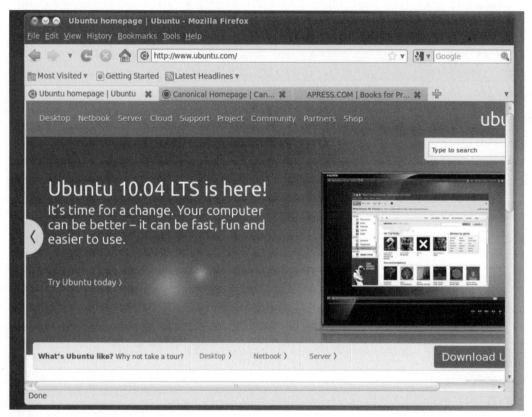

Figure 11-6. Mozilla Firefox

■ **Tip** When Firefox starts, tabs aren't activated. If you would like to keep tabs in view all the time, click Edit ➤ Preferences, click the Tabs button, and then put a check alongside Always Show the Tab Bar.

Firefox is compatible with most of the same add-ons (extensions) that you might have used under the Windows version of the browser. You can download new add-ons from `https://addons.mozilla.org`, or click Tools ➤ Add Ons and select the Get Add-ons icon. In addition, Firefox under Ubuntu can work with Flash animations and multimedia content; the relevant software (including the Flash Player) is installed on demand the first time it's needed. See the instructions in Chapter 17 to learn more.

Audio Playback: Rhythmbox

Ubuntu's multimedia software is uncomplicated and effective. It can play back the majority of audio files, as long as it's properly configured, which is to say after additional software has been installed. We describe how to set up this software in Chapter 16 and if you're thinking of playing audio files on your computer, you may want to read that chapter immediately.

Rhythmbox plays audio files on your computer's hard disk, as well as audio CDs, and it can be started by clicking Applications ➤ Sound & Video ➤ Rhythmbox Music Player. Figure 11-7 shows it in action.

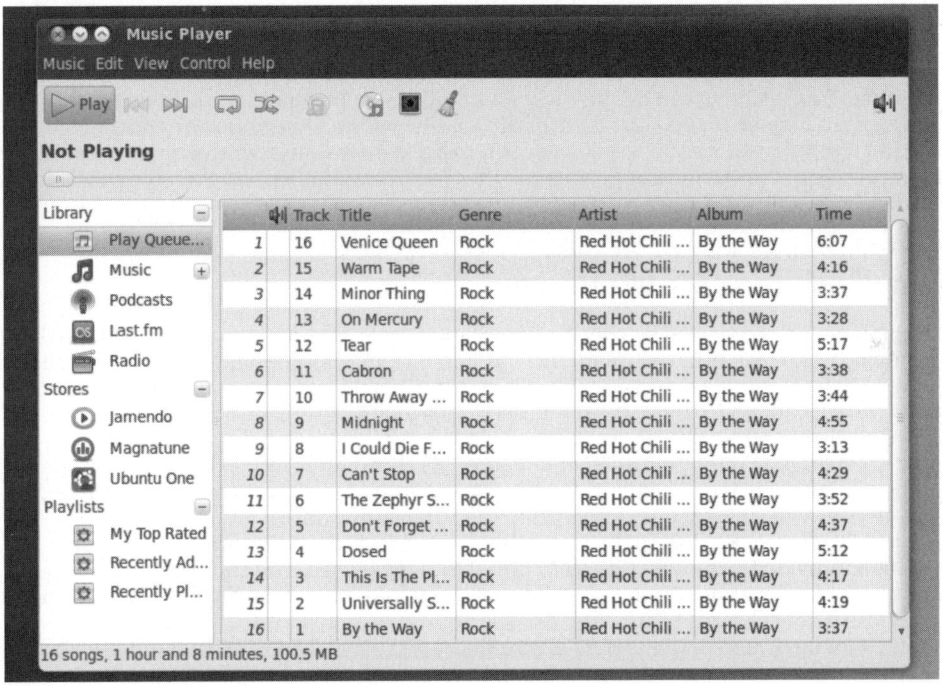

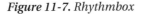

Figure 11-7. Rhythmbox

When you run Rhythmbox for the first time, it's a good idea to configure it to find and then catalog your music collection. You might be used to this kind of functionality with other applications like iTunes, and you can do it by clicking Music ➤ Import Folder. After the initial file cataloging has taken place, whenever Rhythmbox runs you will find your tracks listed by artist or name, providing they have the relevant tag information embedded in them (such as ID3 tags in MP3 music). Ensure that the Music link in the list at the left of the program window is selected. If you already have a large established collection, you can also set Rhythmbox to index that by clicking Edit ➤ Preferences and looking under the Music tab. Next to the Library Location section, click the Browse button and navigate to the folder containing your music. Click the Watch My Library for New Files option to have the software automatically index your collection.

■ **Note** Unlike iTunes, Rhythmbox can't play Digital Rights Management (DRM)-protected files, including standard tracks bought through the iTunes Music Store. iTunes, Amazon.com, and others offer music not encumbered with DRM, and these, as well as music you've ripped from CDs, will play perfectly.

To start playing a music track, double-click it in the list. To make the player smaller so that it doesn't dominate the screen, click View ➤ Small Display.

When an audio CD is inserted, you're asked whether you want to open it with Rhythmbox. Assuming you do, you'll find it listed on the left of the program window under the Devices heading. It is identified by its name because the name of the CD and the track listing are automatically looked up in online databases. To rip the tracks to your own personal music collection, just right-click the CD icon and click Extract to Library. Note that, unless you have specifically added MP3 support, Rhythmbox will rip tracks to Ogg format. This is similar to MP3 in quality, but otherwise incompatible. Choosing an audio format is covered in Chapter 16. You can control the volume within Rhythmbox by clicking the volume icon at the top right of the program window, or you can use the volume control applet, which is located at the top-right side of the Ubuntu Desktop, near the clock. Simply click and then drag the slider to adjust the volume.

Movie Playback: Totem Movie Player

Totem movie player, which can be started by clicking Applications ➤ Sound & Video ➤ Movie Player, is able to handle the majority of video files you might own, as long as some additional software is installed. Totem can also play back DVD movies, which, again, requires the installation of software. We cover setting up this software in Chapters 16 and 17 if you intend to play back video files and DVDs, these chapters should be your first port of call.

Like Rhythmbox, Totem is an uncomplicated application. As shown in Figure 11-8, the video plays on the left side of the window. A playlist detailing movies you have queued appears on the right side. You can remove this, to give the video more room, by clicking the Sidebar button.

You can control video playback by using the play/pause, fast-forward, and rewind buttons at the bottom left. In addition, provided a compatible video format is being played, you can use the Time bar to move backward and forward within the video file. You can switch to full-screen playback by clicking View ➤ Fullscreen. To switch back, simply press the Esc key.

Provided the software described in Chapter 17 is installed, DVD playback will start automatically as soon as a disc is inserted, and you should be able to use the mouse with any onscreen menus. In addition, you can skip between chapters on the disc by using the Go menu, and also return to the DVD's main or submenu systems. To switch between the various languages on a DVD (if applicable), click Sound ➤ Languages and choose from the list.

Figure 11-8. Totem movie player

CD/DVD Burning: Brasero/Nautilus CD/DVD Creator

As soon as you insert a blank writeable disc, whether it's a CD or DVD, Ubuntu detects it and offers a handful of choices: Do Nothing, Open Folder, and Open Disc Burner.

The first option should be obvious, whereas the second option starts Nautilus's CD/DVD burning mode. This is a simple disc-burning interface where files can be dragged into the window and subsequently burned to data CD/DVD.

However, the third option—Open Disc Burner—is most useful. This activates Ubuntu's dedicated CD/DVD-burning software, Brasero, which is able to create data CD/DVDs, as well as audio and video CDs. Brasero, shown in Figure 11-9, can also copy some kinds of discs.

If you want to start Brasero manually, you'll find it on the Applications ➤ Sound & Video menu. When the Brasero interface appears, select from the list whichever kind of project you want to create. For example, to create an audio CD, click the Audio Project button. Then drag and drop your music files onto the program window and click the Burn button. Keep an eye on the meter at the bottom right. This is like a progress bar; when the green portion is full, the disc is full. Note that you can't write certain audio files, like MP3s, to CDs unless you have the relevant codecs installed. See Chapter 16 to learn more.

Using the Nautilus CD/DVD Creator is similar to using Brasero. Just drag and drop files onto the window to create shortcuts to the files. When it comes time to burn, Nautilus copies the files from their original locations. When you've finished choosing files, click the Write to Disc button. Unfortunately, you won't see a warning if the disc's capacity has been exceeded until you try to write to the disc. However, by right-clicking an empty space in the Nautilus window and selecting Properties, you can discover the total size of the files. Remember that most CDs hold 700MB, and most DVD+/-R discs hold around 4.7GB (some dual-layer discs hold twice this amount; see the DVD disc packaging for details).

■ **Tip** Most modern CD/DVD recorders utilize burn-proof technology, which helps ensure error-free disc creation. To activate this for the Nautilus CD/DVD Creator, open a terminal window (Applications ➤ Accessories ➤ Terminal) and type **gconf-editor**. When the program starts, click Edit ➤ Find, and then type **burnproof**. Make sure there's a check in Search Also in Key Names. In the search results at the bottom of the window, click the first result (/apps/nautilus-cd-burner/burnproof) and make sure there's a check in burnproof at the top right of the window. Then close the configuration editor.

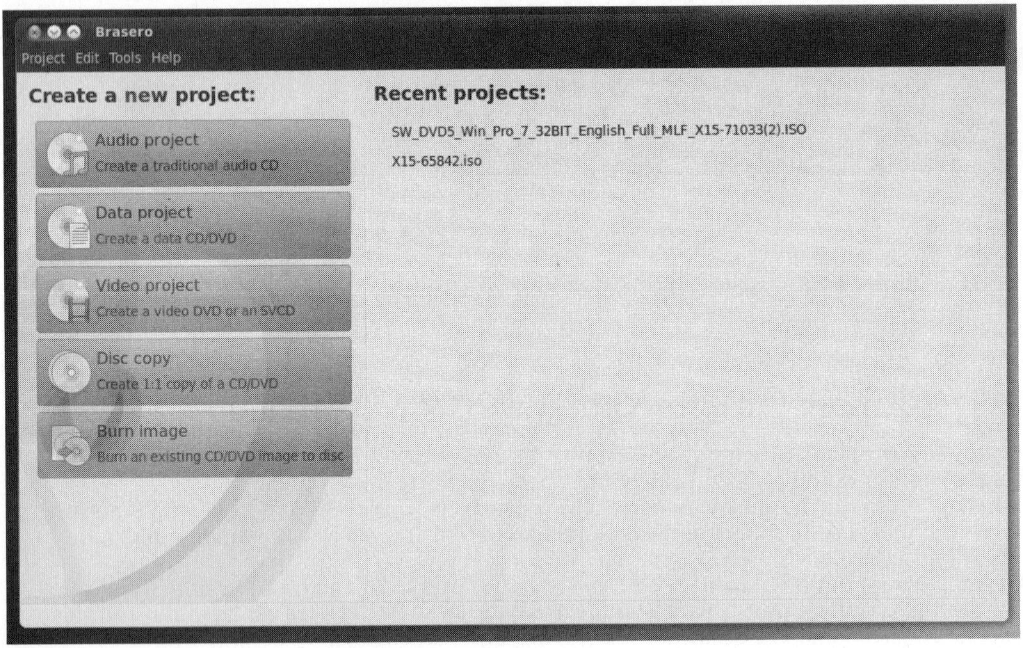

Figure 11-9. Nautilus CD/DVD Creator and Brasero

Photo Editing: F-Spot and GIMP

Ubuntu offers photo-editing tools on par with professional products like Adobe Photoshop. It's certainly more than powerful enough for tweaking digital camera snapshots.

F-Spot is covered in depth in Chapter 18. In this section we give you a brief introduction to GIMP, which has to be installed with Ubuntu Software Center because it's no longer a default application.

To start GIMP, choose Applications ➤ Graphics ➤ GIMP Image Editor. After the program is running, you'll notice that its main program component is a large toolbar on the left side of the screen. On the right are certain floating palettes, while in the middle is the main image-editing program window. This can be maximized to fill the Desktop, and this is a good idea if you want to make serious use of GIMP.

To open a picture, choose File ➤ Open and select your image from the hard disk. After an image file is opened, you can manipulate it by using the tools on the toolbar (which are similar to those found in other image editors). On the bottom half of the main program window are the settings for each tool, which can be altered, usually via click-and-drag sliders.

To apply filters or other corrective changes, right-click anywhere on the image to bring up a context menu with a variety of options. For example, simple tools to improve brightness and contrast can be found on the Colors submenu, as shown in Figure 11-10.

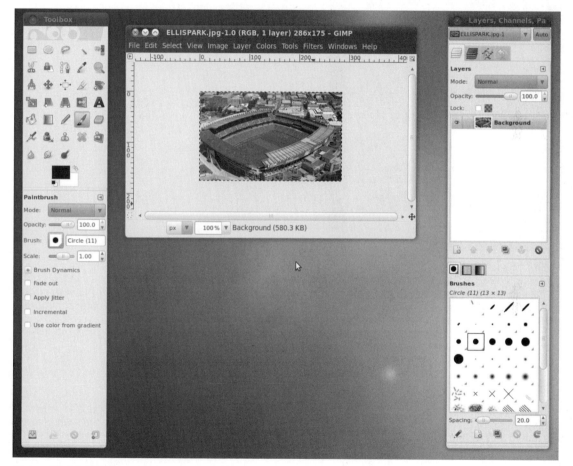

Figure 11-10. GIMP

Other Handy Applications

Many additional applications might prove useful on a day-to-day basis. Here we review some of the more common ones.

Calculator

The GNOME Calculator (also known as Gcalctool) can be found on the Applications ➤ Accessories menu. In its default mode, shown in Figure 11-11, it shouldn't present any challenges to anyone who has ever used a real-life calculator.

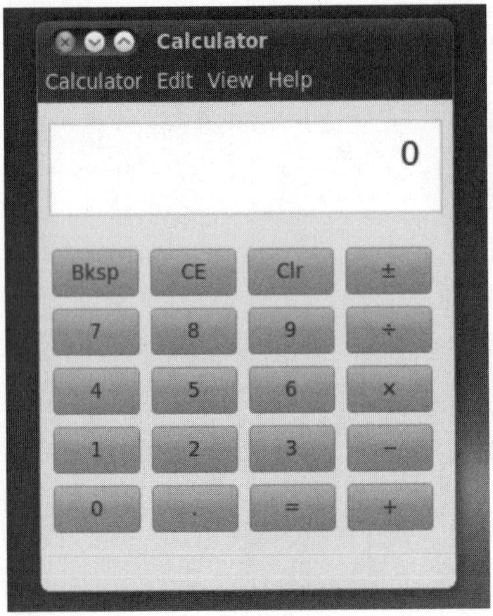

Figure 11-11. *GNOME Calculator*

Calculator also has other modes that you can switch into by using the View menu. Perhaps the three most useful modes for general use are Advanced, Financial, and Scientific. All offer calculator functions relevant to their settings. The Advanced mode is simply a more complicated version of the basic Calculator. It can store numbers in several memory locations, for example, and can also carry out less-common calculations, such as square roots and reciprocals.

Archive Manager

Archive Manager (also known as File Roller), shown in Figure 11-12, is Ubuntu's archive tool. It's the default program that opens whenever you double-click .zip files (or .tar, .gz, or .bzip2 files, which are the native archive file formats under Linux).

To extract files from an archive, select them (hold down the Ctrl key to select more than one file) and then click the Extract button on the toolbar.

To create an archive on the fly, select files or folders in a Nautilus file browser window, right-click the selection, and select Create Archive. Give the archive a name, and the archive will be created. To add new files to an existing archive, double-click an archive file and then drag and drop files into the Archive Manager window. When you've finished, simply close the Archive Manager window.

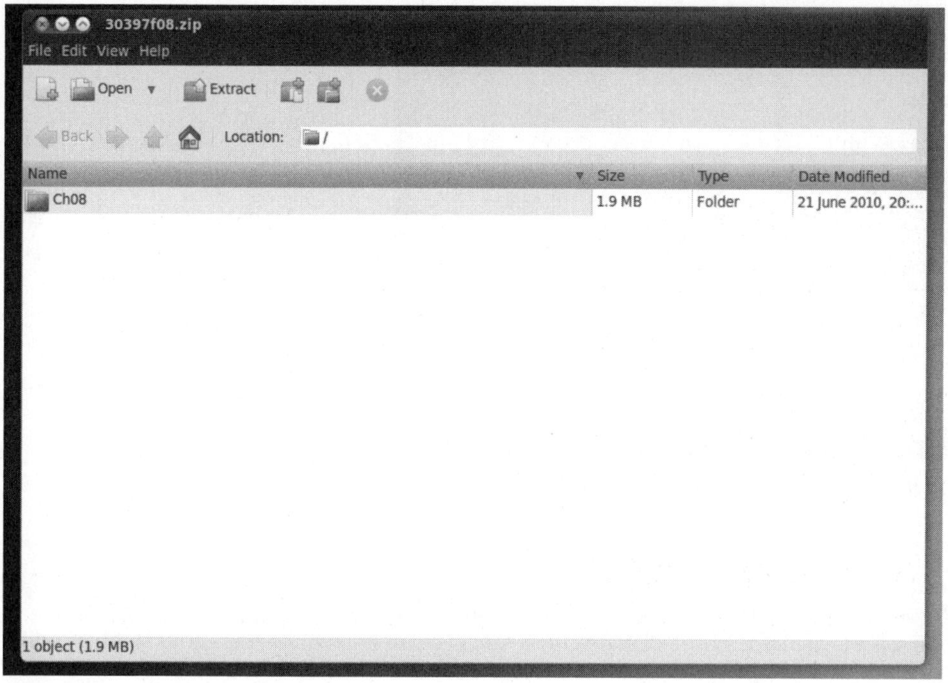

Figure 11-12. Archive Manager

Dictionary

You can use the Dictionary tool to look up the definitions of words in the *Collaborative International Dictionary of English*. This dictionary is based on a 1913 edition of *Webster's Revised Unabridged Dictionary*, but with some additional modern definitions. The Dictionary tool is useful for quick lookups, although if you want a precise and modern definition of a word, you might consider using a more contemporary source.

You'll find the Dictionary program on the Applications ➤ Office menu. Type the word in the Look Up text box at the top of the window, and its definition will appear in the area below, as shown in Figure 11-13. As soon as you start typing, the program will begin to look up the word in the dictionary, and this can cause a momentary delay before the letters appear on your screen.

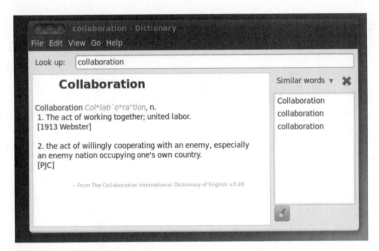

Figure 11-13. Dictionary

Empathy Instant Messaging Client

Empathy is the instant messaging software provided with Ubuntu. Unlike most other messaging programs, Empathy isn't exclusive to one chat protocol. You can use it to connect to GTalk, Jabber, MSN, AOL/ICQ, Yahoo!, Facebook Chat, and many other services. The program can be found on the Applications ➤ Internet menu.

Details for setting up Empathy are in Chapter 14. After the program is up and running, you can chat with any of your buddies by double-clicking their icon, as shown in Figure 11-14.

The rest of the program can be administered by right-clicking the notification area icon that appears when the program starts. For example, you can change your status or sign off from there. You can also use the Me menu, explained more thoroughly in Chapter 15, to change the status of all your Chat accounts at once.

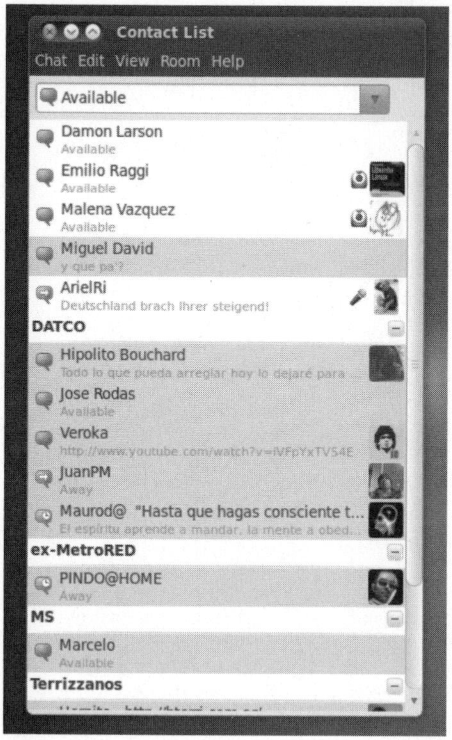

Figure 11-14. Empathy

Ekiga

Ekiga provides Internet telephony (known as Voice over IP, or VoIP) via the SIP and H.323 protocols. It also provides video conferencing, and is compatible with all major features specified within SIP and H.323, such as holding, forwarding, and transferring calls. Ekiga can be found on the Applications ➤ Internet menu.

To activate the camera mode for a video conference, click the webcam icon on the left side of the window. To text chat, click the top icon on the left side of the window. When the program starts, it walks you through setup via a wizard. Simply answer the questions with your details. After the program is up and running, as shown in Figure 11-15, type the URL of the person you would like to call into the address bar and click Call.

Note that Ekiga is not compatible with proprietary VoIP software, such as Skype. To learn how to install Skype under Ubuntu, see Chapter 14.

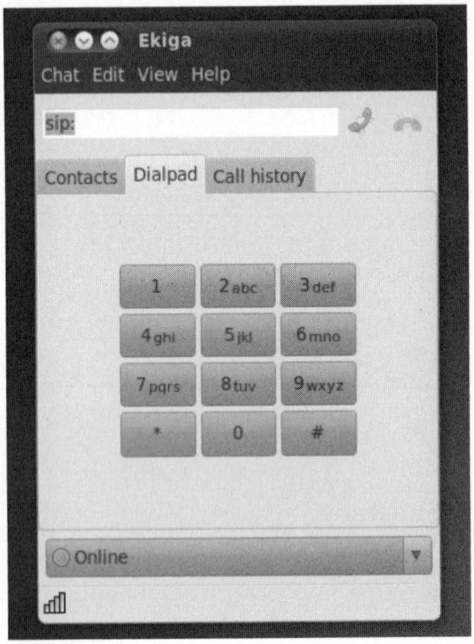

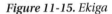

Figure 11-15. Ekiga

Games

Ubuntu comes with a great selection of simple games, including Mines, shown in Figure 11-16. The equivalent of the Windows Minesweeper game, Mines can be found on the Applications ➤ Games menu. The rules are identical, too: on each grid are several hidden mines, and it's your job to locate them. After you've clicked one square at random, you'll see a series of empty squares and several with numbers in them. Those with numbers indicate that a bomb is near. Your job is to deduce where the bombs are and then mark them by right-clicking them. You have to do this as quickly as possible because you're being timed.

To change the grid size, click Settings ➤ Preferences. Your choices are Small, Medium, Large, and Custom.

There are of course a lot of games to play within Ubuntu. We cover the subject in more depth in Chapter 19.

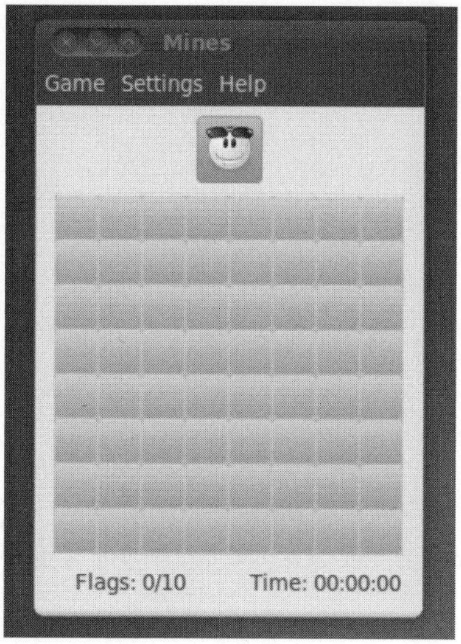

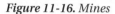

Figure 11-16. Mines

Windows Applications

Although Ubuntu doesn't officially support Windows applications, the Wine project is attempting to add a degree of compatibility and is currently good enough to run many of the most common Windows applications. Wine can be installed by using Ubuntu Software Center, and then applications can be installed by using the standard Windows installer.

Although not every application will work, Wine supports quite a lot of software, including Microsoft Office XP, Spotify (shown in Figure 11-17), Photoshop 7, and even some games. See www.winehq.org for more information.

We discuss how to install Windows applications with Wine in Chapter 20.

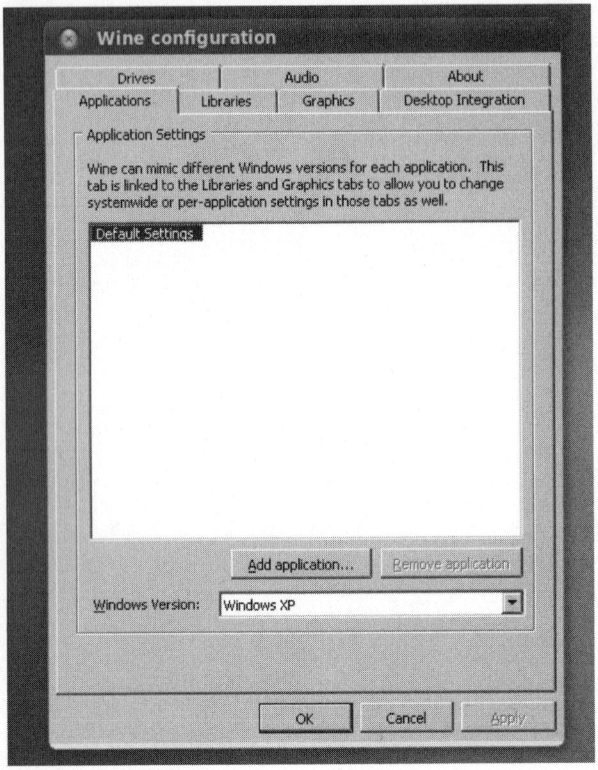

Figure 11-17. Wine

Summary

In this chapter, you've taken a look at some Ubuntu programs that provide vital functions that you might have used daily under Windows. The aim was to get you started with this software as quickly as possible by pointing out key features. You've seen how some programs mirror the look and feel of their Windows counterparts almost to the letter, whereas others resolutely strike out on their own path. It takes just a little time to become familiar with Ubuntu software, and then using these programs will become second nature.

In the next chapter, we move on to more fundamental Ubuntu tasks: manipulating files. However, once again, this is not too dissimilar from the Windows experience, which makes getting used to the system very easy.

CHAPTER 12

■ ■ ■

Working with Text Files

Windows views text files as just another file type, but to Ubuntu (and to the whole Linux family in fact), they are the very fabric of which the system is made. Configuration files and program documentation are stored as plain text. This is clearly different from Windows, where any information you're supposed to read will likely be contained in a Windows help file, a rich text format (RTF) file, or even a Microsoft Word document.

So important are text files to Linux that for a long time you could have been caught in a heated debate . . . over which text editor was the best! And while traditionally text files were managed with command-line tools and text editors, the focus of this chapter is on introducing graphical tools such as gedit. No doubt one day you will get to grips with command-line text editors such as Vim, Emacs, or even both—but right now the thing is to get you up and running with Lucid Lynx!

It's worth mentioning that text files under Linux usually don't have a file extension. Unlike with Windows or other OSs, the .txt file extension is rarely used. Sometimes a .conf extension is added to plain text configuration files, but more often text files have no extension at all.

Text: A History Lesson

Given this reliance on text and text files, it has always been very important for Linux administrators and power users alike to have powerful text-manipulation tools at their fingertips.

■ **Tip** Most program README files, along with other assorted documentation, can be found in a directory named after the program in question within the /usr/share/doc directory.

Piping and Redirecting

When you execute a command in a terminal window (which was—and for many people still is—an everyday task), output is usually produced in the form of a text stream. So the same techniques that apply to text files can be also used on this output, with a simple operation called *piping*. Piping is the process of sending the output of a command as the input for another command, usually a text-manipulation tool. That output is then manipulated as if it were a file. Powerful!

We'll illustrate this with an example using grep. grep is a tool that takes text as its input, searches and tries to match a regular expression or piece of text, and prints the lines that contain that regular expression or text. If you issue the following command in a terminal window (which you can open through Applications ➤ Accessories ➤ Terminal):

```
grep Linux operatingsystems.txt
```

grep will look for the text "Linux" in the file `operatingsystems.txt` and print only the lines that contain that text. So grep works with text files to filter lines in a file based on criteria you set.

But what if you want to do the same thing not to a text file, but to the output of a command? You use piping, which is expressed by the character |. It instructs a command to send its output to another command (and to the second command to take that as its input). For example, if you want to find a particular process—say, the process gedit (processes are listed with the ps command)—you'd type the following at the command line:

```
ps -d | grep gedit
```

This command will show you information about the gedit process (if it is running).

Another way of attaining a similar end is by means of *redirecting*—expressed with the character >. Redirecting means sending the output of a command to a text file. So the preceding task could be fulfilled by executing two commands: one for listing process information (and redirecting its output) and the other to display only the lines that pertain to a certain process:

```
ps -d > processes.txt
```

```
grep gedit processes.txt
```

STANDARD INPUT AND OUTPUT

If you've read any of the Ubuntu man pages, you might have seen references to *standard input* and *standard output*. Like many things in Linux, this sounds complicated, but is merely a long-winded way of referring to something that is relatively simple (although the terms have specific meanings to programmers). Standard input is simply the device that programs running under Ubuntu normally take input from. In other words, on the majority of desktop PCs, when you're using the command-line shell, standard input refers to the keyboard. However, it's important to note that it could also refer to the mouse or any other device on your system capable of providing input; even some software can take the role of providing standard input.

Standard output is similar. It refers to the device to which output from a command is usually sent from software. In the majority of cases at the command line, this refers to the monitor screen, although it could be any kind of output device, such as your PC's sound card and speakers.

The man page for the `cat` command says that it will "concatenate files and print on the standard output." In other words, for the majority of desktop Ubuntu installations, it will combine (concatenate) any number of files together and print the results on the screen. If you specify just one file, it will display that single file on your screen.

In addition to hardware devices, input can also come from a file containing commands, and output can also be sent to a file instead of the screen, or even sent directly to another command. This is just one reason why the command-line shell is so flexible and powerful.

As shown in Table 12-1, there are a number of text-manipulation tools that are not only useful, but that make you love them once you get to know them. The power behind grep, sed, or AWK is hardly replaced by graphical interfaces or fancy touchscreens. These tools can be imitated, but never replaced. Like many other features of Linux, they have been inherited from UNIX. Just as a reference, let's introduce you to some of these tools; should you ever become an Ubuntu guru, you'll learn how to use them in more depth and you'll become a huge fan. Guaranteed!

Table 12-1. List of Traditional Text-Manipulation Tools

Command	Description
grep	The grep command searches for regular expressions or text patterns in a text file or command output, and prints only matching lines. The name is derived from "global/regular expression/print." Use grep if you want to filter lines based on the presence of a word.
sed	Short for "stream editor," as its name implies, this transforms a text stream based on specified rules and criteria. Use sed if you want to search and replace a word in a text file or modify the output of a command.
awk	AWK, whose name derives from the family names of its creators (Alfred Aho, Peter Weinberger, and Brian Kernighan), is a powerful text-manipulation programming language. As Alfred Aho puts it, "*AWK is a language for processing files of text. A file is treated as a sequence of records, and by default each line is a record. Each line is broken up into a sequence of fields, so we can think of the first word in a line as the first field, the second word as the second field, and so on. An AWK program is of a sequence of pattern-action statements. AWK reads the input a line at a time. A line is scanned for each pattern in the program, and for each pattern that matches, the associated action is executed.*" It is used, for example, to print specified columns of a text file.
cat	This is a UNIX command used to display and concatenate text files. You can, for example, merge two text files into a third file.
head	This is used to display just the first lines of a text file.
tail	This is used to display just the last few lines of a text file.
more	This is a command-line utility used to display the contents of a text file one screen at a time.
less	This command lets you move backward in the document.
sort	This tool is used to sort the lines in a text file or stream in forward or reverse order.
diff	This tool is used to compare two text files and print the differences between them. It's useful if you are comparing, for example, two versions of the same source code.

■ **Note** The less and more commands are sometimes known as *pagers* because of their ability to let you scroll through pages of text. You might still hear them referred to as such in the wider Linux community, although the term has fallen out of use.

Bash is an incredibly capable tool when it comes to text manipulation, and some of its tool set offers modest word processing–like functionality. It's no wonder that some people live their lives working at the Bash prompt and have no need of sophisticated GUI tools!

Table 12-2 lists some more text-processing tools that you can use on the command line. Along with the commands are listed any command options needed to make them work in a useful way. Some commands rely on redirection and piping, which were explained earlier in this chapter.

■ **Note** Most text-processing tools under Bash were created for programmers, so some options might seem a little odd when you read the man pages. However, all the tools are extremely flexible and offer functions for every kind of user.

Table 12-2. Useful Text-Processing Commands

Function	Command	Notes
Spell-check	aspell -c *filename*	Highlights any questionable words within *filename*, and offers a choice of replacements, rather like a standard word processor's spell-checker. Press X if you wish to exit after spell-checking starts.
Single word spell-check	look *word*	Looks up *word* in the dictionary; if the word is displayed in the output, the word has been found. If not, the word hasn't been found. Note that this command returns loose matches—searching for test, for example, will return every word beginning with test (testing, testimony, testosterone, and so forth).
Word count	wc -w *filename*	Outputs the number of words in *filename*. Used without the -w command switch, wc outputs the number of lines, followed by the word count, followed by the number of bytes in the file.
Remove line breaks	fmt *filename* > *newfile*	Creates *newfile*, removing breaks at the ends of lines in *filename*. Double line breaks between paragraphs aren't affected. Adding the -u command switch removes instances of double spaces too.
Remove duplicate lines	uniq *filename* > *newfile*	Creates *newfile* from *filename* but removes duplicate lines.

Function	Command	Notes
Join two files	paste *file1* *file2* > *file3*	Creates *file3* by joining *file1* and *file2* side by side (effectively creating two columns of text). Each line is separated by a tab.
Word wrap	fold -sw20 *filename* >↵ *newfile*	Creates *newfile* from *filename*, wrapping lines at the specified 20 characters (increase/decrease this value for shorter/longer lines). Note that the -s switch ensures that lines don't break across words, even if this means exceeding the specified character count.
Add line numbers	nl *filename* > *newfile*	Creates *newfile* from *filename*, adding line numbers to the beginning of each line.
Sort list	sort *file1* > *file2*	Creates *file2* from *file1*, sorting its contents alphanumerically (technically, it sorts according to ASCII, so some symbols appear above numbers). For obvious reasons, this command works best on lists.

If none of this makes sense to you, it doesn't matter, because you will seldom need to use this knowledge for everyday tasks. But it is an interesting insight to know that there's more to Linux than meets the eye!

The Text Editor Wars

A variety of text editors can be used within the shell, but three stand out as being ubiquitous: ed, Vim, and Emacs. The first in that list, ed, is by far the simplest. That doesn't necessarily mean that it's simple to use or lacks powerful features, but it just doesn't match the astonishing power of both Vim and Emacs. To call Vim and Emacs simple text editors is to do them a disservice, because both are extremely powerful interactive environments. In particular, Emacs is considered practically an OS in itself, and some users of Linux treat it as their shell, executing commands and performing everyday tasks, such as reading and sending e-mail from within it. There are entire books written solely about Emacs and Vim.

■ **Tip** A fourth shell-based text editor found on many Linux systems is nano. This offers many word processor–like features that can be helpful if you've come to Linux from a Windows background.

The downside of all the power within Emacs and Vim is that both packages can be difficult to learn to use. They're considered idiosyncratic by even their most ardent fans. Both require the user to learn certain unfamiliar concepts, as well as keyboard shortcuts and commands.

Although there are debates about which text editor is better and which is best, it's generally agreed that Vim offers substantial text-editing power but isn't too all-encompassing. It's also installed by default on Ubuntu. On Ubuntu, Emacs must be installed as an optional extra. Both text editors are normally available on virtually every installation of Linux or UNIX. We'll concentrate on using Vim here.

It's important to understand that Vim is an update of a classic piece of software called vi. In fact, there are many versions and updates of vi. The original program, once supplied with UNIX, is rarely used nowadays. Vim is the most commonly used clone; Vim stands for *vi improved*. Another version is elvis (http://elvis.the-little-red-haired-girl.org). However, most people still refer to Vim and elvis as vi, even though they are entirely new pieces of software.

■ **Note** There used to be a constant flame war between advocates of vi and Emacs, as to which was better. This could be quite a vicious and desperate debate, and the text editor you used was often taken as a measure of your character! Nowadays, the battle between the two camps has softened, and the Emacs vs. vi debate is considered an entertaining cliché of Linux and UNIX use. When users declare online which text editor they prefer, they often include a smiley symbol to acknowledge the once-fevered emotions.

Working with Text Files

Fortunately, you don't need to learn how to use those tools if you don't feel like it, because Ubuntu comes equipped with a powerful, and yes, *graphical*, text-editing tool: gedit. gedit is in fact the default text editor for the GNOME desktop environment, so you can find it in other distributions of Linux such as Fedora and SUSE.

Introducing gedit

The basic interface of gedit, as you can see in Figure 12-1, is quite similar of that of Notepad, and in many regards the two applications work very much alike. But gedit has some salient features, such as plug-in support, that raise it above the crowd of simple text-editing tools like Notepad. You'll see that there are a lot of available plug-ins for gedit that will enable you to do things you can only dream of doing with other text editors. In this respect, it is a tool that honors the history of Linux; it isn't just a simple GUI replacement for Vim or Emacs.

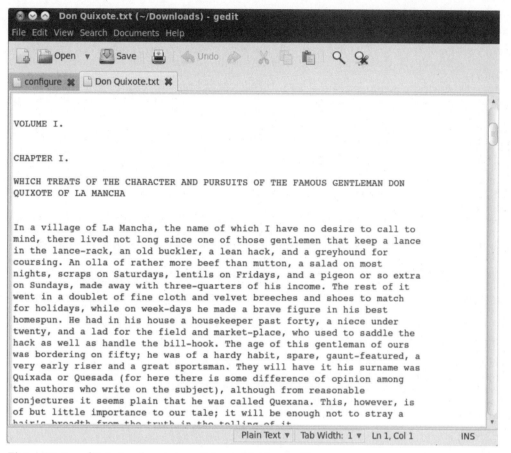

Figure 12-1. gedit: A simple yet powerful graphical text editor

One of the neat features is the ability to work with tabs, just like in your favorite web browser. Each tab is an open text file. So when you are, for example, writing a script or taking notes, you can have *Don Quixote*, the classic novel by Spanish writer Miguel de Cervantes Saavedra, open in another tab to take short breaks from work!

The gedit window has the following elements:

Menubar: The menubar gives you access to all gedit commands.

Toolbar: Using the toolbar you can perform common tasks such as creating, opening, and saving text files.

Display area: The display area is where the action is! This is where the text is actually displayed.

Statusbar: The statusbar, shown at the bottom of the window, displays information about current activity and contextual menus.

Side Pane: The side pane displays a list of open documents, and other information depending on which plug-ins are enabled. By default, the side pane is not shown. To show it, choose View ➤ Side Pane.

Bottom Pane: The bottom pane is used by some programming-related plug-ins to display its output. By default, the bottom pane is not shown. To show it, choose View ➤ Bottom Pane.

To start gedit, simply go to Applications ➤ Accessories ➤ gedit Text Editor, or right-click a text file and select "Open with gedit." It is also very likely that if you double-click a text file it will automatically be opened with gedit.

Opening gedit with those methods assumes that you will edit the file with your everyday user account. But what if you want to edit a configuration file to which only superusers have access? Normal users will only be able to open it in read-only mode, meaning that they will be unable to save the changes they make. To edit configuration files, press Alt+F2 to invoke the Run Command dialog box and type **gksu gedit** in the text field. After entering your password, gedit will open with root-like privileges.

The basic operations are simply explained. You have the buttons on the toolbar and the options in the menus. To create a new file, just click File ➤ New, and a new tab will be created with a blank document (the same happens if you click the New button on the toolbar). To open an existing file, click File ➤ Open…, and a dialog box will let you browse for the text file to open. Finally, click File ➤ Save to store the results of your work to the disk.

Once you have the desired file in your display area, you can begin to work as with any text editor. You can write new text, select chunks of text and copy it to the clipboard, or paste text from other sources. You cannot apply formatting to parts of the file, since gedit is only a text editor, not a word processing tool such as OpenOffice.org's Writer. What you save are text files, and because of this gedit is fully interoperable with Notepad.

gedit saves the history of recently opened files, which you can see by expanding the File menu or clicking the small arrow next to the Open button in the toolbar. If you click a file, it will open once again.

Working with gedit

Working with gedit is just a matter of entering text in the display area and saving the file from time to time. While simple, it does offer plenty of options that can make your tasks easier and more enjoyable.

The menubar gives you access to all the operations that can be performed with gedit. Table 12-3 lists all the options available in the menubar. You can open a test file and play a little with those options to familiarize yourself with them. You can also use the Personalize dialog box to modify the program's general behavior.

Table 12-3. The Menubar Options

Menu	Option	Notes
File	New	Creates a new text file from scratch.
	Open…	Allows you to browse your disk and open an existing text file.
	Save	Stores the changes you have made to the file on the disk. You need to have write permissions on the file to do this.
	Save As…	Allows you to save your file with a different name or to an alternate location. It's useful if you don't have write permissions on the file or if want to save several versions of the same file.
	Revert	Undoes all changes made to the document since the last time you saved it.

Menu	Option	Notes
	Print Preview	Displays how the document will be printed. As this is not a word processor, there wouldn't be much surprises here, but at least you would be able to anticipate how many pages the document has.
	Print...	Actually prints the file.
	List of files	Lists the recently opened files. Click a file to open it again.
	Close	Closes only the current document. You will be asked whether you want to save it beforehand.
	Quit	Quits gedit. All documents can be saved beforehand.
Edit	Undo	Undoes the last change.
	Redo	Redoes the last undone change.
	Cut	Copies the selected text to the clipboard and deletes it from the file.
	Copy	Copies the selected text to the clipboard without deleting it from the file.
	Paste	Inserts the contents of the clipboard into the current file.
	Delete	Deletes the selected text from the file without copying it to the clipboard.
	Select All	Selects all text in the file so you can later copy, cut, or delete it.
	Preferences	Gives you access to the Preferences dialog box (explained later in this chapter).
View	Toolbar	Shows or hides the toolbar. It is selected by default.
	Statusbar	Shows or hides the statusbar. It is selected by default.
	Side Pane	Shows or hides the side pane. It is disabled by default.
	Bottom Pane	Shows or hides the bottom pane. It is disabled and grayed out by default. Some programming functions will allow you to enable it.
	Fullscreen	Switches to full-screen mode for easier editing. Change back to normal mode by pressing F11.
	Highlight Mode	Allows you to highlight portions of the text based on the type of file you are editing. gedit is sometimes used to create or edit scripts and other types of structured text files. To make it easier, you can tell gedit what type of file you are creating, and it will automatically recognize special words and display them with different colors, thus making it easier to identify them. By default, Plain Text mode is selected.

Menu	Option	Notes
Search	Find...	Allows you to find all occurrences of a specific piece of text. It opens a dialog box in which you can enter the search term and select from several options (also available in the Replace dialog box), as follows: *Match case*: Only searches for occurrences of the string that match the text and the case of the search term. *Match entire word only*: Only finds occurrences of the string that match the entire search term. *Search backwards*: Searches backward toward the beginning of the document. *Wrap around*: Searches to one end of the document and then continues the search from the other end of the file. All occurrences of the search term within the document will be highlighted, and the cursor will be positioned at the first one found.
	Find Next	Moves the cursor to the next occurrence of the search term.
	Find Previous	Moves the cursor to the previous occurrence of the search term.
	Incremental Search...	Allows you to search as you type, as most modern browsers. As soon as you begin entering the search term, it will start creating the list of occurrences, more specific as more characters are entered. Press Ctrl+G to move the cursor to the next occurrence, and Ctrl+Shift+G to move to the previous one.
	Replace...	Allows you to search for a term and replace all or some of its occurrences.
	Clear Highlight	Removes the highlighting from all occurrences of the search term.
	Go to Line...	Moves the cursor to a specific line.
Document	*Various options*	Allows you to navigate through your open files or save them at the same time.
Help	*Various options*	Allows you to get more help.

It is worth noting that sometimes additional options will be available at each menu. It depends on which plug-ins you have enabled. Plug-ins, which are fully explained later in this chapter, extend the basic functionality of gedit, allowing you to do more. They can also extend the basic interface—for example, creating a new menu called Tools. So gedit is very extensible.

The Preferences dialog box, which you can access through the Edit menu, allows you to change how text is displayed, and to enable or disable plug-ins. There are four different tabs in the dialog box:

View: The View options allow you to configure how text is displayed.

- *Text Wrapping:* Select the "Enable text wrapping" option to have long lines of text flow into paragraphs instead of running off the edge of the text window. This avoids having to scroll horizontally. Select the "Do not split words over two lines" option to make the Text Wrapping option preserve whole words when flowing text to the next line. This makes text easier to read.

- *Line Numbers:* Select the "Display line numbers" option to display line numbers on the left side of the gedit window.

- *Current Line:* Select the "Highlight current line" option to highlight the line where the cursor is placed.

- *Right Margin:* Select the "Display right margin" option to display a vertical line that indicates the right margin. Use the "Right margin at column" spin box to specify the location of the vertical line.

- *Bracket Matching:* Select the "Highlight matching bracket" option to highlight the corresponding bracket when the cursor is positioned on a bracket character.

Editor: The Editor options allow you to configure how text is edited and to automatically backup files.

- *Tab Stops:* Use the Tab Width spin box to specify the width of the space that gedit inserts when you press the Tab key. Select the "Insert spaces instead of tabs" option to make gedit insert the specified number of spaces instead of a tab character when you press the Tab key.

- *Auto Indentation:* Select the "Enable auto indentation" option to make the next line start at the indentation level of the current line.

- *File Saving:* Select the "Create a backup copy of files before saving" option to create a backup copy of a file each time you save the file. The backup copy of the file contains a ~ at the end of the filename. Select the "Autosave files every … minutes" option to automatically save the current file at regular intervals. Use the spin box to specify how often you want to save the file.

Font & Colors Preferences: The options on this tab allow you to specify the font in which text is displayed, and the color of the text and background.

- *Font:* Select the "Use default theme font" option to use the default system font for the text in the gedit text window. The "Editor font" field displays the font that gedit uses to display text. Click the button to specify the font type, style, and size to use for text.

- *Color Scheme:* You can choose a color scheme from the list of color schemes.

Plugins: Plug-ins are very powerful features that enable you to turn on or off certain advanced features of gedit. They are configured by selecting the check box next to the plug-in name in the Active Plugins list. The complete list of default plug-ins is given in Table 12-4.

Table 12-4. *List of Default Plug-Ins*

Plug-In	What It Does	How To Use It
Change Case	Changes the case of the selected text	When enabled, the option Change Case is added to the Edit menu. Choose it to change the case of the selected text.
Devhelp Support	Displays context-sensitive help from development manuals	When enabled, you can select text and press F2 or click Tools ➤ Show API Documentation to search for that text in developer's manuals and reference material.
Document Statistics	Displays statistics about the current document and selected text	Select the option Tools ➤ Document Statistics.
External Tools	Executes external tools and sends the output to the file	You can use the default external tools available from the Tools ➤ External Tools option. For example, if you choose to run a command such as `ls -l`, the output of that command will be sent to the text file. You can also create your own external tools.
File Browser Pane	Adds a file browser to the side pane	Enable the side pane in the view panel. A folder icon will be displayed at the bottom showing a new tab with the places on your hard disk. Browse to the file you want to open and double-click it.
Insert Date/Time	Inserts the date and time into the text	Select the place where you want to insert the date and time, and click the Edit ➤ Insert Date and Time… option. A format must be selected.
Modelines	Allows you to set editing preferences for individual documents, and supports Emacs-, Kate-, and Vim-style modelines	Insert the modelines for Emacs, Kate, or Vim at the start or end of the document. Preferences set using modelines take precedence over the ones specified in the Preferences dialog.
Python Console	Transforms the bottom panel into an interactive Python console	Enable the bottom panel in the View menu.
Quick Open	Lets you open documents in your Home directory very quickly	Select the File ➤ Quick Open option.
Snippets	Allows you to store frequently used pieces of text, called *snippets*, and insert them quickly into a document	You manage snippets through the Tools ➤ Manage Snippets option. You associate a snippet with a trigger. Pulling the trigger inserts the text.

Plug-In	What It Does	How To Use It
Sort	Sorts selected lines alphabetically (based on ASCII codes)	Select the lines and click the Edit ➤ Sort… option.
Spell Checker	Allows you to search the document for spelling errors and correct them	Go to the Tools menu and either choose to check the spelling immediately or enable the automatic spell-checker. You can also set the language.
Tag	Provides a method to easily insert commonly used tags/strings into a document without having to type them	Go to View ➤ Side Pane, and select the tab with the plus (+) sign. You'll see a list of available categories for tags (e.g., HTML – Tags). Double-clicking a tag will insert it in the text.
Text Encryption	Performs encryption operations on text	Select the text to encrypt and go to Edit ➤ Encrypt… (note that you must have created an encryption key, as detailed in Chapter 8).

As you can see, gedit includes by default a lot of useful plug-ins. But what would be the use of plug-ins if they were not extensible? As you might expect, there are a lot more plug-ins available both at the official Ubuntu repositories and from alternative sources.

Additional plug-ins are available, for example, in the package gedit-plugins, which you can install by using the Ubuntu Software Center. Third-party plug-ins are available from several sources as well. You can check the page http://live.gnome.org/Gedit/Plugins for information about available plug-ins.

Comparing Multiple Files with Diffuse

Another graphical tool that can come in very handy at times is the Diffuse Merge Tool. It combines many of the functionalities already seen in command-line tools such as paste of diff. It lets you, for instance, compare line-by-line two or even three text files, and it spots the differences for you so you can merge the contents of a file into the other. It's very useful if, for example, you are comparing two versions of a program's source code—or if you're a teacher, two exams from different students.

Diffuse is not installed by default, but is easy to get. Simply open the Ubuntu Software Center and search for "Diffuse." The Diffuse Merge Tool will be the first on the list, so simply click Install and wait (for more details about software installation, see Chapter 20). The Diffuse application launcher is available from Applications ➤ Programming.

As you can see in Figure 12-2, Diffuse divides the main pane into two or three windows to enable side-by-side comparison of text files, and highlights the lines with differences.

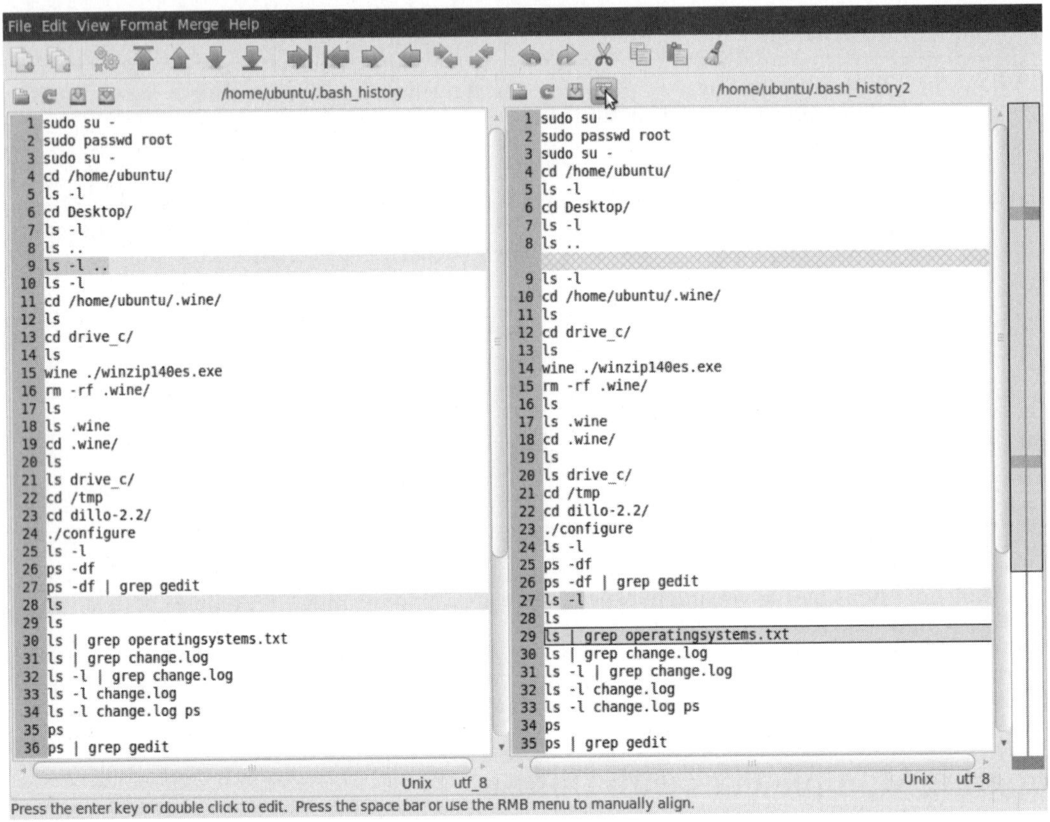

Figure 12-2. The Diffuse Merge Tool combines the power of many command-line tools.

The third element in the main pane, at the right of the documents, is the comparison summary. The summary shows all the documents, and illustrates which lines have differences (in red) and which have been manually edited (in green). You can move from one section of the documents to another simply by moving the location bar in the comparison summary.

Once you've reviewed the differences, you can choose to modify one of the files in accordance to the other. Use the buttons on the toolbar to copy text from one document to the other. The name of modified documents will be appended with an asterisk (*) at the end; this means that the file has been changed since the last save. Make sure you save your files from time to time to avoid losing your work.

Summary

In this chapter, we showed how text files can be manipulated. In many ways, the Bash shell is built around manipulating text, and we presented various tools created with this goal in mind. We then talked about how text file editors were once the most important applications for Linux users.

With Ubuntu, the need for everyday use of such tools is greatly reduced. Nonetheless, Ubuntu includes a powerful and expandable text editor: gedit. It comes out of the box with many features not found in its Notepad counterpart, and new plug-ins are added to the list all the time. In conjunction with the Diffuse Merge Tool, it covers most of your needs for text file manipulation.

## CHAPTER 13

Making the Move to OpenOffice.org

You might be willing to believe that you can get a complete operating system for no cost. You might even be able to accept that this offers everything Windows does and much more. But one stumbling block many people have is believing that a Microsoft Office–compatible office suite comes as part of the zero-cost bundle. It's a step too far. Office costs hundreds of dollars—are they expecting us to believe that there's a rival product that is free?

Well, there is, and it's called OpenOffice.org. It is a suite, meaning that it is a bundle of many applications, most of which come preinstalled with Ubuntu, as well as most other Linux distributions. This makes it the Linux office suite of choice. It's compatible with most Microsoft Office files too, and even looks similar and works in a comparable way to previous "classic" releases of Office (i.e., those prior to Office 2007), making it easy to learn. What more could you want?

Similarities to Microsoft Office

OpenOffice.org started life as a proprietary product called StarOffice, created by a German company called StarDivision. Sun Microsystems (now part of Oracle) subsequently bought StarDivision and released the source code of StarOffice in order to encourage community development. This led to the creation of the OpenOffice.org project, a collaboration between open source developers and Sun. This project has released several new versions of OpenOffice.org, and at the time of this writing, the current version is 3.2. This is the version supplied with Ubuntu 10.04.

■ **Note** Although Sun opened StarOffice's source code, it continued to sell it, along with some useful extras such as fonts, templates, and technical support. When Oracle bought Sun, StarOffice was rebranded as Oracle Open Office. To the naïve onlooker, it will seem that Oracle is beginning to charge for OpenOffice.org. But this is not so, and it cannot be, because OpenOffice.org is an open source application and a community project that's licensed under the GPL. Oracle can package it and charge for the extra functionality, but the core software will remain free.

OpenOffice.org features a word processor, a spreadsheet program, a presentation a package, a drawing tool (vector graphics), a web site creation tool, a database program, and several extras. As such, it matches Microsoft Office almost blow by blow in terms of core functionality. See Table 13-1 for a comparison of core packages.

Table 13-1. How the Office and OpenOffice.org Suites Compare

Microsoft Office	OpenOffice.org	Function
Word	Writer	Word processor
Excel	Calc	Spreadsheet
PowerPoint	Impress	Presentations
Visio	Draw[a]	Technical drawing/charting
FrontPage	Writer[b]	Web site creation
Access	Base[c]	Database
Equation Editor	Math	Formula Editor

[a] Draw is a vector graphics creation tool akin to Adobe Illustrator. Creating flowcharts or organizational diagrams is one of many things it can do. It is found on the Applications ➤ Graphics menu.

[b] Writer is used for word processing and HTML creation; when switched to Web mode, its functionality is altered appropriately.

[c] Writer and Calc can be coupled to a third-party database application such as MySQL or Firebird; however, OpenOffice.org also comes with the Base relational database. This must be installed separately—see Chapter 20.

You should find that the functionality within the packages is duplicated too, although some of the very specific features of Microsoft Office are not in OpenOffice.org. But OpenOffice.org also has its own range of such tools not yet found in Microsoft Office!

■ **Tip** One extremely useful feature provided with OpenOffice.org, but still missing from Office 2007, is the ability to output high-quality PDF files.

OpenOffice.org does have a couple of notable omissions. Perhaps the main one is that it doesn't offer a directly comparable Outlook replacement. However, as we discuss in Chapter 14, the Evolution application offers a highly capable reproduction of Outlook, with e-mail, contacts management, and calendar functions all in one location. In Ubuntu, you'll find Evolution on the Applications ➤ Office menu. Evolution isn't directly linked to OpenOffice.org (although it's possible to share some Evolution contacts data with OpenOffice.org applications), but it retains the overall Ubuntu look, feel, and way of operating.

OpenOffice.org Key Features

Key features of OpenOffice.org include the ability to export documents in Portable Document Format (PDF) across the entire suite of programs. PDF files can then be read on any computer equipped with PDF display software, such as Adobe Acrobat Reader.

In addition, OpenOffice.org features powerful accessibility features that can, for example, help those with vision disabilities use the programs more effectively. For those who are technically minded, OpenOffice.org can be extended very easily with a variety of plug-ins (see `http://extensions.services.openoffice.org`) that allow the easy creation of add-ons using many different programming languages.

Although OpenOffice.org largely mirrors the look and feel of Microsoft Office releases prior to the 2007 version (i.e., those releases of Office prior to the major interface overhaul that's found in Office 2007), it adds its own flourishes here and there. This can mean that some functions are located on different menus, for example. However, none of this poses a challenge for most users, and OpenOffice.org is generally regarded as easy to learn.

■ **Note** Studies carried out by Sun Microsystems, the corporate sponsor of OpenOffice.org, have shown that it's easier for people to switch to OpenOffice.org from an older version of Office than it is for them to move to Office 2007, which introduces radical interface changes. For more information and to learn more about similar studies, see `www.openoffice.org/product/studies.html`.

File Compatibility

In addition to providing core feature compatibility, OpenOffice.org is able to read files from Microsoft Office. A great effort has been made in version 3.2 to add compatibility for Office 2007 formats and password-protected files (i.e., `.docx`, `.xlsx`, and `.pptx` files). Nonetheless, you should always test your files, because sometimes results are less than perfect. However, improvements are being made all the time, and this is just one more reason why you should update Ubuntu frequently to ensure that you have the latest versions of the OpenOffice.org software.

Although file compatibility problems are rare for most simple to moderately complex documents, two issues occasionally crop up when opening Microsoft Office files in OpenOffice.org:

VBA compatibility: OpenOffice.org has partial support for Microsoft Office Visual Basic for Applications (VBA) macros, although work is being undertaken to strengthen this aspect. OpenOffice.org uses a similar but incompatible internal programming language. Such macros are typically used in Excel spreadsheets designed to calculate time sheets, for example. Unfortunately, you won't know whether your VBA macros will work until you give them a try in OpenOffice.org, although the macros will be preserved within the document no matter what (provided you continue to save in the original Microsoft Office format and don't, for example, save the document in an OpenOffice.org file format instead).

■ **Note** If compatibility with VBA macros is a deal breaker for you, and you've yet to install Ubuntu, you might try your documents containing VBA macros in the Windows version of OpenOffice.org. This will enable you to see how well they work in advance. You can download the Windows version from `www.openoffice.org`.

Document formatting: When you create well-polished documents and beautiful presentations, the last thing you want is to lose all your work when you move the files from one computer to another. Sadly, this is often the reality when files are shared between Microsoft Office and OpenOffice.org. Although files can be opened, some formatting may be lost, diminishing the desired visual impact. Sometimes the problem is due to lack of fonts, and we talk about this issue later in this chapter. On other occasions, when you want to distribute your own work, you could just export it as a PDF file, as shown following. Also, you should always test presentations for full compatibility without assuming they will look exactly the same in the different programs. Opening a file is just half the job!

If you find that OpenOffice.org isn't able to open an Office file saved by your colleagues, you can always suggest that they too make the switch to OpenOffice.org. They don't need to be running Ubuntu to do so. Versions are available to run on all Windows platforms, as well as the Mac, and are available from www.openoffice.org.

■ **Note** Two versions of OpenOffice.org are available for Mac OS X: the standard release, which at the time of this writing is still rather new and not fully tested, and NeoOffice, which has been adapted to run natively within Mac OS X. For more details, see www.neooffice.org.

As with the Ubuntu version, versions of OpenOffice.org available for other operating systems are entirely free of charge. Indeed, for many people who are running versions of Office they've installed from "borrowed" CDs, OpenOffice.org offers a way to come clean and avoid pirating software. For more details and to download OpenOffice.org, visit www.openoffice.org.

After your colleagues have made the switch, you can exchange files using OpenOffice.org's native format, or opt to save files in the Microsoft Office file formats (.doc, .xls, .ppt, etc.). Figure 13-1 shows the file type options available in OpenOffice.org's word processor component's Save As dialog box.

■ **Note** OpenOffice.org also supports Rich Text Format (RTF) text documents and comma-separated value (CSV) data files, which are supported by practically every office suite program ever made.

When it comes to sharing files, there's another option: saving your files in a non-Office format such as PDF or HTML. OpenOffice.org is able to export documents in both formats, and most modern PCs equipped with Adobe Acrobat or a simple web browser will be able to read them. However, although OpenOffice.org can open and edit HTML files, it can export documents only as PDF files, so this format is best reserved for files not intended for further editing.

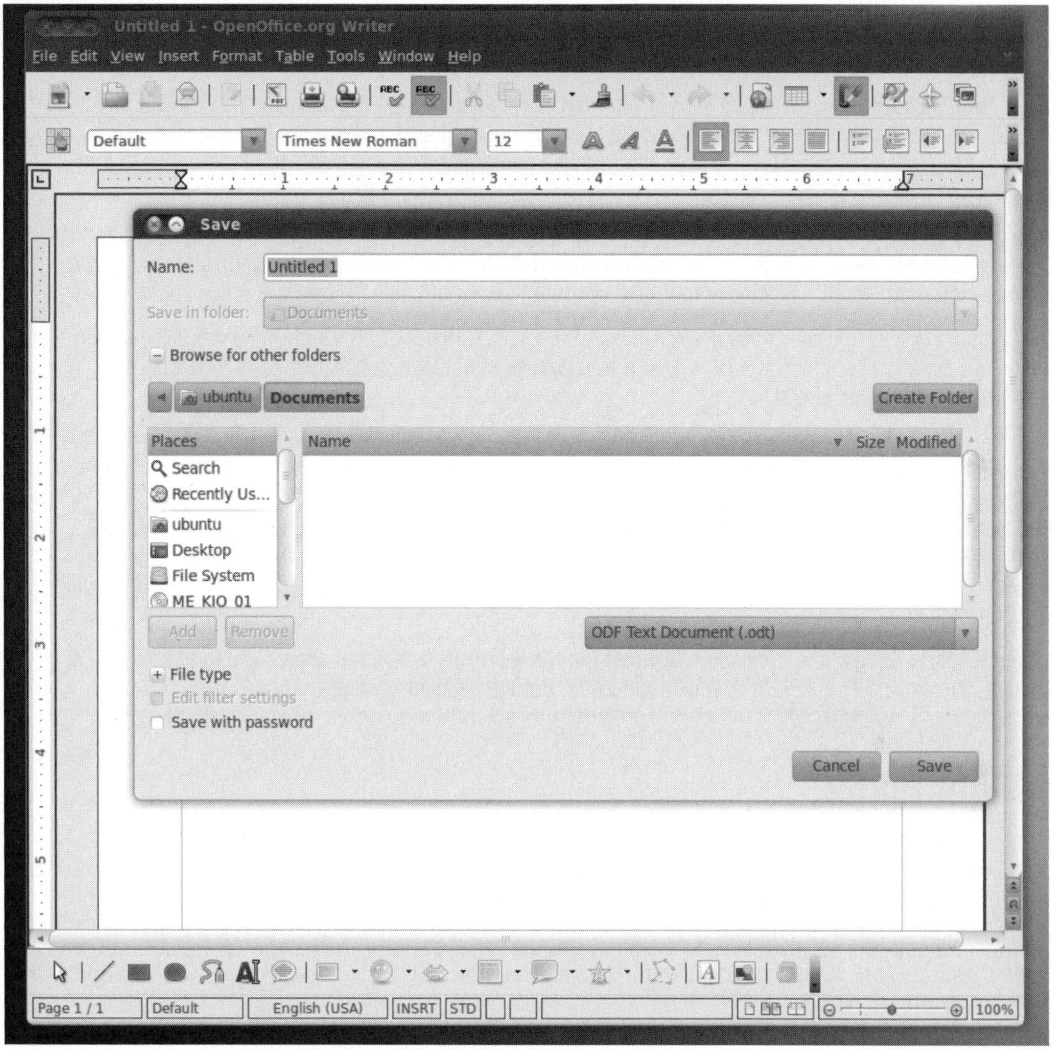

Figure 13-1. *All the OpenOffice.org components are compatible with Microsoft Office file formats.*

OPEN DOCUMENT FORMAT

One of the principles behind all open source software is the idea of open file formats. This means that if someone creates a new open source word processor, that person also makes sure that the technology behind the file format is explained, so that other people can adapt their programs to read or save in that file format.

To meet the goals of open source software, the OASIS OpenDocument Format (ODF) was created, and this is utilized in OpenOffice.org. This is a completely open and free-to-use office document file format that all software suites can adopt. The idea is that ODF will make swapping files between all office suites easy.

While earlier versions of OpenOffice.org relied on ODF 1.1, in October 2008, OpenOffice.org 3.0 adopted ODF 1.2 as its default file format. ODF 1.2 is in the process of being standardized, so in this regard OpenOffice.org is a step ahead.

There have been changes recently regarding Microsoft support for ODF files. Traditionally, Microsoft hasn't supported ODF file formats within its productivity suite, so Sun Microsystems developed a plug-in that enabled you to open ODF files with Microsoft Office. This changed with the release of Microsoft Office 2007 Service Pack 2 (SP2), in which ODF version 1.1 gained support. But since the OpenOffice.org 3.2 default file format is ODF 1.2, you may still have problems opening documents produced with OpenOffice.org in Microsoft Office. It is likely that when ODF 1.2 becomes standardized, Microsoft will add its support to its Office suite.

In the meantime, Oracle has launched a new plug-in for Microsoft Office that allows you to open ODF 1.2 files with Microsoft Office XP, 2000, 2003, and 2007, but this plug-in isn't free.

The Right Fonts

One key to compatibility with the majority of Microsoft Office files is ensuring that you have the correct fonts. This is an issue even when using Windows. It's common to open an Office document and find the formatting incorrect because you don't have the fonts used in the construction of the document.

Although most Windows systems have many fonts, most people tend to rely on a handful of core fonts, which are defaults on most Windows installations: Arial, Tahoma, Verdana, Trebuchet MS, and Times New Roman. (MS Comic Sans might also be included in that list, although it isn't often used within business documents.)

You can obtain these fonts and install them on your Ubuntu system in several ways. Here we cover two methods: copying your fonts from Windows and installing Microsoft's TrueType core fonts. The latter method is by far the easier way of undertaking this task.

■ **Tip** As an alternative to installing Microsoft fonts, you might install the Liberation fonts. These are open source fonts designed to be metrically identical to Arial, Times New Roman, and Courier. In other words, in theory at least, the letter *A* in one of the aforementioned Microsoft fonts should occupy the same space (and therefore display the same on the screen and when printed) as the letter *A* in the matching Liberation font. You can install the Liberation fonts by installing the `ttf-liberation` package. To learn about package installation, see Chapter 20.

Copying Windows Fonts

If you dual-boot Ubuntu with Windows, you can delve into your Windows partition's font folder and copy every font you have available under Windows. This method is useful if you wish to copy *all* the fonts you use under Windows, such as those installed by third-party applications. If you wish to get just Arial and Times New Roman, you might want to skip ahead to the next section.

■ **Caution** Installing Windows fonts under Ubuntu is a legal gray area. Technically speaking, there's no reason why you shouldn't be able to use the fonts under Ubuntu. Purchasing Windows as well as any software running on it should also mean you purchased a license to use the fonts, and there's no restriction on how or where you use them. But the situation is far from clear. You'd be well advised to read the Windows End User License Agreement (EULA) for more guidance. This can usually be found in the packaging for your computer.

To copy your Windows fonts, follow these steps:

1. Click the entry on the Places menu for your Windows partition, so it is mounted and its icon appears on the desktop.

2. Create a folder named `.fonts` in your Home folder. It will be used to store your personal selection of fonts.

3. In the Nautilus window displaying the Windows directories, navigate to your Windows fonts folder. The location of this varies depending on which version of Windows you're using. On our Windows Vista test computer, it was located in the `Windows/Fonts` directory, but on our Windows XP Home test machine, it was located in the `WINDOWS/Fonts` directory. Remember that case sensitivity is important under Ubuntu!

4. Still in the window displaying your Windows font directory, click View ➤ List, and then click the Type column header in the window so that the list is sorted according to file extensions. Scroll down to the list of TrueType fonts and select them all. This can be done by clicking the first, holding down Shift, and then clicking the last.

5. Click and drag all the TrueType fonts to the Nautilus window displaying your personal font directory. The fonts will be copied across and installed automatically. In some of our tests, this happened instantly, and there was no indication (such as a dialog box) that copying had happened.

6. Close any open program windows and start the programs again. You should find that your Windows fonts are now available.

Installing TrueType Core Fonts

If you don't want to undertake the font-copying maneuver, you can download and install Microsoft's TrueType core fonts. This package contains common Windows fonts, including Arial and Times New Roman.

■ **Note** These fonts were made legally available by Microsoft in 1996 for use under any operating system—for more details, see http://en.wikipedia.org/wiki/Core_fonts_for_the_Web.

Here's how it's done (note that these instructions assume that your computer is online):

1. Click Applications ➤ Ubuntu Software Center. Enter your password to continue.

2. In the Quick Search text field at the top of the program window, type **msttcorefonts**. Select Microsoft Core Fonts and click Install.

3. Close all program windows, click System ➤ Quit, and opt to log out of the system. Then log back in again. You should now find that the Windows fonts are available in all applications, including OpenOffice.org, as shown in Figure 13-2.

Figure 13-2. Vital Microsoft fonts are just a download away, courtesy of the Ubuntu Software Center.

OTHER LINUX OFFICE SOFTWARE

OpenOffice.org is widely regarded as one of the best Linux office suites, but it's not the only one. Its main competitor is KOffice. KOffice tightly integrates into the KDE desktop and mirrors much of its look and feel. It includes a word processor, a spreadsheet, a presentation package, a flowcharting tool, a database access tool, graphical tools, and much more. As with OpenOffice.org, in most cases you can load and save Microsoft Office files. For more details, see the KOffice home page at `www.koffice.org`. It's available with Ubuntu too. Just use the Synaptic Package Manager to search for and install it.

In addition, there are several open source office applications that aren't complete office suites. For example, AbiWord is considered an excellent word processor, which packs in a lot of features but keeps the user interface simple. It's partnered by Gnumeric, a spreadsheet application that is developed separately (although both aim to be integrated into the GNOME desktop environment). For more details, see `www.abisource.com` and `www.gnome.org/projects/gnumeric`, respectively. You can also find both of these programs in the Ubuntu software repositories (use the Ubuntu Software Center to search for them).

Introducing the Interface

If you've ever used an office suite such as Microsoft Office, you shouldn't find it too hard to get around in OpenOffice.org. As with Microsoft Office, OpenOffice.org relies primarily on toolbars, a main menu, and separate context-sensitive menus that appear when you right-click. In addition, OpenOffice.org provides floating palettes that offer quick access to useful functions, such as paragraph styles within Writer.

Figure 13-3 provides a quick guide to the OpenOffice.org interface, showing the following components:

Menu bar: The menus provide access to most of the OpenOffice.org functions.

Standard toolbar: This toolbar provides quick access to global operations, such as saving, opening, and printing files, as well as key functions within the program being used. The standard toolbar appears in all OpenOffice.org programs and also provides a way to activate the various floating palettes, such as the Navigator, which lets you easily move around various elements within the document.

Formatting toolbar: As its name suggests, this toolbar offers quick access to text-formatting functions, similar to the type of toolbar used in Microsoft Office applications. Clicking the Bold icon will boldface any selected text, for example. This toolbar appears in Calc, Writer, and Impress.

Ruler: The ruler lets you set tabs and alter margins and indents (within programs that use rulers).

Status bar: The status bar shows various aspects of the configuration, such as whether Insert or Overtype mode is in use. The information and options offered vary depending on which application is in use. Within Writer, for example, a slider to the right of the status bar allows the quick changing of the document's zoom level. If using Calc, you'll see a Sum area that shows the numeric total of any selected cells.

Document area: This is the main editing area.

Most of the programs rely on the standard and formatting toolbars to provide access to their functions, and some programs have additional toolbars. For example, applications such as Impress (a presentation program) and Draw (for drawing vector graphics) have a drawing toolbar, which provides quick access to tools for drawing shapes, adding lines, and creating fills (the blocks of color within shapes).

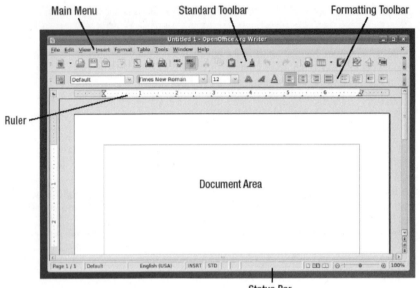

Figure 13-3. The OpenOffice.org interface has several components.

Customizing the Interface

You can select which toolbars are visible on your screen, as well as customize those that are already there. You can also add new toolbars and customize the OpenOffice.org menus. The color scheme of OpenOffice.org can be altered to your tastes, and you can also alter various trivial elements of the interface, such as the size of the icons.

Adding Functions to Toolbars

The quickest way to add icons and functions to any toolbar is to click the small arrow at the right of a toolbar and select the Visible Buttons entry on the menu that appears. This will present a list of currently visible icons and functions, along with those that might prove useful on that toolbar but are currently hidden. Any option already visible will have a check next to it.

Additionally, you can add practically any function to a toolbar, including the options from the main menus and many more than those that are ordinarily visible. Here are the steps:

1. Click the small down arrow to the right of a toolbar and select the Customize Toolbar option.

2. In the Customize dialog box, click the Add button in the Toolbar Content section to open the Add Commands dialog box, as shown in Figure 13-4.

3. Choose a category from the list on the left to see the available commands in the list on the right. The categories of functions are extremely comprehensive. For example, under the Format category, you'll find entries related to specific functions, such as increasing font sizes or setting a shadow effect behind text. Those categories are self explanatory for the most part.

4. Select the function you want to add on the right side of the Add Commands dialog box and then click the Add button.

5. After you've finished making your choices, click the Close button. You'll then see your new function in the list of icons in the Customize dialog box, under the Toolbar Content heading. The last new icon you chose will be automatically selected.

6. Click and drag up or down in the list to move the new function left or right on the toolbar itself (you'll see the toolbar update when you release the mouse button). Alternatively, you can highlight the icon and click the up and down arrows next to the list. To temporarily hide the new icon, or any other icon, remove the check from alongside it.

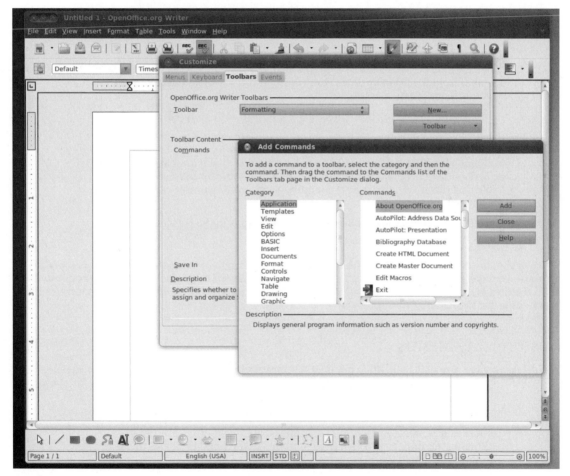

Figure 13-4. Adding a new function to the toolbar is very easy within OpenOffice.org.

Many functions that can be added are automatically given a relevant toolbar icon, but you can choose another icon for a function by selecting the icon in the list in the Customize dialog box, clicking Modify, and then selecting Change Icon. You can also use this method to change an icon that already appears on a toolbar.

■ **Note** To delete an icon from a toolbar, click the two small arrows to the right of the toolbar and then select the Customize Toolbar option. Select the icon you want to remove, click the Modify button, and choose to delete it.

Adding a New Toolbar

If you want to add your own new toolbar to offer particular functions, you'll find it easy to do. Here are the steps:

1. Click the small down arrow to the right of any toolbar and select Customize Toolbar from the list of options. Don't worry—you're not actually going to customize that particular toolbar!

2. In the Customize dialog box, click the New button at the top right.

3. Give the toolbar a name. To make the toolbar permanent, keep the default entry in the Save In field, which should read "OpenOffice.org." To have the toolbar "attach" to the currently open document so that it appears only when that document is opened, select the document's name in the Save In field. Note that this is effective only if documents are saved in native OpenOffice.org file formats.

4. Populate the new toolbar, following the instructions in the previous section.

5. After you've finished, click the OK button.

You should see your new toolbar either beneath or to the right of the main toolbars. If it is located to the right, you may have to click and drag its move handle at the left of the toolbar to reposition it so that all its features are visible. To hide the toolbar in the future, click View ➤ Toolbars, and then remove the check alongside the name of your toolbar.

Customizing Menus

You can also customize the OpenOffice.org menus. Here are the steps:

1. Choose Tools ➤ Customize from the menu bar.

2. In the Customize dialog box, select the Menus tab at the top left.

3. Choose which menu you wish to customize from the Menu drop-down list. Submenus are indicated with a pipe symbol (|). File | Send indicates the Send submenu located in the File menu, for example.

4. Select the position where you wish the new function to appear on the menu by selecting an entry in the Menu Content Entries list, and then click the Add button.

5. Add commands to the menu, as described earlier in the "Adding Functions to Toolbars" section.

The up and down arrows in the Customize dialog box enable you to alter the position of entries on the menu. You could move those items you use frequently to the top of the menu, for example.

You can remove an existing menu item by highlighting it in the Customize dialog box, clicking the Modify button, and then clicking Delete.

If you make a mistake, simply click the Reset button at the bottom right of the Customize dialog box to return the menus to their default state.

Personalizing the Look and Feel

You can alter the color scheme used in OpenOffice.org by clicking Tools ➤ Options, and then clicking the Appearance entry under the OpenOffice.org heading on the left of the dialog box that appears. Each of the programs in the OpenOffice.org suite has its own heading in the Custom Colors list. To alter a particular color setting, click the drop-down alongside that particular entry under the Color Settings heading.

To alter how toolbars appear (i.e., the size of the icons), click the View option under the OpenOffice.org heading. This preference panel also lets you set the default zoom level under the Scaling heading when starting new documents. You can also deactivate font antialiasing, which can help make some fonts look truer to life compared to printed output, although this option is one of personal preference.

Configuring OpenOffice.org Options

In addition to the wealth of customization options, OpenOffice.org offers a range of configuration options that enable you to make it work exactly how you wish (although it should be pointed out that the default configuration is fine for most users). Within an OpenOffice.org program, choose Tools ➤ Options from the menu to open the Options dialog box, as shown in Figure 13-5.

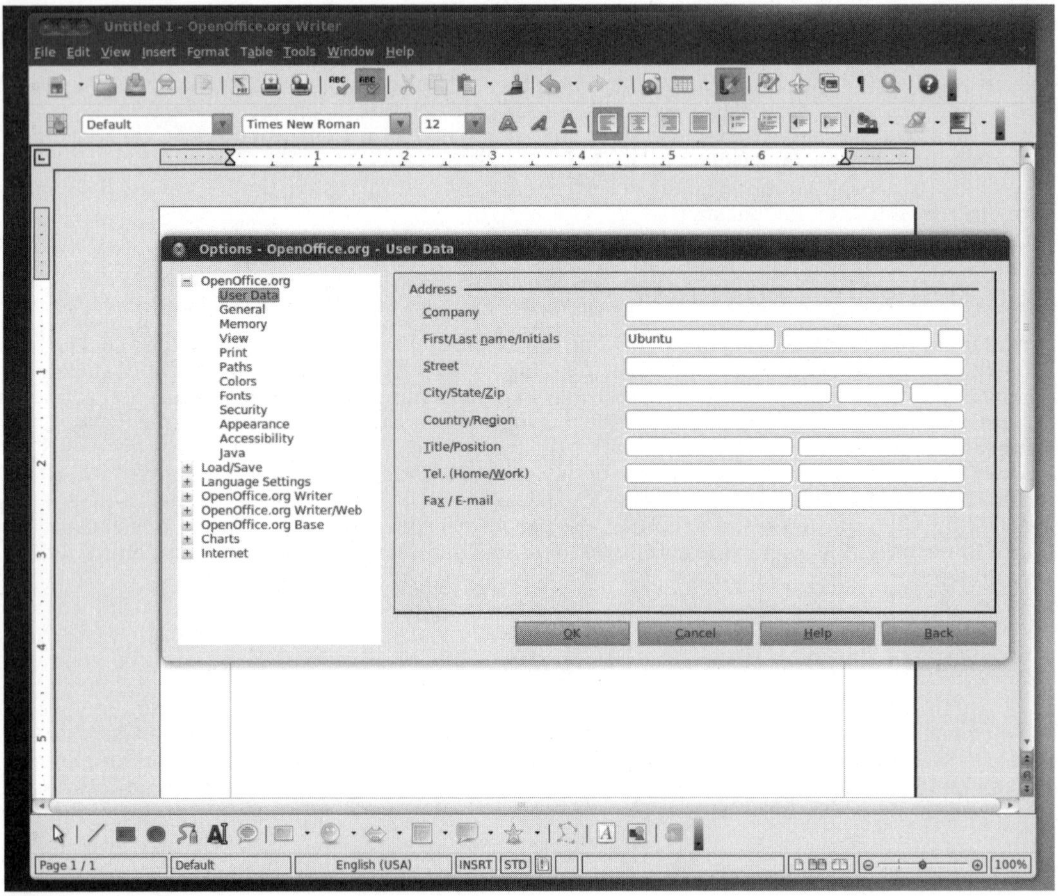

Figure 13-5. Access OpenOffice.org's main configuration options by choosing Tools ➤ Options.

Most of the configuration options offered within each program apply across the suite, but some settings are specific to each program, in which case you'll find them listed under their own heading on the left of the dialog box.

Using OpenOffice.org Core Functions

Although the various programs within OpenOffice.org are designed for very specific tasks, they all share several core functions that work in broadly similar ways. In addition, each program is able to borrow components from other programs in the suite.

Using Wizards

One of the core functions you'll find most useful when you're creating new documents is the wizard system, which you can access from the File menu. A wizard guides you through creating a new document by answering questions and following a wizard-based interface. This replaces the template-based approach within Microsoft Office, although it's worth noting that OpenOffice.org is still able to use templates.

A wizard will usually offer a variety of document styles. Some wizards will even prompt you to fill in salient details, which they will then insert into your document in the relevant areas.

Note that within some components of OpenOffice.org, such as Writer, the wizards offered on the File menu won't work unless Java Runtime Environment (JRE) software is installed. This can be done quickly and easily by closing any open OpenOffice.org applications, opening the Ubuntu Software Center (Applications ➤ Ubuntu Software Center), and installing the following programs:

- Standard Java or Java-compatible runtime (`default-jre`)

- Office productivity suite (arch-independent Java support files [`openoffice.org-java-common`])

You will need to type your password when prompted. The software will probably be in the 200MB range, so it might take a while to download. Installation is automatic; after it has finished, close the Ubuntu Software Center and log out. When you log in again, open any OpenOffice.org application to test the installation by starting a wizard.

■ **Note** In case you're wondering why this useful software isn't included by default, you can blame the fact that it's over 200MB. Put simply, it just won't fit on the Ubuntu installation CD-ROM.

Getting Help

OpenOffice.org employs a comprehensive help system, complete with automatic context-sensitive help, called the Help Agent, which will appear if the program detects you're performing a particular task. Usually, the Help Agent takes the form of a lightbulb graphic, which will appear at the bottom-right corner of the screen. If you ignore the Help Agent, it will disappear within a few seconds. Clicking it causes a help window to open. Alternatively, you can access the main searchable help file by clicking the relevant menu entry.

■ **Tip** To permanently disable the Help Agent, open any OpenOffice.org application and click Tools ➤ Options, and then select the General heading under the OpenOffice.org heading within the dialog box that appears. Remove the check from the Help Agent box on the right of the program window.

Additionally, OpenOffice.org applications have a useful "What's This?" help option that provides point-and-click help. To activate it, select the entry on the Help menu, and then hover the cursor over any interface option that you want to learn about. After a second or two, a detailed help bubble will appear, providing an explanation. To cancel it, just click anywhere.

Inserting Objects with Object Linking and Embedding

All the OpenOffice.org programs are able to use Object Linking and Embedding (OLE). This effectively means that one OpenOffice.org document can be inserted into another. For example, you might choose to insert a Calc spreadsheet into a Writer document.

The main benefit of using OLE over simply copying and pasting the data is that the OLE item (referred to as an *object*) will be updated whenever the original document is revised. In this way, you can prepare a report featuring a spreadsheet full of figures, for example, and not need to worry about updating the report when the figures change. Figure 13-6 shows an example of a spreadsheet from Calc inserted into a Writer document.

Whenever you click inside the OLE object, the user interface will change so that you can access functions specific to that object. For example, if you had inserted an Impress object into a Calc document, clicking within the object would cause the Calc interface to temporarily turn into that of Impress. Clicking outside the OLE object would restore the interface back to Calc.

You can explore OLE objects by choosing Insert ➤ Object ➤ OLE Object. This option lets you create and insert a new OLE object, as well as add one based on an existing file. To ensure that the inserted OLE object is updated when the file is, select the Link to File check box in the Insert OLE Object dialog box.

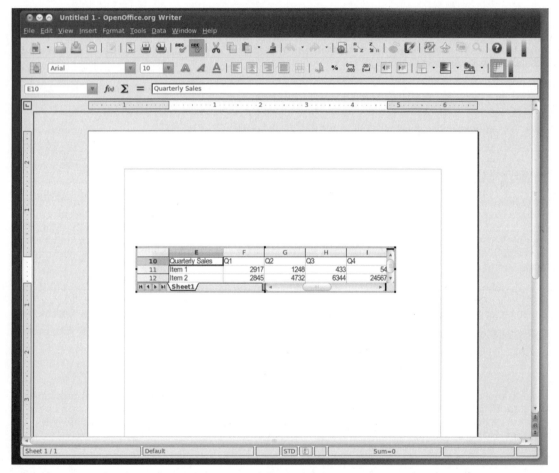

Figure 13-6. OLE lets you incorporate one OpenOffice.org document into another.

Creating Macros

OpenOffice.org employs a powerful BASIC-like programming language, which you can use to create your own functions. Although this language is called BASIC, it is several generations beyond the BASIC you might have used in the past. OpenOffice.org's BASIC is a high-level, object-oriented environment designed to appeal to programmers who wish to quickly add their own functions to the suite.

However, it's possible for any user to record a series of actions as a macro, which is then automatically turned into a simple BASIC program. This can be very useful if you wish to automate a simple, repetitive task, such as the insertion of a paragraph of text, or even something more complicated, such as searching and replacing text within a document.

To record a macro, choose Tools ➤ Macros ➤ Record Macro. After you've selected this option, any subsequent actions will be recorded. All keyboard strokes and clicks of the mouse will be captured and turned automatically into BASIC commands. To stop the recording, simply click the button on the floating toolbar. After this, you'll be invited to give the macro a name (look to the top left of the dialog box). Then click Save. You can then run your macro in the future by choosing Tools ➤ Macros ➤ Run Macro. Simply expand the My Macros and Standard entries at the top left of the dialog box, click Module1, select your macro in the list on the right, and click Run.

Saving Files

OpenOffice.org uses the OpenDocument range of file formats. The files end with an .ods, .odt, .odp, or .odb file extension, depending on whether they've been saved by Calc, Writer, Impress, or Base, respectively. The OpenDocument format is the best choice when you're saving documents that you are likely to further edit within OpenOffice.org. However, if you wish to share files with colleagues who aren't running Ubuntu, another Linux version, or OpenOffice.org under Windows or Mac OS X, the solution is to save the files as Microsoft Office files. To save in this format, just choose that option from the File Type drop-down list in the Save As dialog box. If your colleague is running an older version of OpenOffice.org or StarOffice, you can also save in those file formats.

Alternatively, you might wish to save the file in one of the other file formats offered in the File Type drop-down list. However, saving files in an alternative format might result in the loss of some document components or formatting. For example, saving a Writer document as a simple text file (.txt) will lead to the loss of all of the formatting, as well as any of the original file's embedded objects, such as pictures.

To avoid losing document components or formatting, you might choose to output your OpenOffice.org files as PDF files, which can be read by the Adobe Acrobat viewer. The benefit of this approach is that a complete facsimile of your document will be made available, with all the necessary fonts and on-screen elements included within the PDF file. The drawback is that PDF files cannot be loaded into OpenOffice.org for further editing, so you should always save an additional copy of the file in the native OpenOffice.org format. To save any file as a PDF throughout the suite, choose File ➤ Export as PDF. Then choose PDF in the File Type drop-down box, as shown in Figure 13-7.

■ **Tip** You can obtain a plug-in for OpenOffice.org that allows the opening and subsequent editing of PDF files. For more details, see http://extensions.services.openoffice.org/project/pdfimport.

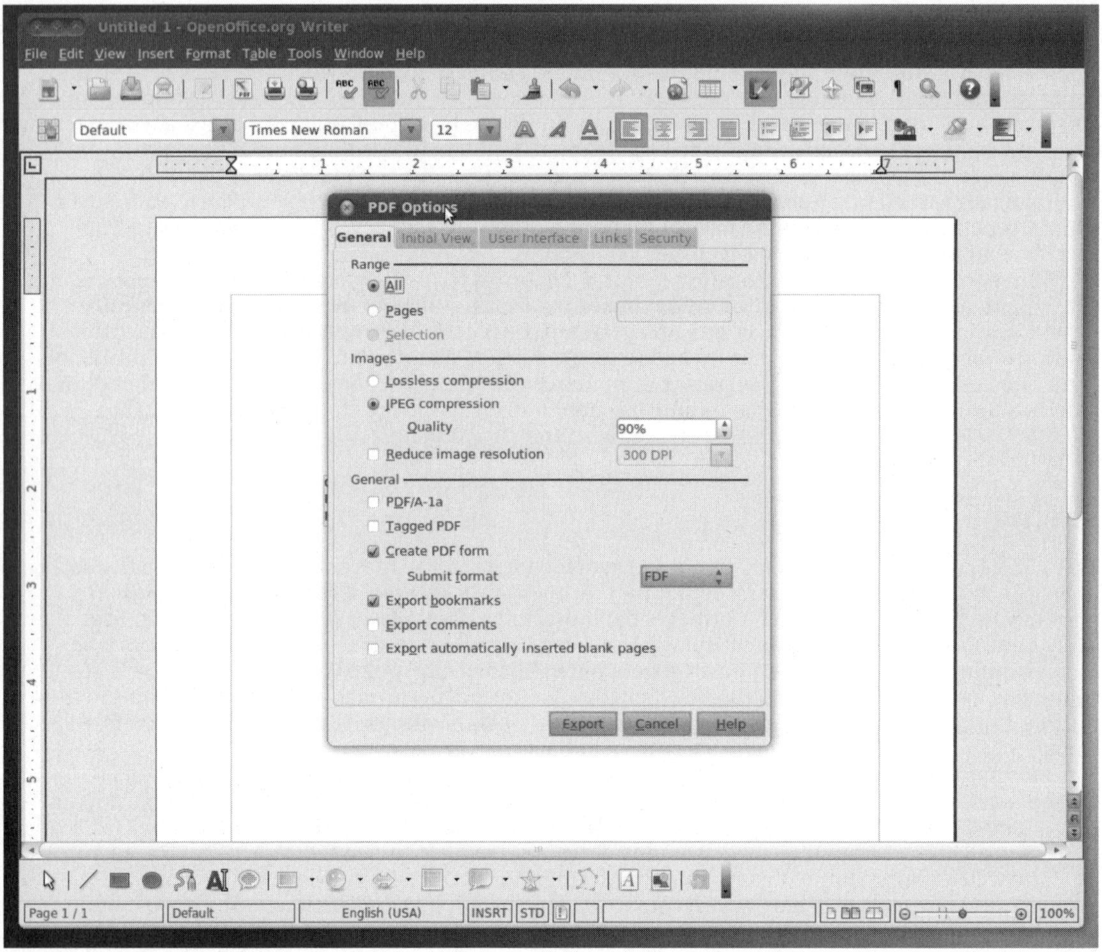

Figure 13-7. All the programs in the suite can export files in Adobe PDF format.

Beginning OpenOffice.org Applications

Beyond the common features just explained, each OpenOffice.org application has its own set of specific functionality that allows it to perform its tasks more effectively. Although this book isn't intended to be a full manual of each of them (there are such books out there; we recommend *Beginning OpenOffice 3*, by Andy Channelle [Apress, 2008]), you will find some useful guidance in the following pages that will let you get started with the most popular applications: the word processor, the spreadsheet application, and the presentation application.

OpenOffice.org Word Processor: Writer

The word processor is arguably the most popular element within any office suite. That said, you'll be happy to know that OpenOffice.org's Writer component doesn't skimp on features. It offers full text-editing and formatting functionality, along with powerful higher-level features such as mail merge. Its most basic function is of course to allow you to write. Having said that, a powerful word processor must also be able to help you give your documents the right look and feel and to check whether your spelling and grammar are correct. Luckily for you, Writer is one such application.

Figure 13-8 shows the most salient features of the Writer interface.

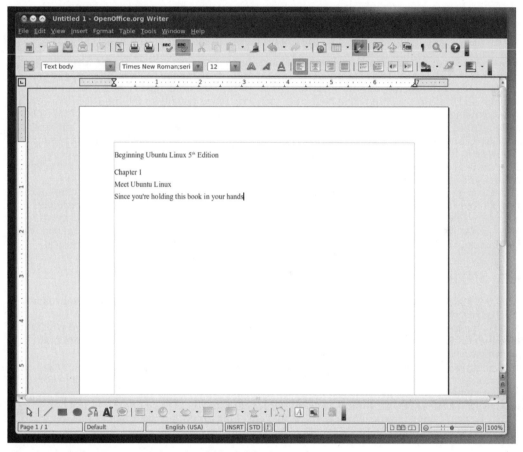

Figure 13-8. The Writer interface should look familiar to anyone with Word 2003 or earlier.

Formatting Text

As in Microsoft Word, formatting text can be done either by applying predefined styles or changing individual aspects of the text, such as font or size. But Writer is much more built around styles than Microsoft Word—enough to make some tasks much easier when you use this functionality.

There are five levels of styles and formatting:

Character: This applies formatting to the selected portion of the text. You will mainly use the formatting toolbar (explained later in this section) to apply formatting at this level.

Paragraph: This allows you to apply formatting for the entire paragraph (i.e., a block of text separated from its neighbors by line breaks).

Frame: Frames are floating boxes into which text or graphics can be inserted. New frames can be created by clicking the entry on the Insert menu. You can apply styles and formatting to all of the content in a frame.

Page: This applies formatting for the entire page, or elements in it, such as footnotes. Most usefully, it allows you to set left- or right-facing pages, which can be useful when creating documents that will be turned into a printed book.

List: This allows you to choose between different bullet point and numbering styles.

The easiest and more straightforward method of applying formatting is by using the formatting toolbar, which is just above the ruler and main document area. By using the toolbar buttons, you can select the type of font you wish to use, its point size, its style (normal, bold, italics, etc.), and more. As with elsewhere in Ubuntu, a tooltip will appear over each icon when you hover the mouse cursor over it.

Instead of using the formatting toolbar, you can format text by using the context menu. Right-click the text you want to format, and a context menu will present options for the font, size, style, alignment, and line spacing. The context menu also enables you to change the case of the highlighted characters—from uppercase to lowercase and vice versa. You can also select the Character, Paragraph, Page, or Numbering/Bullets options for a more complete set of formatting options related to each of those levels (you need to right-click over a frame to make the Frame option appear).

You can also open the Styles and Formatting palette by clicking the button located at the left of the formatting toolbar. The Styles and Formatting palette offers a variety of predefined formatting styles that you can apply to selected text or enable before you begin adding text. You can select the level at which you want to apply the style (Paragraph, Character, Frame, Page, or List), and click the Close button when you have finished. You can also create new styles by clicking the New Styles from Selection button.

Checking Spelling and Grammar

Writer provides features to help clarify your documents, including a spell-checker and a thesaurus. A grammar checker, while not installed by default, can be added as an extension.

Writer is able to automatically spell-check as you type. Any words it considers misspelled will be underlined in red. You can choose from a list of possible corrections by right-clicking the word and selecting from the context menu. You can also add the word to your personal dictionary.

You can change the language of the spell-checker by selecting Tools ➤ Options, and then selecting Language Settings. In Default Languages for Documents, select your local variation. This will become the default for all new documents.

Checking grammar works in a similar way. Any sentences that OpenOffice.org thinks use bad grammar will be underlined in green. Bear in mind that checking for perfect grammar requires human intelligence, and the rules relied on by OpenOffice.org's grammar checker are far from perfect.

Inserting Pictures

Inserting any kind of graphic—a graph, digital camera photo, drawing, or any other type of image—is easy. Simply choose Insert ➤ Picture ➤ From File.

After you've inserted a picture, you can place it anywhere on the page. When you select the picture, a new toolbar appears. This toolbar contains various simple image-tweaking tools, such as those for altering the brightness, contrast, and color balance of the image. Additionally, by clicking and dragging the green handles surrounding the image, you can resize it.

Graphics that are imported into Writer must be anchored in some way. In other words, they must be linked to a page element so that they don't move unexpectedly. By default, they're anchored to the nearest paragraph break, which means that if that paragraph moves, the graphic will move too. Alternatively, by right-clicking the graphic, you can choose to anchor it to the page, paragraph, or character it is on or next to.

The context menu also includes a Wrap option, which lets you set the type of text wrap you want to use. By default, Optimal Page Wrap is selected. This causes the text to wrap down just one side of the picture—the side on which the picture is farthest from the edge of the page. Alternatives include No Wrap, which means that the graphic will occupy the entire space on the page; no text is allowed on either side of it.

Working with Tables

Often it's useful to present columns of numbers or text within a word processor document. To make it easy to align the columns, OpenOffice.org offers the Table tool. This lets you quickly and easily create a grid in which to enter numbers or other information. You can even turn tables into simple spreadsheets, and tally rows or columns via simple formulas.

To insert a table, click and hold the Table icon on the standard toolbar (which runs across the top of the screen beneath the menu). Then simply drag the mouse in the table diagram that appears until you have the desired number of rows and columns, and release the mouse button to create the table.

Whenever your cursor is inside the table, a new toolbar will appear, offering handy options, like the ability to add rows and columns, split an existing cell, alter the styling of a cell, and create a sum cell in which you add the contents of other cells. Once again, simply hover your mouse over each button to find out what it does via a tooltip.

Adding Headers and Footers

You may want to add headers and footers to long documents to aid navigation. They appear at the top and bottom of each page, respectively, and can include the document title, page number, and other information. Headers and footers are created and edited independently of the main document, although they can utilize the same paragraph styles as the main document.

As you might expect, inserting headers and footers takes just a couple of clicks. Choose Insert ➤ Header ➤ Default or Insert ➤ Footer ➤ Default, depending on which you wish to insert (documents can have both, of course). Writer will then display an editing area where you can type text to appear in the header or footer. For more options, right-click in the area, select Page, and then click the Header or Footer tab. Here you can control the formatting and nature of the header or footer. Clicking the More button will let you apply borders or background colors.

You might wish to insert page numbers that will be updated automatically as the document progresses. OpenOffice.org refers to data that automatically updates as a *field*. You can insert a wide variety of fields by choosing from the submenu that appears when clicking Insert ➤ Fields.

To use multiple headers and footers, you need to define them in page styles. In the Styles and Formatting palette (of which we have already spoken), select the Page element and edit the Left Page or Right Page element.

Working Collaboratively

If you work in an office environment, it's unlikely that you'll ever be the only person to read or edit a document you create. Most documents tend to get shared between individuals, especially if you're working in a group or as part of a project. The people behind OpenOffice.org are aware of this, and there are two features in particular that can aid collaborative working: recording changes and notes.

Recording changes: Known as Track Changes in most Microsoft Word products, this feature causes Writer to remember any edits and highlight them within documents. To record changes within a document, click Edit ➤ Changes ➤ Record. From that point on, any additions made to the document will appear in a different color. Any deletions will stay in place but will be crossed out (note that this will adversely affect the document layout, especially if you opt to reject any deletions later). Any formatting changes that aren't accompanied by actual additions or deletions of the text will be highlighted in bold. The changes made by each individual who edits the document will appear in a different color within the document. To accept or reject changes, click Edit ➤ Changes ➤ Accept or Reject.

Inserting a note: To insert a note, first either highlight the text or object (such as a picture) that you'd like the note to be attached to, or simply position the cursor where you want the note to be, and then click Insert ➤ Note. This will make a "sticky note" appear in the margin at the right of the page that you can type a comment within. The note will be attached to the point of insertion by a dotted line. To delete a note, right-click it and select the relevant option from the menu.

OpenOffice.org Spreadsheet: Calc

Calc, shown in Figure 13-9, is the spreadsheet component of OpenOffice.org. Like most modern spreadsheet programs, it contains hundreds of features, many of which few average users will ever use. However, it doesn't abandon its user-friendliness in the process, and remains very simple for those who want to work on modest calculations, such as home finances or mortgage interest payments. In terms of features, Calc is in many regards practically a clone of Excel, and anyone who has used Microsoft's spreadsheet program will be able to get started with Calc immediately.

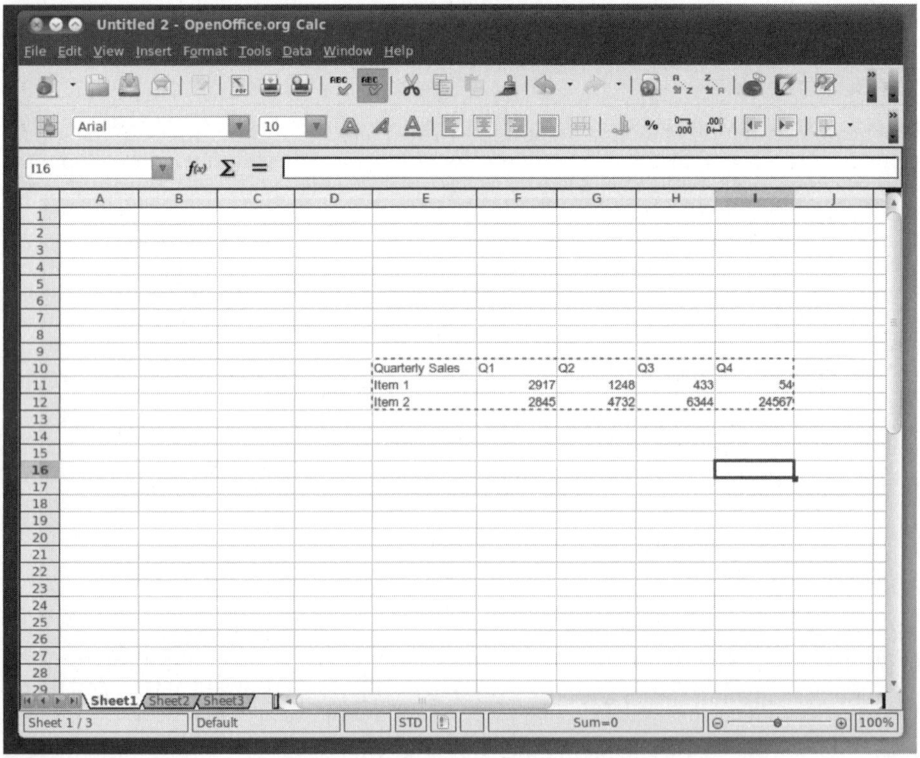

Figure 13-9. Calc has a look and feel common to most spreadsheet programs.

Entering and Formatting Data

As with all spreadsheets, entering data into a Calc document is simply a matter of selecting a cell and starting to type. Although by default cells "expect" to contain numbers, they can be configured to contain various types of data, such as dates or currency. This means that Calc will automatically attempt to set the correct formatting for the cell, if necessary, and also display an error if the wrong type of data is entered (or if the data is entered in the wrong format). Setting the correct cell type is vital with certain types of formulas that might refer to the cell—a formula that requires dates as input won't work if the cells are not set to the Date format, for example.

To change the cell format, ensure that the cell(s) are selected and then click Format ➤ Cells. Ensure that the Numbers tab is selected in the dialog box, and select the format type from the Category list.

Note You might find that Calc is clever enough to automatically detect the nature of the data you're entering and set the cell formatting automatically. For example, if you enter a date, Calc will set the format of the cell to Date.

However, the default cell format type is Number. As you might expect, this anticipates numbers being entered in the cell by the user, although it's worth noting that text can also be entered without an error message appearing (but you will almost certainly see an error later if you try to involve that cell in a formula!). It's also worth noting that Number-formatted cells into which text is entered *aren't* automatically formatted as Text cells.

A handful of symbols are not allowed in a number cell if you use the cell to enter plain text. For example, you cannot enter an equal sign (=), because Calc will assume that this is part of a formula.

Tip To enter any character into a Number-formatted cell, including an equal sign followed by a digit, precede it with an apostrophe ('). The apostrophe itself won't be visible within the spreadsheet, and whatever you type won't be interpreted in any special way; it will be seen as plain text.

Entering a sequence of data across a range of cells can be automated. Start typing the sequence of numbers (or words), highlight them, and then click and drag the small handle to the bottom right of the last cell. This will continue the sequence. You'll see a tooltip window, indicating what the content of each cell will be.

Cells can be formatted in a variety of ways. For trivial formatting changes, such as selecting a different font or changing the number format, you can use the formatting toolbar. For example, to turn the cell into one that displays currency, click the Number Format: Currency icon (remember that hovering the mouse cursor over the icon will reveal a tooltip). You can also increase or decrease the number of visible decimal places by clicking the relevant formatting toolbar icon.

For more formatting options, right-click the individual cell and select Format Cells from the menu. This displays the Format Cell dialog box, where you can change the style of the typeface, rotate text, place text at various angles, and so on. The Borders tab of the Format Cell dialog box includes options for cell gridlines of varying thicknesses, which will appear when the document is eventually printed out.

Deleting and Inserting Data and Cells

Deleting data is also easy. Just highlight the cell or cells with the data you want to delete and then press the Delete key. If you want to totally eradicate the cell along with its contents, right-click it and select Delete. This will cause the data to the sides of the cell to move in. You'll be given a choice on where you want the cells to shift from to fill the space: left, right, above, or below.

To insert a new cell, right-click where you would like it to appear and select Insert. Again, you'll be prompted about where you want to shift the surrounding cells in order to make space for the new cell.

Working with Functions

Calc includes a large number of formulas. In addition to simple and complex math functions, Calc offers a range of logical functions, as well as statistical and database tools. Certain formulas can also be used to manipulate text strings, such as dates.

You can get an idea of the available functions by clicking the Function Wizard button on the Formula bar. (This reads *f(x)* and is located just below the formatting toolbar.) This will bring up a categorized list of formulas, along with brief outlines of what function the formula performs. If you would like more details, use the help system, which contains comprehensive descriptions of most of the formulas, complete with examples of the correct syntax. Just click the Help button and then type the name of the function into the Search text field.

You can reuse formulas simply by cutting and pasting them. Calc is intelligent enough to work out which cells the transplanted formula should refer to, but it's always a good idea to check to make sure the correct cells are referenced.

Sorting Data

Within a spreadsheet, you may want to sort data according to any number of criteria. For example, you might want to show a list of numbers from highest to lowest, or rearrange a list of names so that they're in alphabetical order. This is easy to do within Calc.

Start by highlighting the range of data you wish to sort. Alternatively, you can simply select one cell within it, because Calc is usually able to figure out the range of cells you want to use. Then select Data ➤ Sort from the main menu. Calc will automatically select a sort key, which will appear in the Sort By drop-down list. However, you can also choose your own sort key from the drop-down menu if you wish, and you can choose to further refine your selection by choosing up to two more sort subkeys from the other drop-down menus.

Using Filters

The filter function in Calc lets you selectively hide rows of data. The spreadsheet user can select which criteria to use to filter the rows, or select Autofilter to choose from a drop-down list that appears in the cell at the top of the column.

Using filters can be useful when you're dealing with a very large table of data. It helps isolate figures so you can compare them side by side in an easy-to-follow format. For example, you could filter a table of sales figures by year.

To use the filter function, start by highlighting the data you wish to see in the drop-down list. Make sure the column header for the data is included too. If you're using the filter feature on a table of data, this selection can be any row or column within the table, although it obviously makes sense to use a column that is pertinent to the filtering that will take place. After you've selected the data to filter, choose Data ➤ Filter ➤ Autofilter. Click Yes if asked whether you want the first line to be used as the column header. You should find that, in place of the column or row header, a drop-down list appears. When a user selects an entry in the list, Calc will display only the corresponding row of the spreadsheet beneath.

To remove a filter, choose Data ➤ Filter ➤ Remove Filter.

Creating Charts

Charts are useful because they present a quick visual summary of data. Calc produces charts through a step-by-step wizard, so it becomes very easy indeed. You need to highlight the data you want to graph and choose the Insert ➤ Chart menu option.

A wizard dialog box appears, and a rough draft of the chart appears behind. You can click and resize the chart at this point, although this is best done after the chart has been properly created.

Just follow the wizard to create the graph. You can select the chart type, define the range of cells to be used, and write a title for your chart. After you've created a chart, you can alter its size by clicking and dragging the handles at the corners and edges. Depending on the type of chart, you might also be able to change various graphical aspects by double-clicking them. However, keep in mind that the graph is actually a picture, so the properties you can edit are limited (e.g., you can only do simple things like changing the color and size of various elements).

The chart is linked to your data. Whenever your data changes, so will your chart. This is done automatically and doesn't require any user input.

OpenOffice.org Presentation: Impress

Impress, shown in Figure 13-10, is the presentation package within OpenOffice.org. At first glance, it appears to be the simplest of the key OpenOffice.org components, and also the one that most borrows the look and feel of some versions of Microsoft Office. However, delving into its feature set reveals more than a few surprises, including sophisticated animation effects and drawing tools. Impress can also export presentations as Adobe Flash–compatible files, which means that many Internet-enabled desktop computers around the world will be able to display the files, even if they don't have Impress or even Microsoft PowerPoint installed.

Creating a Quick Presentation

As soon as Impress starts, it will offer to guide you through the creation of a presentation by using a wizard. This makes designing your document a matter of following a few steps.

You'll initially be offered three choices: Empty Presentation, From Template, and Open Existing Presentation. Templates in Impress consist of two parts: the design elements, such as backgrounds, and the slide structure, which provides a range of slide styles. After clicking the Create button in the wizard, which you can do at any point in the wizard, Impress will launch. The first step is to choose a layout for your initial slide. You can preview these on the right side of the program window. A variety of design concepts are available, ranging from those that contain mostly text to those that feature pictures and/or graphs.

Working in Impress

You'll notice three main elements in the program window, from left to right. The following list describes these panes and how you work with them:

Slides pane: This pane shows the slides in your presentation in order, one beneath the other. Simply click to select whichever slide you want to work on, or click and drag to reorder the slides. To create a new slide, right-click in a blank area on the Slides pane and select the option from the small menu that appears. Right-clicking any existing slide will present a range of options, including one to delete the slide. The Slides pane can be torn off the main interface and positioned anywhere on the screen. To dock it back once again, hold down the Ctrl key and double-click the space next to where it reads "Slides."

Main work area: This is in the middle of the program window; it lets you edit the various slides, as well as any other elements attached to the presentation, such as notes or handout documents. Simply click the relevant tab at the top of the work area. The tabs are as follows:

- *Normal*: This is a simple full-scale preview of the slide as it will appear within the presentation, and is entirely editable. Items can be clicked and moved around.

- *Outline*: Here you can roughly draft headings for each slide. The intention of this view is to let you quickly brainstorm ideas, or simply get ideas down as quickly and efficiently as possible. Pressing Enter after each line within the outline creates a new slide according to the heading you've just typed.

- *Notes*: This lets you prepare printed notes that you may want to provide with the printed version of the presentation. Every slide can have a page of notes attached to it. After the Notes view is selected, a letter-sized page will be shown. The top half will contain a preview of the slide, while the bottom half will contain a text area for typing notes.

- *Handout*: This lets you set the formatting of the handouts (i.e., the printed version of the presentation designed to be given to the audience). Each sheet of printed paper can contain between one and nine slides, depending on the selected design. To alter the layout of the handout, either click and drag the elements within the preview, or select a different design in the Layouts preview on the right of the program window.

- *Slide Sorter*: The Slide Sorter tab shows thumbnail previews of the slides side by side, effectively in chronological order. You can click and drag each to reorder, or right-click each slide to change its properties (such as changing the transition effect).

Tasks pane: Here you can access the elements that will make up your presentation, such as slide layouts, animations, and transition effects. Select the slide you wish to apply the elements to in the Slides pane, and then click the effect or template you wish to apply in the Tasks pane. In the case of animations or transitions, you can change various detailed settings relating to the selected element. As with the Slides pane, this can be undocked, but it has a View menu for redocking it to the window (pressing Ctrl while double-clicking also works).

In addition, Impress has a Drawing toolbar, which appears at the bottom of the screen. This lets you draw various items on the screen, such as lines, circles, and rectangles, and also contains a handful of special-effects tools, which we'll discuss later in this chapter, in the "Applying Fontwork" and "Using 3D Effects" sections.

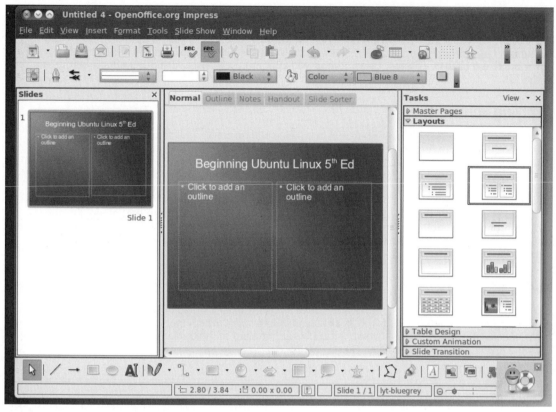

Figure 13-10. The main sections of the Impress interface

You can hide each on-screen item by clicking the View menu and then removing the check next to it. Alternatively, by clicking the vertical borders between each pane, you can resize the pane and make it either more or less prominent on the screen. This is handy if you wish to temporarily gain more work space but don't want to lose sight of the previews in the Slides pane, for example.

Animating Slides

All elements within Impress can be animated in a variety of ways. For example, you might choose to have the contents of a particular text box fly in from the edge of the screen during the presentation. This can help add variety to your presentation and perhaps even wake up your audience, but be aware that too many animations can look unprofessional. They should never get in the way of your message.

Setting an animation effect is simply a matter of clicking the border of the object you wish to animate in the main editing area so that it is selected, selecting Custom Animation in the Tasks pane, and then clicking the Add button. In the dialog box that appears, select how you want the effect to work.

With each animation, you can select the speed you wish it to play at, ranging from very slow to fast. Simply make the selection at the bottom of the dialog box.

After the animation has been defined and you've clicked OK, it will appear in a list at the bottom of the Custom Animation pane. You can choose to add more than one animation to an object by clicking the Add button again (ensuring the object is still selected in the main editing area). The animations will play in the order they're listed. You can click the Change Order up and down arrows to alter the order.

To fine-tune an effect you've already created, double-click it in the list to open its Effect Options dialog box (you can even add sound effects here). Under the Timing tab, you can control what cues the effect, such as a click of a mouse, or whether it will appear in sequence with other effects before or after in the list.

Applying Fontwork

The Fontwork tool lets you manipulate text in various playful ways, such as making it follow specific curved paths. You can find this tool on the drawing toolbar, located at the bottom of the program window. (It's the icon that's an *A* in a frame.)

When you click the icon, the Fontwork Gallery dialog box appears, offering a choice of predefined font effects. Don't worry if they're not quite what you want, because after you make a choice, you'll be invited to fine-tune it.

After you've made the selection, the dummy text *Fontwork* will appear on the screen. Editing the text is simple: just double-click the *Fontwork* text and type your own words (note that, confusingly, the text will appear underneath the fontwork itself, rather than in a dialog box). When you've finished, click outside the Fontwork selection.

Using 3D Effects

In addition to Fontwork effects, Impress includes a powerful 3D tool, which can give just about any on-screen element a 3D flourish (this tool is also available in some other OpenOffice.org applications). To use it, create a text box or shape by using the Drawing toolbar at the bottom of the screen. Then right-click the text box or shape and select Convert ➤ To 3D.

■ **Note** The 3D option is designed simply to give your object depth. If you want to create a genuine 3D object that you can rotate in 3D space, select 3D Rotation Object.

You can gain much more control over the 3D effect by right-clicking it and selecting 3D Effects.

Exporting a Presentation As a Flash File

If you plan to put your presentation online, or you want to send it to a colleague who doesn't have Impress or PowerPoint installed, outputting your presentation as a Flash animation could be a good idea. The process is simple. Just choose File ➤ Export, and then select Macromedia Flash (SWF) in the File Type drop-down list (SWF is the Flash file extension, which stands for Shockwave Flash). No further configuration is necessary.

In order to play the file, it needs to be opened within a web browser that has Flash Player installed. This can be done by choosing File ➤ Open on most browsers, although you can also drag and drop the SWF file onto the browser window under Microsoft Windows. There shouldn't be much of a problem with compatibility, because Flash Player is ubiquitous these days. If the web browser doesn't already have Flash installed, it's easy to download and install it (see www.adobe.com/products/flashplayer).

When the Flash file is opened in a web browser, the presentation starts. You can progress through it by clicking anywhere on the screen.

Summary

This chapter gave a general introduction to OpenOffice.org, providing an overview of what you can expect from the programs within the suite. In particular, we focused on the extent of the suite's similarities with Microsoft Office and discussed issues surrounding file compatibility with Microsoft Office. We also looked at how Windows fonts can be brought into Ubuntu, which aids in successfully importing and creating compatible documents.

We gave you a crash course on the options that can be applied globally and also on the salient features of the most important applications within the suite: Writer, Calc, and Impress.

CHAPTER 14

■■■

Communicating with Others

Being online is all about staying in touch, and Ubuntu is no slouch in this regard. Ubuntu offers a wide range of applications, including a full-featured e-mail program, called Evolution, as well as an instant messaging client called Empathy, which allows you to connect to the most popular instant messaging sites, such as GTalk and MSN.

You can install a Skype client that allows you to connect to the popular service to make voice and video calls to other Skype users or to telephones; and you can install an open source alternative to Skype called Ekiga.

Introducing Evolution

Evolution is considered the "official" GNOME desktop e-mail program, and the Evolution interface retains the same look and feel as many elements of the Ubuntu desktop.

Evolution is similar to Microsoft Outlook: in addition to being a powerful e-mail client, it incorporates contact management, a calendar, a to-do list, and a memo function. It is a first-class business tool. Evolution is even able to connect to Microsoft Exchange (2000 and later) groupware servers and synchronize with contact and calendar data, in addition to fetching e-mail. Of course, it can also connect to standard POP3/SMTP e-mail servers, as well as IMAP, Novell GroupMail, and a handful of other mail server technologies. This means it is compatible with practically every e-mail system in common use today.

Evolution consists of five components: Mail, Contacts, Calendars, Memos, and Tasks. These are interconnected but operate as separate modes within the program. Each mode can be selected by using the switcher located at the bottom-left side of the program window. Simply click the button for the mode you wish to use. The program window, toolbar, and menu system will change to accommodate whichever mode is selected. Figure 14-1 shows the program in the default Mail mode.

■ **Tip** You can shrink the switcher component to small icons or even just text buttons by selecting from the choices on the View ➤ Switcher Appearance submenu.

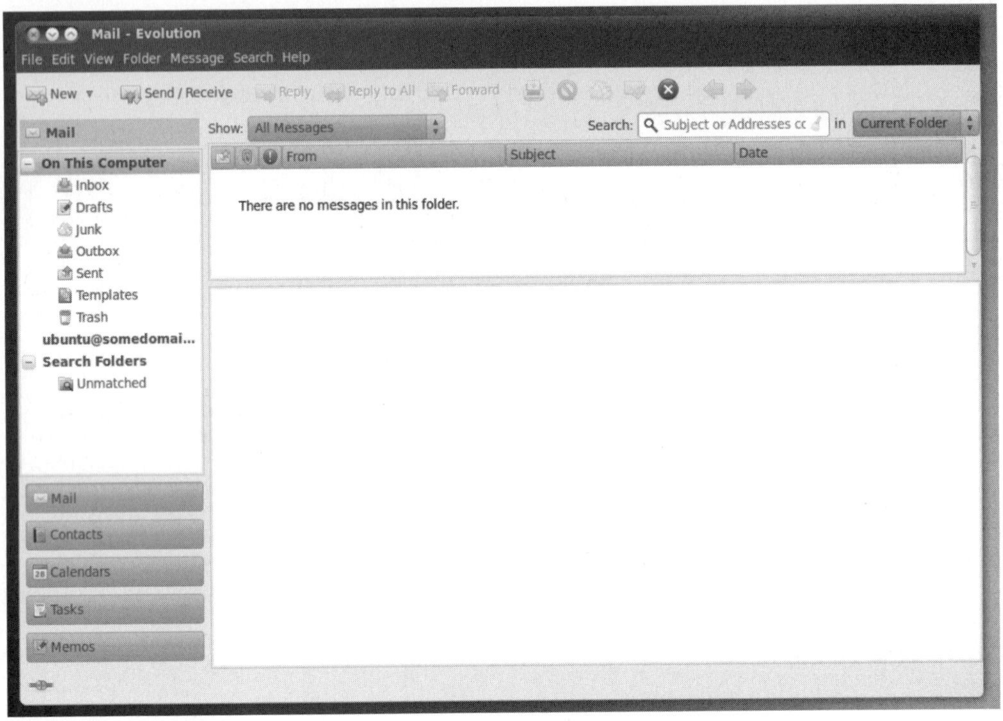

Figure 14-1. You can switch between Evolution's modes by clicking the buttons at the bottom left of the program window.

The five Evolution modes work as follows:

Mail: The e-mail component is at the heart of Evolution, and all the functions you might be used to are available here. After the Mail mode is selected, you'll find the mail folders at the top left of the program window. These include the Inbox and Sent folders, along with any other mail folders you create. On the right is the list of e-mail messages, and beneath this is the message preview pane, where the body of any message you select will be displayed. Above the message list is the search box, which works like most e-mail search routines: type the relevant word(s) and press Enter. Notable icons running along the top of the window include the New button, which will let you compose an e-mail message, and the Send/Receive button, which will download new messages and also send any messages in the Outbox folder. By default, Evolution checks for new mail when the application is launched and every 10 minutes thereafter, though this behavior is configurable for each account under the Edit ➤ Preferences menu.

Contacts: Tied in with the mail function but acting as a separate and powerful entity on its own, Contacts mode lets you store every pertinent detail about colleagues, friends, and others. After the mode is selected, you'll see the various contact folders at the left side of the program window. For most users, there will be just one, named Personal, but if you specified a groupware server during setup, you will also be able to connect to this by clicking its entry. You can also create new address books (e.g., if you have a collection of addresses for work and one for personal information). Simply right-click beneath the existing address book, select the New Address box, and fill out the form. The type On This Computer will create a new book on your machine. At the top right is the list of contacts. Clicking any contact displays that individual's information at the bottom of the window, in the contact information area. The search bar at the top of the window, beneath the toolbar, lets you quickly search for contacts by name. The New button on the toolbar lets you create a new contact, where you can enter a wealth of data. To edit an existing entry, double-click its entry and fill in the additional details. This kind of information is useful for a variety of tasks, so it's particularly useful that Evolution's Contacts mode can be used as a data source in OpenOffice.org.

Calendars: Calendars mode is arguably Evolution's second most useful function (after e-mail). You can add events in half-hour increments and view your schedule in day, week, work week, and month views by clicking the relevant button on the toolbar (work week view presents just five days in the view). After the mode is selected, you'll find the various calendars you can access at the top left of the program window. For most users, the Personal calendar will be the principal one, but you can also access shared calendars, including Google Calendar, here. Assuming the default day view is in operation, beneath this you'll see the monthly calendar and, in the middle of the program window, the appointment list, with half-hour entries covering the working day. By default, the current day is shown. To select a different day, simply double-click the day in the month view or click the Go To button on the toolbar and use the widget to find the date. You can switch among day, week, and month appointment views by clicking the labeled buttons on the toolbar. On the right of the window, any tasks or memos that have been created are displayed, as described next.

Memos: The best way to think of Evolution's Memos mode is as a personal notepad. After Memos mode is selected, the list of memos will appear on the right side of the screen, and the memo contents will appear at the bottom. Memos can consist of virtually any amount of text, along with attachments. They're ideal for jotting down notes during phone calls, for example. Again, you can use the list on the left pane of the application to create categories for memos (e.g., you can break things down by client, job, or interest).

Tasks: Effectively, this is a simple to-do list. After the mode is selected, your tasks will be listed on the right side of the program window. Beneath this will be details of any selected task. If you're a fan of the Getting Things Done method of task management, the left-pane Tasks list is the ideal companion because you can create lots of lists and then populate the main window with tasks to be accomplished.

Basic E-Mail Tasks

Evolution's e-mail functionality is arguably the heart of the program. Although it offers many features, it is quite simple to use. If you've ever used any other mainstream e-mail client, such as Microsoft Outlook, you have a head start.

This section describes how to accomplish several everyday tasks within the e-mail component of Evolution. When you start Evolution, the e-mail mode is selected automatically. However, if it isn't, or if you've switched to a different mode within the program, simply click the Mail button at the bottom left of the program window.

Configuring E-Mail Access

Before starting, you'll need to find out the addresses of the mail servers you intend to use. In the case of POP3 and IMAP mail accounts, you'll need to know the incoming and outgoing server addresses (outgoing may be referred to as *SMTP*). In the case of Microsoft Exchange, you'll need to know the Outlook Web Access (OWA) URL and, optionally, the Active Directory/Global Address List server. With Novell GroupWare, you'll simply need to know the server name. You'll also need to know your username and password details for the incoming and possibly outgoing mail servers.

After gathering the necessary information, follow these steps to configure Evolution:

1. Start the Evolution e-mail client by clicking the little envelope beside the date and time, and selecting the Set Up Mail option. Alternatively, you can choose Applications ➤ Office ➤ Evolution Mail and Calendar.

2. When Evolution starts for the first time, you'll be invited to enter your configuration details via a wizard. Click the Forward button.

3. The next screen offers an option to restore Evolution settings from backup. This is a convenient option for migrating accounts from one Evolution client to another. Because this is your first time using Evolution, you can simply ignore this option by clicking the Forward button.

   You will be asked for your name and the e-mail address you wish to use within Evolution. These are what will appear in outgoing messages. Beneath this is a check box that you should leave selected if you want the account you're about to create to be the default account. In nearly all situations, this will be the correct choice. You can also fill in the Reply-To and Organization information if you wish, but these fields can be left blank. They're not usually displayed by most e-mail clients. Click the Forward button to continue.

4. The next screen asks for details of the receiving (incoming) mail server that you want to use, as shown in Figure 14-2. First, select the server type from the drop-down list. If you don't know which option to go with, select POP. This is by far the most common type of incoming mail server currently in use.

   Additional configuration fields will appear when you make the selection of server type. Enter the server address and username in the relevant fields. Click Check for Supported Types to find out what kind of authentication security, if any, your mail server uses. Following this, you should find that the details are filled in automatically. Click Forward to continue.

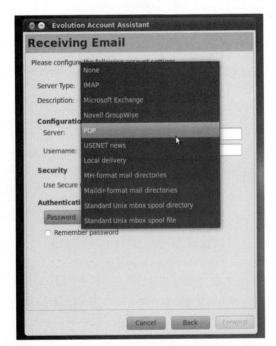

Figure 14-2. *Evolution can work with a variety of mail servers, including POP3, Microsoft Exchange, and IMAP.*

5. You might need to enter your mail password, depending on which server type you chose. In some cases, you'll need to type this later when you download your mail for the first time. Click Forward to continue.

6. You're given the chance to choose between various additional options, such as how often you want Evolution to check for new mail or whether you want to delete mail from the server after it has been downloaded. Unless you have been told otherwise or have special requirements, it should be OK to leave the default settings as they are. If you use a Microsoft Exchange server, you may need to enter the Active Directory/Global Address List server details here. Click Forward to continue.

7. Depending on the server type you chose, you might now need to fill in the outgoing (SMTP) server address. Type this into the Server field. If your SMTP server requires authentication, put a check in the relevant box and then enter your username. Once again, you can click the Check for Supported Types button to automatically fill in the authentication details. Click Forward to continue.

8. You're invited to enter a name for the account. This is the account name you will see when you use Evolution. The default is your e-mail address, but you can type something more memorable if you wish. Click Forward to continue.

9. Finally, choose your location, which will have the effect of automatically defining your time zone. This will ensure that e-mail messages are correctly time-stamped. You can choose your location from the Selection drop-down list (choose the nearest large city in your time zone), or click your location on the map. As during initial installation of Ubuntu, the map will zoom in when you click continents, allowing you to more precisely click the place where you live. Click Forward to continue, and then click the Apply button to finish the wizard.

Sending and Receiving E-Mail

After Evolution has been set up correctly to work with your e-mail servers, you can simply click the Send/Receive button on the toolbar to connect to the server(s) and both send and receive e-mail.

You may need to enter your password if you didn't enter it during setup. You can select the Remember Password check box in Account Preferences (Edit ➤ Preferences) to avoid having to type your password again, but the password will then be stored on your hard disk, posing a security risk if other people have access to your PC.

■ **Note** Although e-mail is normally sent as soon as you click the Send button after composing it, if the sending has been delayed for any reason (such as being offline at the time), it will take place as soon as you click the Send/Receive button. Until that point, it will be held in the Outbox folder on the left side of the program window. You may need to choose File ➤ Work Online if you've been composing e-mail in offline mode.

Any outstanding mail is sent first, and then the receiving procedure is started. As shown in Figure 14-3, a status dialog box will tell you how many messages there are and the progress of the download.

Clicking the Cancel button will stop the procedure (although some messages may already have been downloaded). When you get a new e-mail message, an envelope icon will blink in the notification area in the top right of the desktop, and a small window will appear to tell you that you have mail.

Figure 14-3. You'll see a progress bar display whenever you click the Send/Receive button.

E-MAIL SIGNING AND ENCRYPTION

In Chapter 8, you learned how to use the Seahorse application to set up a public key pair. This allows you to encrypt e-mail messages destined for other people, so that only they can read the messages (provided you have their public key). The application also enables you to digitally sign your own e-mail, so recipients can be sure messages came from you (provided they have *your* public key). If you've followed the instructions to set up the key pair, and uploaded it to a key server, you now need to configure Evolution to use it. After doing this, and when you send a new e-mail message, you can select whether you wish to encrypt the e-mail and/or digitally sign it.

Remember that setting up encryption is *not* obligatory, and relatively few people in the wider world use e-mail encryption or signing.

Assuming you've already set up an account within Evolution, here's the procedure for configuring Evolution for encryption and digital signing:

1. Click Edit ➤ Preferences, ensure that the Mail Accounts icon is selected on the left side of the window, and select your mail account in the list on the right side of the window. Then click the Edit button. In the dialog box that appears, click the Security tab.

2. You now need to find your PGP key ID by using Seahorse. Click Applications ➤ Accessories ➤ Passwords and Encryption Keys. Locate your key in the list under the My Personal Keys tab, and look under the Key ID heading. You should see an eight-character hexadecimal number, like F0C1B52A. Write this down, remembering that any 0 you see is a zero, not the letter *O*.

3. Switch back to the Evolution dialog box and type the PGP key ID you found into the PGP/GPG Key ID box. If you want every e-mail message you send to be digitally signed automatically, which is a good idea (the message itself *won't* be encrypted, so even if the recipients are not using encryption, they will still be able to read it), ensure there's a check in the Always Sign Outgoing Messages When Using This Account box. Then click OK and close the parent Preferences dialog box.

Encrypting outgoing messages, or signing them if you haven't selected to automatically do so, is easy. When composing a new message, click the Security menu entry and select either PGP Sign or PGP Encrypt (or both). Remember that you'll need to have imported the recipient's public key via Seahorse if you want to encrypt a message addressed to that person, or you'll see an error. If you sign a message, upon sending it, you'll be prompted to enter the PGP passphrase you entered when you created the key pair back in Chapter 8.

If, upon sending an e-mail message, you see the error message "Failed to execute GPG: Broken pipe," it's likely you mistyped your key ID when you configured Evolution. Try again.

If you receive a message that has been encrypted using your public key, Evolution will automatically prompt you to enter your PGP passphrase to decrypt it. This is the passphrase you entered when creating your key pair back in Chapter 8.

When you receive a message from someone who uses digital signing, and you have that person's public key, the message should contain a green bar along the bottom containing the words *Valid signature*. If you see words to the effect that the signature is invalid, or if the signature is missing, you should be suspicious and independently verify the authenticity of the e-mail message.

Reading E-Mail

Simply click an e-mail message to view it in the preview pane at the bottom of the screen. Alternatively, you can double-click a message to open it in its own program window (selecting a message and pressing Enter will have the same effect).

As with most e-mail clients, any unread messages in the list appear in bold, and messages that have been read appear in ordinary type. By default, each message is marked as read after 1.5 seconds, but you can alter this value. To change it, click Edit ➤ Preferences, click the Mail Preferences icon in the Preferences dialog box, click the General tab, and then change the value under the Message Display heading. A value of 0 will cause the mail to switch to "read" status as soon as it's clicked, which can be useful if you want to quickly clear a lot of messages.

You can also mark many messages as read by highlighting them all, right-clicking an individual one, and selecting Mark As Read from the menu that appears. You can select multiple messages in the usual way: Shift-click to select a consecutive list, or Ctrl-click for nonconsecutive selections. The Show drop-down menu, above the e-mail list, can be used to display only unread mail, which is great if you have a lot of messages that you're not going to read and want to mark them as read or delete them.

Deleting Messages

You can delete messages by highlighting them and pressing the Delete key. Alternatively, right-click any message (or a selection of them) and select Delete. The message will then be moved to the Trash folder. To empty the Trash folder, right-click the folder and select Empty Trash, as shown in Figure 14-4.

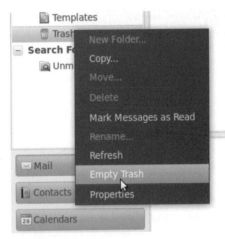

Figure 14-4. To permanently delete messages, right-click the Trash folder and select Empty Trash.

If you move any messages from folder to folder, as described later in the "Sorting and Filtering Messages" section, a copy of the mail will end up in the Trash folder. This is because Evolution doesn't literally move messages. Instead, it copies them from the old to the new location and deletes the original. This can be a little disconcerting at first, but there's nothing to worry about. The mail message will remain wherever you moved it, and it won't disappear.

Flagging Messages

You can flag messages in a variety of ways to help remind you of their status or purpose. The simplest form of flagging is to mark a message as important: right-click the message and select Mark As Important, or click in the space beneath the Important column (this is located to the left of the From column). This will add an exclamation mark symbol alongside the message.

Alternatively, you can add several different flags by right-clicking a message and selecting Mark for Follow Up. The choices, which can be selected from the Flag drop-down list in the dialog box that appears, range from Do Not Forward to No Response Necessary and Review. This heading will then appear in the message preview at the bottom of the window whenever the message is selected.

If you prefer a simple color-coding scheme, you can mark up a message by right-clicking it and selecting Label. Then assign a color. As you'll see, each color relates to a key word or phrase. You can edit both the colors and the key phrases by clicking Edit ➤ Preferences, clicking Mail Preferences on the left of the dialog box, and clicking the Labels tab.

IMPORTING OUTLOOK E-MAIL VIA THUNDERBIRD

Earlier in the book, we discussed a method of exporting e-mail from various Microsoft e-mail programs, which use proprietary formats, so that it can be imported under Ubuntu. To recap, you can install the Mozilla Thunderbird e-mail client under Windows, import your e-mail into it from Outlook or Outlook Express, and then export Thunderbird's mailbox (.mbox) files for *importing* within Evolution.

If you followed these instructions and now have the .mbox files ready for use with Evolution, it's easy to import them. Click File ➤ Import. In the Import dialog box, click the Forward button and then select Import a Single File. Click Forward again and click the Filename drop-down list. This will open a file-browsing dialog box, in which you can locate the .mbox file and click Open. If you have more than one .mbox file, you'll need to import each one manually. The Automatic entry in the dialog box refers to the file type and will select the correct file type by file extension.

Composing a Message

Creating a new e-mail message is as simple as clicking the New button at the top left of Evolution's program window. Fill in the To and Subject details as usual, and then type in the main body of the message.

To add a CC or BCC, click the To button, and select addresses from your contacts list in the dialog box that appears (selecting the CC or BCC button as appropriate). Alternatively, if you would like to have the CC and BCC fields visible and available at all times, click their entries under the View menu of the Compose a Message window.

As with most Microsoft mail programs, new e-mail can be sent either as plain text or as HTML. Plain text mode is the default. To switch to HTML, click the entry on the Format menu. The advantage of HTML mail is that you can vary the style, size, and coloring of text, so you can emphasize various words or paragraphs, as illustrated in Figure 14-5. In addition, if you click Insert ➤ Image, you can insert pictures from the hard disk. Other options on the Insert menu let you insert tables, dividing lines (click the Rule menu entry), and web links.

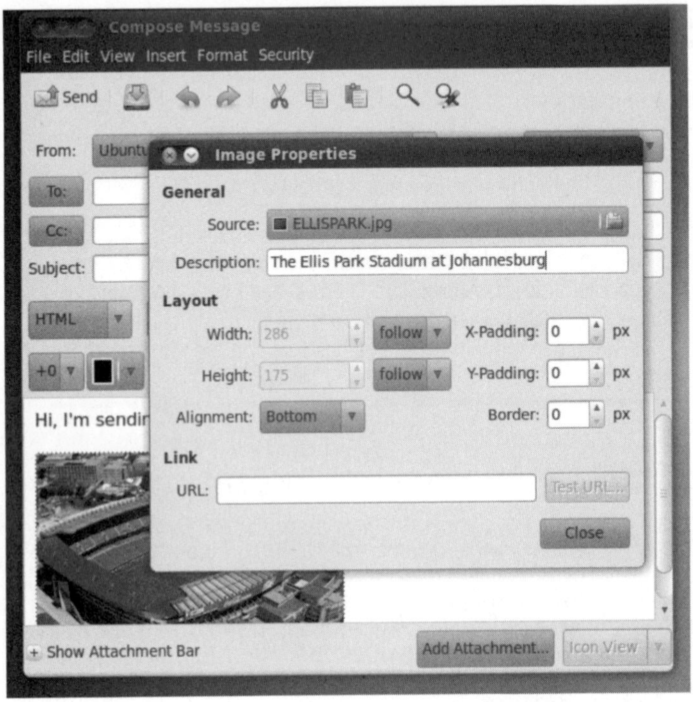

Figure 14-5. *New messages can be formatted in HTML, allowing you to format text and even add images to your messages.*

The disadvantage of HTML e-mail is that the person receiving the message will need an HTML-compatible e-mail program to be able to read it (though most common e-mail programs can handle HTML e-mail just fine). Your mail is also more likely to be tagged as spam by the recipient's server, because of the widespread abuse of HTML and images in mail by spammers.

■ **Tip** Many people in the Linux community frown on HTML-formatted e-mail and prefer plain text messages.

Words are automatically spell-checked in the new e-mail, and are underlined in red if the spell-checker thinks they are incorrect. To correct the word, right-click it and then select the correct spelling from the list provided.

By default, if you chose the English language during the installation of Ubuntu, the Evolution spell-checker will offer only an English (American) dictionary. You can switch to other English dialects (e.g., British, Canadian, or Australian English) by choosing Edit ➤ Preferences in the main Evolution window, clicking the Composer Preferences icon, and then clicking the Spell Checking tab. Select an alternative dictionary or multiple dictionaries by selecting the check boxes to the left of the dictionary names.

While composing an e-mail, you can switch languages by choosing Edit ➤ Current Languages in the menu of the Compose Message window. If the language you require is not listed, this means that you need to install an additional Aspell dictionary package with the Ubuntu Software Center. These dictionary packages usually have a two-letter suffix indicating the language that they support; for example, aspell-fr is the French dictionary package. You'll need to quit and restart Evolution before the new language is visible.

■ **Note** The aspell-fr package also includes the Swiss French variation of the language.

Creating an E-Mail Signature

E-mail signatures are the blocks of text that appear automatically at the end of new e-mail messages you compose. They save you the bother of typing your name and contact details each time. To create an e-mail signature, follow these steps:

1. Click Edit ➤ Preferences. Select Composer Preferences from the left side of the dialog box and click the Signatures tab.

2. Click the Add button at the top right of the dialog box.

3. In the Edit Signature dialog box, type what you want to appear as your signature. The signature can be in either plain text or HTML (click Format ➤ HTML for the latter). Don't forget that in HTML mode, you can insert lines (Insert ➤ Rule), which can act as a natural divider at the top of your signature to separate it from the body of the e-mail, as shown in Figure 14-6.

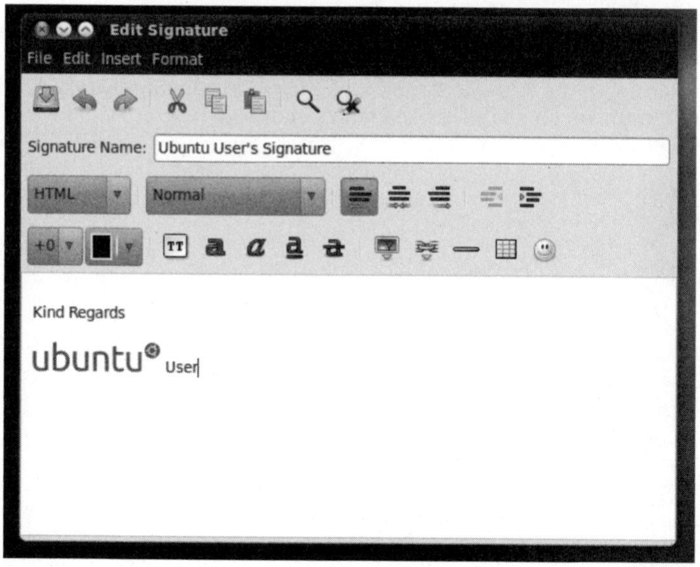

Figure 14-6. Creating an e-mail signature saves you from having to type your contact details each time.

4. Click the Save and Close icon at the top left.

5. Click Mail Accounts in the Preferences dialog box, and double-click your mail account in the list on the right side.

6. In the dialog box that appears, ensure that the Identity tab is selected and click the Signature drop-down list. Click the signature you just created.

7. Click OK and then Close in the Preferences dialog box. Your new signature will then automatically appear in new messages. It's possible to create multiple signatures—for instance, one for work and one for personal e-mail—and then choose the appropriate signature when writing your e-mail.

Advanced E-Mail Tasks

Evolution offers several features that can help you to organize your e-mail. You can create new folders, as well as filter, sort, and search through your messages.

Creating New Folders

If you want to better organize your e-mail, you can create your own folders, which will then appear in the list on the left side of the program window.

To create a new top-level folder, which will appear in the list alongside the standard folders (Inbox, Junk, Outbox, etc.), right-click On This Computer and select New Folder. Then make sure that On This Computer is selected in the folder view of the dialog box that appears. Type a name and click Create.

You can also create second-level folders, which will effectively be "inside" other folders and will appear indented below their parent folder within the list. For example, you might want to create a series of folders within the main Inbox folder to sort your mail from various individuals or organizations. To do this, right-click Inbox, select New Folder, and give the folder a name in the dialog box that appears, as shown in Figure 14-7. After the new folder has been created, click the chevron next to Inbox to expand the display to show your new subfolder.

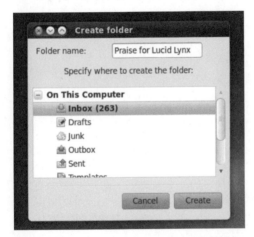

Figure 14-7. You can create your own folders to better organize your mail.

You can then drag and drop messages into the new folders, or you can simply right-click them, select Move to Folder, and select the folder from the dialog box that appears. This can be useful if you wish to select a handful of messages by holding down the Ctrl key. All you need to do then is right-click one of them and select Move to Folder.

You can also copy messages from one location to another, thus producing two copies of the same message. Simply right-click the message, select Copy to Folder, and select the folder from the list. Alternatively, you can hold down the Ctrl key while you drag the message to the new location.

Dealing with Junk E-Mail

Evolution includes intelligent junk mail filtering. Any mail that Evolution thinks is spam or junk mail will end up in the Junk folder. When you first start using Evolution, you should check the folder regularly, because there's a chance Evolution might have made a mistake. However, this is a good thing, because by right-clicking the message and selecting Mark As Not Junk, the Evolution junk mail filter will be able to better understand what to consider as junk in your particular Inbox.

In a similar way, if you find that Evolution misses junk e-mail, and it ends up in your Inbox, you can right-click it and select Mark As Junk. Alternatively, select it and click the Junk icon on the main toolbar.

To empty the Junk folder, select all the messages (Ctrl+A), right-click, and select Delete. Bear in mind that, as with any folder, after the messages are deleted, they will appear in the Trash, and you can restore them from there if necessary.

■ **Note** The junk mail filter used in Evolution is a third-party program called Bogofilter (`http:// bogofilter. sourceforge.net`). You can switch Evolution to an alternative spam filter, which some consider more powerful, called SpamAssassin (`http://spamassassin.apache.org`). To do so, install the `spamassassin` package. Restart Evolution, click Edit ➤ Preferences, click the Mail Preferences icon in the dialog box that appears, and click the Junk tab. Then select SpamAssassin from the Default Junk Plugin drop-down list. While on that preferences page, it's also a good idea to select the Do Not Mark Messages As Junk If Sender Is In My Address Book check box. When you are finished, click OK and then Close to return to the main Evolution program window.

Sorting and Filtering Messages

You can filter incoming messages according to practically any criteria, including who sent the message, its subject line, words within the body of the mail, its size, and whether it has attachments. Coupled with the ability to create folders, this allows you to automatically sort messages as soon as they're received.

To set up filters, click Edit ➤ Message Filters. Click the Add button and, in the Rule Name box, start by giving the new rule a descriptive name by which you'll be able to recognize it in the future. You might think this isn't important, but you may create tens, if not hundreds, of filters, so being able to identify filters will be very helpful.

As shown in Figure 14-8, the Add Rule dialog box is split into two halves: Find Items That Meet the Following Conditions and Then. As implied by the labels, if the selected conditions are met, then the selected actions will take place.

The Find Items part is used to identify the mail. You can select to filter based on almost any criteria, such as who appears in the Sender field of the message, words that appear on the Subject line, the date sent, and so on. Simply select what you require from the drop-down list directly beneath the Add Condition button. In most cases, you'll then need to specify details for the filter. For example, if you select to filter by the address of the individual sending the e-mail, you'll need to provide that e-mail address.

■ **Tip** Several If rules can be created. For example, you could create a rule to filter by the address of the sender, and then click the Add Condition button to create another rule to filter by text in the Subject line. If you click If All Conditions Are Met in the Find Items drop-down list, the mail will be filtered only if both conditions are met. If you click If Any Conditions Are Met from the drop-down list, the mail will be filtered if either condition is met.

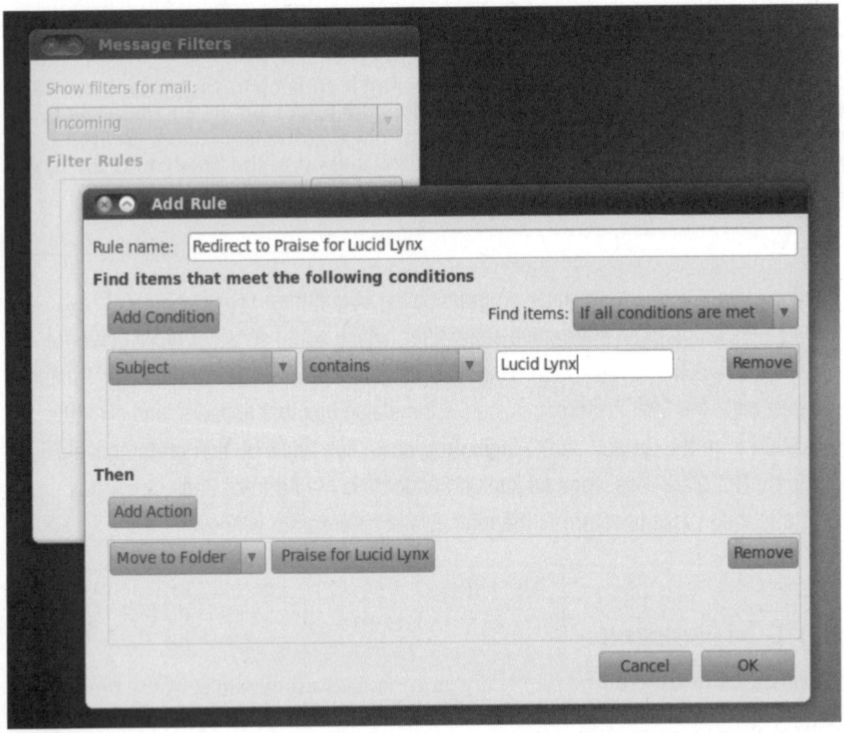

Figure 14-8. Creating message filters lets you automatically organize your e-mail as soon as it's received.

After you've set the Find conditions, you need to select from the Then section of the dialog box. This tells Evolution what to do with the filtered mail. The obvious course of action is to move the e-mail to a particular folder, which is the default choice, but you can also delete the e-mail, set a particular flag, beep, or even run a particular program! As with the rules for finding items, you can set more than one condition here, so you can have Evolution beep and then delete the message, for example. When designing filters, it's good practice to finish with a Then option of Stop Processing because one message may be filtered into a folder and then have other operations performed on it.

Creating Search Folders

Evolution's search folders feature is a more powerful alternative to message filters. Using search folders, you can filter mail based on a similar set of criteria, but you can choose to include messages in the results that might be *associated* with the filtered messages. For example, if you choose to filter by a specific individual's e-mail address, you can choose to have any replies you sent to that person included in the results, rather than simply messages received from her. In addition, you can apply search folders to specific e-mail folders on an ongoing basis, rather than all incoming e-mail.

It's important to note, however, that a search folder isn't a filter. The messages aren't moved into the new folders. They stay where they are in your Inbox (or any other folder they might be contained in). Despite the name, search folders are actually little more than saved searches. They just *act* like filters. However, search folders are dynamically updated—if a message is deleted from the Inbox folder, for example, it will also stop appearing in any relevant search folder.

You can create a new search folder by clicking Edit ➤ Search Folders and then clicking the Add button. As with creating message filters, clicking the drop-down box beneath the Add button will let you select filtering criteria. The choices are broadly similar to those for message filters, in that you can filter by e-mail address, size of e-mail, message body, and so on. At the bottom of the dialog box, you can choose to search specific folders (the default), all local folders, or all active remote folders (which includes any of your mail stored on a server elsewhere).

In the Include Threads drop-down box, you can select what kind of results you would like the search to return:

- None simply returns e-mail messages matching the criteria.

- All Related returns every single message that is associated with the criteria.

- Replies returns results that include replies to the messages returned via the filter.

- Replies and Parents returns results that include replies and also any initial message that you or others might have sent that inspired the message included in the filter results.

- No Reply or Parent returns results that include only initial messages sent to you.

Search folders results are listed under Search Folders on the left side of the Mail mode window. The search folders feature is very powerful and worth spending time investigating.

TIPS FOR USING EVOLUTION E-MAIL

In many ways, Evolution is similar to e-mail programs you might have used in the past, but it also has a few of its own quirks and idiosyncratic ways of working. Here are a handful of preferences you might want to set to have Evolution behave in a more familiar way:

- *Forward e-mail inline*: If you attempt to forward a message, Evolution will attach it to a new message as a file. The person receiving the e-mail will then need to double-click the file to view the forwarded e-mail, which can be confusing. The solution is to make Evolution forward the message *inline*, which is to say that Evolution will quote it beneath the new mail message, like Microsoft e-mail programs. To do this, click Edit ➤ Preferences, click Composer Preferences on the left side of the dialog box, click the Forward Style drop-down list, and select Inline.

- *Change the plain text font*: Any messages sent to you in plain text format, rather than HTML, will appear in the message preview pane in a Courier-style font. To have messages display in a more attractive and readable typeface, click Edit ➤ Preferences, select Mail Preferences on the left side of the dialog box, and then remove the check from Use the Same Fonts As Other Applications. In the Fixed Width Font drop-down list, select an alternative font. The standard Ubuntu font is called Sans and is a good choice.

- *Always create HTML e-mail*: Evolution defaults to plain text e-mail for any new messages you create. If you want to always create HTML messages, click Edit ➤ Preferences, click Composer Preferences on the left side of the dialog box, and then put a check alongside Format Messages in HTML.

- *Empty trash on exit*: To automatically get rid of deleted messages each time you quit Evolution, click Edit ➤ Preferences, click Mail Preferences on the left side of the dialog box, and put a check alongside Empty Wastebasket Folders on Exit. Then select how often you would like this to happen from the drop-down list: every time you quit Evolution, once per day, once per week, or once per month.

- *Vertical message window*: As an alternative to positioning the message preview window beneath your messages, Outlook lets you position the message at the right of the message list, thus forming three vertical columns (folders, messages, and preview). To switch to this view under Evolution, click View ➤ Preview ➤ Vertical View.

Contacts

Evolution includes a powerful contact manager component that can catalog information about individuals. At its most basic, the contact manager stores e-mail addresses for use within the e-mail component of Evolution, but you can enter significant additional data about each individual, including addresses, phone numbers, fax numbers, and even a photograph for easy identification. This should allow Evolution to become your sole personal information manager.

To switch to the Contacts mode, click the button at the bottom-left side of the program window. Once in the Contacts mode, you can view information in several ways. Click View ➤ Current View to choose from the following views:

Address Cards: This is the default view and shows the contacts as virtual index cards arranged alongside each other at the top of the program window. Click the scrollbar beneath the cards to move through them.

List View: This shows the contact information as a simple list, arranged vertically, with various elements of the contact's personal information listed alongside, such as phone numbers and e-mail addresses.

By Company: This organizes the data in a similar way to List view but sorted by the company the contacts work for (if such data has been entered into the contact entries).

Adding or Editing Contact Information

By far, the best way of initially building up your contacts list is to right-click e-mail addresses at the head of messages, in Mail mode, and select Add to Address Book. Make sure the address book selected is Ubuntu One if you want your contact information to be synchronized to your personal space in the

Internet; read the next chapter to learn more about this service. This will add a simple contact record consisting of the individual's name and e-mail address.

When using Microsoft mail applications, simply replying to an e-mail from an individual is enough to add that contact to your address book. Evolution is capable of this behavior too, but the feature isn't activated by default. To set this up, click Edit ➤ Preferences, click Mail Preferences on the left side of the dialog box, and click the Automatic Contacts tab. Next, put a check in the box marked Automatically Create Entries in the Address Book When Responding to Messages. From the Select Address Book for Automatic Contacts drop-down list, select Personal. In the same dialog box, you can synchronize contacts from the Pidgin instant messaging client so that Evolution is brought up to date with your Pidgin contacts, and vice versa. You can then edit the contact details by double-clicking the entry in Contacts mode. This will let you enter a variety of information, as shown in Figure 14-9. To import a photo for this contact, click the top-left icon. You can use any picture here, and you don't need to worry about its size, because it will be resized automatically by Evolution (although its aspect ratio will be preserved). The imported photo will appear in the lower area of the Contacts window when you click the contact's name.

If you add a new contact and the details are substantially similar to those of another contact already on the system, the software will give you the opportunity to merge the two contacts into a single profile.

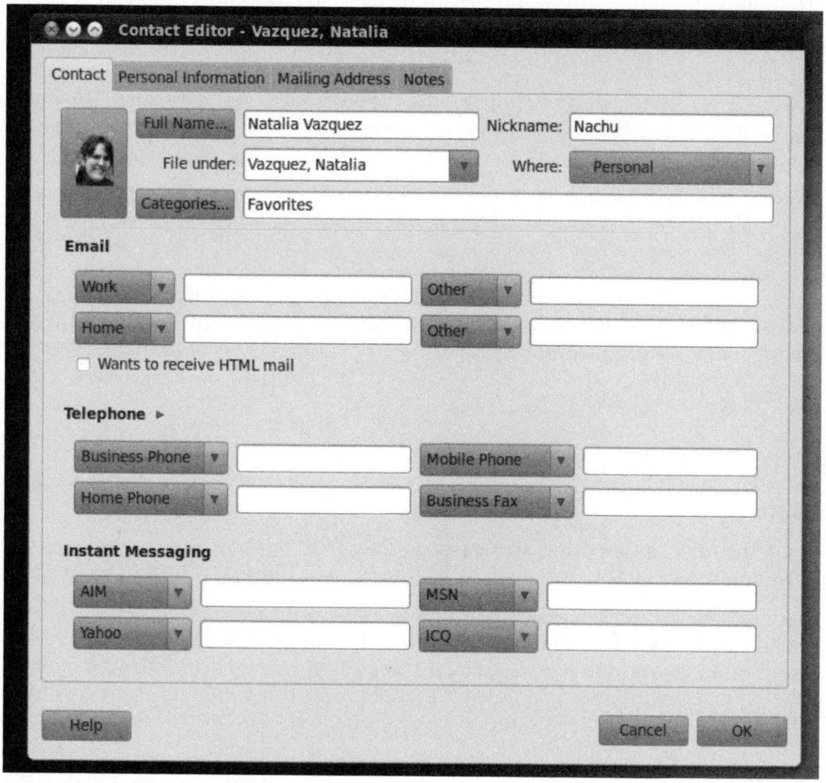

Figure 14-9. A lot of information can be entered for each contact, and, by clicking the button at the top left, you can also add a photograph.

Creating a Contact List

Contact lists are simply lists of e-mail addresses. After a list is created, you can right-click its entry in the contacts list, and then choose to send a message to the list or forward it to someone else as a vCard. The obvious use of contact lists is for sending e-mail messages to a particular group of people.

■ **Note** A vCard is a virtual business card. Effectively, it's a small file that contains personal information. vCards can also contain pictures and audio clips. They're understood by practically all business-level e-mail programs, including Microsoft Outlook and Apple OS X's Mail program.

To create a contact list, click the small down arrow next to the New button in Contacts mode, and select the option from the list. Give the list a name in the relevant box, and simply click and drag contacts from the main program pane onto the bottom of the Contact List Editor pane. This will automatically add their names and e-mail addresses. Alternatively, you can type their e-mail addresses manually into the field under the Members heading, and then click the Add button, which can be useful if the individual isn't in your contact list.

By selecting the Hide Addresses When Sending Mail to This List check box, you can ensure that the e-mail addresses are added to the BCC field of a new message, so people on the list don't see the others on the list.

Calendars

The Calendars mode of Evolution allows you to keep an appointments diary. Entries can be added in half-hour increments to the working day, and you can easily add events to days that are weeks, months, or even years in advance. Viewing a day's appointments is as simple as clicking its entry in the month view at the top right of the program window.

Specifying Appointment Types

You can make the following three types of diary entries:

Appointments: These are events in your diary that apply to you only. You might have a meeting with a colleague, for example, or you might simply want to add a note to your diary to remind you of a particular fact.

All-day appointments: A training day or a holiday could be entered as an all-day appointment. However, all-day events don't block your diary, and you can still add individual appointments (after all, just because your day is taken up with an event doesn't mean you won't need to make individual appointments during the event). All-day events appear as a light-blue bar at the top of the day's entry in your diary.

Meetings: Meetings are like appointments, but you also have the option of inviting others to attend. The invitations are sent as iCal attachments to e-mail, so users of Microsoft Outlook should be able to reply to them (provided Outlook is properly configured; see the program's documentation for details, and note that iCal is sometimes referred to by the specification number RFC 2446/2447). After receiving a meeting invitation, an individual can click to accept or decline. When Evolution receives this response, the individual's acceptance or declination will be automatically added to the diary entry.

Adding or Editing a Diary Entry

These instructions assume that Calendars mode is set to Day view, which shows a full working day diary alongside a monthly calendar. To ensure Day view is selected, click the Day icon on the main toolbar running across the top of the screen. Day view is the default calendar view under Evolution. The other choices are Week, Month, and Work Week (which shows appointments during the week in daily columns). If you switch to another view, Evolution will always work in that view until you change back again.

To add a new diary entry, simply select the day in the monthly calendar on the left, and then select the time the appointment is to start in the day viewer. Then right-click and choose an appointment, an all-day event (this is called an all-day appointment on the New button on the toolbar), or a meeting. To edit an existing diary entry, double-click its entry in the list.

■ **Note** When you right-click in Calendars mode, you'll also see an option to add a task. Adding a task in Calendars mode automatically links it to the selected day and time. Task items due on the current day are marked in dark blue.

At its most basic, all an appointment needs in order to be entered into your diary is some text in the Summary field, as shown in Figure 14-10. By default, appointments and meetings are assumed to last for half an hour, but you can adjust this by using the arrows in the Hour and Minutes sections. For longer appointments, such as a holiday or conference that may last days or weeks, use the drop-down labeled For, select Until, and then define a finishing date or time.

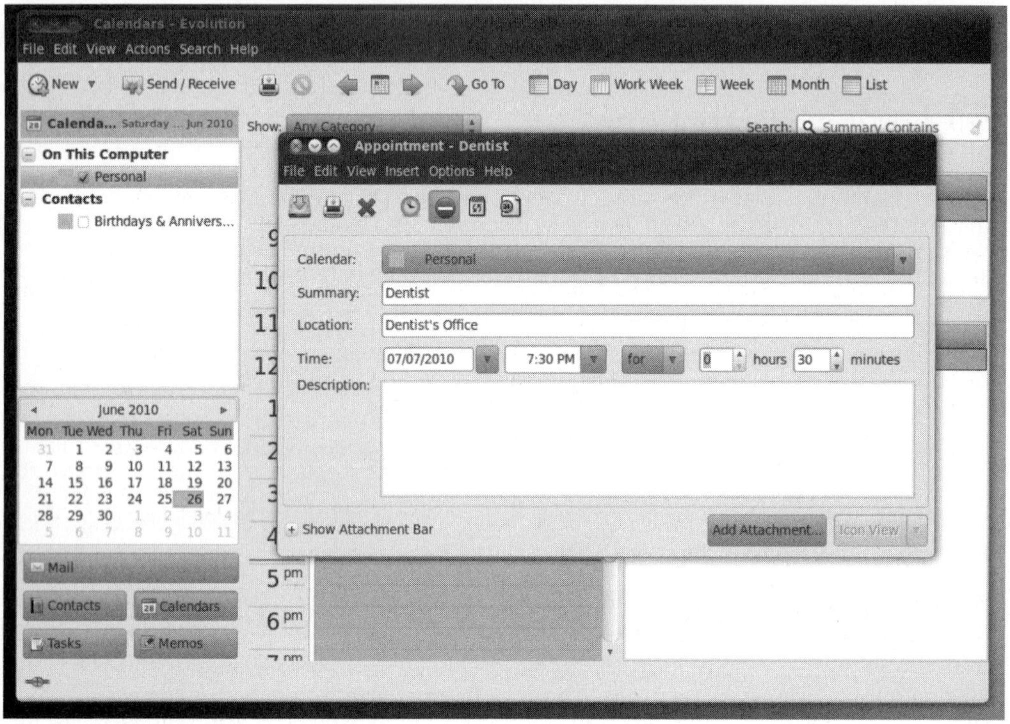

Figure 14-10. *When creating a new appointment, you can add all the details you need, but don't forget to set how long it lasts!*

By clicking the Recurrence button on the toolbar (note that not all buttons are visible in the default program width), you can set the appointment to be booked into your diary according to certain intervals. Start by putting a check in the This Appointment Recurs box, and then select a time interval. For example, selecting "1 week" will mean that the appointment is booked into your diary automatically on a weekly basis. After this, select a day of the week for the recurring appointment. Following this, you must specify the number of recurrences. You can specify an ending date for the appointment or select Forever. In the calendar view at the bottom of the dialog box, you'll be able to see how this looks. Days in bold are those that have appointments.

It's also possible to set exceptions, as when the meeting might skip a week. This could be useful to work around holidays, for example. Simply click the Add button, and then type a date or click the down arrow to select the date from a calendar. Finally, you can also add attachments to an appointment—a meeting agenda, minutes, and so forth—by clicking the Attach button and locating the appropriate file.

When you're finished, click the Close button to add the details of the recurring event to the appointment.

In the case of meeting appointments, you can click the Add button to invite others to the meeting via iCal invitations, which will be sent out by e-mail as soon as you've finished creating the appointment. Simply click the Add button, and in the empty field that appears, start typing the contact name of the individual you want to invite. If the person is already in your contacts list, the name will be automatically completed, but you can also type individual e-mail addresses. By clicking the entry under the Role heading, you can alter the role of the individual. The choices are Chair, Required Participant, Optional Participant, Non-Participant (i.e., somebody you want to inform about the meeting but who doesn't need to attend), and Unknown (for all other instances).

Clicking the Free/Busy button will open a new dialog box showing who can and can't attend, according to replies to the invitations sent out (obviously, this is a feature you'll be using after you initially create an appointment). On the left side of the dialog box, you will see the list of attendees and also their status: whether they've accepted, declined, or sent a busy/tentative reply (in which case you might choose to reschedule the meeting).

Additional Calendars

For those with complicated lives, Evolution can manage multiple calendars sourced from either your local machine or from an online service such as Google Calendar. Moreover, each one can be assigned a different color so you can see how events clash (or not) at a glance. To create a new local calendar, right-click the Calendars pane (on the left) and select New. Choose On This Computer from the drop-down, provide a name for the new calendar, and choose a color. When you create a new event, specify the appropriate calendar, and the event will be highlighted in its color.

You can also add a Google calendar by following the preceding instructions but choosing Google from the drop-down. Supply your Google credentials and then choose a calendar from those available. Again, you can define a color to apply to this calendar, as in Figure 14-11. The Google option is limited to viewing information added to the web service, so you can't add events by using Evolution, but this is a great way to access some of the many public calendars (such as national holidays and football match fixture lists) available on the Internet.

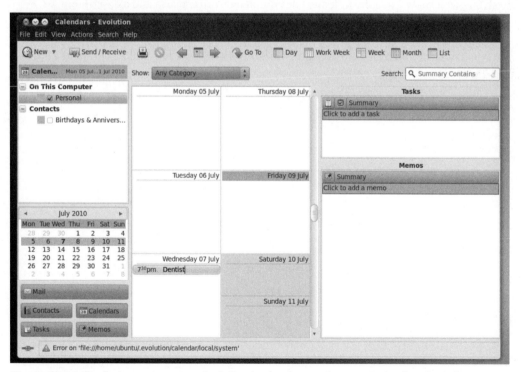

Figure 14-11. *Evolution can manage both local calendars and remote calendars from the Internet, making it ideal for creating and sharing group calendars.*

Memos and Tasks

The Memos and Tasks modes are the simplest components within Evolution. Memos mode allows you to jot down simple notes, and Tasks mode allows you to create a to-do list.

In both modes, which can be selected by clicking their buttons at the bottom left of the screen, the program window consists simply of an area where you can click to add a new memo/task, a list area, and a preview area, which will show any details of the currently selected task.

■ **Note** Memos created in Evolution can also be opened in Tomboy, the default GNOME desktop note-taking application.

In the case of Tasks mode, after you've made an entry, clicking the check box alongside it will mark it as completed. Completed items appear with a strike-through.

To add a new memo or task, click the bar that reads Click to Add a Memo (or Task), type a description, and then press Enter. You will be able to enter more tasks or memos in the same field.

Double-clicking a task or memo allows you to fine-tune its details. For example, you can add a due date for a task, so you'll know when the task must be completed. You can also add a description for future reference and attach files by clicking the relevant button on the toolbar. By clicking the Status Details button in the Task Details dialog box, you can also set a percentage figure for completion of the task, as well as its priority, ranging from low to high. By adding these details, a quick scan over your tasks will give you a good idea of which jobs are overdue, which need attention, and which will stand a little procrastination.

After you've added these details, right-click the Summary bar (at the top of the main window) and select Add a Column. You can now drag and drop elements onto the main window to get a better view of your tasks, as in Figure 14-12.

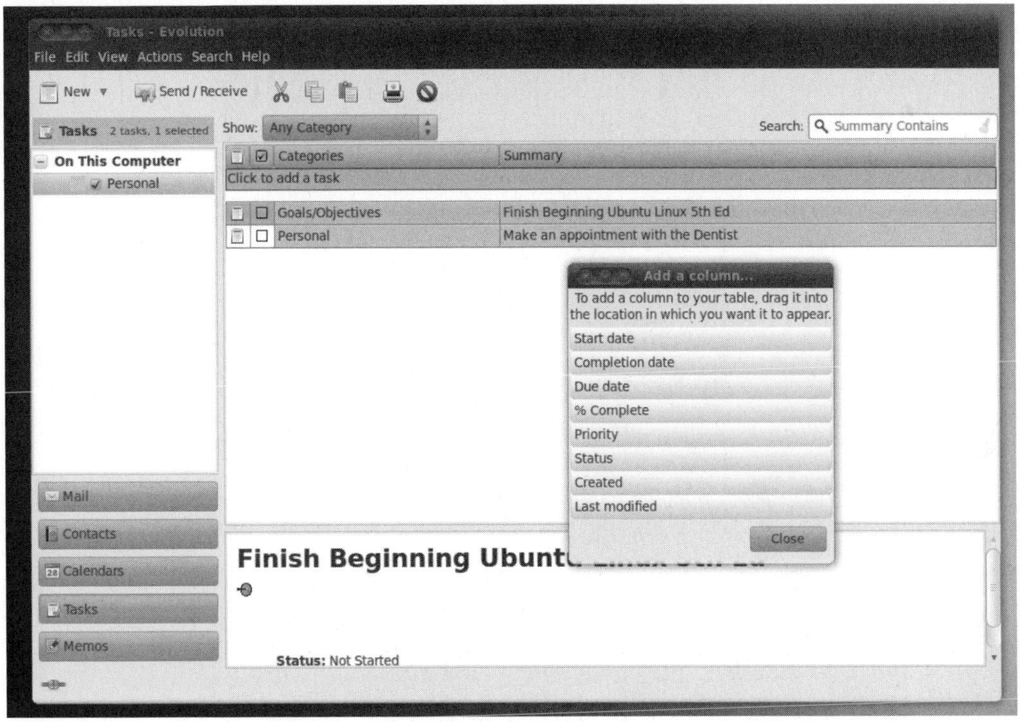

Figure 14-12. Tasks mode lets you catalog chores that you want to do during the day.

Configuring Instant Messaging

Instant messaging is a way of chatting with other people in real time. It's as if you were having a phone conversation, but you're typing instead of speaking. You can talk to one other person or a whole group of people and sometimes share files with them.

The instant messaging program under Ubuntu, Empathy, offers the same functions and works in an almost identical way to programs that you might have used under Windows. It supports virtually all the popular chat standards, such as ICQ/AOL, Google Talk, Yahoo, and MSN (Hotmail/Passport). It assumes that you already have an account with each service, which will likely be the case if you've used instant messaging programs under Windows. You can have as many accounts as you wish and log to all of them at the same time. You can see the contacts from all your instant messaging accounts in the same list and can chat with them at the same time. Using the Me menu, you can set your status for all your accounts at the same time. This is useful, as it provides a single instant messaging application that allows you to chat with users from different networks.

To configure your accounts (referred in Lucid terminology as *chat accounts)*, click the little envelope located next to the date and time in the top panel, and select Set Up Chat. The Welcome to Empathy wizard will appear. If you select the option "Yes, I'll enter my account details now" and click Forward, you will be prompted to enter your account details, as shown in Figure 14-13.

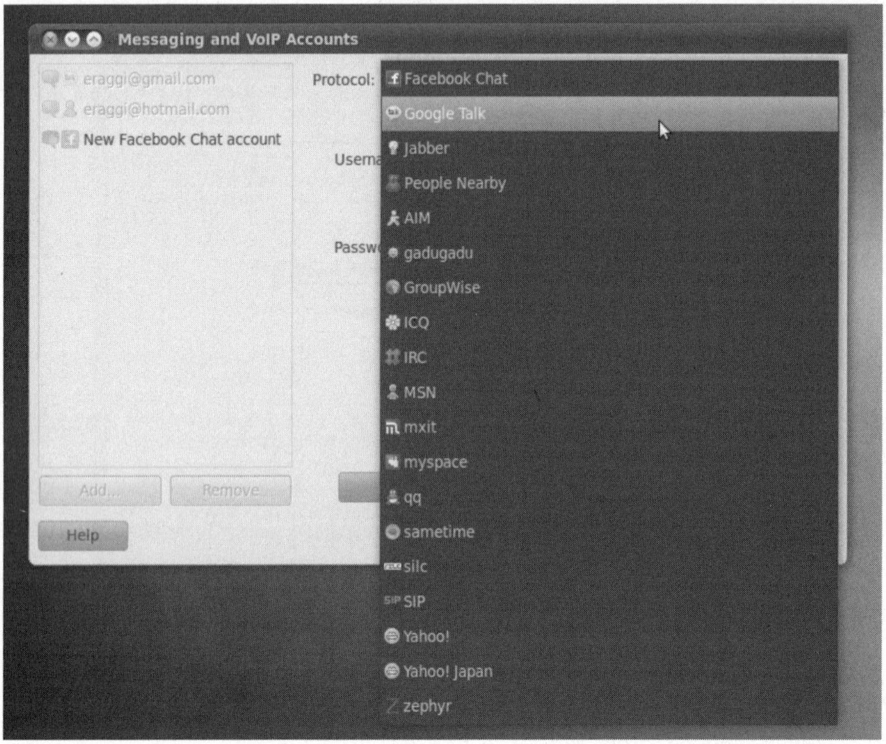

Figure 14-13. Empathy can communicate with users across a range of different protocols.

There are a lot of instant messaging services to which you can connect, as listed in Table 14-1.

Table 14-1. Instant Messaging Services That Can Be Used with Empathy

Instant Messaging Service	Description
Facebook Chat	This is a Facebook feature that allows users to chat with other Facebook users. It requires a Facebook account.
Google Talk	Google Talk, or GTalk, is a free instant messaging service provided by Google.
Jabber	Jabber.org was the first instant messaging service based on the open protocol XMPP (Extensible Messaging and Presence Protocol). It has been running since1999.
AIM	This is the well-known AOL Instant Messenger.
Gadu-Gadu	This is a Polish instant messaging service—the most popular in its home country.

Instant Messaging Service	Description
GroupWise	GroupWise is messaging and collaboration software that supports, among other things, instant messaging.
ICQ	ICQ was the first Internet-wide instant messaging service, launched in 1996. Its name is pronounced *I seek you*.
MSN	This is the popular service provided by Microsoft. It is typically used with MSN Messenger, now rebranded as Windows Live Messenger.
mxit	This is a free instant messaging service whose user base is mainly in South Africa.
MySpace	MySpace is a social networking website (the most popular before Facebook came along) that includes an instant messaging service.
QQ	Tenecent QQ, hosted in QQ.com, is the most popular free instant messaging service in mainland China, with more than 800 million users. Originally known as OICQ, or Open ICQ, its mascot is a penguin.
Sametime	IBM Lotus Sametime is a unified communications and collaboration product for the enterprise that includes instant messaging among its capabilities.
SILC	This is the Secure Internet Live Conferencing protocol, which provides secure conferencing services. Its development is coordinated by the SILC Project, which also maintains the public SILC network.
SIP	The Session Initiation Protocol (SIP) is widely used for controlling multimedia communication sessions such as voice and video calls.
Yahoo	This is an instant messaging service provided by Yahoo free of charge and used with Yahoo accounts.
Yahoo Japan	This is the Japanese affiliate of Yahoo.
Zephyr	Zephyr is an instant messaging protocol created at MIT as part of Project Athena. It is still in use today by some universities.

If you're working in a small office without an Internet connection but you want to send instant messages to your coworkers, you can use the People Nearby feature by selecting the "No, I just want to see people online nearby for now" option from the Welcome to Empathy wizard. You will need to provide a full name and an alias and instruct your fellows to do the same. You will then be able to chat with them without installing a server.

Once you have configured your accounts, you will see all your contacts in Empathy's main window, the Contact List. You can change the status of all of your accounts at the same time by using the drop-down list located beneath the menus, or by using the Me menu online status list.

Installing Skype

Skype, shown in Figure 14-14, is used by millions of people around the world to make Internet telephone calls via Voice over IP (VoIP). This is a complicated way of saying that voice calls are transmitted across the Internet. Using Skype, it's possible to call other Skype users for free, or to call various phone numbers around the world, usually for a small charge.

Installing Skype is easy, and the Skype developers have even created a software repository from which it can be installed. This means that you'll be informed via Update Manager whenever a new version of Skype becomes available.

To add the Skype repository, click System ➤ Administration ➤ Software Sources. Click the Other Software tab in the window that appears, and then click the Add button. In the APT Line text box, type the following:

```
deb http://download.skype.com/linux/repos/debian/ stable non-free
```

Note the spaces between debian/ and stable, and between stable and non-free. Click the Add Source button. Click Close, and then click the Reload button in the dialog box that appears.

After you have done that, you can use the Ubuntu Software Center for installing Skype. Just search for Skype and click Install when the application appears in the list.

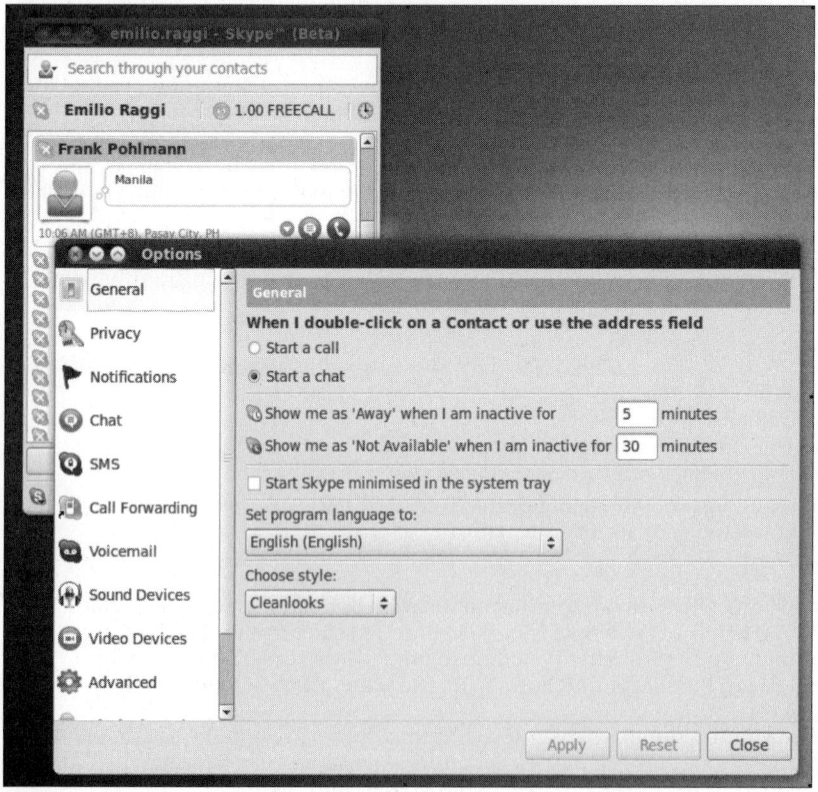

Figure 14-14. *It's easy to install Skype under Ubuntu, and it works almost exactly as it does under Windows or Macintosh.*

After the software is installed, click Applications ➤ Internet ➤ Skype to start it. Using Skype under Linux is very similar to using it under Windows or Macintosh. You'll find excellent documentation at www.skype.com.

■ **Tip** To configure your audio input device (e.g., microphone), right-click the Speaker icon at the top right of the desktop and select Open Volume Control. Then click and drag the Microphone slider as necessary. You may need to unmute the input by removing the red cross next to the speaker icon below the Microphone slider.

Ekiga

Ekiga, an open source alternative to Skype, offers a similar feature set. It can be installed using the Ubuntu Software Center and is available from Applications ➤ Internet ➤ Ekiga Softphone. When the software is launched for the first time, you'll be prompted to create an Ekiga.net account, which will give you a SIP address (the VoIP equivalent of an e-mail address) and an option to purchase call-out credit. After you've signed into the service, it works in a similar way to Skype, with a buddy list and, as shown in Figure 14-15, a standard numerical dial pad for calling land lines or mobile numbers. Ekiga's integration with the Ubuntu desktop is very good—for example, you can receive alerts in the notification area if one of your contacts makes a call to you.

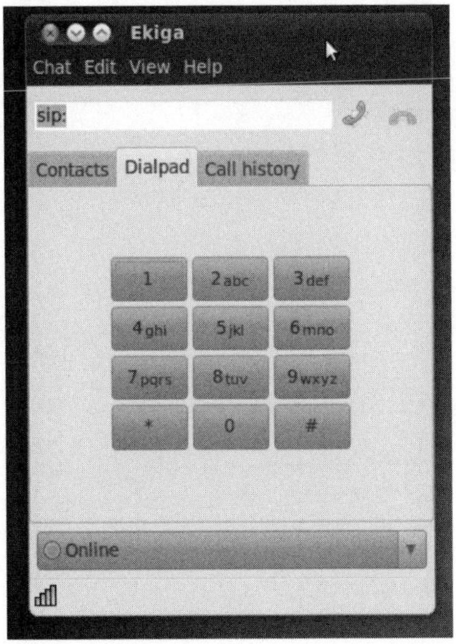

Figure 14-15. Ekiga is an open source alternative to Skype.

Summary

This chapter has been a whistle-stop tour of Evolution's main features. You've looked at e-mail creation and organization, contacts management, working with the appointments calendar, and editing the task list and memos. Evolution is a powerful program. Be sure to take a look at its help documentation (Help ➤ Contents) to learn more about it.

This chapter also discussed the instant messaging client and how it integrates with the Me menu. The next chapter will go into greater detail about this new feature and what can you do with it.

CHAPTER 15

■ ■ ■

Social Networks and Cloud Computing

From the very beginning, computer networks were about more than just connecting devices. They were about connecting people.

The day two computers first got connected, a communication path between two human beings was formed. As the number of connections increased, more and more people were sharing information, experiences, and their lives. Today, of course, we have the web. With its ubiquity, the possibilities are bounded only by our collective imagination.

Social networks have emerged to harness the commincation power of the web. You want to get back in touch with your old classmates from high school? Check. You want to create a virtual business card and relate to colleagues? Check. You want to publish your activities so people know what you are doing all the time? Check.

However, administering your online persona can be an overwhelming task. Social networking sites are currently self-centered and poorly, if at all, integrated, so you have to check and update them one by one.

What we need are applications that do the heavy work for us and let us concentrate on what we want to publish and where—not on how to do it.

A second web trend has emerged: so-called *cloud computing*. As the processing power and storage capacity of the Internet as a whole rises exponentially, so do the benefits of running applications and saving data online, rather than doing so on your own PC. We are in the middle of a computing revolution in which the core processing unit is no longer the individual PC, but the "cloud" of connected devices.

Today, more and more sites provide free space to store personal information in the cloud, whether in order to share with others (for example, a photo in an album you create), or just to have an online copy of your private data.

In this chapter, we talk about how Ubuntu can leverage those two trends and make our online life a lot easier and pleasant.

■ **Note** One of the main applications you will be using with social networks and cloud-based services is your favorite web browser. Most browsers that you can use with Ubuntu are very well suited for social networking. In this chapter we talk about other applications that connect directly to the Internet to perform specific tasks, using its resources as if they were local to your PC.

Social Networking Applications

In the last few years, the use of social networks has experienced staggering growth. Sites like Twitter and Facebook serve millions of users per day and generate terabytes of data.

WELCOME TO WEB 2.0

Social network sites are part of a greater movement called *web 2.0.*

The "first" Internet (web 1.0) offered us mainly static content, provided by the site owner. The user consumed that content typically by using a web browser. Web 1.0 sites included newspapers, magazines, and corporate or e-commerce sites. The user could read the pages, buy something online, and if the site allowed she could post a comment to an existing web page. The user was strictly a consumer.

Web 2.0, on the other hand, is a platform to *share*—to share interests, photos, video, status, and any other information that we deem interesting. There is no "main publisher," and when there is a centralized authority, its role is mainly to set the rules and enforce them, not to produce content. Think YouTube, Wikipedia, Twitter, and Facebook.

Several types of sites are considered part of the "Web 2.0," including but not limited to:

- *Wikis*: These are sites that allow users to create content in the form of sets of interrelated web pages, often with a common subject. It is well suited for documentation of specific topics and for encyclopedias, the most famous being Wikipedia.

- *Blogs*: A blog (short for *web log*) is a service that allows a user or set of users to *post* content, forming a web page of continuous posts sorted in chronological order (showing the newest post first). Derivations of the original blog concept are photoblogs and Microblogging sites (which set a size limit for posts).

- *Social networks*: These are sites that allow users to create profiles and connect to other users to share information and interests. Those connected users are typically called *friends*. The content shared is often divided into private and public content, private content being available only through authorized connections.

Ubuntu 10.04 was designed to be "social from the start," which means that it integrates with social networks seamlessly. In the first section of this chapter we look at some of the applications you can use for this purpose.

Introducing the MeMenu

Lucid Lynx includes a new applet located in the top panel, next to the Date and the Shutdown button, as is shown in Figure 15-1. It is the MeMenu, and it was so important for the developing team that its interface was sketched by Mike Shuttleworth himself. The MeMenu is the cornerstone of a strategy to make you feel like there is no real difference between your local account and your online persona; they are one and the same. Once you log in to Ubuntu, you are online!

The MeMenu allows you to set status for instant messaging (IM) accounts and to broadcast posts to all your social networks, including Twitter and Facebook.

Not all sections are shown by default; some only appear after you have configured certain types of accounts.

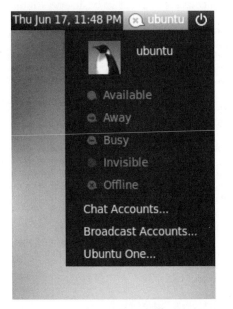

Figure 15-1. The MeMenu allows you to set IM status and to broadcast to your social networks.

Title: The Title section includes an icon representing the online status of your IM accounts, and your short name as specified in About Me (see Chapter 9). It could be that your multiple Chat accounts will have different statuses; in that case, the icon appears as a thick dash—or as disabled if no Chat account has been created.

Me: The Me section contains a photo and your full name, as specified in About Me.

Broadcast: The Broadcast section consists of a text box. It is shown only if you have created at least one Broadcast account. You can enter text in the box, and it's posted to all checked Broadcast accounts the moment you press Enter. Be aware that some social networks limit the number of characters of your posts (Twitter's tweets are limited to 140 characters; Facebook status updates can run to 420 characters).

IM Status: The IM Status section lets you set the status for multiple Chat accounts. You have several options: Available, Away, Busy, Invisible, and Offline. Selecting one option sets all Chat accounts to that status.

Account Configuration: The Account Configuration section lets you associate your online accounts with your profile. You can create both Chat accounts and Broadcast accounts. There's also a pointer to Ubuntu One, a cloud-based storage service about which we will talk later in this Chapter.

The MeMenu relies on Empathy (already seen in Chapter 14) for Chat accounts and on Gwibber (more about it later) for Broadcast accounts. Those applications should be installed if you want to create accounts of each type.

Microblogging with Gwibber

Gwibber is a microblogging client for the GNOME desktop environment that you can use to access Twitter, Facebook, and other social networking sites.

Microblogging is a complex cultural phenomenon, but in itself consists of only two basic operations: to post content, and to read other users' posts (called *following*, as on Twitter). It is the aggregation of millions of such operations a day that renders microblogging so interesting.

As the number of social network sites continues to grow, it is hard for users to keep up the pace. We want our posts to have the greatest impact, so we need to send it to every single microblogging site available, just to make sure no one misses it. On the other hand, we want to receive the most relevant content, no matter where it was originally posted. We can't stick to a single service, we must use them all.

Without tools that help us with these tasks, to fulfill that simple objective we would have to update every site manually, using a web browser, and then check them one by one to see if there is some interesting stuff. We would rarely have time to do this.

Someone once said: "I will work 24 hours a day, and nights too." That sentiment also seems to apply to social networking.

Here's where Gwibber comes in. It allows you to post to multiple sites at the same time, and follow content from different sources. Whereas the MeMenu can post short messages to some microblogging sites, Gwibber lets you also read other people's threads.

Gwibber is installed by default and can be found at Applications ➤ Internet as Gwibber Social Client. If for some reason you don't have it, you can install it by going to Applications ➤ Ubuntu Software Center. Click Get Free Software in the left pane and select the category Internet. Browse the list of available applications and select Gwibber. Click Install to begin installation (refer to Chapter 20 for further information on how to install or remove software).

The basic interface, as shown in Figure 15-2, is quite simple.

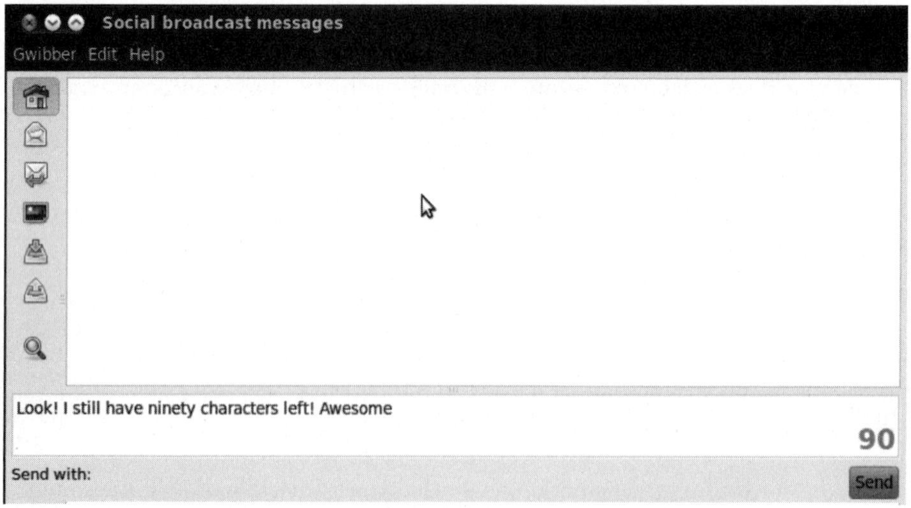

Figure 15-2. Gwibber lets you configure multiple social networking sites.

At the top is a menu that contains only three entries: Gwibber, Edit, and Help.

The main section is divided into two panes: the Streams pane, where you can see your mailboxes, and the Details pane, where the selected mailbox actual posts are shown.

At the bottom, the Broadcast text box is shown, along with icons representing each of your microblogging accounts. You can enter your thoughts into this text box, and when you press the Enter key they will be automatically posted online. You can select which sites to post the message to by enabling or disabling the icons in the Send with: area. If the microblogging sites have a restriction for post's length, the number of remaining characters available will be displayed at the right inside the text box. Very handy!

Gwibber supports many social networking sites, as listed in Table 15-1, but for Gwibber to work with them you must first have an account created for that site, and in some cases you must explicitly allow Gwibber to access your information.

Table 15-1. *Services Supported by Gwibber*

Name	Description	URL
Twitter	Very popular microblogging site. Posts have a maximum length of 140 characters and are known as *tweets*. You can read other people's posts (if they are public), and become a *follower* of them. Even Barack Obama has a Twitter account.	http://www.twitter.com
Identi.ca	Open source social network and microblogging site. Similar to Twitter, it also has a 140-character limit per post, but implements many original features.	http://identi.ca
FriendFeed	FriendFeed is a real-time feed aggregator. You can create your own feed and configure it to retrieve information from several sources, and it will synchronize the information and provide a single point of entry to all your content.	http://friendfeed.com
Facebook	Maybe the best-known social network site, Facebook allows users to connect to friends, post messages, receive comments, and engage in multiple forms of shared activities.	http://www.facebook.com
Digg	Allows users to discover and rank Internet content. When a user *Diggs* a web page, it is sent to a ranking system. Other users can vote up or down the page, and sort it based on popularity.	http://www.digg.com
StatusNet	An open source microblogging service formerly known as Laconica. Similar to Twitter, but aimed at providing distributed communications by allowing enterprise and individual installations.	http://status.net
Flickr	Popular image hosting and sharing site owned by Yahoo!	http://www.flickr.com
Qaiku	Microblogging and photo-sharing site with multilingual support, lets you search content filtered by language.	http://qaiku.com

Once you have created your microblogging accounts, you're ready to add them to Gwibber. Select Edit ➤ Accounts and click the Add… button. Select the account type from the list and click Add. Depending on the type of account you add, you will be asked for various information.

For each account you configure, you will have a new group in the Streams pane. You can display all the posts from all your sites by selecting the Home section, or view more specific streams of posts by selecting the mailbox of the specific site. You have also the Search sections, in which you can look for specific text in the social networks to see what other people are saying about a particular topic. From now on, you can read other people's posts, create your own messages and post them online, and master the social network from a single, easy-to-use application.

Cloud-Based Services

In the last few years ever-increasing processing and storage capacity led to reduction of their costs. It soon became evident how much efficiency could be gained just by outsourcing those resources to the cloud.

WELCOME TO CLOUD COMPUTING

In parallel with the Web 2.0 movement, a second trend is showing its strength in the Internet today: cloud computing.

The term *cloud* itself refers to the image of a cloud used in network engineering to depict a public network that is outside the administrative boundaries of an organization and over which it has no control. The Internet is the biggest of those networks.

In the distributed computing model of the past 20 years or so, the core processing unit was the individual PC. It was a self-contained unit that stored applications and data. Users could connect to other PCs and even the Internet, but that was optional.

As more and more bandwidth became available, and storage and processing costs plummeted, it became apparent that the efficiency that could be gained by centralization was humongous. It wasn't long before companies and organizations started to offer cloud-based services, be they storage, applications, or both.

Today, the shift to the cloud is becoming more evident than ever. Even Google has announced a new OS whose only function is to connect to the Internet and run web-based applications, and Microsoft offers hosted versions of some of its most popular server software, such as Exchange and SharePoint. In a short time, the core processing unit won't be the PC, but the whole of the Internet.

Ubuntu, or Linux for that matter, is not a cloud-centric operating system the way Google Chrome OS is. It still relies on the local PC for most of its operations. Nonetheless, Lucid Lynx comes equipped with some functionality that allows you to have the best of both worlds, by making the most of your PC's hardware resources, while being able to use cloud-based services transparently.

Storing Your Data Online with Ubuntu One

Ubuntu One is an online storage and synchronization service operated by Canonical Ltd. This means it provides you with space in the cloud and synchronizes its content with your computers.

It is not the first service of this kind to have hit the market. Dropbox and Live Mesh have similar functionality. Nonetheless, it has certain characteristics that make it a good choice for Ubuntu users, namely its capacity for synchronizing notes and contacts between several computers (in addition to just storing files). Currently, only Ubuntu clients are supported.

Ubuntu One subscriptions come in two flavors. A basic subscription is available for free, and it enables you to store up to 2GB of personal information on Ubuntu One servers. If you need more space, you can upgrade your subscription to a 50GB plan, for a monthly fee (at the time of writing, the fee was $10 a month).

In order to use Ubuntu One, you must first subscribe to the service and then configure your computers to connect and synchronize files, notes, and contacts.

Subscribing to Ubuntu One

Follow these instructions to create your account and subscribe to the free Ubuntu One service.

1. Access the site at `http://one.ubuntu.com.`

2. Click "Sign in."

3. You will need a Launchpad account. Launchpad is a web development tracking tool maintained by Canonical. Its login services are also used with Ubuntu One.

    • If you already have a Launchpad account, just enter your e-mail address. Enter your password and click Continue.

    • If you don't, press the "New account" button. Click Continue to create the account. A confirmation will be sent to the specified address. Follow the link in the mail and fill the registration form. You will have to specify a display name and a password in order to complete the account creation process.

4. Select the option Subscribe. You will be presented with the available options. If you choose a free plan, you can finish the subscription process. If the plan has a monthly fee, you will have to provide a valid credit card.

5. Confirm that the subscription option is correct and then click Agree & Subscribe.

■ **Caution** Ubuntu One is a free service and as such is very useful. But you should carefully read its Terms of Service and its Privacy Policy, available here: `https://one.ubuntu.com/terms/` and here `https://one.ubuntu.com/privacy/` and make sure they don't affect the use you will give to the service. Make sure you understand that Ubuntu One is not a replacement for regular backups, since Canonical Ltd. cannot be held responsible for lost information.

Configuring your Computer to Synchronize Files

After the subscription is created, you need to configure your computer for synchronization. The Ubuntu One client software is installed by default in Lucid Lynx.

1. Access the Ubuntu One client software, available at the bottom of the MeMenu list.

2. The Ubuntu One Preferences dialog box opens. If you click "Manage account," a web browser will open, asking you to log in to Launchpad if you have not already done so.

3. After you are logged in to Launchpad, you will need to confirm access to the service from your computer. Add the computer name to the list.

Once you have configured your computer for synchronization, you are ready to start using the service.

You will notice in Nautilus that there is a folder with the name Ubuntu One in your /home directory (see Figure 15-3). Every file that is copied or moved to that folder will be synchronized to Ubuntu One and to every other computer that you associate with the same Launchpad account.

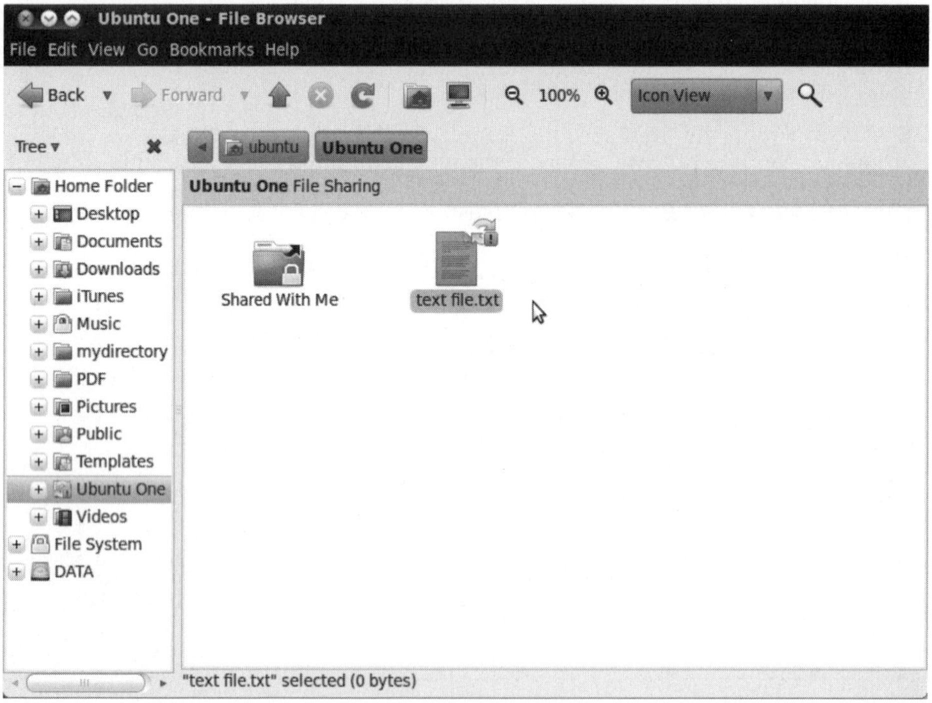

Figure 15-3. The Ubuntu One folder inside Nautilus.

A notification will appear when Ubuntu One is synchronizing files, and when it finishes doing so. You can also share folders with other Ubuntu One users. To do this, right-click a subfolder of UbuntuOne in Nautilus and select the option Share on Ubuntu One. You will need to provide the e-mail address of the person you want to share the folder with, and that e-mail account must be associated with an Ubuntu One subscription.

If other people share their folders with you, you will see them in the subfolder Shared with Me, inside Ubuntu One in Nautilus.

■ **Note** It might happen someday that you want to cancel your Ubuntu One subscription. If you do, the information will be deleted from Ubuntu One, but not from your computer. If you have a free plan it will be deleted immediately, whereas a paid subscription will remain active until the end of the current billing period.

Synchronizing Notes

Another kind of information that you can synchronize with Ubuntu One is Tomboy Notes. Tomboy is an application that allows you to take notes, which comes installed by default in Lucid Lynx. Each note consists of a title and a body.

To configure the application follow these steps:

1. Access the Tomboy Notes application, available in Applications ➤ Accessories.

2. Once the application opens, click the Edit menu and select Preferences.

3. Click the Synchronization tab and select the options shown in Figure 15-4. Click the Connect to Server button.

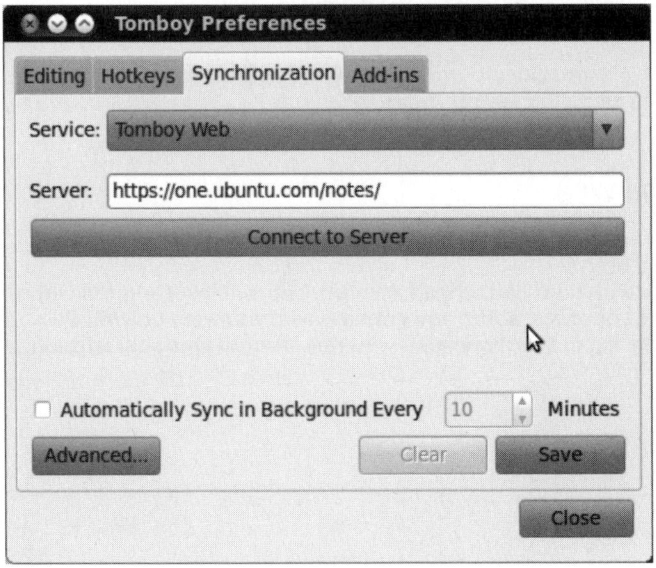

Figure 15-4. Tomboy Notes Synchronization options.

4. Notice that a web page opens in your default browser. You will be prompted to log in to Launchpad and authorize your computer, just as you do when synchronizing files.

5. If login and authorization are successful, you will receive a message telling you so.

6. Go back to Tomboy and click Save to start synchronizing notes.

From that point onwards, your notes will be synchronized to Ubuntu One, and from there to any other computers that you configure with the same Launchpad account.

You can force synchronization by expanding the Tools menu and choosing the option Synchronize Notes.

Synchronizing Evolution Contacts

You can also synchronize Evolution contacts (for an introduction to Evolution, see Chapter 14).

1. Open Evolution, available in Applications ➤ Office. If this is the first time you open Evolution, you will need to create an account.

2. Select to Always Allow the application and the synchronization service to access your default keyring.

3. Access the Contacts section of Evolution.

4. Only contacts residing in the CouchDB ➤ Ubuntu One Address Book will be synchronized. If you already have contacts created in other address books, you can copy them by expanding the Action menu and clicking on the option Copy All Contacts to… Select CouchDB ➤ Ubuntu One as the destination Address Book.

5. You can also set the CouchDB ➤ Ubuntu One Address Book as the default by selecting its properties and checking the option "Mark as default address book."

Accessing Your Information on the Web

Now that you have configured synchronization, you don't need your PC to access your information stored on Ubuntu One. All you need is a web browser.

Go to http://one.ubuntu.com and log in with your Launchpad account. You will be presented with a web page where you can view, edit, or delete your files, notes, and contacts as if you were on your PC (see Figure 15-5). You can also administer the list of PCs associated with this Ubuntu One subscription.

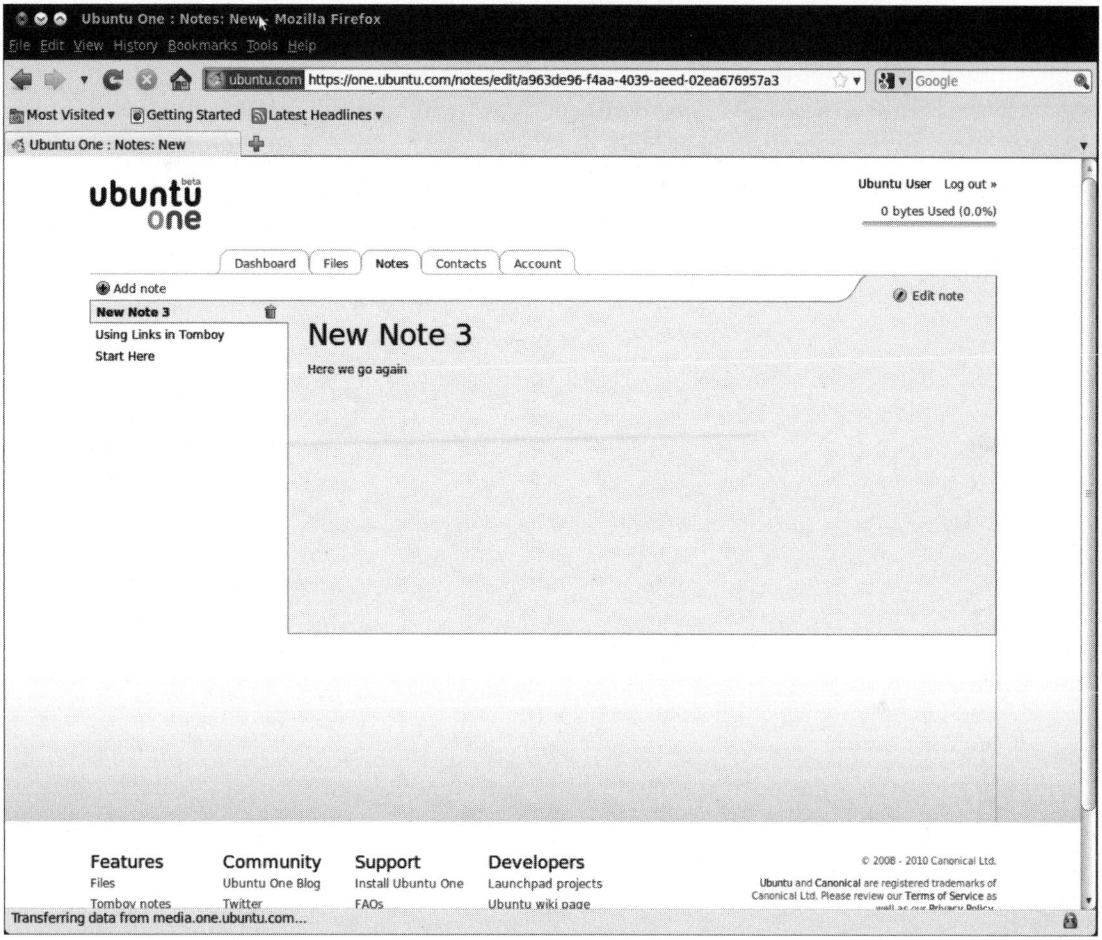

Figure 15-5. *The Ubuntu One web page.*

Sending Photos to the Cloud with F-Spot

Chapter 18 explains how to use F-Spot to administer your photos.

What's important to say at this point is that until Lucid Lynx, your photos stayed on your hard drive. There was no integration with cloud-based services or social network applications like Flickr or Facebook.

The new version of F-Spot makes it easy to keep our web albums up to date by enabling photo uploading directly from the application, without even having to use a browser.

Before you can upload your photos, you must create an account in some web album application. Just click Photo ➤ Export to…and select your online photo gallery to upload your content.

Summary

The Internet is constantly evolving. Ubuntu evolves with it, allowing the user to unleash its power without losing control of the PC. Ubuntu is designed so you can think of our online persona as the same as your local account, and of the cloud as a resource of your PC.

The web browser is no longer the only portal to the Internet. Many more applications are prepared to connect directly to the Internet and do things like upload photos and post to a blog.

CHAPTER 16

■ ■ ■

Digital Audio

Today's PC is a multimedia powerhouse, and it's hard to come across a home computer that doesn't have at least a pair of speakers attached. Some people take this to extremes and have surround-sound speakers on their computers, as well as large widescreen monitors for crystal-clear, high-definition video playback.

The stability of Linux makes Ubuntu a rock-solid general-purpose multimedia system, Audio and video playback software is installed by default, with nearly 300 additional programs for production and consumption of digital media available for free in the Sound & Video section of the Ubuntu Software Center.

In this chapter, you'll learn how to listen to your existing MP3s and CDs on your Ubuntu system, and how to explore a world of new sounds via streaming audio, podcasts, and music stores. In the next chapter, you'll learn how to manage video playback.

Issues Surrounding Multimedia Playback

Since the advent of digital distribution, record companies and content producers have sought ways of restricting the ability of users to copy music and films. This usually means digital rights management (DRM), which often has the side effect of restricting playback of various media formats on noncommercial operating systems, as the DRM required to play back some music and video needs to be licensed. Audio and video playback technologies such as MP3 and MPEG are patented in countries that allow software to be patented, such as the United States. A *patent* protects the implementation of an idea, as opposed to *copyright*, which protects the actual software. Patents are designed to restrict distribution of a particular technology, which implements an idea or concept, unless permission is granted, usually via a payment to the license holder.

Because Linux is based on the sharing of computing technology and knowledge, organizations like Ubuntu (and Canonical, the company behind Ubuntu) are fundamentally and philosophically opposed to software patents. For this reason, as well as to avoid the risk of patent infringement lawsuits, they take care not to distribute such software, which is why MP3 playback is not supported by default within Ubuntu, for example. This doesn't make playback of popular music and video files impossible, but it means that, out of the box, Ubuntu does not have the facility to play these formats. It is up to the user to download and install some extra software to do so if he or she wishes, although this is actually pretty easy as the process is automated.

■ **Note** It isn't the job of this book to dictate a position for you on the ethics of using software that has been patented. That's something you must do on your own. It's a complicated issue, but Wikipedia has a good summary of the arguments: http://en.wikipedia.org/wiki/Software_patent.

Much more devastating than patenting is DRM, a technology tied into audio or video playback software. It's designed to control how, where, when, and on what device you can play certain media. For example, until recently Apple's iTunes DRM scheme meant that you could play back movies and some audio tracks bought from iTunes only on the iPod range of devices (including the Apple TV and iPhone range of devices) or using the iTunes software. DVD and Blu-ray disc players include forms of DRM, called the Content Scrambling System (CSS) and Advanced Access Content System (AACS), respectively, which prevent users from playing DVDs on computers unless special software is purchased. With Apple's move away from DRM, and Amazon's DRM-free MP3 store, the situation for audio tracks is getting better, but nearly all movie files remain affected.

As a community that celebrates openness, many Linux users and developers mistrust any technology that attempts to restrict their rights to use software in particular ways. Moreover, the relatively small user base and the preference for free rather than proprietary software has meant that no mainstream vendor has ported its DRM technology to Linux on the desktop. This means, for instance, that movies purchased via iTunes will not work on a Linux desktop.

■ **Note** Companies *do* make their DRM software available on Linux, only it tends to be developed for inclusion in set-top boxes, DVD players, HD televisions, MP3 players, and Internet-connected media players. One exception—and it's one you may want to consider if you're concerned with the legal issue of DVD playback—is CyberLink's $49.95 PowerDVD software, which is available to buy from Canonical's online store (http://shop.canonical.com).

Linux and other open source projects are very resourceful and are often able to reverse-engineer technology formats in order to get around DRM or patent issues. But the laws in many countries—the United States is a particularly strident example—prohibit reverse-engineering in this way. In addition, the laws in some countries seek to prohibit use of software resulting from this process.

The good news is that programmers have also come up with open and free alternatives to proprietary formats. Examples include the Ogg Vorbis media format, which is every bit as good as MP3 but is unencumbered by patent issues. We look at using Ogg Vorbis later in this chapter, in the "Choosing a Format" section; it's an excellent way of avoiding issues surrounding patenting. On the video side, no open source video format is yet in widespread use, but with Mozilla, Opera, Adobe, Google and many other vendors now backing the royalty-free WebM video format, the picture is likely to change very fast.

As an end user migrating to Ubuntu from Windows or Mac OS X, it's likely you'll want to add support for MP3 and popular video file playback formats, at least until you can switch over to free and open file formats. In this and the next chapter, we're recommending that you install additional software to use in concert with Ubuntu's built-in media players. Some of that software may have issues surrounding patenting, and in one case, is designed to break the encryption that protects the content on DVD movie discs. Although we can't of course provide you with any legal guarantee for your particular jurisdiction, you may be reassured to know that, to our knowledge, no end user has ever had any legal hassle as a result of installing and using this software.

■ **Note** The United States and Japan both have laws allowing software to be patented. Most other countries, including those within the European Union, do not currently allow software patents.

Playing Audio Files

Audio playback under Ubuntu is normally handled by the Rhythmbox Music Player. This is a feature-packed piece of software that can play back audio files, podcasts, Internet radio, and even CDs. However, Totem, the Ubuntu movie player, can also play back digital audio files.

Like many modern music players, Rhythmbox can also manage your music collection, arranging it into a library so you can locate songs easily and create playlists. This makes it a better choice for playback if you have many digital audio files, although Totem is good for quick playback of individual files, such as auditioning those you've just downloaded.

Out of the box, Ubuntu supports playback of Ogg Vorbis and FLAC across all its audio playback applications. These are two open audio file formats, which you learn more about in the "Choosing a Format" section later in this chapter.

To play back other music file formats, such as the ubiquitous MP3 format, additional software known as *codecs* must be installed. A codec handles the decoding of multimedia files, both audio and video. The word is a shortened version of *coder-decoder*. For any digital multimedia file type you want to play on your computer, you need an appropriate codec. In addition, if you want to create your own multimedia files—for example, to create MP3s from CD audio tracks—you might need to download an additional codec that allows the *encoding* of files.

Installation of codec software is largely automated in Ubuntu. However, the issue of patenting continues to have an impact on the distribution of codecs. Several audio codecs available for Linux, contained in various `gstreamer-plugins` software packages, are not licensed with the patent holders. This is of little issue to you as an end user. It's a practical concern only for the distributors of the codecs, because the laws of some countries state that it's their duty to pay patent licensing fees. It's just something you should be aware of. Fully licensed codecs are available for many formats via the commercial Fluendo plug-in suite, which is available from the Canonical store.

MULTIMEDIA PLAYBACK COMPONENTS

In simple terms, three software components are needed for multimedia playback under Ubuntu:

- *Player application:* This is the software that's used to listen to music or display videos. It's the part of the multimedia system that you interact with. Under Ubuntu, Totem movie player is used to play back video, and Rhythmbox is used to handle audio. However, if you install the KDE desktop, Dragon Player is used to play back movies, and Amarok handles audio playback.

- *Multimedia framework:* This is the behind-the-scenes middleman that puts the player application in touch with the codec plug-ins. The multimedia framework preferred by Ubuntu is called GStreamer; KDE is able to use a choice of backends, including GStreamer and Xine. The multimedia framework is a background component of your system, and you won't come into direct contact with it, apart from when you're initially configuring your system for media playback. However, it's important to note that more than one multimedia framework can be installed, because this is sometimes necessary to utilize certain codecs. In Chapter 17, you learn how to install additional software in order to fully support DVD playback under Ubuntu.

- *Codec plug-ins:* Codecs are the small pieces of software that handle multimedia file decoding. Codecs do all the hard work—the number crunching. Most multimedia file formats are compressed, to make for smaller file sizes, and the codec's job is to expand the files again so they can be played back on your computer. Some codecs also work the other way around by shrinking files; if you rip CD tracks to MP3, or convert DVD videos to movie files on your hard disk, you will need to shrink them for ease of storage.

Under Ubuntu, the GStreamer multimedia framework is installed by default, along with a handful of codecs.

Installing Codecs in a Single Package

There is an extremely simple way to install support for all of the common multimedia codecs that aren't distributed by default in Ubuntu. It's a package called Ubuntu Restricted Extras.

With a single click, this package will bring in support for MP3 and the common proprietary video formats, including the Flash plug-in in Firefox, and as a bonus it will install the Microsoft TrueType core fonts (such as Times New Roman and Arial) and OpenJDK, a free/open source version of Java. (The proprietary Sun JDK/JRE is available as an alternative from the Canonical Partner Repository).

To get this very convenient bundle of software onto your system, enter the Ubuntu Software Center, which you'll find in the Applications menu, and type **restricted extras** in the search bar. Select Ubuntu Restricted Extras from the results list, click the Install button, and enter your password when prompted.

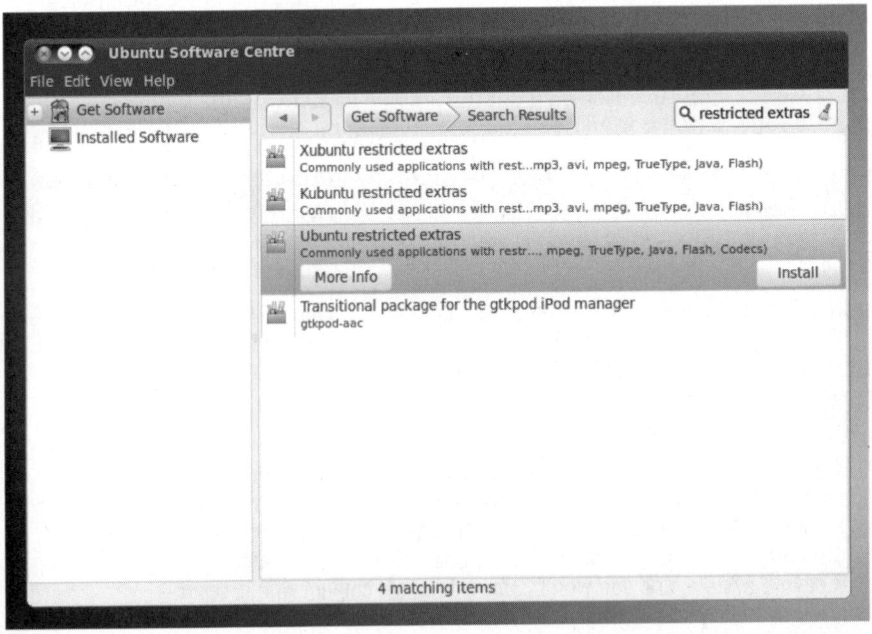

Figure 16-1. Installing the Ubuntu Restricted Extras package in the Ubuntu Software Centre is the easiest way to get support for the most commonly used digital audio and video formats.

Once the Ubuntu Restricted Extras is installed, all of Ubuntu's playback software will automatically support MP3 files, including Totem, Rhythmbox, and any other playback software you install that is designed for the GNOME Desktop.

This is made possible because, behind the scenes, all of Ubuntu's audio and video playback is underpinned by the GStreamer multimedia framework. Once the codec-supporting plug-ins have been installed into GStreamer, as a user you won't come into direct contact with GStreamer, but the benefit of having this integrated system in the background is that you install plug-ins only once for the entire system.

Installing Codecs when Required

Even if you don't get around to installing Ubuntu Restricted Extras, Ubuntu's multimedia applications will automatically suggest which codecs to download and install when you attempt to play a multimedia file that's in a restricted format, such as MP3.

Here we walk through what happens when you try to play an MP3 on an Ubuntu system that hasn't yet had the required codec installed. The same procedure will apply when you try to play back any unsupported audio or video file format; all that will differ is the choice of codecs offered to you.

1. Copy an MP3 file to your computer.

2. Double-click the MP3 file.

3. Totem movie player will start up, but because the underlying GStreamer framework doesn't yet include support for MP3 files, a dialog box will appear, asking whether you want to look for a suitable plug-in to play the file. Click the Search button to do so. The process is automated, but your computer will need to go online if it isn't already.

4. The Install Multimedia Codecs dialog box will eventually appear, offering a choice of plug-ins to install. You'll rarely be offered an individual codec to install. Most are bundled together with similar codecs allowing the playback of other file formats. As you can see in Figure 16-2, for playback of MP3 files we were offered the GStreamer Ugly plug-ins bundle, GStreamer FFmpeg, and the GStreamer Fluendo MP3 plug-in. Although there are three choices, and therefore obviously some overlap in functionality, all three check boxes are selected by default, and you can safely accept this and click the Install button. Ubuntu will handle any overlapping functionality automatically in the background. It's always best to install as many codecs as possible when offered the chance, because that means your computer will be suitably equipped for playback of virtually any file type.

5. As soon as you click the Install button, Ubuntu will ask you to confirm the choice and will explain that use of the software might be restricted in certain countries, although with certain provisos. Read through the dialog box and either cancel or confirm your choice, depending on whether you think the rules explained apply to you.

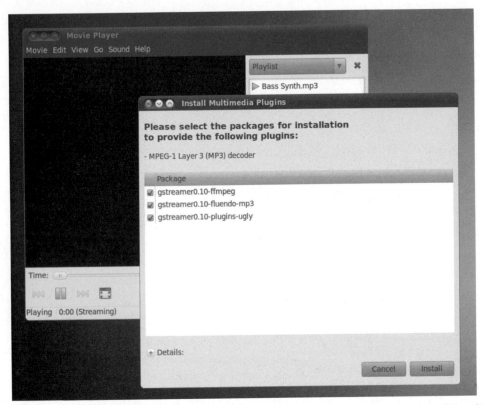

Figure 16-2. Ubuntu recommends codec packages to install so you can play your multimedia files.

6. Click the Confirm button in the dialog box. Because you are about to install software, you'll need to enter your password when prompted. Note that, although you appeared to select three packages, you actually selected to install package *bundles*, containing many individual packages. On the progress bar, you will see that quite a few individual packages are being downloaded—about 20 on our test computer!

7. The files will download and install automatically. After the process has completed, a dialog box will tell you that everything has been successful.

8. Playback of the file should start automatically in the player application. Every piece of playback software within Ubuntu will now automatically support MP3 files, including Totem, Rhythmbox, and any other playback software you install that relies on the GStreamer framework (this will include any playback software designed for the GNOME Desktop).

FLUENDO MP3 CODEC

As mentioned, some codecs available for Ubuntu have certain legal issues surrounding the patenting of software. However, you might be pleased to hear that one audio codec available for Ubuntu *is* licensed with the MP3 patent holder and therefore washes cleaner than clean: the Fluendo MP3 codec. In an act of generosity, the Fluendo company paid the MP3 technology license and made its own decoder freely available for all Linux users. For more information, see `www.fluendo.com/shop/product/fluendo-mp3-decoder`.

The Fluendo codec doesn't avoid the ethical considerations surrounding using patented technology, as discussed early in this chapter, but it does leave you in the best possible position. However, the Fluendo codec can be used only to *decode* MP3 audio. It can't be used to *encode* MP3s, so if you want to rip tracks to MP3 from audio CDs, you will have to use the less legally precise GStreamer plug-in packages (or, better still, encode your audio files using the open source Ogg Vorbis format, which avoids patenting issues and doesn't require installing *any* additional plug-ins!).

So if you simply want to listen to your existing MP3 tracks, intending to embrace open source audio file formats from this point onward, the Fluendo codec is all you need. To install it, open the Ubuntu Software Center (Applications ➤ Ubuntu Software Center) and enter **gstreamer fluendo mp3** in the search box. One result will be returned: `gstreamer0.10-fluendo-mp3`. Click the Install button and enter your password when prompted. After the software is installed, MP3 files should play in both Totem and Rhythmbox.

Using Rhythmbox Music Player

Both Rhythmbox Music Player and Totem Movie Player can be used for audio file playback under Ubuntu. Rhythmbox is best if you have a lot of tunes, because it can catalog and manage your collection. You'll find it on the Applications ➤ Sound & Video menu.

The first step when running Rhythmbox for the first time is to let it index your music files. As soon as it starts up, Rhythmbox will automatically start indexing any files in the Music folder (in Places), so it's a good idea to copy your music collection into that folder if you haven't done so already. But you can also make Rhythmbox index any music you have located elsewhere. To do so, click Music ➤ Import File or Music ➤ Import Folder. Then navigate to your music tracks on the hard disk. You can select more than one file or folder by Shift-clicking or Ctrl-clicking, just as in Windows.

Note that, unlike iTunes or some other comparable programs, Rhythmbox doesn't copy your music to its own library folders when cataloging your files. Instead, it merely creates an index of the files you already have.

If you subsequently move or delete any files, Rhythmbox might get confused. This can be resolved by clicking Music ➤ Import Folder and rebuilding the index (for single files, click Music ➤ Import File).

■ **Tip** If disk space is a concern, and your audio files are in a Windows partition, you could simply leave the files there, rather than copy them across. Rhythmbox will still be able to index them. You just need to navigate to your Windows partition, which you should have as a shortcut under Places (otherwise, it will be in `/media/disk`).

Rhythmbox starts in browse mode, which means that your music files are listed at the bottom of the program window. In roughly the middle-left of the program window, you'll find a listing of the artists behind the MP3s in your collection. On the right, you'll see the album that the music track is taken from (provided that information is included in the music file itself, such as the MP3 ID3 tags). Figure 16-3 shows an example of a Rhythmbox window.

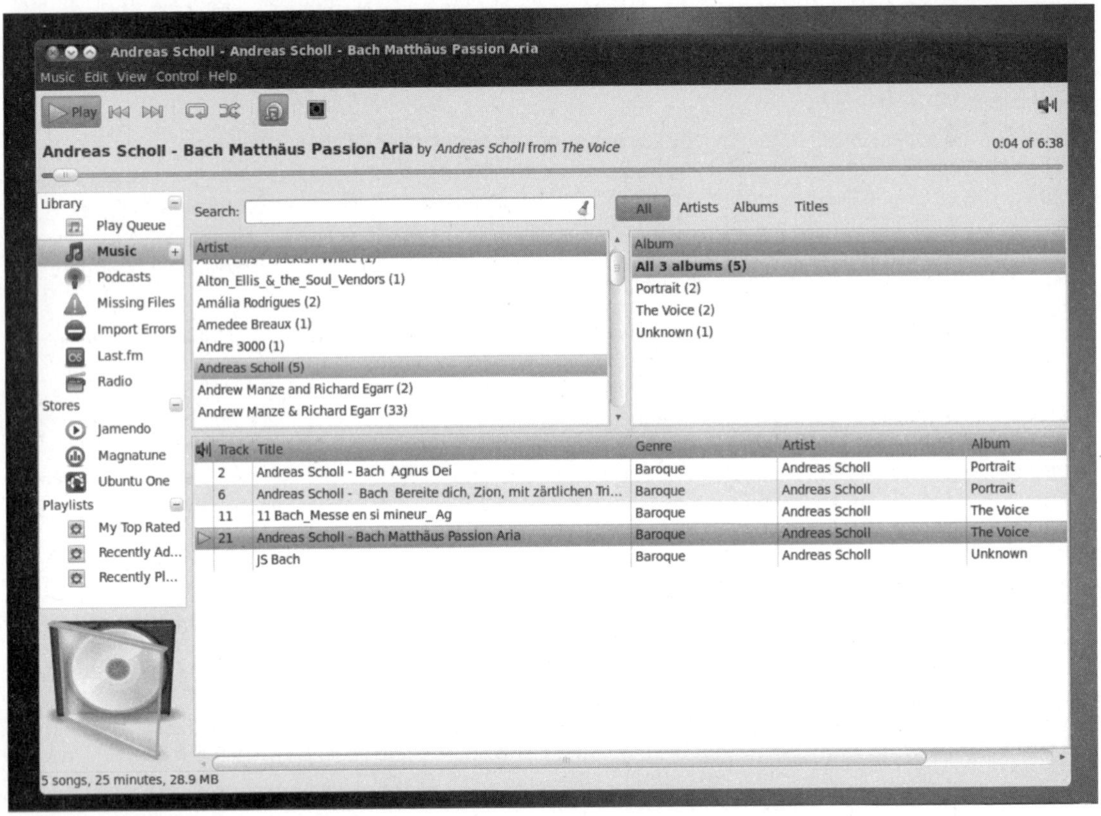

Figure 16-3. Rhythmbox will organize your music tracks by artist or album.

Clicking the Browse button on the toolbar (whose icon is a compact disc overlaid with some musical notes) will remove the Artist and Album lists and present simply a list of the tracks in your collection. You can click on the headings of this list to order it by title, genre, artist and album alphabetically. The default sort order is by artist.

Playing a track is simply a matter of double-clicking it in the list. After the track is finished, Rhythmbox will play the next track in the MP3 file list. At the top of the Rhythmbox window are transport controls that let you pause or play the track, skip tracks, repeat tracks, or switch to shuffle play (that is, random track selection). The Play button combines the functions of play and pause. So if you want to pause or stop the track that's currently playing, you click the Play button. Slightly strange decision by the Rhythmbox developers there, but easy enough to get used to!

You can toggle displaying visual effects with the Visualization button. The display output is shown in the main window by default. The controls for customizing the effects are available at the bottom of the visual effects display and are made visible when you hover your mouse over the visual effects. You have the option to change the nature of the visualization effect; the quality of the effect; and whether the effect will be displayed within Rhythmbox, in a different window, or in full-screen mode.

Beneath the transport controls and the artist/track name information is a slider that shows the progress through the current song and lets you cue forward and backward by clicking and dragging.

To create a new playlist, click Music ➤ Playlist ➤ New Playlist (or press Ctrl+N). A new icon will appear under the Playlists heading in the left pane of Rhythmbox, with the words "New Playlist" highlighted. Type a name for your new playlist and press Enter. To add tracks to the playlist, click Music under the Library heading in the pane on the far left side of the program window, and then drag and drop files onto your new playlist entry. To start playing the tracks in the playlist, select it and double-click the first track in the list.

Portable audio players are well supported by Rhythmbox. If you plug in an MP3 player or iPod, Ubuntu will pop up a window asking you what application you would like to launch. Open Rhythmbox is the default, and you can safety check the Always Perform This Action check box and click OK. An icon representing your digital audio player will now appear under the Devices heading in the left pane of Rhythmbox. If you click the icon, the contents of your device should appear, and you should be able to play songs from it. You can transfer music from your computer to your player by clicking the Music icon in the left pane, selecting the track or tracks you would like to copy, and dragging them to the icon for your digital audio player. To transfer from player to computer, click your player icon and drag tracks to the Library icon under Music in the left panel. When you've done your copying and you'd like to unplug your device, don't forget to right-click the device icon and select Eject.

■ **Note** When you double-click an audio file in a File Browser window, Ubuntu will start Totem Movie Player rather than Rhythmbox Music Player. This is quick if you want to preview tracks, but to have them automatically opened in Rhythmbox when you double-click them, you need to change the Open With preferences. This is easily done: Right-click any MP3 file in a File Browser window, select Properties, and click the Open With tab. Click the radio button alongside Rhythmbox's entry in the list to select it as the default application and then click the Close button.

Purchasing from Online Music Stores

Rhythmbox allows you to purchase albums from the Jamendo, Magnatune, and Ubuntu One online music stores. Jamendo works on the principle of Creative Commons (see `http://creativecommons.org`), so many tracks are free of charge, although you can donate money if you want.

Under the Stores heading on the leftmost pane of the Rhythmbox window, click Magnatune or Jamendo. You'll see a brief introduction to the store while the catalog is downloaded. After the catalog is downloaded (indicated by the status bar at the bottom right of the program window), you will be able to browse through the available tracks, as if they were on your own computer. They will be sorted by artist and track name. Double-clicking each track will download and play a high-quality preview.

■ **Note** The first time you try to browse music on the Jamendo or Magnatune labels, Rhythmbox will have to download the full artist catalogs. Jamendo currently has nearly 20,000 artists, so this will take a few minutes even on a broadband connection. You might want to fix yourself a beverage while you wait!

The main toolbar of Rhythmbox has changed in the latest Ubuntu release. Several new icons appear, allowing you to purchase and download the album, buy a physical CD, or learn more about the artist.

The Ubuntu One music store behaves more like a web page embedded within the Rhythmbox window, and you can start browsing it straight away, as long as you're connected to the Net.

Using the Jamendo Store

Songs from Jamendo are free to listen to, download, and share. Jamendo allows any artist to upload his or her music under one of the "some rights reserved" licenses published by Creative Commons. Fans can join the Jamendo community free of charge, write reviews, and share music with other members, and if you'd like to support an artist with a donation, Jamendo makes it easy to do that.

■ **Tip** Not only can you download the tracks from Jamendo, but you can also remix many of them or use snippets of them in your own music. All of this is because of the artists' choice to use Creative Commons licenses. Many of them opt for a license which permits you to do exactly what you want with their music, as long as you credit the original artist and pass on the same rights to other people if you redistribute your work.

If you want to download an album, select a song in the music list that is included in the album you would like to download, and then click the Download Album button on the toolbar. Firefox will visit a URL that includes a BitTorrent tracker file—effectively, a small file that opens the Transmission BitTorrent client built into Ubuntu. BitTorrent will then attempt to download the entire album.

■ **Note** BitTorrent is a unique file-sharing system designed to share bandwidth. Depending on your hardware setup, you might need to alter your router or firewall settings for it to work efficiently. For more information, see `www.dessent.net/btfaq/`.

If you want to make a donation to an artist, select a song in the music list that the artist performed, right-click it, and select Donate to Artist, or click the Donate to Artist button on the toolbar. Firefox will direct you to a web site where you can fill in a form to complete your donation by Paypal or credit card.

Purchasing from Magnatune

Magnatune operates on a different basis from Jamendo. Like a traditional record label, Magnatune is picky about its artists, with only a few hundred on its books, but, unlike a regular label, it lets you the customer try before you buy.

With Magnatune, you can preview any song in its entirety through your Rhythmbox player without paying a penny. At the end of each song you listen to, you will hear an announcement telling you the name of the track and artists, and inviting you to become a member of Magnatune.

■ **Tip** You can learn more about artists by viewing their Magnatune web pages. Click a relevant track and click the Artist Information button on the toolbar. This will automatically load the relevant page in Firefox.

By signing up as a Magnatune member, for US$15 per month, you can download any of the music featured on the label, in a choice of different formats, including high-quality variable bitrate MP3, high quality Ogg Vorbis, and perfect quality WAV or FLAC, which are ideal for burning to CD.

This is not only a great deal for the listener, but also for the artists, who get paid 50 percent, split evenly from what you listen and download.

To join, right-click on any song in the Magnatune index and select Purchase Album from the context menu. This will open Magnatune's web site in Firefox, which will take you through the sign-up process. Once you're a member, you will be able to right-click any song in the Magnatune listing and select Download Album to get your own fully-licensed, legitimate copy of the album in excellent quality.

Purchasing from Ubuntu One

While Jamendo and Magnatune follow very new business models, giving less well-known artists a chance to get heard and paid, Ubuntu's sponsor Canonical thinks that Linux users should also be able to get their hands on mainstream, commercially available music.

To this end, Canonical has started a new music store as part of its Ubuntu One personal cloud service. Backed by 7digital, a major player in digital media services, the Ubuntu One music store gives you access to commercially published music from major and independent labels at competitive prices, in the same way as you would expect from iTunes or the Amazon music store.

Browse the Ubuntu One music store catalog within Rhythmbox to see what's available from your favorite artists and preview snippets of songs. When you find a song or album you want to buy, click the Download button. This will take you to a basket, from which you can check out or carry on browsing for more songs to buy.

When you click the Checkout button, a page will open in Firefox from which, if you haven't already signed up to Ubuntu One, you will be able to create an account and make your purchase. All the music you buy from the store will be in high-quality 256kbps MP3 format, and will appear in your Rhythmbox library under the Music heading, as well as in your Music folder of course. You can play it through Rhythmbox, sync it to your MP3 player, and burn it to CD as many times as you want.

A very cool, perhaps unique feature of the Ubuntu One music store is that any music that you purchase is automatically copied to your Ubuntu One "personal cloud" (meaning storage on Ubuntu One's servers), and is instantly available to any other computer on which you enable your Ubuntu One account.

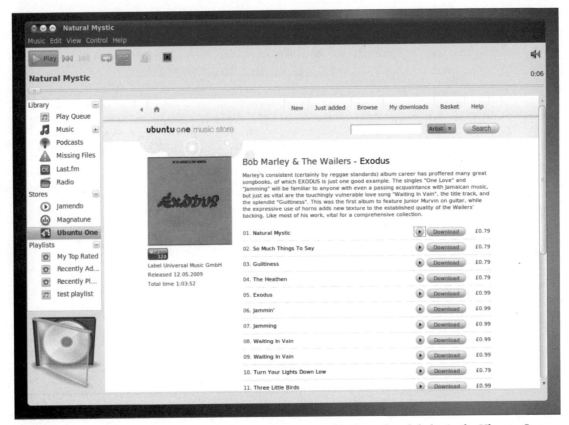

Figure 16-4. Ubuntu users can now buy music from major and independent labels via the Ubuntu One music store that's integrated into Rhythmbox.

Tuning In to Online Radio Stations

With Rhythmbox, you can listen to a number of predefined Internet radio stations or add your own. Provided the MP3 codec software is installed, as discussed earlier, Rhythmbox is compatible with streaming MP3-based playlists, such as those listed at http://shoutcast.com.

To view a handful of stations that have been pre-programmed into Rhythmbox for demonstration purposes, click the Radio heading in the list on the left side of the Rhythmbox window. To listen to a radio station with Rhythmbox, double-click its entry in the list.

To add a new station, do the following: Visit the web page of the radio station you want to listen to in Firefox and copy the stream's link to your clipboard. You can typically do this by right-clicking the Listen Live or similar link (in Shoutcast it's the blue play button) and selecting Copy Link Location. In Rhythmbox, right-click the Radio icon under the Library listing on the left pane and select New Internet Radio Station. A window will pop up, into which you can paste the station link and click Add. The new station will now appear in the track listing, and you can double-click to play it. The title will be the link itself (http:// etc.), so if you would like to change it to the human-readable name of the station, right-click on it, select Properties, edit the station title and click Close.

■ **Tip** There's a great plug-in for Rhythmbox that adds the whole Shoutcast streaming radio catalogue as a heading in your Library. Go to `http://code.google.com/p/rhythmbox-shoutcast/` to download the plug-in and follow the simple installation instructions you'll find there. We found we had to restart Rhythmbox a couple of times for the plug-in to start working, but it's worth that for having the choice of thousands of stations from all around the world.

Listening to Podcasts

Podcasts are audio files that are distributed by RSS (Real Simple Syndication). This sounds complicated, but it's actually quite simple. When you're subscribed to a particular podcast, the audio files are downloaded automatically in the background, so that the latest episodes will always be available. This makes keeping up with the latest podcasts effortless. Most podcasts take the form of MP3 files, but any audio file format can be used.

In terms of content, podcasts range from simple spoken blog entries, usually created by individuals, to podcasts that are more akin to radio shows and involve interviews. Some professional radio stations even release entire shows as podcasts, with the British Broadcasting Corporation (BBC) leading the charge (`www.bbc.co.uk/podcasts`).

Rhythmbox is able to handle podcast subscriptions under Ubuntu, and you can add a new subscription by clicking the Podcasts heading in the leftmost pane of Rhythmbox. Then right-click a blank spot in the track listing area, select New Podcast Feed, and enter the URL. However, a much easier way of adding a podcast is to use Firefox to browse to the link.

Conveniently, Rhythmbox is fully compatible with the iTunes podcast format, which is perhaps the most prevalent podcast format at the present time. On the web page where the link is located, click the subscribe link for iTunes users. This will open a dialog box inviting you to choose to open the podcast. Ensure that Rhythmbox is selected, click the Remember My Choice check box, and click OK. Rhythmbox will then download the podcast feed, showing all the titles of the episodes that are available. To listen to an episode, double-click it in the track listing or right-click and select Download Episode. A progress bar in the Status column will show how the download is going. Double-click to listen to the episode.

■ **Tip** You can start listening to a podcast before it has completely downloaded.

If only an RSS link is provided for the podcast (usually indicated on a web site by the orange RSS button), after you click it Firefox will offer to subscribe to the link itself, using its Live Bookmarks feature. To change this behavior so that in future RSS links will open in Rhythmbox, click the drop-down link alongside Subscribe to This Podcast Using, and click Choose Application. A file browser window will appear, headed Choose Application. In the top left corner of this window there is an icon of a pencil. Click this, and a Location text box will appear below, within which you should type **/usr/bin/rhythmbox** and click Open, as shown in Figure 16-5. The Choose Application window will disappear. Back in Firefox, put a check in the box alongside Always Use Rhythmbox to Subscribe to Podcasts and then click Subscribe Now in the Firefox program window.

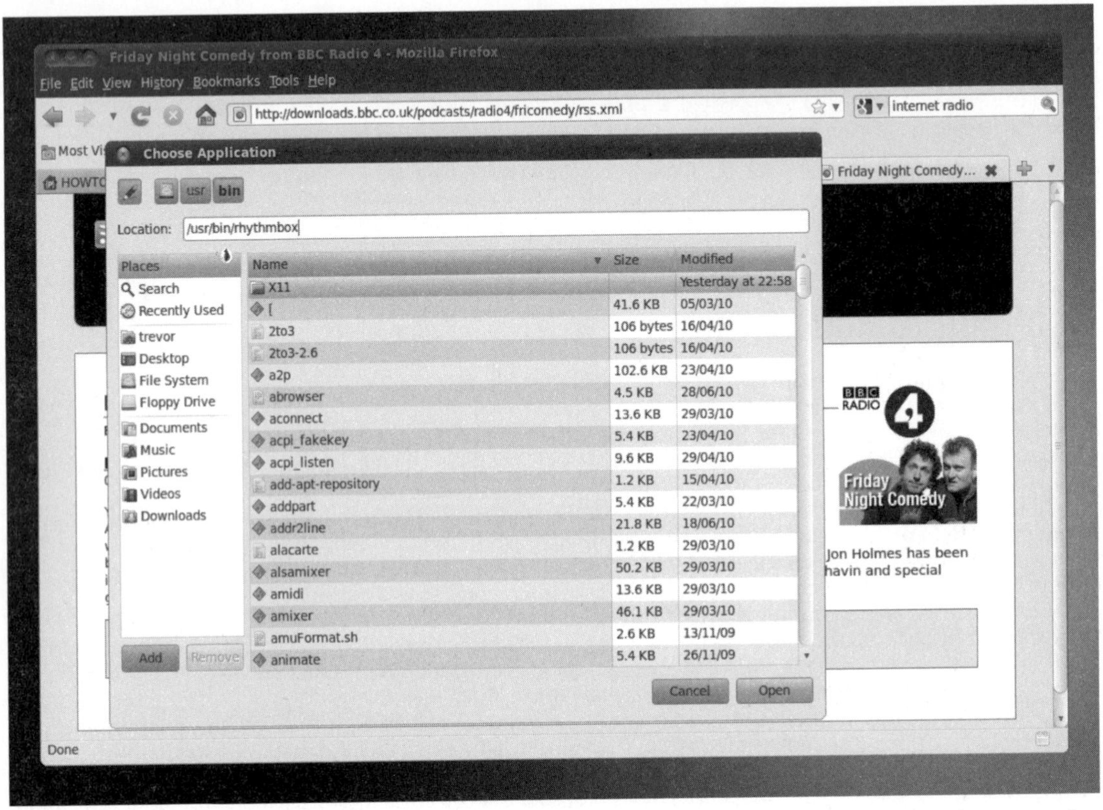

Figure 16-5. To make Rhythmbox handle RSS podcast feeds that you click on in Firefox, you have to make a slightly fiddly one-off change to Firefox's preferences.

Listening to Audio CDs and Ripping Tracks

Playing back audio CDs is simple. Just insert the CD, and you should see a prompt asking which application you want to open the CD with. The two key choices are to open the CD in Rhythmbox, which will enable playback and ripping of the CD tracks to disk, or to open the Brasero software, which lets you to copy the disc.

For simple playback, selecting Rhythmbox is the best option. You can ensure that Rhythmbox starts automatically in the future when you insert an audio CD by selecting the Always Perform This Action check box.

After Rhythmbox has started, click the name of the CD in the leftmost pane (look under the Devices heading) and then click the Play button on the toolbar. It might take a few seconds for the name of the CD to be looked up online and, provided you're online, the track and artist information will be looked up automatically, so you should find a complete listing, and perhaps even an image of the CD inlay, within the bottom left of the Rhythmbox program window.

To cue backward and forward in the currently playing track, click and drag the slider beneath the transport buttons.

To eject the disc, press the button on the front of the drive. If this doesn't work, either click the toolbar icon within Rhythmbox or right-click the Audio Disc desktop icon and select Eject Volume.

■ **Tip** As with all GNOME applications, hover the mouse cursor over each button to display a tooltip that describes what it does.

If you find that the track listing information is incorrect, as can sometimes happen with online lookups, you can correct it by right-clicking the track name and selecting Properties. Then type the correct details in the dialog box that appears.

Converting audio tracks on a CD into digital music files you can store on your hard disk for personal use is informally known as *ripping*.

■ **Note** Because of the way audio CDs work, you can't simply insert the disc and then drag and drop the tracks onto your hard disk. They must be converted first.

Before you start to rip CDs, however, you need to decide the format in which you wish to store the audio files.

Choosing a Format

You have several basic choices for audio file formats, the main ones being Ogg Vorbis, FLAC, and MP3. Let's look at what each has to offer:

Ogg Vorbis: This is the free software alternative to MP3. Unless you have a trained ear, you won't be able to tell the difference between a Vorbis and an MP3 file. (If you *do* have a trained ear, you may find Vorbis better!) The two technologies generate files of around the same size, an average of 4MB to 5MB per song, though you may get a slightly better compression rate with Vorbis. The advantage of Vorbis is that it's completely open source technology, so there isn't the ethical burden of using patented MP3 software and, therefore, working against the interests of the open source software movement. The downside of Vorbis is that not all portable audio players support it (though many do, including players from SanDisk, Cowon, Bang & Olufsen, LG, and iriver—see the list at http://wiki.xiph.org/index.php/PortablePlayers). Other operating systems like Windows will need some additional software installed if you want to play Vorbis files on them (see www.vorbis.com/setup).

FLAC: This stands for Free Lossless Audio Codec, and it's the choice of the audiophile. Vorbis and MP3 are lossy formats, which means that some of the audio data is lost in order to significantly shrink the file. FLAC doesn't lose any audio data but still manages to compress files to a certain degree (although they're still much larger than an equivalent MP3 or Ogg file). FLAC scores points because it's an open format, like Vorbis, but you'll face the same issues of support in portable audio players and other operating systems (unless additional software is installed; see http://flac.sourceforge.net).

Speex: Originally designed purely for Voice over IP (VoIP), Speex was created for speech encoding. As such, it concentrates on audio frequencies generated during ordinary conversation. Aside from the fact that Speex is an open codec that claims to not employ any patented software methods, there really isn't any reason to use it, even if you're ripping speech tracks from a CD. It is built for transmission across low-bandwidth connections (or small file sizes). If hard-disk capacity is an issue, you might consider it, but Ogg and MP3 are better suited in virtually all situations. The Speex file extension is .spx.

WAV: This is perhaps the oldest audio file format. It uses the `.wav` file extension, which you may have seen in use on Microsoft Windows computers. WAV files are usually completely uncompressed and lossless. However, that doesn't necessarily mean they're high quality; as with any kind of audio encoding, the sampling and bit rate can be set to any value desired. For example, Ubuntu includes a default `.wav` encoding profile of low quality that can be used when encoding speech. Although WAV files tend to be supported on most computing platforms, the downside is file size. Uncompressed WAV files can be massive, even those with low-quality settings. If uncompressed audio is your aim, FLAC offers a far better alternative.

MP3: This is by far the most popular music file format, and practically everyone who owns a computer has at least a handful of MP3 tracks. This means software support for MP3 playback is strong, and of course, most portable audio players are built around the MP3 standard. The only problem for you, as a Linux user, is the issue of surrounding patents, as explained at the beginning of this chapter. Using the MP3 format goes against a lot of what the Linux and open source movement stands for. But in the end, the choice is yours. If you want to rip to MP3, make sure you have installed the Ubuntu Restricted Extras package as described in the "Installing Codecs in a Single Package" section earlier in this chapter.

Ripping Tracks

When you're ready to rip some music, insert the audio CD and then start Rhythmbox (if it isn't already running). Select the disc under the Devices heading, as mentioned earlier in the directions for playing back audio CDs. The check boxes to the left of each listed track will automatically be checked. Uncheck any tracks that you don't want to rip. Now right-click the disc under the devices heading and select Extract to Library, or alternatively you can click the Extract button on the main toolbar.

It's possible to play the audio CD while you rip it, but in our opinion that's best avoided!

■ **Tip** By default the buttons on the Rhythmbox Music Player's toolbar aren't labelled, making it tricky to guess what they all mean, especially when their layout and functions change depending on what music source is selected. To make everything clearer, go to Edit ➤ Preferences and, in the Toolbar Button Labels drop-down, choose one of the options with text included.

As the tracks are ripped to your hard disk, you will see a progress display at the bottom right of the Rhythmbox program window. Audio tracks will be saved in a directory named after the artist and album title, within your Music folder in Places.

MAKING MUSIC AND RECORDING AUDIO

Most PCs come with sound cards that are capable of making music. You can use many open source programs, designed for both amateurs and professionals alike, to create music or record and edit audio.

Arguably the crown jewel of Linux audio at the moment is Ardour, a professional-quality digital audio workstation that rivals the functionality of Pro Tools and Logic in the proprietary software world. It is a complex program, and depends on JACK, a low-latency sound server which lets multiple applications connect to one audio device and share audio between each other. MusE and Rosegarden are also well worth investigating. Like all modern MIDI sequencers, these programs let you record audio tracks, effectively turning your PC into a recording studio.

It's also possible to run virtual synthesizers on your PC, which turn even the most basic sound card into a powerful musical instrument. Examples include Bristol and FluidSynth.

If you're interested in only audio recording and processing, Sweep and Audacity are worth a look. In addition to audio recording and playback, both feature graphical waveform editing and powerful filters.

All of the packages mentioned here are available on Ubuntu, and you can install them via the Ubuntu Software Center.

A specialized distribution called Ubuntu Studio has been developed by volunteers, with multimedia creation specifically in mind. It comes with a "real-time" kernel to reduce audio stutters, and the tricky work of configuring the JACK sound server configuration is already taken care of.

For an authoritative overview of audio production on Linux, we recommend getting hold of a copy of *Crafting Digital Media* by Daniel James, published by Apress.

Creating Your Own CDs

You can create audio CDs using Brasero, which aims to be a complete CD-burning suite, like Nero under Microsoft Windows. It's also possible to create audio CDs using only Ubuntu's File Browser, but Brasero offers finer control over the process of compiling and burning your disc.

Start by inserting a blank CD. A dialog box will appear, asking what you want to do with the CD. The default choice of Open CD/DVD Creator isn't what you want, because it will start the File Browser's data CD creator, which is designed to write files to disc. Instead, click Open With Other Application from the drop-down list and select Brasero Disc Burner from the list of applications that appears. Then, in the parent dialog box, select Open Brasero Disc Burner from the drop-down list, if it isn't already selected. To always have Brasero start automatically when a blank disc is inserted, select the Always Perform This Action check box before clicking OK.

When Brasero's main window appears, it will by start with a new Data project by default. To switch to an audio CD project, click Project ➤ New Project ➤ New Audio Project.

The program is very simple to use:

1. Using a File Browser window (Places ➤ Music), browse to where the audio files are located and click and drag them onto the Brasero program window. The files can be Ogg, FLAC, or MP3 files (if you installed the MP3 playback software, as described in the "Installing Codecs" section earlier in this chapter). Note that the Fluendo codec will also work for burning CDs from MP3 tracks.

2. You'll see the track listing build up in the window where you dropped the selected tracks. In addition, at the bottom of the program window, you'll see the estimated size of the project, shown in minutes. You'll need to check the size of the CD you're using on its packaging, but most blank CD-R discs can hold a maximum of between 70 and 80 minutes of audio.

3. Click and drag each track to rearrange them, if necessary, to create an ideal running order, as shown in Figure 16-6. When you're satisfied with the track listing and are sure you haven't exceeded the maximum allowed total time for the disc, click the Burn button to prepare your disc for burning.

4. In the Disc Burning Setup dialog box, click the Properties button if you want to alter any details about the actual burning process, such as the burn speed. However, the default settings are usually OK. Click the Burn button to start the write procedure. First, the tracks are converted to pure audio files, and their volume levels adjusted so no track is louder than any other (something known as *normalization*). Then they're actually burned to disc. This can take some time. When Brasero finishes with the burning, the CD will be ejected.

■ **Note** Depending on the quality of the blank CD, you might not be able to write audio CDs at full speed. If this is the case, Brasero will stop during the writing process with an error message. You'll need to adjust the burn speed. To do so, in the Disc Burning Setup dialog box, click the Properties button and choose a more conservative speed from the Burning Speed drop-down list.

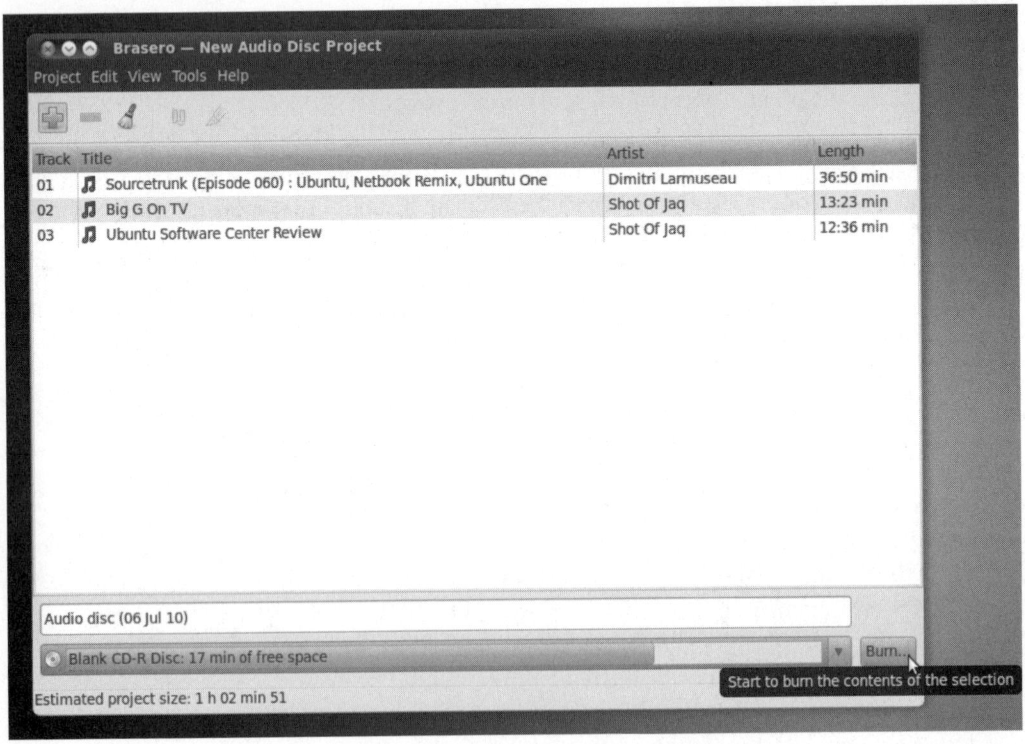

Figure 16-6. Brasero makes it easy to create CDs from digital audio files.

Recording from a Microphone

To enable you to capture live audio, using either your laptop's built-in microphone or an external microphone plugged into the appropriate input, Ubuntu includes a simple program called Sound Recorder. You'll find it on the Applications ➤ Sound & Video menu.

When Sound Recorder starts, you'll first want to check that you are getting a level from your microphone. In the File menu, select Open Volume Control. This will open Sound Preferences in a separate window. (As we saw in the Configuring Sound Cards section in Chapter 7, these controls can also be accessed by clicking on the volume icon in the top panel and selecting Sound Preferences, or via System ➤ Preferences ➤ Sound). Click the Input tab and ensure that Mute is not checked. Speak into the microphone and adjust the Input Volume slider until an acceptable level registers in the Input Level meter (see Figure 16-7). When you're happy with the level, close Sound Preferences.

Next, choose your preferred audio file format from the Record As drop-down menu. By default, "CD Quality, Lossy (.ogg type)" is selected. This is the free Ogg Vorbis format discussed earlier in the "Choosing a Format" section. Alternative formats offered are AAC, FLAC, MP2, MP3, WAV, and Speex. On our test system, Ogg Vorbis worked well, but test recordings made in any other format failed to play back. Your mileage may vary.

Next, select Save As from the File menu and give your recording a name. When you're ready to record, click the red Record icon in the toolbar or press Ctrl+R on your keyboard. To stop the recording, click the square stop icon or press Ctrl+X. To play back, click the green Play button or press Ctrl+P.

That's pretty much all there is to Sound Recorder. It's a very bare-bones . If you'd like a much more fully-featured audio recording program, with the facility to record multiple tracks, edit your recordings, and apply hundreds of sophisticated effects, open the Ubuntu Software Center and install Audacity.

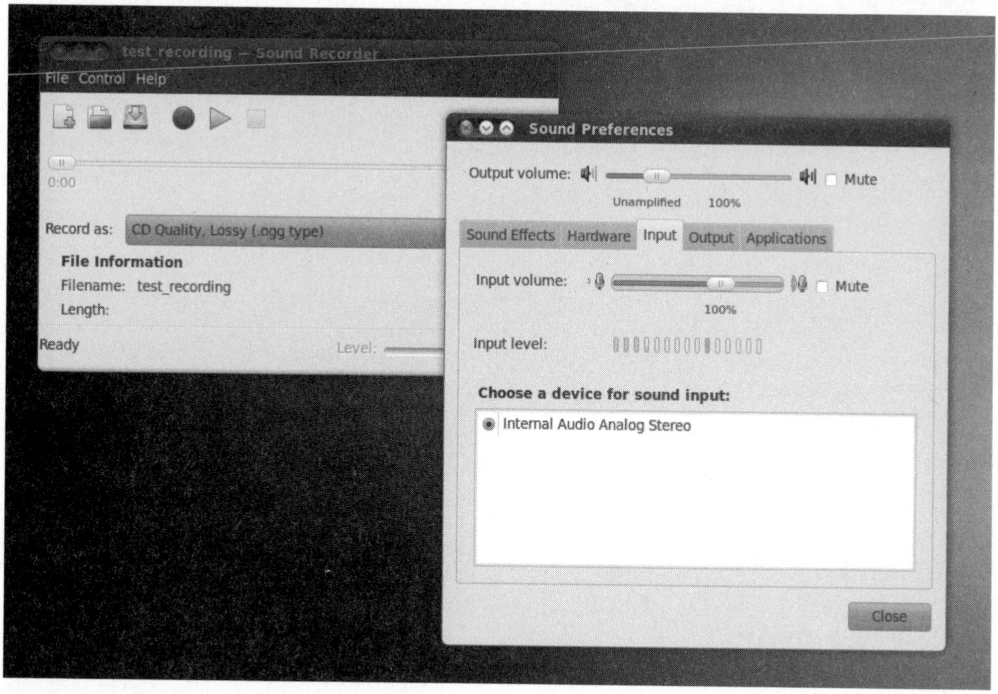

Figure 16-7. Before using Sound Recorder, you'll want to make sure you're getting a good input level from your microphone.

367

Summary

This chapter has covered the audio functions built into Ubuntu and shown how, by downloading a few extra system files, you can play back the majority of audio files in existence. We started by discussing the moral and legal dilemmas associated with multimedia playback on a computer. Then we moved on to how to install the necessary codec files on your computer, before discussing how you can listen to music files, CDs, and online radio stations.

We closed by showing how you can convert CDs into music files, and then the inverse of this: how you can create CDs from audio files.

In Chapter 17, you'll look at playing back movies and online animations when using Ubuntu.

Movies and Multimedia

Watching movies and TV shows on computers is becoming increasingly popular. Most PCs now ship with hardware capable of playing back DVDs. Web sites such as YouTube and Vimeo provide thousands of clips for viewing via your web browser, and Netflix On Demand and Hulu deliver high-quality films and TV shows directly to your PC.

Ubuntu provides support for visual entertainment. As with audio playback (discussed in the previous chapter), you'll need to install some additional codecs to access certain types of files. And just as with audio playback codecs, multimedia applications suggest which movie playback codecs to download and install when you attempt to play unsupported multimedia files. This chapter explains how easy it is to set up Ubuntu for watching videos, DVDs, and TV on your computer, as well as playing web site Flash animations and videos.

Installing Playback Software

Like the other multimedia software provided with Ubuntu, its video playback application, the Totem movie player, is basic but effective and does the job well. However, because of patenting issues, Totem doesn't support all video formats out of the box, although for some of them it's not hard to add support by installing the right codecs. In Table 17-1 you find an overview of some of the most common video formats and their current status in Totem.

Table 17-1. Totem and Popular Movie File Formats

Format	Typical File Extensions	Web Site	Notes
Windows Media Player	.wmv, .wma, .asx, .asf	www.microsoft.com/ windows/windowsmedia	Windows Media Player format is the default for most Windows users. Although it's possible to play Windows Media Player files under Ubuntu (files in WMP1, WMP2, and WMP3 formats), you won't be able to play DRM-restricted files (those that rely on the download and installation of a certificate), such as those from the increasing number of movie rental sites.
RealVideo	.rm, .ram	www.real.com	By downloading the GStreamer plug-in package when prompted, you can play back RealVideo files in Totem. However, you can also download a Linux version of RealPlayer.

Format	Typical File Extensions	Web Site	Notes
QuickTime	.mov, .qt	www.quicktime.com	QuickTime is Apple's default media format and has gained ground on both Windows and Macintosh computers. As with Windows Media Player file playback, you won't be able to play DRM-restricted files.
DivX	.avi, .divx	www.divx.com	The DivX format is one of the most popular formats for those in the Internet community who like to encode their own movies. It's renowned for its ability to shrink movies to very small sizes.

Video and audio playback within the Firefox web browser are handled via the Totem browser plug-in (In Firefox, see Tools ➤ Add Ons ➤ Plugins for a list of currently installed plug-ins. These plug-ins work in exactly the same way as the Windows Media Player and QuickTime browser plug-ins work under Windows. This is set up automatically during initial installation of Ubuntu and is also compatible with the GStreamer codec plug-ins after they are installed. However, when you try to retrieve streaming content, many web sites attempt to probe your setup to ensure that you have the required media player software, and they may balk when they can't find Windows Media Player or QuickTime. This makes playback difficult, although more and more sites are switching to video playback via Flash Player. Additionally, some web sites use Java applets to present content. You can install support for both Flash and Java through Firefox.

Next we cover how to install codecs for movie file formats, as well as how to install the Linux version of RealPlayer and support for Flash and Java.

Installing Codecs

The codecs for video playback are created by the open source community and are therefore entirely free of copyright issues, but it is claimed that some utilize patented technology. As you might expect, this makes for another legally gray area. It's unlikely that the patent holders sanction the distribution of the codecs in countries that allow software to be patented. As with audio playback codecs, you will need to decide whether the caveats shown by Ubuntu during the installation of the codecs apply to you.

■ **Note** Most of the movie playback codecs used under Ubuntu are provided by the excellent FFmpeg Project (http://ffmpeg.mplayerhq.hu). This endeavor is part of the MPlayer Project, which aims to create an open source media player and platform, separate from GStreamer or Xine (used under the GNOME and KDE desktops, respectively). However, as with all open source projects, it is both possible and encouraged to take and reuse just the FFmpeg codec software, which is what the Ubuntu developers have done to bring support for a wide range of movie and audio formats to Ubuntu.

As stated earlier, codec installation for new file formats is automated (so long as you're online), just as with audio codecs. In fact, if you followed the instructions to install the MP3 codecs in the previous chapter, including the GStreamer ffmpeg video plug-in codec, then your system may already have support for the movie formats. In that case, the video file you've chosen to view will just start playing—you won't be prompted to download anything extra.

Here is the procedure for adding codecs to play a multimedia file:

1. From Nautilus, double-click a movie file.

2. The Totem movie player application will start and prompt you to search for a suitable codec. (As noted, the movie will just start playing if you already have the necessary codec.) Click the Search button.

3. Ubuntu will search for the applicable codec. After it has finished searching, the Install Multimedia Codecs dialog box will appear, prompting you to select from the list of codecs.

4. You can read through the descriptions to know which codec to choose, if more than one is offered. As with audio playback codecs, it's usually a good idea to select all the codecs offered, to get the broadest range of support. Ubuntu will handle any functionality overlap in the background, so don't worry about installing two or more sets of codecs that seemingly do the same job. Check the options you want and click the Install button.

5. Ubuntu will ask you to confirm the installation of restricted software. Read through the conditions and warnings. If you want to continue, click Confirm. Otherwise, click the Cancel button to choose not to install the codec (meaning that your system will not be able to play the files).

6. Back in the Install Multimedia Codecs dialog box, click the Install button again.

7. Supply your password in the authorization dialog box and click OK to proceed with the installation.

8. Ubuntu will download and install the packages. After you have been notified that the packages have been installed successfully, click the Close button. At this point, your multimedia file will play in Totem.

Installing RealPlayer 11

RealPlayer 11 is a media playback application designed for Linux, Windows, and Macintosh OS X, written by Real Networks. It gives you access to a range of media. Although the software has been available for Linux and Ubuntu for some years, its installation still occasionally causes confusion. There are a couple of ways to install the software, but we're going to use a native .deb package file that automates much of the process:

1. Open a browser and go to www.real.com/linux. From the main page click Download DEB installer and accept the default suggestion to open the file with the GDebi package installer.

■ **Note** the RealPlayer application you are downloading in this procedure is available in a 32-bit version only. If you have installed the 64-bit version of Ubuntu, you cannot use RealPlayer (at the time of this writing).

2. After the 7MB package has downloaded, it should automatically launch the .deb installation procedure. Click to install and then read through and acknowledge the end-user license.

3. The software will now begin to install. During the process it will download other pieces of software to sort out dependencies, which can take some time. However, it will also pause at one point, waiting for you to configure the mail system for the software. Just click the Terminal disclosure arrow below the progress bar, click into the black window, and press 1 to select the first option.

4. After the software has finished installing, it will create icons under the Applications ➤ Sound and Video menu and will also set up the helpers for Firefox. The first time you run the software, it will do a network speed test and will install additional packages (see Figure 17-1) and will then be ready to go.

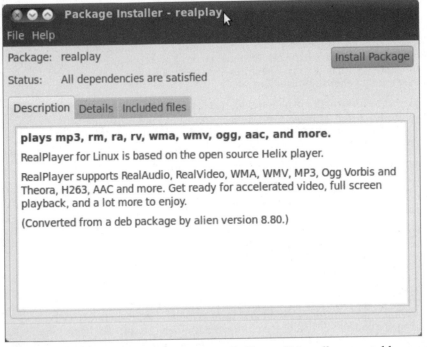

Figure 17-1. After RealPlayer has been installed by a self-installer executable, you must run through its setup program to install the browser plug-in.

■ **Tip** To see which plug-ins are installed under Firefox, type **about:plugins** in the address bar.

Adding Flash Support

Flash is a multimedia plug-in used for animations, games, and video playback on web sites. It is a standard requirement on modern Internet-equipped computers, and finding commercial sites that don't utilize it in some way is becoming difficult. For example, YouTube (www.youtube.com) uses Flash for the playback of video files, as shown in Figure 17-2.

Adobe is the originator of the Flash technology and makes a version of its proprietary Flash Player web browser plug-in especially for Linux, which can be easily installed under Ubuntu. You can also choose to install one of two open source Flash players: Swfdec or Gnash. Of the three, Adobe's own Flash Player offers the best all-round compatibility with web sites of all kinds—general, video, games, and animations. Swfdec is perhaps the best open source choice, although it specializes primarily in video playback, such as that offered by YouTube or the BBC (www.bbc.co.uk). Gnash may be the weakest of the three (at the time of this writing), but may be worth investigating if you prefer to use open source software and find that Swfdec doesn't work correctly with your favorite web sites. Be aware, though, that open source Flash solutions are running behind compared to the possibilities of commercial Flash players. For the best Flash experience, use Adobe Flash.

Figure 17-2. Flash is increasingly popular on video playback sites such as YouTube.

■ **Note** Sadly, there isn't a Linux version of the Shockwave Director browser plug-in. If you really need to have access to Shockwave sites under Linux, consider using CrossOver Professional (www.codeweavers.com) to install the Windows version. But be aware that CrossOver Professional is a commercial product, meaning you have to pay for it.

Installing a Flash Plug-in

As with multimedia codecs, Flash support is installed on demand and is entirely automated. However, this time, installation takes place from within the Firefox browser, as follows:

1. The first time you visit a web site that uses Flash, a yellow bar will appear at the top of the browser window, informing you that you need to install a missing plug-in. Click the Install Missing Plugins button.

2. In the Plugin Finder Service dialog box, click your choice of plug-in and then click the Next button. You're asked whether you want to install additional software. Click the Yes button.

3. The software is downloaded and installed in the background automatically. After installation has completed, click the Finish button to close the Plugin Finder Service dialog box. The browser will then display the Flash content.

4. Some users may find that this method doesn't work and that the plug-in is not available. In this case, go to www.adobe.com, click the link for Get Adobe Flash Player, select the appropriate version to download (.deb for Ubuntu 8.04+), and then install as with the RealPlayer software earlier. Note that you'll be prompted to close down all browsers during the installation procedure.

Removing a Flash Plug-in

If you want to remove a Flash plug-in—perhaps because it doesn't work correctly and you want to try an alternative—open the Synaptic Package Manager (System ➤ Administration) and search for gnash to remove Gnash, swfdec to remove Swfdec, or flashplugin-nonfree to remove Adobe's Flash Player. Click the check box alongside the entry in the list and select Mark for Removal from the menu that appears. (If you want to remove Gnash, you'll need to mark both gnash and gnash-common for removal.) Then click Apply on the main toolbar. Close Synaptic when the removal is complete.

Following this, whenever you visit a site requiring Flash, you will again be prompted to install a Flash plug-in. You can then select a different option from the list.

Adding Java Support

Java is a software platform that some programs use. The intention is that Java is cross-platform, which means that software developed for, say, Microsoft Windows will also work on Linux and Macintosh. Because of this, some web sites use Java applets—small programs embedded into the web page—to present interaction, animation, and even movies.

To access web sites that employ Java applets, you'll need to install the Java Runtime software along with a browser plug-in. Previously, Java would have been a separate installation, but since Sun Microsystems released the software under an open source license, it has been available to distribution developers and hence is now included in the Ubuntu software repositories. The simplest way to install is to open Synaptic Package Manager, do a search for **Java**, and then select Sun Java6 JRE for installation. Other options will automatically be selected, including the binaries and plug-ins for Firefox, and you can just click Apply to install the software.

Watching Movies

The Totem movie player application (Applications ➤ Sound and Video ➤ Movie Player) is used to play back video under Ubuntu, as shown in Figure 17-3.

Figure 17-3. Totem handles movie file playback under Ubuntu and is simple but effective.

To play a movie file on your hard disk, simply double-click its icon. This will automatically start Totem and play the video, if Totem has the appropriate codecs, as shown in Figure 17-4. If not, Totem will suggest which codecs to download and install, as explained earlier in the chapter.

■ **Tip** By default, all video files will play in Totem, including RealMedia. To change this so that RealPlayer handles its own file types, right-click any RealPlayer movie file, select Properties, click the Open With tab, and click Add. Locate RealPlayer in the list, click the Add button, and then make sure the radio button alongside RealPlayer is selected.

Using Totem is easy, and the interface has only a handful of options. At the bottom left of the screen are the transport controls that enable you to pause, play, and move forward and backward in the video file. Alternatively, you can right-click the video window and select the controls from there.

Above the controls is the Time bar. You can usually drag the slider to move through the video, but not all files support this function. You might find that some dragging is allowed, but you're not able to click a new place in the Time bar and have the counter jump to that position.

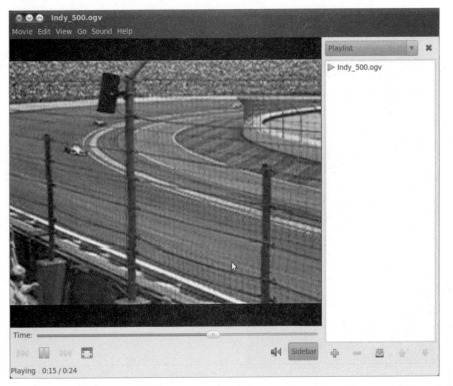

Figure 17-4. Totem can play just about every kind of movie file, such as QuickTime, Windows Media Player, DivX, and Ogg (or .ogv) files, as shown here.

At the right of the program window is a playlist. You can queue several video files to be played in sequence by simply dragging and dropping movies from a Nautilus file browser window. You can hide the playlist by clicking the Sidebar button. This gives nearly all of Totem's program window to the playback window. To play the video full screen, thereby hiding the desktop and Totem controls, press the F key. To return to the program window, press Esc (or press F again). In full-screen mode, you can start and stop the video by pressing the spacebar.

To adjust the image quality, click Edit ➤ Preferences and then click the Display tab in the Preferences dialog box. You can make adjustments by clicking and dragging the Brightness, Contrast, Saturation, and Hue sliders. If a video is playing in the background, the changes are shown as you make them.

■ **Tip** If you find you have problems with video playback, such as Totem showing an error message about another application using the video output, try the following: click System ➤ Preferences ➤ Terminal, and at the prompt, type **gstreamer-properties**. Click the Video tab, and in the Plugin drop-down list under Default Output, select Xwindows (No XV).

OPEN SOURCE MOVIE FILE FORMATS

A number of promising open source movie file formats are in development. Some are more mature than others, but few see widespread use at the moment. All promise much for the future. Many consider the following three formats the chief contenders:

- Xvid (www.xvid.org) is a reworking of the popular DivX MPEG-4–based file format. Unfortunately, Xvid uses technology covered by patents in some parts of the world, so the project exists in a legally gray area. Xvid is able to encode movies to relatively small file sizes (a 90-minute movie can fit on a CD). Despite small file sizes, this format maintains good image and sound quality. In theory, it should also be possible to play Xvid movies by using any MPEG-4 codec, such as DivX or QuickTime.

- Ogg Theora (www.theora.org) is being developed by the Xiph.org Foundation, the people behind the Ogg Vorbis audio codec project that's a favorite among Linux users. As such, it promises to be a completely open source project. Although the technology, again, is covered by patents, Xiph.org has promised never to enforce them, meaning that anyone in the world can use Theora without charge.

- HTML 5 is currently being developed by the World Wide Web Consortium (W3C). Like all its predecessors, from HTML 1.0 onwards, it is supposed to become the dominant web markup language. HTML 5 has explicit support for audio and video. Some parts are stable, others are not, but its video support is being developed vigorously and should be stable by the end of 2010.

Watching DVDs

DVD movie discs are protected by a form of DRM called CSS. This forces anyone who would like to create DVD playback software or hardware to pay a fee to the DVD Copy Control Association, an industry organization set up to protect DVD movie technology.

Nearly all Linux advocates are scornful of any kind of DRM system. Although it is possible to purchase playback software created by Fluendo and CyberLink through Ubuntu's online store, few appear to be willing to support what they see as restrictive software technology.

Some open source advocates reverse-engineered DVD protection and came up with the DeCSS software. This bypasses the CSS system and allows the playback of DVD movies under practically any operating system. Sadly, DeCSS is caught in a legal quagmire. The Motion Picture Association of America (MPAA) has attempted to stop its distribution within the United States, but has so far failed. Some experts suggest that distributing DeCSS breaks copyright laws, but there has yet to be a case anywhere in the world that proves this. Nor has there been a case proving or even suggesting that using DeCSS is in any way illegal.

Ubuntu doesn't come with DeCSS installed by default, but you can download and install the software by issuing a simple command, following the installation of a software package. Here is the procedure:

1. Choose System ➤ Administration ➤ Synaptic Package Manager.

2. Click Search and search for **libdvdread4**. In the list of results, click the check box alongside the package and click Mark for Installation. Click Apply on the main toolbar. Close Synaptic.

3. Open a terminal window (Applications ➤ Accessories ➤ Terminal). Type the following in the terminal window to download and install the DeCSS component:

   ```
   sudo /usr/share/doc/libdvdread4/install-css.sh
   ```

4. After the command has completed, you can close the terminal window.

■ **Note** You must ensure that Synaptic and Update Manager are closed before typing the command to install the DeCSS software. It will fail if either program is running.

After you've installed DeCSS, just insert a DVD, and Totem will automatically start playing it, as shown in Figure 17-5.

■ **Note** If the relevant codecs aren't installed when you insert a DVD, you will be prompted to install them, as with all kinds of multimedia file playback.

If the movie doesn't start playing automatically, double-click the disc's icon on the desktop. In the Nautilus file browser window, click the Open Movie Player button.

Unfortunately, there is a slight limitation to playing DVD movies within Totem: the chapter menus don't work, so you can't navigate from chapter to chapter in the disc. Additionally, in our tests, we noticed that DVD playback can be a little glitchy. To get around both these issues, you can install the totem-xine package. This installs a separate but otherwise identical version of the Totem movie player that utilizes the Xine multimedia framework. Then you can choose between using the standard version of Totem, which relies on the GStreamer multimedia framework, or the Xine version of Totem. Installing the totem-xine package also installs Xine versions of the codecs you need for virtually all multimedia file playback, meaning no extra configuration is necessary.

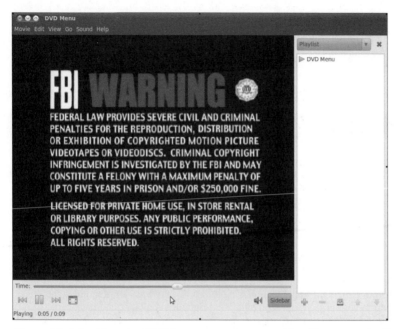

Figure 17-5. Just insert a DVD in your computer, and it will automatically play in Totem.

■ **Note** You might be wondering why we didn't just advise you to install totem-xine back at the beginning of this chapter, if it installs all the codecs you need. The method we recommend installs codecs for the GStreamer multimedia framework, rather than just Totem. GStreamer is used by *all* the GNOME desktop multimedia software. This means that if you install a different GNOME movie player in the future, it will automatically have support for all the file formats you've already added to Ubuntu. In contrast, the totem-xine package is rather self-contained and installs codecs for only the Xine framework, which isn't supported elsewhere under Ubuntu (but is the default framework under KDE).

To install the totem-xine package, start the Synaptic Package Manager (System ➤ Administration) and click the Search button. Search for **totem-xine**. Click the check box alongside the entry in the results list and select to install it. As you'll see from the warning dialog box, installing totem-xine also installs a lot of other packages, including the necessary codecs for playback of virtually all multimedia files. This is fine.

From now on, you'll need to run the Xine version of Totem to play DVD movies. You'll have to do this before you insert the DVD movie disc, to avoid the standard version of Totem attempting to play it. To run the Xine version of Totem, you can use either of these methods:

Run it from a terminal window: Click Applications ➤ Accessories ➤ Terminal and type **nohup totem-xine**.

Create a new launcher: Right-click the desktop, select Create Launcher, and in the Command text box, type **totem-xine**. In the Name box, type something like **Totem (Xine)** for easy identification, and then click OK.

■ **Tip** To find out which version of Totem you're using—GStreamer or Xine—click Help ➤ About in Totem. You'll see either "Movie Player using xine-lib," in the case of Xine, or "Movie Player using GStreamer," in the case of GStreamer.

MOVIE EDITING

The field of Linux movie-editing software is developing, and only a handful of programs are available for the nonprofessional user. One of the best is Kino (www.kinodv.org), which is available in the Ubuntu software archives. Although far from being a professional-level program, Kino allows competent users to import and edit videos, apply effects, and then output in either MPEG-1 or MPEG-2 format.

If you're looking for something more powerful, but also more complicated, Cinelerra is worth a look (http://heroinewarrior.com/cinelerra.php3). Just follow the instructions at http://cvs.cinelerra.org/ getting_cinelerra.php#hardy to install a version of Cinelerra for Ubuntu.

For those who want something a little simpler, the PiTiVi (www.pitivi.org) project is attempting to build a piece of software akin to Apple's iMovie. The possibilities that are offered by PiTiVi are limited, but you can use it to apply simple movie editing to your video films. You can find a default installation of PiTiVi in Applications ➤ Sound and Video ➤ PiTiVi Video Editor. After starting it, PiTiVi shows the screen that you can see in Figure 17-6.

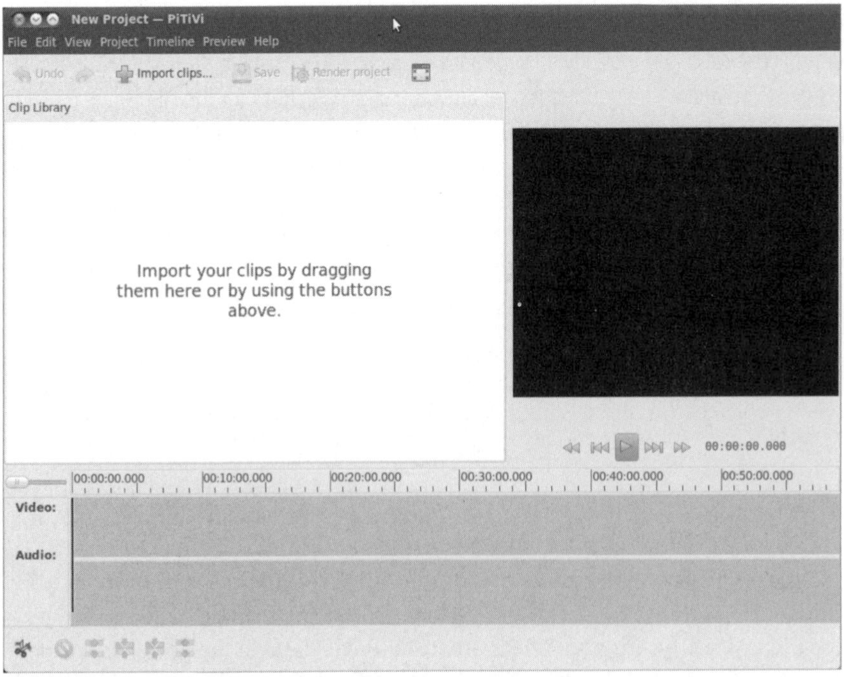

Figure 17-6. *PiTiVi offers a simple solution for Video editing on Ubuntu.*

Basically, all you can do with PiTiVi is put video clips together to join them in a new file. There are no other editing features, neither is it possible to write to another output format as the default PiTiVi format. If you're interested in using this application, you can drag and drop your movie files to the pane in the upper left corner. That makes them available for further editing in PiTiVi. From this location, you next drag them to the time line. By dragging several clips to the timeline, you can compose your own video and that is basically it.

Another approach to movie editing, is to go web-based. An example of this is Adobe's Premiere Express (available through the Photobucket picture-sharing service), which is designed specifically for online video editing and distribution. It works very well under Ubuntu with the Flash plug-in.

Professional moviemakers don't just use software that comes with normal desktops. Quite a few use Linux all the time, particularly when it comes to adding special effects to movies. Movies like *Shrek 2*, *Stuart Little*, and the *Harry Potter* series all benefited from the CinePaint software running under Linux! For more details, see www.cinepaint.org.

Watching TV

If you have a TV card, you may be able to use it to watch TV under Ubuntu. Ubuntu doesn't come with a TV tuner application by default, but you can download the tvtime program from the software repositories by using the Synaptic Package Manager.

Checking for Video Input

Ubuntu includes the Video for Linux project, an extension to the Linux kernel, to allow many popular TV and video-capture cards to work. You can find out whether yours is compatible by opening a terminal window (Applications ➤ Accessories ➤ Terminal) and typing **gstreamer-properties**. In the dialog box that appears, click the Video tab and click the Test button in the Default Input part of the window. If you see a video window without an error message, your TV card is compatible. If you receive an error message, your card probably isn't compatible.

■ **Note** Getting Video for Linux to work can be troublesome, but there are a lot of resources out there to help. You can start by visiting www.linuxtv.org and www.exploits.org/v4l/.

Installing tvtime

To download and install tvtime, open the Synaptic Package Manager (System ➤ Administration), click the Search button, and enter **tvtime** as a search term. In the list of results, click the entry for the package, mark it for installation, and then click Apply.

When the download has completed, you'll be asked a number of questions during the configuration process. First, you need to choose your TV picture format. Users in the United States should choose NTSC. Users in the United Kingdom, Australia, and certain parts of Europe should choose PAL. To find out which TV system your country uses, look up your country at www.videouniversity.com/standard.htm.

You also need to choose your geographical area from the list so that tvtime can set the correct radio frequency range for your TV card.

After the program is installed, you'll find it on the Applications ➤ Sound & Video menu. Using the program is straightforward, but if you need guidance, visit the program's web site at http://tvtime.sourceforge.net.

■ **Tip** If you're interested in setting up a low-cost personal video recorder (PVR) and entertainment system, you may want to install MythTV by using the Synaptic Package Manager. For more information, check out *Practical MythTV: Building a PVR and Media Center PC* by Stewart Smith and Michael Still (Apress, 2007).

Summary

In this chapter, you looked at how you can watch movies on your PC. You've seen how you can update Ubuntu to work with the most popular digital video technologies, such as Windows Media Player and QuickTime.

In addition, you looked at how you can view online multimedia such as Flash animations on your computer, and learned how you can watch TV on your PC.

In the next chapter, you'll take a look at image editing under Ubuntu. You'll learn about one of the crown jewels of the Linux software scene: GIMP.

■■■

## CHAPTER 18

Digital Photos

The PC has become a vital tool in the field of photography. In fact, you're unlikely to find any photographer—professional or amateur—who doesn't use a PC somewhere in his or her work.

Ubuntu includes a number of applications for cataloging and editing images. Chief among these is GIMP (GNU Image Manipulation Program), which compares favorably with professional software such as Photoshop. But there are also applications for more casual users. This chapter begins with a brief tour of F-Spot, an application ideal for cataloging and managing image collections and also doing some basic edits, before introducing GIMP. The GIMP is not part of the default Lucid install, but you can quickly and easily install it via the Ubuntu Software Center.

Downloading and Cataloging Images

Before you can undertake any image editing, you need to transfer the images to your PC. Depending on the source of the pictures, there are a variety of methods of doing this, but in nearly every case, the work of importing your photos can be handled by F-Spot. But before we cover F-Spot, let's briefly recap the various methods of transferring images to your PC, some of which were outlined earlier in this book.

Connecting Your Camera

Most modern cameras use memory cards to store pictures. If you have such a model, when you plug the camera into your PC's USB port, you should find that Ubuntu instantly recognizes it. An icon should appear on the Desktop, and double-clicking it should display the memory card's contents in a Nautilus window. Along the top of the window, you'll see an orange bar reading, "This media contains digital photos" alongside a button marked Open F-Spot Photo Manager. Clicking this button starts F-Spot, with which you can copy the images to your hard disk, as explained in the next section. Of course, you can also drag and drop pictures to your hard disk manually using Nautilus.

In the unlikely event that your camera doesn't appear to be recognized by Ubuntu, you might have more luck with a generic USB memory card reader, which will make the card appear as a standard removable drive on the Desktop. These devices are relatively inexpensive and can usually read a wide variety of card types such as SD, XD, and CompactFlash (CF), making them a useful investment for the future. Some new PCs even come with card readers built in, but they often are hard to address in Linux environments. Most generic USB card readers should work fine under Linux, though, as will most new digital cameras.

■ **Caution** Before detaching your camera or removing a photo card, you should right-click the Desktop icon and select Safely Remove. This tells Ubuntu that you've finished with the device. Using this method to eject the device ensures that all data is written back from memory to the photo card. Failing to eject in this way could cause data errors, as information may be partially written back to the card, or transfers between the two devices may not have finished.

If you're working with print photos, negative film, or transparencies, you can use a scanner and the Simple Scan program (Applications ➤ Graphics ➤ Simple Scan Image Scanner) to digitize them, as explained in Chapter 7.

Importing Photos Using F-Spot

F-Spot is designed to work in a similar way to applications you may have encountered under Windows or Mac OS X, such as iPhoto or Picasa. After you run F-Spot (Applications ➤ Graphics ➤ F-Spot Photo Manager), or after you click the Open F-Spot Photo Manager button that appears along the top of a Nautilus file browser window when you insert a memory card or attach your digital camera, the F-Spot Import window will appear. (Depending on your configuration, the Import window may appear within a file browser.) For some devices, though, this doesn't happen automatically. If, for instance, you attach your mobile phone to your computer, you may have it attached as a disk device by default. To import photos in that case also, use the Import button in F-Spot to browse to the appropriate device and import your pictures from there.

The Import window contains a preview of the pictures stored in your camera, the option to tag the pictures, and the target directory where the photos will be copied. If you have no camera attached, you'll see some default pictures that are available in the F-Spot program directory. While working on your camera, by default, all the pictures are selected. You can deselect and select photos by using the standard selection techniques (Ctrl-click or Shift-click). Embedded tags are very useful in filtering and searching for pictures, as discussed in the "Tagging Images" section a little later in the chapter. The default target directory where the photos will be copied is Photos in your /home directory, but you can change it to any directory you want.

To import the pictures from your camera to your hard disk, just click the Import button. F-Spot will import your photos in the target location, in directories named after the year, month, and day the photos were originally taken.

Importing pictures from a mounted Windows partition, or any other folder on your computer's hard disk is easy. Click Photo ➤ Import. In the Import window, click the Import Source drop-down list and then click Select Folder. Using the file browser, navigate to the Windows directory containing your images and then click Open. (Don't double-click the directory, because that causes F-Spot to open the directory in the file browser.) After you've selected the folder, F-Spot displays thumbnail previews of the images, and this might take some time. Keep your eye on the orange status bar. When this indicates "Done Loading," you can click the Import button to import all the images in one go, or Ctrl-click to select photos in the left side of the window and then click the Import button.

If you're importing the photos from a particular event, this is also a great time to define a set of tags for the whole set (which will save having to manually tag pictures later) Using tags makes it much easier to find back your photos later. Of course, a well-organized directory tree containing your photo albums might suit you as well. As with photos from a camera, by default, F-Spot copies the images into a directory it creates within your /home directory, called Photos. Therefore, after you've imported the photos, you can delete the originals from the Windows partition if you want.

■ **Tip** You may be familiar with Picasa from Google. This software is available for Ubuntu from `http://picasa.google.com/linux/`. One advantage of Picasa is that it integrates well with Google's own photo-sharing service and also has a plug-in that allows one-click uploading from your library to Facebook.

After the photos have been imported, the main F-Spot window will appear. On the left are the default tags and a list of any tags added to imported files. On the right is the picture preview window, which can be set to either Browse or Edit Photo mode. You can switch between these two modes by using the buttons on the toolbar. You can also view an image full screen or start a slide show that will cycle through the images in sequence.

Above the picture window is the timeline. By clicking and dragging the slider, you can move backward and forward in the photograph collection, depending on when the pictures were taken. Each notch on the timeline represents a month in the year marked beneath the timeline. The graphs on the timeline give a general idea of how many photographs were taken during that particular month (or, indeed, if *any* were taken during a particular month). The arrows to the left and right of the timeline can be used to expose a different set of months.

Tweaking Photos

F-Spot offers you all you need to do basic photo editing. By either double-clicking an image or selecting an image and clicking Edit Photo on the toolbar, you can tweak images by cropping them, adjusting brightness and contrast, or setting the color saturation/balance. The available tools appear in a docked toolbar, replacing the default tags pane, as shown in Figure 18-1. In addition, you can convert images to black-and-white or sepia tone, and you can remove red-eye caused by an indoor flash. All of this can be achieved by clicking the buttons under the image. (Hovering the mouse cursor over an icon will cause a tooltip to appear, explaining what the button does.) Simple rotations on single images or multiple selections can be performed by using the Rotate Left and Rotate Right buttons on the toolbar.

Figure 18-1. Any edits to the image are made live, so it's a good idea to move the adjustment dialog box out of the way.

You can also add a comment in the text field below the image. This is then attached to the image for future reference and can act as a useful memory aid.

A note of caution is required when tweaking images with F-Spot, because there is no traditional undo mechanism. However, F-Spot keeps a copy of the original image alongside the modified one, which you can access by clicking Photo ➤ Version ➤ Original. It's possible to create a new version of the image complete with modifications by clicking Photo ➤ Create New Version. You can then name this separately and, if necessary, continue to edit while retaining both the original and the intermediate version. You can do this as many times as you want, perhaps to save various image tweaks to choose the best one at a later date.

Tagging Images

F-Spot's cataloging power comes from its ability to tag each image. A *tag* is simply a word or short phrase that can be attached to any number of images, rather like a real-life tag that you might find attached to an item in a shop. After images have been tagged, you can then filter the images by using the tag word. For example, you could create a tag called *German vacation*, which you would attach to all images taken on a trip to Germany. Then, when you select the German vacation tag, only those images will be displayed. Alternatively, you could be more precise with tags—you could create the tags *Dusseldorf* and *Cologne* to subdivide pictures taken on the vacation.

If your collection involves a lot of pictures taken of your children at various stages during their lives, you could create a tag for each of their names. By selecting to view only photos tagged with a particular child's name, you could see all the pictures of that child, regardless of when or where they were taken.

Images can have more than one tag. A family photo could be tagged with the words thanksgiving, grandma's house, family meal, and the names of the individuals pictured. Then, if you searched using any of the tags, the picture would appear in the list.

A handful of tags are provided by default: Favorites, Hidden, People, Places, and Events. To create your own tags, right-click under the tag list on the left of the F-Spot program window and select Create New Tag. Simply type in the name of the new tag in the dialog box and click OK.

If you tagged items on importing, these will appear under the Import Tags parent. Drag and drop these tags to the appropriate parent tag (Germany under Places, for example).

■ **Note** Tags can have *parents*, which can help organize them. For instance, you might put the names of family members under the People parent tag, or put Birthday under the Events parent. You can reveal or hide child tags by clicking the disclosure arrow next to the parent.

Tags can also have icons attached to them. An icon based on the first photo that is tagged will automatically be added to the tag name, but to manually assign one, right-click it in the list and select Edit. Next, in the Edit Tag dialog box, click the icon button and select from the list of icons under the Predefined heading.

To attach a tag to a picture, simply right-click it (in either the Browse or Edit Photo mode) and click its entry on Attach Tag.

To filter by tag, double-click the tag in the tag list, as shown in Figure 18-2. To remove the filtering, right-click the tag in the orange bar at the top of the display and select Remove from Search.

F-Spot has a good range of export options for when you want to share your pictures with the wider world. You'll find these under the Photo ➤ Export To option, and supported services include Picasa Web Albums, SmugMug, and Flickr. When using Flickr, F-Spot even includes an option to turn your tags into Flickr tags during the upload process.

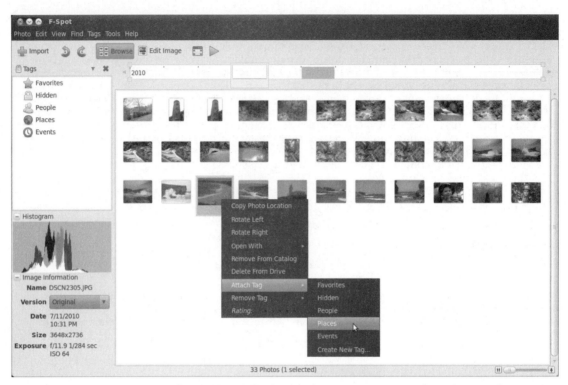

Figure 18-2. *Tag an image by right-clicking and selecting the appropriate entry from the Attatch Tag option.*

Using GIMP for Image Editing

GIMP is an extremely powerful image editor that offers the kind of functions usually associated with top-end software like Adobe Photoshop. Although GIMP is not aimed at beginners, those new to image manipulation can get a lot from it, though it may demand a little more work than the limited options available in F-Spot.

The program relies on a few unusual concepts in its interface, which can catch many people off guard. The first of these is that each of the windows within the program, such as floating dialog boxes or palettes, gets its own panel entry. In other words, the GIMP's icon bar, image window, settings window, and so on have their own buttons on the Ubuntu Desktop panel alongside your other programs, as if they were separate programs.

■ **Note** GIMP's way of working is called a Single Document Interface, or SDI. It's favored by a handful of programs that run under Linux and seems to be especially popular among programs that let you create things. If your taskbar is getting a little crowded, edit its Preferences to "Always group windows."

Because of the way GIMP runs, before you start up the program it's a wise idea to switch to a different virtual desktop, which you can then dedicate entirely to GIMP.

Having installed GIMP via the Ubuntu Software Center, click Applications ➤ Graphics ➤ GIMP Image Editor to launch the application. You'll be greeted by what appears to be a complex assortment of program windows.

Now you need to be aware of a second unusual aspect of the program: its reliance on right-clicking. Whereas right-clicking usually brings up a context menu offering a handful of options, in GIMP it's the principal way of accessing the program's functions. Right-clicking an image brings up a menu offering access to virtually everything you'll need while editing. Ubuntu offers the latest version of GIMP, 2.6.8 (as of this writing), which includes a more traditional menu bar in the main image-editing window, so you can choose your preferred method of working.

The main toolbar window, shown in Figure 18-3, is on the left. This can be considered the heart of GIMP, because when you close it all the other program windows are closed too. Version 2.6 also introduces a blank window that is visible when no image is open. This means that the traditional menus are available at all times. Closing this window also causes the entire application to close. The menu bar on the toolbar window offers most of the options you're likely to use to start out with GIMP. For example, File ➤ Open opens a browser dialog box in which you can select files to open. It's even possible to create new artwork from scratch by choosing File ➤ New.

■ **Tip** To create vector artwork, a better choice is a program like Inkscape (www.inkscape.org), which can be downloaded via the Ubuntu Software Center (to learn about software installation, see Chapter 20).

Beneath the menu bar in the main toolbar window are the tools for working with images. Their functions are described in Table 18-1, which lists the tools in order from left to right, starting at the top left.

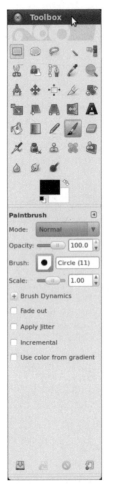

Figure 18-3. GIMP's main toolbar window

Table 18-1. GIMP Image-Editing Tools

Tool	Description of Use
Rectangle Select	Click and drag to select a rectangular area within the image. This selected area can then be copied and pasted into a different part of the image or turned into a new layer.
Ellipse Select	Create an oval or a circular selection area within the image, which you can then copy and paste.
Free Select	Click and draw with the mouse to create a hand-drawn selection area. Your selection should end where it started. If not, GIMP will draw a straight line between the start and end of the selection, which makes it easy to create geometric selections.

Tool	Description of Use
Select by Color	Works like the Fuzzy Select tool, but creates a selection across the entire image based on the color you select. In other words, selecting a black T-shirt will also select a black signpost elsewhere in the picture if the hues are similar.
Scissors Select	Another "magical" tool that lets you create a selection by clicking on various points within an image, with the program joining the points together based on the color differences between the two points. This means that you can select the outline of a car by clicking a few points around the edge of the car and, provided the color of the car is different from the background, GIMP will work out the color differences and select the car's shape automatically.
Foreground Select	Lets you automatically create an intricate selection of an object in the foreground of a picture, via a three-step process. Click to draw roughly around the foreground object as with the Free Select tool. (Be careful you don't stray into the object; if you do, momentarily select a different tool, which will cancel the selection, and try again.) Then release the mouse button and draw across the main areas of the object by using a kind of paintbrush tool. For example, if the object is a face, draw a little on the skin and hair. The trick is to cover areas that have different color ranges, because that's how GIMP detects the edges. You'll see that the background—the area that *won't* be selected—is masked out in blue tint. If any of the foreground object is masked, draw on it to add it to the selection area. You can subtract from the selection area by Ctrl-clicking. When you're happy with the selection, press Enter.
Paths	Draws Bezier curves in order to create *paths*, which are akin to selections and can be saved for use later in the image-editing process. Just click and drag to draw a curve. Each extra click you make will define a new curve, which will be joined to the last one. To turn the path into a selection, click the button at the bottom of the toolbar.
Color Picker	Lets you see the RGB, HSV, or CMYK values of any color within the image. Simply click the mouse within the image.
Zoom	Click to zoom into the image, right-click to see various zoom options, and hold down the Alt key while clicking to zoom out.
Measure	Measures distances between two points (in pixels) and also angles. Just click and drag to use it. The measurements appear at the bottom of the image window.
Move	Click and drag to move any selection areas within the image, as well as rearrange the positioning of various layers.
Alignment	Allows you to align layers to other objects relative to each other. To choose a layer, click an object within the preferred layer. To select several layers, Shift-click objects inside the preferred layers. In the tool options of the Alignment tool, select how the layer or layers will be aligned relative to other layers or image objects. Alignment includes left, center horizontal, right, top, center vertical, and bottom, with an option to use offsets as well.

Tool	Description of Use
Crop	Click and drag to define an area of the image to be cropped. Anything outside the selection area you create will be discarded.
Rotate	Rotates any selections you make and can also rotate entire layers. It opens a dialog box in which you can set the rotation numerically. Alternatively, you can simply click and drag the handles behind the dialog box to rotate by hand.
Scale	Known in some other image editors as *transform*, this lets you resize the selection area or layer. It presents a dialog box for entering numeric values, or you can click and drag the handles to resize by hand.
Perspective	Lets you transform a selection by clicking and dragging its four corners and independently moving them without affecting the other corners. In this way, a sense of perspective can be emulated.
Flip	Flips a selection or image so that it is reversed on itself, either horizontally (click) or vertically (Ctrl-click).
Text	Click the image to add text.
Bucket Fill	Fills a particular area with solid color or pattern, according to the color or pattern selected in the color box or fill type box below.
Blend	Creates a gradient fill based on the foreground and background colors. Just click and drag to add the fill. Hold down Ctrl to force the blend along predefined angles, including horizontal and vertical.
Pencil	Lets you draw individual pixels when zoomed in, or hard-edge lines when zoomed out. Simply click and drag to draw freehand, and hold down Shift to draw lines between two points. Again, holding down Ctrl constrains the angle of the lines.
Paintbrush	Lets you draw on the picture in a variety of brush styles to create artistic effects. A brush can also be created from an image, allowing for greater versatility.
Erase	Rather like the Paintbrush tool in reverse, deletes whatever is underneath the cursor. If layers are being used, the contents of the layer beneath become visible.
Airbrush	Like the Paintbrush tool, it draws on the picture in a variety of styles. However, the density of the color depends on the length of time you press the mouse button. Tap the mouse button, and only a light color will appear. Press and hold the mouse button, and the color will become more saturated.
Ink	Like the Paintbrush tool, except that, rather like an ink pen, the faster you draw, the thinner the brushstroke.
Clone	Allows you to copy one part of an image to another via a brush. The origin point is defined by Ctrl-clicking.

Tool	Description of Use
Healing	Typically used to remove unwanted irregularities, such as pimples, scars, and blemishes in a person's face. Ctrl-click an ideal source similar to the area that needs to be healed and then draw over the blemish, which will disappear. Effectively, the Healing tool is a Clone tool that has some intelligence built in to aid intermixing of the sample area and the area you're drawing over.
Blur/Sharpen	Clicking and drawing on the image will spot blur or sharpen the image, depending on the settings in the tool options area, in the lower half of the toolbar.
Smudge	As its name suggests, clicking and drawing with this tool smudges the image, rather like rubbing a still-wet painting with your finger.

Directly beneath the image-editing tool icons, on the left, is an icon that shows the foreground and background colors that will be used when drawing with tools such as the Paintbrush. To define a new color to be used for either of these, double-click either the foreground (top) or background (bottom) color box.

Beneath these icons, you'll see the various options for the selected tool. The brush selector lets you choose the thickness of the brushstrokes and patterns that are used with various tools. Simply click each to change them. By using the buttons at the bottom of the window, you can save the current tool options, load tool options, and delete a previously saved set of tool options. Clicking the button on the bottom right lets you revert to the default settings for the tool currently being used (useful if you tweak too many settings!).

If you use particular options regularly, use the disclosure arrow on the right edge of the context-sensitive part of the toolbox to add a tab to the window. When you begin to experiment, having the Layers tab available here is useful, but you can add and remove as many as you like.

The Basics of GIMP

After you've started GIMP (and assigned it a virtual desktop), you can load an image by choosing File ➤ Open. The browser dialog box offers a preview facility on the right side of the window.

You will probably need to resize the image window, or change the zoom level, so the image fits within the remainder of the screen. You can then use the Zoom tool (see Table 18-1) to ensure that the image fills the editing window, which makes working with it much easier. Alternatively, you can click the Zoom drop-down list in the lower left part of the image window.

You can save any changes you make to an image by right-clicking it and selecting File ➤ Save, or create a new, named version of the picture by using Save As. You can also print the image from the same menu.

Before you begin editing with GIMP, you need to be aware of some essential concepts that are vital in order to get the most from the program:

Copy, cut, and paste buffers: Unlike some Windows programs, GIMP lets you cut or copy many selections from the image and store them for use later. It calls these saved selections *buffers*, and each must be given a name for future reference. Create a new buffer by using any of the selection tools to select, and then right-clicking within the selection area and selecting Edit ➤ Buffer ➤ Copy Named (or Cut Named). Pasting a buffer back is a matter of right-clicking the image and selecting Edit ➤ Buffer ➤ Paste Named.

Paths: GIMP paths are not necessarily the same as selection areas, although it's nearly always possible to convert a selection into a path and vice versa (right-click within the selection or path, and look for the relevant option on the Select menu: Select ➤ To Path, or Select ➤ From Path, as shown in Figure 18-4). In general, paths allow the creation of complex shapes, rather than the simple geometric shapes offered by the selection tools. You can save paths for later use or take one from one image and apply it to another. To view the Paths dialog box, right-click the image and select Dialogs ➤ Paths.

■ **Tip** Getting rid of a selection or path you've drawn is easy. In the case of a path, simply click any other tool or some other part of the canvas, and the path disappears. To get rid of a selection, use any selection tool to quickly click once on the image, being careful not to drag the mouse while doing so.

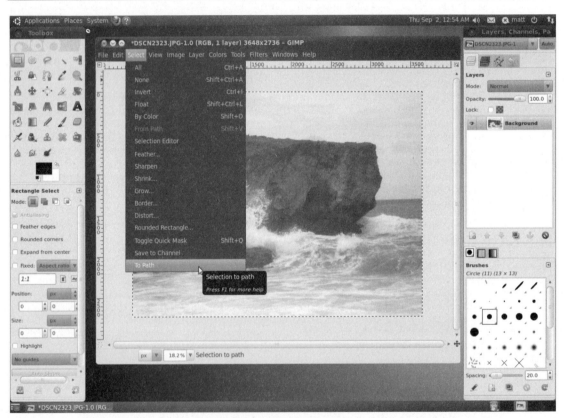

Figure 18-4. Paths allow for more elaborate and intricate selections, such as those that involve curves.

Layers: In GIMP (along with most other image-editing programs), *layers* are like transparent sheets of paper that are placed on top of the image. Anything can be drawn on each individual transparent sheet, and many layers can be overlaid in order to create a complicated image. Layers also let you cut and paste parts of the image between them. Though layers might be thought of as high-end, they're great if you need to add text to an image; the text is added to a new layer, which can then be moved or resized simply. The Layers dialog box, shown in Figure 18-5, appears by default, but if you closed it earlier, you can open it again by right-clicking the image and selecting Dialogs ➤ Layers. The layers can be reordered by clicking and dragging them in the dialog box. In addition, the blending mode of each layer can be altered. This refers to how it interacts with the layer below it. For example, you can change its opacity so that it appears semitransparent, thereby showing the contents of the layer beneath. You can also define how the colors from different layers interact by using the Mode drop-down list. The Layers menu also offers an option to collapse all of the layers back down to a single image (Layers ➤ Merge Visible Layers or Flatten Image).

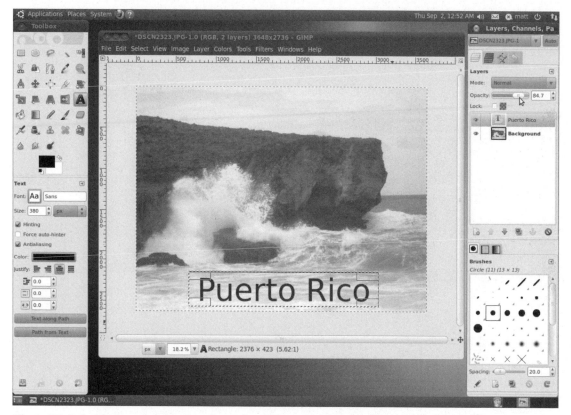

Figure 18-5. *Set the opacity of various layers by clicking and dragging the relevant slider in the Layers dialog box.*

Making Color Corrections

The first step when editing most images is to correct the brightness, contrast, and color saturation. This helps overcome some of the deficiencies that are commonly found in digital photographs or scanned-in images. To do this, right-click the image and select Colors. You'll find a variety of options to let you tweak the image, allowing you a lot of control over the process.

For simple brightness and contrast changes, selecting the Brightness-Contrast menu option opens a dialog box in which you can click and drag the sliders to alter the image. The changes you make will be previewed on the image itself, so you should be able to get things just right.

Similarly, the Hue-Saturation option lets you alter the color balance and the strength of the colors (the saturation) by clicking and dragging sliders. By selecting the color bar options at the top of the window, you can choose individual colors to boost. Clicking the Master button lets you once again alter all colors at the same time.

The trouble with clicking and dragging sliders is that it relies on human intuition. This can easily be clouded by a badly calibrated monitor, which might be set too dark or too light. Because of this, GIMP offers another handy option, which can ensure that the whites in your image are white and that your blacks are truly black: Levels. To access the Levels feature, right-click the image and select Colors ➤ Levels. This presents a chart of the brightness levels in the photo and lets you set the dark, shadows, and highlight points, as shown in Figure 18-6. Three sliders beneath the chart represent, from left to right, the darkest point, the midtones (shadows), and the highlights within the picture. The first step is to set the dark and light sliders at the left and right of the edges of the chart. This will make sure that the range of brightness from the lightest point to the darkest point is set correctly. The next step is to adjust the middle slider so that it's roughly in the middle of the highest peak within the chart. This will accurately set the midtone point, ensuring an even spread of brightness across the image.

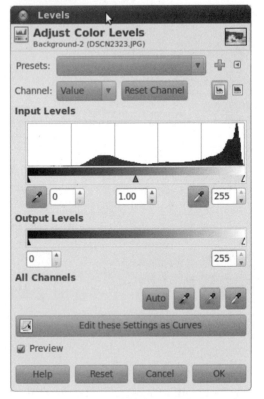

Figure 18-6. The Levels function can be used to accurately set the brightness levels across an image.

A little artistic license is usually allowed at this stage, and depending on the effect you want in the photo, moving the midtone slider a little to the left or right of the highest peak might produce more-acceptable results. However, be aware that the monitor might be showing incorrect brightness or color values.

Cropping and Healing

After you've adjusted the colors, you might want to use the Crop tool to remove any extraneous details outside the focus of the image. For example, in a portrait of someone taken from a distance away, you might choose to crop the photo to show only the person's head and shoulders, or you might separate a group of people from their surroundings, as shown in Figure 18-7.

Figure 18-7. You can use the Crop tool to focus on one part of a picture or introduce a dramatic new shape.

The Healing tool is great for removing small blemishes, not just on people, but also dust from an unclean lens or scratches on an old scanned photo. Start by using the Zoom tool to close in on the area. If the blemish is small, you might need to go in quite close. Then try to find an area of the image that is clear and from which you can copy. Ctrl-click that area. Then click and draw over the blemish. The crosshair indicates the area from which you're copying.

Applying Filters

To take you beyond basic editing, GIMP includes a selection of filters that can add dramatic effects to your images. Filters are applied either to the currently selected layer or to a selection within the layer. To apply a filter, right-click the image and choose the relevant menu option. If you don't like an effect you've applied, you can reverse it by choosing Edit ➤ Undo, or by pressing Ctrl+Z.

The submenus offer filters grouped by categories, as follows:

Blur: These filters add various kinds of blur to the image or selection. For example, Motion Blur can imitate the effect of photographing an object moving at speed with a slow shutter. Perhaps the most popular blur option is Gaussian Blur, which has the effect of applying a soft and subtle blur and is great for creating drop shadows.

Enhance: The Enhance effects are designed to remove various artifacts from an image or otherwise improve it. For example, the Despeckle effect attempts to remove unwanted noise within an image (such as flecks of dust in a scanned image). The Sharpen filter discussed in the previous section is located here, as is Unsharp Mask, which offers a high degree of control over the image-sharpening process.

Distort: As the name of this category of filters suggests, the effects available distort the image in various ways. For example, Whirl and Pinch allow you to tug and push the image to distort it (imagine printing the image on rubber and then pinching or pushing the surface). This category also contains other special effects, such as Pagecurl, which imitates the curl of a page at one corner of the picture.

Light and Shadow: Here you will find filters that imitate the effects that light and shadow can have on a picture, such as adding sparkle effects to highlights or imitating the lens flare caused by a camera's lens.

Noise: This collection of filters is designed to add speckles or other types of artifacts to an image. These filters are offered within GIMP for their potential artistic effects, but they can also be used to create a grainy film effect—simply click Scatter RGB—or white noise.

Edge-Detect: This set of filters can automatically detect and delineate the edges of objects within an image. Although this type of filter can result in some interesting results that might fall into the category of special effects, it's primarily used in conjunction with other tools and effects.

Generic: In this category, you can find a handful of filters that don't seem to fall into any other category. Of particular interest is the Convolution Matrix option, which lets you create your own filters by inputting numeric values. According to GIMP's programmers, this is designed primarily for mathematicians, but it can also be used by others to create random special effects. Simply input values and then preview the effect.

Combine: Here you'll find filters that combine two or more images into one.

Artistic: These filters allow you to add paint effects to the image, such as making it appear as if the photo has been painted in impressionistic brushstrokes or painted on canvas. Figure 18-9 shows an example of applying the Oilify filter for an oil painting effect.

Decor: This section has some interesting rendered effects such as coffee stains, bevels, and outlines that can be applied to images or layers.

Figure 18-8. *The Artistic effects can be used to give images an oil painting effect.*

Map: These filters aim to manipulate the image by treating it like a piece of paper that can be folded in various ways and stuck onto 3D shapes (a process referred to as *mapping*). Because the image is treated as if it were a piece of paper, it can also be copied, and the copies placed on top of each other to create various effects.

Render: Here you'll find filters designed to create new images from scratch, such as clouds or flame effects. Most of the options here will completely cover the underlying image with their effect, but others, such as Difference Clouds, use the base image as part of its source material.

Web: Here you can create an image map for use in a web page. An *image map* is a single image broken up into separate hyperlinked areas, typically used on a web page as a sophisticated menu. For example, an image map is frequently used for a geographical map on which you can click to get more information about different regions. There's also a useful Slice tool, which can be used to break up a large image into smaller parts for display on a web page.

Animation: These filters aim to manipulate and optimize GIF images, which are commonly used to create simple animated images for use on web sites.

Alpha to Logo: These filters are typically used to create special effects for text. They are quite specialized and require an in-depth knowledge of how GIMP works, particularly the use of alpha channels.

■ **Tip** If you like GIMP, you might be interested in *Beginning GIMP: From Novice to Professional, Second Edition* by Akkana Peck (Apress, 2009). This book offers a comprehensive, contemporary, and highly readable guide to this software.

GIMPSHOP

GIMP is one of the most powerful programs available for Linux, but not everyone is enamored of its user interface. One bone of contention for some is that GIMP uses almost completely different terminology from that used by Adobe Photoshop.

One developer became so annoyed by this that he created a new version of GIMP called GIMPshop (www.gimpshop.com). This is ostensibly exactly the same as the GIMP program, but the names of the tools have been changed to match those of Photoshop (or the simpler Photoshop Elements program). In a similar way, many of the GIMP's right-click menu entries have also been changed so that they're identical to Photoshop's menu options.

The freedom to adapt programs in this way is one of the benefits of open source software. The ability to take program code and create your own version is the foundation of Linux.

GIMPshop isn't available via the Ubuntu Software Center, but the Linux version offered for download at the GIMPshop web site can be installed under Ubuntu. After you've downloaded the package, see Chapter 20 to learn how software installation works under Ubuntu.

A second Photoshop-like fork of the software is called GimPhoto (/www.gimphoto.com), but it is based on an older version of the software.

Sharpening

One handy trick that can improve your photos, when used with care, is to use the Sharpen filter. This has the effect of adding definition to the image and reducing any slight blur caused by camera shake or poor focusing. To apply the Sharpen filter, right-click the image and select Filters ➤ Enhance ➤ Sharpen.

As shown in Figure 18-8, a small preview window shows the effect of the sharpening on the image (you might need to use the scrollbars to move to an appropriate part of the image, or resize the preview by clicking and dragging the bottom-right corner). Clicking and dragging the slider at the bottom of the dialog box alters the severity of the sharpening effect. Too much sharpening can ruin a picture, so be careful. Try to use the effect subtly.

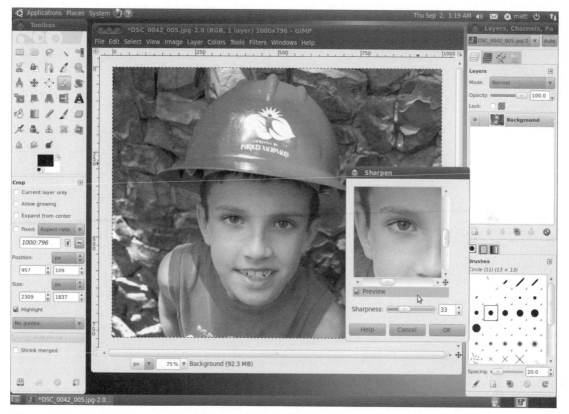

Figure 18-9. Sharpening an image can give it better definition, but keep checking the preview.

Summary

In this chapter, you've taken a look at working with images under Ubuntu. First you looked at the F-Spot photo manager tool. F-Spot lets you easily import pictures, catalog them, and make some adjustments. Then you learned how to edit your images by using GIMP, one of the best programs available for the task under any OS. As with most areas, we could have selected many more applications to cover such as Google's Picasa, digiKam, and gphoto2, but F-Spot and GIMP provide perfect tools for both users and uses across the spectrum.

CHAPTER 19

■ ■ ■

Playing Games

Playing games in Ubuntu might be seen by some people as an awkward idea, and many more may think that you will be lucky if you find at most a Space Invaders-like game. It is not widely recognized as a mainstream gaming platform like PlayStation, Xbox or Wii, and it's not as popular as Windows. But Ubuntu does, you might say, under-promise and over-deliver. You'll be surprised by the sheer amount of possibilities that the casual gamer has at hand.

In this chapter we first examine what games Ubuntu has to offer by default and in its official repositories. Those are games developed specifically for Linux and that are at some level endorsed by Canonical, the company behind Ubuntu. There are also other sources of games for Ubuntu, not officially acknowledged, which can provide many hours of fun.

But the gaming world is changing rapidly, and many people find that web- and Adobe Flash-based games are all they need. And we'll learn how to make those available under Ubuntu. Unleashing the power of Flash-based games will open you the door to an awesome source of free entertainment.

One cannot deny that Windows is a popular gaming platform, and that many games for Windows are available. So you might be in a position in which you want to switch to Ubuntu because you think it is a great OS, but are afraid that you will lose the possibility of playing with your favorite Windows games. What if we tell you that you can have your cake and eat it too? What if you can have the OS of choice (Ubuntu) and your games at the same time and computer? As you see in this chapter, such thing is possible.

So start warming up your thumbs, because at the end of this chapter there'll be action!

Linux Games

As with any type of application, Ubuntu has a bunch of games installed by default and many other readily available at the Ubuntu Software Center. You will usually find games in the Applications ➤ Games menu.

Official Sources

The most basic game package is gnome-games, which is installed by default (and is available at the Ubuntu Software Center). It includes 16 simple games, ranging from Chess to Mahjongg, and from Sudoku to Four-in-a-row. You can see the full list in Table 19-1; those are games designed to give you a rewarding break from work. In five minutes you can be relieved from your stress and go back to your tasks with your batteries renewed. But be careful, because those games are well known for their addictive power! They will certainly help you get through a lazy day. Who hasn't spent hours at the office playing Minesweeper (Ubuntu's version is called Mines)?

■ **Tip** You will not find gnome-games if you look for it in the Games department in the Ubuntu Software Center. Being a metapackage, you'll find it either in Get Software or in the Provided by Ubuntu folder.

Table 19-1. GNOME Games: That's Entertainment!

Command	Description
Aisleriot	Aisleriot is a compilation of over 80 different solitaire card games, from Freecell and Klondike to Clock Patience.
Chess	A chess game. Need we say more?
Five or More	GNOME version of Color Lines. Arrange the balls to form lines of five or more and they will disappear. Meanwhile, more balls keep appearing.
Four-in-a-Row	Play against the computer in an attempt to form a line of four balls.
Iagno	The GNOME version of Reversi. The goal is to control the largest number of disks on the board.
Klotski	A series of sliding block puzzles. Try and solve them in the least number of moves.
Lights Off	Lights Off is a puzzle game, where the objective is to turn off all of the tiles on the board. Each click toggles the state of the clicked tile and its non-diagonal neighbors.
Mines	The popular logic puzzle minesweeper. Find mines on a grid using hints from squares you have already cleared.
Mahjongg	A tile-based solitaire game with an Asian flavor. Remove tiles in matching pairs to dismantle elaborately designed stacks.
Nibbles	Pilot a worm around a maze trying to collect diamonds while avoiding the walls and yourself. With each diamond your worm grows longer and navigation becomes more and more difficult. Playable by up to four people.
Quadrapassel	Tetris-like game.
Robots	The classic game where you have to avoid a hoard of robots who are trying to kill you. Each step you take brings them closer toward you. Fortunately they aren't very smart and you also have a helpful teleportation gadget.
Swell Foop	Swell Foop is a puzzle game. The goal is to remove as many objects as possible in as few moves as possible. Objects that are adjacent to each other get removed as a group. The remaining objects then collapse to fill in the gaps and new groups are formed. You cannot remove single objects.

Command	Description
Sudoku	The Japanese game that became a sensation in the last few years.
Tali	An ancient Roman game.
Tetravex	A puzzle game where you have to match a grid of tiles together. The skill level ranges from the simple two by two up to the seriously mind-bending six by six grid.

There are plenty more games in the default repositories. Just open the Ubuntu Software Center and browse to the Games department, shown in Figure 19-1. There are close to 500 games to choose from!

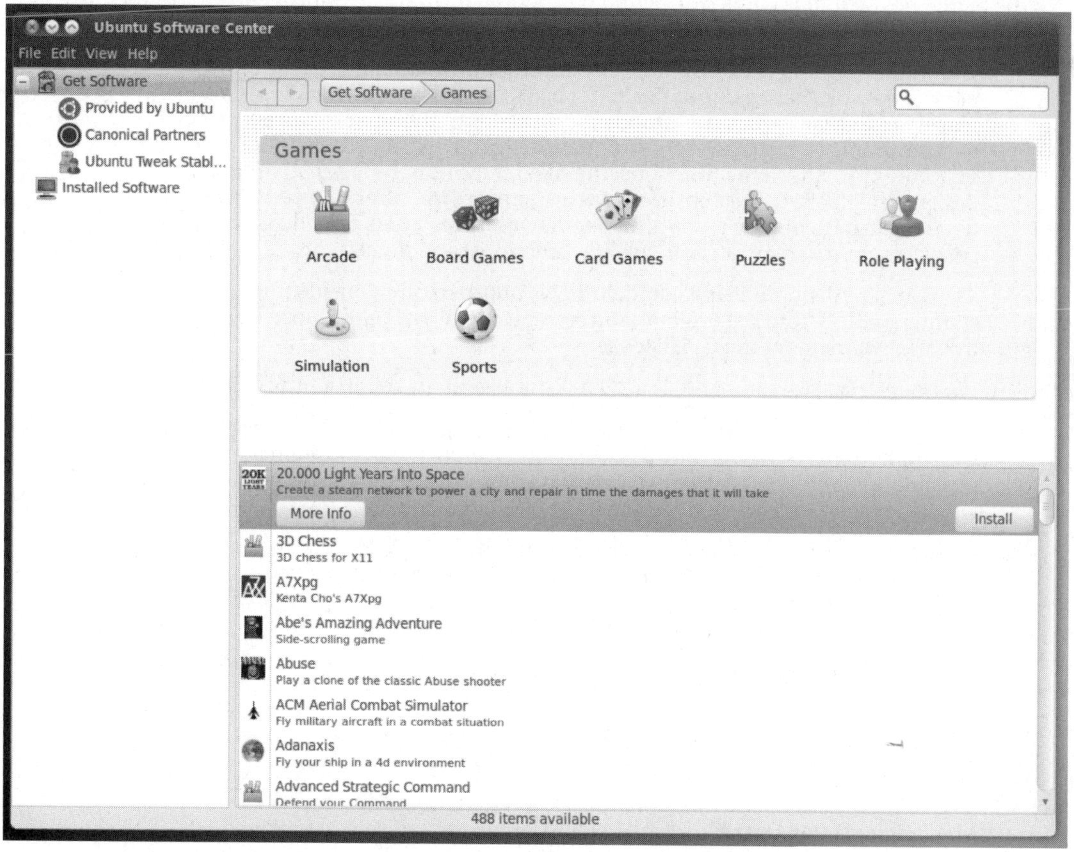

Figure 19-1. Search through the Games department and you'll find many jewels.

Two games even made it to the initial Featured Applications list:

- *Frozen Bubble:* Frozen Bubble is a clone of the popular Puzzle Bobble game, in which you attempt to shoot bubbles into groups of the same color to cause them to pop. The game mainly consists of firing randomly chosen bubbles across the board. If the shoot ends up having a clump of at least three bubbles of the same color, they all pop. If some bubbles were stuck only on the popping clump, they fall. In one-player mode, the goal is to pop all the bubbles on the board as quickly as possible. In two-player or network mode, you have to get your opponent to "die" before you.

- *Pingus:* Pingus is a free clone of the popular Lemmings game. Your goal is to guide a horde of penguins through a world full of obstacles and penguin traps to safety. Although penguins (unlike lemmings) are rather smart, they sometimes rely on you to save them.

Some of the most popular Linux games find their home too in the Ubuntu repositories. Before ditching Ubuntu as a gaming platform, try out these games. You will be surprised!

- *Tremulous:* Tremulous is a free, open source game that blends a team-based first-person shooter (FPS) game with elements of a real-time strategy (RTS) game. Players can choose from two unique races, aliens and humans. Players on both teams are able to build working structures in-game like an RTS game. These structures provide many functions, the most important being *spawning*. The designated builders must ensure there are spawn structures or other players will not be able to rejoin the game after death. Other structures provide automated base defense (to some degree), healing functions, and much more.

- *Alien Arena:* Alien Arena is a standalone 3D first-person online deathmatch shooter crafted from the original source code of Quake II and Quake III, released by id Software under the GPL license.

- *Warzone 2100:* Warzone 2100 is a 3D real-time strategy set on a future Earth.

- *Extreme Tux Racer:* Racer is a racing game featuring Tux, the Linux mascot. The goal of the game is to slide down a snow- and ice-covered mountain as quickly as possible, avoiding the trees and rocks that will slow you down. Collect herrings and other goodies while sliding down the hill, but avoid fish bones.

- *SuperTux:* Super Tux is a classic 2D jump and run sidescroller game in a style similar to the original Super Mario games. Super Tux features 9 enemies, 26 playable levels, software and OpenGL rendering modes, configurable joystick and keyboard input, new music, and completely redone graphics.

- *Frets on Fire:* Frets on Fire is a game of musical skill and fast fingers. The aim of the game is to play guitar with the keyboard as accurately as possible.

- *FreeCiv:* FreeCiv is a Civilizations-like game in which you are the leader of an entire civilization in the search of progress and world domination.

- *Pysol:* Pysol is a collection of more than 1,000 solitaire games, ranging from Mahjong to Hanoi Puzzle.

Are your engines getting ready for gaming now? Would you have believed there were so many great games available for free, just clicks away? Well, buckle up, because this ride is just starting!

Additional Sources

Ubuntu being part of a community, it is only natural that the official source of games is not the only one. As explored in Chapter 20, you can add new, unofficial repositories to your list and download programs from them. Games are no exception. If you browse the web and the Ubuntu Forums you will find plenty of information about additional sources for installing games. In this section we examine one of those sources, so you become familiar with the idea.

The site we will be accessing is http://www.PlayDeb.net, shown in Figure 19-2.

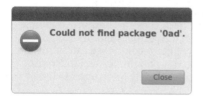

Figure 19-2. PlayDeb.net *is one of many sources of additional games.*

You can click Games and browse the list of games available. But when you see one that you like and click "Install this now" and follow the instructions on screen, you might soon get the error message shown in Figure 19-3. Why?

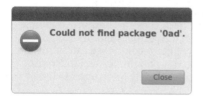

Figure 19-3. *An error message when trying to install from* PlayDeb.net.

In order to be able to install games from PlayDeb.net, you should add the repository to your software sources. Repositories, covered with greater detail in Chapter 20, are storage locations from which software packages can be downloaded and installed. Let's follow the steps of adding PlayDeb.net as a source. This training will help you when adding any other source of Ubuntu games.

1. Try to install a game from PlayDeb.net and verify if you get an error message.

2. Open System ➤ Administration ➤ Software Sources. Go to the Other Software tab.

3. Click Add… and in the apt line textbox copy the following line :

4. deb http://archive.getdeb.net/ubuntu lucid-getdeb games

5. Click Add Source. Don't close the Software Sources dialog box.

6. Open a web browser and copy the following line in the address bar :

7. http://archive.getdeb.net/getdeb-archive.key

8. You will be prompted to open or save the key file. It will be stored in your Downloads folder.

9. Go back to the Software Sources dialog box and click the Authentication tab.

10. Click Import Key File… and browse to your Downloads folder. Double-click the downloaded key.

11. Click Close. You will be prompted to update the catalog on your computer. Accept.

12. Try to install the game once again. You should be successful this time!

Although PlayDeb.net is just one of many additional sources of games for Ubuntu, this demo is useful because adding software sources is almost always the same two-step process: adding the repository in the Other Software tab, and importing the key in the Authentication tab.

The next time you open the Ubuntu Software Center after reloading the catalog, you should see under Get Software a new entry, GetDeb, along with Provided by Ubuntu and Canonical Partners. If you select GetDeb, the list of available games will be displayed in the main pane. To install a new game, just select it and click Install, as you would for any application.

Congratulations ! You now have access to more than 200 additional games!

Adobe Flash and Web-based Gaming

Many things have been said about the cloud and cloud-based applications—especially about how you will no longer need to install applications locally on your hard drive to use it, because they will always be available online.

In no area is this trend is more obvious and mainstream than in the world of gaming. And when you talk of online gaming, you more often than not come to rely on Adobe Flash. Flash is an animation file format pioneered by Macromedia which continues to be supported by its successor company, Adobe. Flash has been extended to include audio and video content, and programs written in many scripting languages. Despite the advance of other web gaming technologies and of the recent Steve Job's attack on Flash, more and more games based on this technology are created each day and made available online entirely for free. Search for **"free flash game"** in Google or Yahoo, and a seemingly interminable list of sites will be displayed. It's hard to avoid them if you like to play.

But when you try to open those games after installing Ubuntu, you find that Firefox tells you that "Additional plug-ins are required to display all the media on this page," and where the game should be, a broken link is all you get. Many people have thought that that was all for Linux, that they could never be able to play Flash games in Ubuntu. This isn't so.

In fact, there's not one but three different ways of playing Flash files in your Ubuntu computer, but none of them is installed by default. You can see them in your browser if you click the "Additional plugins" bar. They are listed in Table 19-2.

Table 19-2. Flash Players

Player	Description
Adobe Flash Player	A plug-in for web browsers, developed and maintained by Adobe. This is proprietary software.
Swfdec SWF Player	Swfdec SWF Player is a plug-in that integrates Flash player capabilities to the GNOME environment.
Gnash	Gnash is a GNU Flash movie player sponsored by the Free Software Foundation.

If you intend to play online games, we recommend you install Adobe Flash Player. It is available at the Canonical Partners section of the Ubuntu Software Center. Follow these instructions to install the Flash Player:

1. Open Firefox and go to your Flash gaming site. When you try to load a game, the message "Additional plug-ins are required to display all the media on this page" should appear.

2. Close Firefox.

3. Go to Applications ➤ Ubuntu Software Center

4. Expand Get Software in the navigation pane and select the Canonical Partners folder.

5. The application Adobe Flash Plugin 10 should be at the top of the list. Click Install.

6. When it finishes, close the Ubuntu Software Center and open Firefox.

7. Go to your favorite Flash gaming site. Now you shouldn't have any problem.

■ **Tip** You might find Java-based games at some web sites. Although Java's use is less mainstream nowadays than Flash for these kinds of applications, Java is a very popular technology. To play online Java games, make sure you install the application Icedtea Java Plugin in the Ubuntu Software Center.

Installing Windows Games

One of the reasons you might be reluctant to make the switch to Ubuntu is you have made a large investment in Windows games and don't want to throw all that money away, even when finding Ubuntu the superior OS.

This is a very understandable concern, but there is a workaround. Follow us.

Welcome to PlayOnLinux. In Chapter 20 we talk about Wine, a utility that allows you to run Windows applications under Linux. We also point out in that chapter that sometimes those applications are not so easy to install and configure. Many present a bunch of problems requiring expert knowledge and hours of investigation. They may work in the end, but the process can be lengthy and tedious. It's not very encouraging when you only want to play a game.

PlayOnLinux is a frontend for Wine, specialized in making games work out-of-the-box. It takes away from the user the task of preparing the system for a certain application. It is a community-based solution in which different users upload configuration scripts for games to the repositories. When you need to install a game that someone else has installed before, the script is executed and the game is seamlessly installed.

It is worth noting that to install Windows games you will likely need the original CD or DVD and the license key. It is a drag sometimes, but that's how Windows games work. Having a community tool for installing games doesn't make games themselves sharable. Original licensing restrictions still applies.

You can install PlayOnLinux from the official repositories. Just look for it in the Ubuntu Software Center and click Install. Once installed, a shortcut will be created in Applications ➤ Games.

The first time you launch PlayOnLinux it will try to download the game's catalog from the Internet, which can take a few minutes. If a game you're trying to install is not in the catalog, you can try updating it by clicking File ➤ Refresh the repository.

Before you install any application, the main window of PlayOnLinux will be rather empty, as you can see in Figure 19-4. There's where installed games are listed after you install them.

Figure 19-4. PlayOnLinux main window is empty until you install a game.

To install a game, click Install and select the Games category. You'll see the list of compatible games, as shown in Figure 19-5.

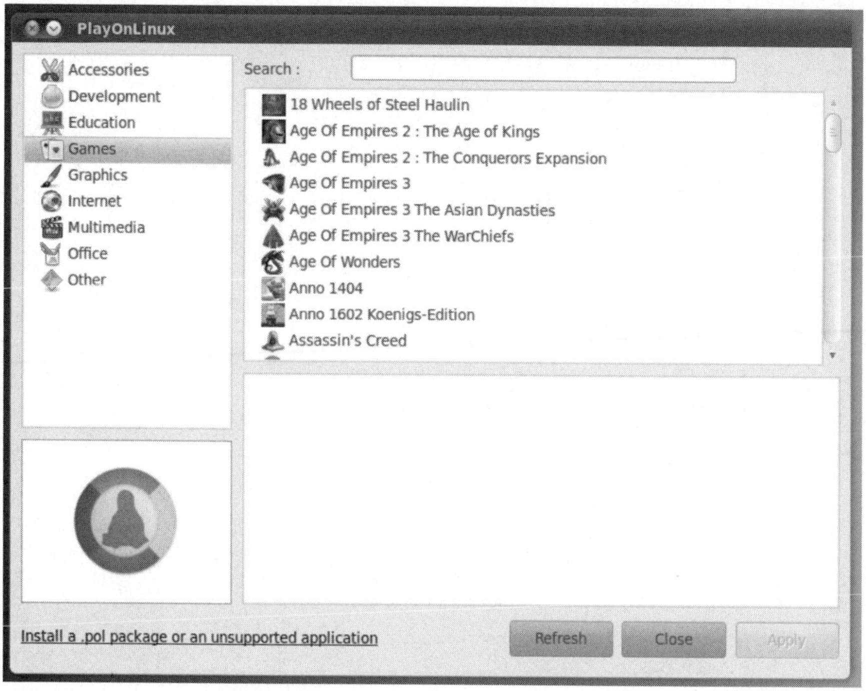

Figure 19-5. The list of PlayOnLinux compatible games

Select the game you want to install and click Apply. The script for that game will begin to run, asking you for the installation media and keys if they apply. At some point the installation wizard for the application starts, the same wizard you can see in Windows. When it finishes, the game is installed.

You will see the game in the PlayOnLinux main window. Just click Run and enjoy!

■ **Tip** As you can see in the Install dialog box, PlayOnLinux can install other types of applications in addition to games. What PlayOnLinux does is to run a script when installing the application. However, games are the main feature of PlayOnLinux.

Summary

In this chapter we opened you the door for a world of games and entertainment. Although many people consider Linux to be a platform for playing with the command-line, this chapter has shown that this is not true. You can find a lot of free games in the official repositories, and many more in the community pages.

You can also play mainstream Flash- and Java-based games online.

And if this is not enough, and you miss your Windows games, PlayOnLinux makes it easy to install them in your Ubuntu box, so you can have the OS of choice without losing your investment in games.

If all these methods fail to satisfy your gaming hunger, maybe it's time to think about buying a console!

## PART 5

Keeping Your System Running

■ ■ ■

## CHAPTER 20

Installing and Removing Software

One of the fun things about running any operating system is the ability to expand it—to add in new software over time to improve your workflow or just enhance entertainment value.

Linux is blessed in this regard, because tens of thousands of software titles are available to meet almost every need.

But for years, the generally accepted idea was that Linux was a great OS, superior in many ways to Microsoft Windows, but that it was too difficult to use. Software installation, continued the argument, was one of the major examples of this difficulty: many people still think that for installing software in Linux you must know how to compile source code! Comparing this to the seemingly straightforward method of getting software for Windows, either online or at a retail store, and then running an installation wizard, Linux was seen as a non-option for the average user.

It is not that Windows applications are easy to get. For starters, you must pay for them, a couple hundred dollars or more in some cases. Then you have restrictions on how you can use them, and it is often hard to follow the rules of what you can or cannot do. You might be infringing the terms of license of your software even without knowing it. It is harder still for companies and individual users alike to determine and prove that the software they are using is legitimate; some vendors asks that you store your license keys or certificates, while others demand an invoice as proof of your purchase. It's up to the vendor.

Another problem is to find the right software. There's no central location where you can find all the software available for Windows. And while there are freeware applications, more often than not you need to download them from less-than-trusted sites prone to bundling malware into their download packages.

This method of application installation was practically rendered obsolete by Apple's Application Store for the iPhone and iPod Touch. This is a secure, centralized, and searchable catalog of applications, available just one click of the mouse away. If the application exists, you just browse or search the store, and the application appears.

But this model has its limitations too, the most important being the tight control Apple enforces in this store, making a developer's job of publishing applications a nightmare.

When the people at Canonical wanted to make an OS for human beings, they soon realized that all the shortcomings of competing models could be overcome based on the foundations of Linux, and of Debian in particular. The result of this effort was the Ubuntu Software Center, first launched for Karmic Koala (Ubuntu 9.10), and revamped for Lucid Lynx. It is a centralized yet extensible catalog for all Ubuntu applications, and is also the subject of the first section of this chapter. If you just want to install applications the easy way, that's all you need to read. Next, a few pages of theory are available, which gives you a clearer view of how the Center works and lays the foundation for the third section of this chapter, in which you learn more methods for installing and working with Ubuntu… and Windows!… applications.

And of course, how to compile source code!

Using the Ubuntu Software Center

Ubuntu has traditionally had many different tools for application installation and management: the Synaptic Package Manager, Add/Remove Programs, the Update Manager, Software Sources... not to mention the command-line tools dpkg and apt. Those were related tools for doing similar tasks around software management. Before undertaking any installation task, you first needed to know which tool to use.

And many developers weren't even coordinated to the extent of making their applications available from a single source. So an effort was to be made in two directions: the making of a single, all-encompassing tool, and the publication of all available software in that tool. Thus the Ubuntu Software Center was born.

Navigating the Ubuntu Software Center

The Ubuntu Software Center is available as the last item in the Applications menu. When opened, it shows a default start page, as shown in Figure 20-1. It is the root of the Get Software item.

Figure 20-1. The structure of the Ubuntu Software Center

The menu bar is a quite straightforward way of performing actions within the Center, but its options are usually disabled. They are made available only at certain times, depending on the section of the Center in which you are.

File: Here you will find the Install and Remove commands, only available when you select a specific application in a list, or when you open the application page itself. Only one of the options will be available at a given time, depending on the current state of the application. The Close option is always available and instructs the Ubuntu Software Center to quit (notice that if there are pending operations in progress, the Center will wait until those are completed to close).

Edit: Many of the options in this menu, like Cut, Copy, Paste, and Delete, are available only when you are entering text in the Search dialog box. The Copy Web Link option is enabled when you select an application from a list or when you open that application's details page and copy the URL of the application to the clipboard, so you can paste it into your browser and access it directly. The Search option is available whenever the Search dialog box is present, and basically focuses on it. And last, the Software Sources option allows you to modify or add locations from which you want to download applications. More about this later in this chapter.

View: Here you can select the scope of the applications which you want to see listed. All Software displays software from all sources. Canonical-Maintained Software displays only software maintained by the company behind Ubuntu.

Help: Here you can access useful help information about the Ubuntu Software Center.

The navigation pane is used to browse the different sections of the Ubuntu Software Center. It has three main elements, of which one is usually hidden. The main page changes depending on the element selected in the navigation pane.

Get Software: This is used mainly to locate and install software in the catalog. This catalog is constructed by using software sources, of which you can see the default two: Provided by Canonical, and Canonical Partners. More items appear under Get Software as you begin to add alternative software sources, as explained later in this chapter. Those two default sources are by far the most secure way of installing applications in Ubuntu—much safer than downloading them from an unknown web site. But someday you may want to install software not officially endorsed by Canonical, and for that it is important to know how to add software sources.

Installed Software: Here you see the list of software already present in your computer, and can remove it. Installed software is recognizable by the checkmark that accompanies its icon in the list. Browse this section if you don't want to install additional software; you could for instance just see what you have installed, or remove an application that is no longer needed (to free up disk space, for instance).

In Progress: When performing actions like installing or removing applications, or updating the software catalog, you will notice in the notifications pane a third element named In Progress. When you select this item, you can see in the main pane the status of each of those actions, along with a progress bar indicating how near to completion the task is. If you are installing an application, for instance, a Cancel button will show up next to the progress bar while downloading the application. Once the installation starts (after download), it cannot be canceled. When all actions have completed, the In Progress element returns to its hidden state.

The status bar usually shows useful information about the number of applications in each section. For example, when selecting Get Software for the first time, it shows the total number of applications in the catalog (32,420 at the time of writing!). If you select a particular department, it shows the number of applications in that department (for instance, the Office department shows 124 applications). When using the Search dialog box, it tells the number of applications that matched the search terms.

Browsing and Searching for Software

To install an application, first you need to find it. This is made easy by the Center's browsing and searching mechanisms, and by the fact that Ubuntu maintains all applications in a catalog containing information about the applications available from all configured software sources.

This catalog is a hierarchical structure organized into departments and sometimes sublevels under them, and is made available in the main pane when you select Get Software in the navigation pane. Each department groups applications with a common objective, and its name is self-explanatory; for example the Games department has games like Mines, and the Office department has applications used mostly at the office, like OpenOffice.org Word Processor (commonly known as Writer). So, just select the department you feel is most likely to have the application you are looking for. If you are just exploring, you can select the Featured Applications link, which takes you to a special list of applications selected by the Ubuntu team.

At the top of the Get Software section in the main pane is the location bar, composed of three items: the Back and Forward buttons, the path bar, and the Search dialog box.

The Back and Forward buttons allow you to navigate the history of the visited pages.

The path bar shows you which part of the hierarchy you are in at the moment, and allows you to navigate to parent levels by clicking in the corresponding part of that bar. For example, clicking Get Software takes you to the start page.

Either by selecting the Featured Applications or by clicking on a department, you access what is known as a software list view. Some departments (like Games, for instance) have sublevels, and this is shown by dividing the main pane in an upper section with the sublevels (which are browsable themselves), and a lower section with the software list view. In this view all related applications are displayed in a series of contiguous rows, as shown in Figure 20-2. You see here the application's icon, name, and short description. You can tell whether an application is already installed by looking at its icon: if a white checkmark inside a green circle is merged with the icon, then your application is already in your system.

■ **Note** Take into account that the software installation media actually resides in repositories maintained by Ubuntu on the web, and that the first thing the Ubuntu Software Center has to do when you click Install is download the software package. If you don't have an Internet connection, you will not be able to install software from those repositories. You can use a CD or DVD instead, or download the application packages to another computer and then locally install them into your computer. Those options are explained later in this chapter.

When you find the application you want to install, just select it from the list and press the Install button that appears at the right end of the application's row. You'll be prompted for your password, and the application will start installing. A progress bar will appear above the Install button, and a new element labeled In Progress will emerge in the navigation pane. Once it has finished installation, the progress bar disappears, the Install button is replaced with a more appropriate Remove button, and the In Progress element disappears. Can you guess how to uninstall your application? Yes, by pressing that Remove button.

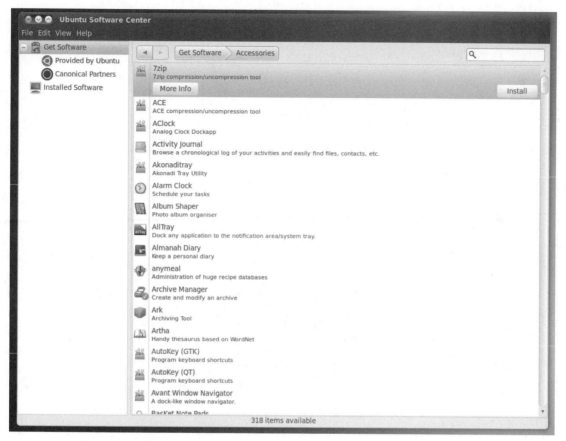

Figure 20-2. *The list of available software for the Accessories department*

If you want to know more about a particular application, just select it from the list and click the More Info button. This takes you to the software item screen, which you can see in Figure 20-3.

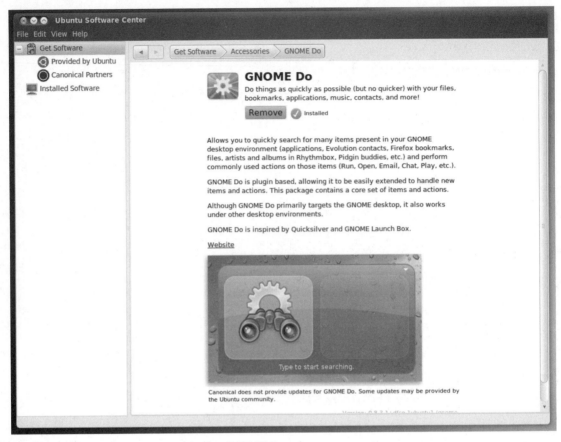

Figure 20-3. The software item screen for GNOME Do

The elements in the software item screen are:

- The application icon.

- The name of the application.

- A short description.

- An Action/Status bar section, in which you can see if the application is already installed, choose to Install or Remove it, and follow the progress bar when performing one of those two tasks.

- A full-length description of what the application does.

- A link to the application's web site.

- Screenshots of the application.

- A description of the availability of updates for the application—whether they are made available by Canonical or by the community, or by nobody.

- Licensing information. Most applications are Open Source, but you will find some proprietary drivers.

- Package name and version.

Click the Back button or the name of the department in the location bar to go back to the list of applications.

Another way of finding an application is by using the Search dialog box, available at the location bar. You need to be aware that searches are targeted at the scope specified by the path bar. This is to say that if you are browsing the Get Software ➤ Education department and search for an application, only applications in that department will show up. The department software list is filtered to show only the applications that match the search terms, and in the status bar the number of matching items is shown.

All operations available at a text box, such as pasting and deleting, can be used in the Search dialog box. The search is performed as you type your text; it is not necessary to press Enter or click on the magnifying glass to execute the query. If you want to remove the filter for the applications, just click the little sweeper that's inside the Search dialog box, at the right.

Does all this seem too easy to be true? Well, it *is* true, and it is all you have to do to install most of the software you will ever need within Ubuntu (as we mentioned before, at the time of writing there were 32,420 applications available at the Center!). But Ubuntu is also a versatile and flexible OS that gives you options. It allows you to install additional software through alternative sources, keep your applications up-to-date, and even use Windows applications. This is explained later in this chapter, but first we need to delve a little deeper into the theory behind Ubuntu software management to understand those processes better.

Software Installation Basics

If the Ubuntu Software Center is a marvel for its beauty and simplicity, the overall Ubuntu software management system is of no lesser merit in what it enables. The Center takes advantage of years and years of previous developments that made it possible, such as the introduction of Debian packages, the apt tool, and software repositories. Let's look at those elements in a little more detail.

Formats of Linux Installation Files

If you visit the web site of a particular Linux application, you may find that it's available to download in a number of different formats. The program will almost certainly be available as *source code*—the original human-readable text that the developer created. But it might also be available as a binary or a package file.

■ **Tip** Linux isn't the only OS for which open source programs are created and used. There are open source projects for both Windows and Apple Macintosh, many of which are hosted at the http://sourceforge.net web site. Many other, less widely used operating systems also rely on open source software to a greater or lesser extent. Ubuntu software is hosted in Launchpad (https://launchpad.net), a web application maintained by Canonical, used also for software development and bug tracking.

Here are the formats by which Linux software is usually distributed:

Source code: Programmers write their software in various programming languages, such as C and C++, and the code that results is known as *source code*. To make source code usable, it must be *compiled* into a *binary*. Because the cornerstone of the Linux philosophy is the sharing of source code, you'll almost always find the source code of a program available at the developer's web site. You can then download and compile this on your own system (or, if you're so inclined, study the source code to further your understanding). Although compiling source code isn't very hard to do, it's more convenient to download either a binary version of the program or a package.

Binary files: You might find that ready-made binary files are available at the developer's web site. In other words, the programmer (or a third party) has taken his or her own source code and, as a service to users of the program, compiled it so that it's ready for use as soon as it's downloaded. For example, this is how Linux versions of the Mozilla Foundation software, like Thunderbird and Firefox, are currently distributed if you download them directly from www.mozilla.com. Sometimes binary files come with scripts to help you install them. However, in most cases, you simply place the files in a convenient location on your hard disk and then run them from there.

■ **Note** In the cases of both source code and binary files, the files usually come in a *tarball*, which is a single archive file containing other files. A tarball isn't, by definition, compressed, but usually either the bzip2 or gzip tool is used to shrink the file, to ease transportation across the Internet.

Self-installing binaries: Some larger programs are made available as self-installing binary files. This comes very close to the way Windows works, because when the file is executed, a GUI-based installation wizard takes you through installation. If you download the standard version of OpenOffice.org (that is, not a version packaged for a particular system) from the official web site (www.openoffice.org), for example, you'll end up with a single 160MB+ file, which you then simply execute from the command line.

Package files: In many cases, you'll find that a package file of the program is available. In this case, someone has compiled the software files and put them all together in a single, easily transported file. Ubuntu package files end with .deb file extensions, but other Linux distributions use other package formats, such as .rpm (Fedora/Red Hat, SUSE Linux, and Mandriva, among others).

■ **Note** As a blanket rule, an installation package created for one distribution isn't compatible with another. It's possible to use a program called alien under Ubuntu, which aims to convert packages between distributions and different package formats, but this should be seen as a last resort because the results may not always be satisfactory. You'll be better off simply obtaining a package specifically designed for your Linux distribution.

Package Management

Of all the preceding formats, packages are by far the most common and popular in the world of Linux. Ubuntu utilizes packages, as do nearly all other distributions. In fact, the Ubuntu installation DVD-ROM contains hundreds of packages, and its various software repositories contain many thousands.

A well-implemented package management system is able to install programs, upgrade them, and uninstall them, all with just a few keystrokes or clicks of the mouse. It vastly reduces the amount of work required to get new software onto your system and makes maintenance tasks such as upgrading software easy too.

It's important to understand what an Ubuntu package file actually is and what it contains. With Windows, an installation .exe file is effectively a piece of software combined with an archive of files. When you run the executable, it triggers a small program contained within it that then unpacks the contents of the file and installs them to the hard disk.

In contrast, package files used by Ubuntu merely contain the program files along with a handful of configuration scripts to ensure that the software is set up correctly. Package files are useless without the various pieces of software already installed on the system that are used to manipulate them and do the hard work of installing, removing, and querying them. This software is known as the *package management system*. In the case of Ubuntu, the package management system has two components: dpkg and apt, which we cover later in this chapter. The Ubuntu Software Center itself is always working with packages, although you never see them.

The use of a package management system has a number of benefits. The package management system builds its own database, so it knows exactly what programs are installed at any one time. Therefore, you can simply query the database rather than search the applications menu or hard disk. The package system also keeps track of version numbers. This gives the user much more control over the software on the system, and it makes updating easy.

The use of a package management system also means that if a program starts to act strangely, its configuration files can simply be refreshed by using the package manager. There's no need to uninstall and reinstall the software, as is so often the case with Windows programs. The clean way in which a package manager uninstalls software makes it very easy to try out, and remove, lots of different software without worrying about the stability of your computer.

Dependency Management

One of the key features offered by any package management system is *dependency management*. Put simply, the package manager ensures that if you install a piece of software, any additional software it relies on to work properly is already present on the system. It the software isn't present, the package manager must either resolve the situation automatically or ask you what to do.

Sometimes the software you want to install might depend on other programs on your system, such as applications that simply add a graphical front end to shell applications, but more often, the dependencies take the form of system libraries. It helps if you realize that not all packages contain software that you, as a user, will make direct use of. Some packages contain nothing but library files— shared pieces of code that are equivalent to .dll files under Windows. The key library on an Ubuntu system is the GNU C Library, without which the Linux kernel couldn't function, which is provided by the libc6 package. But practically every program has its own needs when it comes to library files, and these requirements must be handled by the package manager.

■ **Note** One reason Windows installation files are often so large is that they typically come with all the system files they need, in case they're not already present on the system. This does not make dependency problems disappear, however. Third-party application installers sometimes overwrite existing libraries with versions that are incompatible with the rest of the system.

Dependency management doesn't just mean adding in packages that a piece of software needs. It might also mean *removing* packages already present on your system. This might need to happen if they're incompatible with new software you want to install, something that's referred to as *package conflict*. In addition, sometimes you might want to remove a package that other packages rely on, a situation known as *reverse dependency*. In such a case, the package manager must either stop you from removing that software, to avoid breaking the software that depends on it, or remove the reverse-dependency packages too. In most cases, the package manager ask you what to do.

DEPENDENCY HELL

If you try to install certain software packages, you will very likely find that they depend on other packages, such as software libraries. These must be either already present on the system or installed at the same time for the software to work correctly. In most cases, the Synaptic Package Manager takes care of all this.

Dependency hell, which is far less common than it once was, comes about when chains of dependencies arise, which is to say, when a program you install or remove involves the installation or removal of several other, apparently unrelated pieces of software. For example, let's say you decide to manually install a program called Oscar. You download it and type the command to install it, but you are then told that this depends on another program called BigBird, which isn't installed. Fine, you think, I'll just download and add BigBird to the same installation command. But it then transpires that BigBird has its own dependency of Snuffleupagus. You download and add that too. Alas! Snuffleupagus has its own dependency of MrHooper.

This can carry on for some time, and this is why you should use the Ubuntu Software Center to install and remove software and try to stay within the standard Ubuntu repositories (see the following section). In the preceding example, the Ubuntu Software Center would add in all the dependencies automatically and download and install them at the same time.

Dependency chains like this are a by-product of any package management system. The solution is often simple—just don't remove the software package. After all, hard disks are extremely large nowadays, and space is rarely an issue, so there's little reason to not have software packages you no longer need hanging around.

Software Repositories

As mentioned previously, dpkg and apt take care of package management within Ubuntu. These tools are taken from the Debian distribution of Linux, on which Ubuntu is based.

Debian Package, or dpkg, is the most basic part of the system. It's used to install and uninstall software, and it can also be used to query any individual software packages. It's like the manager in a warehouse who is tasked with knowing exactly what boxes have been stored where. The manager doesn't know where the boxes come from, and he doesn't know anything about packages outside his warehouse. He just manages the boxes that are delivered to him and that are stored in his warehouse.

dpkg is aware of dependency issues and will refuse to fully install a package if the others it needs aren't already installed or supplied at the same time. But it doesn't have the means to fix the situation automatically. This is akin to the warehouse manager's inability to order more boxes if he needs them. That's not his job. He'll just tell you if boxes delivered to him are missing some of their components.

Because of this, there's an additional layer of software that sits on top of dpkg called the Advanced Packaging Tool, or apt. apt is very sophisticated. Its job is to handle dependency management. Try to install some software using apt, and any dependency issues will be worked out for you.

apt can do this because it's designed to work with *software repositories*. Users can search and install packages from these collections of software. More often than not, these software repositories are online, but that's not always the case. The DVD supplied with this book contains the base installation software repository, for example.

■ **Note** As you might already have guessed, the Ubuntu Software Center is simply a GUI front end for the apt system.

It's important to note that apt relies on the dpkg system to take care of the actual installation. Effectively, dpkg and apt are two sides of the same coin.

As you might have realized, the package management system means that Linux software installation/removal is a fundamentally different proposition than handling software under Windows or Mac OS X. If you want to install new software, the first place to look is the Ubuntu software repositories. The online repositories contain most of the popular software available for Linux right now, all packaged for installation under Ubuntu.

It's comparatively rare for an Ubuntu user to visit a web site and download a package file for installation, as is often the case for Windows users. The only time this normally happens is if you can't find what you're looking for in the official repositories. Staying within the standard repositories makes problems less likely.

■ **Tip** Software repositories don't have to be "official," or sanctioned by Ubuntu, to be used under Ubuntu. Sometimes you might opt to add repositories that contain particular software, such as multimedia repositories. This may be necessary because multimedia formats are often licensed under terms that Ubuntu doesn't agree with, so it declines to offer this software from its official repositories. Bear in mind that unofficial repositories aren't necessarily safe.

Out of the box, Ubuntu comes with a couple of software repositories already configured. These allow you to download new software and also update the system online. Ubuntu software repositories are subdivided into various categories and components.

SOFTWARE VERSIONS

Because most Linux software is open source, a curious thing happens when it comes to software versions. Rather than there being just one "official" version of a program, such as with most Windows software (where you must download the official version of the file), many individuals and organizations take the source code, compile it, and make their own package files available for others to use.

For example, virtually all the software installed with Ubuntu has been compiled by Ubuntu developers. This means it can be quite different from what's "officially" available at the programmer's web site. In some cases, the source code is tweaked to fix notorious bugs or apply a different look and feel to the software, so it integrates with the distribution. Often the configuration files are changed so that the software works properly under Ubuntu, such as integrating with other software packages.

The programmer behind the software doesn't mind when such things happen, because this way of working is part and parcel of open source software. In fact, the programmer is likely to encourage such tweaking.

Because of this, the first place to look if you want any additional software is not the developer's web site but the Ubuntu software repositories. If the package is available in the Ubuntu main distribution, you'll get an officially sanctioned Ubuntu release that will fit in with the rest of your system and won't require much, if any, additional work to get it up and running.

Categories of Repositories

Regardless of whether they're online or on a CD/DVD, Ubuntu repositories are strictly categorized according to the type of software they contain:

Main Distribution: This repository contains the packages that are required to install Ubuntu. This repository usually takes its name from the code name for the release and is activated by default. For Ubuntu 10.04, the main distribution repository is called lucid, after the code name for the 10.04 release (Lucid Lynx). In the previous release, the main distribution repository was called karmic, and the next version (Maverick Meerkat) will have the maverick repository. (For more details on Ubuntu code names, see https://wiki.ubuntu.com/DevelopmentCodeNames.)

Security Updates: Sometimes security flaws are so serious that they need to be fixed immediately, within as little as 24 hours of being discovered. If so, the packages concerned will be placed on this server. The Security Updates server isn't about new versions or functionality. It's about fixing security holes rapidly. This repository is also activated by default and is named after the main release title. In the case of 9.04, this means the Security Updates repository is called lucid-security.

Recommended Updates: This repository contains newer versions of the packages in the Main Distribution repository. Like Security Updates, this category also offers bug fixes, but these fixes aren't urgent and are often more substantial than quick patches to fix a critical bug. It is named after the main release title. In the case of 10.04, it is called lucid-updates.

Proposed Updates: This is a special category by which testing releases of updates are made available. There's no reason to use this category unless you want to test packages and help fix bugs (for more information, see https://wiki.ubuntu.com/ HelpingWithBugs). This category is not activated by default. It is named after the main release title, so in the case of 10.04 is named lucid-proposed.

Unsupported (Backport) Updates: The Backports server allows access to software that's intended to go into the next version of Ubuntu but has been packaged for the current version. This software might not have been tested thoroughly and so is suitable only for neophiliacs or those who absolutely need the latest version (perhaps because of a vital new feature it offers). This category is not activated by default. As before, its name is derived from the main release, so in the case of 10.04 is called lucid-backports.

Repository Components

In addition to the categories listed in the previous section, the Ubuntu repositories are further split into *components* (effectively subsections) according to how essential the software is to a basic Ubuntu installation or the license that the software uses. Here are the components under which software is typically filed within a repository (although you should note that a third-party repository might have its own names for repository components, and they might vary from this list):

Main: This section contains nearly all the software that's featured in a basic Ubuntu installation. As such, it's all free software, and every package is supported by Canonical, the company that oversees the Ubuntu project. That means that updates are frequently provided to fix security holes or simply to keep up with latest releases.

■ **Note** *Free software* refers to software that's licensed by using one of the schemes recognized by the Free Software Foundation as being free. The most common example is the GNU Public License (GPL). It doesn't necessarily mean that the software is free of charge, although that's nearly always the case.

Universe: This section might be referred to as "the rest," because it contains the majority of free software available at the present time. Much of it is borrowed from the massive Debian software repository, although the packages are sometimes tweaked to work correctly under Ubuntu before being made available (some people who create Debian packages also create the Ubuntu equivalents). Unlike Main and Restricted, the Universe section is not officially supported by the Ubuntu project, which means there's no guarantee that security flaws will be fixed. Nor is there any guarantee of updates, although most packages are usually updated regularly.

Restricted: Although Ubuntu is mostly free software, it must include some drivers released only in binary form (that is, proprietary) and that, therefore, have license agreements that are not compatible with the goals of free software. That's what you'll find in this section. Some hardware simply won't work fully without software from the Restricted section.

Multiverse: As with the Restricted section, here you'll find software that's released under a software license incompatible with either the letter or spirit of free software. However, unlike the software in the Restricted section, none of the software in Multiverse is considered essential to a default Ubuntu installation.

Source Code: This section contains source code packages. Unless you're a software developer or are thinking of becoming one, this section won't be of much interest.

Partner: This repository contains software offered by vendors who have partnered with Canonical, the company that sponsors the development of Ubuntu. This software is usually commercial and proprietary (that is, not open source). The precise list of software packages offered differs from release to release, but past examples have included virus scanners, media players, and commercial server software.

Now that we've covered the basics of Linux software installation, it's time to talk about additional tools used to manage software that will enable you to perform advanced tasks.

DECODING PACKAGE FILENAMES

Although the filenames of packages might seem like cryptic mumbo-jumbo, they actually tell you a great deal about the file. Let's take a look at the package file of the Eye of GNOME image viewer to explain this:

`eog_2.21.92-0ubuntu1_i386.deb`

The first element of the filename is the name of the program. In this case, Eye of GNOME has been abbreviated to `eog`. Abbreviations like this are quite common, because they decrease the length of the filename. But it's important to note that they will be consistent. For as long as Eye of GNOME is supported as a package under Ubuntu, its package filename will always begin with `eog`.

Following the name of the package is the version number of the program in question: `2.21.92-0`. This is almost always the version number that will appear if you click Help ➤ About when the program is running and is the version number decided on by the developer who created the software.

After the version number is the word `ubuntu`, which indicates that this is a package that has been created specifically for the Ubuntu distribution of Linux. Then you see the build version number of the package: `1`. This is Ubuntu's own version number, indicating how many times the package has been built (created) by the Ubuntu team. Sometimes it's necessary to release an updated build of the same version of a program in order to correct an error that was accidentally introduced in the preceding build version. Sometimes the program is patched by the Ubuntu team to support a new function.

After Ubuntu's build version number is the platform on which the package will run. In this case, `i386` indicates that the package will run on all x86-based processors, from 80386 upward (the 486, Pentium, Pentium II, AMD processors, and so on). Sometimes you might see `i686`, which means that the package has been optimized for Pentium Pro chips and above (Pentium II, III, IV, and AMD's Athlon range of chips). If the package is created for 64-bit desktop processors, `amd64` will appear there. Some packages are for all architectures.

Optimized versions of packages for particular processors are used only when they might bring a performance boost. For example, there are `i686` versions of the Linux kernel and the `libc6` library. Even ordinary programs, like OpenOffice.org, can be optimized for their architectures, but the majority of packages that are used under Ubuntu have the `i386` designation.

Advanced Application Management

There may be times when you need to perform more advanced tasks than just installing or removing software. You might want to have more control over what you install, or enable additional software repositories not included by default. You can update your installed software to use always the most recent version. Or you might need to install software manually from a Debian package. In this section we will look at those and other tasks in depth.

Managing Ubuntu Software Options

You can manage what components of the official repositories to make available to download in your catalog by using the Software Sources tool, available many places: at the main menu in System ➤ Administration ➤ Software Sources, in the Edit menu in the Ubuntu Software Center, and in other places.

Figure 20-4. The Ubuntu Software tab at the Software Sources tool

You can see the Ubuntu Software tab in Figure 20-4. Here you can:

- Select the repository components downloadable from the Internet. You can choose to make available the main, universe, restricted, and multiverse repository components, as well as the source code of the applications (which you will rarely need). We have already talked about those components.

- Select the server from which you will download applications. If you select Other… from the drop-down list, you will see a series of servers from all around the world. If you are unsure which server best suits your needs, click the Select Best Server button and the system will start checking how long it takes for each listed server to respond to its requests, to determine which one is the best selection.

- Select the Installable from CD-ROM/DVD option if you want to install software available directly in the Ubuntu CD or DVD, without an Internet connection. This source will be listed in the Ubuntu Software Center under the Get Software element.

Click Close when finished.

429

Adding Software Sources

Other sources of software available for Ubuntu are out there that you might need or like to set up. You can access them using the Other Software tab in the Software Sources tool, shown in Figure 20-5.

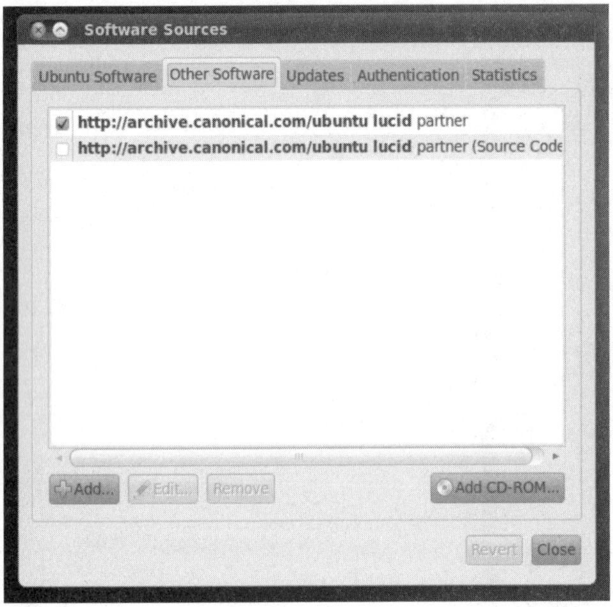

Figure 20-5. The Other Software tab at the Software Sources tool

By default you will see the Canonical partner repositories, of which the main component is selected and the source code component is not. This is the software source listed under Canonical Partners in the Ubuntu Software Center. You can also add PPAs and other software sources.

The PPAs or Personal Package Archives are repositories hosted by Canonical in its Launchpad service, on behalf of third-party developers. A developer can activate a PPA, and Launchpad will generate a unique key to sign any package contained in that PPA. The developer can then submit the source code for its applications, and the people at Canonical build the binaries and packages needed to install the application. Ubuntu users benefits from this collaboration because they can add those PPAs to their software sources and install the applications with Ubuntu Software Center. Note that the software contained in a PPA is considered untrusted by Canonical, so extra care should be taken.

Follow these steps to add a PPA to your software sources:

1. First you need to find the right PPA. You can search for PPAs at the PPAs main page, `https://launchpad.net/ubuntu/+ppas`, or browse to a PPA directly if you know its URL (it will always be contained in the same site). For example, the Chromium web browser's daily build is hosted in `https://launchpad.net/~chromium-daily/+archive/ppa`.

2. Locate the Adding this PPA to your System section. You will see the address of the PPA in the format `ppa:<software_name>/ppa`. For example, for Chromium daily build it is `ppa:chromium-daily/ppa`. Copy that text to the clipboard.

3. Open the Software Sources tool and access the Other Software tab. Press the Add button and paste the PPA's address in the APT line text box. Press Add Source. You will see a URL for the added PPA.

4. The key generated by Launchpad for that PPA will also be imported, as you can see in the Authentication tab in Software Sources (you will see an entry called `Launchpad PPA for <software_name>`)

5. Click Close. The catalog in your hard disk will be updated to take into account the new software source. Click Reload.

Now that the catalog is updated, the software available at that PPA can be installed by using the Ubuntu Software Center. You will see an entry for the PPA under Get Software.

You can also add software sources hosted at other services. You need to know the server name and the component name. Go to the Other Software tab, click the Add… button, and fill the APT line field with the information of the repository, using the following format:

```
deb http://<server>/<repository> lucid <component>
```

Click Add Source and then Close to add the source to the catalog.

Managing Software Updates

As important as installing software is keeping it up-to-date, to avoid security breaches and to take full advantage of new functionality as it is added. Ubuntu can automatically take notice of software that has been updated in the repositories or software sources it knows, and lets you choose your course of action. This is configured by using the Updates tab of the Software Sources tool, shown in the Figure 20-6.

Figure 20-6. The Updates tab at the Software Sources tool

Here you can:

- Select the type of Ubuntu update to allow: Important security updates (lucid-security), recommended updates (lucid-updates), pre-released updates (lucid-proposed) and unsupported updates (lucid-backports). We discuss them earlier in this chapter.

- Configure how often to check for updates (daily, every two days, weekly or every two weeks) and what to do when new versions are found: to install security updates without confirmation, to download all updates in the background, or to only notify when new versions are available.

- Ubuntu will let you know when a new version of the OS itself is made available (which is every six months!). You can select to be warned about "Long term support" (LTS) releases only (which happens every two years), for all normal releases, or never be warned.

Once you have configured to be notified about software updates, it will be a short while until you are prompted to install them. You can do so by opening the Update Manager, a tool located at the System ➤ Administration menu and shown in Figure 20-7.

Figure 20-7. Ubuntu Update Manager

There's the list of available updates, each with a check box next to it that indicates whether you want to install the update or not. It is always recommended to keep your software up-to-date, or at least to install the important security updates as soon as possible to avoid future problems.

Clicking the Check button forces a resynchronization of the software catalog to verify that there are no new updates to install. Once you have reviewed all the updates, you can click the Install Updates button and proceed with the task.

The Synaptic Package Manager in Depth

The Synaptic Package Manager is effectively a graphical front end for the apt system and was the preferred GUI application prior to the Ubuntu Software Center. Although Synaptic has been replaced as the primary source for software installation, it can still be useful if you need more control over the specific packages that get installed into your system. While Ubutu Software Center is a great tool for installing applications, you may feel more comfortable installing system libraries or other files with Synaptic. You can use it to search for and install software. To start this program, click System ➤ Administration ➤ Synaptic Package Manager.

Searching for Software

Before searching for software, it's always a good idea to refresh the package database. This database describes the software contained in the repositories, and it is held on your hard disk. Just click the Reload button on the Synaptic Package Manager toolbar to grab the latest package lists from the various repositories you're subscribed to (which are in your Software Sources). Reloading can take a few minutes on a slow connection, but it ensures that you have access to the latest software within the repositories.

You can search for software in three ways:

Ultra-quick: For a fuss-free instant search, click any entry in the list of packages and then simply start typing. This will match what you type against the package names and sort the list dynamically as you type. This does not let you search through descriptions for keywords, however.

Quick: By typing your search term into the Quick Search field on the main toolbar, you can search through package names and descriptions.

In-depth: For an in-depth search, which lets you search all the information contained within packages, click the Search button on the toolbar. By default, this searches through both package names and the descriptions, but by clicking the Look In drop-down list, you can select to search by other information, such as the version number. You can type either the specific program name or a keyword that may be within the description. For example, if you are looking for graphics drivers for your Nvidia card, but you don't know the name of the package that contains them, you can type **nvidia**.

■ **Tip** You don't need to type whole words in the search field. You can type part of a word or, more commonly, the word in a shortened or alternate form. For example, if you're looking for an e-mail client, it might be more fruitful to simply type *mail client* or even just *mail*. This will then return results containing *e-mail*, *mail*, *mailing*, and so on.

By clicking the Settings ➤ Filters button, you can enhance your search results by creating a filter that removes packages from results that don't meet your requirements. You can filter by criteria such as whether the software is already installed, whether it's new in the repository, and much more. It's advisable to click the New button to create your own filter before starting, as shown in Figure 20-8, rather than editing one that's already there. After a filter has been created, you can apply a filter to search results by clicking the Custom Filters button at the bottom left of the main program window, and then clicking the name of your filter in the list.

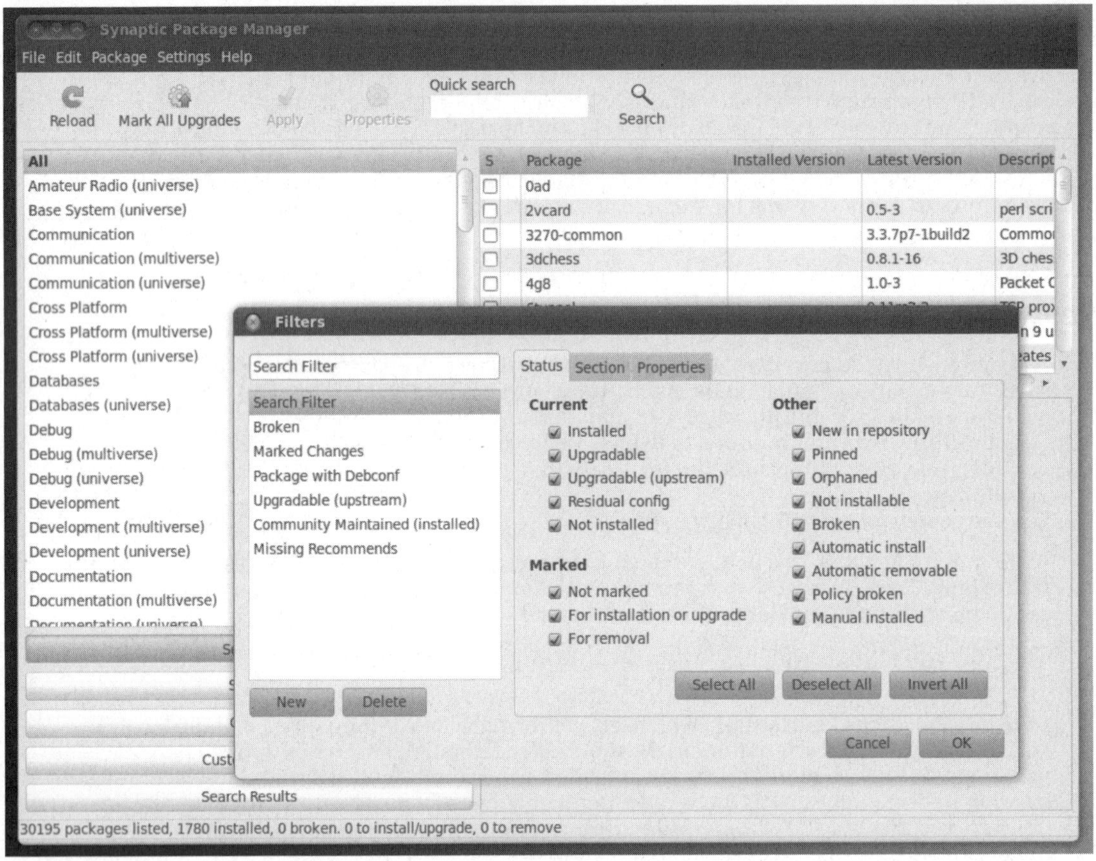

Figure 20-8. *Filters can be used to trim the list of search results according to certain criteria.*

One use of filtering is to remove the check alongside Installed so that you can remove from the search list any packages that might be already on your system.

■ **Note** Filtering can help reduce the number of search results if you use a generic search term, but don't forget to deactivate filtering when you're finished. To do so, click All at the top of the filters list.

In the search results, any packages with the Ubuntu symbol next to them are *supported* packages, which is to say, they're from the Main or Restricted software repositories, as opposed to Universe, Multiverse, or a third-party repository. Therefore, future updates are likely to be offered.

If the check box is green, that means the package is already installed. A star next to the check box means the package is new. You can view the complete range of Synaptic icons by clicking Help ➤ Icon Legend.

By clicking the Get Screenshot button at the top of the description panel, you can view a thumbnail screenshot of the application, if one is available. This can help identify whether the software will fulfill your needs. Clicking the thumbnail when it appears downloads a full-resolution rendition of the screenshot.

Be aware that not all applications presently have screenshots. Some—such as system software or command-line programs that lack a user interface—will never have screenshots because, quite simply, there is nothing to see.

Installing Software

When you click the check box next to a piece of software in the search results and select Mark for Installation, the program will be queued for installation, which will take place as soon as you click the Apply button on the toolbar. If the program has any uninstalled dependencies, you'll also see a dialog box asking you to confirm installing those as well. If you agree, these are automatically added to the list of packages to be installed.

Additionally, if you right-click the file and select Mark Suggested for Installation or Mark Recommended for Installation, you'll see a list of programs that, although not essential to the running of the program in question, will enhance its features to some degree. For example, if you choose to install the VLC media player program, it's also suggested that you install `mozilla-plugin-vlc`, so that VLC can be used as a plug-in for playing media files in Firefox. You don't have to install these recommended programs; the software will run fine without them. But it can often be rewarding if you do so.

▓ **Note** If the software in the recommended and suggested lists is grayed out, that means it's already installed. It's also possible that the package doesn't have any recommended/suggested packages.

After making your selection and clicking the Apply button on the toolbar (bear in mind that you can install more than one piece of software at once), you'll see the Summary dialog box, as shown in Figure 20-9. Here you're once again asked to confirm what needs to be installed. If any software needs to be removed in order to handle dependency issues, you'll be told about this too. Additionally, under the Summary heading, you'll be shown the total size of the files that will be downloaded, as well as the space required on your hard disk.

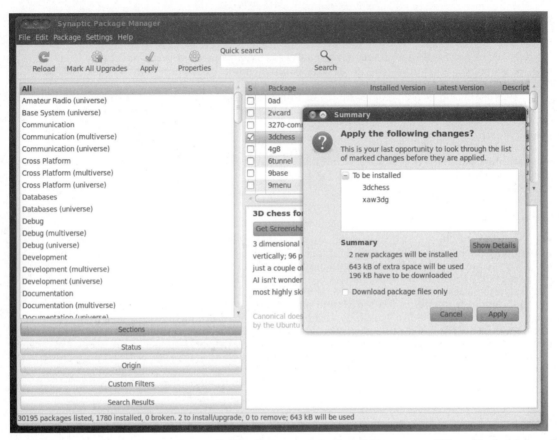

Figure 20-9. *Before any software is installed by the Synaptic Package Manager, you'll be told what it is and asked to confirm the choice.*

At the very bottom of the Summary dialog box, you'll see a check box marked Download Package Files Only. As it suggests, this will download but not install the packages. If you then select the package for installation again in the future, you won't need to download it, and installation will be almost instantaneous (unless a newer version of the package has been released, in which case the newer version will be downloaded and installed).

If you see an Unchanged heading in the Summary dialog box, this means that there are several system updates available that you haven't selected for installation. To install the system updates, click Cancel and then click the Mark All Upgrades button on the toolbar. Then click Apply again. You will then see two separate headings in the Summary dialog box: one listing the upgrades and one listing the new packages you've selected to install.

■ **Note** Of course, you can opt to ignore the fact that updates are available and simply go ahead with installation. Installing updates as soon as possible is advised but not enforced.

METAPACKAGES

Software such as the GNOME desktop actually consists of a number of programs and system libraries, rather than one single piece of software. Therefore, you might be wondering how, as just one example, you might install the KDE desktop under Ubuntu 10.04. Is it necessary to install each component's package manually?

In theory, dependency management should be able to help, and you should be able to select one key part of the KDE desktop system, such as the Konqueror file browser, and have the Synaptic Package Manager take care of the rest. After all, Konqueror will be dependent on other KDE packages.

Alas, this rarely works in reality. Installing Konqueror in this way will indeed install much of the KDE desktop suite, but not everything. Konqueror isn't reliant on Kate, for example, which is the default text editor under KDE. And although the packages will be installed, there's no guarantee that they'll be configured to work correctly as a desktop environment.

Metapackages provide the solution. These are packages that contain configuration files to ensure that the full range of software is installed and configured correctly, and they also have extensive lists of dependencies that include the complete set of packages for the software in question. (The metapackage for KDE is `kdebase`, but if you want the full Kubuntu experience, you should install the `kubuntu-desktop` metapackage.)

Alongside desktop suites, other examples of Ubuntu metapackages include the OpenOffice.org office suite, where the metapackage ensures that all the components of the suite can be easily installed, and the X.org graphical subsystem. To see what metapackages are available, simply search for *metapackage* by using the Synaptic Package Manager or the Ubuntu Software Center.

Removing Software

To remove a piece of software, search for it by name, click the check box alongside it, and then select Mark for Removal. This will remove the software but leave behind any configuration files it created. This means you can install it again in the future, and it will function as it did before removal. However, you can also select Mark for Complete Removal, which will remove the configuration files.

As with installing software, the Synaptic Package Manager attempts to manage dependencies when you remove software, but in this case, it enforces the removal of any software that explicitly relies on that software.

Often the solution is simply not to remove the software package. After all, modern hard disks have huge capacities, and it's unlikely the package will take up much room.

Manually Installing Using Gdebi

Gdebi Package Installer is a simple program designed to facilitate the installation of single packages that you've sourced yourself (that is, that you may have acquired from elsewhere on the Internet). Like Synaptic, it can automatically take care of dependencies by adding them into the total installation tally.

Gdebi runs automatically when you double-click a package file on your hard disk (a file with a `.deb` file extension). It is also offered as the default choice to open package files when you click on a package link within the web browser.

After Gdebi's simple program window appears, there is only one course of action: to click the Install Package button. This will install the software and—if necessary, or possible—automatically download and install the software packages. You'll be told if any dependencies are required, and clicking the Details button will display a list of them.

If the dependency packages are not available in the repositories, the Install Package button is inactive, and the missing dependencies listed. In theory you must now source the missing dependencies manually, but it is very likely that, if they are not available in the repositories, the package in question just isn't intended for either the version of Ubuntu you're using, or even for Ubuntu itself (it might be a package designed for a different derivative of Debian, for example, or even Debian itself).

When Gdebi first runs, you might see a dialog box indicating that the package "is available in a software channel." This means that the software you mean to install is available in Ubuntu's repositories. If so, it might be better for you to install it from there instead, because then you will receive automated updates, as well as a version of the software that's guaranteed to be tweaked so it works fully within Ubuntu's infrastructure.

Installing Windows Applications with Wine

Thousands of free applications. Ease to install. What if this isn't enough? What if you just need that Windows application to do some special task? As with everything in Ubuntu, there's a solution for that.

The solution is Wine. *Wine* (a recursive acronym meaning "Wine Is Not an Emulator") is a software layer capable of running Windows applications on Linux. The project began as early (in Linux lifetime) as 1993, as a way of supporting Windows 3.1 applications on Linux. Today the need of this kind of support is more apparent than ever, so Wine should be one of your biggest allies in your move to Ubuntu.

Why is it so important? Given the fact that Windows is the most popular desktop OS, it is a fact that there are many applications that are developed to work only with that platform. It's sad but it's also true. So many users feel trapped in an expensive OS which they don't want just because they need to run an application. It shouldn't be that way. There's the classic chicken and egg dilemma: few people use Linux because of lack of applications; developers don't port their applications to Linux because there are not enough users. Wine is the tool for breaking this vicious circle.

Installing Wine is fairly easy. Installing Windows applications to run on top of it, on the other hand, can be quite challenging. Not everything works out-of-the-box as you would like. Wine is just a tool that is in continuous development and that takes a great deal of input from its users. The Wine community deserves much credit for evaluating and reviewing applications.

Many users around the world try to install Windows applications on Linux by using Wine and share their experiences in `http://appdb.winehq.org`. Not surprisingly, the most tested applications are actually... games!

We will examine now how to install Wine, how to make its initial configuration, and how to install a sample application. If you have a program that you'd like to see running in your new Ubuntu desktop computer, we recommend browsing the Applications Database for advice on how to make it run. There are almost 9,000 applications in the database, so it is very likely that you will find yours.

Installing and Configuring Wine

Wine can be easily installed using the Ubuntu Software Center. Just search for the application Wine Microsoft Compatibility Layer (if you search for Wine it will be the first of the list) and click Install. As always, you will be prompted for your password to begin the installation.

Once it has finished, a new category will be added to the Applications menu: Wine, with four sub-entries:

Programs: From here you will be able to access the Windows applications you install on Wine. It's like the All Programs menu on Windows.

Browse C: Drive: We mention in Chapter 10 that the Ubuntu file system is different from that of Windows, in that it doesn't use letters to identify drives. So what's this C: drive? It is a virtual folder that Wine creates to make Windows applications feel more at home. Wine creates a hidden .wine folder in your home, and a drive_c folder inside of .wine. Windows applications believe that folder is the root of the C: drive.

Configuring Wine: This tool allows you to configure Wine. You will be able to select the OS that best supports an application, and do advanced tasks as adding system libraries, selecting the graphic settings, adding drives or configuring audio. This is the tool that will help you tweak your applications to make them work.

Uninstall Wine Software: This is the Wine version of Add/Remove Programs. From here you can install or remove Windows software to Ubuntu.

Installing a Windows Application

Now that Wine is up and running, you can install your Windows applications.

The best way to learn how to do it is by giving you an example. It is really easy to do, and on occasion it works out of the box. If it doesn't, you should consult the AppDB or other forums because other people very likely have had the same problems.

In this example we install the application Notepad++, a Notepad replacement used by many developers to write source code. It is an easy-to-install application that will serve our ends well. Those are basic instructions that will work well with most simple software. You will be able to accommodate them to the software you want to install. So here we go:

1. Open Firefox and go to the site http://notepad-plus.sourceforge.net. Click the Download menu.

2. Expand Binary files and click Download Notepad++ executable files.

3. In the download page, make sure you select the Windows installable files. Click it. A dialog box will pop up asking you to open or save the file (it should be an executable file, with the .exe extension. If not, go back to the previous page and verify that you selected the Windows installable program). Download the files to your hard drive.

4. Go to your Downloads folder (this is where Firefox stores the files it gets from the Internet) and right-click the installer you just downloaded. Open the Properties dialog box and in the Permissions tab check the "Allow executing file as program" box. Click Close.

5. Right-click the file and select the option Open with Wine Windows Program Loader.

6. The normal installation wizard, familiar to all Windows users, will show up. Follow it until the application is installed.

7. Voila! The application is now installed. It will open automatically. From now on you will find it in Applications ➤ Wine ➤ Programs ➤ Notepad++

An alternate method is to use go to Applications ➤ Wine ➤ Uninstall Wine Software. The Add/Remove Software dialog box will appear. Click the Install... button and select the executable file that will install the software. Follow the wizard as you would have done with the first method.

When you're positive that you will no longer need the application, you can remove it from your system with the same tool. Select the application from the list and press the Remove... button. Follow the wizard to uninstall the application.

In this way, installing Windows applications seems quite straightforward. In some cases, though, it isn't so easy. Fortunately there's always the Ubuntu community to help!

Installing from Source

Some years ago, the only way to install many software packages in a UNIX system was from source code, a process known as *compiling*. This was because most people edited the source code themselves, or at least liked to have the option of doing so. Nowadays, innovations such as the Debian package management system make compiling all but redundant for the average user. But knowing how to compile a program from source is still a good Linux skill to have. In some cases, it's your only option for installing certain programs, because you may not be able to find a packaged binary or because the packagers have not yet created binary versions of their latest cutting-edge release.

Program compilation is usually handled at the command prompt, so make sure you read Appendix A before moving forward. It's not the kind of thing you would do via a GUI program.

Installing the Compiler Tools

Before you can compile from source, you need to install several items of software: the make program, which oversees the process of creating a new program, and the GNU Compiler Collection (GCC), which does the hard work of turning the source code into a binary. In addition, if the software relies on certain library files, you'll need to install development (dev) versions of them, as well as the libraries themselves if they're not already installed. For example, if you're compiling a program to run under the GNOME desktop, you'll need development versions of the GTK2+ libraries.

Under Ubuntu, it's possible to install all the program-compilation tools you need by installing the build-essential metapackage. You can use the Synaptic Package Manager or the Ubuntu Software Center.

In the remaining pages of this chapter we will talk about a generic process for source code compilation and installation. It does not reference any software in particular, but it does work with most applications.

Unpacking the Source Tarball and Solving Dependencies

Let's take a look at installing a program from source. You usually download the application's source code package from the developer's site on the web. The name of the package will reference the application name and version number, for instance: applicationx-2.0.4.tar.gz. The .tar.gz extension (or .tgz in some cases) is because of the fact that source code files comes in a packaged and zipped file.

The first thing you have to do is to unpack it. From the command line go to the directory where you saved your .tar.gz file (if you downloaded it using Firefox, it will probably be in your Downloads folder), and run the following command (with the appropriate filename of course):

```
tar xzvf applicationx-2.0.4.tar.gz
```

This will create a subdirectory named application-2.0.4. Move to it with the following command:

```
cd applicationx-2.0.4
```

In this folder you should find a file named either README or INSTALL. Read it very carefully to check for dependencies or other useful information.

```
less README
```

If you find that the software has any dependencies, you can install the required packages by using either the Synaptic Package Manager or the Ubuntu Software Center.

■ **Note** Unlike binary packages, source code is rarely designed with one specific Linux distribution in mind—or even with Linux in mind! With a little work, it might even be possible to compile it under Windows!

Compiling

Now comes the exciting process of compiling the program! This is a three-step process, with three commands that you have to execute in sequence:

```
./configure
```

The first command starts the configure script, created by the application's programmer, which checks your system to ensure that it meets the requirements. In other words, it checks to make sure the dependencies are present. It also checks to make sure you have the correct software that's required to actually compile a program, such as GCC and make.

It's when the configure script is running that something is most likely to go wrong. In that case, more often than not, the error message will tell you that you're missing a dependency, which you must then resolve.

■ **Note** Some configure scripts are very thorough and check for components that the program you're trying to install might not even need because, for example, they may just be alternative packages for doing the same job. Because of this, you shouldn't worry if, as the text scrolls past, you see that various components are missing. Unless configure complains about it when it has finished, it's not a problem.

```
make
```

The next command, make, takes care of the actual program compilation. When you run this, the screen will fill with what might look like gibberish, but this is merely the output of the GNU compiler. It provides a lot of valuable information to those who know about such things, but you can largely ignore it. However, you should keep your eyes peeled for any error messages. It's possible that the configure script did not check your system thoroughly enough, and you might be missing an important system component—in which case, make will halt.

■ **Note** It is possible that both the make and the make install commands report error messages, but that the applications works after installation nonetheless. The moral of the story is that software compilation is something of a black art, with error messages designed for programmers, and not all error messages are fatal.

Alternatively, the program simply might not be able to compile on your system without some tweaking to the Makefile (the file that make uses). If such a situation arises, the best plan is to visit the web site of the developer of the software and see whether there's a forum you can post to. Alternatively, check if the developer has an e-mail address you can contact to ask for help.

```
sudo make install
```

Eventually, the compilation will stop with a number of exit messages. Then the final command must be run: make install. This needs to be run with superuser powers, because its job is to copy the binary files you've just created to the relevant system directories. In addition, any documentation that comes with the program is also copied to the relevant location on your system.

After the three commands have completed, you should be able to run the program by typing its name at the command prompt.

■ **Note** You'll probably need to add your own icon for the application to the desktop or Applications menu (see Chapter 9 for more details on the procedure to do this). Source packages are usually designed to be installed on any version of UNIX running a variety of desktop managers. In the past, it was difficult for the developer to know where to create desktop shortcuts, but now organizations like freedesktop.org (http://freedesktop.org) are standardizing the process.

Summary

This chapter described how to install software under Ubuntu. We looked at how this differs from Windows software installation, and how the Debian package management system is designed to make life easier.

You learned how to use the Ubuntu Software Center and Synaptic Package Manager to install software from the official repositories, and how to use the different tools for more complex scenarios. Finally, you looked at how programs can be compiled from their source code, which is a fundamental process for all versions of Linux.

■ ■ ■

## CHAPTER 21

Understanding Linux Users and File Permissions

Most modern operating systems work with user accounts to grant people access to the system, and Ubuntu is no exception. You might not have noticed this—if during installation or when you personalized your system you selected the option to allow automatic logins, you are taken directly to your desktop when you boot your PC, thus masking the fact that a user is actually logging into the system.

So, whether you're aware of it or not, you always have a user account inside Ubuntu. Your user account will have a defined set of attributes that will distinguish it from other user accounts: for example, a name and a Home folder. But it also will be a member of a group. Being a member of certain groups allows access to portions of the system that would be otherwise hidden, because groups can enable permissions to access and manipulate files on your hard disks. And, since all configuration in Ubuntu is stored in files (see Chapter 10), those permissions will allow it to change the system itself.

Understanding User and Group Accounts

We've already stated that to interact with Ubuntu you need a user account. However, there's more to the story than that. For example, there are situations in which you might need more than one user account. Either in the office or at home there may be more than one person that uses the computer, and you surely will want to keep your personal configuration and data separate from theirs. That's when the need for additional user accounts arises. This section will explain what a user account is, how to create it, and how to work with groups.

Users and Groups

Each person who wishes to log into Ubuntu must have a user account. This will define what that user can and cannot do on the system, with specific reference to files and folders. Because Ubuntu is effectively one large file system (even hardware devices are files; see Chapter 10), user permissions lie at the heart of controlling the entire system. They can limit which user has access to which hardware and software, and therefore control access to various PC functions.

Each user also belongs to a group. Groups have the same style of permissions as individual users. File or folder access can be denied or granted to a user, depending on that person's group membership.

■ **Note** As in real life, a group can have many members and can be based around various interests. In a business environment, this might mean that groups are created for members of the accounting department and the human resources department. By changing the permissions on files created by the group members, each group can have files that only the group members can access (although, as always, anyone with superuser powers can access all files).

On a default Ubuntu system with just a handful of users, the group concept might seem somewhat redundant. However, the concept of groups is fundamental to the way Ubuntu works and cannot be avoided. Even if you don't use groups, Ubuntu still requires your user account to be part of one.

In addition to actual human users, the Ubuntu system has its own set of user and group accounts. Various programs that access hardware resources or particular sets of files are part of these groups. Setting up system users and groups in this way makes the system more secure and easier to administer.

Root User

On most Linux systems, the root user has power over the entire system. Root can examine any file and configure any piece of hardware. Root typically belongs to its own unique group, also called root.

Ubuntu is different from most Linux distributions in that the root account isn't used by default. Instead, certain users—including the one set up during installation—can "borrow" root-like, or superuser, powers by simply typing their login password. This is done by preceding commands with sudo or gksu at the command-line prompt, or as needed when using GUI programs that affect system settings. For some programs, including Users and Groups (System ➤ Administration ➤ Users and Groups), you need to click an Unlock button to gain superuser powers. Until you unlock the Users and Groups program, most of the buttons are grayed out and unusable.

If you wish, you can activate the root user account on your system for administration purposes. To activate the root account, use the following command in a terminal window (see Appendix A for details on issuing commands in a terminal window):

```
Sudo  passwd root
```

After typing your own login password, you'll be invited to define a password for the root user. Because of its power, the root user can cause a lot of accidental damage, so by default Ubuntu prevents you from logging in as root. Instead, you can switch to being the root user temporarily from an ordinary user account by using the Switch From option in the Shutdown menu. This will leave your session open while letting you open an additional session as any user (e.g., root).

You will be prompted for the root password and then given root powers for as long as you need. When you've finished, log out and return to your ordinary user account.

■ **Tip** You can tell when you're logged in as the root user because in the Me menu your name is "root." This should be seen as a warning that you now have unrestricted control over the system, so be careful what you type, and double-check everything before pressing Enter!

If you enable the root password in the name of security, it might be a sensible precaution to then disable sudo, thus preventing nonadmin users from playing with things they shouldn't. To do this, you'll need to edit the file /etc/sudoers. There will be a line (shown in Figure 21-1) that reads as follows:

```
%admin  ALL=(ALL) ALL
```

Comment this out with a # sign and save the file. This, of course, will all need to be done using root privileges, so use gksudo gedit in the Run Applications dialog box (accessible by pressing Alt+F2) to launch the text editor, and then navigate to and open the file. Also make sure you've set up the root password, as shown earlier, before you do this.

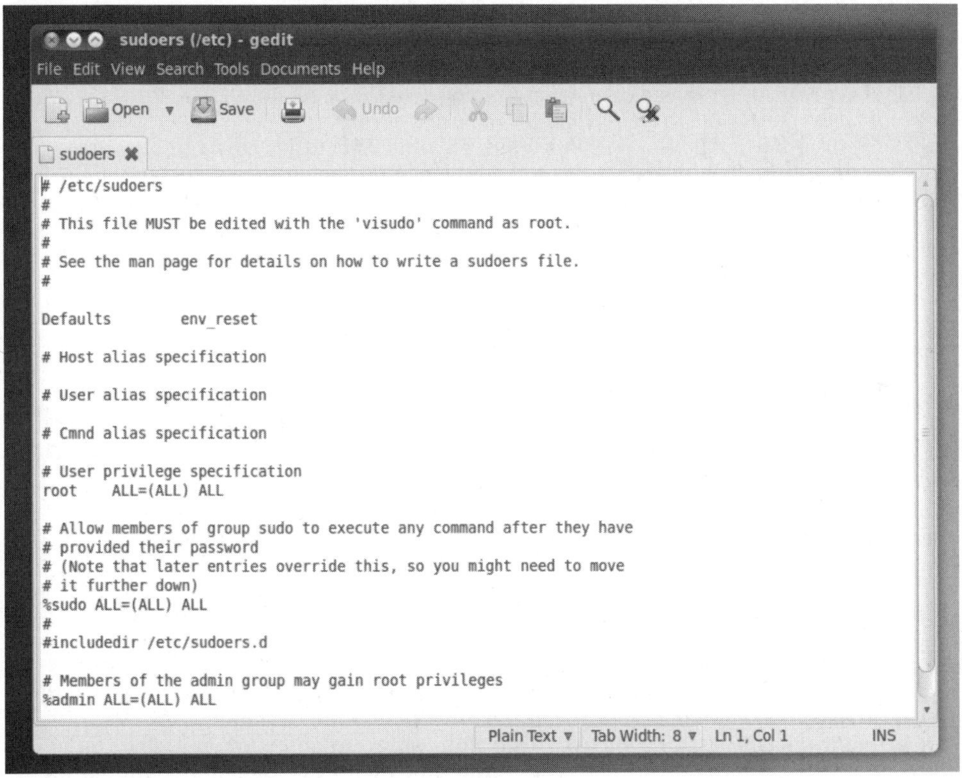

Figure 21-1. Be very cautious when editing these files.

Users and File Permissions

The concepts of users and permissions are as important to Ubuntu as the idea of a central and all-encompassing file system. In fact, the two are implicitly linked.

When initially installing Linux, you should have created at least one user account. By now, this will have formed the day-to-day login that you use to access Linux and run programs.

Although you might not realize it, as a user you also belong to a group. In fact, every user on the system belongs to a group. Under Ubuntu, ordinary users belong to a group based on their usernames (under other versions of Linux, you might find that you belong to a group called users).

■ **Note** Groups are yet another reminder of Ubuntu's UNIX origins. UNIX is often used on huge computer systems with hundreds or thousands of users. Putting each user into a group makes the system administrator's job a lot easier. When controlling system resources, the administrator can control groups of users rather than hundreds of individual users. On most home user PCs, the concept of groups is a little redundant because there's typically a single user, or at most two or three. However, the concept of groups is central to the way that Linux handles files.

A standard user account under Ubuntu is typically limited in what it can do. As a standard user, you can save files to your own private area of the disk, located in the /home directory, but usually nowhere else. You can move around the file system, but some directories are strictly out of bounds. In a similar way, some files are read-only, so you cannot save changes to them. All of this is enforced using file permissions.

Every file and directory is owned by a user. In addition, files and directories have three separate settings that indicate who within the Linux system can read them, who can write to them, and, if the files in question are *runnable* (usually programs or scripts), who can run (execute) them. In the case of directories, it's also possible to set who can browse them, as well as who can write files to them. If you try to access a file or directory for which you don't have permission, you'll be turned away with an "access denied" error message.

Root vs. Sudo

Most versions of Linux have two types of user accounts: standard and root. Standard users are those who can run programs on the system but are limited in what they can do. The root user has the complete run of the system, and as such, is often referred to as the *superuser*. The root user can access and/or delete whatever files it wants. It can configure hardware, change settings, and so on.

Most versions of Linux create a user account called root and let users log in as root to perform system maintenance. However, for practical as well as security reasons, most of the time the user should be logged in as a standard user.

Ubuntu is different in that it doesn't allow login as the root user. Instead, it allows certain users, including the one created during installation, to temporarily adopt root-like powers. You will already have encountered this when configuring hardware. As you've seen, all you need to do is type your password when prompted in order to administer the system.

This way of working is referred to as *sudo*, which is short for *superuser do*. Most applications that require root privileges will ask you for your password if you are a sudoer (i.e., a standard user with permission to act as root in specific circumstances). Other applications might not require that you have root privileges, but you might want to open them as root from time to time. Good examples of this are Nautilus and gedit—maybe you want to completely remove a deleted user's Home folder and you can't do that as a standard user. For this you use Gksudo, which is a graphical front end to the sudo command (which will let you adopt root powers at the shell prompt—simply preface any command with sudo and type your password when prompted in order to run it with root privileges). If you open the Run Application dialog box (press Alt+F2) and type **gksudo Nautilus**, you will be able to browse the file system as root. Or, if you want to edit a file to which only root has write privileges, run gksudo gedit. Ubuntu remembers when you last used sudo, too, so it won't annoy you by asking you again for your password within 15 minutes of its first use.

In some ways, the sudo system is arguably slightly less secure than using a standard root account. But it's also a lot simpler. It reduces the chance of serious errors too. Any command or tweak that can cause damage will invariably require administrative powers, and therefore requires you to type your password or preface the command with gksudo or sudo. This serves as a warning and prevents mistakes.

UIDs and GIDs

Although we talk of user and group names, these are provided only for the benefit of humans. Internally, Ubuntu uses a numerical system to identify users and groups. These are referred to as user IDs (UIDs) and group IDs (GIDs), respectively.

Under Ubuntu, all the GID and UID numbers below 1,000 are reserved for the system. This means that the first nonroot user account created during installation will probably be given a UID of 1000. In addition, any new groups created after installation are numbered from 1,000. The first user you add has a UID of 1000 and a GID of 1000, the second user a UID of 1001, and so on.

■ **Note** UID and GID information isn't important during everyday use, and most commands used to administer users, groups, and file permissions understand the human-readable names. However, knowing about UIDs and GIDs can prove useful when you're undertaking more complicated system administration, such as setting up a restricted system for children or scripting.

Adding and Deleting Users and Groups

The easiest and quickest way to add a new user or group is to use the Users and Groups tool under the System ➤ Administration menu. Of course, you can also perform these tasks through the command line.

Adding and Deleting Users

To add a new user, choose System ➤ Administration ➤ Users and Groups. Next, click Add. In the authentication window, supply your password and click Authenticate. You'll see the Create New User dialog box, as shown in Figure 21-2.

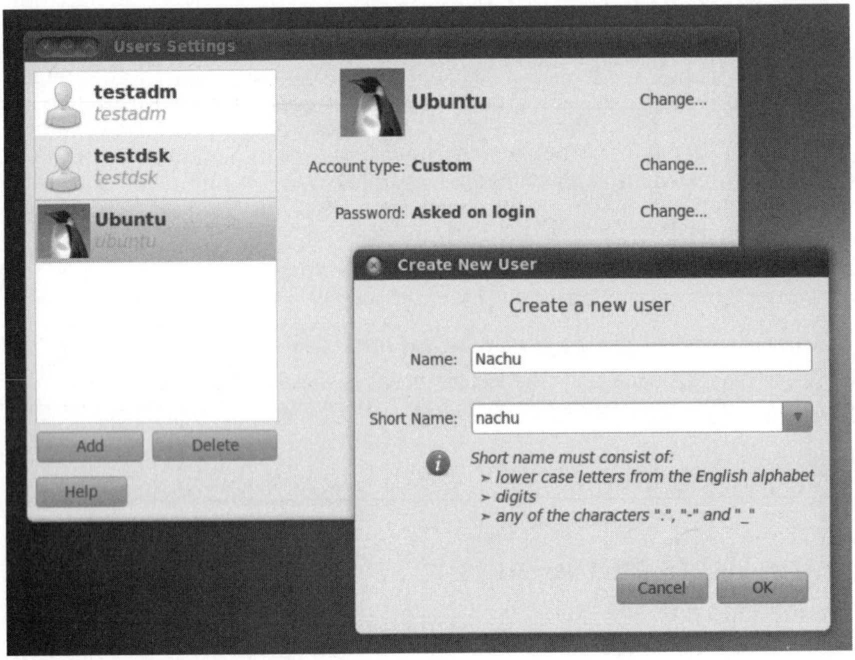

Figure 21-2. Adding new users and groups is easy with the Users and Groups program.

Fill out the fields on the Account tab, and optionally the Contact, User Privileges, and Advanced tabs, as follows:

Create a new user: As during initial installation (see Chapter 5), you're invited to enter a username as well as a real name. The username is how the user is identified to the system, while the real name is how the user will be identified to other users. By default they are set to the same. Press OK when done.

Changing user password for: You can set the user's password by hand or let the system generate a random password for you. In either case, make sure to remember the password to give it to the person that will use the user account. You can also select the option to let the user to log into his session without entering the password. Press OK when finished.

Once the user has been created, you can set additional settings by selecting the user from the list and clicking the various options at the left of the User Settings window.

Account type: You can select the profile you want the user to have: Administrator, Desktop User, or Custom. Users with the Administrator profile can use sudo or gksu to administer the system. Although desktop users can't use these commands, they do have access to most other system resources. For most users, the Desktop User profile is a good choice. You cannot select the Custom profile for a user account, but if you manually change its privileges (more about this shortly), this profile is selected automatically.

Password: An initial password for the user is required, but you can change it any time you want with the Users and Groups tool (as long as you have the required privileges). You can enter it in the text box (and confirm it below) or let the system generate a random password from letters and numbers, but this may be harder for the user to remember.

If you click the Advanced Settings button, more options will be available, as follows:

Contact Information: Here you can enter contact information for the user. This is not obligatory.

User Privileges: The settings on this tab offer much more control over what a user can and cannot do on the system. Here you can prevent users from using certain hardware, such as the 3D capabilities of graphics cards, or modems. You can also control whether the user is able to administer the system. Simply put a check alongside any relevant boxes.

Advanced: Here you can alter additional settings, if you wish, relating to the technical setup of the account on the system. If you're not sure about these parameters, it's best to leave the default settings alone. You can disable the account from here, and it will no longer be available for login. You might like to change the main group for the user as well. By default, the user will belong to a newly created group based on the user's own username. For example, if you add the user john, he will be added to the group john. This private group approach enforces a more stringent policy regarding personal file access. Alternatively, you could create a single group and assign several users to that group for file-sharing purposes. We'll discuss adding and removing groups in the next section.

■ **Caution** Many groups are listed in the Main Group drop-down list. Nearly all of these relate to the way the Linux operating system works and can be ignored (you can see the list of groups in Table 21-1). You should never delete any of these groups or add new users to them. This may make the system unstable and/or insecure.

Deleting a user is simply a matter of highlighting the username in the list within the main Users and Groups window and clicking the Delete button. Note that you can choose to either delete the user's Home folder or to keep the files. You might want to access the files yourself and make a backup of them before completely removing the Home folder.

Creating and Deleting Groups

Adding a group is simply a matter of clicking the Manage Groups button in the Users and Groups program window (System ➤ Administration ➤ Users and Groups). After clicking the Add button, you'll be prompted to give the group a name. The GID will be filled in for you automatically, but you could choose a different number if you have good reason to do so. (Remember to use a number above 1,000 to keep in line with the way Ubuntu operates.)

It isn't essential that you add users to the group then and there, but a list of users is provided at the bottom of the dialog box. Put a check alongside any user to grant that user access to your group.

■ **Note** Bear in mind that users can be members of more than one group, although all users have a main group that they belong to, from which the GID is assigned to files they create.

As with user accounts, deleting a group is simply a matter of highlighting it in the list and clicking the Delete button. You should ensure that the group no longer has any members before doing this, because Ubuntu won't prevent you from removing a group that has members (although it will warn you that this is a bad thing to do).

■ **Note** Ubuntu appears to offer protection against the havoc caused by deleting a group that is the main group of users on your system. When we deleted an entry that was the main group of a different user and then logged in as that user, the group was automatically re-created! You shouldn't rely on this kind of protection, however, and should always check before deleting a group.

Table 21-1. *System Groups Within Ubuntu*

Group	Definition
adm	Used for system logging
dialout	Required for use of serial port devices, such as older modems
cdrom	Allows the user to access the CD/DVD-ROM
plugdev	Allows the user access to removable storage, such as card readers, digital cameras, and so on
lpadmin	Allows the user to administer the printer
admin	Gives the user system administration abilities (superuser powers)
sambashare	Facilitates sharing files with others across the network

As you might have guessed, to manually add a user under Ubuntu, not only must you create a group and then add the user to it, but you must also add that user to the required selection of supplementary groups. Some are considered mandatory for effective use of the computer, such as plugdev, while others are optional, depending on how much freedom you want to afford the new user.

Adding and Changing Passwords

On a default Ubuntu installation, ordinary users are able to change their own passwords by using the Users and Groups tool. Select your user account from the list and click the Change button next to the Password field. You will be prompted with the Change User Password window, shown in Figure 21-3, in which you must enter your current password and select the new one, with the same options as when you originally created the account.

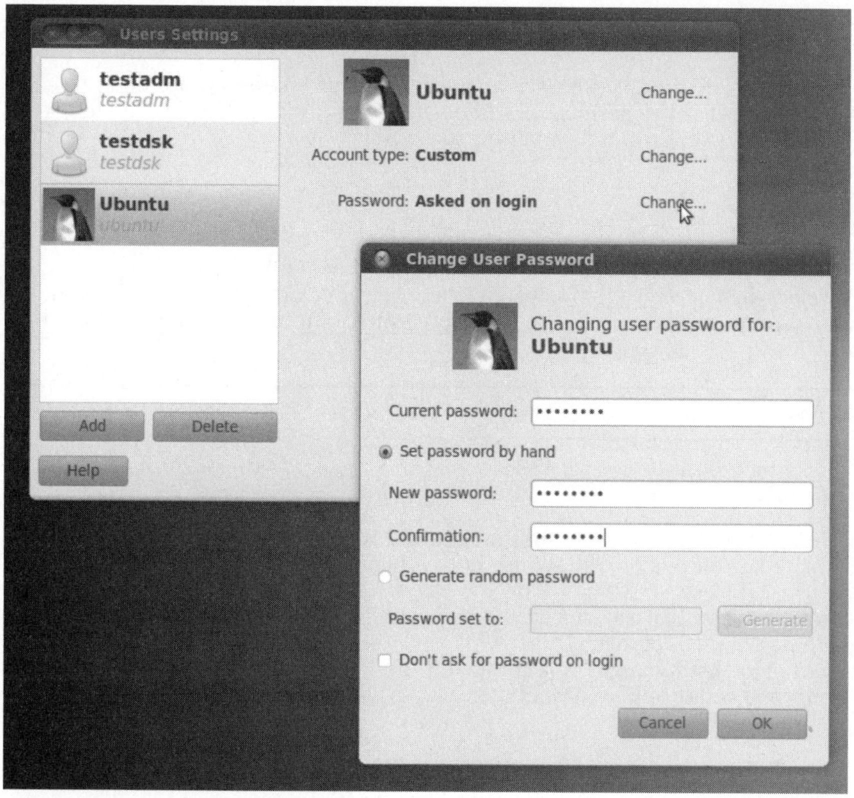

Figure 21-3. The Change User Password window

You need root privileges to change other users' passwords, but the procedure is the same. For obvious security reasons, Ubuntu won't allow blank passwords. (It might allow you to set a blank password, but then it won't let that user log in—this is an interesting way of disabling a user account).

You can enter just about anything as a password, but you should bear in mind some common-sense rules. Ideally, passwords should be at least eight characters long and contain letters, numbers, and even punctuation symbols. You might also want to include both uppercase and lowercase letters, because that makes passwords harder to guess.

■ **Tip** You can temporarily switch into any user account by using the Switch From option on the Shutdown menu. In this way your session will be kept open. If you log out, on the other hand, the session will be closed and you'll need to save your open documents to keep them for future use.

Understanding File and Folder Permissions

One of the main reasons why users and groups exist is manage different permissions for different people. Each file and folder on your disk has permissions associated with it, along with a user and group who own it. Without permissions, a user cannot do anything to a file.

Viewing Permissions

Within Nautilus, is easy to see the users and groups who own a file or folder and the permissions associated with it. Simply select the List view; then select the View ➤ Visible Columns option from the menu and check the Owner, Group, and Permissions boxes. Here's an example of one line of a file listing from our test PC:

Name	Owner	Group	Permissions
Myfile	ubuntu - Ubuntu	ubuntu	-rw-r--r--

In the Permissions column are the permissions for the file or folder. The permission list usually consists of the characters r (for read), w (for write), x (for execute), and/or – (meaning none are applicable).

The Owner column lists the owner of the file (ubuntu in this example) and the group that has permission to access the file (in this case, Ubuntu).

The file permissions part of the listing might look confusing, but it's actually quite simple. To understand what's going on, you need to split it into four groups, as illustrated in Figure 21-4.

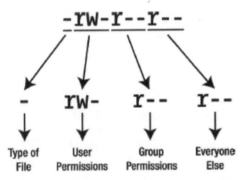

Figure 21-4. *The file permissions part of a file listing can be broken down into four separate parts.*

The four groups are as follows:

Type of file: This character represents the file type. A standard data file is indicated with a hyphen (-). Most files on your system fall into this category. A d shows that the entry is not a file, but a directory. Table 21-2 lists the file type codes.

User permissions: Next come the permissions of the person who owns the file. The three characters indicate what the person who owns the file can do with it. The owner of a file is usually the user who created it, although the owner can be changed later on. In this example, rw- is shown. This means that the owner of the file can read (r) and write (w) to the file. In other words, she can look at it and also save changes to it. However, there's a hyphen after the rw, which indicates that the user cannot execute the file. If this were possible, there would be an x in this spot instead.

Group permissions: After the owner's permissions are the permissions given to the specified group that the file is assigned to. This is indicated by another three characters in the same style as those for user permissions. In the example, the group's permission is r--, which means that the members of the specified group can read the file but don't have permission to write to it, because there's a hyphen where the w would normally appear. In other words, as far as they're concerned, the file is read-only.

Everyone else's permissions: The last set of permissions indicates the permissions of everyone else on the system (other users in other groups). In the example, they can only read the file (r); the two hyphens that follow indicate that others cannot write to or execute the file.

Table 21-2. File Type Codes

Code	File Type
-	Standard file
d	Standard directory
l	Symbolic link (a shortcut to another file)
p	Named pipe (a file that acts as a conduit for data between two programs)
s	Socket (a file designed to send and receive data over a network)
c	Character device (a hardware device driver, usually found in /dev)
b	Block device (a hardware device driver, usually found in /dev)

As with Windows, programs are stored as files on your hard disk, just like standard data files. On Linux, program files need to be explicitly marked as being executable. This is indicated in the permission listing by an x. Therefore, if there's no x in a file's permissions, it's a good bet that the file in question isn't a program or script (although this isn't always true for various technical reasons).

To make matters a little more confusing, if the entry in the list of files is a directory (indicated by a d), then the rules are different. In this case, an x indicates that the user can access that directory. If there's no x, the user's attempts to browse to that directory will be met with an "access denied" message.

File permissions can be difficult to understand, so let's look at a few real-world examples. These examples assume that you're logged into Linux as the user ubuntu.

Typical Data File Permissions

Here's the first example:

Name	Owner	Group	Permissions
myfile2	ubuntu - Ubuntu	Ubuntu	-rw-rw----

You know that this file is owned by user ubuntu because that username appears in the Owner column. Also notice that the group Ubuntu has access to the file, although precisely how much depends on the permissions.

From left to right, the initial file permission character is a hyphen, which indicates that this is an ordinary file and has no special characteristics. It's also not a directory.

After that is the first part of the permissions, rw-. These are the permissions for the owner of the file, ubuntu. You're logged in as that user, so this file belongs to you, and these permissions apply to you. You can read and write to the file but not execute it. Because you cannot execute the file, you can infer that this is a data file, not a program (there are certain exceptions to this rule, but we'll ignore them for the sake of simplicity).

Following this is the next part of the file permissions, rw-. This tells you what members of the group Ubuntu can do with the file. It's fairly useless information if you're the only user of your PC, but for the record, it tells you that anyone else belonging to the group Ubuntu can also read and write the file but not execute it. If you're not the only user of a computer, group permissions can be important. The "Altering Permissions" section, coming up shortly, describes how to change file permissions to control who can access files.

Finally, the last three characters tell you the permissions of everyone else on the system. The three hyphens (---) mean that they have no permissions at all regarding the file. There's a hyphen where the r normally appears, so they cannot even read it. The hyphens afterward tell you they cannot write to the file or execute it. If they try to do anything with the file, they'll get a "permission denied" error.

Permissions on a User's Directory

Here's another example:

Name	Owner	Group	Permissions
mydirectory	ubuntu - Ubuntu	ubuntu	drwxr-xr-x

The list of permissions starts with d, which tells you that this isn't a file but a directory. After this is the list of permissions for the owner of the directory (ubuntu), who can read files in the directory and also create new ones there. The x indicates that you can access this directory, as opposed to being turned away with an "access denied" message. You might think being able to access the directory is taken for granted if the user can read and write to it, but that's not the case.

Next are the permissions for the group members. They can read files in the directory but not write any new ones there (although they can modify files already there, provided the permissions of the individual files allow this). Once again, there's an x at the end of their particular permission listing, which indicates that the group members can access the directory.

Following the group's permissions are those of everyone else. They can read the directory and browse it, but not write new files to it, as with the group users' permissions.

Permissions on a Directory Owned by Root

Here's the last example:

Name	Owner	Group	Permissions
root	root - root	root	drwx------

You can see that the file is owned by root. Remember that in this example, you're logged in as ubuntu and your group is Ubuntu.

The list of permissions starts with a d, so you can tell that this is actually a directory. After this, you see that the owner of the directory, root, has permission to read, write, and access the directory.

Next are the permissions for the group: three hyphens. In other words, members of the group called root have no permission to access this directory in any way. They cannot browse it, create new files in it, or even access it.

Following this are the permissions for the rest of the users. This includes you, because you're not the user root and don't belong to its group. The three hyphens mean you don't have permission to read, write, or access this directory. In other words, it's out of bounds to you, probably because it contains files that only the root user should access!

Altering Permissions

You can easily change permissions of files and directories within Nautilus. You must be the owner of a file to change its permissions (or you can be root, of course; remember to use Gksudo in the Run Applications dialog box to open Nautilus with root privileges). Just right-click a file and select Properties.

Figure 21-5 shows the Permissions tab of a file. You can set permissions for the owner, group, or everybody else. The available permissions are None (no access), Read-Only, and Read and Write. The permissions are applied automatically when you select them; if you keep your Nautilus windows open and visible behind the file properties window, you will see this, as the permissions get updated almost instantly.

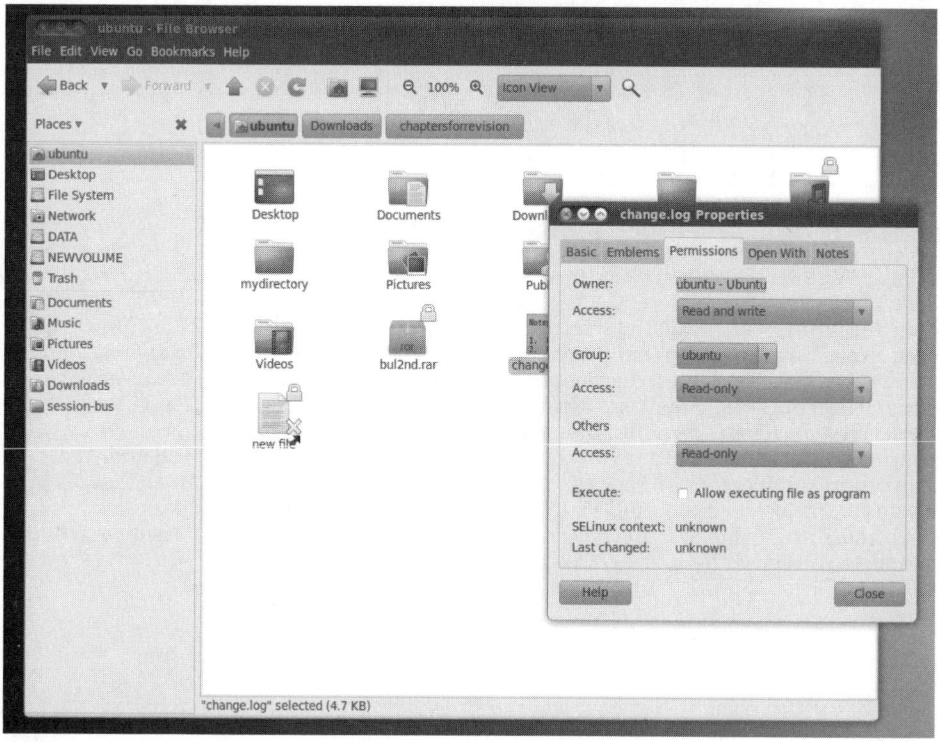

Figure 21-5. The file Permissions tab

You can enable the Execute permission by checking the "Allow executing file as program" check box. It applies for the owner, group, and other users alike.

The permissions on a folder are somewhat more complicated, as shown in Figure 21-6.

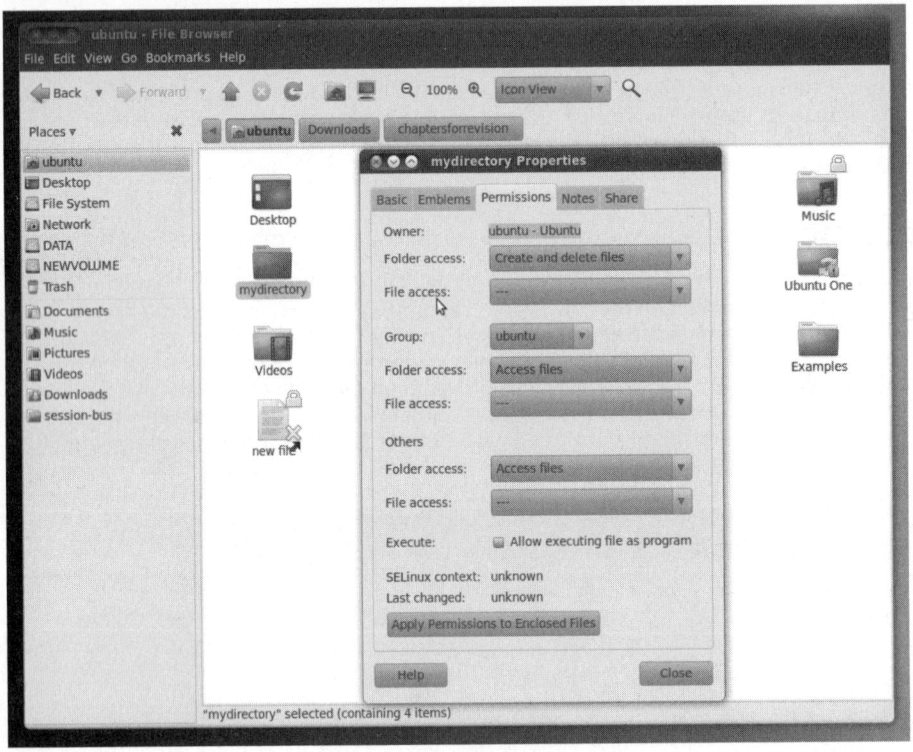

Figure 21-6. *The folder Permissions tab allows you to change its files' permissions as well.*

You can change the group of the folder by selecting the one you want in the Group drop-down list.

There are three levels of folder access that you can set at any particular folder for the owner, the group, and everybody else: List Files Only (which really allows read access to the folder), Access Files (which allows read and execute access), and Create and Delete Files (which allows read, write, and execute access). You can also change the permissions applied to the files contained in the folder by selecting the appropriate level in each of the "File access" dialog boxes: Read-Only or Read and Write. Check the "Allow executing file as program" box to set the Execute permission on contained files. Click the Apply Permissions to Enclosed Files button to propagate the changes down into the hierarchy.

To change the ownership of a file or folder, you need to have root privileges, so make sure you open Nautilus with Gksudo. In the Owner field, select the user.

■ **Tip** Directory permissions are rather strange in that it's easy to set confusing and even illogical permissions. Generally speaking, the day-to-day rules you should follow are simple. If you wish to stop a particular user from accessing a directory, remove all permissions—Read, Write, and Execute (rwx). If you wish to make a directory read-only, leave the Read and Execute permissions in place, but remove the Write permission (r-x). It's even possible to make a directory write-only, by leaving the Write and Execute permissions in place and removing the Read permission (-wx). However, it's rare that you would want to do this.

NUMERIC FILE PERMISSIONS

In this chapter, we've discussed file permissions exclusively in terms of their abbreviations: r for Read, w for Write, and x for Execute. This is known as *symbolic notation*, and its goal is to make file permissions intuitive and easy for the user to understand. However, UNIX and Linux file permissions are traditionally expressed as *octal notation*. File permissions are expressed as a series of three numbers ranging from 0 to 7, each of the three numbers representing the Read, Write, and Execute permissions for user, group, and other assignations of the file or directory.

For example, a file with a permission listing of -rwxr-xr-- can be expressed as 754 in octal notation, and a file permission of -rwxrwxrwx can be expressed as 777.

This sounds more complicated than it is. It's enough to know that Read permissions have a value of 4, Write permissions have a value of 2, and Execute permissions have a value of 1. Permissions can be "added together" to make a larger number: Read and Write permissions have a value of 6, for example (4 + 2). The "full" file permission setting (rwx) has a value of 7 (4 + 2 + 1).

In fact, octal notation can consist of four digits, because—as with symbolic notation—a total of four permission groups can be set: Read, Write, and Execute, and also special file permissions such as the sticky bit, SetUserID, and SetGroupID. However, in most cases octal notation file permissions are expressed as three digits.

It should be kept in mind that, for most tasks, it's not necessary to use octal notation. Symbolic notation is usually enough, and has the added bonus of being less likely to induce a migraine. However, when changing some system settings (e.g., the umask variable that controls what permissions newly created files have), it's often necessary to specify an octal value. Additionally, some Linux and UNIX technical documentation prefers to specify octal notation instead of the more modern symbolic notation.

■ **Tip** You can view the octal notation by adding the column in Nautilus. Select View ➤ Visible Columns, and check the box next to Octal Permissions.

CREATING FILE SHORTCUTS

We touched on the idea of file system shortcuts in Chapter 9, when we discussed creating launchers on the GNOME desktop. The problem with launchers is that they are recognized only within GNOME. In other words, they mean nothing when you're using the command prompt (or virtually any other program that loads/saves files, with the exception of some programs created specially for the GNOME desktop environment).

The Ubuntu file system offers two types of genuine shortcuts, which it refers to as *file links*. They are *symbolic links* and *hard links*.

Symbolic links are the most commonly used. A symbolic link is similar to a Windows shortcut in that a small file is created that "points toward" another file. Unlike a Windows shortcut, however, the symbolic link isn't a real file—it exists at the file system level, so it can't be viewed in a text editor, for example.

You can spot a symbolic link in a file listing in Nautilus because it has a small arrow pointing upward and to the right, and if you are in List view, the Type column indicates that it is a link to a file. If you right-click the link and open its Properties window, you can see on the Basic tab the field link target to find out which is the original file.

A hard link is more complex and requires some understanding of how files work. In simple terms, all files consist of a pointer and actual data. As you might expect, the pointer tells the file system where on the disk to find the data. Creating a hard link effectively creates an additional pointer to the data that has exactly the same attributes as the original pointer, except with a different name. Performing any operation on the linked file will perform that operation on the original file. Additionally, there will be no obvious sign that the hard link isn't a genuine file, apart from the fact that the *link count*—a property of files—will be greater than 1. This indicates that more than one file *links* to the data. Maybe now you can see why people prefer to use the more obviously detectable symbolic links!

To create a symbolic link, just right-click a file and select the option Make Link. You can move the link wherever you want; it will still point to the correct file.

The new link has odd file permissions. It claims to have Read/Write/Execute permissions for everybody (rwxrwxrwx), but actually, because it's a link, it mirrors the permissions of the file it links to. So if you attempt to access a shortcut that links to a file you don't have permission to access, you'll see the appropriate error message.

Summary

In this chapter you got to know two important elements of the Ubuntu experience, largely derived from its UNIX and Linux predecessors: users and permissions. These are important concepts that lay the foundation of the security implemented in Ubuntu. Through users, people can have their own experiences, configurations, data, and permissions. An important characteristic is that every user account can have its own files and set permissions on them. What files a user can change determines in brief what that user can do with the system.

We discussed the differences between root and standard users, and how to allow temporary access to root's privileges. We showed you the steps to create users and group accounts, and investigated the sometimes puzzling notation for file and folder permissions. Once you've mastered the basics, you should be ready to set permissions on your own.

CHAPTER 22

■ ■ ■

Optimizing Your System

You'll soon find out that Ubuntu offers great performance and relatively few stability problems, especially as compared to some other operating systems. (For instance, Linux file systems generally don't need to be defragmented, unless you have NTFS or FAT32 partitions to take care of). But you can always make it even better. If you still run into any performance issues, or if you simply want to get the most out of your system, this chapter is for you. You don't *have* to apply the topics it discusses; by default Ubuntu already works great without applying any optimizations to it, so you can skip it if you're satisfied with how your system runs. More often than not, the chapter discusses hacks—clever methods of making things work in a nonstandard fashion. But as your experience of Ubuntu might have already taught you, such hacks are the lifeblood of Linux. One of the strengths of Linux is the ability to delve under the hood and change absolutely any aspect of the way it works. So even if the topics in this chapter are not essential, we recommend that you read the chapter carefully and consider applying its tips.

Speeding Up Booting

Since Ubuntu 6.10 (Edgy Eft), Ubuntu has been using a boot routine called Upstart that effectively optimizes itself. Upstart is responsible for starting services and has been greatly enhanced with the release of 10.04. You can learn more about Upstart at http://upstart. ubuntu.com. However, you can still tweak performance by enabling startup scripts to run in parallel instead of one after the other. This works well for multithreaded, multicore processors like Intel's Core 2 Duo and AMD's Athlon 64 X2. It won't make the computer start instantly, but it will save a few seconds each time you boot.

To configure running startup scripts in parallel, you need to edit the /etc/init.d/rc file. You can load this file into the Gedit text editor by typing the following in a terminal window:

```
gksu gedit /etc/init.d/rc
```

Look for the line that begins with CONCURRENCY near the top of the file, as shown in Figure 22-1, and change the value from none to shell. Save the file and reboot the computer. If you see no improvement in boot speed, you can change this value back to CONCURRENCY=none if you want.

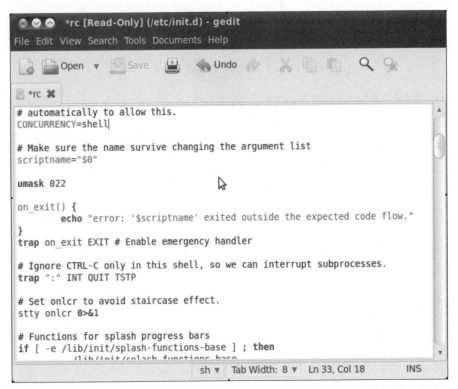

```
# automatically to allow this.
CONCURRENCY=shell

# Make sure the name survive changing the argument list
scriptname="$0"

umask 022

on_exit() {
        echo "error: '$scriptname' exited outside the expected code flow."
}
trap on_exit EXIT # Enable emergency handler

# Ignore CTRL-C only in this shell, so we can interrupt subprocesses.
trap ":" INT QUIT TSTP

# Set onlcr to avoid staircase effect.
stty onlcr 0>&1

# Functions for splash progress bars
if [ -e /lib/init/splash-functions-base ] ; then
        /lib/init/splash-functions-base
```

Figure 22-1. Parallel execution of scripts in the boot process can be enabled by editing the /etc/init.d/rc
file.

Reducing the Boot Menu Delay

Getting rid of the Grub boot menu delay can save some waiting around in the early stages of the boot
process. The delay can be reduced to 1 second or even eradicated completely. Of course, if you do that
you won't be able to choose which kernel you want to load—or which operating system if you're dual-
booting with Windows (but why would you want to?). Even if Ubuntu is the only OS on your computer,
without the boot menu delay, you won't have the chance to boot into recovery mode or a previously
installed Linux kernel from the Grub menu. So you need to consider whether this is a worthwhile time-
saving measure.

   The boot menu delay is stated in the /etc/default/grub file. You can load this into the Gedit text
editor by typing the following in a terminal window:

```
gksu gedit /etc/default/grub
```

   Look for the line that begins with GRUB_TIMEOUT and change the value to whatever you want. The
units are counted in seconds, so a value of 3 equates to 3 seconds. A value of 0 (zero) will mean the boot
menu won't appear at all, which is not recommended, for the reasons just mentioned. Generally
speaking, a delay of 1 second (1) gives you just enough time to press a key at the appropriate time. This
will cancel the countdown, meaning the boot menu will stay on your screen until you select an option.

■ **Note** When you've finished, save the file and quit Gedit.

Managing GNOME Sessions

Under Windows, you might be used to controlling which programs start up at the same time as the Desktop, by adding or deleting entries in the Start menu's Startup program group. When running Ubuntu, you can control which system applets are started automatically, as well as your personal choice of Desktop applications.

To control which programs start up with the GNOME Desktop, use the Startup Applications Preferences dialog box (gnome-session-properties). To run the program, click System ➤ Preferences ➤ Startup Applications.

Clicking the Startup Programs tab shows the programs that start when GNOME does. You can disable a startup program in the list by unchecking the check box beside it. You definitely should have a thorough look at the applications that are started by default, as it is quite likely that you'll find some that are of no use to you at all.

You should see most or all of the following entries, though our test system had some additional elements added by other applications and services.

Bluetooth Manager: This program is responsible for the Bluetooth applet that can be used to send and receive files, browse other Bluetooth devices, set up Bluetooth services, and manage Bluetooth service settings. You can disable this applet if your system is not Bluetooth-enabled or if you just don't want to use Bluetooth at all.

Certificate and Key Storage: When using secured tools on a local network or the Internet, you'll often receive a certificate that is used to prove the identity of the remote host. You'll receive encryption keys as well. This applet allows you to store all those items in a secure place. So you had better leave it on.

Check for New Hardware Drivers: This tool scans your hardware devices and checks whether new third-party proprietary drivers can be used with them. If a new driver is compatible, this tool provides a facility to download, install, and configure the driver in your computer. If your hardware devices are working perfectly without third-party drivers, or you're uncomfortable using proprietary software, it is safe to disable this program. Otherwise, keep the tool enabled so you can receive driver bug fixes and updates.

Disk Notifications: Your hard disk by default is monitored by the SMART utility. If the current disk state is degrading, SMART will tell you about it. So it makes sense to leave the Disk Notifications option on to make sure that you are updated as soon as something goes wrong on your hard drive. And if you want to switch this option off, use System ➤ Administration ➤ Disk Utility on a regular basis to monitor the current state of your hard disks.

Evolution Alarm Notifier: As its name suggests, this utility ties into Evolution's calendar function in order to notify you of events, such as an appointment that you don't want to forget. If you don't use Evolution or don't use its calendar function, this applet can be disabled.

GNOME Login Sound: As you might have guessed, this plays the Ubuntu welcome music that you hear whenever the GNOME Desktop appears. It can be disabled without causing any problems.

Network Manager: This applet manages your wi-fi, Ethernet, and VPN connections. This is useful for laptop users who connect to several wi-fi networks on the go, as discussed in Chapter 8. You should not disable this program.

NVidia X Server Setting: This program helps you to configure settings for an Nvidia graphics card. As you would have guessed, this program can only be used for Nvidia graphics cards. If you leave it on, you can use this program to change graphics display settings in a convenient way. This is in particular useful if you have to change graphics display settings often—for example, if you regularly use your computer with an external projector.

Personal File Sharing: This application allows users to enable file sharing with other users. This is a convenient program that makes it easy to work together with other users, but at the same time it's also a potential security risk. For that reason, you might want to switch this program off unless you really need it.

Power Manager: This program controls all aspects of GNOME's power management, including the useful hibernate feature that can save the contents of the system's RAM to provide quicker startup. If your computer is a notebook, this tool should be considered essential. If you have a desktop PC and are looking to save power by using hibernate, suspend, or screen blanking after a period of inactivity, you won't want to disable Power Manager. Disabling it will remove the Suspend and Hibernate options from the System ➤ Quit dialog box. So better not switch it off.

Print Queue Applet: This applet provides an interface for you to cancel or repeat printer jobs. It is also responsible for automatically setting up a printer for use when you plug in a printer. You can disable this applet if you will never print from your computer.

Remote Desktop: This background service allows other computers to connect to your computer, after an invitation has been issued (see Chapter 33). If you have no intention of remotely accessing your computer, this service can be disabled.

Secret Storage Service: This is a background component necessary for the application that generates and stores encryption keys. If you do not encrypt files and/or e-mails, this service can be disabled.

Ubuntu One: This item gives access to Ubuntu One, the Ubuntu cloud solution offered by Canonical. Switch it on if you intend to use this service.

Update Notifier: This is the Update Manager tool. You shouldn't disable this applet, because it performs the essential task of checking whether any system updates are available. It runs in the background after it is started and hardly impacts startup time at all. However, if you absolutely must prune valuable milliseconds from startup, you can disable it. You can then check for updates manually, whenever you desire, by clicking System ➤ Administration ➤ Update Manager.

User Folders Update: This tool pops up during the start of your session if you have recently changed the default language (System ➤ Administration ➤ Language Support) of your computer. The tool gives you an option to translate the folder names Desktop, Templates, Public, Documents, Music, Pictures, and Videos in your /home directory to the new default language. You can disable this tool if you don't change your language settings.

Visual Assistance: This utility runs assistive technologies such as the Orca screen reader, magnifier, and Braille application if these tools were enabled in the Assistive Technologies Preferences window (System ➤ Preferences ➤ Assistive Technologies). If you are not using assistive technologies, you can disable this applet.

The Options tab contains a single item labeled Automatically Remember Running Applications When Logging Out, and this is designed to get you back exactly where you started next time you launch the computer. The system has been problematic in previous versions of Ubuntu, but the developers appear to have sorted things out. The exception is Wine-based Windows applications. These didn't seem to automatically start on our test system, but everything else, including KDE applications, worked fine.

■ **Tip** The Startup Programs tab of the Startup Applications Preferences dialog box contains an Add button, which lets you add any program you like to the GNOME startup. You could add Evolution, for example, so that it starts automatically whenever you log in. But it's easier to add currently running applications by using the option on the Options tab.

STOP WAITING FOR AN ADDRESS

If you use an Ethernet or wi-fi connection to access your network, you might find that Ubuntu spends a few seconds during each boot acquiring an Internet address. This is characterized by a long pause while nothing seems to be happening. Therefore, one way to provide an instant speed boost is to give your computer a static IP address. Chapter 8 explains how to configure your network interface.

However, to assign a static address, you'll need to find out what IP address range your router (or other DHCP server) uses. You can discover this by looking at the router's configuration software. Sometimes this is accessed via a web browser. Look for the section of the web interface called DHCP Configuration or something similar.

■ **Note** Before you start assigning a static IP address, bear in mind that static IP addresses are cool if you don't connect to other networks frequently. If you do want to switch easily between networks, don't apply this tip.

Normally, IPv4 local area network addresses are in the 192.168.*x.x* range, where *x.x* can be any series of numbers from 0.0 to 255.255. For instance, you may find that your router uses the 192.168.1.2-255 range. In this case, assigning a static IP address that will work with the router is simply a matter of choosing an IP address in this range. However, this router may hand out addresses sequentially from 2 upward, so it's best to choose an address it's unlikely to reach, even if you happen to have many computers connected to the network. Starting at 50 is a good idea, so you could assign the address 192.168.1.50.

Don't forget that when defining static IP addresses, you need to manually supply the gateway, subnet, and DNS addresses. In the example, the gateway would be 192.168.1.1 (the address of the LAN interface on the router), and the subnet would be 255.255.255.0. The DNS address on a small home network will probably be the same as the gateway address, because the router will usually be set to forward DNS requests by default. This isn't always the case, though, so be sure to check.

BUILD YOUR OWN READAHEAD PROFILE

Ubuntu includes a feature called *readahead*, which is able to order the list of files to be loaded during bootup by their locations on the hard disk. A default readahead list is installed on a standard Ubuntu installation. This is created on a generic PC, but you can build your own version of the list, customized for your own computer.

Here are the steps to create your own readahead list:

1. Reboot Ubuntu, and at the boot menu, highlight the Ubuntu entry and press E. If Ubuntu is the only operating system on your computer (that is, your computer doesn't dual-boot with Windows), you might need to press Shift to see the boot menu when prompted.

2. Highlight the line, beginning with the word `linux` and press E again.

3. Using the right-arrow key, move the cursor to the end of the line. Insert a space and type **profile**. The following is how the entire line read on our test PC; yours may be slightly different (note that the beginning of the line was cropped off because of the resolution of the screen):

   ```
   < quiet splash profile
   ```

4. Press Control-X to boot the computer. This boot will take longer than usual, because the boot profile is being rebuilt. When the computer has booted up, and all disk activity has stopped (which might take a minute or two after the Desktop has appeared), reboot your computer. You should find that bootup is faster.

Prelinking

A lot of Ubuntu software relies on other pieces of code to work. These are sometimes referred to as *libraries*, which is a good indicator of their purpose: to provide functions that programs can check in and out whenever they need them, as if they were borrowing books from a library.

Whenever a program starts, it must look for these other libraries and load them into memory so they're ready for use. This can take some time, particularly with larger and more-complicated programs. Because of this, the concept of *prelinking* was invented. By a series of complicated tricks, the `prelink` program makes each bit of software you might run aware of the libraries it needs, so that memory can be better allocated.

Prelinking claims to boost program startup times by up to 50 percent or more, but the problem is that it's a *hack*—a programming trick designed to make your system work in a nonstandard way. Because of this, some programs are incompatible with prelinking. In fact, some might simply refuse to work unless prelinking is deactivated. At the time of this writing, such programs are in the minority. However, keep in mind that prelinking can be easily reversed if necessary. Alternatively, you might want to weigh whether it's worth setting up prelinking in the first place.

Configuring Prelinking

If you decide to go ahead with prelinking, you'll need to download the relevant software from the Ubuntu software repositories. Open the Ubuntu Software Center and type **prelink** into the search box. Click Install.

Before you can run a prelinking sweep of your system, you need to enable it in one of its configuration files. To do this, type the following in a terminal window:

```
gksu gedit /etc/default/prelink
```

Change the line that reads PRELINKING=unknown to PRELINKING=yes. Then save the file and quit Gedit. To run a prelinking scan of your system, simply issue this command:

```
sudo prelink -a
```

This will prelink practically all the binary files on your system and may take some time to complete. You may also see some error output, but you don't need to pay attention to it.

Prelinking was automatically added as a daily cron job when you installed it, so any new programs you add will be automatically prelinked.

Deactivating Prelinking

If you find that prelinking makes a particular application malfunction or simply stop working, you can try undoing prelinking. To do this, find out where the main binary for the program resides and issue the prelink command with the --undo command option. For example, to remove prelinking from the Gedit text editor program, you could type the following:

```
whereis gedit
```

This command will show that the gedit binary is found at the location /usr/bin/gedit in the file system. Next, attempt to undo prelinking on the binary:

```
sudo prelink --undo /usr/bin/gedit
```

However, this may not work, because some programs might rely on additional binaries on the system. Therefore, the solution might be to undo prelinking for the entire system, which you can do by typing the following:

```
sudo prelink -ua
```

After this, you should remove the prelink package, via the Ubuntu Software Center, to stop it from running again in the future (or manually remove its cron entry).

■ **Caution** Prelinking is dangerous, as services and programs may stop working if you use it. If it works, your computer will be faster. But be prepared to do some additional manual work to undo prelinking for some of the programs on your computer.

OPTIMIZING THE KERNEL

You can download the Linux kernel source code and compile your own version of it. This gives you total control over the kernel configuration, so you can leave out parts you don't want in order to free memory. On current kernels however, you won't often need to compile your own kernel. The Linux kernel is modular; so it just won't load components that are not going to be needed. But still, you can compile your kernel to leave out certain components completely.

By recompiling, you can also set certain optimization settings, such as creating a version of the kernel specifically built for your model of CPU. On the other hand, the mere fact of recompiling your kernel allows you to learn a lot about the way it works. So even if it's not really useful for better performance, it may give you a better understanding of the way Linux works.

Although compiling a kernel is a simple procedure, you'll need to answer many complex questions and have an in-depth knowledge of the way Linux works. You could also have a model of a working kernel to crib from, which is a great way to avoid some growing pains while teasing out optimal kernel compilation settings.

In addition, compiling your own kernel brings with it several issues. The first is that it may not work with any binary modules that you have installed, such as graphics cards or wireless drivers. You can opt to update these yourself, but this adds to the complexity.

The second problem is that Ubuntu is built around precompiled kernels. Several software packages expect to work with the precompiled kernel, and in addition, Ubuntu may occasionally download an updated prepackaged kernel automatically as part of the system update feature and override the one you've created. If there are any security problems with the kernel version you compiled, you'll need to recompile a new kernel from scratch (or patch the one you have). This means you'll have to keep an eye on the security news sites and take action when necessary.

Your customized kernel may also fail to automatically detect newly supported hardware, meaning you'll have to acquire and load the drivers manually.

That said, compiling a kernel is an excellent way of learning how Linux works, and if it all goes well, the sense of achievement is enormous.

Some people choose to download the kernel source code from the official Linux kernel site, `www.kernel.org`. However, it makes more sense to download the official Ubuntu release, because this will be tailored for the way your system works. Using the Synaptic Package Manager, simply search for `linux-source`.

You can find several guides to compiling your own kernel online, but we recommend the following posting on the Ubuntu forums web site, which looks at compiling a kernel under Ubuntu: `https://help.ubuntu.com/community/Kernel/Compile`.

Optimizing the Kernel

Whereas precompiling the kernel is not really the way to make your system faster, optimization of the kernel does help. In the file system of your computer, you'll find lots of files in the /proc/sys and the /sys directories. The /proc/sys directory relates to kernel settings, while the /sys directory is more to do with the devices you are using. Optimizing an Ubuntu system by tuning these files is specialist work, but let's just give you one example, which is about the scheduler.

The scheduler is the kernel component that handles I/O requests. Basically, the scheduler can do only one thing at a time: it can read data blocks, or it can write them. As an administrator, you can specify what it should do. The scheduler setting is applied to each device that is installed in your computer. For your hard disk, which in most cases uses the name /dev/sda, you can find the setting in the file /sys/block/sda/queue/scheduler. To display the current contents of this file, use the command cat /sys/block/sda/queue/scheduler:

```
root@texas:/sys/block/sda/queue# cat scheduler

noop anticipatory deadline [cfq]
```

As you can see, in the file you can use four different values:

- noop: The scheduler doesn't do anything with I/O but gives it directly to the I/O controller. This is a useful setting if your computer uses a fast RAID controller.

- anticipatory: If the scheduler gets a request to read a block, it will read ahead the next couple of blocks. This optimizes your computer to do fast reads.

- deadline: The scheduler will wait as long as it can to write data to disk. By doing this, it can write the data as efficient as possible, which will make writes on your computer faster.

- cfq (complete fair queueing): This value does nothing to optimize I/O on the scheduler, which gives an equal share to read and write requests.

By default, the scheduler is set to cfq, which makes sense for desktop systems. If however you are reading data most of the time, your computer's performance will benefit from selecting the anticipatory setting. On the other hand, a computer that writes more than that it reads (which is typically not the case for a desktop computer) will benefit from setting the deadline option.

To change the setting from the command line you need to echo the new value into the configuration file. To do this, using root permissions, use for example echo anticipatory > /sys/block/sda/queue/scheduler. This immediately applies the new value:

```
root@texas:/sys/block/sda/queue# echo anticipatory > scheduler
```

After doing this, start some intensive read activity on your computer (like watching a movie file that is installed on your hard disk). You might see some improvement.

Freeing Up Disk Space

After using Ubuntu for some time, you might find that the disk begins to fill up. You can keep an eye on disk usage by clicking System ➤ Administration ➤ System Monitor and looking under the File Systems tab or using the following command in a terminal window:

```
df -h
```

Either method will show the free space in terms of megabytes or gigabytes for each partition, also expressed as a percentage figure. If the disk does start to get full, you can take steps to make more space available.

Emptying the /tmp Folder

An easy way to regain disk space is to empty the /tmp folder. Like its counterpart in the Windows operating system, this is the folder in which temporary data is stored. Some applications clean up after themselves, but others don't, leaving behind many megabytes of detritus. To check if this is the case on your computer, you can use the du -hs command from a terminal, which gives a summary of used disk space in this folder.

Because the /tmp folder is accessed practically every second the system is up and running, to empty it safely, it's necessary to switch to run level 1. This ensures that few other programs are running and avoids the risk of deleting data that is in use. Before doing this, make sure you've closed all programs that you are working in, because switching the run level will close all active programs! First, switch to the text console by pressing Ctrl+Alt+F1. Then enter these commands to switch to run level 1:

```
sudo killall gdm
sudo telinit 1
```

A recovery menu will appear. Select the Drop to Root Shell Prompt option. Then enter the following to empty the /tmp folder and reboot:

```
rm -rf /tmp/*
reboot
```

■ **Tip** On a similar theme, don't forget to empty the Trash. This can hold many megabytes of old data. If you see an error message about permissions when emptying the Trash, you can do so manually from a terminal window. Simply type **sudo rm -rf ~/..local/share/Trash/{files,info}/** to get the job done.

Emptying the Cache of Package Files

You might also choose to clear out the Advanced Packaging Tool (APT) cache of old .deb package files. On a system that has been very frequently updated, this can free many megabytes (possibly gigabytes) of space.

You can empty the cache by typing the following command in a terminal window:

```
sudo apt-get clean
```

Note The files concerned are held in the following directory: `/var/cache/apt/archives/`. Alternatively, you can use the `apt-get autoclean` command; this simply removes any package files that are no longer available on the main repository server (that is, those that are out-of-date) but leaves any that you might need in the future. Using this command is considered a much safer way to remove unwanted package files.

If you want to restore any packages later, simply locate them in the Synaptic Package Manager list, click the check box, and click Mark for Reinstallation. This will cause the package to be downloaded, installed, and configured.

Removing Unused Software

If you still need disk space, consider uninstalling unused programs. As you've learned, you can manage software through the Ubuntu Software Center.

To remove a package, search for it in the Installed Software section and click the Remove button. However, it's not a good idea to simply scroll down the list and remove anything that seems dispensable.

As always, removing software can create dependency problems, so you might find yourself limited in what software you can actually remove.

It's also worth periodically issuing the `sudo apt-get autoremove` command, which will remove any unused dependency packages on the system. Theoretically, these will always be removed provided `apt-get autoremove` is used when specifying packages to uninstall, but the way Ubuntu is updated might mean that a handful of unused dependencies hang around after they're no longer needed.

If you find you're adding and removing lots of software, you might find an application such as BleachBit (`http://bleachbit.sourceforge.net/`) quite useful. This can remove clutter that takes up space and could contain private information that would be best cleared away. You can download BleachBit through the Synaptic Package Manager, and it will appear under the Applications ➤ System Tools menu. You can run the software either as a normal user (which makes it harder to mess things up), or as root. To use it, simply scroll down the list and select the parts you'd like to remove (for instance, the cookies from Firefox), and then click the Delete button. Clicking the Preview button will give you a good idea of what is going to be removed and the amount of space it's likely to save.

Summary

In this chapter, you looked at streamlining your installation of Ubuntu. This involves speeding up the boot procedure by running boot scripts in parallel, and decreasing the boot menu delay, along with a handful of other tricks. You also looked at optimizing your hard disk settings to allow for greater speed when loading and saving files.

Additionally, we discussed prelinking programs so that they load faster, recompiling the kernel so that it's optimized for your system, and freeing disk space by various means.

In the next chapter, you learn how to perform backups to safeguard your data.

■ ■ ■

## CHAPTER 23

Backing Up Data

Every computer user knows that backing up data is vital. This is usually because every computer user has lost data at some point, perhaps because of a corrupted file or an accidental deletion.

Some of the people behind UNIX were highly aware of such occurrences, and built in several advanced and useful backup tools. These have been mirrored within Linux, with the result that creating and maintaining backups is easy.

In this chapter, you first look at what data should be backed up and then explore two ways to make backups: via the Simple Backup utility and the command line.

What Data Should You Back Up?

Data on your system can be classified into three broad types: program data, configuration data, and personal data. It's traditionally reasoned that backing up all types of data is inefficient, because it would mean backing up many gigabytes of information regularly. Because of this, you usually want to back up the latter two types of data: configuration and personal. The theory is that if your PC is hit by a hard-disk-wrecking disaster, you can easily reinstall the OS from the CD or DVD. Restoring your system from backup is then simply a matter of ensuring that the configuration files are back in place, so your applications work as you would like them to, and your personal data is once again made accessible.

Practically all the personal configuration data for programs you use every day, as well as your personal data, is stored in your /home directory (although the configuration files for software used systemwide are usually stored in the /etc directory).You might also want to consider locating your /home directory in a separate partition, for additional security.

If you take a look in your /home directory, you might think that the previous sentence is incorrect. On a freshly installed system, the directory appears largely empty, apart from a handful of directories for music, photos, and so on. However, most, if not all, of the configuration files are hidden; their directory and filenames are preceded with a period (.), which means that Linux doesn't display them in a standard directory listing.

To view hidden files and folders in the Nautilus file manager, choose View ➤ Show Hidden Files. This can be quite an eye-opener when you see the masses of data you didn't even realize were there, as shown in the example in Figure 23-1.

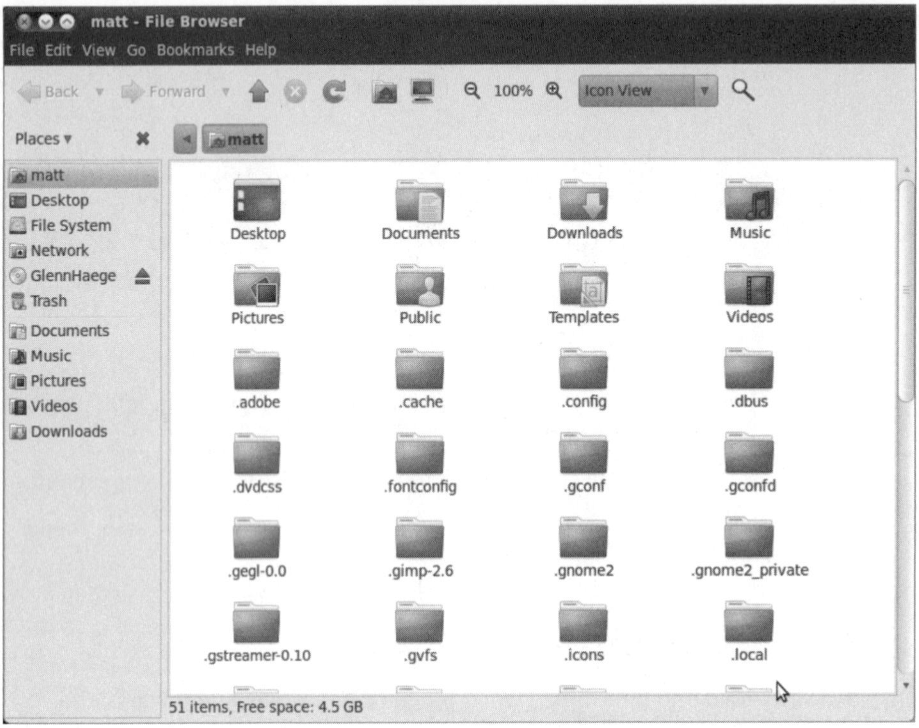

Figure 23-1. Most of the configuration files for programs are hidden—literally—in your /home directory.

The configuration files held in your /home directory relate solely to your user account. Any other users will have their own configuration files, entirely independent of yours. In this way, all users can have their own configuration settings for various applications, which can be backed up independently.

Under Ubuntu, you can back up both configuration data and personal files by using Simple Backup, which can be downloaded from the Ubuntu software repositories.

Keep in mind that there's little point in making backups if you leave the resultant archive files on your hard disk. For full backup protection, the archives should be stored elsewhere, such as on an external hard disk, network mount, or CD/DVD-ROM. Consider using GNOME's CD/DVD Creator (click Applications ➤ Accessories ➤ CD/DVD Creator on the Main Menu).

Using Simple Backup

Simple Backup is a series of programs that enable quick and easy backup and restoration of personal data, as well as system configuration files. Its output, which takes the form of backup directories containing an archive of the files, plus configuration data, can be written to your hard disk (or a network mount attached to it), or to a remote Internet location, such as an FTP server.

Simple Backup was created courtesy of the Google Summer of Code sponsorship scheme and was designed with the help of Ubuntu developers. To install Simple Backup, open the Ubuntu Software Center (Applications ➤ Ubuntu Software Center) and then search for sbackup. Click the entry Simple Backup Config in the list of results and click Install. You'll then find entries for Simple Backup Config and Simple Backup Restore on the System ➤ Administration menu.

Backing Up Data via Simple Backup

To configure a backup, choose System ➤ Administration ➤ Simple Backup Config. You'll see the Backup Properties dialog box, as shown in Figure 23-2. Using this dialog box, you can choose the files that Simple Backup backs up, as well as when it does so. After you've made your changes, click the Save button. Do this before making a backup. If scheduled backups are set, it's sufficient to save the changes and quit the program. The backup jobs will take place automatically, in the background, at the set times.

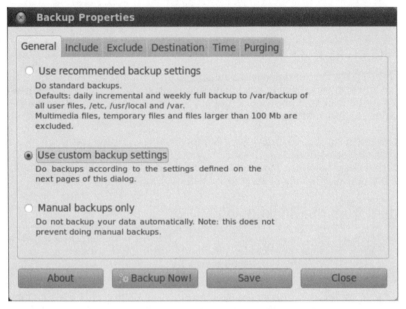

Figure 23-2. Simple Backup can work automatically or with custom settings you specify.

As listed on the General tab of the Backup Properties dialog box, Simple Backup can operate in three modes:

Use recommended backup settings: This is by far the best choice for fuss-free operation. Simple Backup will perform a daily backup of your /home directory, as well as the vital system data held in /etc, /usr/local, and /var. However, it will deliberately exclude any multimedia files (because of their large size), along with any temporary files and files of any type that exceed 100MB (again for size reasons). By default, the backup directory created is placed in /var/backup.

Use Custom Backup Settings: This is effectively the same as the recommended backup, and includes the same list of file inclusions and exceptions, but you can edit the settings manually. For example, you might choose to include MP3 files, rather than excluding them. The custom backup option lets you alter where the eventual backup directory is saved and the time when the backup is made.

Manual Backups Only: This effectively deactivates Simple Backup, so that it no longer periodically backs up files. However, you can still click the Backup Now! button to manually perform a backup according to the settings on the other tabs of the Backup Properties dialog box.

> ■ **Note** Simple Backup doesn't create a new backup each time it runs, because that would take too long. The first time it runs, a full backup is taken, but those created afterward are *incremental backups*, and only files that are new or that have changed are backed up. The backup directory created during the first run is given the file extension `.ful`, while the backup directories created after this have the extension `.inc`. As you might expect, if the original `.ful` backup directory can't be found, a new full backup will be created.

Including Files and Folders in the Backup Job

Assuming that you've chosen a custom backup, and therefore are able to alter the backup settings, clicking the Include tab in the Backup Properties dialog box enables you to specifically define directories and files that you want to include in the backup. Simply click the Add File or Add Directory button and then browse to the relevant location (to add a directory, you need to click to open it before clicking the Open button).

Bear in mind that adding a directory does so recursively, which means that any directories contained within that directory are also backed up. For this reason, you don't need to specifically add your /home/<username> directory, because the entire /home directory is included in the backup by default. This means the backup will also include all other users' directories within /home too.

Excluding Files and Folders from the Backup Job

You have a wide range of choices when it comes to excluding files and folders from the list. Directories can be excluded based on their location. Files can be excluded based on location, type, or size.

Clicking the Exclude tab in the Backup Properties dialog box reveals a set of side tabs on the left side of the program window which enable you to exclude items from the backup as follows:

Paths: To exclude a specific file or folder, click this side tab. As with including files, click the Add File or Add Directory button and then browse to the relevant location.

File Types: To exclude certain types of files, click this side tab, as shown in Figure 23-3. After clicking the Add button, you'll see that you can choose from a brief list of standard file types or filter by file extension (such as `.mp3` for MP3 files or `.zip` for compressed Zip files). If you want to back up your multimedia files, remove the corresponding file type entries from this list.

Regex: If you're competent at using regular expressions, you can use them to specify extremely precise rules by clicking this side tab.

Max Size: Any files larger than the stated size on this tab aren't backed up. By removing the check next to the Do Not Backup line, you can deactivate this feature (although that could lead to massive backup files, which would take a long time to generate).

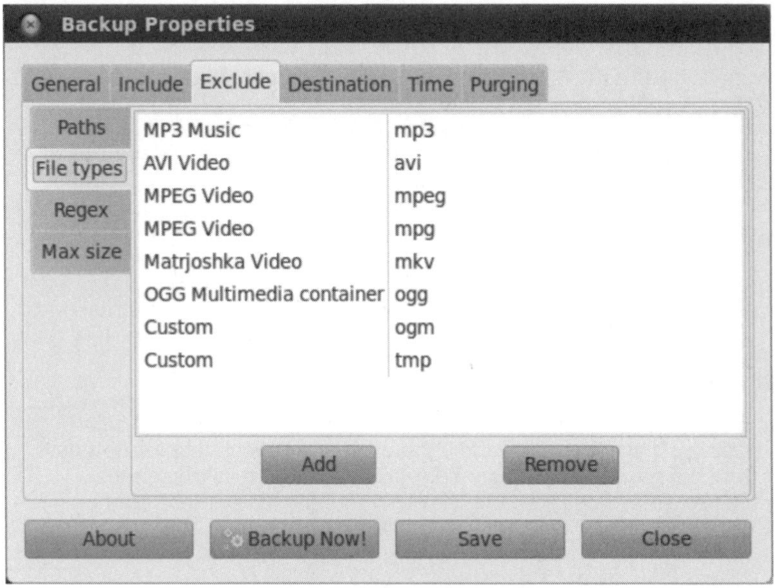

Figure 23-3. Excluding certain types of large files leads to far smaller backup files.

Changing the Backup Directory Destination

By default, the backup directory created by Simple Backup is stored in the /var/backup directory. By clicking the Destination tab in the Backup Properties dialog box, you can choose to save it in a different location on your hard disk. Of course, if you have a network mount, you can also opt to save it there. In most cases, we advise that you use /var/backup to store the newly created backup files, and copy the files to their permanent destinations later. You might even choose to do this periodically and automatically. By following the instructions in Chapter 24, which explain how to schedule tasks, you could set up a cron job to automatically copy the files to a network mount or removable storage device.

■ **Note** Remember that Simple Backup creates incremental backups, so you should copy *all* the backup directories and files within /var/backup to the external storage device, rather than just the latest one.

You can even transfer the backup directory across the Internet via SSH file transfer or the less secure FTP standard. To do so, simply enter the protocol, username, password, and URL in the following format:

```
sftp://username:password@mysite.com/remotedirectory
```

It's important to precede the address with the protocol you intend to use: sftp:// for SSH or ftp:// for FTP.

Changing the Time Period Between Backups

Clicking the Time tab in the Backup Properties dialog box lets you set the frequency of the backup. You can opt to back up hourly, daily, weekly, or monthly. You can also set the exact time of the backup if necessary. For example, you could set a backup to take place every week on a Tuesday at 12.30 p.m. Simply select the interval period from the Do Backups drop-down list and then select from the Day of Month, Day of Week, Hour, and Minute lists, as necessary. Simple Backup uses the system scheduler, cron (discussed in more detail in Chapter 24). The use of cron means that Simple Backup doesn't need to be running all the time for the backup to take place. Simple Backup is started and stopped automatically in the background as needed.

You can also elect to perform a full backup after a certain number of days have passed (up to 1,000). A full backup means that Simple Backup creates a new complete backup, rather than incremental ones.

Purging Old Backup Files

By clicking the Purging tab in the Backup Properties dialog box, you can opt to automatically delete old backup directories. This saves on storage space. Purging can be done either by specifying a cutoff date, so that any backup archive older than the specified number of days is deleted, or it can be done logarithmically. This means that the program keeps just one backup out of the many that might be created in a week, month, and so on. All others are deleted. For obvious reasons, you should use the purging option with care!

Restoring Data via Simple Backup

If the worst happens, and you need to restore any number of files from the backup, you can click System ➤ Administration ➤ Simple Backup Restore.

The first step is to select the location of the backup directories. If the backups aren't contained in /var/backup, click "Use custom" and either type the path into the field or click the file browser button and locate the backup directories and click Apply. Then click the Available Backups drop-down list to choose a backup directory from which to restore. The directory names contain the dates and times the backups were made, and it makes sense to choose the latest (unless you want to revert to an older version).

After the backup has been selected, the files that the backup archive contains are displayed. Each directory has a small triangle to its left, which you can click to expand the directory and show its contents.

After you've found the file(s) or directories you want to restore, highlight them and click the Restore button. But beware, because this will rewrite the files and directories to their original locations—files or directories already there with matching filenames will be overwritten!

If you want to restore the files to a different location, click the Restore As button and then choose a folder. Simple Backup stores its information in a standard .tar.gz file within the selected directory when you back up. This means it's possible, if necessary, to manually access the information in the backup.

■ **Caution** Restored files and directories are owned by root. This is because Simple Backup runs with superuser powers. Therefore, one of the first things you have to do is to change the ownership and group of the file to what they were originally. See Chapter 21 for more details about file ownership and how to change it.

Creating and Compressing Archives

Although Simple Backup allows the uninitiated to make quick and regular backups, there are many other ways to package a folder and store it as a single file. Linux users often create archives in the form of `.tar` files. *tar* stands for Tape ARchive and refers to backing up data to a magnetic tape backup drive. Originally designed for backing up files with UNIX operating systems, it has also become a standard method of transferring files across the Internet, particularly with regard to source files or other installation programs.

■ **Note** Linux comes with a couple more backup commands, which you might choose to use. They are `cpio` and `pax`. Both aim to improve on `tar` in various ways, but neither is broadly supported at the moment. `cpio` is installed by default under Ubuntu, and `pax` can be found via the Ubuntu Software Center. Examine their `man` pages for more details.

Creating Archives with Nautilus

An archive is a file that can act as a container for other files. The most common type of archive in Linux is the `.tar` file, but there are many others. Usually you'll use archive files to pack together the contents of a folder, for example, your `/home` directory. Although you can archive a single file, it's not very useful! Some of the archive types even compress the information so it consumes less space in your disk or is downloaded faster when posted to a web site.

To create an archive file, open Nautilus and browse to the parent of the folder you wish to archive. Right-click the folder and select the option Compress... The Compress dialog box will open.

You can set the name of the destination file and select the type. You have a few options to choose from, each with its specific functionality. Table 23-1 briefly describes each of those options. Some archive types allow you to password-protect its contents so you can add a layer of security to the information. Only users provided with the password will be able to access your files. Additionally, you can select the location in which the new archive file will be created. By default it is in the same path as the folder you are archiving.

Table 23-1. Types of Files to Create with the Compress Dialog Box

File Extension	Compressed?	Password-Protected?	Description
`.ar`	No	No	AIX small indexed archive
`.cbz`	Yes	Yes	ZIP Archived Comic Book
`.jar`	No	No	Java archive
`.tar`	No	No	Uncompressed `tar` archive
`.tar.bz2`	Yes	No	`tar` archive compressed with `bzip2`, higher compression ratio than `gzip`

File Extension	Compressed?	Password-Protected?	Description
`.tar.gz`	Yes	No	tar archive compressed with `gzip`, faster operation than `bzip2`
`.tar.lzma`	Yes	No	tar archive compressed with the LZMA algorithm
`.zip`	Yes	Yes	WinZip archive

When you create an archive from a folder, the operation is automatically recursive, so it adds all subdirectories to the same archive.

Folders and files added to the archive have the initial forward slash removed from their paths. So, rather than store a file in the archive as this:

```
/home/keir/Mail/file1
```

the file will be stored as follows:

```
home/keir/Mail/file1
```

The difference between the two forms concerns us when the files are extracted from the archive. If the files had the initial slash, to the particular file would be restored to `/home/keir/Mail/file1`. If there were already a file of that name in that location, it would be overwritten. With the leading slash removed, a new directory is created wherever you choose to restore the archive. In this example, it creates a new directory called `home`, and then a directory called `keir` within that, and so on.

Managing Archive Files

Once you have created an archive file, you can manage its contents just using the File Roller, an archive manager for GNOME that is preinstalled with Ubuntu.

Viewing the Contents of an Archive File

To open an archive with the File Roller, browse to its location in the disk within Nautilus and right-click the archive. Select Open with Archive Manager from the context menu.

The File Roller opens, displaying the content of the archive file. You have several options to get more information about the file or change the way its content is displayed, for example as follows:

- Click File and select Test Integrity to check whether or not the archive is corrupted.

- Click File and select Properties to view information about the archive, such as location, the date in which it was modified, the size and compression ratio, and so on.

- Click View and select whether you want to see all files as if they were in the same folder (View All Files, Ctrl+1), or if you want to respect the folder structure in which the files are stored (View as a Folder, Ctrl+2).

- Click View and select Folders (or press F9) to split the navigation pane and display the folder hierarchy to the left for easier browsing of big and complex archives.

■ **Tip** A popular compressed archive file type is `rar` files. You usually manage them with WinRar in Windows. To add support for `rar` files to the File Roller, install the package `unrar` using the Ubuntu Software Center. Another package, `rar`, lets you archive and compress in additional formats using Nautilus (`.bz2`, `.cbr`, `.lzma`, `.rar`).

Extracting Folders and Files

You can extract one or more folders or files from an archive, or even its whole contents, to the folder you choose. Just select the folder/s and/or file/s you need and click the Extract button. The Extract dialog box is displayed. Here you can select the destination folder in which you will extract your files. You can also specify whether you will be extracting all the files contained in the archive, or only specific files within it. Under Actions, you have some options for changing the behavior of the extract operation:

Re-create folders: When selected, the whole folder structure will be recreated in the destination directory. Files within subfolders will be placed into the corresponding directory. If this option is left unchecked, all files will be extracted to the root of the folder you specify as a destination.

Overwrite existing files: When selected, files stored in the destination folder which have the same name as a file being extracted will be deleted. If it is unchecked, files with conflicting names will not be extracted.

Do not extract older files: This option is used in conjunction with "Overwrite existing files" and works only if that option is selected as well. When selected, if there is a conflict between an existing file and one being extracted, only the file with the most recent modification date will be saved.

Saving the File to a CD-R/RW or to a DVD-R

After the `.tar` file has been created, the problem of where to store it arises. As we mentioned earlier, storing backup data on the same hard disk as the data it was created to back up is useless, because any problem that might affect the hard disk might also affect the archive. You could end up losing both sets of data!

If the archive is less than 700MB, it should be possible to store it on a CD-R or CD-RW. If the backup file is larger than 700MB, you might want to burn the backup file to DVD, using a DVD-R/RW drive.

■ **Note** Remember that Ubuntu has a very capable CD/DVD burning tool called Brasero. To access it, click Applications ➤ Sound & Video ➤ Brasero. Note that although it's listed as a multimedia application, it is in fact capable of burning all types of data discs. To get started, just click the Data Project button. Then simply drag the backup file(s) onto the program window and click the Burn button at the bottom right.

You can access a special folder named CD/DVD Creator by using a launcher located in Applications ➤ Accessories in the Main Menu. This opens Nautilus. A banner is shown in which you are instructed to copy the files you want to burn to a CD. When you are finished doing so, you can click on the Write to Disk button to start the write operation.

Of course, you need to insert a valid CD or DVD into the optical drive of your computer and make sure it can write such disks. If Ubuntu detects that there is no valid and writable disc in the optical drive, it will give you the option to store your content in the form of a disc image with the extension `.iso`. That format is widely used and broadly recognized by most operating systems.

In any case, you should eject your disc and insert it again in order to be able to read it.

Summary

In this chapter, you looked at making backups. First, you saw where in the Linux file system your personal files and other vital data are stored. Then you looked at how the Simple Backup tool can be used to back up system configuration and personal data. You next learned how to create and manage archives to back up any kind of data. Finally, you learned how to burn CDs and DVDs of your backup files from within Nautilus.

In the next chapter, we look at how tasks can be scheduled to occur at various times under Ubuntu.

## CHAPTER 24

Scheduling Tasks

In this book, you've learned about various tasks you can perform to keep Ubuntu running smoothly. Although some of these tasks require human intervention, many—such as backing up your important files or clearing the clutter from the tmp folder to ensure that you always have enough free disk space—can be automated relatively easily by using the methods in this chapter. This will give you more time to do other stuff and will also ensure that those vital tasks are carried out regularly and without fail. They can be run either periodically or as one-time tasks.

Scheduling with GNOME Scheduler

Under Linux, the traditional way of scheduling tasks, such as creating an archived file of a particular folder, is via the cron daemon. This works on behalf of the user to automate individual jobs and is also used by the system to run its own maintenance tasks. The cron command is useful for scheduling heavy loads at a time when you know the system will be underused.

For cron to run system tasks, it reads a file called /etc/crontab. Traditionally, cron starts soon after bootup and sits in the background while you work, checking every minute to see whether a task is due. As soon as one comes up, cron commences the task and then returns to a waiting status.

Users have their own crontab file, which is stored by username in the /var/spool/cron/crontabs/ directory. This directory is owned by root, and normal users can't view each other's crontab. The user's crontab file is updated in a text editor, but you need either a special command or a program to help you do it. This is when GNOME Scheduler comes to help.

GNOME Scheduler is a graphical interface that allows you to edit the crontab file, either for the root user (if you have enough privileges) or for yourself.

It is not installed by default, so you'll have to use the knowledge acquired in Chapter 20 about installing software and grab the program named Scheduled Tasks. You can search for that name in Ubuntu Software Center and click install when the program is listed.

Once installed, you'll find it at Applications ➤ System Tools ➤ Scheduled tasks. By default, it will run under your user account and allow you to schedule your own personal tasks. If you want to schedule tasks for the root user, you should run it with elevated privileges. Okay, it's not obvious how to do that. An easy way is by following these instructions:

1. Go to Applications ➤ System Tools and right-click "Scheduled tasks."

2. Select the option "Add this launcher to desktop."

3. Go to your Desktop and right-click on the new Scheduled tasks icon.

4. Select Properties.

5. The "Scheduled tasks Properties" dialog box will open. Edit the Command box, adding gksudo at the beginning of the command. It should end up like this, as shown in Figure 24-1:

```
gksudo /usr/bin/gnome-schedule
```

6. Click Close. When you double-click the Scheduled tasks icon on your Desktop, you should be prompted with your password because you're trying to elevate your privileges and act as root.

7. Congratulations! You can now edit the root user's own crontab. With the root user you can actually edit the crontab of any user. Take into account that this will only work if you are a sudoer, as described in Chapter 21.

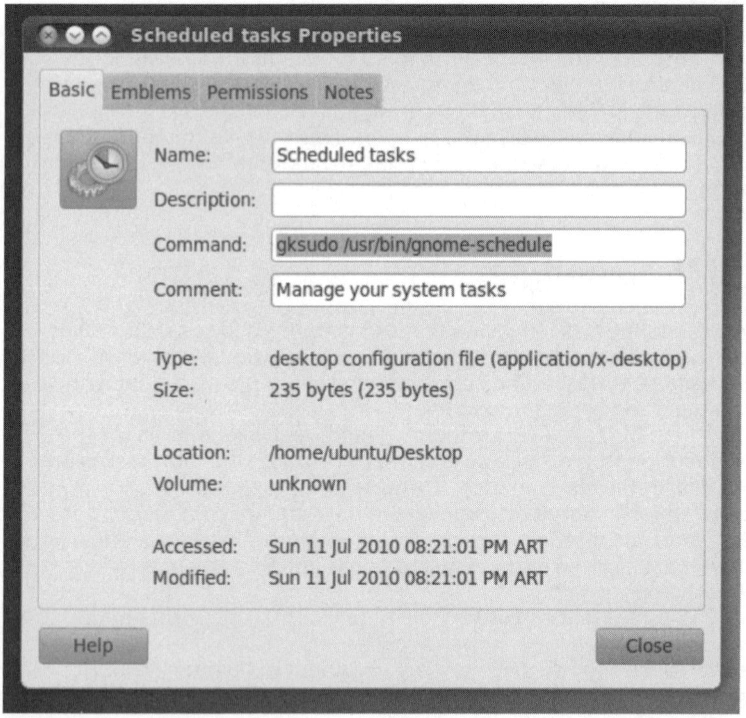

Figure 24-1. Adding gksudo *to an application launcher enables you to run it with elevated privileges, if you have the rights to do so.*

Creating a Recurrent Task

Creating a new scheduled task is easy with GNOME Scheduler.

One of the most common types of scheduled tasks is the *recurring* task. This is a command or program that you want to run on a periodic basis—for example, the cleaning of certain folders or your system's backup. You don't want to run those tasks just once, but to configure them and be at ease because you know they're running without your intervention.

To create a recurrent task, open GNOME Scheduler and click New. The Add a Scheduled Task dialog box will open. Select the option A task that launches recurrently.

You will see the Create a New Scheduled Task dialog box, shown in Figure 24-2.

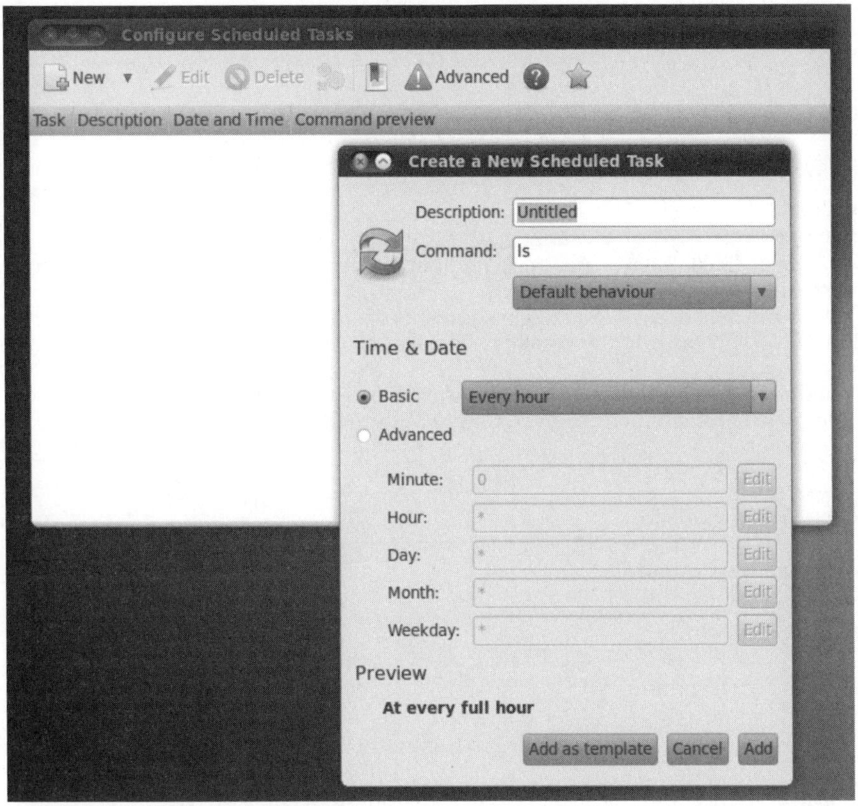

Figure 24-2. Creating a new scheduled task.

You can give your task a description that will allow you to remember what that task was created for. You can use spaces or special characters in your description.

As the name implies, there are two critical components to create a scheduled task: the task and the schedule. The task tells your system what to do; the schedule, when to do it.

In Linux the task is defined by a command or a script. You cannot configure multiple lines of commands inside the scheduled task; if what you want to do is too complex for a single line, you should create a script.

GNOME Scheduler is very versatile regarding how you define the time at which the task will run and its periodicity. You can play around in the section Time & Date of the Create a New Scheduled Task dialog box until you find the perfect schedule for your task. In the Preview section, a human-readable translation of the schedule is displayed so you can be sure that your inputs produce the desired results.

The Basic option allows you to select from six simple schedules: every minute, every hour (at every full hour), every day (at 00:00), every week (on every Monday at 00:00), every month (at 00:00 on day 1), or at reboot. The minute is the minimum schedule time frame, so you cannot schedule a task to run every 15 seconds.

The Advanced lets you to be a little more imaginative. As every UNIX and Linux administrator can tell you, the crontab has five time fields that you can configure: Minute, Hour, Day, Month, and Weekday (0 being Sunday, 1 Monday, and so on). You can fill every one of them or just one. All the fields are combined by the system by using the AND operator. That means that all conditions must be met for the command to run. For example, in the following configuration:

- Minute: 0
- Hour: 15
- Day: *
- Month: *
- Weekday: *

The task will run every day at 15:00 (3 p.m.). Again, remember to check the Preview section to verify that the schedule you are creating matches your intentions.

You can press the Edit button beside each field to get some more options; for example, if you want a task to run only on working days, you can edit the Weekday field and specify the range from 1 (Monday) to 5 (Friday).

What you do with the Edit button can also be done by manually editing each field with the convention shown in Table 24-1. The examples are given for the Minute field.

Table 24-1. Task Conventions

Expression	Description
*	Run the task at every minute
5	Run the task at minute 5
*/5	Run the task every five minutes
5-15	Run the task every minute from minute 5 to minute 15
5-15/5	Run the task every five minutes from minute 5 to minute 15
5,14,37	Run the task at minutes 5, 14, and 37

When done, click the Apply button, and the task will be scheduled to run at the specified times. In order for it to happen, it's not necessary that the Scheduled Tasks program to be open, because it is the cron daemon which handles the execution of the task itself, and it starts automatically with the system.

But what happens if the PC is turned off when the task was meant to run? Well, it's embarrassing to say, but what happens is that it just won't run. That's why you have another options to schedule a task, for example, anacron, which we talk about later in this chapter. Let's cover first the option to create a one-time task.

Scheduling One-Off Tasks

What if you want to schedule a one-time-only task quickly? For this, you can also use the GNOME Scheduler.

For this type of scheduled task, the GNOME Scheduler doesn't rely on the cron daemon, but on the at command. The at command is useful when you have to schedule a task to occur in a specific moment in time only once.

To do so, go to Applications ➤ System Tools ➤ Scheduled tasks, click the New button, and select the option "A task that launches one time." The Create a New Scheduled Task dialog box, shown in Figure 24-3, will appear.

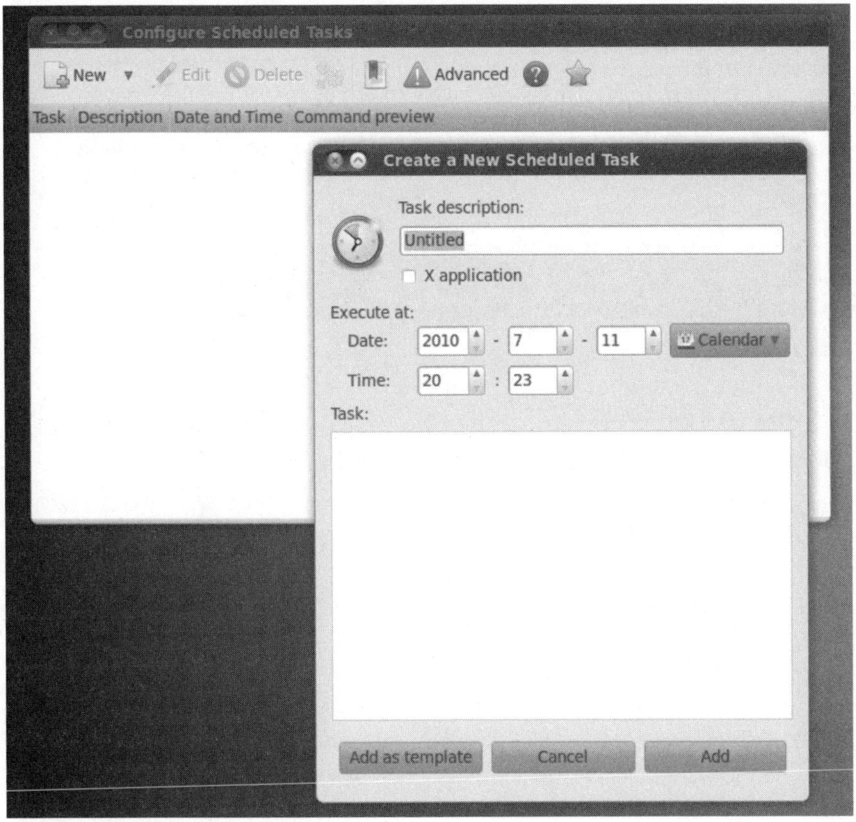

Figure 24-3. Creating a one-time task.

As you can see, adding a job is as easy as selecting a date in a calendar. Give the task a description, select a date and time, and type in the command. Then click Add to make it real.

You might have noticed when creating either a recurring or a one-time task a button with the legend "Add as template" in the Create a New Scheduled Task window. This button lets you to store the configuration for a task without actually scheduling it. It comes in handy when you have several tasks with similar configurations: you can create a template and then base on it to create the tasks.

■ **Note** To use a template, in the GNOME Scheduler main window click the Manage Templates button. Select the template and click the Use template button. Make the necessary changes and click Apply to create the task.

Scheduling with anacron

If cron (and the GNOME Scheduler for that matter) has an Achilles heel, it is that it expects your computer to be up and running all the time. If you schedule a task for around midnight and your computer isn't switched on at that time, the task simply won't run.

anacron was created to fix this problem (see Figure 24-4). It also can run scheduled tasks, but unlike cron, it doesn't rely on exact times or dates. Instead, it works on the principle of time periods. For example, tasks can be set to run every day. In fact, tasks can be set to run every x number of days, regardless of whether that's every two days or every hundred thousand. It also doesn't matter if the computer is shut down and rebooted during that time; the task will be run only once in the specified time period. In addition, tasks can be specifically set to run at the beginning of each month, regardless of the length in days of each month.

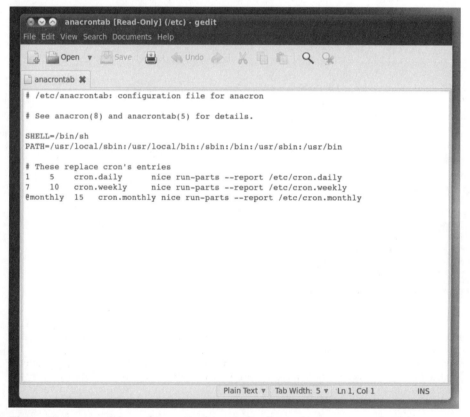

Figure 24-4. anacron *is used to run tasks periodically, such as every couple of days.*

anacron is primarily designed to be used for system maintenance, and the /etc/anacrontab file holds the details of the tasks. Unlike with crontab, each user doesn't have his own anacrontab file. However, there's no reason why you can't add your own commands to the main anacrontab file. This file can be modified in any text editor, and you don't need to use a special command or program (as with crontab), although you'll need to adopt superuser (root) powers.

■ **Note** The /etc/anacrontab file runs scripts contained in the directories /etc/cron.daily, /etc/cron.weekly, and so on, depending on when the tasks are meant to run (every day, week, or month). The average user never needs to bother with systemwide anacron jobs. Programs create their own entries as and when necessary.

Each line in anacrontab takes the following form:

```
days    delay    name of task    command
```

The days field holds the number of days in between the running of the task. To set the task to run every day, you would enter **1**. To make the task run every nine days, you would add **9**. To set it to run monthly, you would type **@monthly**.

The delay field tells anacron how long to wait before running the task, specified in minutes. This is necessary because anacron is run at boot time by default. If it were to run all the scheduled tasks simultaneously, the machine could grind to a halt under the load. A delay of 5 minutes is usually adequate, although if some tasks are already scheduled to run on the same day before that task, you should allow enough time for them to finish.

The name of task field is for your personal reference and shouldn't contain either slashes or spaces. (Hint: Separate words with underscores or periods.)

The command field is, as with crontab, the shell command that should be run.

The fields can be separated by blank spaces or by tabs.

■ **Note** anacron is run as the root user, so if you do add your own entry to anacrontab, any files it creates will be owned by root too. If you use anacron to create a backup of your /home directory, for example, the resultant backup file will be owned by root. You will have to take back the ownership of your files later, as seen in Chapter 21.

Let's look at an example of an anacrontab entry:

```
1    15    backup_job    tar -cjf /home/ubuntu/mybackup.tar.bz2 /home/ubuntu
```

This will run the specified tar command every day (because 1 is in the days field), and with a delay of 15 minutes after anacron is first run.

anacron is run automatically every time you boot, but you can also run it manually by simply typing it at the command prompt (with superuser powers):

```
sudo anacron
```

Summary

In this brief chapter, you looked at how you can schedule tasks under Ubuntu, which essentially means making programs run at certain times. You've learned to schedule recurring tasks, one-time tasks, and tasks that run on specific time periods.

CHAPTER 25

■■■

Accessing Computers Remotely

One area where Linux particularly excels is in its support for networking, including across the Internet. If you want to learn about how networks operate on a fundamental level, Linux is an ideal choice, because it puts you in direct contact with the technology.

The widespread integration and support for networking extends to several useful system tools, which let you access Linux across any kind of network, including the Internet. In fact, it's even possible to access a Linux machine running on a different continent, just as if you were sitting in front of it!

This chapter presents the many ways you can access an Ubuntu computer remotely. You might need to do so, for example, if you want to administer your computer from another PC or to help another person who is using Ubuntu in his own computer. In addition, we look at ways that you can use Ubuntu to access almost any other computer, including Windows PCs.

Using Secure Shell

The history of UNIX has always featured computers connecting to other computers in some fashion, whether they were dumb terminals connecting to a mainframe computer or UNIX machines acting as nodes on the fledgling Internet. Because of this, a wide variety of techniques and protocols were invented to allow computers to communicate and log in to each other across networks. However, although these still work fine over the modern Internet, we're now faced with threats to the privacy of data. In theory, any data transmitted across the Internet can be picked up by individuals at certain key stages along the route. If the data isn't protected in any way, it can be easily intercepted and read.

To counter such an occurrence, the ssh suite of programs was created. Although these programs started as open source, they gradually became proprietary. Therefore, several newer open source versions were created, including the one used on the majority of Linux distributions (including Ubuntu): OpenSSH.

The goal of ssh is to create a secure connection between two computers. You can then do just about any task, including initiating a shell session so you can use the remote computer as if you were sitting in front of it, or copying files to and from the remote machine. ssh uses various techniques at both ends of the connection to encrypt not only the data passing between the two machines, but also the username and password.

■ **Note** This chapter refers to remote and local machines. The *remote* machine is the computer you're connecting to across the network or Internet. The *local* machine is the one you're sitting in front of. These two terms are widely used in networking documentation.

Logging In to a Remote Computer

The most basic type of ssh connection is a remote login. This gives you a command prompt on the remote computer, as if you had just sat down in front of it and logged in to a text console.

But before you can log in to any machine via ssh, you need to be sure the remote computer is able to accept ssh connections. This means that it needs to be running the ssh server program (called a *service* or *daemon*), and also that its firewall has an open port for incoming connections.

The two major components of OpenSSH are the *client* and the *server*. Some distributions install both packages and run the server component all the time. However, only the client component of OpenSSH is installed under Ubuntu by default. To install the server component, and therefore access your Ubuntu system remotely, you need to open the Ubuntu Software Center (Applications ➤ Ubuntu Software Center) and search for openssh-server. An application named secure shell (SSH) server, for secure access from remote machines, will be at the top of the list. Click to install it. Configuration is automatic, although if you're using the Ubuntu firewall (see Chapter 8), you will need to configure an incoming rule to open port 22, the standard port for ssh connections. Take into account that for security reasons the SSH port is often changed from this default value to some other, less obvious to an attacker.

■ **Tip** If you use Firestarter, as described in Chapter 8, you can simply select the default incoming ssh rule. There's no need to manually specify a port number.

Initiating an ssh session with a remote machine is usually achieved by typing something similar to the following at a command prompt on the local machine:

```
ssh <username>@<IP address>
```

In other words, you specify the username you want to log in as, as well as the IP address of the remote machine. If there's a fully qualified domain name (FQDN) for the system you want to access, you could specify that instead of the IP address.

■ **Note** An FQDN is the hostname of a system plus its Internet address, such as mycomputer.example.com. Unless you have had this function specifically set up for you by a system administrator, you'll probably have to connect via its IP address. However, if you rent a web server, you might be able to ssh into it by using the domain name of the server.

You'll be prompted for your password, which, obviously, is the password for the account you're trying to log in to on the remote computer.

When you log in for the first time, you'll see the following message:

```
The authenticity of the host <host IP address> can't be established
```

Figure 25-1 shows an example. This means that the remote computer's encryption key hasn't yet been added to your PC's store file. However, after you agree to the initial login, the encryption key will be added, and it will be used in the future to confirm that the remote computer you're connecting to is authentic.

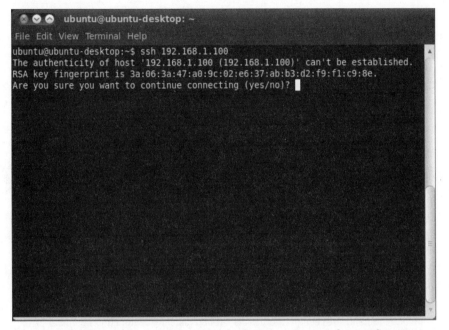

```
ubuntu@ubuntu-desktop: ~
File  Edit  View  Terminal  Help
ubuntu@ubuntu-desktop:~$ ssh 192.168.1.100
The authenticity of host '192.168.1.100 (192.168.1.100)' can't be established.
RSA key fingerprint is 3a:06:3a:47:a0:9c:02:e6:37:ab:b3:d2:f9:f1:c9:8e.
Are you sure you want to continue connecting (yes/no)?
```

Figure 25-1. When logging in via ssh for the first time, you need to confirm acceptance of the encryption key.

■ **Note** There's a fine line between security concern and paranoia. Connecting to a remote machine for the first time and accepting its ssh key is considered insecure by some people, because you cannot be 100 percent sure that the remote machine is the one you want to connect to. It might have been swapped for a different machine by crackers. In addition, the key might be intercepted on its journey to you. Because of this, those who are highly security conscious can use the ssh-keygen program or Seahorse (see Chapter 8) to create a key on the remote machine first, and then import it to the local machine before logging in. See the ssh-keygen man page or www.openssh.com for more details.

After confirming that you want to make the connection, you're invited to enter the password for the user account under which you initiated the ssh connection. After this is done, you should find yourself with a shell login on the remote computer. You can run the same commands as usual and perform identical tasks.

The machine you're logged in to will show no symptoms of being used remotely. It isn't like the movies, where what you type on your local machine is somehow mirrored on the remote machine for all to see. However, obviously, if a user of the remote machine were to view her network connections using something similar to the netstat command, then she would see another computer attached via ssh.

To end an ssh session, simply type **exit** to return to the command prompt on your own machine. You can also press Ctrl+D to log out.

■ **Tip** There's a version of the ssh client that runs on a variety of non-Linux operating systems, making it possible to log in to your Ubuntu machine from a Windows computer. The program is called PuTTY and can be downloaded from www.chiark.greenend.org.uk/~sgtatham/putty/ and many mirrors of this site around the world. PuTTY is also available for Linux, and you can install it using Ubuntu Software Center. It is useful to access another Linux machines without having to open a terminal window each time. Another graphical front-end for ssh and scp is SecPanel, also available in Ubuntu Software Center.

MANAGING REMOTE SESSIONS

Whenever you open any kind of shell to enter commands and run programs, you might have noticed that any commands you start running last only as long as the shell window is open. When the shell window is closed, any task running within it ends too. This is because the shell is seen as the "owner" of the process, and when the owner dies, any processes it started also die.

When using ssh to start a remote shell session, this also applies. Whenever you log out, any tasks you were running are ended. This can be annoying if, for example, you've started a lengthy download on the remote machine. Effectively, you must remain logged in via ssh until the download has finished.

To get around this, you can use the handy screen program. This isn't specifically designed to be an aid to remote logins, but there's no reason why it cannot be used in such a situation.

The screen program effectively starts shell sessions that stick around, even if the shell window is closed or the ssh connection is ended or lost. After logging in to the remote computer via ssh, you can start a screen session by simply typing the program name at the prompt: screen. After choosing a color scheme when prompted, which can help remind you that you're running a screen session, there won't be any indication that you're running a screen session. There's no taskbar at the bottom of the terminal window, for example. screen works completely in the background.

Let's consider what happens when you detach and then reattach to a screen session. To detach from the screen session, press Ctrl+A and then Ctrl+D. You'll then be returned to the standard shell and, in fact, you could now disconnect from your ssh session as usual. However, the screen session will still be running in the background on the remote computer. To prove this, you could log back in and then type this: screen -r. This will resume your screen session, and you should be able to pick up quite literally where you left off; any output from previous commands will be displayed.

To quit a screen session, you can either type exit from within it or press Ctrl+A and then \ (backslash key).

The screen program is very powerful. To learn more about it, read its man page. To see a list of its keyboard commands, press Ctrl+A, and then type a question mark (?) while screen is running.

Transferring Files Between Remote Computers

The ssh utility brings with it two basic ways of transferring files between machines: scp and sftp. scp is fine for smaller file transfers, but if you want to copy a lot of files, sftp is probably a better choice.

Using scp

Strictly speaking, scp is merely a program that copies files from one computer to another in a secure fashion by using the underlying ssh protocol. You don't have to be logged in to another computer via ssh to use it. For example, if you were merely browsing your own computer and wanted to transfer a file to a remote computer, you could type the scp command in the following form:

```
scp myfile <username>@<IP address>:/home/username/
```

The IP address is the IP address of the computer to which you want to send the file. In other words, you must first specify the local file you want to copy across, and then provide the login details for the remote computer in the same format as with an ssh login. Then, after a colon, you specify the path on the *remote* computer where you would like the file to be copied.

■ **Note** If it helps, consider the latter part of the scp command after the filename as one large address: first you provide your username, then the computer address, and then the path.

Using the command when you *are* logged in to another computer via ssh works in exactly the same way. Let's consider an example: Assume there are two computers: A and B. You have a user account on each one. So sitting at the keyboard of A, you establish an ssh connection with B by typing the following:

```
ssh <username>@computer_B
```

This lets you log in to B as if you were sitting in front of it. You spot a file called spreadsheet.xls that you want to copy to your local machine (A). You therefore issue the following command:

```
scp spreadsheet.xls <username>@computer_A:/home/username/
```

This will copy the file from computer B to computer A and place it in the /home/*username*/ directory.

■ **Tip** With scp, you can copy entire directories too. Simply add the -r command option, like so: scp -r mydirectory <username>@<IP address>:/path/.

Using sftp

To copy a lot of files to or from a remote computer, the sftp program is the best solution, because it uses the same secure connection already described. If you've ever used a shell-based FTP program, you'll feel right at home, because sftp isn't very different.

You can initiate an `sftp` session by using this command format:

```
sftp <username>@<IP address>
```

The same rules as when you're logging in with `ssh` apply, both in terms of formatting the login command and also confirming the encryption key if this is the first time you've logged in.

The `sftp` commands are fairly basic. For example, to copy a file from the remote machine, simply type this:

```
get <filename>
```

This will copy the file into the directory you were in on the local machine before you started the `sftp` session.

By specifying a path after the filename, the file will be copied to the specified local directory, as in this example:

```
get spreadsheet.xls /home/keir/downloaded_files/
```

Sending files from the local machine to the remote machine is just as easy:

```
put <filename>
```

By specifying a path after the filename, you can ensure that the file is saved to a particular remote path.

One useful thing to remember is that any command preceded by an exclamation point (!, called a *bang* in Linux-speak) is executed on the local machine as a shell command. So, if you wanted to remove a file on the local machine, you could type this:

```
!rm -rf <filename>
```

Simply typing a bang symbol (the familiar exclamation mark) on its own starts a shell session on the local machine, so you can perform even more tasks. When you're finished, type **exit** to return to the `sftp` program.

For a list of popular `sftp` commands, see Table 25-1.

Table 25-1. Common sftp Commands

Command	Function
Cd	Change the remote directory
Lcd	Change the local directory
Get	Download the specified file
Mget	Download multiple specified files
Ls	List the remote directory
Lls	List the local directory

Command	Function
Mkdir	Create a directory on the remote machine
Lmkdir	Create a directory on the local machine
Put	Upload the specified file to the remote machine
Mput	Upload multiple specified files to the remote machine
Pwd	Print the current remote directory
Rmdir	Delete the remote directory
Rm	Delete the remote file
Exit	Quit sftp
!command	Execute the specified command on the local machine
!	Start a temporary local shell session (type **exit** to return to sftp)
Help	Show a list of commands

Accessing GUI Applications Remotely

So far, we've looked at connecting to a remote machine by using command-line tools. But Ubuntu is based around the graphical desktop, so is there any way of running, say, a Nautilus file browser window so you can manipulate files on the remote machine? Yes!

The graphical subsystem of Linux, X, is designed to work across a network. In fact, if you run Linux on your desktop PC, X *still* works via a loopback network within your machine (meaning that network commands are sent out but addressed to the very same machine on which they originated). Because of this, it's possible to make programs on a remote machine run on a local machine's X server. The actual work of running the application is handled by the *remote* machine, but the work of displaying the graphics is handled by the *local* machine.

■ **Caution** X connections across a network can be a little slow and certainly not as snappy as running the same application on the local machine. This lag can become irritating after a while.

Running X Applications on a Remote Computer

Unfortunately, X server communications aren't typically encrypted, so if one machine were to simply connect to an X server over a network (or even the Internet), the data transfer would be unencrypted and open to eavesdroppers.

But ssh once again comes to the rescue. You can configure ssh so that X applications on the remote computer can be run on the local machine, with the data sent through the ssh connection. Log in to the remote machine by using ssh, but also specify the -X flag:

```
ssh -X <username>@<IP address>
```

When you're logged in, you can simply start any application by typing its name as usual. The only difference is that the program will appear on the screen of the local machine, rather than on the remote machine, as shown in Figure 25-2.

Using X across the Internet or even a local network isn't very fast, and you can expect delays when you open menus or if the screen must frequently redraw. However, it can prove very useful, if you need for example to install a program by using a Wizard, or if you need to run a graphical application such as Gedit.

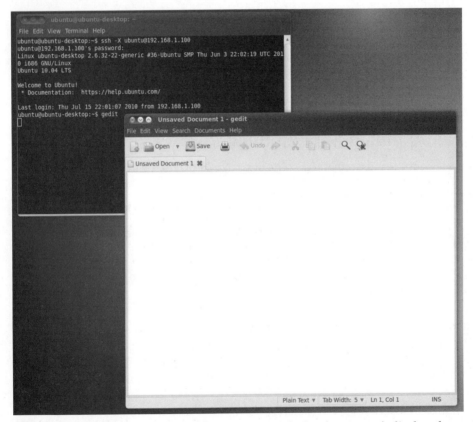

Figure 25-2. Although the Gedit *window appears on the local computer's display, the application is actually running on the remote machine.*

Accessing Ubuntu via Remote Desktop

A less secure but more convenient way to access your Ubuntu PC's desktop applications across a network is to use Ubuntu's Remote Desktop feature. The advantage of this method is that the entire Desktop of the remote computer appears in a window on the local computer's Desktop.

Remote Desktop uses the Virtual Network Computing (VNC) software to share the Desktop. *Sharing* is the key word because, effectively, anyone who connects will take control of the main Desktop. They will control the mouse and keyboard input. This is a great way of helping a friend in need!

However, there are a couple of important differences compared to accessing X across an ssh connection:

- Although the password is sent encrypted, the rest of the VNC data transfers aren't. Complete encryption is possible by using special versions of VNC, or via an OpenSSH tunnel, but this can be difficult to set up on the Windows end of the connection.

- The remote Desktop isn't blanked, so anyone standing in front of the computer will be able to see what you're doing. This could present a security/privacy risk.

If you're prepared to put up with these caveats, then allowing Remote Desktop access on a computer is easy. Here's the procedure:

1. Click System ➤ Preferences and then click Remote Desktop. In the Sharing section of the dialog box, put a check alongside Allow Other Users to View Your Desktop and ensure that there's a check in the box alongside Allow Other Users to Control Your Desktop, as shown in Figure 25-3. In the Security section, you can choose whether the user can confirm each connection and whether you want to set a password. Both options add to the security of your system, although the confirmation option will mean that someone will have to be at the computer to authorize an incoming connection.

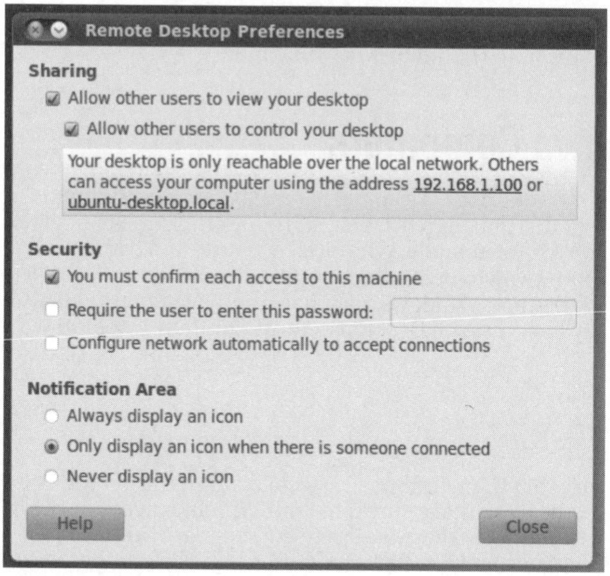

Figure 25-3. Ubuntu's Remote Desktop feature lets you share your Desktop, but isn't as secure as making an X server connection across ssh.

■ **Note** Ignore the information in the dialog box about how users can view your desktop. Instead, you should find out your computer's IP address and use that.

---

2. On the computer from which you want to connect to the remote Desktop, click Applications ➤ Internet ➤ Remote Desktop Viewer.

■ **Note** Remote Desktop Viewer also includes the option to connect to computers with `ssh`, not only VNC.

---

3. With any luck, you'll see the remote computer listed in the panel on the left of the program window. Just select it and double-click. If it isn't listed, click the Connect button. Select VNC as the Protocol. In the Host field, enter the IP address of the computer you want to connect to. Under the Connection Options heading within the dialog box, you can select to run the session full-screen (which is to say, let the remote Desktop entirely take over the local computer's screen); opt to create a connection whereby you only view the remote Desktop, rather than control it; and opt to scale the remote Desktop, so it shrinks to fit within the program window. After you've made your choices, click Connect.

4. You'll be prompted to enter the password, if one is applicable, and you should then see the remote computer's Desktop in a window.

After you've finished with the Remote Desktop session, press Ctrl+Alt to release the cursor and simply close the window's tab, or click the Close button to terminate the connection.

Connecting to Remote Windows Computers

The Terminal Server Client program (Applications ➤ Internet ➤ Terminal Server Client) allows you to connect to a variety of remote Desktop server programs and, in particular, Windows 7, Vista, XP, or 2000 computers via the Remote Desktop Protocol (RDP). Unfortunately, Windows XP Home and earlier versions of Windows don't support RDP connections, which means that they aren't able to run an RDP server and allow other computers to access their Desktops. Windows Vista Basic and Vista Premium also suffer from this limitation. However, there is a way to access the Desktop of these computers remotely by using some add-in software.

Connecting to Windows 7 and Vista

Before initiating the connection, you should ensure that the Windows 7 or Vista computer is set for incoming remote connections, if you haven't already. First, make sure that your Windows account has a password—Terminal Server Client won't be able to connect otherwise. Next, ensure that Windows Remote Desktop feature is activated. Click the Start button, right-click Computer, and click Properties. In the window that appears, click the Remote Settings link on the left side. In the dialog box that appears, click Allow Connections from Computers Running Any Version of Remote Desktop (Less Secure), and then click Apply.

■ **Note** These instructions assume that you intend to connect using a Windows administrator username and password. If not, you'll need to click the Select Users button and add the user accounts you wish to use.

Back on the Ubuntu computer, click Applications ➤ Internet ➤ Terminal Server Client. When the program is running, in the Computer field, type either the IP address of the machine or its FQDN. You don't need to type the username, password, or any other details. Click Connect, and a new window should appear, in which you should see a login prompt. You should then log in to Windows, using your username and password.

Connecting to Windows XP Professional, 2000, and NT

Here we use an XP Professional machine as an example, but the instructions are also valid for Windows 2000 and NT.

First, make sure the Windows XP computer is configured to allow incoming RDP connections. To configure it, right-click My Computer and select Properties. In the System Properties dialog box, click the Remote tab, and make sure "Allow users to connect remotely to this computer" is selected, as shown in Figure 25-4. The Windows computer to which you want to connect may also need to be updated with the latest service packs, particularly in the case of a Windows 2000 computer.

To connect, use the Terminal Server Client program, which is on the Applications ➤ Internet menu. When it's running, in the Computer field type either the IP address of the machine or its FQDN (if applicable). You don't need to type the username, password, or any other details. Click Connect, and a new window should appear, in which you should see an XP login prompt. You should then log in to Windows, using your username and password.

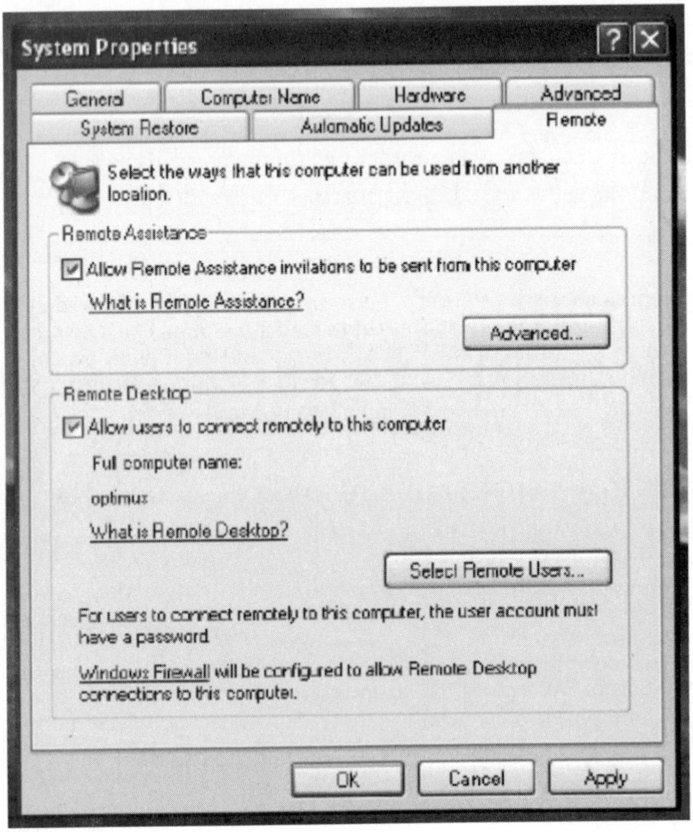

Figure 25-4. You need to enable the option under Remote Desktop to access Windows XP Professional machines using RDP and the Terminal Server Client program.

■ **Caution** If you haven't set a password for your user account on the Windows machine, you won't be able to log in. This is a quirk of the Windows XP RDP system. The solution is simple: use the User Accounts applet within the Windows Control Panel to assign yourself a password.

Connecting to Other Computers

You can download a VNC server for just about any OS. Windows and Linux are supported, as is Mac OS X. In fact, a VNC server will run on any Windows computer, from 95 upward. After it's installed, you can then use the Terminal Server Client program within Ubuntu to connect to that computer's remote desktop.

■ **Note** Any computer that's running the VNC Viewer program can access a computer running a VNC server (including the one set up by Ubuntu's Remote Desktop feature). Various VNC Viewer programs are available for Linux, Windows, Mac OS X, and other operating systems, including the likes of PocketPC. Just search the Web by using **VNC Viewer** as a search string to find viewer programs.

Of course, you'll have the same insecurities and lack of Desktop blanking that plague VNC connections to an Ubuntu Desktop, as described previously. But if you're prepared to accept this, you'll be pleased to hear that setting up the VNC server on the Windows machine is easy. TightVNC, available from www.tightvnc.com, is one of the best variations of VNC around. You should download the self-installing package for Windows. During installation, you'll be asked whether you want to register TightVNC as a system service. Click the check box alongside this option. This will activate the VNC server every time the computer starts.

After the program is installed, the server configuration program will appear. You should change the password by overtyping the default in the Password field.

Connecting to the remote Windows machine is also a piece of cake. On the Ubuntu system, open Remote Desktop Viewer (Applications ➤ Internet ➤ Remote Desktop Viewer) and click the Connect button. Type the remote computer's IP address into the Host field and then click Connect. There's no need to fill in any of the other details. You'll be prompted for the remote computer's VNC server password and, after you enter this, the remote Desktop will appear in a window.

Summary

In this chapter, you looked at how you can access your Ubuntu computer remotely across the Internet. You examined how you can access the computer as if you were sitting in front of it, using the ssh program. This allows you to start a command-line prompt and even run GUI programs from the remote computer.

In addition, we discussed how the screen program can be used to keep sessions alive across various logins, and how you can transfer files by using the sftp and scp programs. Then you looked at how to use the Remote Desktop Viewer and Terminal Server Client tools to access the Desktop of remote Windows computers.

■ ■ ■

## CHAPTER 26

Taking Control of the System

By now, you should be starting to realize that the shell offers an enormous amount of power when it comes to administering your PC. The BASH shell commands give you quick and efficient control over most aspects of your Linux setup. However, the shell truly excels in one area: controlling the processes on your system.

If you are only running a home computer, you may not have to pay much attention to processes. However, if you are running a shared machine or a network, controlling processes can be essential for administration of your system. You can tidy up crashed programs, for example, or even alter the priority of a program so that it runs with a little more consideration for other programs. Unlike with Windows, this degree of control is not considered out of bounds. This is just one more example of how Linux provides complete access to its inner workings and puts you in control.

■ **Tip** This chapter concentrates on using the Terminal to provide powerful control over your system. If you'd rather avoid working in the Terminal but would still like to view and control processes, you can do so in the Processes tab of the System Monitor program (System ➤ Administration ➤ System Monitor). Extra functions are available via the right-click context menu.

Viewing Processes

A *process* is one instance of a software program, with its associated state. When the user runs a program one or many processes might be started, but they're usually invisible unless the user specifically chooses to manipulate them. You might say that programs exist in the world of the user, but processes belong in the world of the system.

Processes can be started not only by the user, but also by the system itself to undertake tasks such as system maintenance, or even to provide basic functionality, such as the GUI system. Many processes are started when the computer boots up and then they sit in the background, waiting until they're needed (such as programs that provide printing functionality). Other processes are designed to work periodically to accomplish certain tasks, such as ensuring that system files are up to date.

You can see what processes are currently running on your computer by running the top program. Running top is simply a matter of typing the command at the shell prompt.

As you can see in Figure 26-1, top provides comprehensive information and can be a bit overwhelming at first sight. However, the main area of interest is the list of processes (which top calls *tasks*).

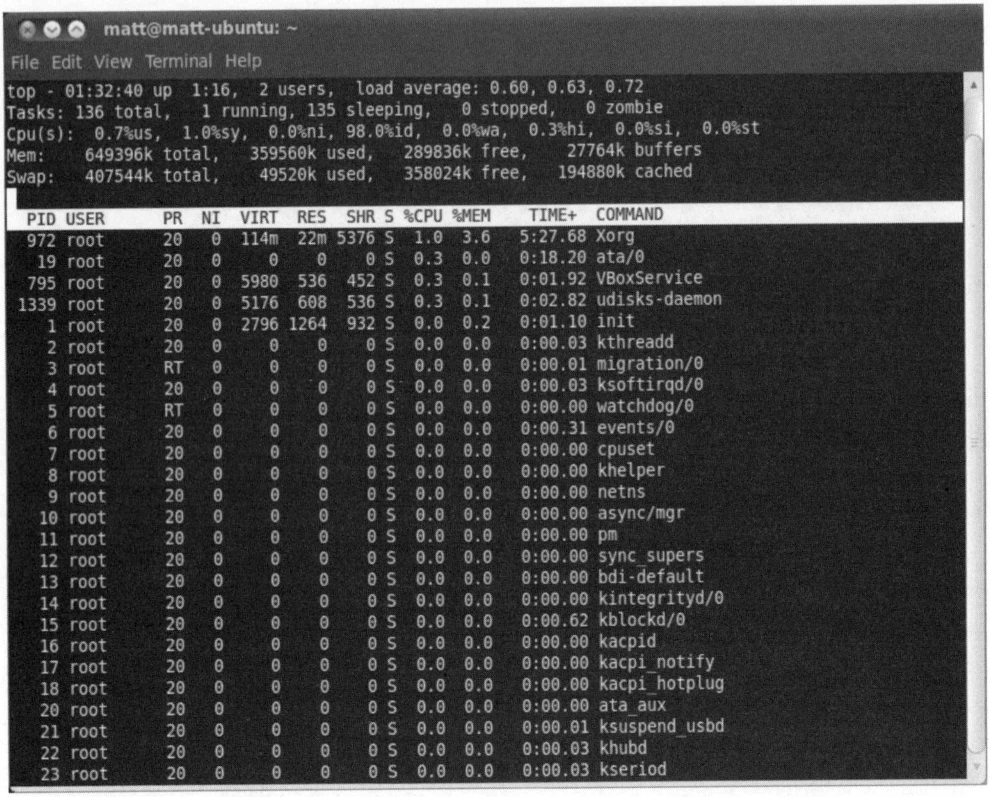

Figure 26-1. *The* top *program gives you an eagle-eye view of the processes running on your system.*

Here's an example of a line taken from top on our test PC, shown with the column headings from the process list:

```
PID USER PR NI VIRT RES SHR S %CPU %MEM TIME+ COMMAND

5499 root 15 0 78052 25m 60m S 2.3 5.0 6:11.72 Xorg
```

A lot of information is presented here, as described in Table 26-1.

Table 26-1. The top *Program Process Information*

Column	Description
PID	The first number is the Process ID (PID). This is the unique number that the system uses to track the process. The PID comes in handy if you want to kill (terminate) the process (as explained in the next section of this chapter).
USER	This column lists the owner of the particular process. As with files, all processes must have an owner. A lot of processes are owned by the root user. Some of them are system processes that need to access the system hardware, which is something only the root user is allowed to do. Other processes are owned by root for protection; root ownership means that ordinary users cannot tamper with these processes. Other processes are owned by ordinary users. On a network, you might see several instances of the same command running at the same time, each owned by a different user.
PR	This column shows the priority of the process (that is, how important it is compared to other processes, and therefore how much attention it will gain from the CPU). This is a dynamic number, showing where the particular process is in the CPU queue at the present time.
NI	This column shows the "nice" value of the process on a scale from -20 to 19. This refers to how charitable a process is in its desire for CPU time. A high figure here (up to 19) indicates that the process is willing to be interrupted for the sake of other processes. A negative value means the opposite: the process is more aggressive than others in its desire for CPU time. Some programs need to operate in this way, and this is not necessarily a bad thing.
VIRT	This column shows the amount of virtual memory used by the process.[a]
RES	This column shows the total amount of physical memory used.[a]
SHR	This column shows the amount of shared memory used. This refers to memory that contains code that is relied on by other processes and programs.
S	This column shows the current status of the task. Generally, the status will either be *S* (Sleeping), or *R* (Running). Most processes will be sleeping, even ones that appear to be active. Don't worry about this; it just reflects the way the Linux kernel works. A *Z* in this column indicates a zombie process (a child of a process that has been terminated).
%CPU	This column shows the CPU use, expressed as a percentage.[b]
%MEM	This column shows the memory use, again expressed as a percentage. Note that this figure can vary considerably, depending on what the process is currently doing.[b]
TIME+	This column shows a measure of how long the process has been up and running.
COMMAND	This shows the actual name of the process itself.

[a] Both *VIRT* and *RES* are measured in kilobytes, unless an *m* appears alongside the number—in which case, you should read the figure as megabytes.

[b] The *%CPU* and *%MEM* entries tell you in easy-to-understand terms how much of the system resources a process is taking up.

This list will probably be longer than the screen has space to display, so top orders the list of processes by the amount of CPU time the processes are using. Every few seconds, it updates the list. You can test this quite easily. Open a Nautilus file-browsing window (Places ➤ Home) and then let your PC rest for a few seconds, without touching the mouse or typing. Then click an icon in the Nautilus window. You'll see that the process called nautilus leaps to the top of the list (or appears very near the top).

Near the top of the list will probably be Xorg. This is the program that provides the graphical subsystem for Linux; making the mouse cursor appear to move around the screen and drawing program windows requires CPU time.

■ **Tip** Typing **d** while top is running lets you alter the *update interval*, which is the time between screen updates. The default is 3.0 seconds, but you can reduce that to 1 second or even less if you want (that is, a fraction of a second, such as 0.5). However, a constantly updating top program starts to consume system resources and can therefore skew the diagnostic results you're investigating. Because of this, a longer, rather than shorter, interval is preferable.

It's possible to alter the ordering of the process list according to other criteria. For example, you can list the processes by the quantity of memory they're using, by typing **M** while top is up and running. You can switch back to CPU ordering by typing **P**.

To quit top, type **Q**.

RENICING A PROCESS

You can set how much CPU time a process receives while it's actually running. This is done by *renicing* the process. It isn't something you should do on a regular basis, but it can prove handy if you start a program that then uses a lot of system resources and makes the system unbearably slow.

The first thing to do is to use top to spot the process that needs to be restrained and find out its PID number. Renicing is best done as the root user, because in order to protect the system, limitations are placed on what ordinary users can set in terms of CPU scheduling. Run top as root by typing **sudo top** (although be careful—with top running as root, you can kill any process!). The PID will be listed on the left of the program's entry on the list.

Once you know this, type **r** and then type in the PID number. You'll then be asked to specify a renice value. The scale goes from −20, which is considered the highest priority, to 19, which is considered the lowest. Zero is the median value, and most new user-started processes are given a value of 0. Therefore, using a value of 19 will ensure that a process stops hogging system resources. However, instead of simply resetting the priority to 19, you should err on the side of caution if you suspect you might be renicing an important process. Check the current niceness, and make only small changes at a time.

After you make adjustments, you should find that some responsiveness has returned to the system, although how much (if any) depends on the nature of the programs you're running.

You might be tempted to bump up the priority of a process to make it run faster, but this may not work the way you want because of complexities in the Linux kernel. In fact, it might cause serious problems. Therefore, you should renice with care and only when you must.

Renicing can also be carried out via the `renice` command at the prompt, avoiding the need to use `top`. Also useful is the `nice` command, which can be used to set the initial priority of a process before it starts to run. To learn more, see the man pages for `renice` and `nice`.

Controlling Processes

Despite the fact that processes running on your computer are usually hidden away, Linux offers complete, unrestricted control over them. You can terminate processes, change their properties, and learn every item of information there is to know about them.

This provides ample scope for damaging the currently running system but, in spite of this, even standard users have complete control over processes that they personally started (one exception is zombie processes, described a bit later in this section). As you might expect, the root user (or any user who adopts superuser powers) has control over all processes that were created by ordinary users, as well as those processes started by the system itself.

The user is given this degree of control over processes in order to enact repairs when something goes wrong, such as when a program crashes and won't terminate cleanly. It's impossible for standard users to damage the currently running system by undertaking such work, although they can cause themselves a number of problems.

Note This control over processes is what makes Linux so reliable. Because any user can delve into the workings of the kernel and terminate individual processes, crashed programs can be cleaned up with negligible impact on the rest of the system.

Killing Processes

Whenever you quit a program or, in some cases, when it completes the task you've asked it to, it will terminate itself. This means ending its own process and also that of any other processes it created in order to run. The main process is called the *parent*, and the ones it creates are referred to as *child* processes.

Tip You can see a nice hierarchical display of which parent owns which child process by typing **pstree** at the command-line shell. It's useful to add the -p command option (that is, `pstree -p`). This adds the PIDs to the output. It's worth piping this into the `less` command so you can scroll through it: type **pstree | less**. We explain piping in the next chapter.

Although this termination should mean that your system runs smoothly, badly behaved programs sometimes don't go away. They stick around in the process list. Alternatively, you might find that a program crashes and so isn't able to terminate itself. In rare cases, some programs that appear otherwise healthy might get carried away and start consuming a lot of system resources. You can tell when this happens because your system will start slowing down for no reason, as less and less memory and/or CPU time is available to run actual programs.

You can get rid of these troublesome processes by logging out then immediately logging back in, but an even simpler way to handle them is to kill the process and terminate it manually. This is easily done by using top. The first task is to track down the crashed or otherwise problematic process. In top, look for a process that matches the name of the program, as shown in Figure 26-2. For example, the Mozilla Firefox web browser generally runs as a process called firefox-bin.

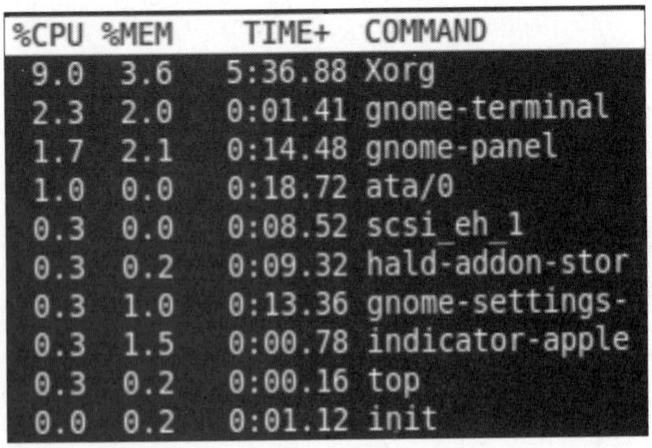

%CPU	%MEM	TIME+	COMMAND
9.0	3.6	5:36.88	Xorg
2.3	2.0	0:01.41	gnome-terminal
1.7	2.1	0:14.48	gnome-panel
1.0	0.0	0:18.72	ata/0
0.3	0.0	0:08.52	scsi_eh_1
0.3	0.2	0:09.32	hald-addon-stor
0.3	1.0	0:13.36	gnome-settings-
0.3	1.5	0:00.78	indicator-apple
0.3	0.2	0:00.16	top
0.0	0.2	0:01.12	init

Figure 26-2. You can usually identify a program by its name in the process list.

■ **Caution** You should be absolutely sure that you know the correct process before killing it. If you get it wrong, you could cause other programs to stop running.

Because top doesn't show every single process on its screen, tracking down the trouble-causing process can be difficult. A handy tip is to make top show only the processes created by the user you're logged in under. This will remove the background processes started by root. You can do this within top by typing **u** and then entering your username.

After you've spotted the crashed process, make a note of its PID number, which will be at the very left of its entry in the list. Then type **k**. You'll be asked to enter the PID number. Enter that number and then press Enter once again (this will accept the default signal value of 15, which tells the program to terminate).

The process (and the program in question) should disappear. If it doesn't, the process you've killed might be the child of another process that also must be killed. To track down the parent process, you need to configure top to add the PPID field (for the *parent process ID*) to its display. To add this field, type **f** and then **b**. Press Enter to return to the process list. The PPID column will appear next to the process name on the right of the window. It simply shows the PID of the parent process. You can use this information to look for the parent process within the main list of processes.

■ **Note** No magic is involved in killing processes. All that happens is that `top` sends them a "terminate" signal. In other words, it contacts them and asks them to terminate. By default, all processes are designed to listen for commands such as this; it's part and parcel of how programs work under Linux. When a program is described as *crashed*, it means that the user is unable to use the program itself to issue the terminate command (such as Quit). A crashed program might not be taking input, but its *processes* will probably still be running.

The trick here is to make sure that the parent process isn't something that's vital to the running of the system. If it isn't, you can safely kill it. This should have the result of killing the child process you uncovered prior to this.

■ **Caution** In both the PPID and PID fields, you should always watch out for low numbers, particularly one-, two-, or three-digit numbers. These are usually processes that started early on when Linux booted and that are essential to the system.

Controlling Zombie Processes

Zombie processes are those that are children of processes that have terminated. However, for some reason, they failed to take their child processes with them. Zombie processes are rare on most Linux systems.

Despite the name, zombie processes are harmless. They're not actually running and don't take up system resources. However, if you want your system to be spick-and-span, you can attempt to kill them.

In the top-right area of `top`, you can see a display that shows how many zombie processes are running on your system, as shown in Figure 26-3. Zombie processes are easily identified because they have a Z in the status (S) column within `top`'s process list. To kill a zombie process, type **k** and then type its PID. Then type **9**, rather than accept the default signal of 15.

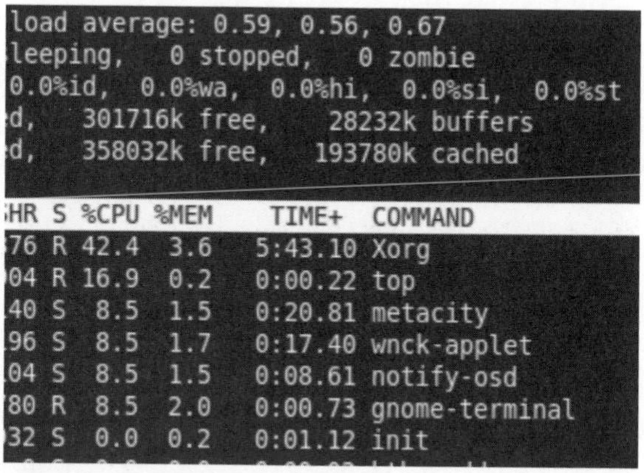

```
load average: 0.59, 0.56, 0.67
leeping,    0 stopped,    0 zombie
0.0%id,  0.0%wa,  0.0%hi,  0.0%si,  0.0%st
d,   301716k free,    28232k buffers
d,   358032k free,   193780k cached

HR S %CPU %MEM    TIME+   COMMAND
76 R 42.4  3.6   5:43.10 Xorg
04 R 16.9  0.2   0:00.22 top
40 S  8.5  1.5   0:20.81 metacity
96 S  8.5  1.7   0:17.40 wnck-applet
04 S  8.5  1.5   0:08.61 notify-osd
80 R  8.5  2.0   0:00.73 gnome-terminal
32 S  0.0  0.2   0:01.12 init
```

Figure 26-3. *You can see at a glance how many zombie processes are on your system by looking at the top right of* top's *display.*

In many cases, zombie processes simply won't go away. When this happens, you have two options. The first is to restart the program that is likely to be the zombie's owner, in the hope that it will reattach with the zombie, and then quit the program. With any luck, it will take the zombie child with it this time. Alternatively, you can simply log out and log in again, or reboot. But it's important to note that zombie processes are harmless and can be left in peace on your system!

Using Other Commands to Control Processes

You don't always need to use top to control processes. A range of quick and cheerful shell commands can diagnose and treat process problems.

The first of these is the ps command. This stands for *process status* and will report a list of currently running processes on your system. This command is typically used with the aux command options (there's no need to provide a dash before the options, as with most commands):

```
ps aux
```

This will return a list something like what you see when you run top. If you can spot the problematic process, look for its PID and issue the following command:

```
kill <PID number>
```

For example, to kill a process with a PID of 5122, you would type this:

```
kill 5122
```

If, after that, you find the process isn't killed, then you should use the top program, as described in the previous sections, because it allows for a more in-depth investigation.

Another handy process-killing command lets you use the actual process name. The killall command is handy if you already know from past experience what a program's process is called. For example, to kill the process called firefox, which is the chief process of the Firefox web browser, you would use the following command:

```
killall firefox
```

■ **Caution** Make sure you're as specific as possible when using the killall command. Issuing a command like killall bin will kill all processes that might have the word bin in their name!

CLEARING UP CRASHES

Sometimes a crashed process can cause all kinds of problems. The shell you're working at may stop working, or the GUI itself might stop working properly.

In cases like this, it's important to remember that you can have more than one instance of the command-line shell up and running at any one time. For example, if a process crashes and locks up GNOME Terminal, simply start a new instance of GNOME Terminal (Applications ➤ Accessories ➤ Terminal). Then use top within the new window to kill the process that is causing trouble for the other terminal window.

If the crashed program affects the entire GUI, you can switch to a virtual console by pressing Ctrl+Alt+F1. Although the GUI disappears, you will not have killed it, and no programs will stop running. Instead, you've simply moved the GUI to the background while a shell console takes over the screen. Then you can use the virtual console to run top and attempt to kill the process that is causing all the problems. When you're ready, you can switch back to the GUI by pressing Ctrl+Alt+F7.

If you know the name of the program that's crashed, a quick way of getting rid of it is to use the pgrep command. This searches the list of processes for the program name you specify and then outputs the PID number. So if, say, Nautilus had frozen, you could type pgrep nautilus. Then you would use the kill command with the PID number that's returned.

Controlling Jobs

Whenever you start a program at the shell, it's assigned a job number. *Jobs* are quite separate from processes and are designed primarily for users to understand what programs are currently doing on the system.

You can see which jobs are running at any one time by typing the following at the shell prompt:

```
jobs
```

When you run a program, it usually takes over the shell in some way and stops you from doing anything until it's finished what it's doing. However, it doesn't have to be this way. Adding an ampersand symbol (&) after the command will cause it to run in the background. This is not much use for commands that require user input, such as vim or top, but it can be handy for commands that churn away until they're completed.

For example, suppose that you want to decompress a large Zip file. For this, you can use the unzip command. As with Windows, decompressing large Zip files can take a lot of time, during which time the shell would effectively be unusable. However, you can type the following to retain use of the shell:

```
unzip myfile.zip &
```

When you do this, you'll see something similar to the following, although the four-digit number will be different:

```
[1] 7483
```

This tells you that unzip is running in the background and has been given job number 1. It also has been given process number 7483 (although bear in mind that when some programs start, they instantly kick off other processes and terminate the one they're currently running, so this won't necessarily be accurate).

■ **Tip** If you've ever tried to run a GUI program from the shell, you might have realized that the shell is inaccessible while it's running. After you quit the GUI program, the control of the shell is returned to you. By specifying that the program should run in the background with the & (ampersand symbol), you can run the GUI program and still be able to type away and run other commands.

You can send several jobs to the background, and each one will be given a different job number. In this case, when you want to switch to a running job, you can type its number. For example, the following command will switch you to the background job assigned the number 3:

```
%3
```

You can exit a job that is currently running by pressing Ctrl+Z. It will still be there in the background, but it won't be running (officially, it's said to be *sleeping*). To restart it, you can switch back to it, as just described. Alternatively, you can restart it but still keep it in the background. For example, to restart job 2 in the background, leaving the shell prompt free for you to enter other commands, type the following:

```
%2 &
```

You can bring the command in the background into the foreground by typing the following:

```
fg
```

When a background job has finished, something like the following will appear at the shell:

```
[1]+        Done unzip myfile.zip
```

Using jobs within the shell can be a good way of managing your workload. For example, you can move programs into the background temporarily while you get on with something else. If you're editing a file in vim, you can press Ctrl+Z to stop the program. It will remain in the background, and you'll be returned to the shell, where you can type other commands. You can then resume vim later on by typing **fg** or typing **%** followed by its job number.

■ **Tip** Also useful is Ctrl+C, which will kill a job that's currently running. For example, if you previously started the unzip command in the foreground, pressing Ctrl+C will immediately terminate it. Ctrl+C is useful if you accidentally start commands that take an unexpectedly long time to complete.

NOHUP

What if you want to start a command running in a terminal window, but then want to close that terminal window? As soon as you close the window, any processes started within it are also closed. Try this now—type **gcalctool** at the prompt to start the Calculator application and then quit the terminal window.

This happens because, when you quit, the parent process sends any process that it started a hang-up signal. Some processes are designed to ignore the hang-up signal, so in the preceding example not every process will quit when the terminal window does, but most will. As you might expect, the hang-up signal is a remnant of the way UNIX used to work many years ago, when people dialed into computers across slow connections; it is designed to stop processes from continuing to consume resources after the user has hung up the phone and thereby ended the session!

To get around processes quitting like this, you can use the nohup command. This stands for *no hang-up*, and in simple terms, it tells the command you specify to stick around, even after the process that started it has ended (technically, the command is told to ignore the SIGHUP signal). However, commands run via nohup can still be killed in the usual way.

To use nohup, simply add it before the command, for example:

```
nohup unzip myfile.zip
```

If the command requires sudo or gksu powers, add either of these after the nohup command.

Any command output (including error messages) is sent to the file nohup.out, which you can then view in a text editor. Note that if you run a command via nohup using sudo or gksu, the nohup.out file will have root privileges. If that's the case, you will also have to delete the nohup.out file via sudo before you can use nohup again as an ordinary user—because otherwise, nohup will be unable to overwrite the root-owned nohup.out.

Summary

This chapter has covered taking complete control of your system. You looked at what processes are, how they're separate from programs, and how they can be controlled or viewed by using programs such as top and ps. In addition, you explored job management under BASH. You saw that you can stop, start, and pause programs at your convenience.

In the next chapter, we take a look at several tricks and techniques that you can use with the BASH shell to finely hone your command-line skills.

## PART 6

Appendixes

APPENDIX A

■ ■ ■

Introducing the BASH Shell

As you learn in Chapter 1, strictly speaking, the word *Linux* refers to just the kernel, which is the fundamental, invisible program that runs your PC and lets everything happen. However, on its own, the kernel is completely useless. It needs programs to let users interact with the PC and do cool stuff, and it needs a lot of system files (also referred to as *libraries*) to provide vital functions.

The GNU Project provides many of these low-level pieces of code and programs. This is why many people refer to the Linux OS as GNU/Linux, acknowledging that without the GNU components Linux wouldn't have gotten off the starting blocks.

The GNU Project provides various shell programs too. A *shell* is what the user interacts with on a day-to-day basis, whether by mouse or keyboard. The word originates from the fact that the shell is the outer layer of the OS, which encapsulates the kernel (and in some instances protects it by filtering out bad user commands). Some shells offer graphical functionality but, in general, the word *shell* is understood to mean text-only interfaces. These text shell programs are also known as *terminal programs*, and they're often colloquially referred to as *command-line prompts*, in reference to the most important component they provide. This kind of shell lets you take control of your system in a quick and efficient way.

Although using the shell is not strictly necessary nowadays, because almost everything can be done in Ubuntu using the graphical interface, it remains true that by using the shell you become the true master of your own system. This appendix introduces the BASH shell, which is the default shell on Ubuntu systems.

What Is the BASH Shell?

The best way of explaining the BASH shell to a Windows user is to compare it to the DOS command prompt. It lets you issue commands directly to the OS via the keyboard without needing to mess around with the mouse and windows (although it is sometimes possible to use the mouse within a BASH shell to copy and paste text, and sometimes to control simple text-based menus). The big difference is that the BASH shell has commands for just about everything you might do on your system, whereas the DOS command prompt is mostly limited to tools capable of manipulating and viewing files and directories.

In the old days, the DOS command prompt was also the visible layer of an entire operating system in which DOS programs were designed to be run. However, the shell is merely one of the many ways of accessing the Linux kernel and subsystems. It's true that many programs are designed to run via the BASH shell, but technically speaking, most actually run on the Linux OS, and simply take input and show their output via the BASH shell.

The instinctive response of a longtime Windows user is to be wary of the BASH shell, because it presents an entirely new way of working and a new set of concepts to learn. There's no denying that the shell provides plenty of challenges for the newbie user, but the rewards it brings—both in terms of sense of achievement, as well as making users more effective at controlling their computers—more than outweigh the initial difficulties.

Linux finds itself with the BASH shell largely because Linux is a clone of UNIX. In the early days of UNIX, the text-based shell was the *only* way for users to control the computer. Typing in commands directly is one of the most fundamental ways of controlling any type of computer and, in the evolutionary scale, comes straight after needing to set switches and watch blinking lights in order to run programs.

That the BASH shell can trace its history back to the early days of UNIX might sound like a tacit indication that the BASH is somehow primitive—far from it. It's one of the most efficient and immediate ways of working with your computer. Many people consider the command-line shell to be a fast, efficient way of using a computer that has yet to be superseded by a better method.

■ **Note** When you run a shell on a Linux system, the system refers to it as a `tty` device. This stands for *teletypewriter*, a direct reference to the old system of inputting data on what were effectively electronic typewriters connected to mainframe computers. These, in turn, took their names from the devices used to automate the sending and receiving of telegrams in the early part of the 20th century.

Most Linux distributions come with a choice of different shell programs. However, the default shell for most Linux systems is BASH, as is the case with Ubuntu. *BASH* stands for *Bourne Again SHell*. The name is a pun and alludes to the origins of Bash as a rewrite of the Bourne shell, a tried-and-tested program from the heyday of UNIX in the late 1970s.

The other shells available include PDKSH (Public Domain Korn SHell, based on Korn Shell, another early UNIX shell) and ZSH (Z SHell), a more recent addition. These are usually used by people who want to program Linux in various ways or by those who simply aren't happy with BASH.

■ **Note** Discussing the technical differentiators between shells is beyond the scope of this book, but you'll find an excellent comparison at Wikipedia: `http://en.wikipedia.org/wiki/Comparison_of_computer_shells`.

The BASH shell is considered by many to be the best of all worlds in that it's easy enough for beginners to learn, yet is able to grow with them and offer additional capabilities as necessary. BASH is capable of scripting, for example, which means you can even create your own simple programs.

Why Bother with the Shell?

You might have followed the instructions in this book and consider yourself an expert in Linux. But the real measure of a Linux user comes from your abilities at the shell.

Most modern Linux distributions prefer you to use the GUI to do nearly everything. To this end, they provide GUI tools for just about every task you might want to undertake. Ubuntu is strong in this regard, and you can configure a lot of things from the Desktop (as this book helps to prove).

However, it's well worth developing at least some command-line shell skills, for a number of reasons:

It's simple and fast: The shell is the simplest and fastest way of working with Ubuntu. As just one example, consider the task of changing the IP address of your network card. You could right-click the NetworkManager icon, select the relevant menu option, and then work your way through the Network Connection dialog box options. That will take at least a minute or two if you know what you're doing, and perhaps longer if it's new to you. Alternatively, you could simply open a shell and type this:

```
ifconfig eth0 192.168.0.15 up
```

It's versatile: Everything can be done via the shell—from deleting files, to configuring hardware, to creating MP3s. A lot of GUI applications actually make use of programs you can access via the shell, although it isn't always the case that you'll find a GUI program that does the job of a well-crafted shell command. Sometimes you simply have to use the shell for a particular task.

It's consistent among distributions: All Linux systems have shells and understand the same commands (broadly speaking). However, not all Linux systems have Ubuntu's graphical configuration programs. SUSE Linux uses its own GUI configuration tool, as does Mandriva Linux. Therefore, if you ever need to use another system or decide to switch distributions, a reliance on GUI tools means learning everything from scratch. Knowing a few shell commands can get you started instantly.

It's crucial for troubleshooting: The shell offers a vital way of fixing your system should it go wrong. Your Linux installation might be damaged to the extent that it cannot boot to the GUI, but you'll almost certainly be able to boot into a shell. A shell doesn't require much of the system other than the ability to display characters on the screen and take input from the keyboard, which most PCs can do even when they're in a sorry state. This is why most rescue floppy disks or CDs offer shells to let you fix your system.

It's useful for remote access: One handy thing about the shell is that you don't need to be in front of your PC to use it. Programs such as ssh let you log in to your PC across the Internet and use the shell to control it (as described in Chapter 25). For example, you can access data on a remote machine, or even fix it when you're unable to be at the machine's location. This is why Linux is preferred on many server systems when the system administrator isn't always present on the site.

It's respected in the community: Using a shell earns you enormous brownie points when speaking to other Linux users. It is what professionals use, because it gives you greater power and control.

Seen in this light, learning at least a handful of shell commands is vital to truly mastering your PC. The drawback when using a command-line shell is that it's not entirely intuitive. Take for instance the command discussed earlier that changes the network card's IP address:

```
ifconfig eth0 192.168.0.15 up
```

If you've never used the shell before, it might as well be Sanskrit written on the side of an ancient tomb. What on Earth does ifconfig mean? And why is the word up at the end?

▓ **Note** If you're curious, the command tells the network card, called by Linux eth0, to adopt the specified IP address. The word up at the end merely tells it to activate—to start working now. If the word down were there instead, it would deactivate! Don't worry about understanding all this right now; later in this appendix, we explain how you can learn about every Linux command.

Learning to use the shell requires learning terms like these. Hundreds of commands are available, but you really need to learn only about 10 or 20 for everyday use. The comparison with a new language is apt because, although you might think it daunting to learn new terminology, with a bit of practice it will all become second nature. After you've used a command a few times, you'll know how to use it in the future. And as we discuss later, lots of built-in help is available. The main thing to realize is that the shell is your friend. It's there to help you get stuff done as quickly as possible. When you become familiar with it, you'll see that it is a beautiful concept. The shell is simple, elegant, and powerful.

When Should You Use the Shell?

The amount of use the Linux shell sees is highly dependent on the user. Some Linux buffs couldn't manage without it. They use it to read and compose e-mail, and even to browse the Web (usually using Mailutils and the Lynx program, respectively).

However, most people simply use it to manage files, view text files (such as program documentation), run programs, and administer the system. All kinds of programs—including GUI and command-line—can be started from the shell. As you learn in Chapter 20, unlike with Windows, installing a program on Ubuntu doesn't necessarily mean the program automatically appears on the Applications menu. In fact, unless the installation routine is specifically made for the version of Linux you're running, this is unlikely.

■ **Note** Unlike with DOS programs, Ubuntu programs that describe themselves as *command-line* are rarely designed to run solely via the command-line shell. All programs are like machines that take input at one end and output objects at the other. Where the input comes from and where the output goes to is by no means limited to the command line. Usually, with a command-line program, the input and output are provided via the shell, and the programmer makes special dispensation for this, but this way of working is why GUI programs often use what might be considered shell programs. You'll often find that a GUI program designed to, for example, burn CDs, will also require the installation of a command-line program that actually does the hard work for it.

There's another reason why the shell is used to run programs: you can specify how a particular program runs before starting it. For example, to launch the Totem movie player in full-screen mode playing the `myvideofile.mpg` file, you could type this:

```
totem --fullscreen myvideofile.mpg
```

This saves the bother of starting the program, loading a clip, and then selecting the full- screen option. After you've typed the command once or twice, you'll be able to remember it for the next time. No matter how much you love the mouse, you'll have to admit that this method of running programs is very efficient.

When you get used to using the shell, it's likely you'll have it open most of the time behind your other program windows.

Getting Started with the Shell

You can start the shell in a number of ways. The most common is to use a terminal emulator program. As its name suggests, this runs a shell inside a program window on your Desktop.

You can start GNOME Terminal, the built-in GNOME shell emulator, by clicking Applications ➤ Accessories ➤ Terminal.

You'll see the terminal window—a blank, violet window that's similar to a simple text editor window. When you run the terminal for the first time, at the top of it will be a handful of lines telling you about the sudo command. We explain the importance of this in Chapter 21, but right now there's no need to worry about it.

Below this is the most important component of the terminal window: the *command prompt*—a few words followed by the dollar symbol ($). On our test system, this is what we see:

ubuntu@ubuntu-desktop:~$

■ **Note** The first part is the username—the user account we created during installation and use to log in to the PC. After the @ sign is the hostname of the PC, which we also chose when installing Ubuntu. The hostname of the PC isn't important on most home systems, but assumes relevance if the PC is part of a network. The @ sign tells us that we are running user ubuntu on the computer with the hostname ubuntu-desktop.

After the colon is the current directory you're browsing. In this example, the tilde symbol (~) appears instead of an actual path or directory name. This is merely Linux shorthand for the user's /home directory. In other words, wherever we see a ~ on our test PC, we read it as /home/ubuntu/. After this is the dollar symbol ($), which indicates being currently logged in as an ordinary user, as opposed to the root user. However, unlike most other Linux distributions, Ubuntu doesn't use the root account during day-to-day operations, so this is a moot point. Finally, there is a cursor, and this is where you can start typing commands!

■ **Note** If you were to log in as root, a hash (#) would appear instead of the $ prompt. This is important to remember, because often in magazines and some computer manuals, the use of the hash symbol before a command indicates that it should be run as root. In addition, if you select the recovery option of the installation CD, you'll be running as root, and a hash will appear at the prompt. See Chapter 21 for more information about the root user.

Running Programs

When we refer to *commands* at the shell, we're actually talking about small programs. When you type a command to list a directory, for example, you're starting a small program that will do that job. Seen in this light, the shell's main function is to simply let you run programs—either those that are built into the shell, such as ones that let you manipulate files, or other, more-complicated programs (including those that you've installed yourself).

The shell is clever enough to know where your programs are likely to be stored. This information was given to it when you first installed Ubuntu and is stored in a system variable.

■ **Note** A *variable* is the method Linux uses to remember things such as names, directory paths, or other data. Many system variables are vital for the running of Ubuntu. These variables can be seen by typing **set** at the command prompt.

The information about where your programs are stored and therefore where Ubuntu should look for commands you type in, as well as any programs you might want to run, is stored in the PATH variable. You can take a look at what's currently stored there by typing the following:

```
echo $PATH
```

Don't forget that the difference between uppercase and lowercase letters matters to Ubuntu, unlike with Windows and DOS.

The echo command merely tells the shell to print something onscreen. In this case, you're telling it to "echo" the PATH variable onto your screen. On our test PC, this returned the following information:

```
/usr/local/sbin:/usr/local/bin:/usr/sbin:/usr/bin:/sbin:/bin
```

Several directories are in this list, each separated by a colon.

Don't worry too much about the details right now. The important thing to know is that whenever you type a program name, the shell looks in each of the listed directories in sequence. In other words, when you type **ls**, the shell will look in each of the directories stored in the PATH variable, starting with the first in the list, to see whether the ls program can be found. The first instance it finds is the one it will run. (The ls command gives you a directory listing, as described in the "Listing Files" section later in this chapter.)

But what if you want to run a program that is not contained in a directory listed in your PATH? In this case, you must tell the shell exactly where the program is. Here's an example:

```
/home/ubuntu/myprogram
```

This will run a program called myprogram in the /home/ubuntu directory. It will do this regardless of the directory you're currently browsing, and regardless of whether there is anything else on your system called myprogram.

If you're already in the directory where the program in question is located, you can type the following:

```
./myprogram
```

So, just enter a dot and a forward slash, followed by the program name. The dot tells BASH that what you're referring to is "right here." Like the tilde symbol (~) mentioned earlier, this dot is BASH shorthand.

■ **Note** Some of the most basic commands are built into the BASH program and aren't stand-alone programs. Examples include the command to change directory (cd) and the aforementioned echo command. Logically enough, these commands are known as BASH *built-ins*. Should you type such a command, BASH will not search the PATH directories to find the command because there is no need. You can find out whether a command is a built-in by preceding it with type—for example, type cd.

Getting Help

Each command usually has help built in, which you can query (a little like typing /? after a command when using DOS). This will explain what the command does and how it should be used. In most cases, you'll see a hypothetical example of the command in use, along with the range of command options that can be used with it. For example, you can get some instant help on the ifconfig command by typing this:

```
ifconfig --help
```

The --help option is fairly universal, and most programs will respond to it, although sometimes you might need to use a single dash. Just type the command along with --**help** to see what happens. You'll be told if you're doing anything wrong.

In addition, most commands have technical manuals that you can read to gain a fairly complete understanding of how they work. Virtually every Ubuntu setup has a set of these man pages, which can be accessed by typing this:

```
man <command>
```

However, man pages are often designed for experienced Ubuntu users who understand the terminology.

Some commands also have info pages, which offer slightly more down-to-earth guides. You can read these by typing this:

```
info <command>
```

If a command isn't covered by the info system, you'll be shown the default screen explaining basic facts about how the info command works.

Note that both man and info have their own man and info pages, explaining how they work. Just type man man or info info. We explain how to read man and info pages in Appendix C.

Running the Shell via a Virtual Console

As noted earlier, you can start the shell in a number of ways. The most common way among Linux diehards is via a virtual console. To access a virtual console, press Ctrl+Alt and then press one of the function keys from F1 through F6 (the keys at the top of your keyboard).

Using a virtual console is a little like switching desks to a completely different PC. Pressing Ctrl+Alt+F1 will cause your GUI to disappear and the screen to be taken over by a command-line prompt (don't worry—your GUI is still there and running in the background). You'll be asked to enter your username and your password to log in.

Any programs you run in a virtual console won't affect the rest of the system, unless they're system commands specifically designed to affect other programs. (This can be very useful—as discussed in Chapter 26, one way to rescue a crashed GUI program is to switch to a virtual console and attempt to terminate the program from there.)

You can switch back to the GUI by pressing Ctrl+Alt+F7. Don't forget to quit your virtual console when you're finished with it, by typing **exit**.

BOOTING INTO THE SHELL

If you're really in love with the shell, you can choose to boot into it, avoiding the GUI completely.

Stopping Ubuntu from running a GUI upon booting is simply a matter of stopping the program that appears when Ubuntu boots—GDM. This provides the login window that appears and starts the whole graphical subsystem. An easy way to do this is by renaming the configuration file: gdm.conf.

```
sudo mv /etc/init/gdm.conf /etc/init/gdm.disabled
```

This prevents GDM from ever starting. Next time you boot your computer you will be taken to the command-line shell. To enable GDM again just rename the file back to its original name.

```
sudo mv /etc/init/gdm.disabled /etc/init/gdm.conf
```

Working with Files

So let's start actually using the shell. If you've ever used DOS, you have a head start over most shell beginners, although you'll still need to learn some new commands and forget some entrenched ones! Table A-1 shows various DOS commands alongside their Ubuntu equivalents. This table also serves as a handy guide to some BASH commands, even if you've never used DOS. At the end of this appendix, you'll find a comprehensive list of useful shell commands, together with explanations of what they do and examples of typical usage. Perhaps it's obvious, but most commands are abbreviations of the words that describe their function. The cp command copies files, for example, and the rm file removes files. This can often help identify commands when you first encounter them, and also aid in memorizing.

Table A-1. DOS Commands and Their Shell Equivalents

Command	DOS Command	Linux Shell Command	Usage
Copy files	COPY	cp	cp <filename> <new location>
Move files	MOVE	mv	mv <filename> <new location>
Rename files	RENAME	mv	mv <old filename> <new filename> [a]
Delete files	DEL	rm	rm <filename> [b]
Create directories	MKDIR	mkdir	mkdir <directory name>

Command	DOS Command	Linux Shell Command	Usage
Delete directories	DELTREE/RMDIR	rm	rm -rf <directory name>
Change directory	CD	cd	cd <directory name>
Edit text files	EDIT	vi	vi <filename>
View text files	TYPE	less	less <filename> [c]
Print text files	PRINT	lpr	lpr <filename>
Compare files	FC	diff	diff <file1> <file2>
Find files	FIND	find	find -name <filename>
Check disk integrity	SCANDISK	fsck	fsck [d]
View network settings	IPCONFIG	ifconfig	ifconfig
Check a network connection	PING	ping	ping <address>
View a network route	TRACERT	tracepath	tracepath <address>
Clear screen	CLS	clear	clear
Get help	HELP	man	man <command> [e]
Quit	EXIT	exit	exit

[a] The BASH shell offers a *rename* command, but this is chiefly used to rename many files at once.

[b] To avoid being asked to confirm each file deletion, you can add the -*f* option. Be aware that the *rm* command deletes data instantly, without the safety net of the Recycle Bin, as with the GNOME desktop.

[c] Use the cursor keys to move up and down in the document. Type **Q** to quit.

[d] This is a system command and can be run only on a disk that isn't currently in use. To scan the main partition, you'll need to boot from the installation CD and select the rescue option. Then issue the fsck command.

[e] The info command can also be used.

CREATING ALIASES

If you've ever used DOS, you might find yourself inadvertently typing DOS commands at the shell prompt. Some of these will actually work, because most distribution companies create command aliases to ease the transition of newcomers to Linux.

Using aliases means that whenever you type certain words, they will be interpreted as meaning something else. However, an alias won't work with any of the command-line switches used in DOS. In the long run, you should try to learn the BASH equivalents. You can create your own command aliases quickly and simply. Just start a BASH shell and type the following:

```
alias <DOS command>='<Linux shell command>'
```

For example, to create an alias that lets you type `cls` instead of `clear`, type this:

```
alias cls='clear'
```

Note that the Ubuntu command must appear in single quotation marks. Also note that the `dir` command is already implemented under Ubuntu as a separate command that functions almost identically to the Linux `ls` command, although it's intended for only brief file listings. In most cases, it's far better just to use the `ls` command.

To make aliases permanent, you need to add them to your `.bashrc` file.

Open the file in the Gedit text editor by typing the following:

```
gedit .bashrc
```

At the bottom of the file, add new lines for all the aliases you want to make permanent. Simply type the command shown previously. Save the file when you've finished.

Note that the aliases won't go into effect until you open a new terminal window or reboot the computer.

Listing Files

Possibly the most fundamentally useful BASH command is `ls`. This lists the files in the current directory. If you have a lot of files, they might scroll off the screen. If you're running GNOME Terminal, you can use the scrollbar on the right side of the window to view the list.

Having the files scroll off the screen can be annoying, so you can cram as many as possible onto each line by typing the following:

```
ls -m
```

The dash after the command indicates that you're using a command option. These are also called command-line *flags* or *switches*, and they modify how a command works. Nearly all shell commands have options. In fact, some commands won't do anything unless you specify various options. In the case of the `ls` command, only one dash is necessary, but some commands need two dashes to indicate an option.

■ **Note** Technically speaking, using two dashes before a command option is a relatively modern convention introduced by the GNU Project in the 1980s. Prior to this, UNIX used a single dash for command options. Thus, two dashes usually indicate GNU-specific command options. However, this is a moot point nowadays because even versions of UNIX, such as Mac OS X, tend to use the GNU BASH shell.

You can see a list of all the command options for ls by typing the following (ironically, itself a command option):

```
ls --help
```

Once again, the output will scroll off the screen, and you can use the window's scrollbars to examine it.

With most commands, you can use many command options at once, as long as they don't contradict each other. For example, you could type the following:

```
ls -lh
```

This tells the ls command to produce "long" output and also to produce "human-readable" output. The long option (-l) lists file sizes and ownership permissions, among other details (permissions are covered in the next chapter). The human-readable option (-h) means that rather than listing files in terms of bytes (such as 1,029,725 bytes), it will list them in kilobytes, megabytes, gigabytes, and so on. Notice that you can simply list the options after the dash; you don't need to give each option its own dash.

■ **Caution** Don't forget that case-sensitivity is vitally important in Ubuntu! Typing **ls -L** is not the same as typing **ls -l**. Each will produce different results.

Copying Files and Directories

Another useful command for dealing with files is cp, which copies files. You can use the cp command in the following way:

```
cp myfile /home/ubuntu/
```

This will copy the file to the location specified. In this example, the filename and location are technically known as *arguments*. Anything that you specify a command should work with is referred to as an argument, and this can often be important when you try to figure out what the man pages are saying about how a command works.

One important command-line option for cp is -r. This stands for *recursive* and tells BASH that you want to copy a directory and its contents (as well as any directories within this directory). Most commands that deal with files have a recursive option.

■ **Note** Only a handful of BASH commands default to recursive copying. Even though it's extremely common to copy folders, you still need to specify the -r command option most of the time.

One curious trick is that you can copy a file from one place to another but, by specifying a filename in the destination part of the command, change its name. Here's an example:

```
cp myfile /home/ubuntu/myfile2
```

This will copy myfile to /home/ubuntu, but rename it as myfile2. Be careful not to add a final slash to the command when you do this. In the example here, doing so would cause BASH to think that myfile2 is a directory.

This way of copying files is a handy way of duplicating files. By not specifying a new location in the destination part of the command, but still specifying a different filename, you effectively duplicate the file within the same directory:

```
cp myfile myfile2
```

This will result in two identical files: one called myfile and one called myfile2.

Moving Files and Directories

The mv command is similar to cp, except that rather than copying the file, the old one is effectively removed. You can move files from one directory to another, for example, like this:

```
mv myfile /home/ubuntu/
```

You can also use the mv command to quickly rename files:

```
mv myfile myfile2
```

The mv command can be used to move a directory in the same way as with files. However, there's no need to use a command option to specify recursivity, as with other commands.

For instance, to move the directory /daffodil into the directory /flowers, you could type the following (assuming both directories are in the one you're currently browsing):

```
mv daffodil/ flowers/
```

Note the use of the slash after each directory.

To rename directories, simply leave off the slashes. To rename the directory /daffodil to /hyacinth, for example, you could type the following:

```
mv daffodil hyacinth
```

■ **Note** Getting technical for a moment, moving a file in Linux isn't the same as in Windows, where a file is copied and then the original deleted. Under Ubuntu, the file's absolute path is rewritten, causing it to simply appear in a different place in the file structure. However, the end result is the same.

Deleting Files and Directories

But how do you get rid of files? Again, this is relatively easy, but first a word of caution: the shell doesn't operate any kind of Recycle Bin. After a file is deleted, it's gone forever. (There are utilities you can use to recover files, but these are specialized tools and aren't to be relied on for everyday use.)

Removing a file is achieved by typing something like this:

```
rm myfile
```

It's as simple as that.

In some instances, you'll be asked to confirm the deletion after you issue the command. If you want to delete a file without being asked to confirm it, type the following:

```
rm -f myfile
```

The f command option stands for *force* (that is, force the deletion).

If you try to use the rm command to remove a directory, you'll see an error message. This is because the command needs an additional option:

```
rm -rf mydirectory
```

As noted earlier, the r stands for *recursive* and indicates that any folder specified afterward should be deleted, in addition to any files it contains.

■ **Tip** You might have used wildcards within Windows and DOS. They can be used within Ubuntu, too. For example, the asterisk (*) can be used to mean any file. So, you can type rm -f * to delete all files within a directory, or type rm -f myfile* to delete all files that start with the word myfile. But remember to be careful with the rm command. Keep in mind that you cannot salvage files easily if you accidentally delete them!

WORKING WITH FILENAMES THAT HAVE SPACES

If, at the command prompt, you try to copy, move, or otherwise manipulate files that have spaces in their names, you'll run into problems. For example, suppose you want to move the file picture from germany.jpg to the directory /mydirectory. In theory, the following command should do the trick:

```
mv picture from germany.jpg mydirectory/
```

But when we tried it on our test Ubuntu setup, we got the following errors:

```
mv: cannot stat 'picture': No such file or directory
mv: cannot stat 'from': No such file or directory
mv: cannot stat 'germany.jpg': No such file or directory
```

In other words, BASH had interpreted each word as a separate file and tried to move each of them! The error messages tell us that BASH cannot find the file picture, from, or germany.jpg.

There are two solutions. The easiest is to enclose the filename in quotation marks (either double or single), so the previous command would read as follows:

```
mv "picture from germany.jpg" mydirectory/
```

The other solution is to precede each space with a backslash. Known as *escaping the character*, this tells BASH you're including a *literal character* in the filename. In other words, you're telling BASH not to interpret the space in the way it usually does, which is as a separator between filenames or commands. Here's how the command looks if you use backslashes:

```
mv picture\ from\ germany.jpg mydirectory/
```

The backslash can also be used to stop BASH from interpreting other symbols in the way it usually does. For example, the less-than and greater-than symbols (<>) have a specific meaning in BASH, but they're allowed in filenames. So to copy the file <bach>.mp3 to the directory /mydirectory, you could type the following:

```
cp /<bach/>.mp3 mydirectory/
```

Generally speaking, however, simply enclosing filenames in quotation marks is the easiest approach. Often you might find that filenames under Linux avoid using spaces completely by using hyphens or underscore characters instead, or by simply not including the space characters and running the words into each other (for example, thirdquarterreport.doc).

Changing and Creating Directories

Another handy command is cd, for *change directory*. This lets you move around the file system from directory to directory. Say you're in a directory that has another directory in it, named mydirectory2. Switching to it is easy:

```
cd mydirectory2
```

But how do you get out of this directory after you're in it? Try the following command:

```
cd ..
```

The .. refers to the *parent* directory, which is the one containing the directory you're currently browsing. Using two dots to indicate this may seem odd, but it's just the way that Ubuntu (and UNIX before it) does things. It's one of the many conventions that UNIX relies on and that you'll pick up as you go along.

To switch to the root of the file system, you would type the following:

```
cd /
```

■ **Tip** BASH always remembers the last directory you were in, and you can switch to it instantly by typing cd -.

You can create directories with the mkdir command:

```
mkdir mydirectory
```

What if you want to create a new directory and, at the same time, create a new directory to contain it? Simply use the -p command option. The following command will create a new folder called flowers and, at the same time, create a directory within /flowers called /daffodil:

```
mkdir -p flowers/daffodil
```

RELATIVE AND ABSOLUTE PATHS

A *path* is simply the description of where in the file system a particular file or folder lives—for example, /home/ubuntu/Music/britneyspears.mp3. Paths come in two forms: absolute and relative. The differences are simple.

An *absolute path* shows the location of the file from the ground up—from the root of the file system, specifying each individual folder along the way. The preceding example (/home/ubuntu/Music/britneyspears.mp3) is an absolute path. There's an elementary way of identifying them: absolute paths always begin with a forward slash, which indicates the root of the file system.

A *relative path* is one that's expressed relative to the currently browsed directory. That might be a little difficult to understand, so here's an example. We already know that, when used with the cd command, two dots (..) refer to the parent directory of the one currently being browsed. With this in mind, what if the user Frank was browsing /home/Frank/Music and wanted to switch to the /etc directory, which contains configuration files? He could simply type cd /etc, thereby specifying the absolute path. That's certainly the simplest method. But he also could specify a relative path as follows:

```
cd ../../../etc
```

In other words, he's specified the parent of the current directory, then the parent of that directory, and finally the parent of *that* directory! That takes him all the way back to the root of the file system, so finally he specifies the /etc directory, which is where he wants to be.

You can move from any position in the file system to anywhere else by specifying a relative path, and the same technique works when you're manipulating files by copying, moving, and so on. To be honest, specifying an absolute path is usually the simplest option, but relative paths can prove surprisingly useful in some situations.

Using Autocompletion

The Tab key is your best friend when using the shell, because it will cause BASH to automatically complete whatever you type. For example, if you want to run Ubuntu's web browser, you can enter **firefox** at the command line. However, to save yourself some time, you can type **fir** and then press Tab. You'll then find that BASH fills in the rest for you. It does this by caching the names of the programs you might run according to the directories listed in your $PATH variable.

Of course, autocompletion has some limitations. On our Ubuntu test system, typing **loc** didn't autocomplete the useful locate command. Instead, it caused BASH to beep. This is because on a default Ubuntu installation, there is more than one possible match. Pressing Tab again immediately shows those matches. Depending on how much you type (how much of an initial clue you give BASH), you might find there are many possible matches.

In this case, the experienced BASH user simply types another letter, which will be enough to distinguish the almost-typed word from the rest, and presses Tab again. With any luck, this should be enough for BASH to fill in the rest.

Autocompletion with Files and Paths

Tab autocompletion also works with files and paths. If you type the first few letters of a folder name, BASH will try to fill in the rest. This also obviously has limitations. There's no point in typing **cd myfol** and pressing Tab if there's nothing in the current directory that starts with the letters myfol. This particular autocomplete function works by looking at your current directory and seeing what's available.

Alternatively, you can specify an initial path for BASH to use in order to autocomplete. Typing **cd /ho** and pressing Tab will cause BASH to autocomplete the path by looking in the root directory (/). In other words, it will autocomplete the command with the directory /home. In a similar way, typing **cd myfolder/myfo** will cause BASH to attempt to autocomplete by looking for a match in myfolder.

If you want to run a program that resides in the current directory, such as one you've just downloaded, for example, typing ./, followed by the first part of the program name, and then pressing Tab should be enough to have BASH autocomplete the rest. In this case, the dot and slash tell BASH to look in the current directory for any executable programs or scripts (programs with x as part of their permissions) and use them as possible autocomplete options.

BASH is clever enough to spot whether the command you're using is likely to require a file, directory, or executable, and it will autocomplete with only relevant file or directory names.

Viewing Available Options

The autocomplete function has a neat side effect. As we mentioned earlier, if BASH cannot find a match, pressing Tab again causes BASH to show all the available options. For example, typing **ba** at the shell and then pressing Tab twice causes BASH to show all the possible commands starting with the letters *ba*. On our test PC, this produces the following list of commands:

```
badblocks  baobab  basename  bashbug

banner  base64  bash  batch
```

This can be a nice way of exploring what commands are available on your system. You can then use each command with the --help command option to find out what it does, or browse the command's man page.

When you apply this trick to directory and filename autocompletion, it's even more useful. For example, typing **cd** in a directory and then pressing the Tab key twice will cause BASH to show the available directories, providing a handy way of retrieving a brief directory listing. Alternatively, if you've forgotten how a directory name is spelled, you can use this technique to find out prior to switching into it.

Other Autocompletion Examples

Under Ubuntu, but not under most Linux distros, you can also use Tab autocomplete with other commands. In fact, anywhere you might think autocomplete will prove useful, you'll probably find it works. For example, when installing software by using the apt-get command you can type a little of the package name you'd like to install, and then hit Tab to have it autocompleted. As when exploring commands by using the Tab key (as explained earlier), this is a neat way of exploring what packages are available.

You will also find that Tab autocomplete works with the man command, used to view technical documentation. Just type **man** and then a little of the command you're interested in, before hitting Tab to autocomplete.

Using Keyboard Shortcuts

Your other good friends when using BASH are the Ctrl and Alt keys. These keys provide shortcuts to vital command-line shell functions. They also let you work more efficiently when typing by providing what most programs call keyboard shortcuts.

Shortcuts for Working in BASH

Table A-2 lists the most common keyboard shortcuts in BASH (there are many more; see BASH's man page for details). If you've explored the Emacs text editor, you might find these shortcuts familiar. Such keyboard shortcuts are largely the same across many of the software packages that originate from the GNU Project. Often, you'll find an option within many Ubuntu software packages that lets you use Emacs-style navigation, in which case, these keyboard shortcuts will most likely work equally well.

Table A-2. Keyboard Shortcuts in BASH

Shortcut	Description
Navigation	
Left/right cursor key	Moves left/right in text
Ctrl+A	Moves to beginning of line
Ctrl+E	Moves to end of line
Ctrl+right arrow	Moves forward one word
Ctrl+left arrow	Moves left one word
Editing	
Ctrl+U	Deletes everything behind cursor to start of line
Ctrl+K	Deletes from cursor to end of line
Ctrl+W	Deletes from cursor to beginning of word
Alt+D	Deletes from cursor to end of word
Ctrl+T	Transposes characters on left and right of cursor
Alt+T	Transposes words on left and right of cursor

Shortcut	Description
Miscellaneous	
Ctrl+L	Clears screen (everything above current line)
Ctrl+U	Undoes everything since last command[a]
Alt+R	Undoes changes made to the line[b]
Ctrl+Y	Undoes deletion of word or line caused by using Ctrl+K, Ctrl+W, and so on[c]
Alt+L	Lowercases current word (from the cursor to end of word)

[a] In most cases, this has the effect of clearing the line.

[b] This is different from Ctrl+U, because it will leave intact any command already on the line, such as one pulled from your command history.

[c] This allows primitive cutting and pasting. Delete the text and then immediately undo, after which the text will remain in the buffer and can be pasted with Ctrl+Y.

Shortcuts for System Control

In terms of the control over your system offered by keyboard commands, pressing Ctrl+Z has the effect of stopping the current program. It suspends the program until you switch back into it or tell it to resume in another way, or manually kill it.

In the same style, pressing Ctrl+C while a program is running will quit it. This sends the program's process a termination signal, a little like killing it by using the top program. Ctrl+C can prove handy if you start a program running by accident and quickly want to end it, or if a command takes longer than you expected to work and you cannot wait for it to complete. It's also a handy way of attempting to end crashed programs. Some complicated programs don't take too kindly to being quit in this way, particularly those that need to save data before they terminate. However, most should be okay.

Ctrl+D is another handy keyboard shortcut. This sends the program an end-of-file (EOF) message. In effect, this tells the program that you've finished your input. This can have a variety of effects, depending on the program you're running. For example, pressing Ctrl+D on its own at the shell prompt when no program is running will cause you to log out (if you're using a GUI terminal emulator like GNOME Terminal, the program will quit). This happens because pressing Ctrl+D informs the BASH shell program that you've finished your input. BASH then interprets this as the cue that it should log you out. After all, what else can it do if told there will be no more input?

Although it might not seem very useful for day-to-day work, Ctrl+D is vital for programs that expect you to enter data at the command line. You might run into these as you explore BASH. If you ever read in a man page that a program requires an EOF message during input, you'll know what to press.

Using the Command History

The original hackers who invented the tools used under UNIX hated waiting around for things to happen. After all, being a hacker is all about finding the most efficient way of doing any particular task.

Because of this, the BASH shell includes many features designed to optimize the user experience. The most important of these is the *command history*. BASH remembers every command you enter (even the ones that didn't work!) and stores them as a list on your hard disk.

During any BASH session, you can cycle through this history by using the up and down arrow keys. Pressing the up arrow key takes you back into the command history, and pressing the down arrow key takes you forward.

The potential of the command history is enormous. For example, rather than retype that long command that runs a program with command options, you can simply use the cursor keys to locate it in the history and press Enter.

■ **Tip** Typing !-3 will cause BASH to move three paces back in the history file and run that command. In other words, it will run what you entered three commands ago.

On our Ubuntu test system, BASH remembers 500 commands. You can view all of the remembered commands by typing **history** at the command prompt. The history list will scroll off the screen because it's so large, but you can use the scrollbars of the GNOME Terminal window to read it. To view the last 20 commands, type **history 20**. You can specify any number here, in fact. Each command in the history list is assigned a number. You can run any of the history commands by preceding their number with an exclamation mark (!), referred to as a *bang*, or sometimes a *shriek*. For example, you might type **!923**. On our test system, command number 923 in the BASH history is cd .., so this has the effect of switching us into the parent directory.

Command numbering remains in place until you log out (close the GNOME Terminal window or end a virtual console session). After this, the numbering is reordered. There will still be 500 commands, but the last command you entered before logging out will be at the end of the list, and the numbering will work back 500 places until the first command in the history list.

■ **Tip** One neat trick is to type two bangs: !!. This tells BASH to repeat the last command you entered.

Rather than specifying a command number, you can type something like **!cd**. This will cause BASH to look in the history file, find the last instance of a command line that started with cd, and then run it.

Pressing Ctrl+R lets you search the command history from the command prompt. This particular tool can be tricky to get used to, however. As soon as you start typing, BASH will autocomplete the command based on matches found in the history file, starting with the last command in the history. What you type appears before the colon, while the autocompletion appears afterward.

Because BASH autocompletes as you type, things can get a little confusing when you're working with the command history, particularly if it initially gets the match wrong. For example, typing **cd** will show the last instance of the use of cd. This might not be what you're looking for, so you must keep typing the command you do want until it autocompletes correctly. Alternatively, you can hit Ctrl+R to cycle through older examples of the particular command that you've started typing.

Piping and Directing Output

It's not uncommon for a directory listing or output from another command to scroll off the screen. When using a GUI program such as GNOME Terminal, you can use the scrollbars to view the output, but what if you are working at the bare command-line prompt?

By pressing Shift+Page Up and Shift+Page Down, you can "scroll" the window up to take a look at some of the old output, but very little is cached in this way, and you won't see more than a few screens. A far better solution is to pipe the output of the directory listing into a text viewer. Another useful technique is to redirect output to a file.

Piping the Output of Commands

Piping was one of the original innovations provided by UNIX. It simply means that you can pass the output of one command to another, which is to say the output of one command can be used as input for another.

This is possible because shell commands work like machines. They usually take input from the keyboard (referred to technically as *standard input*) and, when they've done their job, usually show their output on the screen (known as *standard output*).

The commands don't need to take input from the keyboard, and they don't need to output to the screen. Piping is the process of diverting the output before it reaches the screen and passing it to another command for further processing.

Let's assume that you have a directory that is packed full of files. You want to do a long directory listing (ls -l) to see what permissions various files have. But doing this produces reams of output that fly off the screen. Typing something like the following provides a solution:

```
ls -l | less
```

The | symbol between the two commands is the *pipe*. It can be found on most US keyboards next to the square bracket keys (near the Enter key—you'll need to hold down the Shift key to get it).

What happens in the example is that ls -l is run by the shell, but rather than sending the output to the screen, the pipe symbol (|) tells BASH to send it to the command that follows—to less. In other words, the listing is displayed within less, where you can read it at your leisure. You can use Page Up and Page Down or the arrow keys to scroll through it. After you quit less, the listing evaporates into thin air; the piped output is never stored as a file.

In the previous section, you saw how you can use the history command to view the command history. At around 500 entries, its output scrolls off the screen in seconds. However, you can pipe it to less, like so:

```
history | less
```

You can pipe the output of any command. One of the most common uses is when searching for a particular string in the output of a command. For example, let's say you know that, within a crowded directory, there's a file with a picture of some flowers. You know that the word *flower* is in the filename, but you can't recall any other details. One solution is to perform a directory listing and then pipe the results to grep, which is able to search through text for a user-defined string (see Chapter 12):

```
ls -l | grep -i 'flower'
```

In this example, the shell runs the ls -l command and then passes the output to grep. The grep command then searches the output for the word *flower* (the -i option tells it to ignore uppercase and lowercase). If grep finds any results, it will show them on your screen.

The key point to remember is that grep is used here as it normally is at the command prompt. The only difference is that it's being passed input from a previous command, rather than being used on its own.

You can pipe more than once on a command line. Suppose you know that the filename of the picture you want includes the words *flower* and *daffodil*, yet you're unsure of where they might fall in the filename. In this case, you could type the following:

```
ls -l | grep -i flower | grep -i daffodil
```

This will pass the result of the directory listing to the first grep, which will search the output for the word *flower*. The second pipe causes the output from grep to be passed to the second grep command, where it's then searched for the word *daffodil*. Any results are then displayed on your screen.

Redirecting Output

Redirecting is like piping, except that the output is passed to a file rather than to another command. Redirecting can also work the other way: the contents of a file can be passed to a command.

If you wanted to create a file that contained a directory listing, you could type this:

```
ls -l > directorylisting.txt
```

The angle bracket (>) between the commands tells BASH to direct the output of the ls -l command into a file called directorylisting.txt. If a file with this name exists, it's overwritten with new data. If it doesn't exist, it's created from scratch.

You can add data to an already existing file by using two angle brackets:

```
ls -l >> directorylisting.txt
```

This will append the result of the directory listing to the end of the file called directorylisting.txt, although, once again, if the file doesn't exist, it will be created from scratch.

Redirecting output can get very sophisticated and useful. Take a look at the following:

```
cat myfile1.txt myfile2.txt > myfile3.txt
```

As you learned in Chapter 12, the cat command joins two or more files together. If the command were used on its own without the redirection, it would cause BASH to print myfile1.txt on the screen, immediately followed by myfile2.txt. As far as BASH is concerned, it has joined myfile1.txt to myfile2.txt and then sent them to standard output (the screen). By specifying a redirection, you have BASH send the output to a third file. Using cat with redirection is a handy way of combining two files.

It's also possible to direct the contents of a file back into a command. Take a look at the following:

```
sort < textfile.txt > sortedtext.txt
```

The sort command simply sorts words into alphanumeric order (it actually sorts them according to the ASCII table of characters, which places symbols and numbers before alphabetic characters). Directly after the sort command is a left angle bracket, which directs the contents of the file specified immediately after the bracket into the sort command. This is followed by a right angle bracket, which directs the output of the command into another file.

■ **Tip** To see a table of the ASCII characters, type **man ascii** at the command-line prompt.

There aren't many instances in day-to-day usage where you'll want to use the left angle bracket. It's mostly used with the text-based mail program (which lets you send e-mail from the shell), and in shell scripting, in which a lot of commands are combined together to form a simple program.

REDIRECTING STANDARD ERROR OUTPUT

Standard input and standard output are what BASH calls your keyboard and screen. These are the default input and output methods that programs use unless you specify something else, such as redirecting or piping output and input.

When a program goes wrong, its error message doesn't usually form part of standard output. Instead, it is output via *standard error*. Like standard output, this usually appears on the screen.

Sometimes it's beneficial to capture an error message in a text file. This can be done by redirecting the standard error output. The technique is similar to redirecting standard output:

```
wodim --scanbus 2> errormessage.txt
```

The wodim command is used to burn CDs, and with the --scanbus command option, you tell it to search for CD-R/RW drives on the system, something that frequently results in an error message if your system is not properly configured.

After the initial command, you see the redirection. To redirect standard error, all you need to do is type **2>**, rather than simply **>**. This effectively tells BASH to use the second type of output: standard error.

You can direct both standard output and standard error to the same file. This is done in the following way:

```
cdrecord --scanbus > error.txt 2>&1
```

This is a little more complicated. The standard output from wodim --scanbus is sent to the file error.txt. The second redirect tells BASH to include standard error in the standard output. In other words, it's not a case of standard output being written to a file, and then standard error being added to it. Instead, standard error is added to standard output by BASH, and then this is written to a file.

Using Brace Expansion

The ultimate labor-saving trick at the command-line is brace expansion.

Put simply, anything within braces ({}) is substituted within the specified filename. The following will create new directories called PhotosGermany, PhotosEngland, and PhotosSpain:

```
mkdir Photos{Germany,England,Spain}
```

In other words, the mkdir command takes the word Photos and combines it with Germany, England, and Spain, creating three new directories.

If you also wanted to create a directory called Photos, with no country after it, you could do so via brace expansion by specifying a comma with nothing before it. Here's a repeat of the same command with this in place, followed by a file listing showing the results:

```
mkdir Photos{,Germany,England,Spain}
```

```
$ ls

Photos   PhotosEngland   PhotosGermany   PhotosSpain
```

A numeric or alphabetic range of expansions can be specified by using two dots (..). You will have observed that this is different from wildcards, where the dash is used to indicate a range. The following will create directories called PhotosA, PhotosB, PhotosC, and so on, all the way to Z:

```
mkdir Photos{A..Z}
```

BASH Command Index

This appendix provides a whistle-stop tour of commands that can be used at the BASH shell. This is a highly selective listing, intended to provide a guide to commands that see day-to-day use on average desktop systems. In a similar fashion, although some command options are listed, they're strictly limited to those that receive regular deployment.

The description of each command is deliberately simple. Note that the quantity of space given to a command is not an indication of its importance or usefulness. To this end, each command listed with an asterisk after its name offers far more than its brief description indicates. In such cases, we strongly advise that you refer to the command's man page for more information.

Various conventions are used in the list:

- You should substitute your own details wherever italicized words appear.

- Commands that can and might be run by ordinary users are preceded with a dollar sign ($).

- Commands that require root privileges (the use of sudo) are preceded with a hash symbol (#).

Commands that present dangers to the system through misuse are clearly marked. Such commands should not be used without research into the command's usage and function.

Table A-3. *Common BASH Commands*

Command	Description	Typical Command Options	Examples of Use
$ alias	Create or display command aliases		alias *list*=ls
$ alsamixer	Alter audio volume levels		alsamixer
$ apropos	Search man pages for specified words/phrases		apropos "*word or phrase*"
$ apt-cache	Search, query, and otherwise manipulate the APT database cache (see aptget)	search: Search for specified package (regexes may be used; see Chapter 15) showpkg: Show information about specified package depends: Show package dependencies of specified package, and show other packages that can meet that dependency	apt-cache search *packagename*

Command	Description	Typical Command Options	Examples of Use
# apt-get	Multifunction tool used to install, remove, and otherwise administer software packages, according to the APT database	install: Search for and install specified package from repositories (as specified in /etc/apt/sources.list) update: Update or build package database by contacting package repositories upgrade: Attempt to upgrade all current installed packages with new versions dist-upgrade: Attempt to upgrade all currently installed packages, automatically and aggressively resolving package conflicts; often used to upgrade entire distro to new version remove: Opposite of install; removes packages clean: Remove any old package installation files that are stored on hard disk -f: Attempt to fix broken package dependencies (used with install or remove) force-yes: Override any errors and thereby bypass apt-get's protective measures. Dangerous option—use with care!	apt-get install packagename
$ bzip2	Compress specified file (replaces original file with compressed file and gives it .bz2 file extension)	-d: Decompress specified file -k: Don't delete original file -t: Test; do a dry run without writing any data	bzip2 *myfile*
$ bzip2 recover	Attempt recovery of specified damaged .bz2 file		bzip2recover *myfile* *.tar.bz2*
$ cal	Display calendar for current month (or specified month/year)		cal 4 2005
$ cat	Display a file onscreen or combine and display two files together		cat *myfile*

Command	Description	Typical Command Options	Examples of Use
$ cd	Change to specified directory		cd /usr/bin
$ cdparanoia *	Convert CD audio tracks to hard disk files	-B: Batch mode; convert all tracks to individual files -S: Set CD read speed (2, 4, 8, 12, and so on; values relate to CD-drive spin speed; used to avoid read errors)	cdparanoia -S 8 -B
# wodim *	Burn audio or CD-R/RW data discs (the latter usually based on an ISO image; see mkisofs)	-dev=: Specify the drive's device number (can be discovered by running wodim with the scanbus option) scanbus: Scan to see which CD-R/RW drives are present and return device numbers -speed=: Specify the write speed (2, 4, 6, 8, and so on) -v: Verbose output; obligatory for feedback on wodim's progress	wodim dev=0,0,0 -speed=16 -v myfile.iso
# cfdisk *	Dangerous! Menu-based disk-partitioning program		cfdisk /dev/hda
# chgrp	Change group ownership of a file/directory	-R: Recursive; apply changes to subdirectories	chgrp mygroup myfile
$ chmod	Change permissions of a file/directory (where a = all, u = user, g = group, and r = read, w = write, x = executable)	-R: Recursive; apply to subdirectories reference=: Copy permissions from specified file	chmod a+rw myfile
$ chown	Change file ownership to specified username	-R: Recursive; apply to subdirectories	chown username myfile1
# chroot	Change the root of the file system to the specified path		chroot /home/mydirectory
# chvt	Switch to the specified virtual terminal (equivalent of holding down Ctrl+Alt and pressing F1–F6)		chvt 3

Command	Description	Typical Command Options	Examples of Use
$ clear	Clear terminal screen and place cursor at top		clear
$ cp	Copy files	-r: Recursive; copy subdirectories and the files therein -s: Create symbolic link instead of copying	cp *myfile1 directory/*
$ crontab	Edit or display the user's crontab file (scheduled tasks)	-e: Edit the crontab file (create/amend) -l: List crontab entries -r: Delete the crontab file -u: Specify a user and edit their crontab file	crontab -e
$ date	Display the date and time		date
$ df	Display free disk space within file system	-h: Human readable; display sizes in KB, MB, GB, and TB, as appropriate -l: Restrict to local file systems, as opposed to network mounts	df -h
$ diff	Display differences between specified files	-a: Consider all files text files (don't halt when asked to compare binary files) -i: Ignore lowercase and uppercase differences	diff *myfile1 myfile2*
$ diff3	Display differences between three specified files		diff3 *myfile1 myfile2 myfile3*
$ dig	Look up IP address of specified domain		dig *mysite.com*
$ dmesg	Display kernel message log		dmesg
# dosfsck *	Check and repair MS-DOS– based file hard disk partition (see also fsck)	-a: Repair without asking user for confirmation -r: Repair file system, asking user for confirmation when two or more repair methods are possible -v: Verbose; display more information	dosfsck -rv */dev/hda4*

Command	Description	Typical Command Options	Examples of Use
# dpkg	Install, remove, and otherwise administer local installation packages (on your hard disk); see also apt-get	-i: Install specified package -r: Remove (uninstall) specified package -I: Show info about specified package ignore-depends=*packagename*.*deb*: Don't halt on package dependency issues (dangerous!)	dpkg -i *packagename*.*deb*
# dpkg-reconfigure	Reconfigure an already installed package		dpkg-reconfigure *packagename*
$ du	Show sizes of files and folders in kilobytes	-h: Human readable; produce output in MB, GB, and TB -s: Summary; display totals only for directories rather than for individual files	du -h /*home*/*myuser*
$ eject	Eject a removable storage disk	-t: Close an already open tray	eject /*media*/*dvd-rom*
$ ex *	Start a simple text-editor program used principally within shell scripts		ex *myfile*.*txt*
$ exit	Log out of shell (end session)		exit
$ fdformat	Low-level format a floppy disk (this won't create a file system; see also mkfs)		fdformat /*dev*/*fd0*
# fdisk *	Dangerous! Hard disk partitioning program	-l: List partition table	fdisk /*dev*/*hda*
$ fg	Bring job running in background to foreground		fg 1
$ file	Display information about specified file, such as its type		file *myfile*

Command	Description	Typical Command Options	Examples of Use
$ find *	Find files by searching directories (starting in current directory)	-maxdepth: Specify the number of subdirectory levels to delve into, starting from 1 (current directory) -name: Specify name of file to search for -type: Specify file types to be returned; -type d returns directories, and -type f returns only files	find -name "myfile"
$ free	Display information about memory usage	-m: Show figures in MB -t: Total the columns at bottom of table	free -m
# fsck *	Check file system for errors (usually run from rescue disc)		fsck /dev/hda1
$ ftp *	FTP program for uploading/downloading to remote sites		ftp ftp.mysite.com
$ fuser	Show which processes are using a particular file or file system	-v: Verbose; detailed output	fuser -v myfile
$ genisoimage *	Create ISO image file from specified directory (usually for burning to disc with wodim)	-o: Options; this must appear after command to indicate that command options follow -apple: Use Mac OS extensions to make disc readable on Apple computers -f: Follow symbolic links and source actual files -J: Use Joliet extensions (make ISO compatible with Windows) -R: Use Rock Ridge extensions (preferred Linux CD-ROM file system) -v: Verbose; display more information (-vv for even more info)	mkisofs -o isoimage.iso -R -J -v mydirectory

Command	Description	Typical Command Options	Examples of Use
$ grep *	Search specified file for specified text string (or word)	-i: Ignore uppercase and lowercase differences -r: Recursive; delve into subdirectories (if applicable) -s: Suppress error messages about inaccessible files and other problems	grep "phrase I want to find" myfile.txt
# groupadd	Create new group		groupadd mygroup
# groupdel	Delete specified group		groupdel mygroup
$ groups	Display groups the specified user belongs to		groups myuser
$ gzip	Compress files and replace original file with compressed version	-d: Decompress specified file -v: Verbose; display degree of compression	gzip myfile
# halt	Initiate shutdown procedure, ending all processes and unmounting all disks	-p: Power off system at end of shutdown procedure	halt -p
# hdparm *	Dangerous! Tweak or view hard disk settings		hdparm /dev/hda
$ head	Print topmost lines of text files (default is first 10 lines)	-n: Specify number of lines (such as -n 5)	head myfile.txt
$ help	Display list of common BASH commands		help
$ history	Display history file (a list of recently used commands)		history
$ host	Query DNS server based on specified domain name or IP address	-d: Verbose; return more information -r: Force name server to return its cached information rather than query other authoritative servers	host 82.211.81.166
$ hostname	Display localhost-style name of computer		hostname

Command	Description	Typical Command Options	Examples of Use
$ id	Display username and group info of specified user (or current user if none specified)		id *myuser*
# ifconfig *	Display or configure settings of a network interface (assign an IP address or a subnet mask, and activate/deactivate it)	down: Disable interface (used at end of command chain) netmask: Specify a subnet mask up: Enable interface (used at end of command chain)	ifconfig eth0 *192.168.0.10* netmask *255.255.0.0* up
$ info *	Display info page for specified command		info *command*
# init	Change current run level		init *1*
$ jobs	Display list of jobs running in background		jobs
$ kill	Kill specified process		kill *1433*
$ killall	Kill process(es) that have specified name(s)	-i: Confirm before killing process -v: Verbose; report if and when successful	killall *processnumber*
$ last	Display details of recent logins, reboots, and shutdowns		last
$ ldd	Display system files (libraries) required by specified program		ldd */usr/bin/program*
$ less	Interactively scroll through a text file	-q: Quiet; disable beeps when end of file is reached or other error encountered -i: Ignore case; make all searches case insensitive unless uppercase letters are used	less *myfile.txt*
$ ln	Create links to specified files, such as symbolic links	-s: Create symbolic link (default is hard link)	ln -s *myfile1 myfile2*

Command	Description	Typical Command Options	Examples of Use
$ lpr	Print file (send it to the printer spool/queue)	-V: Verbose; print information about progress of print job	lpr *myfile.txt*
$ lpstat	Display print queue		Lpstat
$ ls	List directory	-a: List all files, including hidden files -d: List only directory names rather than their contents -h: Human readable; print figures in KB, MB, GB, and TB -l: Long list; include all details, such as file permissions -m: Show as comma-separated list	ls -h *mydirectory*
# lsmod	Display currently loaded kernel modules		Lsmod
$ lsof	Display any files currently in use	-u: Limit results to files used by specified user	lsof -u *username*
$ man	Display specified command's manual		man *command*
$ md5sum	Display MD5 checksum (normally used to confirm a file's integrity after download)		md5sum *myfile*
# mkfs *	Dangerous! Create specified file system on specified device (such as a floppy disk)	-t: Specify type of file system	mkfs -t *vfat /dev/fd0*
# modinfo	Display information about kernel module		modinfo *modulename*
# modprobe	Insert specified module into the kernel, as well as any others it relies on	-k: Set module's autoclean flag so it will be removed from memory after inactivity -r: Remove specified module as well as any it relies on to operate	modprobe *modulename*
$ more	Interactively scroll through text file (similar to less)		more *myfile.txt*

Command	Description	Typical Command Options	Examples of Use
# mount *	Mount specified file system at specified location	-o: Specify command options, such as rw to allow read/write access; various types of file systems have unique commands	mount /dev/hda4 /mnt
$ mv	Move (or rename) specified files and/or directories	-b: Back up files before moving -v: Display details of actions carried out	mv myfile mydirectory/
$ netstat *	Show current network connections		netstat -a
$ nice	Run specified command with specified priority	-n: Specify priority, ranging from the highest priority of – 20, to 19, which is the lowest priority	nice -n 19
$ nohup	Run specified command and continue to run it, even if user logs out		nohup command
$ passwd	Change user's password		Passwd
$ ping	Check network connectivity between local machine and specified address	-w: Exit after specified number of seconds (such as -w 5)	ping mydomain.com
$ printenv	Display all environment variables for current user		Printenv
$ ps *	Display currently running processes	a: List all processes (note that command options don't require preceding dash) f: Display ownership of processes by using tree-style graphics u: Limit results to processes running for and started by current user x: Include processes in results not started by user but running with the user ID	ps aux
$ pwd	Display current directory		Pwd
# reboot	Reboot computer		Reboot

Command	Description	Typical Command Options	Examples of Use
$ renice	Change a process's priority while it's running (see nice)		renice 19 10704
$ rm	Delete single or multiple files and/or directories	-r: Recursive; delete specified directories and any subdirectories -f: Force; don't prompt for confirmation before deleting (use with care!)	rm -rf mydirectory
# rmmod	Delete module from kernel		rmmod modulename
# route *	Add and create (or view) entries in routing table (see ifconfig)		route add default gw 192.168.1.1
$ runlevel	Display current run level		runlevel
$ screen *	Program that runs pseudo shell that is kept alive regardless of current user login	-ls: Display list of currently running screen sessions -R: Reattach to already running screen session or start new one if none available	screen
$ sftp *	Secure Shell FTP; like FTP but running over an ssh connection (see ssh)		sftp username@192.168.1.14
$ shred	Overwrite data in a file with gibberish, thereby making it irrecoverable	-u: Delete file in addition to overwriting -v: Verbose; show details of procedure -f: Force permissions to allow writing if necessary	shred -fv myfile
$ sleep	Pause input for the specified period of time (where s = seconds, m = minutes, h = hours, d = days)		sleep 10m
$ smbclient *	FTP-style program with which you can log in to an SMB-based (Windows) file share		smbclient //192.168.1.1/

Command	Description	Typical Command Options	Examples of Use
$ sort	Sort entries in the specified text file (default is ASCII sort)		sort myfile.txt -o sorted.txt
$ ssh *	Log in to remote computer by using secure shell		ssh username@192.168.1.15
$ startx	Start GUI session (if GUI isn't already running)		startx
$ su	Temporarily log in as specified user; log in as root if no user specified (provided root account is activated)	-: Adopt user's environment variables, such as $PATH	su
$ sudo	Execute specified command with root privileges		sudo *command*
$ tac	Display specified text file but in reverse (from last to first line)		tac *myfile.txt*
$ tail	Display final lines of specified text file	-n: Specify number of lines to display (such as -n4)	tail *myfile.txt*
$ tar *	Combine specified files and/or directories into one larger file, or extract from such a file	-c: Create new archive -j: Use bzip2 in order to compress (or decompress) files -f: Specifies filename (must be last in chain of command options) -r: Add files to existing archive -x: Extract files from existing archive -z: Use gzip to compress (or decompress) files	tar -zcf *myfile* *.tar.gz mydirectory*
$ tee	Display piped output and also save it to specified file		ls -lh| tee *listing.txt*
$ top *	Program that both displays and lets the user manipulate processes		top

Command	Description	Typical Command Options	Examples of Use
`$ touch`	Give specified file current time and date stamp; if it doesn't exist, create a zero-byte file with that name		`touch` *`myfile`*
`$ tracepath`	Discover and display network path to another host		`tracepath` *`192.168.1.20`*
`$ umask`	Set default permissions assigned to newly created files		`umask u=rwx,g=r,o=`
`# umount`	Unmount a file system		`umount` *`/media/cdrom`*
`# useradd`	Add new user	`-m`: Create home directory for user	`useradd -m` *`username`*
`# userdel`	Delete all mention of user in system configuration files (effectively deleting the user, although files owned by the user might remain)	`-r`: Remove user's /home directory	`userdel -r` *`username`*
`$ unalias`	Remove specified alias	`-a`: Remove all aliases (use with care!)	`unalias` *`command`*
`$ uname`	Display technical information about current system	`-a`: Display all basic information	`uname -a`
`$ unzip`	Unzip a Windows-compatible Zip file	`-l`: Display archive content but don't actually unzip	`unzip` *`myfile.zip`*
`$ uptime`	Display uptime for system, as well as CPU load average and logged-in users		`uptime`
`$ vim` *	Text editor program		`vim`
`$ wc`	Count the number of words in a file		`wc` *`myfile.txt`*

Command	Description	Typical Command Options	Examples of Use
`$ whatis`	Display one-line summary of specified command		`whatis command`
`$ whereis`	Display information on where a binary command is located, along with its source code and man page (if applicable)	-b: Return information only about binary programs	`whereis -b command`
`$ xhost`	Configure which users/systems can run programs on the X server	+: When followed by a username and/or system name, gives the user/system permission to run programs on the X server; when used on its own, lets *any* user/system use the X server -: Opposite of +	`xhost +`
`$ xinit`	Start elementary GUI session (when not already running a GUI)		`xinit`
`$ zip`	Create Windows-compatible compressed Zip files	-r: Recursive; includes all subdirectories and files therein -u: Updates Zip with specified file -P: Encrypts Zip with specified password -v: Verbose; display more information -#: Set compression level (from 0, which is no compression, to 9, which is highest)	`zip -r myfile .zip mydirectory`
`$ zipgre p`	Searches inside Zip files for specified text string		`zipgrep " search phrase myfile .zip`

∎∎∎

Glossary of Linux Terms

This appendix provides brief explanations of common terms used in the Linux and UNIX environments. These include technical terms, as well as conventions used in the Linux community. Because of space limitations, this glossary is somewhat selective but still should prove a lasting reference as well as a helpful guide for those new to Linux.

Cross-referenced terms are highlighted in italics.

Symbols

.

In the context of file management at the *command-line prompt*, this symbol refers to the current directory.

..

In the context of file management at the *command-line prompt*, this symbol refers to the parent directory of that currently being browsed.

/

In the context of file management at the *command-line prompt*, the forward slash refers to the *root* of the file system; it also separates directories in a path listing.

~

In the context of file management at the *command-line prompt*, the tilde refers to a *user*'s home directory.

|

The pipe symbol is used at the *command-line prompt* to *pipe* output from one *command* to another.

>

When used at the *command-line prompt*, the right angle bracket indicates that output should *redirect* into a file.

<

When used at the *command-line prompt*, the left angle bracket indicates that a *command* should accept input from a file (see *redirect*).

#

When it appears at the *command-line prompt*, this symbol usually indicates that the *user* is currently logged in as *root*.

$

When it appears at the *command-line prompt*, the dollar sign usually indicates that the *user* is currently logged in as an ordinary user. (Note that some versions of *Linux/ UNIX* use % or > instead of $.)

?

The question mark is a wildcard character indicating that any character can be substituted in its place; this symbol is typically relevant only at the *command-line prompt*.

*

The asterisk is a wildcard character indicating that zero or more characters can appear in its place; this symbol is typically relevant only at the *command-line prompt*.

*nix

Popular but unofficial way of describing the family tree that comprises *UNIX* and its various clones, such as *Linux* and *Minix*.

A

administrator

A *user* on the system with ultimate power to configure the system. Usually under standard *Linux* installations, this is another word for either the *root user* or one who has adopted that user's powers temporarily.

AIX

IBM's *proprietary* form of *UNIX* that runs on the company's proprietary hardware, as well as *commodity* hardware based around AMD and Intel processors. Nowadays, IBM is slowly deprecating AIX in favor of *Linux*.

alias

Method of creating a *user*-defined *command* that, when typed, causes another command to be run or a *string* to be expanded.

Apache

Popular *open source* web *server* software that runs on *UNIX*, *Linux*, and other operating system platforms. Considered responsible in part for the rise in popularity of Linux in the late 1990s.

applet

Small program that, in the context of the *Ubuntu* Desktop, runs as part of a larger program and offers functions that complement the main program. The *GNOME* desktop incorporates several applets, and—technically speaking—all features or elements of the panels are applets, including even the main menus.

APT

Advanced Packaging Tool; the underlying system by which software is managed and installed on *Ubuntu* and *Debian Linux* systems. *Shell* commands beginning with apt, such as apt-get, are used to install new software from various repositories. Under Ubuntu, the Synaptic Package Manager program provides a *GUI* method of using APT.

archive

Any file containing a collection of smaller files, compressed or otherwise (see also *tar*).

B

BASH

Bourne Again SHell. The most common *shell* interpreter used under *Linux* and offered as the default on many Linux systems. Based on the older Bourne sh software.

binary executable

Another way of referring to a program that has been compiled so that it can be used day to day. See also *compilation*.

block device

How the *Linux kernel* communicates with a *device* that sends and receives blocks of data; usually a hard disk or removable storage device. See also *character device*.

BSD UNIX

Berkeley Software Distribution UNIX; form of *UNIX* partially based on the original UNIX *source code* but also incorporating recent developments. BSD is *open source* and *free* for all to use and share, with practically no restrictions. There are various forms of BSD UNIX, such as FreeBSD, NetBSD, and OpenBSD. BSD doesn't use the *Linux kernel* but runs many of the same programs. Some of the programs offered within the Linux OS come from BSD.

bzip2

Form of file compression. Together with the older and less-efficient *gzip*, it is a popular form of file compression under *Linux* and the equivalent to Zip compression under Windows. Files employing bzip compression are usually given a `.bz2` file extension (*tar* files are usually given the double file extension `.tar.bz2`, or occasionally just `.tbz`). See also *tar*.

C

C

Programming language in which much of the *Linux kernel* is written, as were later versions of *UNIX* before it. C was created by some of the same people who created UNIX, and its development mirrors that of UNIX.

C++

Object-oriented programming language; originally designed to be an enhancement to *C*, but now seen as a popular alternative.

C#

Modern programming language, which uses similar syntax to *C*, created by Microsoft and re-created on *Linux* via the Mono project.

character device

How Linux refers to a *device* that sends/receives data asynchronously. For various technical reasons, this typically refers to the *terminal* display. See also *block device*.

checksum

Mathematical process that can be applied to a file or other data to create a unique number relative to the contents of that file. If the file is modified, the checksum will change, usually indicating that the file in question has failed to download correctly or has been modified in some way. The most common type of checksum program used under *Linux* and *UNIX* is `md5sum`.

client

Shorthand referring to a computer (or software) that connects to a *server*.

closed source

The reverse of *open source*, in which the *source code* is not available for others to see, share, or modify. See also *proprietary*.

code

See *source code*.

command

Input typed at the *shell* that performs a specific task, usually related to administration of the system and/or the manipulation of files.

command-line prompt

See *shell*.

commodity

In the context of hardware, describes PC hardware usually based around Intel or AMD processors that can be bought off the shelf and used to create sophisticated computer systems (as opposed to buying specially designed hardware). One reason for *Linux*'s success is its ability to use commodity hardware.

community

The general term for the millions of *Linux users* worldwide, regardless of what they use Linux for or their individual backgrounds. By using Linux, you automatically become part of the community.

compilation

The practice of creating a binary file from *source code*, usually achieved using the `./configure`, `make`, `make install` series of *commands* and *scripts*.

config file

Configuration file; any file that contains the list of settings for a program. Sometimes it's necessary to edit config files by hand by using programs such as *vi* or *Emacs*, but often the program itself will write its config file according to the settings you choose.

copyleft

The legal principle of protecting the right to share a creative work, such as a computer program, using a legally binding license. Copyleft also ensures that future iterations of the work are covered in the same way.

cracker

Someone who breaks into computer systems to steal data or cause damage. The term is not necessarily linked to *Linux* or *UNIX* but was created by the *community* to combat the widespread use of *hacker* in this sense. The word *hacker* has traditionally defined someone who merely administers, programs, and generally enjoys computers.

cron

Background *service* that schedules tasks to occur at certain times. It relies on the `crontab` file.

CUPS

Common UNIX Printing System; set of programs that work in the background to handle printing under *UNIX* and *Linux*.

curses

Library that lets software present a semigraphical interface at the *shell*, complete with menu systems and simple mouse control (if configured). The version of curses used under *Linux* and *UNIX* is called `ncurses`.

CVS

Concurrent Versions System; application that allows the latest version of software packages to be distributed over the Internet to developers and other interested parties. Nowadays Git or Subversion are preferred instead and work along similar lines.

D

daemon

See *service*.

Debian

Community organization that produces *distributions* of *free software* operating systems, including *Linux*. Because it is a nonprofit organization run by passionate free software advocates, it is considered the most ethically sound of all Linux outfits. Many distributions, including *Ubuntu*, use Debian as the basis for their software because of its claimed reliability, relative simplicity, and certain sophisticated features, such as the *APT* software management system.

dependency

A way of referring to system files or other software that a program requires in order to run. If the dependencies are not present during program installation, a program might refuse to install.

device

Linux shorthand describing something on your system that provides a function for the *user* or that the system requires in order to run. This usually refers to hardware, but it can also describe a virtual device that is created to provide access to a particular Linux function.

directory

What Windows refers to as a folder; areas on a hard disk in which files can be stored and organized.

distribution

A collection of software making up the *Linux* operating system; also known as a *distro*. The software is usually compiled by either a company or organization. A distribution is designed to be easy to install, administer, and use by virtue of it being an integrated whole. Examples include *Ubuntu*, SUSE *Linux*, *Red Hat*, and *Debian*.

distro

Shorthand for *distribution*.

documentation

Another way of describing written guides or instructions; can refer to online sources of help as well as actual printed documentation.

dpkg

Debian package management system; *shell command* that can be used to administer software under *Ubuntu* and *Debian*. However, the *APT* system, which uses dpkg, is the preferred method of installing software.

E

Edubuntu

Official spin-off of the main *Ubuntu* project that features educational software along with a child-friendly user interface and classroom administration software. Unlike other spin-off projects, such as *Xubuntu* and *Kubuntu*, Edubuntu features the same *GNOME* interface as the main Ubuntu release, and much of the same software.

Emacs

Seminal text editor and pseudo-*shell* beloved by *UNIX* aficionados; can be used for programming tasks, simple word processing, and much more. This editor has cultural significance as one of the core pieces of software offered by the *GNU Project*. Emacs was originally developed principally by *Richard Stallman*. See also *vi*.

environment

Shorthand referring to a *user*'s unique *Linux* configuration, such as *variables* that tell the *shell* where programs are located.

F

FAT32

File Allocation Table 32-bits; file system offered by Windows 98, Me, 2000, and XP. *Linux* can both read and write to FAT32 file systems. See also *NTFS* and *VFAT*.

Firefox

Web browser program used under *Ubuntu* and produced by the *Mozilla Foundation*.

FLOSS

Free, libre, or open source software; used within the *community* to describe all software or technology that, broadly speaking, adheres to the ethical approach of *open source* software and/or *free software*, as well as its legal guidelines.

FOSS

Free or *open source* software; alternative term for *FLOSS*.

free

When used to describe software or associated areas of technology, *free* indicates that the project abides by the ethical (if not legal) guidelines laid down by the *GNU Project*. It doesn't necessarily indicate that the software is free in a monetary sense; its meaning is quite different from freeware.

Free software

Software in which the *source code*—the original listing created by the programmer—is available for all to see, share, study, and adapt to their own needs. This differs from the concept of *open source*, because the right of others to further modify the code is guaranteed via the *GNU Public License* (GPL) software license (or a compatible license). For various reasons, in some instances free software does not include the source code (although the software can still be legally decompiled), but this is rare.

Free Software Foundation

Nonprofit organization founded by *Richard Stallman* to effectively sponsor the creation of the *GNU* operating system, and further the aims and goals of *free software* (including the legal documents, such as the *GPL*). It is considered the home of the free software ideal and GNU itself. Sometimes abbreviated as FSF.

G

GCC

GNU Compiler Collection; programs used when creating *binary executable* files from *source code*. Formerly called GNU C Compiler.

GID

Group ID; numbering system used by the operating system to refer to a *group*.

GIMP

GNU Image Manipulation Program; high-powered image-editing program that runs under *Linux*, *UNIX*, Windows, and other operating systems. Often preceded by the definite article: The GIMP.

GNOME

A *GUI*-based desktop *environment* used by *Ubuntu* as well as several other *distributions*. It uses the GTK+ libraries. The name was originally created as an acronym standing for GNU Network Object Model Environment, but now the term is considered a word and not an acronym. See also *KDE*.

GNU

GNU's Not UNIX; seminal operating system project initiated by *Richard Stallman* in 1983 and intended to form a *free software* clone of *UNIX*. See *GNU Project*.

GNU/Linux

Another name for the operating system referred to as *Linux*. The name GNU/Linux gives credit to the vast quantity of *GNU Project* software that is added to the *Linux kernel* within a *distro* to make a complete operating system. As such, GNU/Linux is the preferred term of many *free software* advocates.

GNU Project

Organization created by *Richard Stallman* in order to further the aims of *free software* and create the body of software that makes up the *GNU* operating system.

GNU Public License

Software license principally created by *Richard Stallman* in order to protect software *source code* against *proprietary* interests and ensure that it will always be shared. It does this by insisting that any source code covered by the GNU Public License (GPL) must remain licensed under the GPL, even after it has been modified or added to by others. The *Linux kernel*, as well as much of the software that runs on it, uses the GPL. There are several versions of the GNU Public License that refine its requirements and limitations (notably versions 2 and 3), and several variations designed for other uses; key examples include the Lesser GPL (*LGPL*), which relinquishes some requirements of the GPL and is usually used with *library* software, and the GNU Free Documentation License that, as its name suggests, is usually used to license technical literature, such as manuals.

GPL

See *GNU Public License.*

grep

Global regular expression print; powerful *shell command* that lets you search a file or other form of input by using *regular expressions*. Because of the ubiquity of the grep program, many *Linux* and *UNIX* users refer to searching as *grepping*. To *grep a file* is to search through it for a *string*.

group

Collection of *users* under one heading (group name) to facilitate system administration.

GRUB

GRand Unified Bootloader; boot manager program that offers a menu from which you can choose which operating system you wish to boot. It's needed to load the *kernel* program and thereby initiate the *Linux* boot procedure.

GUI

Graphical user interface; describes the software that provides a graphical system to display data and let you control your PC (usually via a mouse).

guru

One who is experienced and knowledgeable about *Linux/UNIX* and is willing to share his or her knowledge with others. In a perfect world, every *newbie* would have his or her own guru.

gzip

One of the two preferred forms of file compression used under *Linux*. Files employing gzip compression usually have a `.gz` file extension. See also *bzip2*.

H

hack

Ingenious and/or extremely efficient solution to a problem, particularly within the programming world.

hacker

Term used within the *community* to describe anyone who enjoys computers and possesses some skill therein, either in a professional capacity or as a hobby. A positive and highly valued term, the word is distinct from connotations of maliciously breaking into computers propagated by the media. See also *cracker*.

host

Shorthand referring to any computer that acts as a *server* to another computer. See also *client*.

HP-UX

Hewlett-Packard's *proprietary* form of *UNIX* designed to work on its own hardware platform.

Hurd

Kernel developed by the *GNU Project* and originally intended to form the centerpiece of the *GNU* operating system. However, with the arrival of the *Linux kernel*, its necessity was lessened, and it is now arguably a minor project. It's not associated with the Linux kernel in any way.

I

info

Source of *documentation* accessible from the *shell*; an alternative to the more established *man page* system. Also known as Texinfo.

init

With most versions of *Linux*, init is the program that is automatically run after the *kernel* has finished loading, and therefore early in the boot procedure. It's responsible for effectively starting the operating system. Under *Ubuntu*, a system called *Upstart* is used instead, but it is 100 percent backward-compatible with the way init works, to the extent that those not knowing Upstart was in use would not realize the difference.

init.d

Collection of startup *scripts* that make up the components of a *run level*. Under *Ubuntu*, these are found at /etc/init.d. *Symbolic links* to selected init.d scripts are contained in folders within /etc/init.d that are named after *run level* numbers, such as rc0.d, rc1.d, rc2.d, and so on.

initrd

Initial RAM disk; system used by the *Linux kernel* to load *modules* that are essential for the kernel to be able to boot, such as disk controllers.

inode

Part of the usually invisible file system structure that describes a file, such as its ownership permissions or file size.

ipchains

Now-deprecated component of version 2.2 of the *Linux kernel* that allows the creation of network security setups, such as firewalls or port-forwarding arrangements. Note that some *distros* still prefer to use ipchains. See also *iptables*.

iptables

Component of versions 2.4 and 2.6 of the *Linux kernel* that allows powerful network security setups via the configuration of netfilter. Chiefly used in the creation of firewalls, but can be used for more elementary arrangements such as network address translation (NAT) routers. *Ubuntu* offers a far more user-friendly command-line tool called ufw that aids configuration of iptables.

J

job

How the *BASH shell* refers to a running program in order to facilitate administration by the *user*.

journaling

File system technology in which integrity is maintained via the logging of disk writes.

K

KDE

K Desktop Environment; *GUI* and set of additional programs used on various *distros*, such as Mandriva and a variation of *Ubuntu* called *Kubuntu*.

kernel

Essential but ordinarily invisible set of programs that run the computer's hardware and provide a platform on which to run software. In the *Linux* operating system, the kernel is also called Linux, after its creator, *Linus Torvalds*.

kernel panic

Error message that appears when the *kernel* program in *Linux* cannot continue to work. In other words, a polite way of indicating a crash or, more often, a problem arising from *user* misconfiguration. This is most often seen when booting up after making incorrect changes to the system.

kludge

Community slang describing an inelegant way of making something work, usually not in a way that is generally accepted as being correct. Pronounced *kloodge*.

Kubuntu

Version of *Ubuntu* that substitutes the *GNOME* desktop *environment* for *KDE*.

L

LAMP

Acronym describing a series of programs that work together to provide a complete *Linux*-based web-hosting *environment*. Stands for *Linux, Apache, MySQL,* and PHP, Python, or Perl (the last three in the list are scripting languages; see *script*).

LGPL

Lesser GPL; version of the *GNU Public License* (GPL) in which some use restrictions are slackened at the expense of various freedoms laid down by the main GPL. The LGPL is mostly used for *library* files.

library

General term referring to *code* that programs need to run and that, once in memory, is frequently accessed by many programs (leading to the phrase "shared library"). The most common and vital library is glibc (GNU C Library), created by the *GNU Project* and the fundamental building block without which *Linux* could not operate. *GNOME* relies on the GTK+ libraries, among others.

link

File system method of assigning additional filenames to a block of data that represents a file; also known as a "hard link." See also *symbolic link*.

Linux

(1) A *kernel* program created by *Linus Torvalds* in 1991 to provide an inexpensive operating system for his computer, along with other components.

(2) The entire operating system discussed in this book, although many argue (perhaps quite rightly) that this is inaccurate, and use the term *GNU/Linux* instead, to give credit to the inclusion of many components of the *GNU* operating system.

Linux Foundation

A nonprofit organization that aims to further the adoption of the *Linux* operating system, and as such is sponsored by many corporations that utilize the Linux OS as part of their business, such as IBM and Novell. It is considered the spiritual home of Linux, if such a distinction can be made, and employs *Linus Torvalds*, the originator and leader of the Linux *kernel* project.

local

Shorthand referring to the *user*'s PC or a device directly attached to it (as opposed to *remote*).

localhost

Network name used internally by *Linux* and software to refer to the *local* computer, distinct from the network.

M

man page

Concise technical *documentation* accessible from the *shell* that describes a *command* and how it should be used.

Minix

Created by Andrew Tanenbaum, this operating system is a rough clone of *UNIX*. It was the operating system that *Linus Torvalds* had in mind when devising *Linux,* and which acted as an early development platform for him.

module

Program *code* that can be inserted or removed from the *kernel* in order to support particular pieces of hardware or provide certain kernel functions. Drivers under Windows perform the same function.

mount

To add a file system so that it is integrated (and therefore accessible) within the main file system; applies to external file systems, such as those available across networks, as well as those on the *local* PC, such as the hard disk or CD/DVD-ROMs.

Mozilla Foundation

Organization founded by Netscape to create *open source* Internet software, such as web browsers and e-mail clients; originally based on the Netscape *source code*. At the time of this writing, it produces the *Firefox* and Camino web browsers, the Thunderbird e-mail and Usenet client, the Bugzilla bug-tracking software, as well as other programs. The underlying web-browsing engine software used by many Mozilla Foundation products is known as Gecko.

MySQL

Popular and powerful *open source* database application. See also *LAMP*.

N

newbie

Term used to describe anyone who is new to *Linux* and therefore still learning the basics. It's not a derogatory term! See also *guru*.

NFS

Network File System; reliable and established method of sharing files, printers, and other resources across a network of *UNIX*-based operating systems. See also *Samba*.

NTFS

NT File System; file system offered by Windows NT, 2000, XP, and Vista. It is usually fully accessible under *Linux*, although some distributions do not allow writing to NTFS *partitions*. See also *FAT32*.

O

open source

(1) Method and philosophy of developing software whereby the *source code*—the original listing created by the programmer—is available for all to see. Note that open source is not the same as *free software*; describing software as open source doesn't imply that the code can be shared or used by others (although this is often the case).

(2) A community of *users* or any project that adheres to open source values and/or practices.

OpenOffice.org

Open source office suite project created with the continuing input of Sun Microsystems (now part of Oracle) and based on *code* Sun contributed to the open source *community*. Oracle commercializes a proprietary version called Oracle Open Office (previously known as StarOffice).

P

partition

Subdivision of a hard disk into which a file system can be installed.

PID

Process ID; the numbering system used to refer to a *process*.

pipe

Method of passing the output from one *command* to another for further processing. Piping is achieved within the *shell* by typing the | symbol.

POSIX

Portable Operating System Interface; various technical standards that define how *UNIX*-like operating systems should operate and to which the *Linux* operating system attempts to adhere.

PPP

Point-to-Point Protocol; networking technology that allows data transfer across serial connections such as telephone lines. In other words, it's the technology that lets you connect to your Internet service provider by using a modem.

process

The way the system refers to the individual programs (or components of programs) running in memory.

proprietary

Effectively, software for which a software license must be acquired, usually for a fee. This usually means that the *source code* is kept secret, but it can also indicate that the source code is available to view but not to incorporate into your own projects or share with others.

R

Red Hat

Well-known company that produces *distributions* of *Linux*.

redirect

Used to send the output of a *command* into a particular file. This also works the other way around: the contents of a particular file can be directed into a command. Redirection is achieved within the *shell* by using the left and right angle brackets (< and >), respectively.

regex

See *regular expression*.

regular expression

Powerful and complex method of describing a search *string*, usually when searching with tools such as *grep* (although regular expressions are also used when programming). Regular expressions use various symbols as substitutes for characters or to indicate patterns.

remote

Indicates a computer or *service* that is available across a network, including but not limited to computers on the Internet (as opposed to *local*).

root

(1) The bottom of the *Linux* file system directory structure, usually indicated by a forward slash (/).

(2) The /root directory in the bottom of the file system, which is effectively the root user's personal directory.

(3) The hard disk *partition* on which operating system files are installed, sufficient to boot Linux; under *Ubuntu* the root partition contains all operating system and user data files.

(4) The *user* on some versions of *UNIX* or Linux who has control over all aspects of hardware, software, and the file system.

(5) Used to describe a user who temporarily takes on the powers of the root user (via the sudo command, for example).

RPM

Red Hat Package Manager; system used to install and administer programs under *Red Hat*, *SUSE Linux*, and some other *distributions*. The equivalent of *APT*.

RTFM

Read the Fine manual/*man page*; exclamation frequently used online when a *newbie* asks for help without having undertaken basic research.

run level

Describes the current operational mode of *Linux* (typically, the *services* that are running). Run level 1 is single-user mode (a stripped-down system with minimal running services); run levels 2 through 5 provide a *GUI*; run level 6 is reboot mode (switching to it will cause the computer to terminate its processes and then reboot); run level 0 is shutdown (switching to it will cause the PC to shut down). Under *Ubuntu* and most derivatives of *Debian*, run level 2 is the default.

S

Samba

Program that re-creates under *UNIX* or *Linux* the Microsoft *SMB*-based system of sharing files, printers, and other computer resources across a network. It allows Linux to become a file or printer *server* for Linux and Windows computers, and also allows a Linux *client* to access a Windows-based *server*.

scalable

Term describing the ability of a single computer program to meet diverse needs, regardless of the scale of the potential uses. The *Linux kernel* is described as being scalable because it can run supercomputers as well as handheld computers and home entertainment devices.

script

Form of computer program consisting of a series of *commands* in a text file. Most *shells* allow some form of scripting, and entire programming languages such as Perl are based around scripts. In the context of the *Linux* OS, shell scripts are usually created to perform trivial tasks or ones that frequently interact with the *user*. Shell scripts have the advantage that they can be frequently and easily modified. The Linux boot process relies on several complex scripts to configure essential system functions such as networking and the *GUI*. See also *init* and *Upstart*.

server

(1) Type of computer designed to share data with other computers over a network.

(2) Software that runs on a computer and is designed to share data with other programs on the same PC or with other PCs across a network.

service

Background program that provides vital functions for the day-to-day running of *Linux*; also known as a *daemon*. Services are usually started when the computer boots up and as such are constituent parts of a *run level*.

shell

Broadly speaking, any program that creates an operating *environment* in which you can control your computer. The *GNOME* Desktop can be seen as a shell, for example. However, it's more commonly understood within *UNIX* and *Linux* circles as a program that lets you control the system by using *command*s entered at the keyboard. In this context, the most common type of shell in use on Linux is *BASH*.

Shuttleworth, Mark

Entrepreneurial South African businessman who, as a long-term *Debian hacker*, devised and financially supports *Ubuntu* via his company, Canonical Ltd.

SMB

Server Message Block; network technology for sharing files, printers, and other resources. See also *Samba*.

Solaris

Form of *UNIX* sold by Sun Microsystems (now part of Oracle); runs on *proprietary* hardware systems as well as on *commodity* systems based on Intel and AMD processors. Available in an entirely *open source* rendition called OpenSolaris.

source code

The original program listing created by a programmer. Most programs that you download are precompiled—already turned into *binary executables* ready for general use—unless you specifically choose to download and compile the source code of a program yourself.

SSH

Secure SHell; program that lets you access a *Linux*/*UNIX* computer across the Internet. SSH encrypts data sent and received across the *link*.

SSL

Secure Sockets Layer; form of network data transfer designed to encrypt information for security purposes. It's used online for certain web sites and also within *Linux* for certain types of secure data exchange.

Stallman, Richard M.

Legendary *hacker* who founded the *GNU Project* and created the concept of *copyleft*, as well as the software license that incorporates it: the *GNU Public License* (GPL). See also *Linus Torvalds*.

standard error

Linux and *UNIX* shorthand for the error output provided by a *command*.

standard input

Linux and *UNIX* shorthand for the *device* usually used to provide input to the *shell*. For the majority of desktop PC *users*, this refers to the keyboard.

standard output

Linux and *UNIX* shorthand for the *device* usually used to display output from a *command*. For the majority of desktop PC *users*, this refers to the screen.

string

A word, phrase, or sentence consisting of letters, numbers, or other characters that is used within a program and is often supplied by the *user*.

sudo

Program that runs under *UNIX* and *Linux* by which ordinary *users* are temporarily afforded *administrator* rights. *Ubuntu* relies on sudo as the exclusive way for users to administer the system. The equivalent command to start *GUI* applications under Ubuntu is gksu.

SVG

Scalable Vector Graphics; vector graphics technology. SVG is actually an XML markup language designed to create 2D graphics, increasingly used for *Linux* desktop icons and web graphics.

swap

Area of the hard disk that the *Linux kernel* uses as a temporary memory storage area. Desktop or *server* Linux differs from Windows in that it usually requires a separate hard disk *partition* in which to store the swap file.

symbolic link

Type of file akin to a Windows shortcut. Accessing a symbolic link file routes the *user* to an actual file. See also *link*.

sysadmin

Systems administrator; a way of describing the person employed within a company to oversee the computer systems. In such an *environment*, the sysadmin usually is the *root* user of the various computers.

System V

Variant of *UNIX* used as a foundation for modern forms of *proprietary* UNIX.

T

tainted

Describes a *kernel* that is using *proprietary modules* in addition to *open source* modules. Can also refer to insecure software.

tar

Tape ARchive; software able to combine several files into one larger file in order to back them up to a tape drive or simply transfer them across the Internet. Such files are usually indicated by a `.tar` file extension. Note that a `tar` file isn't necessarily compressed; the *bzip2* and *gzip* utilities must be used if this is desired.

TCP/IP

Transmission Control Protocol/Internet Protocol; standard protocol stack used by most modern operating systems to control and communicate across networks and also across the Internet (as opposed to NetBEUI, commonly available on older versions of Windows, and IPX/SPX, used on Novell's NetWare operating system).

terminal

Another word for *shell*.

TeX

Method and set of programs for typesetting complex documents. Invented prior to word processors and desktop publishing software, and now considered a specialized tool for laying out scientific texts. An updated version of the program called LaTeX is also available.

Torvalds, Linus

Finnish programmer who, in 1991, created the initial versions of the *Linux kernel*. Since then, he has utilized an international network of volunteers and staff employed by various companies who help produce the kernel. Torvalds himself contributes to and oversees the efforts and is employed by the *Linux Foundation*.

tty

TeleTYpewriter; shorthand referring to underlying *Linux* virtual *devices* that allow programs and *users* to access the *kernel* and thereby run programs.

Tux

The name of the penguin character that is the *Linux* mascot. The original Tux graphic was drawn by Larry Ewing.

U

Ubuntu

Linux distribution with several unique characteristics. Ubuntu is designed primarily for desktop use (although other versions are available, including some for *server* hardware and for handheld computers). It is intended for use by individuals in any location in the world, so it has strong multiple-language support. It's run by the *Ubuntu Foundation*, which is financially backed by *Mark Shuttleworth*. Each release is guaranteed to be supported for 18 months, or three years in the case of long-term support (LTS) releases (five years in the case of server releases).

Ubuntu Foundation

Organization set up by *Mark Shuttleworth* and his company, Canonical Ltd., to provide an official home for the *Ubuntu* distribution of *Linux*.

UID

User ID; numbering system used by the operating system to refer to a *user*.

UNIX

Seminal operating system created as a research project in 1969 by Kenneth Thompson and Dennis Ritchie at Bell Labs (later AT&T). Because it was initially possible to purchase the *source code* for a fee, subsequent revisions were enhanced by a variety of organizations and went on to run many mainframe and minicomputer systems throughout the 1980s, 1990s, and up to the present. Nowadays, UNIX is fragmented and exists in a variety of versions. Perhaps most popular is its *open source* rendition, *BSD UNIX,* which has seen many developments since the source code was first released. This means that BSD UNIX no longer exists but has instead diversified into a number of separate projects. *Proprietary* versions are also available, including *Solaris*, *HP-UX*, and *AIX*.

Upstart

Replacement for *init*, the software that effectively boots *Ubuntu* into a useable state whenever the computer is switched on or rebooted. However, Upstart goes beyond the design goals of init, and can stop and start various *services* (and also monitor them) on the fly while the system is up and running.

user

The way the operating system refers to anyone who accesses its resources. A user must first have a user account set up, effectively giving that user his or her own private space on the system. In addition to actual human users, an average *Linux* system has many other user accounts created to let programs and *services* go about their business. These are usually not seen by human users.

V

variable

A changeable value that stores a certain data type (such as a number, date, or *string*), remembering it for future reference by the system or *script* it is defined by. Variables defined by and for the *Linux kernel* are vital to it.

verbose

Command option that will cause it to return more-detailed output (or, in some cases, to return actual output if the command is otherwise "quiet"); usually specified by adding the -v command option.

VFAT

Virtual File Allocation Table; technical name of Microsoft's FAT file system offered under Windows and also on removable storage devices such as flash memory cards.

vi

Arcane text editor and pseudo-*shell* beloved by *UNIX* aficionados that can be used for creation of text files or programs. Traditionally, UNIX *users* either love or hate vi; some prefer *Emacs*. Nowadays new and improved versions of vi are available, such as vim, used under *Ubuntu*.

W

Wine

Short for Wine Is Not an Emulator; software that re-creates the Windows application programming interface (API) layer within *Linux* and lets *users* run Windows programs.

workspace

X terminology referring to a *GUI* desktop.

X

X

Short for X Window; software that controls the display and input devices, thereby providing a software foundation on top of which Desktop managers like *GNOME* are able to run.

X11

Version 11 of the *X* software, currently in use on most desktop *Linux* systems.

XFree86 Project

Organization that creates *X* software. At one time, every *distribution* of *Linux* used XFree86 software, but most now use similar software from the *X.org* organization.

xinetd

The *service* responsible for starting various network servers on the computer.

XMMS

Audio player program.

X.org

Organization that produces the *X* Window software and, in particular, a set of programs called *X11*. X11 is used on most modern distributions of *Linux*. It is backed by a number of *UNIX* and Linux industry leaders.

xterm

Simple program that allows you to run a *shell* under *X*. This program has the advantage of being available on most *Linux* systems that offer a *GUI*.

Xubuntu

Version of *Ubuntu* that utilizes the XFCE4 desktop *environment* instead of *GNOME*.

APPENDIX C

■ ■ ■

Getting Further Help

So you've read through this book and have a good working knowledge of Linux. Ubuntu is running exactly as you want it to, and things are going okay. But then you hit a brick wall. Perhaps you want to perform a task but simply don't know how. Or maybe you know roughly what you need to do but don't know the specifics. Although this book tries to be as comprehensive as possible, it can't cover every eventuality.

You need to find some help, but where do you turn? Fortunately, many sources of information are available to those who are willing to help themselves. Linux contains its own series of help files in the form of man and info pages, and these are good places to start. In addition, some programs come with their own documentation. If neither of these sources provides the help you need, you can head online and take advantage of the massive Linux community around the world.

Read the Manual!

Before asking for help online, it's important that you first attempt to solve your problems by using Linux's built-in documentation. If you go online and ask a question so simple that it can be answered with a little elementary research, you might find people replying with the pithy admonition *RTFM*. (This stands for *Read The <expletive> Manual* or, in more refined company, *Read The Fine Manual*). In other words, do some basic research and then come back if you're still stuck.

It's not that people online don't want to help. It's that they don't like it when people are too lazy to help themselves and expect others to do even the slightest work for them. Although not all Linux people you encounter will take such a hard line, doing a little homework first can provide answers to a lot of questions, removing the need to ask others. This is particularly true when it comes to the fundamentals.

Documentation typically comes in three formats: man pages, info pages, and README files.

Man Pages

man pages are the oldest form of UNIX documentation. In the old days, after an individual had created a piece of software, he or she would write a brief but concise man page in order to give others a clue as to how to operate it. The programmer would come up with a few screens of documentation that could be called up from the command prompt. This documentation would outline what the software did and list all the ways in which it could be used.

Nowadays, depending on the software package, man pages are sometimes created by technical writers, but the concept of providing essential information still applies. man pages under Linux provide all the information you need about how to use a particular command or piece of software.

Sounds great, doesn't it? Alas, there's a problem: man pages are written by software engineers *for* software engineers. They expect you to already understand the technology being discussed. This is illustrated very well by the man page for wodim, software that can be used to burn CD images to disc. You can view this man page by typing man wodim at the command prompt.

The first line of the man page states, "Wodim is used to record data or audio compact discs on an Orange Book CD-recorder or to write DVD media on a DVD-recorder."

Most of that is clear, but what do they mean by *Orange Book*? They don't explain. (If you're curious, head over to http://searchstorage.techtarget.com/sDefinition/0,,sid5_gci503648,00.html.)

Farther down in the man page, you see, "Wodim is completely based on SCSI commands . . . Even ATAPI drives are just SCSI drives that inherently use the ATA packet interface as [a] SCSI command transport layer."

What's SCSI, or ATAPI for that matter? Again, the man page doesn't explain. (By the way, they're methods of interfacing with storage devices attached to your computer.)

But why should man pages explain as they go along? Their function is to describe how to use a piece of software, not to provide a beginner's introduction to technology. If they did that, a single man page could run to hundreds of pages.

In other words, man pages are usually not for complete beginners. This isn't always the case and, because Linux sees widespread usage nowadays, man pages are sometimes created with less knowledgeable users in mind. But even so, the format is inherently limited: man pages provide concise guides to using software. Luckily, there are some tips you can bear in mind to get the most from a man page. But before you can use those tips, you need to know how to read a man page.

How to Read a Man Page

To read a man page, you simply precede the command name with man. For example, to read the man page of wodim, a piece of software used to write ISO images to CD-R/RW discs, type the following command:

```
man wodim
```

This opens a simple text viewer with the man page displayed. You can use the cursor keys to move up and down line by line, or you can use the Page Up and Page Down keys (these are sometimes labeled Pg Up and Pg Dn) to move page by page. You can search by pressing the forward slash key (/). This highlights all instances of the word you type. You can search for other examples of the word in the document by pressing the N key (pressing Shift+N will search backward). The average man page will include many headings, but the following are the most common:

Name: This is the name of the command. There will also be a one-sentence summary of the command.

Synopsis: This lists the command along with its various command options (sometimes known as *arguments* or *flags*). Effectively, it shows how the command can be used. It looks complicated, but the rules are simple. First is the command itself. This is in bold, which indicates it is mandatory. This rule applies to anything else in bold: it must be included when the command is used. Anything contained within square brackets ([ ]) is optional, and this is usually where you will find the command options listed. A pipe symbol (|) separates any command options that are exclusive, which means that only one of them can be used. For example, if you see [apple|orange|pear], only one of apple, orange, or pear can be specified. Usually at the end of the Synopsis listing will be the main argument, typically the file(s) that the command is to work on and/or generate.

Description: This is a concise overview of the command's purpose.

Options: This explains what the various command options do, as first listed in the Synopsis section. Bearing in mind that command options tell the software how to work, this is often the most useful part of the man page.

Files: This lists any additional files that the command might require or use, such as configuration files.

Notes: If this section is present (and often it isn't), it sometimes attempts to further illuminate aspects of the command or the technology the command is designed to control. Unfortunately, Notes sections can be just as arcane as the rest of the `man` page.

See Also: This refers to the `man` pages of other commands that are linked to the command in question. If a number appears in brackets, that means the reference is to a specific section within the `man` page. To access this section, type **man *<section no.>* command**.

Although there are guidelines for the headings that should appear in `man` pages, as well as their formatting, the fact is that you may encounter other headings, or you may find nearly all of them omitted. Some `man` pages are the result of hours, if not days, of effort; others are written in ten minutes. Their quality can vary tremendously.

Tips for Working with Man Pages

The trick to quickly understanding a `man` page is decoding the Synopsis section. If you find it helps, split the nonobligatory command options from the mandatory parts. For example, `wodim`'s `man` page says that you *must* specify the dev= option (it's in bold), so at the very least, the command is going to require this:

```
wodim dev=X <filename>
```

Then you should skip to the Options section and work out which options are relevant to your requirements. While you're there, you'll also need to figure out what the dev= command option requires.

Although the command options contained in square brackets in the Synopsis section are, in theory, nonobligatory, the command might not work satisfactorily without some of them. For example, with `wodim`, we use the -speed command option, which sets the burn speed, and also the -v option, which provides verbose output (otherwise, the command runs silently and won't display any information onscreen, including error messages!).

Another handy tip in decoding `man` pages is understanding what standard input and standard output are. In very simple terms, standard input (`stdin`) is the method by which a command gets input— the keyboard on most Linux setups. Standard output (`stdout`) is where the output of a command is sent, which is the screen on most Linux setups. Often a `man` page states that the output of a command will be sent to standard output—in other words, unless you specify otherwise, its output will appear onscreen. Therefore, it's necessary to specify a file to which the data will be sent, either by redirecting the output, or by using a command option to specify a file. For example, the `genisoimage` command can be used to create ISO images from a collection of files for subsequent burning to CD. But unless the -o option is used to specify a filename, `genisoimage`'s output will simply be sent to standard output—it will appear on the screen.

Finally, here's the best tip of all for using `man` pages: don't forget that `man` has its own `man` page. Simply type `man man`.

Info Pages

`man` pages date from the days of relatively primitive computers. Back then, most computers could only display page after page of text and allow the user to scroll through it. In addition, memory and disk space were scarce, which is why some `man` pages are incredibly concise— fewer words take up less memory.

The Texinfo system is a valiant attempt by the GNU Project to overcome the shortfalls of `man` pages. Often this is referred to as `info`, because that's the command used to summon Texinfo pages (normally, you type **info *command***).

For starters, `info` pages are more verbose than the equivalent `man` pages, and that gives the author more space to explain the command or software. This doesn't necessarily mean that `info` pages are easier to understand, but there's a better chance of that being the case.

Second, info pages contain hyperlinks, just like web pages. If you move the cursor over a hyperlinked word, usually indicated by an asterisk (*), you can proceed to a related page. In a similar sense, pages are linked together so that you can move back and forth from topic to topic.

The bad news is that the man page system is far more popular and established than Texinfo. A programmer who creates a new application, unless the program is part of the GNU Project, will not likely bother with an info page but will almost certainly produce a man page.

In fact, in many cases, typing **info *command*** will simply bring up the man page, except in the software used to browse info pages.

However, nearly all the GNU tools are documented by using info pages, either in their own pages or as part of the coreutils pages. For example, to read about the cp command and how to use it, you can type this:

```
info coreutils cp
```

To browse through all sections of the coreutils pages, type this:

```
info coreutils
```

Because man pages are so established, everyone expects to find one for every utility. So most utilities that have info pages will also have man pages. But in such a case, the man page will state near the end that the main documentation for the utility is contained in an info page, and you may find it more fruitful to use that instead.

Navigating through info pages is achieved via the keyboard and is something of an art. But, as you might expect, there's a user-friendly guide to using info: just type **info info**. Remember that words preceded with an asterisk are hyperlinks, and you can jump from link to link using the Tab key.

README Files and Other Documentation

Some programs come with their own documentation. This is designed to give users the information they need to get started with the program (as opposed to the man page, which is a concise and complete guide to the software). Alternatively, program documentation sometimes gives a brief outline of the program's features.

The files are usually simple text, so they can be read in any text editor or word processor, and are typically called README. Under Ubuntu, these documents are usually stored in a program-specific directory within /usr/share/doc (although a small minority of programs use /usr/doc).

Not all programs are friendly enough to provide such documentation, but even so, you'll still find a directory for the software in /usr/share/doc. This is because the software might also come with a getting started guide written by the Ubuntu package maintainer. Such guides detail specifics of using the software under Ubuntu, such as where configuration files are located or how the program interoperates with other software on the system. Sometimes this documentation is written by a Debian package maintainer, because nearly all Ubuntu software has its origins in the Debian project (www.debian.org).

In addition, the directory will probably contain copyright information, explaining the software license used by the software, as well as a CHANGELOG, which is a text file listing features that have been added to each release of the software. The directory might contain some other files too, detailing where to send information about bugs, for example.

Viewing the README documentation is easy. For example, for the sudo command, you could type this:

```
cd /usr/share/doc/sudo
less README
```

Sometimes the README documentation is in a compressed tarball, in which case it will have either a `.tar.gz` or a `.tar.bz2` file extension. However, `less` is clever enough to realize this and extract the document for reading.

Getting Help Online

If you can't figure out the answer by referring to the documentation, you have little choice other than to look online. Fortunately, Linux benefits from a massive community of users, all of whom are usually willing to help each other.

The best way of getting help is to visit a forum. There you can post messages for others to reply to. Alternatively, you might choose to sign up for a mailing list. This is a way of sending e-mail to several hundreds, if not thousands, of people at once. Any individual can then reply. Mailing lists often have the benefit of allowing personal attention and interaction, but this comes at the expense of each subscriber receiving a whole lot of mail.

Forums

The official Ubuntu project forums are located at `www.ubuntuforums.org`. You'll find forums for just about every need, from security to beginner's issues, but the most popular by far is the one devoted to the current release of Ubuntu. Look in the General Help forum if your question isn't specifically related to one of the other technology areas listed.

Before you can post, you need to register by providing an e-mail address. This is required to keep down the quantity of unwanted junk postings to the forum.

You might think it fine to post a new question immediately after registering, but don't forget the simple RTFM rules mentioned at the beginning of this appendix: if you don't do elementary research first and try to solve your own problem, you may elicit a hostile response from the other posters, especially if your question is one that comes up time and time again and has been answered several times.

So, first use the comprehensive search facility provided with the forums. For example, if you're looking for advice on getting a Foomatic D1000 scanner working, use that as a search term and see what comes up. The chances are that you won't be the first person who has run into problems with that piece of hardware, and someone else may have already posted a solution.

Often you need to read the full thread to find an answer. Someone may start by asking the same question as you and, with the help and guidance of the forum members, finds a solution, which is given several messages later.

In addition, some individuals write their own HOWTO guides when they figure out how to do something. These are normally contained in the Tutorials & Tips forum, under the Other Community Discussions heading.

If you're unable to find a solution by searching, consider posting your own question. Keep your question simple, clear, and concise, because no one likes reading through acres of text. If possible, provide as many details about your system as you can. You will almost certainly want to provide the version number of the Linux kernel you're using, for example. You can find this version number by typing the following in a GNOME Terminal window:

```
uname -sr
```

In addition, any other details you can provide may prove handy. You definitely should mention the version of Ubuntu you're using, which is Lucid Lynx (often referred to simply as *Lucid*). If you're asking about hardware, give its entire model name and/or number. Don't just ask for help with a Foomatic scanner. Ask for help with a Foomatic D1000 scanner, model number ADK1033, Revision 2. If you're asking about a piece of software, provide its version number (to find that, click Help ➤ About).

Sometimes in their replies, other forum members may ask you to post further details or to provide log files. If you don't understand the question, simply ask the poster to give you more details and, if necessary, instructions on what to do. Just be polite. Explain that you're a newbie. If you think the question is extremely obvious, say so—apologize for asking what may be a stupid question, but explain that you've tried hard to answer it yourself but have failed.

Don't forget that the Ubuntu forums include the Absolute Beginner Talk forum, where fundamental questions are asked all the time.

Mailing Lists

Using the forum's search function also has the advantage of searching the archives of the mailing lists.

Mailing lists have a number of advantages and disadvantages. The advantages are that a mailing list provides an excellent way to learn about Ubuntu. All you have to do is read through the e-mail messages you receive in order to partake of a constant information drip-feed. In addition, some mailing lists are designed to make public announcements, so you'll find it easy to learn about the latest happenings in the Ubuntu community.

Mailing lists also have a terrific sense of community. They offer a neat way of getting to know other Ubuntu users and talking to them. E-mails often drift off-topic into humor and general discussion.

The disadvantages of mailing lists are that you can easily receive in excess of 200 messages a day, depending on which mailing list you join (although you can also opt to receive period digests of recent messages; these arrive in the form of a single daily, weekly, or monthly e-mail). Even if you have a moderately fast Internet connection, that quantity of messages can take a long time to download. In addition, you'll need to sort out any personal or business e-mail from the enormous quantity of mailing list traffic (although the mailing list messages usually have the list title in square brackets in the subject field; you can therefore create a mail rule that sorts the mail according to this).

You can learn more about the Ubuntu mailing lists at `https://lists.ubuntu.com`.

Other Official Sites

The Official Ubuntu Documentation is an ongoing community effort to create simple and effective instructions on the use of Ubuntu. In truth, there is nothing presently on the site that isn't already described in this book, so its usefulness for you is limited, but it might be ideal to send the link to a friend or relative who's new to Ubuntu. In addition, you might want to take a look at the Ubuntu wiki: `https://wiki.ubuntu.com`. Once again, this is largely community generated. It contains a whole world of fascinating information about Ubuntu, but can be somewhat difficult to navigate and tends to be aimed at higher-level Ubuntu users, such as developers. However, it's an excellent place to learn "off-the-wall" Ubuntu knowledge, such as how to get Ubuntu working with particular hardware.

Third-Party Sites

Of course, the Ubuntu project doesn't have a monopoly on sites that discuss Ubuntu. Several third-party web sites are worth at least an occasional visit, and other forum web sites are devoted to Linux.

One we visit on a regular basis is the Ubuntu Geek blog: `www.ubuntugeek.com`. Written by a team of dedicated Ubuntu experts, this blog is packed full of tips for all levels of Ubuntu users. In addition, we like to visit `http://linuxhelp.blogspot.com`, which is a similar blog written by a Linux user who uses Ubuntu and likes to share tips and techniques.

Perhaps the king of third-party Ubuntu sites is Ubuntu Guide: `http://ubuntuguide.org`. This contains brief instructions on how to do a variety of common tasks under Ubuntu, such as installing certain types of software or administering particular hardware. It covers a lot of the same ground as this book, but is still worth investigating if you want to browse through some excellent tips and advice.

One site to check on a regular basis for news about future releases of Ubuntu and upcoming applications is OMG! Ubuntu!, which you can find at `http://www.omgubuntu.co.uk`. There you can the most up-to-date information about the development of new software, new trends in the development of Ubuntu, and analyses of the future of Ubuntu.

Finally, one of the best Linux forums and general advice sites can be found at `www.linuxquestions.org`. This has a forum dedicated specifically to Ubuntu, but also contains hundreds more devoted to just about every aspect of Linux, including forums for beginners.

■ ■ ■

Exploring the DVD-ROM and Other Ubuntu Versions

The DVD-ROM supplied with this book contains the main Ubuntu 10.04 release (Lucid Lynx), along with sister versions of Ubuntu that use different desktop environments, including Kubuntu and Xubuntu. Additionally, we have included the alternate installer version of Ubuntu, which can be useful if your PC hardware is incompatible with the main Ubuntu installation routine.

This appendix provides details about the many and varied Ubuntu derivations, along with instructions on how to utilize them.

Version Numbers, Code Names, and Support

Each version of Ubuntu has a version number and a code name. The version number is simply the year of release, followed by the month. The release made in April 2008 has the version number 8.04, for example.

The code name is how Ubuntu is referred to informally, especially among community members, and is set by Mark Shuttleworth, the creator of Ubuntu. Code names tend to involve animals and are usually humorous. The 6.06 version of Ubuntu was code-named Dapper Drake, for example. The 8.04 release was code-named Hardy Heron. People often just use the first word of the code name, especially on Internet forums. For example, the 8.04 release is often referred to as *Hardy*.

This book was written using version 10.04, code-named Lucid Lynx, as a base. This version was released in April 2010. It was the most recent version at the time of this writing.

Each successive version of Ubuntu brings improvements, such as newer versions of software packages. However, not all versions of Ubuntu are created equal when it comes to online updates, as provided by the Update Manager program. All versions of Ubuntu come with free software updates for a set period, usually 18 months, after which users are expected to upgrade (for free) to the most recent version at that time.

However, versions 6.06, 8.04 and now 10.04 also have the epithet LTS, which stands for *Long-Term Support*. The freely available software updates for 8.04 will last until 2011, and for 10.04 until 2013, some three years after the initial release. Support for the 6.06 release expired in early 2009. LTS releases are made approximately every two years, so the next LTS release will presumably be 12.04 (not code-named yet).

■ **Note** If you use the Ubuntu 10.04, 8.04, or 6.06 release on a server system, support will last for five years.

The intention behind the Long-Term Support releases is that they should be used by those who want a proven and stable Linux operating system, and don't care about newer features in the latest releases of Ubuntu. For example, in a corporate environment, some of the new features provided in more recent versions of Ubuntu might require additional staff training, so an unchanging release may prove appealing.

UPGRADING TO A NEWER VERSION OF UBUNTU

Ubuntu works on a six-month release cycle, and this means a new version of Ubuntu comes out every half year. By the time you read this, a new release of Ubuntu may be available, and you might choose to update to it.

You can update to a newer version of Ubuntu in two ways: by burning the ISO image to a CD or by upgrading online.

You can download the ISO image of the latest release from www.ubuntu.com/getubuntu/download and burn it to CD. Then insert the CD when Ubuntu is up and running. You'll be asked whether you want to upgrade to the latest version using the Synaptic Package Manager or Ubuntu Software Center. This process is automated. Of course, you can then use the same CD to install Ubuntu afresh on any other computer.

To upgrade online, open a terminal window (Applications ➤ Accessories ➤ Terminal) and type the following two lines, pressing Enter after each one:

```
sudo apt-get update
sudo apt-get dist-upgrade
```

This will download all the packages for the latest release of Ubuntu, if one is available, and attempt to update your system. Updating in this way involves less downloading, because your computer will get only the packages it needs, although it's still likely that several hundred megabytes will need to be downloaded.

Often when a newer version of Ubuntu becomes available, you may find a pop-up window appearing, asking whether you want to upgrade. In this case, upgrading is as simple as agreeing to the prompts and using Update Manager to complete the procedure. You will have to reboot when the upgrade has finished.

Other Versions of Ubuntu

In addition to the main Ubuntu releases, several Ubuntu derivations are available. You might refer to these as *spin-off projects*. They are created by taking the main Ubuntu release as a base and then adding software, usually in the form of an alternative Desktop environment. Some support alternative hardware platforms but are otherwise identical to the main release.

Some spin-off projects are officially sponsored, which is to say they are developed as part of the wider Ubuntu project, and development work on them is paid for by Canonical, the corporate sponsor of Ubuntu. However, others are strictly community projects, developed largely by enthusiasts. Some of their software packages might be found in the Universe software repositories, however. This section describes how to install the Ubuntu derivatives that are included on the DVD-ROM disc supplied with this book. It then provides some details about the Kubuntu, Xubuntu, and Edubuntu versions. Table D-1 lists the major Ubuntu projects at this time.

Table D-1. *Versions of Ubuntu*

Ubuntu Version	Description	Level of Support
Ubuntu Desktop	The main topic of this book, it is an edition of Ubuntu targeted at desktop computers and uses the GNOME Desktop environment by default. It comes preloaded with a great range of applications. For more details see http://www.ubuntu.com/desktop.	Official edition
Ubuntu Server	A release of Ubuntu designed for server computers. To this end, it includes software for easy installation of the Apache web server, for example, or the Samba file server software. It does not feature a graphical user interface, although it shares the same repositories as the main release, so a GUI can be added later. For more, see www.ubuntu.com/server.	Official edition
JeOS	An efficient variant of the Ubuntu Server edition, configured specifically to run on virtual appliances. It is no longer available as a separate ISO image, but it can be selected during Ubuntu Server installation. For more information visit https://help.ubuntu.com/10.04/serverguide/C/jeos-and-vmbuilder.html.	Official edition
Ubuntu Netbook Edition	An edition of Ubuntu targeted to the small Netbook computers. It uses more efficiently reduced Desktop space, has a different selection of default software, and is ideal for web browsing and e-book reading. To learn more visit www.ubuntu.com/netbook.	Official edition
Ubuntu alternate installer	Same as the standard release of Ubuntu but employs a text-mode installer that can help bypass some graphical problems. This is included as an ISO image on the DVD-ROM that comes with this book (ubuntu-10.04-alternate-i386.iso). For more information, visit www.ubuntu.com/desktop/get-ubuntu/alternative-download.	Official edition
Kubuntu	Same as the main Ubuntu release, except that it uses the KDE desktop (www.kde.org). This is included as an ISO image on the DVD-ROM that comes with this book (kubuntu-10.04-desktop-i386.iso). To read more, see www.kubuntu.org.	Recognised derivative
Xubuntu	Same as the main Ubuntu release, except that it uses the Xfce Desktop Environment (www.xfce.org). This is included as an ISO image on the DVD-ROM that comes with this book (xubuntu-10.04-desktop-i386.iso). To learn more you can visit www.xubuntu.org.	Recognised derivative

Ubuntu Version	Description	Level of Support
Edubuntu	Same as the main Ubuntu release but with a child-friendly interface along with the addition of some educational software. See `http://edubuntu.org/` for more details.	Recognised derivative
Mythbuntu	Version of Ubuntu designed for computers containing TV/video processing cards. It is built around the MythTV digital video recording software and features the Xfce Desktop Environment. For more details, and to download the project ISO image, visit `www.mythbuntu.org`.	Recognised derivative
Ubuntu Studio	A version of the standard Ubuntu release that includes multimedia editing tools. For more information, see `http://ubuntustudio.org`.	Recognised derivative
KubuntuKde3Lucid	A remix of Lucid Lynx created with only KDE3/Trinity installed, for the convenience of users who are not quite ready to take the jump to KDE4.x. To read more go to `https://wiki.kubuntu.org/Kubuntu/Kde3/Lucid`.	Community edition
Lubuntu	Lubuntu is a faster, more lightweight and energy-saving variant of Ubuntu using LXDE, the Lightweight X11 Desktop Environment. The Lubuntu team aims to earn official endorsement from Canonical. Visit `http://lubuntu.net/` to get more information.	Community edition
gNewSense	Almost identical to the main release of Ubuntu, although this release features only software that strictly follows the letter and spirit of the GNU Public License and the GNU philosophy. To this end, proprietary software such as hardware drivers, is not included. It is endorsed by the Free Software Foundation. For more details, see `www.gnewsense.org`.	Community edition
Ubuntu PowerPC	Same as the main Ubuntu release but compiled for computers with PowerPC processors, such as G3, G4, or G5 chips, typically found in older Apple Macintosh computers. To download the ISO image, visit `http://cdimage.ubuntu.com/ports/releases/10.04/release/`. You can also find in that location versions for PlayStation 3 and for Itanium-2 computers. It is not officially supported.	Community edition

Installation of Other Versions

Several of the Ubuntu derivatives are included in the DVD-ROM disc supplied with this book, as follows:

- Kubuntu
- Xubuntu
- Alternate installer disc

They are included on the disc in the form of *ISO images*. These are single files that contain the entire contents of the bootable installation CDs. They're designed to be burned to blank CD-R or CD-RW discs, and the user then installs from the disc. If you want to install Kubuntu or Xubuntu, you have two options:

- Start afresh, by burning a CD from the ISO image and installing from it. To learn how to do this on most major operating systems, see the "Creating Bootable CDs from ISO Images" section later in this appendix. See Table D-1 for the filename of the ISO image for each version.
- Upgrade from an existing installation of Ubuntu by using the Ubuntu Software Center.

You can also download other versions, such as Edubuntu, from its respective download page as detailed in Table D-1. To install each version alongside the current Desktop, you'll need to search for and install a particular metapackage by using the Ubuntu Software Center (see Chapter 20 for details on using the Ubuntu Software Center):

- For the main Kubuntu release, install the kubuntu-desktop package. During installation of Kubuntu, you will be prompted for which login manager you wish to use. It's a good idea to stick with gdm (GNOME Display Manager), which is the default choice.
- For Xubuntu, install xubuntu-desktop. This is a metapackage that ensures all the Xfce desktop components are installed alongside the current Desktop environment.

Kubuntu

The standard Ubuntu release, as supplied with this book, relies on the GNOME Desktop Project for its graphical interface (see www.gnome.org). Many other desktop projects exist in the wider Linux world, but perhaps the only one that ranks alongside GNOME in terms of popularity is the KDE (www.kde.org). Kubuntu is simply a version of Ubuntu that eschews GNOME in favor of KDE.

Kubuntu (www.kubuntu.org) retains the same philosophy as Ubuntu, in both its humanitarian aims of being available to all, as well as its more pragmatic aspects, such as always including the latest versions of applications. It also shares many technical features, such as the use of sudo to invoke superuser powers.

■ **Note** Rather than use gksu to invoke sudo powers for graphical applications, Kubuntu uses kdesu. It's used in the same way, however.

The main difference is the software bundled with this variant. When it comes to e-mail, KDE's KMail program is used instead of Evolution, for example, and Konqueror is used for web browsing instead of Firefox (although, of course, Evolution and Firefox can easily be installed via the Ubuntu Software Center after Kubuntu has been installed). Additionally, the Dolphin file manager is used instead of Nautilus. Kopete is the default instant messaging client. The system configuration software is radically different too, with several KDE tools used instead of the GNOME software described in this book. The look and feel, as seen in Figure D-1, is quite different. However, most everything works in a broadly similar way.

After the Kubuntu components have been installed, as described in the previous section, you can opt to boot into Kubuntu by clicking the Options button on the login screen and clicking the Select Session entry. Then select the KDE entry and click the Change Session button. You'll be asked whether you want to always boot into KDE, or just this time. If you select to always boot into KDE but decide to boot into GNOME subsequently, repeat these steps and select GNOME from the list.

Figure D-1. *Kubuntu 10.04*

Xubuntu

Although GNOME and KDE dominate the Desktop interface landscape of Linux and are used in the main Ubuntu and Kubuntu releases, respectively, other projects take a different approach to the graphical desktop. The Xfce Desktop Environment (www.xfce.org) is one of these. It's a streamlined Desktop that retains the good looks of GNOME but is much smaller in terms of memory footprint. This means that a system running Xfce is faster than an equivalent GNOME system. It also means that Xfce can be used on many older computers that don't have the powerful hardware we take for granted nowadays and would struggle with the latest GNOME and KDE releases of Ubuntu.

Because a key component of the Ubuntu Foundation's philosophy is to create an OS that can be used by everyone, regardless of where they are in the world, a version of Ubuntu that can run on older hardware makes a lot of sense. It's unlikely that less-developed countries will have access to the latest expensive computer hardware, for example.

As you might expect, Xubuntu (www.xubuntu.org) is simply a version of Ubuntu that replaces the GNOME Desktop with the Xfce desktop, as shown in Figure D-2. Some key components are still present, such as the Firefox web browser. Other Ubuntu components are swapped for Xfce replacements; for example, the Nautilus file browser is replaced with Thunar.

Despite Xfce's claim to be lightweight, it still offers a high degree of usability and shouldn't be seen as a second-best choice for stripped-down hardware. It's certainly worth trying out if you long for a less cluttered Desktop experience. It also uses many modern GUI aspects we take for granted, such as theming (see Chapter 9) and font antialiasing.

To use the Xfce desktop after it's installed, click the Options button on the login screen and then click the Select Session entry. Next, select Xfce from the list and click the Change Session button. To boot to the standard Ubuntu Desktop after this, simply repeat the steps and select GNOME from the list.

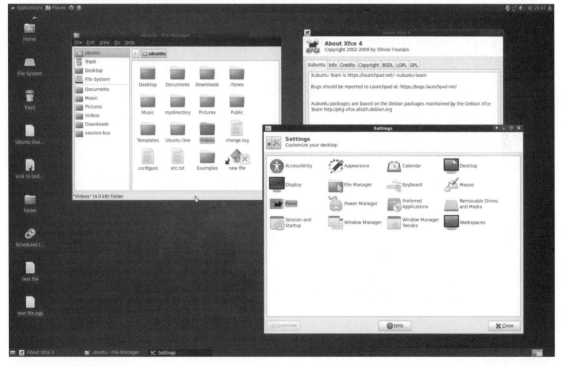

Figure D-2. Xubuntu 10.04

Edubuntu

The Ubuntu philosophy is to make an operating system accessible to everyone, no matter who they are or where they live in the world. Of course, young people are included in this vision, and Edubuntu (`www.edubuntu.org`) is a version of Ubuntu specifically geared toward their needs. This rendition of the standard Ubuntu release has been bolstered by many educational software titles as well as classroom management software, which makes administrating many classroom computers easier for teachers.

In addition, Edubuntu has a friendlier and simpler interface that's designed to appeal to youngsters, although it still utilizes the same Desktop environment as the main Ubuntu release. Actually, two versions are available: one that uses the same GNOME Desktop as the main release and another that is built on the KDE Desktop of Kubuntu.

Edubuntu also features software from the Linux Terminal Server Project (`www.ltsp.org`). This brings the potential for computers without a hard disk to boot Edubuntu from a central server. The intention is to give older computers (unfortunately, the type typically found in educational environments) a new lease on life, even if they're too underpowered to run modern software. Additionally, the terminal server can be used to administer the computers, which is clearly beneficial in a teaching environment.

However, the standard installation of Edubuntu is just like any other Ubuntu configuration, and the software is designed to be installed directly on the hard disk of computers. The following are the chief education titles provided with Edubuntu:

- KDE-Edu programs (`http://edu.kde.org`) include games involving mathematics, languages, science, and other miscellaneous topics. Teachers might also appreciate the inclusion of KEduca, a program designed to create form-based tests and exams.

- GCompris (`http://gcompris.net`) is for children of kindergarten age and introduces them to computer use as well as elementary math and reading skills.

- Tux Paint (`www.tuxpaint.org`) is a user-friendly drawing package full of sound effects and colorful graphics.

The main benefit of Edubuntu for educational establishments is that it's both free of charge and comes with the same kind of update support as Ubuntu. This provides a consistent experience for students and teachers alike.

Because Edubuntu is built on the Ubuntu base, there is no way to "switch between" Edubuntu and Ubuntu. Effectively, Edubuntu is a reconfiguration of Ubuntu with the addition of some educational software and a more kid-friendly theme. To return to a standard Ubuntu setup and deactivate the Edubuntu theme, simply select the Ambiance entry within the Appearances Preferences dialog box. See Chapter 9 for more details on how to switch themes.

To install Edubuntu (without downloading it from `http://edubuntu.org`), choose to install the `edubuntu-desktop` package in the Ubuntu Software Center. There are two versions of Edubuntu: the default based on the GNOME Desktop and another based on the Kubuntu Desktop (`edubuntu-desktop` and `edubuntu-desktop-kde`, respectively). You can choose either from the list of results in the Ubuntu Software Center.

Creating Bootable CDs from ISO Images

The Ubuntu derivatives can be found on the DVD-ROM disc included with this book. It should be obvious from the individual filenames what each ISO file contains, but you can also consult Table D-1.

ISO images are designed to be burned to blank CD-R or CD-RW discs that you boot from in order to install the operating system, just as you booted from the DVD-ROM to install Ubuntu. Alternatively, you can use an ISO image to install the operating system on virtual machines.

Of course, to burn ISO images to CD, you'll need a CD or DVD drive capable of burning discs. These have been available for many years and are standard features on nearly all desktop and notebook computers. You'll also need a blank CD-R or CD-RW disc and perhaps one or two spares in case your first attempt doesn't work. If you opt to use CD-RW discs, these should be blanked prior to use (this can be done with most CD-burning software).

A few rules should be followed whenever burning ISO images:

- Copy the ISO image to your computer's hard disk. Don't try to burn an ISO image directly from a DVD/CD or a network share. The burning software requires quick access to the ISO file, and this isn't possible when it's not on your hard disk.

- If your computer has limited resources, it is not a good idea to use it for heavy tasks while burning ISO images. You should refrain from game playing or video editing, although light computer use should be fine (that is, word processing, web browsing, and so on).

The instructions in the following sections describe how to burn ISO images to CDs when using Ubuntu, Windows, and Mac OS X.

DECODING ISO FILENAMES

ISO filenames for Linux distributions can be a little hard to understand, so here's a quick guide. Let's take the Xubuntu 10.04 ISO filename as a guide. Here it is:

xubuntu-10.04-desktop-i386.iso

This filename consists of four main parts:

- The first part is the name of the distribution. In this case, it's xubuntu, but this could read edubuntu or just ubuntu, for example.

- The second part is the version number of the distribution—10.04.

- The third part is the platform for which the distribution is designed. In this case, this version of Xubuntu is designed for the desktop, but this could read server or alternate, to indicate an alternate install disc.

- The final part, before the .iso file extension, is a description of the computer architecture for which the distribution is made. i386 means the distribution will run on all 32-bit PCs (which is to say, every computer made since around 1990). You might also see amd64 here, which means the distribution is designed to work on 64-bit processors, such as Intel Pentium 4 and AMD Athlon 64–based computers. If you see PowerPC here, it means the distribution is designed to run on PowerPC-based computers, primarily older Apple Macintoshes.

Burning CDs Using Ubuntu

Here are the steps for burning CDs from ISO images when using Ubuntu:

1. Copy the ISO image to the Desktop.

2. Right-click the image on the Desktop and select Write to Disc from the menu that appears.

3. A new dialog box appears. In the Write Speed drop-down list, select the lowest value possible (if you don't see a Write Speed drop-down list, click the Properties button). If you have more than one CD/DVD writer drive installed on your computer, ensure that the correct model is selected from the Write Disc To list.

4. Insert a blank CD-R or CD-RW.

5. Click the Write button to create the CD.

Burning CDs Using Windows Vista/XP

Unlike Ubuntu and Mac OS X, Windows Vista and XP don't contain any built-in ISO burning software. For the purpose of burning ISO images, we recommend that you download and install the freeware ISO Recorder tool from http://isorecorder.alexfeinman.com/isorecorder.htm. Versions are available for both Windows XP and Vista. The following are the steps for burning CDs from ISO images when using the Windows XP version of ISO Recorder:

1. Copy the ISO file to your Desktop.

2. Insert a blank CD-R or CD-RW disc into your drive.

3. Right-click the .iso file on the desktop, select Open With, and then select ISO Recorder from the list.

4. The ISO Recorder program window opens. Click the Properties button.

5. Click and drag the recording speed slider so that the middle number under the slider is 1 (or to the lowest possible number if 1 isn't available). Click OK in the Properties dialog box.

6. Click the Next button in the main ISO Recorder program window. This will start the burning procedure, which might take some time, during which you should avoid using your PC.

Burning CDs Using Windows 7

Windows 7 includes image burning software in its default installation:

1. Copy the ISO file to the Desktop.

2. Insert a blank CD-R or CD-RW disc.

3. Right click the ISO file and select the option "Burn disc image."

4. The program window opens. Select the target drive and check the option to verify the disc after the burning operation.

5. Click the Burn button. This will start the burning procedure. Wait until it's finished and verify that it has completed successfully.

Burning CDs Using Mac OS X

Here are the steps for burning CDs from ISO images when using a Mac OS X system:

1. Copy the ISO file to the Desktop.

2. Insert a blank CD-R or CD-RW disc.

3. In Finder, click Applications ➤ Utilities ➤ Disk Utility.

4. When the program starts, click Images ➤ Burn.

5. Navigate to the ISO file on the Desktop and then click the Burn button in the dialog box that appears.

Index

■■■

■ U

You Need the Companion eBook

Your purchase of this book entitles you to buy the companion PDF-version eBook for only $10. Take the weightless companion with you anywhere.

We believe this Apress title will prove so indispensable that you'll want to carry it with you everywhere, which is why we are offering the companion eBook (in PDF format) for $10 to customers who purchase this book now. Convenient and fully searchable, the PDF version of any content-rich, page-heavy Apress book makes a valuable addition to your programming library. You can easily find and copy code—or perform examples by quickly toggling between instructions and the application. Even simultaneously tackling a donut, diet soda, and complex code becomes simplified with hands-free eBooks!

Once you purchase your book, getting the $10 companion eBook is simple:

❶ Visit **www.apress.com/promo/tendollars/**.

❷ Complete a basic registration form to receive a randomly generated question about this title.

❸ Answer the question correctly in 60 seconds, and you will receive a promotional code to redeem for the $10.00 eBook.

THE EXPERT'S VOICE™

233 Spring Street, New York, NY 10013

Offer valid through 3/11.